Give Us This Day®

DAILY PRAYER FOR TODAY'S CATHOLIC

LIVING LITURGY™

Using this book for small group sharing

Groups using *Living Liturgy*™ for prayer and faith-sharing might begin with the following general format and then adjust it to fit different needs.

OPENING PRAYER
- Begin with a hymn
- Pray the collect for the Sunday or solemnity

GOD'S WORD
- Read aloud the gospel
- Observe a brief period of silence

INDIVIDUAL STUDY, REFLECTION, PRAYER
- Read and consider "Reflecting on the Gospel" or "Living the Paschal Mystery"
- Spend some time in reflection and prayer

FAITH-SHARING
- Use the "Assembly & Faith-sharing Groups" spirituality statements (and the specific liturgical ministry statements if they apply)
- Consider what ways the gospel is challenging you to *live* the liturgy you will celebrate on Sunday

CONCLUDING PRAYER
- Pray the "Model Universal Prayer (Prayer of the Faithful)"
- Pray the Our Father at the end of the intercessions
- Conclude with a hymn

LIVING LITURGY™

Using this book for personal prayer

The best preparation for Sunday celebration of Eucharist is prayer. Here are two suggested approaches for an individual to use this book for personal prayer.

Daily Prayer

MONDAY
- Read the gospel prayerfully

TUESDAY
- Read the gospel again
- Reflect on the statements from "Assembly and Faith-sharing Groups" and let your reflection lead you to prayer

WEDNESDAY
- Read again the gospel
- Read "Reflecting on the Gospel" and let it lead you to prayer

THURSDAY
- Read and study "Living the Paschal Mystery"
- Pray the "Model Universal Prayer (Prayer of the Faithful)"

FRIDAY
- Pray the responsorial psalm
- Read "Connecting the Responsorial Psalm to the readings"

SATURDAY
- Read the gospel and first reading
- Read and study "Focusing the Gospel"
- Reflect on how you have been able to live this gospel during the week

SUNDAY
- Enter fully into the celebration of Eucharist
- Enjoy a day of rest

Prayer as Time and Opportunity Permit

A daily routine of study and prayer is not always possible. As time and opportunity permit:
- Read the gospel prayerfully
- Reflect on "Living the Paschal Mystery"
- Pray the "Model Universal Prayer (Prayer of the Faithful)"

LIVING LITURGY™

LIVING LITURGY™

SPIRITUALITY, CELEBRATION, AND CATECHESIS FOR SUNDAYS AND SOLEMNITIES

Year B • 2015

Joyce Ann Zimmerman, C.PP.S.
Kathleen Harmon, S.N.D. de N.
Rev. John W. Tonkin

LITURGICAL PRESS
Collegeville, Minnesota

www.litpress.org

Design by Ann Blattner. Art by Br. Martin Erspamer, OSB, a monk of Saint Meinrad Archabbey, Indiana.

ISSN 1547-089X

ISBN 978-0-8146-3812-5

☩ CONTENTS

Joyce Ann Zimmerman, C.PP.S., is the director of the Institute for Liturgical Ministry in Dayton, Ohio, and is an adjunct professor of liturgy, liturgical consultant, and frequent facilitator of workshops. She has published numerous scholarly and pastoral liturgical works. She holds civil and pontifical doctorates of theology.

Kathleen Harmon, S.N.D. de N., is the music director for programs of the Institute for Liturgical Ministry in Dayton, Ohio, and is the author of numerous publications. An educator and musician, she facilitates liturgical music workshops and cantor formation programs. She holds a graduate degree in music and a doctorate in liturgy.

John W. Tonkin is a priest of the Archdiocese of Cincinnati who was ordained in 2005. He is the pastor of Sacred Heart Parish in McCartyville, Ohio, has served on a number of archdiocesan and other boards and committees, and is a member of his local ministerial league. He has pursued graduate studies in Sacred Scripture.

USING THIS RESOURCE

Three-year-old Ben was meeting some of his cousins for the first time at a family reunion. He quickly latched onto his older cousin Sam, who allowed Ben to take his hand and pull him around, playing at different things. When it came time to eat and everyone gathered, someone asked Ben with whom he had been playing. He wrinkled up his face in concentration, then broke into a radiant smile as he exclaimed, "A friend." How heartwarming! He didn't know or remember Sam's name, but he knew who Sam had become for him. How descriptive this incident is of where *Living Liturgy*™ might lead us. As we spend time preparing for our participation in the most important event of the week—celebrating the eucharistic liturgy as a memorial of Jesus' saving life, death, and resurrection—we are invited to come to know Jesus ever more deeply as our Friend. We want to open ourselves to let him take our hand and lead us during the week in right and just ways of living. And, yes, perhaps even play a little with him!

With this sixteenth volume of *Living Liturgy*™ we again have a change in team membership. After six years of teamwork, Marianist Fr. Christopher Conlon has retired and is replaced by Archdiocese of Cincinnati priest Fr. John Tonkin. Fr. John is the first priest team member who is a full-time pastor, and he brings to our team prayer and discussions a wealth of pastoral experience. From his studies and love of Sacred Scripture he brings fresh insights to our work. His warm personality, quick humor, and lots of teasing have contributed to making the long team meetings most enjoyable.

As with each of the three teams that have collaborated to write *Living Liturgy*™ over the years, we continue the original purpose: to help people prepare for liturgy and live a liturgical spirituality (that is, a way of living that is rooted in liturgy) which opens their vision to their baptismal identity as the Body of Christ and shapes their living according to the paschal mystery rhythm of self-giving and God's blessing of a share in Jesus' risen Life. The paschal mystery is the central focus of liturgy, of the gospels, and of each volume of *Living Liturgy*™.

A threefold dynamic of daily living, prayer, and study continues to determine the basic structure of *Living Liturgy*™, captured in the layout under the headings "Spirituality," "Celebration," and "Catechesis." This structure continually reminds us that our celebration of liturgy must spill over into a lived spirituality, and that both celebration and spirituality are deepened as we take the time and energy for continual catechesis, for the kind of learning that helps us participate more fully in both liturgy and daily Christian living.

During Ordinary Time of the 2015 liturgical year, we read from Mark's gospel, which is structured around the all-important question of who Jesus is. In chapter 8 Peter responds to Jesus' query, "But who do you say that I am?" with "You are the Messiah" (vv. 29, 30, NABRE). The centurion facing Jesus on the cross after he died exclaimed, "Truly this man was the Son of God!" (15:39, NABRE). Both recognized that Jesus was Someone beyond being human—that he was One with God and our Savior. We know nothing more of the centurion, but we do know that Peter spent the rest of his life witnessing to Jesus' life and saving message. No doubt, Jesus was Peter's Friend. During each liturgical year we are invited to come to know Jesus as our Friend, too.

A FRIEND

NEW TEAM MEMBER

PASCHAL MYSTERY STILL CENTRAL FOCUS

SPIRITUALITY, CELEBRATION, AND CATECHESIS

JESUS: A FRIEND

INTRODUCTION to the Gospel of Mark

The Gospel of Mark, generally recognized as the earliest of the four canonical gospels, was written around the year 70—the year the Romans destroyed the city of Jerusalem. This gospel addresses both Gentiles and Jews and "invites" them to follow Jesus of Nazareth. Its very structure is organized around two confessions of who Jesus is, and so Jesus' identity is a major focus of the gospel.

The first eight chapters of Mark's gospel address the question, Who is Jesus? and they climax in the answer given by Peter at the end of chapter 8: "You are the Messiah," the Christ, the Anointed (NABRE). This first half of Mark's gospel portrays Jesus going up and down Galilee healing and forgiving, eating with sinners, and in amazing ways nourishing people through word and deed. He invites people to follow him not because they are spellbound by his teaching and deeds (more miracles are recorded in Mark than in any other gospel), but because they are willing to live in such ways as to announce to all people the Good News that God has visited the people in a new and unprecedented way in the very Person of Jesus.

The second half of the gospel asks the follow-up question, What does it mean to be the Messiah? Jesus' answer is contrary to popular opinion; the Messiah would not come as a great and successful military leader, but as One who must suffer and die. This very answer is revealed in the reaction of Peter to Jesus as not only surprising but also disturbingly challenging to his disciples. Mark intertwines predictions of Jesus' suffering and death (which the disciples don't understand) with stories of healing those who are blind. The Messiah is the One who gives his life for the people—first in smaller things, for example, by staying with them when they misunderstand and even disappoint him; then in the greatest act of all time, by giving his very life on the cross. This second half of the gospel climaxes not in the disciples acknowledging Jesus as the suffering Messiah, but in the confession of the centurion who gazes on the crucified Jesus: "Truly this man was the Son of God!" (NABRE).

Mark's is the shortest and probably the oldest of the four canonical gospels. It is written in an "earthy" kind of way: Jesus seems to show more "human" reactions—anger, frustration, disappointment—than he does in the other three gospels. In Mark's original version there was almost exclusive emphasis on the suffering entailed in being a disciple of the Messiah; the stories of the resurrection were added later after the appearance of the other three gospels. The gospel's call to discipleship entails the same difficulties, frustrations, and annoyances that Jesus himself endured. But it is precisely by continuing the paschal journey through suffering and death that new Life can be experienced and come to fullness. Mark's Good News is that the Word continues to be made flesh first in Jesus himself, and then through his followers. The risen Jesus continues to dwell among us and within us.

ABBREVIATIONS

LITURGICAL RESOURCES

BofB   *Book of Blessings*. International Commission on English in the Liturgy. Collegeville: Liturgical Press, 1989.

BLS   *Built of Living Stones: Art, Architecture, and Worship.* Guidelines of the National Conference of Catholic Bishops, 2000.

CCC   *Catechism of the Catholic Church.* Washington, DC: USCCB, 2004.

GIRM   *General Instruction of the Roman Missal* (2002/2011).

GNLYC General Norms for the Liturgical Year and the Calendar (1969).

ILM   Introduction to the *Lectionary for Mass* (1981).

SC   *Sacrosanctum Concilium* (The Constitution on the Sacred Liturgy). Vatican II, 1963.

MUSICAL RESOURCES

BB   *Breaking Bread*. Portland, OR: Oregon Catholic Press, annual.

G3   *Gather*, Third Edition. Chicago: GIA Publications, Inc., 2011.

HG   *Hymns for the Gospels*. Chicago: GIA Publications, Inc., 2011.

JS3   *Journeysongs*, Third Edition. Portland, OR: Oregon Catholic Press, 2012.

LMGM2 *Lead Me, Guide Me*, Second Edition. Chicago: GIA Publications, Inc., 2012.

SS   *Sacred Song*. Collegeville: Liturgical Press, 2011–2014.

W3   *Worship*, Third Edition. Chicago: GIA Publications, Inc., 1986.

W4   *Worship*, Fourth Edition. Chicago: GIA Publications, Inc., 2011.

WC   *We Celebrate*. Schiller Park, IL: World Library Publications, 2011–2014.

WS   *Word and Song*. Schiller Park, IL: World Library Publications, 2013.

GIA   GIA Publications, Inc.

OCP   Oregon Catholic Press

STL   *Sing to the Lord: Music in Divine Worship*. Washington, DC: USCCB, 2007.

WLP   World Library Publications

NOTE: The music suggestions made in *Living Liturgy*™ are not intended to be an exhaustive list of suggestions for every Sunday (these are readily available in other publications), but to offer a model and accompanying catechesis for making fruitful liturgical and pastoral choices. This necessarily limits the number of suggestions made, but the model for making musical choices presumes those responsible for music ministry will draw from whatever wider spectrum of resources they have on hand.

SEASON OF ADVENT

SPIRITUALITY

GOSPEL ACCLAMATION
Ps 85:8

R̸. Alleluia, alleluia.
Show us Lord, your love;
and grant us your salvation.
R̸. Alleluia, alleluia.

Gospel

Mark 13:33-37; L2B

**Jesus said to his disciples:
"Be watchful! Be alert!
You do not know when the time will
    come.
It is like a man traveling abroad.
He leaves home and places his servants
    in charge,
    each with his own work,
    and orders the gatekeeper to be on
    the watch.
Watch, therefore;
    you do not know when the lord of the
    house is coming,
    whether in the evening, or at
    midnight,
    or at cockcrow, or in the morning.
May he not come suddenly and find you
    sleeping.
What I say to you, I say to all:
    'Watch!'"**

Reflecting on the Gospel

With today's instant and easy communication technology, it is difficult to imagine not knowing when someone for whom we're waiting will come. We know the exact time when the plane will land, when the car leaves the Interstate, when the guest is arriving at our house. While Christ doesn't exactly communicate by texting us of his every arrival, when our watching for him is alert and wakeful, we begin to see all the signs of his Presence to us *now*. We prepare best for Christ's final coming by the kind of watching we do now and how we grow in our ability to recognize his presence now.

We begin Advent this Sunday not by looking to Christ's first coming into our midst at the Incarnation, but by looking to Christ's return at the end of time. Christ has come, fulfilled his mission, and then, like the "lord of the house" in the gospel, is "traveling abroad." We, "his servants in charge," have each been given our own work to do until Christ returns. And what is our first and most important work? Watching for Christ's coming! We must always remember that the watching is never in vain: our watching hastens encounters with the very One on whom we wait. Our watching and encountering is *now* and in it the past and future meet. Yes, during this wonderful time of the liturgical year we look to the past to remember Jesus' becoming incarnate by the power of the Holy Spirit and dwelling among us, and we look to the future when Christ will come again. But we live *now,* and in this present moment Christ is within us and among us.

Four times in this gospel Christ commands us, "Be watchful!" or "Watch!" While we are to watch for Christ's Second Coming, that future can be elusive for us. What is immediate and manageable is to watch for Christ's coming *now* into our midst. Being watchful and alert for the Second Coming is not enough; we must consciously seek to identify Christ already present *now.* If we are proactively watching for everyday encounters with Christ, he will surely not find us "sleeping," neither now nor when he returns. The Second Coming becomes real for us in our encounters with Christ in the here and now. Christ's glory becomes real for us in our encounter with Christ in the here and now.

Our watching for Christ's coming is heightened by seeing God in the simple, everyday things we do. Our lives often seem to bog down with the endless "sameness" of things. We spend Advent in the time and place we always live, and we still can find Christ anew because he is ever making us anew. When we encounter Christ, we actually encounter who we are now and who we are becoming. The work of Advent is to "Be watchful!" so that we grow in being Christ's Presence for others.

Living the Paschal Mystery

We are the servants left in charge; we are the ones who watch and wait for the master's return. The gospel illustrates for us *how* we are to be during our watching: we are not only to watch *for* Christ, but we *watch Christ*. From him we learn how to reach out to others. Our work is futile when it serves our own ends; it is fruitful when it manifests the very work the Son came to do—bring justice and peace to a weary world. Only by encountering Christ and opening ourselves to his goodness is our weariness soothed, our energy quickened, and our lives expressed in the joy of the Word being made flesh today in us.

Focusing the Gospel

Key words and phrases: Be watchful!, the lord . . . is coming, find you sleeping, Watch!

To the point: Four times in this gospel Christ commands us, "Be watchful!" or "Watch!" While we are to watch for Christ's Second Coming, we also need to watch for Christ's coming *now* into our midst. Being watchful and alert for the Second Coming is not enough; we must consciously seek to identify Christ already present *now.* If we are proactively watching for everyday encounters with Christ, he will surely not find us "sleeping."

Connecting the Gospel

to the first reading: Israel stumbles when they do not actively seek the Lord and keep his commands. Instead of blaming God for letting them wander and have hard hearts, they needed to open their ears and eyes to recognize the great deeds God was doing "for those who wait for him."

to experience: Most of us know what it feels like to be groggy and unalert when we wake up in the morning. It takes a cup of coffee, a hot shower, or a brisk run to fully wake us up. We will be groggy about watching for the Second Coming if we have not fully woken up to Christ's invigorating presence to us now.

Connecting the Responsorial Psalm

to the readings: Psalm 80 was written at a time when Israel had suffered devastating defeat at the hands of an enemy. Their homeland lay in ruins, their way of life destroyed. In anguish they cried out to God who had called them into existence as a people. Part of their cry concerned the person of the king—the "man of your right hand" of verse 18—who embodied God's presence among them and care for them. Restoring the king's strength would restore their identity and way of life as God's chosen people.

The psalm indicates Israel's sense of complicity in their own destruction. In numerous ways they had withdrawn from God; God had merely "delivered [them] up to [their] guilt" (first reading). Yet Israel holds God accountable for their salvation: "make us turn to you," they cry, "and we will be saved." As we pray these verses this Sunday, we need to reflect on how this psalm is our call from our own time and situation. How have we wandered from God's ways (first reading)? How are we in need of redemption? The second reading reminds us the redemption we seek has been given to us in Christ. Like gatekeepers, we must watch diligently for Christ's return (gospel); when we see his face, we will know new life (psalm).

to psalmist preparation: As you prepare to sing this psalm, pray about where in your life you need God to turn you around so that you may see God's face more clearly. How have you wandered from God's ways? What is God doing to bring you back? How is turning back to God part of the work of Advent?

**ASSEMBLY &
FAITH-SHARING GROUPS**
- Christ's Second Coming means to me . . . I watch for it best when . . .
- I find myself truly alert to Christ's Presence now when I . . .
- What helps me recognize Christ's Presence in everyday encounters is . . .

PRESIDERS
When I preside at liturgy, I am best able to recognize Christ's Presence in the word when I . . . in the assembly when I . . . in myself when I . . .

DEACONS
I encounter the Presence of Christ in those I serve when I . . . They encounter Christ in me when . . .

HOSPITALITY MINISTERS
My greeting helps those who come to liturgy be watchful and alert for Christ among us when . . .

MUSIC MINISTERS
When I recognize the Presence of Christ in my daily living, my music making becomes . . .

ALTAR MINISTERS
The manner of my serving at the altar promotes the assembly's discerning Christ's many comings during liturgy when I . . .

LECTORS
My proclamation alerts the assembly to the coming of the Lord when . . .

**EXTRAORDINARY MINISTERS
OF HOLY COMMUNION**
The face of each communicant renews my hope in the coming of the Lord by . . .

Model Penitential Act

Presider: On this first Sunday of Advent we are reminded to be watchful and alert for Christ's Second Coming in future glory. Let us call to mind when we have failed to be watchful and alert . . . [pause]

Lord Jesus, you will come in glory to gather the faithful: Lord . . .

Christ Jesus, you sit in glory at the right hand of your Father: Christ . . .

Lord Jesus, you call us to be watchful and alert for your many comings: Lord . . .

Homily Points

• Watch the ball! Watch the children! Watch for cars! Phrases such as these reveal that for us human beings, the verb "watch" is never passive. It involves alertness, discernment, judgment, quickness, action. We watch not simply with our eyes, but with our hearts, our very being. This is the kind of watching that Jesus in this gospel commands of us.

• Not knowing when the "lord of the house" will return, the servants in the gospel story must constantly watch for his arrival so that all in his house will be in order. We, too, must have our own house in order when Christ the Lord returns. Then he will not find us sleeping, but prepared for his coming in glory.

• We keep our house in order by staying alert to the many ways Christ comes to us now. For example, Christ comes to us in the person who has hurt us and whom we need to forgive; in the unjust situation we ought to have the courage to address; in the opportunity to turn the children's squabble into a learning moment. We learn to look for Christ in persons and situations where we might never dream of seeing him. We watch not simply with our eyes, but with our hearts, our very being.

Model Universal Prayer (Prayer of the Faithful)

Presider: God desires that we share in Christ's glory when he returns at the Second Coming. Let us make our needs known so that we will be ready.

Response:

Lord, hear our prayer.

Cantor:

we pray to the Lord,

For all members of the Church, may they watch with eagerness for the many comings of Christ into their lives . . . [pause]

For all people of the world, may they receive the salvation that Christ's Second Coming promises . . . [pause]

For the sick, the dying, and all those in need, may they keep watch and wait patiently for Christ's Presence and care . . . [pause]

For all of us gathered here, may we spend Advent watching in ever new ways for the coming of the Lord . . . [pause]

Presider: Ever present God, you sent your Son to show us the glory of the salvation you offer us in him. Hear our prayers and keep us alert during this Advent to be ready for Christ's coming. We ask this through that same Christ our Lord. **Amen.**

COLLECT

Let us pray

Pause for silent prayer

Grant your faithful, we pray, almighty God,
the resolve to run forth to meet your Christ
with righteous deeds at his coming,
so that, gathered at his right hand,
they may be worthy to possess the heavenly Kingdom.
Through our Lord Jesus Christ, your Son,
who lives and reigns with you in the unity of the Holy Spirit,
one God, for ever and ever. **Amen.**

FIRST READING

Isa 63:16b-17, 19b; 64:2-7

You, Lord, are our father,
    our redeemer you are named forever.
Why do you let us wander, O Lord, from your ways,
    and harden our hearts so that we fear you not?
Return for the sake of your servants,
    the tribes of your heritage.
Oh, that you would rend the heavens and come down,
    with the mountains quaking before you,
while you wrought awesome deeds we could not hope for,
    such as they had not heard of from of old.
No ear has ever heard, no eye ever seen,
    any God but you
    doing such deeds for those who wait for him.
Would that you might meet us doing right,
    that we were mindful of you in our ways!
Behold, you are angry, and we are sinful;
    all of us have become like unclean people,
    all our good deeds are like polluted rags;
we have all withered like leaves,
    and our guilt carries us away like the wind.
There is none who calls upon your name,
    who rouses himself to cling to you;
for you have hidden your face from us
    and have delivered us up to our guilt.
Yet, O Lord, you are our father;
    we are the clay and you the potter:
    we are all the work of your hands.

RESPONSORIAL PSALM

Ps 80:2-3, 15-16, 18-19

R͡. (4) Lord, make us turn to you; let us see your face and we shall be saved.

O shepherd of Israel, hearken,
    from your throne upon the cherubim,
        shine forth.
Rouse your power,
    and come to save us.

R͡. Lord, make us turn to you; let us see your face and we shall be saved.

Once again, O LORD of hosts,
    look down from heaven, and see;
take care of this vine,
    and protect what your right hand has
        planted,
        the son of man whom you yourself
            made strong.

R͡. Lord, make us turn to you; let us see your face and we shall be saved.

May your help be with the man of your
        right hand,
    with the son of man whom you yourself
        made strong.
Then we will no more withdraw from you;
    give us new life, and we will call upon
        your name.

R͡. Lord, make us turn to you; let us see your face and we shall be saved.

SECOND READING

1 Cor 1:3-9

Brothers and sisters:
Grace to you and peace from God our
        Father
    and the Lord Jesus Christ.

I give thanks to my God always on your
        account
    for the grace of God bestowed on you in
        Christ Jesus,
    that in him you were enriched in every
        way,
    with all discourse and all knowledge,
    as the testimony to Christ was
        confirmed among you,
    so that you are not lacking in any
        spiritual gift
    as you wait for the revelation of our
        Lord Jesus Christ.
He will keep you firm to the end,
    irreproachable on the day of our Lord
        Jesus Christ.
God is faithful,
    and by him you were called to
        fellowship with his Son,
    Jesus Christ our Lord.

✠ CATECHESIS

About Liturgy

Advent penance: Advent is a time for joyful expectation and waiting for the coming of Christ; and this is true and appropriate. This Sunday's first reading from Isaiah, however, also reminds us that we might not want to do away altogether with the penance that has been traditionally associated with Advent. This reading gives us a context for such penance: Christ's judgment that will accompany his coming at the end of time. We are judged according to how "mindful of [God] in our ways" we are. We are sinners and we must turn our faces to God.

Penance helps us to be mindful of God in our lives and helps us become more pliable so that God, the potter, can truly mold us into God's image and likeness. Advent's penance, then, might be directed toward the discipline of watching for God and being mindful of God at the center of our lives. For example, we might consciously look at the face of others and see an image of Christ. Or we might take five minutes each day and just *stop* all our activity to be aware of God's Presence to us. Or we might take the time to read each day the gospel for the next Sunday and begin to see how it motivates right actions for us to choose during each day.

About Liturgical Music

Service music for Advent: Because Advent is a season of quiet expectation, the service music we sing during these weeks should not be as exuberant as what we will sing during the Christmas season. Yet because Advent is joyful, the music need not have the somberness of a Mass setting sung during Lent. The tone and style of the Advent service music needs to be somewhere in between. Furthermore, we need to sing this setting throughout all of Advent, letting it work with the liturgical prayers, colors, and environment to draw our minds and hearts into the season's spirit of expectation, patience, and hope.

Music suggestions: Despite the popular association of "O Come, O Come, Emmanuel" with the opening of Advent, this ancient hymn actually belongs to the final two weeks of this season when the "O" antiphons, upon which it is based, are sung as part of the church's Evening Prayer. During the first two weeks of Advent the liturgy focuses on Christ's coming as King and Judge at the end of time rather than on his coming as Emmanuel in the Incarnation. He is the "lord of the house" for whose return we are to remain alert and ready (see gospel). Examples of songs to sing this Sunday include "Wake, O Wake and Sleep No Longer" (also titled "Sleepers, Wake!"); "The King Shall Come"; and "The Advent of Our God" (also titled "The Advent of our King"), all of which are found in most resources; "Lift Up Your Heads, You Mighty Gates" (BB, JS3, SS); "Come, Lord, and Tarry Not!" (W4, LMGM2); and "Like a Bird" (W4). "As Servants Working an Estate" (W4), written to accord with this Sunday's gospel, would be a good choice during the preparation of the gifts.

NOVEMBER 30, 2014
FIRST SUNDAY OF ADVENT

SPIRITUALITY

GOSPEL ACCLAMATION
Luke 3:4, 6

℟. Alleluia, alleluia.
Prepare the way of the Lord, make
    straight his paths:
all flesh shall see the salvation of God.
℟. Alleluia, alleluia.

Gospel

Mark 1:1-8; L5B

**The beginning of the gospel of
    Jesus Christ the Son of God.**

As it is written in Isaiah the
    prophet:
*Behold, I am sending my
    messenger ahead of you;
he will prepare your way.
A voice of one crying out in
    the desert:
"Prepare the way of the
    Lord,
    make straight his paths."*
John the Baptist appeared in the desert
    proclaiming a baptism of repentance
        for the forgiveness of sins.
People of the whole Judean countryside
    and all the inhabitants of Jerusalem
    were going out to him
    and were being baptized by him in
        the Jordan River
    as they acknowledged their sins.
John was clothed in camel's hair,
    with a leather belt around his waist.
He fed on locusts and wild honey.
And this is what he proclaimed:
    "One mightier than I is coming after
        me.
I am not worthy to stoop and loosen the
    thongs of his sandals.
I have baptized you with water;
    he will baptize you with the Holy
        Spirit."

Reflecting on the Gospel

We often see old war films showing a scene of two uniformed armed forces personnel ringing the doorbell of an average home, the door is opened, and the woman answering sees the soldiers and immediately swoons. No words are needed for her to know the news is dire. These messengers are doing their duty, but it is not a pleasant one. Other messengers are welcomed with open arms and joy, for example, when the boss's secretary brings out the vacation schedule and the laborer has gotten the vacation time requested or when the child brings home an improved report card to the parents. Still other messengers might leave us wondering, uncertain, searching. In this gospel John is the messenger for "One mightier than I [who] is coming after me." His message was new and startling: "He will baptize you with the Holy Spirit." No doubt John's hearers received his message with wondering, uncertain, searching hearts.

John was a desert ascetic whose mission was to prepare the people for a life-transforming change—the Lord is coming! Who is this Lord? One mightier than John. How so? John announces the nearness of salvation; Jesus *is* the salvation. John baptizes with water, Jesus with the Holy Spirit. What does this mean? Jesus' baptism instills God's very Life through the power of the Holy Spirit within us. Baptism with the Holy Spirit transforms our preparation into fulfillment—the Lord has come!

Here is the key to grasping John's message: by our encountering the Lord, our own wondering, uncertainty, and searching about the meaning of John's message is dispelled. John's humility as depicted in the words of this gospel ("One mightier than I") did not rest in a false sense of his own worth, but instead on his own deep conviction about who Jesus is, a conviction that only could come from his having encountered the One whom he proclaimed. Like John, we too must personally encounter the very One whose messengers we, too, are to be. Encounter with the Lord's Presence opens us to the Spirit with whom we've been baptized, enabling us to have greater clarity about the message and the One whom we proclaim by the quality of our own holy living.

Living the Paschal Mystery

John the Baptist diverted attention from himself to Jesus. His ministry was not about himself but about the "One mightier than I [who] is coming after me." He proclaimed repentance, prepared for Jesus, died—this was the pattern of John's life. Actually, it's the pattern of Jesus' life, too: he proclaimed the Good News, prepared the way to the Father, died. Further, it's the pattern of our own paschal mystery living: proclaim the gospel of repentance, prepare for Christ's many comings, die to ourselves.

Our being baptized "with the Holy Spirit" enables us to do the work of God, for by baptism we are grafted onto Christ. In baptism we become heralds, like John, of Christ's redeeming Presence in our world. By our Christian living (blamelessly and with righteousness) we not only point to Christ, but we also make present the Christ who dwells in us. The challenge of Gospel living is ever to seek encounters with Christ, surrender ourselves to the Holy Spirit, cooperate with the divine Life coursing within us. Once we are armed with this kind of divine Presence and power, then we, too, can be messengers, like John, of the Lord's coming for all we meet in our daily Gospel living.

Focusing the Gospel

Key words and phrases: prepare, One mightier than I, baptized you with water, baptize you with the Holy Spirit

To the point: John was a desert ascetic whose mission was to prepare the people for a life-transforming change—the Lord is coming! Who is this Lord? One mightier than John. How so? John announces the nearness of salvation; Jesus *is* the salvation. John baptizes with water, Jesus with the Holy Spirit. What does this mean? Jesus' baptism instills God's very Life through the power of the Holy Spirit within us. Baptism with the Holy Spirit transforms our preparation into fulfillment—the Lord has come!

Connecting the Gospel

to the second reading: The Spirit with whom Jesus baptizes creates for us "new heavens and a new earth." This is part of the life-transforming change that the Lord's coming makes possible and is already a glimpse of the fulfillment of all things at Christ's Second Coming.

to experience: We spend Advent preparing for the Lord's coming and this is appropriate. But Advent is more than a four-Sunday season; it is a whole way of life. Our baptismal lives are characterized by constant preparing for the assured change in us that every coming of Christ brings.

Connecting the Responsorial Psalm

to the readings: A new day is coming when salvation (psalm) will replace sin and servitude (first reading), when God will come with power (first reading) and peace (psalm). A new person is coming, the One who will baptize with the Holy Spirit (gospel). God's own justice will prepare the way (psalm). But so are we to prepare the way (gospel, first reading). We who have been baptized in the Holy Spirit are to be persons of "holiness and devotion" (second reading) whose manner of living heralds the kindness, peace, truth, and justice (psalm) of the new heavens and new earth we so eagerly await (second reading).

to psalmist preparation: How is this psalm a proclamation of the "new heavens and a new earth" God is promising? How through baptism have you already been made part of this new creation by the Holy Spirit? How can your singing of this psalm both announce what has already happened and call the people to prepare for what is yet to come?

ASSEMBLY & FAITH-SHARING GROUPS
- What I need to make straight in my life to prepare the way of the Lord is . . . This changes my life by . . .
- The Lord for me is . . . This Advent I hope to learn that . . .
- The Holy Spirit within me prepares me for . . . moves me to . . . changes me by . . .

PRESIDERS
I am John the Baptist preparing the way of the Lord for others when I . . .

DEACONS
My service to others announces the coming of the Lord when I . . .

HOSPITALITY MINISTERS
When I call to mind that the Holy Spirit dwells within each of those gathering for liturgy, my manner of greeting them looks like . . .

MUSIC MINISTERS
My music making is a pathway to the Lord for me and for others when I . . .

ALTAR MINISTERS
My attentiveness to the details of liturgy witnesses to how I am preparing for the coming of the Lord in that . . .

LECTORS
The manner of my proclamation prepares the assembly to encounter the Word when I . . .

EXTRAORDINARY MINISTERS OF HOLY COMMUNION
My distribution of Holy Communion participates in the coming of "new heavens and a new earth" because . . .

Model Penitential Act

Presider: In the gospel John the Baptist announces that we must prepare for the One coming who will baptize us with the Holy Spirit. Let us examine how well we have lived our baptism this week and allowed the Holy Spirit to change our lives . . . [pause]

Lord Jesus, you come to bring us salvation: Lord . . .

Christ Jesus, you came to baptize us with the Spirit: Christ . . .

Lord Jesus, you will come in the fullness of time in eternal glory: Lord . . .

Homily Points

• What we are expecting radically affects how we prepare. A couple expecting a new baby, for example, prepares a nursery. A family expecting to go on a vacation prepares reservations, clothing, the car. A child expecting the first day of school prepares pencils, notebooks, backpack. The preparation matches the expectation. No matter what our preparation, however, the coming of the Lord always exceeds our expectation.

• John the Baptist is telling the people that the One who is coming will exceed their expectation. He will be mightier than John because he will baptize with the Holy Spirit; his coming will initiate unprecedented, life-transforming change.

• During this Advent are we primarily preparing ourselves for life-transforming change or merely preparing to celebrate a secular Christmas? What are our expectations? How does John the Baptist challenge us with a new set of expectations? Who helps us listen to John and respond? What prepares us to open ourselves to respond more fully to the Spirit with whom we have been baptized? Do our responses show that we know our expectations will be exceeded? What really prepares us for the changes the coming of the Lord will bring into our lives?

Model Universal Prayer (Prayer of the Faithful)

Presider: God always exceeds our expectations when God reaches out to us. So we are confident to make our needs known to such a good God.

Response:

Lord,————— hear our prayer.

Cantor:

we pray to the Lord,

That all members of the Body of Christ hear the challenge of John the Baptist to prepare for the life-transforming changes the coming of the Lord brings . . . [pause]

That all peoples of the world open themselves to the salvation God offers . . . [pause]

That the poor, the lonely, and the homeless experience the coming of Christ through the comfort and care offered by others . . . [pause]

That all of us here present expand our expectation of what the coming of the Lord will bring us . . . [pause]

Presider: O God who sent your divine Son for our salvation, we humbly beg you to hear these prayers and grant what we need to come to fullness of Life with you. We ask this through your Son Jesus Christ. **Amen.**

COLLECT

Let us pray

Pause for silent prayer

Almighty and merciful God,
may no earthly undertaking hinder those
who set out in haste to meet your Son,
but may our learning of heavenly wisdom
gain us admittance to his company.
Who lives and reigns with you in the unity
     of the Holy Spirit,
one God, for ever and ever. **Amen.**

FIRST READING

Is 40:1-5, 9-11

Comfort, give comfort to my people,
     says your God.
Speak tenderly to Jerusalem, and proclaim
     to her
     that her service is at an end,
     her guilt is expiated;
indeed, she has received from the hand of
     the LORD
     double for all her sins.

     A voice cries out:
In the desert prepare the way of the LORD!
     Make straight in the wasteland a
          highway for our God!
Every valley shall be filled in,
     every mountain and hill shall be made
          low;
the rugged land shall be made a plain,
     the rough country, a broad valley.
Then the glory of the LORD shall be revealed,
     and all people shall see it together;
     for the mouth of the LORD has spoken.

Go up onto a high mountain,
     Zion, herald of glad tidings;
cry out at the top of your voice,
     Jerusalem, herald of good news!
Fear not to cry out
     and say to the cities of Judah:
     Here is your God!
Here comes with power
     the Lord GOD,
     who rules by his strong arm;
here is his reward with him,
     his recompense before him.
Like a shepherd he feeds his flock;
     in his arms he gathers the lambs,
carrying them in his bosom,
     and leading the ewes with care.

RESPONSORIAL PSALM
Ps 85:9-10, 11-12, 13-14

℟. (8) Lord, let us see your kindness, and grant us your salvation.

I will hear what God proclaims;
  the LORD—for he proclaims peace to his
      people.
Near indeed is his salvation to those who
      fear him,
  glory dwelling in our land.

℟. Lord, let us see your kindness, and grant us your salvation.

Kindness and truth shall meet;
  justice and peace shall kiss.
Truth shall spring out of the earth,
  and justice shall look down from heaven.

℟. Lord, let us see your kindness, and grant us your salvation.

The LORD himself will give his benefits;
  our land shall yield its increase.
Justice shall walk before him,
  and prepare the way of his steps.

℟. Lord, let us see your kindness, and grant us your salvation.

SECOND READING
2 Pet 3:8-14

Do not ignore this one fact, beloved,
    that with the Lord one day is like a
        thousand years
    and a thousand years like one day.
The Lord does not delay his promise, as
        some regard "delay,"
    but he is patient with you,
    not wishing that any should perish
    but that all should come to repentance.
But the day of the Lord will come like a
        thief,
    and then the heavens will pass away
        with a mighty roar
    and the elements will be dissolved by fire,
    and the earth and everything done on it
        will be found out.

Since everything is to be dissolved in this
        way,
    what sort of persons ought you to be,
    conducting yourselves in holiness and
        devotion,
    waiting for and hastening the coming
        of the day of God,
    because of which the heavens will be
        dissolved in flames
    and the elements melted by fire.
But according to his promise
    we await new heavens and a new earth
    in which righteousness dwells.
Therefore, beloved, since you await these
        things,
    be eager to be found without spot or
        blemish before him, at peace.

☩ CATECHESIS

About Liturgy

The structure of the Lectionary: The Lectionary selections this Sunday offer a good opportunity to reflect on how this important liturgical book was put together. The gospels were selected first, arranged in a three-year cycle with each year focusing on either Matthew, Mark, or Luke (especially evident during Ordinary Time when one of these gospels is read semi-continuously; this year we read from Mark). Rather than having its own year, the Gospel of John is read during key liturgical times such as during the Easter season and in Ordinary Time from the seventeenth to twenty-first Sundays in Year B (this year).

Once the gospels were assigned, then the first readings were chosen to relate to the gospel and they are mostly taken from the Old Testament (a notable exception is during the Sundays of Easter when the first reading is taken from the Acts of the Apostles). During the festal seasons (such as now, during Advent) the second reading is also specially selected to relate to the other two readings, but during Ordinary Time the second reading stands on its own as a semi-continuous reading of one of the New Testament letters over several Sundays. The second reading for this second Sunday of Advent is especially important because it points to the eschatological theme that is notable during the first two weeks of Advent.

Advent and Christ's comings: "Eschatological" is a term that derives from two Greek terms meaning the word of (or science of) the end times. Specifically, it refers to the final fulfillment of all things that will take place at Christ's coming at the end of time, a motif during the last part of the liturgical year and during the first part of Advent. Advent actually celebrates three comings of Christ. Christ's first coming took place in the past (over two thousand years ago!) and celebrates his coming in history. Christ's second coming will take place only in the future and celebrates his coming in final glory (this is the eschatological coming we mentioned above). And, finally, Christ's coming in sacraments takes place in the present and celebrates his coming in mystery.

About Liturgical Music

Music suggestions: On this second Sunday of Advent when we hear the cry of John the Baptist in the desert, "On Jordan's Bank" (found in most resources) is certainly an appropriate entrance song, as is Stephen Pishner's "Prepare! Prepare!" with cantored verses and ostinato refrain (G3). Another excellent entrance song would be Kenneth W. Louis's "Prepare Ye the Way of the Lord" (LMGM2). Michael Joncas's "A Voice Cries Out" (BB, JS3) would work well for the Communion procession, with cantor or choir singing the verses. "Comfort, Comfort, O My People" (found in most resources) relates directly to the first reading and would make a good choice during the preparation of the gifts.

It is important to keep singing songs related to Christ's Second Coming on this Sunday. In addition to suggestions given last Sunday, further examples include "Soon and Very Soon" (found in most resources); "Alleluia! Hurry the Lord Is Near" (BB); and, for Communion, "Jesus, Hope of the World" (WC, WS) with its assembly refrain and call-and-response verses.

DECEMBER 7, 2014
SECOND SUNDAY OF ADVENT

SPIRITUALITY

GOSPEL ACCLAMATION
cf. Luke 1:28

R︎⃫. Alleluia, alleluia.
Hail, Mary, full of grace, the Lord is with you;
blessed are you among women.
R︎⃫. Alleluia, alleluia.

Gospel Luke 1:26-38; L689

The angel Gabriel was sent
    from God
    to a town of Galilee
        called Nazareth,
    to a virgin betrothed to a
        man named Joseph,
    of the house of David,
    and the virgin's name
        was Mary.
And coming to her, he
    said,
    "Hail, full of grace! The
        Lord is with you."
But she was greatly
    troubled at what was
    said
and pondered what sort
    of greeting this might be.
Then the angel said to her,
    "Do not be afraid, Mary,
    for you have found favor with God.
Behold, you will conceive in your womb and
    bear a son,
    and you shall name him Jesus.
He will be great and will be called Son of
    the Most High,
    and the Lord God will give him the throne
        of David his father,
    and he will rule over the house of Jacob
        forever,
    and of his Kingdom there will be no end."

Continued in Appendix A, p. 261.

See Appendix A, p. 261, for the other readings.

FIRST READING
Gen 3:9-15, 20

RESPONSORIAL PSALM
Ps 98:1, 2-3, 3-4

SECOND READING
Eph 1:3-6, 11-12

Reflecting on the Gospel

Sometimes we might be asked to help a friend, and a yes pops out of our mouth before we even think. Later as we write the commitment on our calendar, we might chide ourselves: I'm too busy, I don't have the right skills, I'm afraid I won't meet my friend's expectations. Yet, seldom, if ever, do we call and cancel out. Our yes pops out because of the good and deep relationship we have with our friend, because of a history of being and doing for each other, because of a built-up generosity toward the other. If we would say no, the friend would understand and accept. However, when we say yes the friendship grows and the ease of relationship blossoms even more. These kinds of deep relationships only build over much time and commitment and mutuality. In this feast day's gospel, Mary says yes to the most singular request ever made to a human being. It was not an easy yes. But it was borne out of her relationship with God that had built up over much time and commitment and mutuality.

In Gabriel's address to Mary, the archangel announces what is at the heart of this feast day: "Hail, full of grace! The Lord is with you." Even before assenting to conceiving Jesus by the Holy Spirit, Mary had made "May it be done to me" the abiding habit of her way of relating to God and choosing to do God's will. The relationship between Mary and God had grown all her life to the point where her yes was simply the natural thing for her to do. It didn't take thinking; it was an answer of the heart. When we make choosing to do God's will the abiding habit of our own lives, then like Mary we, too, are filled with God's grace and we, too, bear the Life of the Lord within us.

Rather than shy from God's Presence, Mary welcomed it with her yes. Her emptiness as a virgin is filled by her acceptance of the Lord's coming to her, and a whole new in-breaking of God's Presence happens—of which we receive the inestimable fruits. Surely "nothing [is] impossible for God"! God is present to us and within us just as surely as God was present to and within Mary. No wonder we join with the psalmist and "[s]ing to the Lord a new song, for he has done marvelous deeds."

Living the Paschal Mystery

This is what it looks like when God comes: like Mary, we are surprised; our emptiness (barrenness) is filled; the Holy Spirit overshadows us; our own lifetime habit of yes to God pops out from us and with ease when we have practiced our yes over and over in our daily living. As with Mary, God's coming and our yes to it changes us for life.

The gospels say little about Mary: she bore and gave birth to the Messiah, she was the mother who helped him grow in wisdom and grace, she was with him during his ministry, she stood at the foot of the cross when he was dying. Yet this is enough to know that Mary's yes to God carried far beyond the initial events of conception and birth. Her own everyday living bore out her continual living in and openness to God's Presence. So it is with us. Our everyday living must proclaim that God is present to us and fills us. "How can this be?" Because we are blessed in Christ, adopted as God's own children, chosen, and destined to exist "for the praise of his glory" (second reading). The effect of God's Presence to us is just as astounding as God's coming to Mary. All we need to do is *believe* that we, too, are extended God's fullness of grace. We are faithful to that grace when we say yes to God's will in our everyday lives.

Focusing the Gospel

Key words and phrases: Hail, full of grace! The Lord is with you; conceive in your womb; The Holy Spirit will come upon you; May it be done to me

To the point: In Gabriel's address to Mary, the archangel announces what is at the heart of this feast day: "Hail, full of grace! The Lord is with you." Even before assenting to conceiving Jesus by the Holy Spirit, Mary had made "May it be done to me" the abiding habit of her way of relating to God and choosing to do God's will. When we make choosing to do God's will the abiding habit of our own lives, then like Mary we, too, are filled with God's grace and we, too, bear the Life of the Lord within us.

Model Penitential Act

Presider: Mary was conceived without sin, remained sinless her whole life, and bore Christ our Lord within her. Let us ask God to forgive our sins and make us pure and holy . . . [pause]

Lord Jesus, you are the holy One, the Son of God: Lord . . .

Christ Jesus, you call us to be holy and without blemish before God: Christ . . .

Lord Jesus, you gave us your mother Mary as a model of holiness: Lord . . .

Model Universal Prayer (Prayer of the Faithful)

Presider: God calls us to holiness and gives us what we need to follow his will. And so we make our needs known.

Response:

Lord, hear our prayer.

Cantor:

we pray to the Lord,

That all members of the church imitate Mary's abiding habit of saying yes to whatever Gods asks . . . [pause]

That all people in the world choose to do good and come to the holiness that brings salvation . . . [pause]

That the sick and the dying be comforted by Mother Mary's gentle presence and care . . . [pause]

That all of us gathered here recognize we, too, have found favor with God and witness to this gift by the goodness of our lives . . . [pause]

Presider: Loving God, you called us from the foundation of the world to be holy and blameless in your sight: hear these our prayers that we may remain faithful to this call. We pray through Christ our Lord. **Amen.**

COLLECT

Let us pray

Pause for silent prayer

O God, who by the Immaculate Conception
    of the Blessed Virgin
prepared a worthy dwelling for your Son,
grant, we pray,
that, as you preserved her from every stain
by virtue of the Death of your Son, which
    you foresaw,
so, through her intercession,
we, too, may be cleansed and admitted to
    your presence.
Through our Lord Jesus Christ, your Son,
who lives and reigns with you in the unity
    of the Holy Spirit,
one God, for ever and ever. **Amen.**

FOR REFLECTION

• It is easy for me to say to God "May it be done to me" when . . . It is difficult when . . .

• I realize doing God's will is becoming an abiding habit in me because . . .

• I am aware of God's grace working in me when . . .

Homily Points

• Until something becomes a habit, it can be difficult, challenging, awkward, take much thought and time. For example, a child tries and tries again to learn to tie shoes. When first learning to drive a car, we over-steer, accelerate too quickly and brake too hard, turn corners short or wide. Only perseverance and practice develop within us the skills needed to do these things with ease and grace. The same dynamic of habit formation is essential for us to grow more faithful in doing God's will.

• Mary's yes to God is not a new utterance for her. She could say yes to Gabriel's announcement because she had been saying yes to God's every request all of her life. This is why we celebrate this feast: to honor her fidelity and to hold her up as our model for grace and holiness.

SPIRITUALITY

GOSPEL ACCLAMATION
Isa 61:1 (cited in Luke 4:18)

R̸. Alleluia, alleluia.
The Spirit of the Lord is upon me,
because he has anointed me
to bring glad tidings to the poor.
R̸. Alleluia, alleluia.

Gospel John 1:6-8, 19-28; L8B

A man named John was sent from
    God.
He came for testimony, to testify to
    the light,
  so that all might believe through
    him.
He was not the light,
  but came to testify to the light.

And this is the testimony of John.
When the Jews from Jerusalem sent
    priests and Levites to him
  to ask him, "Who are you?"
  he admitted and did not deny it,
  but admitted, "I am not the Christ."
So they asked him,
  "What are you then? Are you Elijah?"
And he said, "I am not."
"Are you the Prophet?"
He answered, "No."
So they said to him,
  "Who are you, so we can give an answer
    to those who sent us?
What do you have to say for yourself?"
He said:
  "I am *the voice of one crying out in the
    desert,*
  make straight the way of the Lord,
  as Isaiah the prophet said."
Some Pharisees were also sent.
They asked him,
  "Why then do you baptize
  if you are not the Christ or Elijah or the
    Prophet?"
John answered them,
  "I baptize with water;
  but there is one among you whom you do
    not recognize,
  the one who is coming after me,
  whose sandal strap I am not worthy to
    untie."
This happened in Bethany across the Jordan,
  where John was baptizing.

Reflecting on the Gospel

Parents know the different cries of their baby: whether it's a cry of discomfort, hunger, anger. The very sound of the baby's cry includes something of the baby's experience and need. Though not able to speak words yet, the baby nevertheless is quite capable of communicating, and good parents are ever attuned to this constant and revealing self-information that helps them give comfort and security to their little bundle of love. Advent calls us to be ever attuned to the cries around us that testify to the Light come into our midst and that challenge us to encounter Christ in such a way that we cannot hold within ourselves our own cries of recognition and commitment.

After saying clearly who he is not ("Christ or Elijah or the Prophet"), John does say who he is: "I am the voice of one crying out in the desert." "Voice": the audible revelation of self. "Crying out": testifying to core convictions. "Desert": place of barrenness and desolation as well as a place of testing and growth. So who is John? The one who in his very being recognizes the Christ who has come to lead the people into the fullness of light and Life.

Testifying with conviction to the light of Christ must be more than speaking words; the conviction is conveyed—cried out—by the way we choose to live each day. We are to do good works ("bring glad tidings to the poor," "heal the brokenhearted," etc.; first reading). Testifying with conviction also means that we must constantly grow in our relationship to Christ and learn to recognize him even where we might not expect to find him. Yes, sometimes we are like the people in the gospel in that we seek the Messiah but often do not recognize his Presence in our midst. The work of Advent is to intensify our good works so that we become attuned to recognizing Christ here and now; even more, it is the work of our whole Christian lives. As we near the celebration of Christmas, we ourselves must take up John's conviction, John's cry.

Living the Paschal Mystery

Testifying with conviction comes to greater fullness when we have been tried in the various "deserts" of our daily living. Testing confronts us with choices, and making good choices attunes us to Christ's Presence to us in so many ways. This testing brings us growth and liveliness. It helps us see in new ways and cry out with ever greater urgency. What is at stake is recognition of the Messiah-Christ among us.

It's easy and comfortable to recognize Christ in the expected places and ways. When we enter the peace of a church, for example, we expect to find God. When we sit and pray in our homes, we expect to find God and have our prayers answered. All this is good. However, living the paschal mystery means that we take up the mission of Christ ourselves, that we ourselves are to be Christ for others. Especially during these final days before Christmas when everyone is so busy, we can forget that our mission is like John's: to testify to the Light by crying out its Presence in our midst. We do this by how we respond to those around us: take time to listen to the one hurting, visit those who might be forgotten, do with a little less ourselves so others might have more, take time to pray, remember to give thanks, offer a helping hand, reorganize our priorities, praise the God in others.

Focusing the Gospel

Key words and phrases: light, I am the voice of one crying out in the desert, one among you . . . recognize

To the point: After saying clearly who he is not ("Christ or Elijah or the Prophet"), John does say who he is: "I am the voice of one crying out in the desert." "Voice": the audible revelation of self. "Crying out": testifying to core convictions. "Desert": place of barrenness and desolation as well as a place of testing and growth. So who is John? The one who in his very being recognizes the Christ who has come to lead the people into the fullness of light and Life. As we near the celebration of Christmas, we ourselves must take up John's conviction, John's cry.

Connecting the Gospel

to the second reading: Paul admonishes the Thessalonians to "Test everything; retain what is good." Our entire lives are a "desert" where, in the Spirit, we sort out who we are and how we are; we discern what is of the light and what is of darkness.

to experience: We often cry out when we feel pain, are overwhelmed by fear, are overjoyed at a ball game. These are instinctive utterances. To cry out with conviction that Christ the Messiah has come and is in our midst, however, is a conscious choice rooted in our encounters with him.

Connecting the Responsorial Psalm

to the readings: This Sunday's responsorial psalm is taken from the *Magnificat,* Mary's hymn of praise for what God is doing for her and for all people. Mary testifies to the Presence and activity of God within her and within the world. What she sees God doing is concrete: the lowly are being lifted up, the hungry are being filled, mercy is being granted. Like John the Baptist, Mary knew who she was (God's "lowly servant") and who God was (the Almighty who does "great things"). She cannot hold herself back from proclaiming what she knows. She must announce the "glad tidings" of salvation (first reading). As we sing her song, we, too, proclaim who God is and what God is doing. We, too, rejoice in announcing salvation.

to psalmist preparation: As you sing these verses from the *Magnificat,* Mary's words become your words. With Mary, you take up the mission of John the Baptist (gospel) and of Isaiah (first reading). You announce the coming of the Savior and the presence of salvation. How do you believe and live what you announce?

**ASSEMBLY &
FAITH-SHARING GROUPS**
- My "voice," the audible revelation of myself, sounds like . . .
- What brings me to cry out is . . . What brings me to cry out my conviction about Christ is . . .
- The "desert" of my life looks like . . . has led me to . . .

PRESIDERS
I meet my community in the desert when . . . I lead my community out of the desert when . . .

DEACONS
My serving ministry testifies to my belief that Christ is the light of the world when I . . .

HOSPITALITY MINISTERS
The kind of greeting that gives testimony to Christ's Presence among us is . . .

MUSIC MINISTERS
My "voice" reveals the Presence of Christ in my own life when . . . My "voice" reveals that I see Christ in the assembly when . . .

ALTAR MINISTERS
The reverence with which I serve at the altar testifies to my recognition and love of Christ in that . . .

LECTORS
Like John the Baptist, I testify to Christ through public proclamation; what helps me internalize this proclamation more is . . .

**EXTRAORDINARY MINISTERS
OF HOLY COMMUNION**
Those who come to receive Holy Communion testify for me to the Presence of Christ in that . . .

Model Penitential Act

Presider: We hear in today's gospel how clearly John understood himself to be the voice testifying to Christ, the light. For the times when we have failed to be the voice testifying to Christ, let us ask for God's mercy . . . [pause]

Lord Jesus, you are the Light come into our midst: Lord . . .

Christ Jesus, you are the Messiah who comes to save us: Christ . . .

Lord Jesus, you are the One who straightens our path to eternal Life: Lord . . .

Homily Points

• Crying out with conviction can take many forms. Some, such as Martin Luther King Jr., use their voices in effective and powerful ways. Others, such as Rosa Parks, speak through quiet action. Still others, such as the cloistered Thomas Merton, convey conviction through the written word. The manner of crying out is not as important as the conviction behind it.

• John's manner of crying out was direct, bold, courageous, clear, challenging, and effective. His conviction was grounded in the person of the Christ to whom he gave testimony. This conviction was the fruit of his own years of being tested in the desert.

• The "deserts" of our own lives are opportunities testing us and leading us to deeper conviction about who Christ is. For example, the "desert" of a long, debilitating illness tests our trust in God's Presence and care. The "desert" of a failed relationship tests our understanding of love and fidelity, and our willingness to forgive. The "desert" of unemployment and financial stress tests our priorities and values and our willingness to depend on God. Such testing shapes our convictions, helps us encounter Christ in our daily living, and enables us to testify to him with greater authenticity.

Model Universal Prayer (Prayer of the Faithful)

Presider: With the conviction that we will be heard, let us cry out to God for our needs.

Response:
Lord, hear our prayer.

Cantor:
we pray to the Lord,

For all members of the church to grow in their conviction that Christ is the Light of the world and testify to his saving power . . . [pause]

For all peoples of the world to come to the light of salvation . . . [pause]

For those suffering in any way to be comforted and encouraged by the Presence of Christ coming to them through the care of others . . . [pause]

For each of us here to prepare for Christmas by being voices crying out that Christ is among us . . . [pause]

Presider: O God, you hear the prayers of those who cry out to you: hear our prayers, increase our conviction about the saving power of your divine Son, and lead us to testify to his Presence and Life. Who lives and reigns for ever and ever. **Amen.**

Let us pray

Pause for silent prayer

O God, who see how your people
faithfully await the feast of the Lord's
    Nativity,
enable us, we pray,
to attain the joys of so great a salvation
and to celebrate them always
with solemn worship and glad rejoicing.
Through our Lord Jesus Christ, your Son,
who lives and reigns with you in the unity
    of the Holy Spirit,
one God, for ever and ever. **Amen.**

FIRST READING
Isa 61:1-2a, 10-11

The spirit of the Lord God is upon me,
    because the Lord has anointed me;
he has sent me to bring glad tidings to the
      poor,
    to heal the brokenhearted,
to proclaim liberty to the captives
    and release to the prisoners,
to announce a year of favor from the Lord
    and a day of vindication by our God.

I rejoice heartily in the Lord,
    in my God is the joy of my soul;
for he has clothed me with a robe of
      salvation
    and wrapped me in a mantle of justice,
like a bridegroom adorned with a diadem,
    like a bride bedecked with her jewels.
As the earth brings forth its plants,
    and a garden makes its growth spring
      up,
so will the Lord God make justice and
      praise
    spring up before all the nations.

RESPONSORIAL PSALM
Luke 1:46-48, 49-50, 53-54

℟. (Isa 61:10b) My soul rejoices in my God.

My soul proclaims the greatness of the
  Lord;
  my spirit rejoices in God my Savior,
for he has looked upon his lowly servant.
  From this day all generations will call
  me blessed:

℟. My soul rejoices in my God.

the Almighty has done great things for
  me,
  and holy is his Name.
He has mercy on those who fear him
  in every generation.

℟. My soul rejoices in my God.

He has filled the hungry with good things,
  and the rich he has sent away empty.
He has come to the help of his servant
  Israel
  for he has remembered his promise of
  mercy.

℟. My soul rejoices in my God.

SECOND READING
1 Thess 5:16-24

Brothers and sisters:
Rejoice always. Pray without ceasing.
In all circumstances give thanks,
  for this is the will of God for you in
  Christ Jesus.
Do not quench the Spirit.
Do not despise prophetic utterances.
Test everything; retain what is good.
Refrain from every kind of evil.

May the God of peace make you perfectly
  holy
  and may you entirely, spirit, soul, and
  body,
  be preserved blameless for the coming
  of our Lord Jesus Christ.
The one who calls you is faithful,
  and he will also accomplish it.

About Liturgy

Liturgy's link with right living: Christmas is one time of the year when charitable giving is very high. Many families, for example, limit or eliminate altogether their gift exchange and collect the saved money to give to a family in need or to some worthy cause. All of this is very good and laudable, but the first reading challenges us further and reminds us particularly of two things.

First, our charity isn't something that might happen once a year. Charity—genuine caring for others—aptly describes our Christian living. It is something that we must pay attention to every day; we are "anointed" to do good works. Second, our just acts on behalf of others less fortunate than ourselves are clearly linked both to being "clothed . . . with . . . salvation" (first reading) and to the praise of God.

To state this liturgically: liturgy and right living are inextricably linked. The reason for this link rests not only in our intimate relationship with God—which liturgy celebrates in praise and thanksgiving—but also because of our intimate relationship with each other. In liturgy we come together and manifest the Body of Christ; as members we are joined one to another. When one part of the Body hurts, the whole Body hurts. Thus it is only right and just that we do whatever we can to "bring glad tidings to the poor, to heal the brokenhearted, to proclaim liberty to the captives and release to the prisoners" (first reading).

Gaudete *Sunday:* Traditionally the Third Sunday of Advent is called *gaudete* (rejoice) Sunday. The rose vestments for this day are still an option, but since we have a different understanding of Advent (it is not simply about penance with today being a day of rejoicing because we are halfway through the season) it is probably best to retain the royal purple color of Advent for this Sunday. True, penance is appropriate for Advent, but this penance has a different meaning from the penance of Lent; during Advent the reason for penance is as preparation for the final judgment (especially prominent during the first two weeks of Advent).

About Liturgical Music

Music suggestions: The past two Sundays of Advent have kept our eyes looking toward the Second Coming of Christ at the end of time. This Sunday turns our focus toward Christ whose birth as a babe we commemorate on Christmas. This is the Sunday to begin singing "O Come, O Come, Emmanuel." Since this is *gaudete* Sunday, "Awake! Awake, and Greet the New Morn" (found in most resources) would make an appropriate song either at the entrance or after Communion. "O Come, Divine Messiah" (found in most resources) would be suitable at the preparation of the gifts or as the recessional song. Deanna Light and Paul Tate's "Come, Emmanuel" (WC, WS) with its call-response verses would work well for either the entrance or the Communion procession. James Quinn's "O Child of Promise, Come!" (SS) would be suitable during the preparation of the gifts. Other well-known Advent songs which prepare us for the coming of the Christ Child include "Come, O Long Expected [Long-Awaited] Jesus"; "Creator of the Stars of Night"; and "People, Look East."

SPIRITUALITY

GOSPEL ACCLAMATION
Luke 1:38

R͞. Alleluia, alleluia.
Behold, I am the handmaid of the Lord.
May it be done to me according to your word.
R͞. Alleluia, alleluia.

Gospel   Luke 1:26-38; L11B

The angel Gabriel was sent from God
    to a town of Galilee called Nazareth,
    to a virgin betrothed to a man named
        Joseph,
    of the house of David,
    and the virgin's name was Mary.
And coming to her, he said,
    "Hail, full of grace! The Lord is with
        you."
But she was greatly troubled at what was
        said
    and pondered what sort of greeting
        this might be.
Then the angel said to her,
    "Do not be afraid, Mary,
    for you have found favor with God.

"Behold, you will conceive in your womb
        and bear a son,
    and you shall name him Jesus.
He will be great and will be called Son of
        the Most High,
    and the Lord God will give him the throne
        of David his father,
    and he will rule over the house of Jacob
        forever,
    and of his kingdom there will be no end."
But Mary said to the angel,
    "How can this be,
    since I have no relations with a man?"
And the angel said to her in reply,
    "The Holy Spirit will come upon you,
    and the power of the Most High will
        overshadow you.
Therefore the child to be born
    will be called holy, the Son of God.
And behold, Elizabeth, your relative,
    has also conceived a son in her old age,
    and this is the sixth month for her who
        was called barren;
    for nothing will be impossible for God."
Mary said, "Behold, I am the handmaid of
        the Lord.
May it be done to me according to your word."
Then the angel departed from her.

Reflecting on the Gospel

This gospel from Luke is so very familiar to us. In fact, we just heard it a couple of weeks ago on December 8, the solemnity of the Immaculate Conception of the Blessed Virgin Mary. On that day we interpreted the gospel within the context of the feast day, and focused on Mary's holiness as announced by Gabriel's greeting of her: "Hail, full of grace! The Lord is with you." Now, on the Fourth Sunday of Advent when we hear this gospel proclaimed again, we are drawn particularly to Gabriel's annunciation that Mary would, by the power of the Holy Spirit, "conceive in [her] womb and bear a son."

Conception to birth: a time of waiting and anticipation, nurturing life and protecting it, preparing and hoping. Can we not imagine Mary and Joseph quietly sitting together during these wonderful months of pregnancy, wondering about this great mystery, putting their hands on Mary's body and feeling "the child to be born" stirring in her womb? Each kick that a mother (and father) feels in the womb is an annunciation of life. Each movement is an annunciation of life eagerly bursting to come forth. In Mary's womb, the Life stirring is the author of life and salvation, the very "Son of God," announcing that a new in-breaking of God is happening.

God's whole plan of salvation is a perpetual annunciation. In this gospel, there are numerous "annunciations" beyond Gabriel's revealing to Mary that she would conceive "the Son of God." Gabriel makes known that Mary is holy; that the child shall be named Jesus; that the kingdom of this Child would have no end; that this Child is "holy, the Son of God"; that Elizabeth has conceived; that "nothing will be impossible for God"; and that Mary is God's faithful and obedient handmaid. Indeed, perpetual annunciation is God's pattern of relating to us. How do we, then, relate to God? We do so by responding with a yes to God's annunciations in our own lives. God chooses to be known to us, names us holy, and desires that we be filled with God's Life. Our response, like Mary's, must be one of openness and full-throated yes to whatever God asks of us.

God's annunciations of saving Presence can come to us in so many ways. Yes, God speaks to us during times of prayer. But God also speaks to us through the everyday persons and events of our lives, in cries for help and forgiveness or in the jubilation of success and growth. God's annunciations of salvation might be mediated by our struggle to make a just decision or our choice to walk away from a group engaging in negative gossip. Yes is not simply a word. Deepening our relationship with God and others happens when our yes becomes a way of living.

Living the Paschal Mystery

We have only a few days left before we celebrate Christmas, the mystery of God becoming human. Now is the time to rehearse our own yes to God by imitating Mary's faithfulness and obedience to God's annunciations. Perhaps we could consciously think of our holiday greeting to others as a way to make generosity and joy concrete. Perhaps we could take a few minutes out of our busy days to listen for God's word to us, say yes, and then put God's annunciation into action, "enflesh" God's Presence in the goodness of our own lives. God's annunciations are perpetual and beg from us a yes response. Will this Christmas be a time to renew our own commitment to say yes to God and God's offer of salvation?

Focusing the Gospel

Key words and phrases: sent from God, Behold, behold, Behold

To the point: God's whole plan of salvation is a perpetual annunciation. In this gospel, there are numerous "annunciations" beyond Gabriel's revealing to Mary that she would conceive "the Son of God." Gabriel makes known that Mary is holy; that the child shall be named Jesus; that the kingdom of this Child would have no end; that this Child is "holy, the Son of God"; that Elizabeth has conceived; that "nothing will be impossible for God"; and that Mary is God's faithful and obedient handmaid. Indeed, perpetual annunciation is God's pattern of relating to us. How do we, then, relate to God?

Connecting the Gospel

to the first reading: God reveals through the prophet Nathan to King David that his "kingdom shall endure forever." It is from David's offspring and lineage that the Savior of the world will be born. From the beginning of salvation history, God's revelation has prepared us for the greatest annunciation—the Word will become flesh and dwell among us.

to experience: Advent is about both waiting and preparing. We await each new annunciation of God's Presence in our midst and we prepare ourselves to hear, accept, and respond to God's many comings.

Connecting the Responsorial Psalm

to the readings: The verses used for this Sunday's responsorial psalm are disparate quotes from a lengthy psalm telling a painful story of what seems to be infidelity on God's part. Psalm 89 begins with God promising David everlasting love and loyalty. David's throne, God swears, will stand forever; no enemy will ever defeat him. No matter what the behavior of his descendants, God promises, I will never withdraw my love. When David's kingdom is eventually destroyed, then, the people question God's fidelity: "Where are your former mercies, Lord?" they cry (v. 50).

The Lectionary lifts a few verses from Psalm 89 which declare God's love and fidelity to David. The selections are awkward because the direction of their address keeps shifting: sometimes the psalmist speaks to God, sometimes God speaks to the psalmist, and in the refrain the assembly speaks to the world. It is this last shift which is the key liturgically. No matter what happens in history, God's care for us is relentless. Under appearances to the contrary, God remains faithful to the divine promise. The Lord is with us; our Savior is being born among us (gospel). We can sing "forever" of "the goodness of the Lord" (psalm refrain).

to psalmist preparation: In preparing to sing this responsorial psalm, you need to pay careful attention to the shifts in direct address which the verses contain. When are you speaking *to* God? When are you speaking *for* God? Your task will be to communicate both God's love for us and our love for God. How might you do this?

ASSEMBLY & FAITH-SHARING GROUPS

- God announced divine Presence in the lives of David and Mary. I experience God's Presence in my life when . . . through . . . by . . .
- God relates to me in these ways . . . I relate to God in these ways . . .
- I announce the Word made flesh within me for others when . . .

PRESIDERS

My life and ministry announce God's plan of salvation to the people I serve when I . . .

DEACONS

My service announces God's plan of salvation in these ways . . .

HOSPITALITY MINISTERS

My hospitality (both at home and at liturgy) announces the "Lord is with you" when . . .

MUSIC MINISTERS

My music making announces that the Word has been made flesh in my own life when . . .

ALTAR MINISTERS

My attention to details when serving announces God's care and Presence when . . .

LECTORS

My proclamation of the word is an annunciation of my own encounters with God's Presence when I . . .

EXTRAORDINARY MINISTERS OF HOLY COMMUNION

Like Mary, I am a Christ-bearer most effectively when . . .

Model Penitential Act

Presider: God announced to Mary and announces to us now new possibilities of life and salvation. We call to mind the times when we have not heard God speaking to us nor accepted what God offers us . . . [pause]

Lord Jesus, you are holy, the Son of the Most High: Lord . . .

Christ Jesus, you are God's Word of new life: Christ . . .

Lord Jesus, you are the Word made flesh dwelling among us: Lord . . .

Homily Points

• Some "annunciations" are immediately recognizable and easily invoke response. For example, a woman announcing to her husband and parents that she is pregnant elicits a joyful response; an unemployed father announcing to his family that he has finally landed a job elicits relief and hope; a struggling student announcing to parents that he or she passed a difficult exam elicits a celebration. Other annunciations, however, are not so easily evident. We need to keep ourselves open to recognizing and responding to them.

• God announces divine Presence and salvation to us in many ways, but always in ways we can come to recognize and understand. Often those annunciations come through others. Mary learned through Gabriel that she would conceive the Son of God by the power of the Holy Spirit and responded with obedience and trust. Like Mary, we must learn in our daily living to respond with openness and willingness to God's perpetual annunciations to us.

• In our daily living, God may announce to us through a friend's remark that our life is off track and we need to change certain habits and behaviors. Or perhaps a priest or vowed religious asks if we've ever thought about a call to ordination or vows. Or someone in need approaches us and we respond with care. In all these annunciations God is present, calling forth a response from us. How we respond to these messengers from God is how we respond to God.

Model Universal Prayer (Prayer of the Faithful)

Presider: God has announced to us the divine plan of salvation through Jesus Christ. In his name we raise our needs to God.

Response:

Cantor:

May all members of the church open themselves to God's annunciations of salvation and respond with willing hearts . . . [pause]

May world leaders be guided in their decisions by God's plan of salvation for all . . . [pause]

May the poor, the downtrodden, and the suffering have their cares lifted by the response of this community . . . [pause]

May all of us deepen our relationship with God through our responses to God's many annunciations of divine Presence . . . [pause]

Presider: God our Father, you sent your Son into our world to bring us the new life of salvation: hear these our prayers that we might one day enjoy the fullness of life with you. We ask this through Christ our Lord. **Amen.**

COLLECT

Let us pray

Pause for silent prayer

Pour forth, we beseech you, O Lord,
your grace into our hearts,
that we, to whom the Incarnation of Christ your Son
was made known by the message of an Angel,
may by his Passion and Cross
be brought to the glory of his Resurrection.
Who lives and reigns with you in the unity of the Holy Spirit,
one God, for ever and ever. **Amen.**

FIRST READING

2 Sam 7:1-5, 8b-12, 14a, 16

When King David was settled in his palace,
and the LORD had given him rest from his enemies on every side,
he said to Nathan the prophet,
"Here I am living in a house of cedar,
while the ark of God dwells in a tent!"
Nathan answered the king,
"Go, do whatever you have in mind,
for the LORD is with you."
But that night the LORD spoke to Nathan and said:
"Go, tell my servant David, 'Thus says the LORD:
Should you build me a house to dwell in?

"'It was I who took you from the pasture
and from the care of the flock
to be commander of my people Israel.
I have been with you wherever you went,
and I have destroyed all your enemies before you.
And I will make you famous like the great ones of the earth.
I will fix a place for my people Israel;
I will plant them so that they may dwell in their place
without further disturbance.
Neither shall the wicked continue to afflict them as they did of old,
since the time I first appointed judges over my people Israel.
I will give you rest from all your enemies.
The LORD also reveals to you
that he will establish a house for you.
And when your time comes and you rest with your ancestors,
I will raise up your heir after you,
sprung from your loins,
and I will make his kingdom firm.

I will be a father to him,
and he shall be a son to me.
Your house and your kingdom shall
endure forever before me;
your throne shall stand firm forever.'"

RESPONSORIAL PSALM
Ps 89:2-3, 4-5, 27, 29

R̸. (2a) For ever I will sing the goodness of the Lord.

The promises of the LORD I will sing forever;
through all generations my mouth shall proclaim your faithfulness.
For you have said, "My kindness is established forever";
in heaven you have confirmed your faithfulness.

R̸. For ever I will sing the goodness of the Lord.

"I have made a covenant with my chosen one,
I have sworn to David my servant:
forever will I confirm your posterity
and establish your throne for all generations."

R̸. For ever I will sing the goodness of the Lord.

"He shall say of me, 'You are my father, my God, the Rock, my savior.'
Forever I will maintain my kindness toward him,
and my covenant with him stands firm."

R̸. For ever I will sing the goodness of the Lord.

SECOND READING
Rom 16:25-27

Brothers and sisters:
To him who can strengthen you,
according to my gospel and the proclamation of Jesus Christ,
according to the revelation of the mystery kept secret for long ages
but now manifested through the prophetic writings and,
according to the command of the eternal God,
made known to all nations to bring about the obedience of faith,
to the only wise God, through Jesus Christ
be glory forever and ever. Amen.

About Liturgy

Reflecting on the word "mystery": "Mystery" is a favorite theme in the Pauline corpus (see second reading); it was a favored term in the early church. So much so that the early designation for sacraments was "the mysteries" (*mysteria*). We might detect a use of the notion of mystery in three progressively involving ways. First, mystery refers to the plan of salvation that God set in motion from the time of Adam and Eve's first sin. Establishing David's throne forever is one more annunciation in this unfolding plan of salvation. Second, mystery refers to the birth of Jesus Christ; he himself embodies the plan and carries it forward by his death and resurrection. Third, mystery refers to the sacraments by which we share in God's unfolding plan of salvation. This is how we ourselves participate in the establishment of God's everlasting reign. Liturgy is the ritual enactment of God's mystery of salvation. Our full, conscious, and active participation in liturgy is our full-throated yes to God's mystery of salvation. Our yes to liturgy is our "obedience of faith."

Reflecting on the word "mystery" challenges any historical approach to the Advent and Christmas seasons. We await and prepare for Christ, but Christ is already present, too. This Fourth Sunday of Advent specifically turns us to Christmas and tends to blur a clear distinction between seasons. What we celebrate on Christmas (Christ's coming) we celebrate every day—Christ is already present through God's plan of salvation and in us through the sacraments.

About Liturgical Music

Music suggestions: The Basque carol "The Angel Gabriel from Heaven Came" (BB, JS3, W4) retells the story of this Sunday's gospel and would be worth singing during the preparation of the gifts. The strong, marching meter of "Savior of the Nations, Come" makes this classical hymn a good choice for the recessional song. G3 and W4 use the familiar verses; SS offers new verses composed by Delores Dufner. Carl Daw's "Though Famed in Israel's Royal History" (W4) transforms Bethlehem from a famous city in "Israel's royal history" (verse 1) to a "new and willing Bethlehem" built from our lives (verse 4). Tune and length of this piece suggest singing it during the preparation of the gifts. Rory Cooney's setting of the *Magnificat*, "Canticle of the Turning" (G3, W4), has Mary singing her joy that "the world is about to turn!" This would make an energetic and fitting post-Communion song on the last Sunday of Advent just before the world turns with the birth of Christ.

SEASON OF CHRISTMAS

He made himself a pure body,
he clothed himself with it,
and came forth
and clothed our weakness
with glory,
which in his mercy
he brought from the Father.

—St. Ephraim the Syrian
Nineteen Hymns on the Nativity of Christ in the Flesh
Hymn V

SPIRITUALITY

The Vigil Mass

GOSPEL ACCLAMATION
℞. Alleluia, alleluia.
Tomorrow the wickedness of the earth will be
    destroyed:
the Savior of the world will reign over us.
℞. Alleluia, alleluia.

Gospel   Matt 1:1-25; L13ABC

**The book of the genealogy of Jesus Christ,
    the son of David, the son of Abraham.**

**Abraham became the father of Isaac,
    Isaac the father of Jacob,
    Jacob the father of Judah and his
        brothers.
Judah became the father of Perez and
    Zerah,
    whose mother was Tamar.
Perez became the father of Hezron,
    Hezron the father of Ram,
    Ram the father of Amminadab.
Amminadab became the father of Nahshon,
    Nahshon the father of Salmon,
    Salmon the father of Boaz,
    whose mother was Rahab.
Boaz became the father of Obed,
    whose mother was Ruth.
Obed became the father of Jesse,
    Jesse the father of David the king.**

Continued in Appendix A, p. 262

or Matt 1:18-25 in Appendix A, p. 262.

See Appendix A, p. 263, for the other readings.

Reflecting on the Gospel and Living the Paschal Mystery
Key words and phrases from the gospel: righteous man, name him Jesus, save his people, named him Jesus

To the point: Joseph models for us what it means to be in right relationship with God. He wishes to keep the law, but does not want his beloved betrothed to be shamed; he hears the word of God from the angel, and obeys by taking Mary as his wife and naming her Son Jesus. By listening to God and changing his mind (and his course of life), Joseph is a righteous servant of God who directly cooperates in God's saving work.

To ponder and pray: An adage says that it is a woman's prerogative to change her mind. In this gospel, it is the "righteous man" Joseph who changes his mind. Joseph sets aside all his Jewish sense of how to deal with this delicate situation of a pregnant woman who is his betrothed, and instead listens and responds to God's word that changes the very course of history. He not only takes Mary as his wife, but he also gives up his right to choose a name for this Son when he names him Jesus as the angel commanded.

The name Jesus comes from the Hebrew *yehoshuʾa* and means "Yahweh is salvation." It was a common name at Jesus' time and before (Joshua and Hosea, for example). When we look at Jesus' genealogy as recorded by Matthew, however, none of these names appear. To name this newborn baby Jesus seems to indicate that, while the genealogy is given precisely to locate Jesus in the lineage of David, something entirely new is happening. There is a new in-breaking in the royal lineage. A new Prophet of salvation and love is born: a newborn King who is the very Son of God.

The first reading gives us an intimate description of what happens when salvation dawns upon us: we enjoy a whole new relationship with God. Not an ordinary relationship, for God calls us "My Delight." Through the incarnation of Jesus we enter into an intimate relationship with God, an espousal relationship, a relationship that invites us into a love that has never before been experienced, never before been embraced, never before been offered. For this love is a divine love. Indeed, Christmas is a festival of new relationship.

Joseph models for us what it means to be in intimate relationship with God, an espousal relationship that places the will of the divine Lover before all else. He wishes to keep the law, but does not want his beloved betrothed to be shamed; he hears the word of God from the angel, and obeys by taking Mary as his wife and naming her Son Jesus. By listening to God and changing his mind (and his course of life), Joseph is a righteous servant of God who directly cooperates in God's saving work.

The salvation Jesus offers us is a wholeness and well-being that comes from being in an intimate relationship with our divine Lover and with each other. Like Joseph, we are called to be faithful, called to hear God's word and obey it joyfully, called to cooperate with God's plan of salvation. We please our divine Lover when we open ourselves to God's great care, mercy, compassion, forgiveness, and, above all, love. We please our divine Lover when we receive the divine Son and the very revelation of God's offer of salvation. This means that we, too, will be called to change our course of life.

SPIRITUALITY

Mass at Midnight

GOSPEL ACCLAMATION
Luke 2:10-11

R̸. Alleluia, alleluia.
I proclaim to you good news of great joy:
today a Savior is born for us,
Christ the Lord.
R̸. Alleluia, alleluia.

Gospel

Luke 2:1-14; L14ABC

In those days a decree went out
    from Caesar Augustus
  that the whole world should be
    enrolled.
This was the first enrollment,
  when Quirinius was governor of
    Syria.
So all went to be enrolled, each to
  his own town.
And Joseph too went up from
  Galilee from the town of
    Nazareth
  to Judea, to the city of David that is
    called Bethlehem,
  because he was of the house and
    family of David,
  to be enrolled with Mary, his
    betrothed, who was with child.
While they were there,
  the time came for her to have her child,
  and she gave birth to her firstborn son.
She wrapped him in swaddling clothes
  and laid him in a manger,
  because there was no room for them
    in the inn.

Continued in Appendix A, p. 263.

See Appendix A, p. 264, for these readings:

FIRST READING
Isa 9:1-6

RESPONSORIAL PSALM
Ps 96:1-2, 2-3, 11-12, 13

SECOND READING
Titus 2:11-14

Reflecting on the Gospel and Living the Paschal Mystery
Key words and phrases from the gospel: the glory of the Lord shone around them, good news of great joy, a savior has been born for you

To the point: Christmas celebrates more than the birth of a baby; it is a feast of salvation announcing to us that the glory of the Lord is upon us. Christmas calls us to open ourselves to God's glory so that it may shine through us for others.

To ponder and pray: There is perhaps no other gospel story that has been told and retold in so many thousands of ways as this one about the birth of Jesus. Much about it piques our imaginations and quickens our hearts. It is an easy story for children's drama, with lots of characters: mom, dad, a newborn baby, angels, shepherds, sheep, donkeys. We empathize with the hardship of Mary and Joseph: "no room for them in the inn," giving birth to a "firstborn son" in a place less than hospitable, and having to use a manger for a crib. These picturesque and memorable details, however, can limit our appreciation for what we really celebrate. Christmas is less about the birth of a baby and far more about the birth of a divine Savior. It is less about glory and joy of long ago and more about an invitation to us today to enter into the saving mystery God revealed so uniquely in Jesus Christ. It is less about drama and more about the nitty-gritty challenge of living daily the mystery of God among us.

Christmas is a feast of salvation; the Son is sent to bring us from the darkness of sin into the light of glory. Through the prophets we were foretold that "a son is given us." This Son is born to help us walk from the darkness of sin and gloom into the "great light" that illumines our life journey so we walk steadily and faithfully toward God (see first reading). This Son trains us to "reject godless ways and worldly desires" and instead to choose "to live temperately, justly, and devoutly" (second reading). This Son makes for God a new people, those who have been invited into a share of God's glory, God's peace, God's graciousness. Christmas is not a feast for unwrapping earthly gifts; it is a feast for wrapping ourselves in the glory of divine Life brought to us by this Savior Son.

Christmas calls us to give the most important gift of all—the very Life of God—to each other. We have been given the Gift of Jesus, now we share this Gift with others as we continue our life journey. Christmas calls us to open our eyes and see where we ourselves can bring the joy and peace of salvation to those around us. Indeed, the greatest gift we can give others is God's glory, God's Presence.

Christmas affords many opportunities for us to be God's glory through Jesus Christ for others. Most of us go out of our way to be generous to the poor and less fortunate at this time, especially so that the drudgery and worry of not having enough might be allayed at least for a little while. We must also open our eyes to those near and dear to us who might be lonely or depressed, struggling or drained, fearful or discouraged. Sometimes, like the shepherds, we need only to listen. Or, like Joseph, we might accept without question. Or, like Mary, we might say yes to what might be an unspoken request for help. Christmas is a salvation feast that happens every day. May we live our lives in such a way that the glory of God within us shines forth, bringing light into darkness, hope into desperation, and peace into discord.

SPIRITUALITY

Mass at Dawn

GOSPEL ACCLAMATION
Luke 2:14

R̸. Alleluia, alleluia.
Glory to God in the highest,
and on earth peace to those
on whom his favor rests.
R̸. Alleluia, alleluia.

Gospel

Luke 2:15-20; L15ABC

When the angels went away
　　from them to heaven,
　the shepherds said to one
　　　another,
　"Let us go, then, to
　　　Bethlehem
　to see this thing that has taken place,
　which the Lord has made known to
　　us."
So they went in haste and found Mary
　　and Joseph,
　and the infant lying in the manger.
When they saw this,
　they made known the message
　that had been told them about this
　　child.
All who heard it were amazed
　by what had been told them by the
　　shepherds.
And Mary kept all these things,
　reflecting on them in her heart.
Then the shepherds returned,
　glorifying and praising God
　for all they had heard and seen,
　just as it had been told to them.

See Appendix A, p. 264, for these readings:

FIRST READING
Isa 62:11-12

RESPONSORIAL PSALM
Ps 97:1, 6, 11-12

SECOND READING
Titus 3:4-7

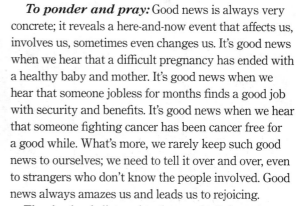

Reflecting on the Gospel and Living the Paschal Mystery

Key words and phrases from the gospel: made known the message, amazed by what had been told, reflecting on them

　To the point: We cannot know or recognize the mystery of salvation by ourselves. God alone makes this mystery known to us. Whether God communicates the message through angels or shepherds or others or even ourselves, the message always begs heartfelt reflection and committed response.

　To ponder and pray: Good news is always very concrete; it reveals a here-and-now event that affects us, involves us, sometimes even changes us. It's good news when we hear that a difficult pregnancy has ended with a healthy baby and mother. It's good news when we hear that someone jobless for months finds a good job with security and benefits. It's good news when we hear that someone fighting cancer has been cancer free for a good while. What's more, we rarely keep such good news to ourselves; we need to tell it over and over, even to strangers who don't know the people involved. Good news always amazes us and leads us to rejoicing.

　The shepherds listened to the angel tell them the good news of Jesus' birth, and then told it to others. But what was the good news they told? Surely not the birth of a baby—that is commonplace enough. Maybe that a baby was born in a stable? Well, that's unusual but it is more fodder for gossip than it is good news. Like Mary, the shepherds must have reflected on the announcement of Jesus' birth in their hearts as they hastened to see for themselves. This reflection took them beyond the birth to a mystery that was worth telling. And retelling.

　The message of good news and this whole festival is "your savior comes!" (first reading). We cannot know or recognize the mystery of salvation by ourselves. God alone makes this mystery known to us. It is for us to take the time to reflect in our hearts on what God is revealing. The shepherds in the gospel model for us openness to the mystery of God's message of salvation. Sometimes we're the hearers of the good news, and our response is simply to reflect on it in our hearts, to wait for God's message to well up within us and become a light that seeks to be expressed. At other times, like the shepherds, we are called to make "known the message" of salvation revealed to us. Then we open ourselves to an encounter with the mystery and share it with everyone we meet. We ourselves, then, become bearers of the Good News.

　None of us will travel to Bethlehem to behold a newborn infant lying in a manger. But all of us travel the road of daily life: when we are called to see the newborn infant in the youngster who needs companionship, the teenager who needs a listening ear, the parent who needs a helping hand, the elder who needs someone to care, the stranger who needs food or shelter. Through us the Lord makes known the message of divine mercy, love, and care. God uses us to lead others to encounter the mystery of Jesus' Presence and the salvation he brings. Our openness to God begins with divine encounter, continues through our reflecting on God's message to us, and comes to fruition in our encounters with others. Our telling the Good News to others is one committed response. Our living the Good News is another. Our *being* the Good News is the fullest response.

SPIRITUALITY

Mass during the Day

GOSPEL ACCLAMATION
R). Alleluia, alleluia.
A holy day has dawned upon us.
Come, you nations, and adore the Lord.
For today a great light has come upon the
    earth.
R). Alleluia, alleluia.

Gospel

John 1:1-18; L16ABC

In the beginning was the
        Word,
    and the Word was with
        God,
    and the Word was God.
He was in the beginning
        with God.
All things came to be through
        him,
    and without him nothing came
        to be.
What came to be through him was life,
    and this life was the light of the
        human race;
    the light shines in the darkness,
    and the darkness has not
        overcome it.
A man named John was sent from God.
He came for testimony, to testify to the
        light,
    so that all might believe through him.
He was not the light,
    but came to testify to the light.

Continued in Appendix A, p. 265

or John 1:1-5, 9-14 in Appendix A, p. 265.

*See Appendix A, pp. 265–266, for the other
readings.*

Reflecting on the Gospel and Living the Paschal Mystery
Key words and phrases from the gospel: In the beginning, life, Word became flesh, his fullness we have all received

To the point: In the beginning, God granted existence to all things by speaking a mighty word. God's desire was that we have life. To this end, God's Word assumed human flesh so that "all the ends of the earth will behold the salvation of our God" (first reading). Because of Christ's birth we have received salvation—the very fullness of God, the very fullness of existence.

To ponder and pray: In July 2012, physicists believed they had discovered the Higgs boson, the so-called "God particle" that is supposedly the building block of life. No doubt there will be decades of more experiments and many discussions about the Higgs boson's existence. Some people disclaim the possibility based on faith in God's singular act of creation. Others have their faith shaken. For believers, the "God particle" has already been revealed to us: "In the beginning was the Word . . . the Word was God . . . the Word became flesh." However scientists want to discuss the beginning of creation, we people of faith know unshakably that God created us out of love, that God willed us to be saved in spite of our own darkness of sin, and that through this divine Word made flesh we "become children of God," partakers of divine Life itself.

The incredible joy of the Christmas message is that the One who was with God and was God from the beginning is now in the world among us (gospel), fully revealed (second reading), and directly seen (first reading). Because of Christ's birth we have received salvation—the very fullness of God, the very fullness of existence. The joy of this festival comes with the realization that the effects of sin are overcome; God is with us and we receive new life, divine Life. This Life is not a particle to be discovered but a relationship that is already revealed to us in Christ Jesus.

Both the first reading and gospel begin with an announcement of salvation: glad tidings, peace, good news (first reading). The reason for the announcement of salvation is given in terms of what God has done on behalf of humanity: given comfort, redeemed, "bared his holy arm" for our salvation (first reading); God "gave power to become children of God" and "from his fullness we have all received" (gospel). This festival is really about the wonders God has done for us through Jesus Christ. Even more stupendous than heralding angels, believing shepherds, and adoring magi is the invitation to each of us to accept the One who is in the world and become sons and daughters who have received the very fullness of God: the Word made flesh. Salvation is an invitation to open ourselves to God's merciful and generous offer of Life, to grow in that Life, and to look forward to that day when we shall be united forever with the Word made flesh who already dwells among and within us.

This season offers many opportunities for each of us to be charitable toward those less fortunate than ourselves. These readings remind us that the goodness we share with others is a continuation and symbol of the goodness God has shared with us in giving us our Savior, Jesus Christ. Every good deed is a testimony to God's loving offer of salvation. This is how God makes salvation known (see responsorial psalm): through us and the works we perform. Christmas isn't a reality for us until we ourselves become the presence of the Word made flesh.

Model Penitential Act

Presider: The great mystery of salvation we celebrate is that God's only-begotten Son became flesh and dwells among us. We pause to ponder this great mystery and reflect on whether we have been open to the salvation God offers . . . [pause]

Lord Jesus, you are the Word made flesh who dwells among us: Lord . . .

Christ Jesus, you are the true light that dispels darkness: Christ . . .

Lord Jesus, you share the glory of the Father, full of grace and truth: Lord . . .

Homily Points

• Very early Christmas morning, little children run to the Christmas tree and see all those pretty wrapped gifts piled under and around it. It doesn't take long, however, for that beautiful, neat, orderly Christmas scene to become a jumbled mass of torn paper, discarded ribbons, and empty boxes. The hidden and anticipated gifts are now revealed, to the children's delight.

• We celebrate on this great feast that the hidden and anticipated gift of salvation is revealed to us in the Word made flesh come to dwell among us. This revelation begs of us encounter and response. We unwrap God's gift of salvation and are delighted with God's offer of peace, life, well-being, wholeness, union with God. We take up a new way of living and being.

• Just as the children toss away the paper, ribbon, and boxes, we, too, must discard whatever is in the way of our receiving God's gift of salvation. We must discard, for example, the sparkle of self-satisfaction, the lure of self-promotion, the smugness of self-righteousness so that we may discover anew each day God's continued Presence and love. Christmas is a feast day of gift, discovery, surprise, encounter, and promise.

Model Universal Prayer (Prayer of the Faithful)

Presider: The God who gives us the gift of salvation will surely hear our prayers.

Response:

Lord, hear our prayer.

Cantor:

we pray to the Lord,

That all members of the church may open themselves to God's many gifts during this holy season of Christmas . . . [pause]

That all peoples of the world may enjoy peace and fullness of life . . . [pause]

That the sick and suffering, the lonely and the homeless may be comforted by Christ who comes to them through the care of others . . . [pause]

That all of us here gathered might come to the fullness of Life that Jesus' birth promises . . . [pause]

Presider: O glorious God, you sent your Son to dwell among us: hear these our prayers that we might open ourselves to your gift of salvation and one day share the fullness of Life with you for ever. We ask this through your Son Jesus Christ our Lord. **Amen.**

COLLECT

(from the Mass during the Day)

Let us pray

Pause for silent prayer

O God, who wonderfully created the dignity
    of human nature
and still more wonderfully restored it,
grant, we pray,
that we may share in the divinity of Christ,
who humbled himself to share in our
    humanity.
Who lives and reigns with you in the unity
    of the Holy Spirit,
one God, for ever and ever. **Amen.**

FOR REFLECTION

• I receive God's message of salvation when . . . through . . . I announce God's message of salvation when . . .

• The new life for which I long is . . . The new life from God I experience this Christmas is . . .

• I express my Christmas joy throughout the year when . . .

✠ SPIRITUALITY

GOSPEL ACCLAMATION
Col 3:15a, 16a

℟. Alleluia, alleluia.
Let the peace of Christ control your hearts;
let the word of Christ dwell in you richly.
℟. Alleluia, alleluia.

Gospel

Luke 2:22-40; L17B

When the days were completed
    for their purification
    according to the law of Moses,
    the parents of Jesus took him
        up to Jerusalem
    to present him to the Lord,
    just as it is written in the law
        of the Lord,
    Every male that opens the
        womb shall be consecrated
        to the Lord,
    and to offer the sacrifice of
    a pair of turtledoves or two
        young pigeons,
    in accordance with the dictate in the
        law of the Lord.

Now there was a man in Jerusalem
    whose name was Simeon.
This man was righteous and devout,
    awaiting the consolation of Israel,
    and the Holy Spirit was upon him.
It had been revealed to him by the Holy
    Spirit
    that he should not see death
    before he had seen the Christ of the
        Lord.
He came in the Spirit into the temple;
    and when the parents brought in the
        child Jesus
    to perform the custom of the law in
        regard to him,
    he took him into his arms and blessed
        God, saying:

Continued in Appendix A, p. 266.

or Luke 2:22, 39-40 in Appendix A, p. 266.

Reflecting on the Gospel

Toddlers seem to need only two words in their vocabulary: "No!" and "Mine!" As soon as they are able they assert themselves forcefully. This is a survival tactic. As the little ones become aware of themselves, their instincts for survival kick in. They grab for whatever they think they need to preserve the precious life they are and to ensure their perceived happiness and well-being. With great patience do parents (and often siblings) teach these little ones that they are not the center of the universe, that the best way to preserve life is to cooperate with the community of people around them, that what ensures happiness and well-being is loving relationships. The family is usually the first community a toddler knows. It is there that relationships become real. It is there that relationships become life-giving.

In this gospel Mary and Joseph bring their forty-day-old Son to the temple "to present him to the Lord." Simeon takes the Child "into his arms" and recognizes him to be "a light for revelation" to all people. The prophetess Anna encounters the One whom she recognizes as "the redemption of Jerusalem." Such lofty words about this tiny Child! The gospel then tells us that the "child grew and became strong." Can we imagine this Child uttering "No!" and "Mine!"? Cannot we presume that Mary and Joseph exercised the same patience with the toddler Jesus as they taught him how to live as a member of their family?

Right relationships in families and other communities don't just happen. They are taught by example, patience, care, and take a lifetime of openness and growth. Holy families (holy communities) are made up of people living in right relationship with each other. Simeon in the gospel is described as "righteous" because he was in right relationship with God ("the Holy Spirit was upon him") and others ("Simeon blessed" Mary and Joseph).

This gospel describes three ways to be righteous. Mary and Joseph bring Jesus to the temple "according to the *law,*" fulfilling their obligation as new parents. Simeon is open to the *Holy Spirit's* Presence, guidance, and revelation to him of the "Christ of the Lord." Anna *spoke prophetically* to others about the redemption that was at hand. Faithfulness to the law, openness to the Holy Spirit, prophetically speaking about what has been revealed deepen our right relationship with God. Families are holy when they, too, act righteously as did Mary and Joseph, Simeon, and Anna.

Living the Paschal Mystery

God so cared for the family of humanity that God gave us the only-begotten Son; we show our acceptance of membership in God's family by caring for each other, by building just and loving relationships, by growing in righteousness. This process of being holy usually begins with our own family members. This feast calls us to care for one another in practical ways. Perhaps this means phoning an elder who lives alone or is in a retirement center or nursing home. Maybe this means sharing toys more generously on the part of little ones (learning words other than "No!" and "Mine!"), or pitching in to help without being asked on the part of adolescents, or husband and wife listening more intently to each other. Emptying self for the sake of the other is what builds up each of us and our families and relationships, and this is being holy. Righteousness is very concrete. So is holiness.

Focusing the Gospel

Key words and phrases: according to the law, righteous, the Holy Spirit was upon him, prophetess . . . spoke about the child to all

To the point: This gospel describes three ways to be righteous. Mary and Joseph bring Jesus to the temple "according to the *law*," fulfilling their obligation as new parents. Simeon is open to the *Holy Spirit's* Presence, guidance, and revelation to him of the "Christ of the Lord." Anna *spoke prophetically* to others about the redemption that was at hand. Faithfulness to the law, openness to the Holy Spirit, prophetically speaking about what has been revealed deepen our right relationship with God. Families are holy when they, too, act righteously as did Mary and Joseph, Simeon, and Anna.

Connecting the Gospel

to the first and second readings: Abram was credited with being "righteous" because he "put his faith in the LORD." By trusting that God would give the childless Abram descendants, by being obedient to God's call to leave his ancestral home, and by offering up Isaac for sacrifice Abram put his faith into action. Righteousness (right relationship with God) is faith in action.

to experience: Right relationship with God is demonstrated through our healthy and good relationships within our families, workplaces, leisure activities. Righteousness is very concrete. So is holiness.

Connecting the Responsorial Psalm

to the readings: These verses from Psalm 105 relate directly to the story told in the first reading. God promises Abraham offspring when it is no longer possible for Sarah to bear children (second reading). Even more, God promises Abraham and Sarah their offspring will outnumber the stars. Their ultimate progeny would be the Child of Mary and Joseph, the "light of revelation" and gift of salvation to all nations (gospel). For God achieves what human beings cannot, and does so not just for a time but for all time, not just for one line of descendants but for all the human family. Indeed, the "Lord remembers his covenant forever" (psalm refrain) with those who are faithful (second reading). For this we, God's holy family, give God thanks.

to psalmist preparation: As you prepare to proclaim this psalm, spend some time reflecting on the God about whom you will be singing. Who is this God who desires to be in covenant with us? Who is this God who remembers us forever? Who is this God who keeps acting in our favor? And who are we because of this God?

**ASSEMBLY &
FAITH-SHARING GROUPS**
- Righteousness means to me . . . Holiness means to me . . .
- I grow in holiness when . . . I help others grow in holiness when . . . Others help me grow in holiness when . . .
- What keeps me from growing in righteousness and holiness is . . .

PRESIDERS
I am led by the Holy Spirit to speak prophetically to my people in these ways . . .

DEACONS
Ways I've grown in righteousness and holiness through my serving others are . . .

HOSPITALITY MINISTERS
The manner of my greeting helps others recognize their holiness when . . .

MUSIC MINISTERS
Music making is an expression of my right relationship with God and others when . . . of my holiness because . . .

ALTAR MINISTERS
My attentiveness to liturgical details "according to the law" helps me grow in my relationship with God and others because . . .

LECTORS
I experience God's word as prophetic when . . . I sometimes neglect to speak out God's word because . . .

**EXTRAORDINARY MINISTERS
OF HOLY COMMUNION**
I see the righteousness and holiness in others when I . . . This makes a difference in my ministry because . . .

Model Penitential Act

Presider: This feast invites us to reflect on our relationships with God, with each other in our own families, and in the broader family of humanity. We pause and ask God to make all of us holier and better family members . . . [pause]

Lord Jesus, you are the awaited consolation and redemption of all people: Lord . . .
Christ Jesus, you are the fullness of Life and holiness: Christ . . .
Lord Jesus, you call us to share in the holiness of the family of God: Lord . . .

Homily Points

• Given any family, if each member were asked to write down five characteristics of that family, how many of these lists would include the word "holy"? Probably not one of them. Is being holy too lofty a goal? too challenging? too improbable? too abstract? too saintly? This gospel tells us otherwise.

• Holiness is as concrete as faithfully being guided by God's laws and other just laws, fulfilling our obligations in life, being open to the Presence and guidance of the Holy Spirit, prophetically speaking out our convictions and faith values, growing in our right relationships with God and others. Ultimately, holiness is a call to live faithfully God's Life that is within us.

• The Holy Family, we know all too well from the gospels, experienced challenges and difficulties just as we do in our own families and lives. They were able to overcome these difficulties because they remained faithful to what God asked of them. Our challenge as holy families and holy people is to discern God's will for us in our lives, respond with courage through the indwelling of the Holy Spirit, and grow in our right relationship with God and others.

Model Universal Prayer (Prayer of the Faithful)

Presider: Let us pray that God may bless all our families, make us holier, and draw us to stronger relationships with the family of all of humanity.

Response:

Lord, hear our prayer.

Cantor:

we pray to the Lord,

That all members of the church strive to create a welcoming and hospitable holy family . . . [pause]

That all peoples of the world grow in holiness by striving for just relationships . . . [pause]

That families suffering loss be comforted, families in need of healing be reconciled, and all families grow in love and care for each other . . . [pause]

That each of us gathered here be open to the Holy Spirit who fashions us into a holy people . . . [pause]

Presider: God our Father, you created the family of humanity to share in your holiness: hear these our prayers that one day we may enjoy the fullness of Life with you. We ask this through Christ our Lord. **Amen.**

COLLECT
Let us pray

Pause for silent prayer

O God, who were pleased to give us
the shining example of the Holy Family,
graciously grant that we may imitate them
in practicing the virtues of family life
     and in the bonds of charity,
and so, in the joy of your house,
delight one day in eternal rewards.
Through our Lord Jesus Christ, your Son,
who lives and reigns with you in the unity
     of the Holy Spirit,
one God, for ever and ever. **Amen.**

FIRST READING
Gen 15:1-6; 21:1-3

The word of the Lord came to Abram in a
     vision, saying:
"Fear not, Abram!
I am your shield;
I will make your reward very great."
But Abram said,
"O Lord God, what good will your gifts
     be,
if I keep on being childless
and have as my heir the steward of my
     house, Eliezer?"
Abram continued,
"See, you have given me no offspring,
and so one of my servants will be my
     heir."
Then the word of the Lord came to him:
"No, that one shall not be your heir;
your own issue shall be your heir."
The Lord took Abram outside and said,
"Look up at the sky and count the stars,
     if you can.
Just so," he added, "shall your descendants
     be."
Abram put his faith in the Lord,
who credited it to him as an act of
     righteousness.

The Lord took note of Sarah as he had
     said he would;
he did for her as he had promised.
Sarah became pregnant and bore
     Abraham a son in his old age,
at the set time that God had stated.
Abraham gave the name Isaac to this son
     of his
whom Sarah bore him.

RESPONSORIAL PSALM

Ps 105:1-2, 3-4, 6-7, 8-9

℟. (7a, 8a) The Lord remembers his covenant for ever.

Give thanks to the Lord, invoke his name;
  make known among the nations his deeds.
Sing to him, sing his praise,
  proclaim all his wondrous deeds.

℟. The Lord remembers his covenant for ever.

Glory in his holy name;
  rejoice, O hearts that seek the Lord!
Look to the Lord in his strength;
  constantly seek his face.

℟. The Lord remembers his covenant for ever.

You descendants of Abraham, his servants,
  sons of Jacob, his chosen ones!
He, the Lord, is our God;
  throughout the earth his judgments prevail.

℟. The Lord remembers his covenant for ever.

He remembers forever his covenant
  which he made binding for a thousand generations
which he entered into with Abraham
  and by his oath to Isaac.

℟. The Lord remembers his covenant for ever.

SECOND READING

Heb 11:8, 11-12, 17-19

Brothers and sisters:
By faith Abraham obeyed when he was
  called to go out to a place
  that he was to receive as an inheritance;
  he went out, not knowing where he was to go.
By faith he received power to generate,
  even though he was past the normal age
  —and Sarah herself was sterile—
  for he thought that the one who had made the promise was trustworthy.
So it was that there came forth from one man,
  himself as good as dead,
  descendants as numerous as the stars in the sky
  and as countless as the sands on the seashore.

Continued in Appendix A, p. 266.

See Appendix A, p. 267, for additional readings.

About Liturgy

Liturgy and holiness: All liturgy is an opportunity to grow in holiness. This means much more than simply "getting grace." It means that liturgy is one concrete way we can open ourselves to God's Presence and give ourselves over to God's action so we can be transformed into ever more perfect members of the Body of Christ. Our growth in holiness begins with God's action within us. It continues with the dismissal from liturgy, when we are sent forth to live holy lives. Liturgy continues as we reach out with gentleness and kindness, justice and peace, forgiveness and reconciliation to those who cross our paths. Liturgy's fruit is God's grace borne out in the holiness of our lives.

Canticle of Simeon: Simeon's prayer in the gospel is called the Canticle of Simeon or the *Nunc dimittis.* This is the proper gospel canticle for night prayer (or Compline) and has been an invariable part of Liturgy of the Hours since about the fourth century. Just as the elderly Simeon could face his death with peace because he knew he had seen the Messiah so, too, when we sing this canticle every night before retiring can we sleep peacefully in the confidence that God will see us through the night, since the terrors of darkness were dispelled when the Light came into the world. It is a wonderful habit to pray this prayer of confidence in God each night.

Advantage of the revised Lectionary: In order to profit from the additions to the readings in the revised Lectionary, we have chosen to go with the proper readings assigned for Year B. The advantage of these extra readings is that they provide different interpretive contexts for liturgy planning and preaching. In this way the feast can stay fresh and meaningful.

About Liturgical Music

Music suggestions: Although hymns which speak of the infant Jesus and/or the Holy Family are always appropriate on this day, the readings of Year B suggest using texts which sing of God's fidelity through the ages to the covenant promises and the faithful response of so many who trusted in that fidelity. "Of the Father's Love Begotten" and "Lo, How a Rose E'er Blooming," both found in most hymn resources, would be good choices on this day.

John Bell's "The Aye Carol" (G3) draws us into the space where the Holy Child lies. In successive verses we gaze at the different persons who form part of this scene, asking ourselves who they are. Who is the baby an hour or two old? Who is the woman with child at her breast? Who is the man who looks on at the door? Who are the people come in from the street? And finally, we choose to enter, to "come to his cradle and come to his cry" with the gift of our "yes," our "aye." The mostly stepwise movement of the melody laid out in gentle triplets captures both our hesitancy and the simplicity with which we must approach. This hymn would be a lovely piece to sing during the preparation of the gifts.

DECEMBER 28, 2014
THE HOLY FAMILY OF JESUS, MARY, AND JOSEPH

✠ SPIRITUALITY

GOSPEL ACCLAMATION
R/. Alleluia, alleluia.
In the past God spoke to our ancestors through
    the prophets;
in these last days, he has spoken to us through
    the Son.
R/. Alleluia, alleluia.

Gospel

Luke 2:16-21; L18ABC

The shepherds went in haste
    to Bethlehem and found
    Mary and Joseph,
    and the infant lying in the
    manger.
When they saw this,
    they made known the
    message
    that had been told them
    about this child.
All who heard it were amazed
    by what had been told them
    by the shepherds.
And Mary kept all these things,
    reflecting on them in her heart.
Then the shepherds returned,
    glorifying and praising God
    for all they had heard and seen,
    just as it had been told to them.

When eight days were completed for
    his circumcision,
he was named Jesus, the name given
    him by the angel
before he was conceived in the
    womb.

See Appendix A, p. 268, for the other readings.

FIRST READING
Num 6:22-27

RESPONSORIAL PSALM
Ps 67:2-3, 5, 6, 8

SECOND READING
Gal 4:4-7

Reflecting on the Gospel

One of the joyful trends of childbirth in this day and age is that the fathers are also present at the birth. The shared love of the wife and husband brought forth this life. Together they celebrate the gift God has given them and the very moment of birth. The gospels telling the Christmas story include Joseph. When the "shepherds went in haste to Bethlehem" they found "Mary and Joseph and the infant lying in the manger." This feast day, however, is not one of Mary *and* Joseph, but of Mary. Yes, Joseph was faithful to God and said yes, as did Mary, to what God asked of him. Yes, Joseph was Jesus' foster father and taught him the Jewish traditions and how to make a living by being a carpenter. But something else is being celebrated with this feast. Mary conceived by the Holy Spirit. This is no ordinary "infant lying in the manger." This infant amazes shepherds and leads all who encounter him to glorify and praise God.

Because Mary is the mother of the "infant lying in the manger," she is also the Mother of God. This infant conceived by the Holy Spirit in Mary's womb is both God and man. No doubt Mary reflected "in her heart" on this great mystery throughout her life, a reflection that preserved her as a holy and faithful mother. Our reflection on the mystery of the incarnation must be so deep as Mary's that it brings us to greater holiness and faithfulness. It must bring us, like the shepherds, to come in haste to encounter the One who deserves all glory and praise.

Honoring Mary as the Mother of God goes beyond the event of her giving birth to the Son of God. By keeping "all these things" and "reflecting on them in her heart," she exhibits a life of encountering God and being open to whatever God asks of her. Like Mary, we must ponder God's entry into our own lives, making the divine Presence the very "stuff" of our hearts. We, too, must be open to whatever God asks of us. Sometimes pondering and reflecting will not resolve all the questions we might have. We do not only say yes to God when we understand perfectly all that God asks of us. No, instead we say yes to God, ponder what God wants of us, and then respond with a yes that is open to wherever God leads us.

Living the Paschal Mystery

Often New Year's resolutions are about such things as losing weight, trying to stop smoking, cleaning up our language, etc. The readings for this festival honoring Mary might challenge us and our resolution-making in another direction. Perhaps this year we might resolve to take time each day to see and hear what God is revealing to us in the ordinary things of our lives: in the grateful smile of a child, in the gift of a compliment, in the unexpected call or visit of a friend. Or our resolution might be to look for encounters with the Son of God in unexpected circumstances and through people whom we might too easily dismiss.

We might also resolve to spend more time, as Mary did, pondering and reflecting in our hearts God's mystery of salvation. We might set aside a special time each day to pray and then stick to it. We might join a faith-sharing group or volunteer to read Scripture to the sight-impaired. The most fruitful Christianity is that lived simply and quietly but steadily and resolutely: dying to self for the sake of a new and better life for others. Our most fruitful reflecting and pondering might lead us to see the Christ in all those we meet.

Focusing the Gospel

Key words and phrases: Mary, infant lying in the manger, reflecting . . . in her heart, conceived in the womb

To the point: Because Mary is the mother of the "infant lying in the manger," she is also the Mother of God. This infant conceived by the Holy Spirit in Mary's womb is both God and man. No doubt Mary reflected "in her heart" on this great mystery throughout her life, a reflection that preserved her as a holy and faithful mother. Our reflection on the mystery of the incarnation must be so deep as Mary's that it brings us to greater holiness and faithfulness.

Model Penitential Act

Presider: At this time when we celebrate the incarnation of the divine Son, the church gives us this festival to honor Mary, the Mother of God. With her, let us ponder the mystery of God's salvation and open our hearts to receive God's grace . . . [pause]

> Lord Jesus, you were conceived by the Holy Spirit in the womb of the Virgin Mary: Lord . . .
>
> Christ Jesus, you are the Son of God and the son of Mary: Christ . . .
>
> Lord Jesus, you are worthy of all glory and praise: Lord . . .

Model Universal Prayer (Prayer of the Faithful)

Presider: On this first day of the New Year let us pray for God's continued blessings on us and the world.

Response:

Lord, hear our prayer.

Cantor:

we pray to the Lord,

May all members of the church, like Mary, ponder and respond faithfully to God's marvelous deeds of salvation . . . [pause]

May all peoples of the world, like the shepherds, come to know God's salvation . . . [pause]

That those who are poor, sick, hungry, diseased, or discouraged may see and hear of God's blessings and peace . . . [pause]

That all of us here gathered, like Mary, may often reflect in our hearts on God's mystery of salvation and grow in holiness and faithfulness . . . [pause]

Presider: O saving God, you sent your Son, born of Mary, to dwell among us: hear our prayers at the beginning of this New Year that we might receive your blessings and live in peace. We ask this through that same Son Jesus Christ our Lord. **Amen.**

FOR REFLECTION

- Those things I keep in my heart and reflect upon are . . .
- Mary, the Holy Mother of God, inspires me to . . .
- I experience coming to greater holiness and fidelity when . . .

Homily Points

• In the Eastern Church the mystery of Mary as the Mother of God is referred to as *Theotokos,* literally, "the one who gives birth to God." This feast day extolls Mary as one who cooperated with God's plan of salvation, even when she did not understand fully what this plan was. She faithfully, however, reflected "in her heart" on God's working in and through her. We, too, must give birth to God in our midst, reflecting in our own hearts about our own role in God's plan of salvation for all people.

• We give birth to God when we, like Mary, listen for God's voice in our lives, respond with our yes to what God asks of us, reflect on God's life in us as we strive to grow in holiness and faithfulness. The mystery of the incarnation is not something we celebrate once a year, but is a mystery we live and make present each day of our lives.

✠ SPIRITUALITY

Gospel Matt 2:1-12; L20ABC

When Jesus was born in
Bethlehem of Judea,
in the days of King
Herod,
behold, magi from the
east arrived in
Jerusalem, saying,
"Where is the newborn
king of the Jews?
We saw his star at its
rising
and have come to do
him homage."
When King Herod heard
this,
he was greatly troubled,
and all Jerusalem with him.
Assembling all the chief priests and the
scribes of the people,
he inquired of them where the Christ was
to be born.
They said to him, "In Bethlehem of Judea,
for thus it has been written through the
prophet:
And you, Bethlehem, land of Judah,
are by no means least among the
rulers of Judah;
since from you shall come a ruler,
who is to shepherd my people Israel."
Then Herod called the magi secretly
and ascertained from them the time of
the star's appearance.
He sent them to Bethlehem and said,
"Go and search diligently for the child.
When you have found him, bring me word,
that I too may go and do him homage."
After their audience with the king they set
out.

Continued in Appendix A, p. 268.

Reflecting on the Gospel

It is the dead of winter now in the northern hemisphere. The days are short, the nights are long. Most of us like to be indoors early where it is warm and safe and light. Darkness is not appealing to us. Once the sun goes down the temperature begins to drop; the creatures of the night emerge; often crime takes place. We tend to associate danger with darkness. But in these readings the "danger" is in the light. It is light that brings us to encounter "the newborn king of the Jews." It is the light of encounter that challenges us, offers us choice, changes us. We ought to run from the light. Instead, the magi embrace it. They follow it. They trust it. Darkness or light? Such stark contrasts. Which do we choose?

This gospel uncovers a number of contrasts: the magi-Gentiles from the east vs. Herod and the Jews of all Jerusalem; the light of the star that guided the magi vs. the darkness of Herod's heart; the "newborn king of the Jews" thought to be found in Jerusalem, the home of Israel's king vs. this Child being found in the small village of Bethlehem; Herod breeding evil in his heart to keep his power and status vs. the magi who paid homage and offered gifts to the Child. Searching for and finding the Christ necessitates a choice in face of contrasts: to accept or reject this new in-breaking of God. Further, there can be no encounter with Christ without a change in us.

Like the magi we, too, will find Christ if we search diligently. God also gives us a light that guides us. What leads us and prompts us to seek the divine is more than simple light, though; it is always God's power to lead us to encounter the divine. The light is Christ, the Light of the world. This divine Light always presents us with a choice: to embrace the gift of salvation, or to remain stuck in our own ways, wallowing in our own self-made darkness, brooding over our own fears of losing what we think is so precious to us. When we choose darkness we are choosing narrowness of vision, limited expectations, confined insight, restricted dreams, checked possibilities. When we encounter the light, embrace it and offer the homage of ourselves, we are choosing broad horizons, fresh anticipation, new openness, worthy ideals, unbounded options. The light changes us because it opens up for us a divine world we cannot imagine but is so attractive that we let go of self in order to allow God to fashion us in this Light that never fades. The magi followed the light, encountered the Light, offered homage to the Light. So must we.

Living the Paschal Mystery

God leads us just as surely as the star led the magi to Bethlehem. We must choose to trust in God's loving Presence and sure guidance. There will be inevitable setbacks and challenges as we struggle with following the light; our everyday lives are filled with obstacles and restlessness which can get us off track. We must "search diligently": God and God's will can be found in many circumstances of our family life, work, and leisure times. Sometimes we must change course and take "another way": conversion is an ongoing milestone in Christian living.

This feast day of the Lord's epiphany reminds us that the light of Christ is a diffuse one; it permeates all the world, diffuses salvation everywhere, and invites all people to live in the light. Our response: give of the treasure of our hearts. Give over our very selves to the light.

Focusing the Gospel

Key words and phrases: magi from the east, King Herod . . . greatly troubled, all Jerusalem, Bethlehem, saw the child, did him homage, offered him gifts

To the point: This gospel uncovers a number of contrasts: the magi-Gentiles from the east vs. Herod and the Jews of all Jerusalem; the light of the star that guided the magi vs. the darkness of Herod's heart; the "newborn king of the Jews" thought to be found in Jerusalem, the home of Israel's king vs. this Child being found in the small village of Bethlehem; Herod breeding evil in his heart to keep his power and status vs. the magi who paid homage and offered gifts to the Child. Searching for and finding the Christ necessitates a choice in face of contrasts: to accept or reject this new in-breaking of God. Further, there can be no encounter with Christ without a change in us.

Connecting the Gospel

to the first reading: The first reading refers to a contrast, too—between darkness and light. In spite of the darkness caused by some of our own choices, God shines divine glory upon us and calls us to "walk by [the] light."

to experience: We tend to live by common sense and logic. Who of us would ever follow a star into the unknown? From the magi we learn that willingness to be guided by unexpected in-breakings of wisdom that come from sudden light, the counsel of others, inspiration, insight, dreams can bring us to unexpected encounters with the Christ.

Connecting the Responsorial Psalm

to the readings: Psalm 72 proclaimed that all kings would pay homage to the king of Israel and all nations would serve him. The reason for such adulation had nothing to do with the personality of the king, but with the belief that he was God's representative. Acting under God's directive and with God's empowerment, the king was the one above all who saw that justice was done for the poor and the oppressed. The king, then, was the personal embodiment of what God had planned for all peoples from the beginning of creation.

For us, this plan is fulfilled in the person of Christ. In him the fullness of God shines (first reading) and the mystery of God's intention is completely revealed (second reading). Christ is the king who will give his very life to save the lives of the poor. May every nation come to adore him!

to psalmist preparation: Much of Psalm 72 is intercessory prayer for the king that he be able to fulfill his mission of implementing God's plan of justice and peace for the poor. Through baptism we have become God's kingly people. This means that all nations will come to adore Christ if we lead them through lives of justice and peace. Your singing of this psalm is not only proclamation of what will be, but also invitation that we, God's kingly people, work to make it happen.

ASSEMBLY & FAITH-SHARING GROUPS
- The contrasts I encounter in my daily living are . . . The choices I make in face of them are . . .
- The star I follow in order to find the Christ in my daily living is . . .
- I most surely encounter Christ when . . . I have been changed in these ways . . .

PRESIDERS
I am best a guiding light for others when I . . . Others guide me in these ways . . .

DEACONS
My serving others is a shining star that leads them to Christ in these ways . . .

HOSPITALITY MINISTERS
My manner of greeting those gathering helps them to encounter Christ during liturgy when I . . .

MUSIC MINISTERS
My music ministry is a light guiding the members of the assembly to . . .

ALTAR MINISTERS
My diligence in serving at the altar manifests my own search for Christ in these ways . . .

LECTORS
My proclamation is an epiphany of Christ to the assembly whenever I . . .

EXTRAORDINARY MINISTERS OF HOLY COMMUNION
My ministry of distributing Holy Communion is homage of the Christ who is present when I . . .

Model Penitential Act

Presider: The magi were guided by the light of God's star to the newborn King. We pause to reflect on how we have sometimes failed to recognize God's light guiding us . . . [pause]

Lord Jesus, you are Light for all nations: Lord . . .

Christ Jesus, you are the manifestation of God's glory: Christ . . .

Lord Jesus, you are worthy of all homage: Lord . . .

Homily Points

• Life is full of contrasts that force us to make choices. For example, we are faced with a choice between eating healthy food and eating junk food; between helping another in need and being selfish with our time; between forgiveness and holding a grudge. Searching for and encountering Christ help us make appropriate choices in these and many other daily circumstances. The choices we make determine the kind of people we are.

• As the magi were open to being guided by the star, so must we be open to the guidance of the light of Christ. This light brings the focus we need to make choices that further the manifestation of Christ in our world.

• Winston Churchill once said, "To improve is to change; to be perfect is to change often." Our encounters with Christ never leave us unchanged, but always draw us into the light so that we can see more clearly the choices we need to make in our own lives in order to come to perfection in Christ. Indeed, the choices we make determine who we are.

Model Universal Prayer (Prayer of the Faithful)

Presider: God gives us everything we need to come to the light of Christ. Illuminated by that light, we pray.

Response:

Lord, hear our prayer.

Cantor:

we pray to the Lord,

That all members of the church reflect the light of Christ and thus lead others to encounter Christ . . . [pause]

That all people of the world may be enlightened by God's guiding Presence and come to salvation . . . [pause]

That those who experience darkness and alienation in their lives may encounter Christ through the goodness of others . . . [pause]

That all of us here gathered may encounter Christ in the good choices we make each day . . . [pause]

Presider: O God, the light of your divine Son gives direction and purpose to our lives. Hear these our prayers that the choices we make each day may bring us closer to fullness of Life and light in Christ. We pray through that same Christ our Lord. **Amen.**

COLLECT

Let us pray

Pause for silent prayer

O God, who on this day
revealed your Only Begotten Son to the
nations
by the guidance of a star,
grant in your mercy
that we, who know you already by faith,
may be brought to behold the beauty of
your sublime glory.
Through our Lord Jesus Christ, your Son,
who lives and reigns with you in the unity
of the Holy Spirit,
one God, for ever and ever. **Amen.**

FIRST READING

Isa 60:1-6

Rise up in splendor, Jerusalem! Your light
has come,
the glory of the Lord shines upon you.
See, darkness covers the earth,
and thick clouds cover the peoples;
but upon you the LORD shines,
and over you appears his glory.
Nations shall walk by your light,
and kings by your shining radiance.
Raise your eyes and look about;
they all gather and come to you:
your sons come from afar,
and your daughters in the arms of their
nurses.

Then you shall be radiant at what you see,
your heart shall throb and overflow,
for the riches of the sea shall be emptied
out before you,
the wealth of nations shall be brought
to you.
Caravans of camels shall fill you,
dromedaries from Midian and Ephah;
all from Sheba shall come
bearing gold and frankincense,
and proclaiming the praises of the LORD.

RESPONSORIAL PSALM
Ps 72:1-2, 7-8, 10-11, 12-13

℟. (cf. 11) Lord, every nation on earth will adore you.

O God, with your judgment endow the
     king,
   and with your justice, the king's son;
he shall govern your people with justice
   and your afflicted ones with judgment.

℟. Lord, every nation on earth will adore you.

Justice shall flower in his days,
   and profound peace, till the moon be no
     more.
May he rule from sea to sea,
   and from the River to the ends of the
     earth.

℟. Lord, every nation on earth will adore you.

The kings of Tarshish and the Isles shall
     offer gifts;
   the kings of Arabia and Seba shall
     bring tribute.
All kings shall pay him homage,
   all nations shall serve him.

℟. Lord, every nation on earth will adore you.

For he shall rescue the poor when he cries
     out,
   and the afflicted when he has no one to
     help him.
He shall have pity for the lowly and the
     poor;
   the lives of the poor he shall save.

℟. Lord, every nation on earth will adore you.

SECOND READING
Eph 3:2-3a, 5-6

Brothers and sisters:
You have heard of the stewardship of
     God's grace
   that was given to me for your benefit,
   namely, that the mystery was made
     known to me by revelation.
It was not made known to people in other
     generations
   as it has now been revealed
   to his holy apostles and prophets by the
     Spirit:
   that the Gentiles are coheirs, members
     of the same body,
   and copartners in the promise in Christ
     Jesus through the gospel.

About Liturgy
Connecting the two great festal seasons: There are hints in this Sunday's gospel which help us connect the two great festal seasons (Advent-Christmas-Epiphany and Lent-Triduum-Easter) as two sides of salvation. (1) The magi saw the "star at its rising"; that is, in the East. This is the direction from which Israel expected the Messiah to come and the direction from which the early church expected Christ to come at the Parousia. (2) King Herod has an exchange with the Jewish leaders, as happened at the trial of Jesus. (3) Jesus manifested himself to Gentiles as an infant, as it was a Gentile (the centurion) who recognized Jesus on the cross as the Son of God. (4) There is fear and a power struggle among the leadership at Jesus' birth as there was at his trial, suffering, and death.

These connections help us realize that the liturgical year is a seamless celebration of the whole mystery of Christ. The year unfolds event by event and invites us to enter into Jesus' paschal journey. But this is not a historical journey; it is a liturgical journey calling us to pattern our lives more closely on that of Jesus. All the various events along our own journey to follow the light of Christ actually collapse into the one mystery of salvation.

About Liturgical Music
Music suggestions: We have many traditional Epiphany songs available to sing on this day, such as, "We Three Kings," "The First Noel," "What Child Is This," "As with Gladness Men of Old," "Songs of Thankfulness and Praise," "What Star Is This," and "How Brightly Shines the Morning Star." Less well-known, and worth introducing into wider use, are such songs as "Famed though the World's Great Cities Be" (HG); "The People Who Walked in Darkness" (W4); "Epiphany Carol" (G3, LMGM2); "Jesus, the Light of the World" (LMGM2); "Behold the Star" (LMGM2); and "Rise Up in Splendor" (WS). Choices will need to be made concerning where in the liturgy a given song best fits the purpose of the rite. Generally, more energetic pieces such as "Jesus, the Light of the World" are well suited to the entrance or the recessional processions. The text of "Epiphany Carol" suggests its use for the entrance procession. The verse-refrain structure of "The People Who Walked in Darkness" would make this piece very singable during the Communion procession with cantor or choir singing the verses and the rest of the assembly joining in on the refrain.

SPIRITUALITY

Gospel

Mark 1:7-11; L21ABC

**This is what John the Baptist
    proclaimed:
    "One mightier than I is coming after
        me.
I am not worthy to stoop and loosen the
    thongs of his sandals.
I have baptized you with water;
    he will baptize you with the Holy
        Spirit."**

**It happened in those days that Jesus
    came from Nazareth of Galilee
    and was baptized in the Jordan by
        John.
On coming up out of the water he saw
    the heavens being torn open
    and the Spirit, like a dove,
        descending upon him.
And a voice came from the heavens,
    "You are my beloved Son; with you I
        am well pleased."**

Reflecting on the Gospel

One element of our baptismal ceremony for babies and children who have not yet reached the age of reason is clothing those being baptized with a white garment. The words accompanying this gesture include "You have become a new creation, and have clothed yourselves in Christ . . . the outward sign of your Christian dignity." The rite goes on to suggest that it "is desirable that the families provide the garments" (Rite of Baptism for Children). Many families have a tradition of using the same baptismal dress for all their children—some families even pass this down through several generations and so the baptismal dress becomes a cherished family heirloom. It then symbolizes a double identity: a member of this particular family who share a common blood bond as well as a member of the family of God, of Christ's Body, who share a Life bond in the Holy Spirit. Baptism, then, is about who we become through our new relationship with God and each other.

The event of Jesus' baptism with water in the Jordan revealed who he already was: the "beloved Son" with whom God was "well pleased." Jesus' baptism did not change his identity, but revealed who he was. John prophesied that Jesus, however, would bring an entirely different baptism, for he would baptize us with the Holy Spirit. The event of our baptism with the Spirit announces to all present who we become: beloved children with whom God is "well pleased." Baptism initiates us into a way of living defined by a relationship of identity. Our whole Christian life is a journey of taking ownership of the ownership God has already taken of us. Through baptism God claims us. Our whole Christian life is a journey of keeping our baptismal garment spotless, living the dignity God has bestowed on us, growing in our identity as the beloved of God, allowing God to lay claim on us, being open to the Spirit who dwells within us.

Our identity is to be "begotten by God" (second reading), God's beloved daughters and sons. Through baptism we become one with Christ. An essential tenet of Christianity is that baptism plunges us into an ongoing way of living whereby our lives are patterned after Christ's. By the indwelling of the Spirit we become adopted sons and daughters of God, God's "beloved," too. By this indwelling—God's very Life—Jesus' life and way of living become our own. Jesus' saving work becomes our own life work.

Living the Paschal Mystery

We are plunged into the baptismal waters and rise out of those waters a new creation grafted onto Christ. We spend our lives growing into our identity as members of the Body of Christ. We spend our lives appreciating what it means to be God's beloved and the kind of life that relationship requires of us. We spend our lives continuing Jesus' saving mission. We spend our lives being the risen Presence of Christ for others. Being Christlike is what our baptismal identity is all about.

At our own baptism we unite ourselves with Christ as his Body (become God's children) and commit ourselves to continue his saving mission. Our lives must be spent being faithful to the relationship with God in Christ through the Holy Spirit which our baptism begins. Our dignity is found in being faithful to our identity and living the Gospel Jesus proclaimed, doing works with which God is "well pleased."

Focusing the Gospel

Key words and phrases: baptize you with the Holy Spirit, Jesus . . . was baptized, my beloved Son, well pleased

To the point: The event of Jesus' baptism with water in the Jordan revealed who he already was: the "beloved Son" with whom God was "well pleased." John prophesied that Jesus, however, would baptize us with the Holy Spirit. The event of our baptism with the Spirit announces who we become: beloved children with whom God is "well pleased." Our whole Christian life is a journey of taking ownership of the ownership God has already taken of us.

Connecting the Gospel

to the second reading: Three times this reading from John's letter speaks of our being "begotten by God." Truly we are of God because of our baptism in the Spirit.

to experience: We tend to think of baptism only as a ritual lasting a few moments. Actually, baptism is an ongoing immersion in the identity and mystery of Jesus and requires lifelong commitment.

Connecting the Responsorial Psalm

to the readings: The responsorial psalm this Sunday is not taken from the Psalter but from the book of Isaiah. The verses are part of a song celebrating God's deliverance of Israel from disaster and destruction. The psalmist proclaims God savior and calls all Israel to spread the news of God's saving intervention to "all the earth."

The salvation God offers is the gift of covenant relationship (first and second readings) celebrated with the fullness of the messianic banquet (first reading). It is the gift of personal relationship with God and one another marked by love (second reading). This gift is free but not without its demand that we change our manner of living (first and second readings). We can accept the gift and take on its demand because, through Jesus, we have been baptized with the Holy Spirit who will give us the strength and courage we need (psalm).

to psalmist preparation: In this Sunday's responsorial psalm you sing about God's gift of salvation. The readings reveal that salvation means our adoption as God's children, our feasting freely at the messianic meal, and our communion with one another. How have you experienced this salvation? How have you enabled others to share in it?

ASSEMBLY & FAITH-SHARING GROUPS
- What Jesus' being called the beloved Son means for me is . . . For me to be the beloved of God means . . .
- God is most pleased with me when I . . .
- For me, the greatest challenge of my baptism is . . . The greatest blessing is . . .

PRESIDERS
When I remember who I am because of my baptism with the Spirit, my presiding becomes . . .

DEACONS
What helps me serve others as an expression of my baptism with the Spirit is . . .

HOSPITALITY MINISTERS
My greeting helps the assembly members believe themselves to be God's beloved when . . .

MUSIC MINISTERS
When I pursue my music ministry knowing I am the beloved of God, the assembly hears . . .

ALTAR MINISTERS
My service at the altar is an expression of my baptismal identity when . . .

LECTORS
My proclamation of God's word challenges the assembly to deeper baptismal living when . . .

EXTRAORDINARY MINISTERS OF HOLY COMMUNION
My manner of distributing Communion helps the communicants take ownership of who they are as God's beloved when . . .

CELEBRATION

Model Rite for the Blessing and Sprinkling of Water
Presider: Dear friends, today we celebrate Jesus' baptism in the Jordan when the heavens were opened, the Spirit descended, and he was revealed as God's beloved Son. We also celebrate the grace of our own baptism and identity as God's daughters and sons.

[*continue with* Roman Missal, *Appendix II*]

Homily Points
• Learning a new skill takes a long time. The aging of a fine wine takes a long time. Getting to know another person well as a beloved and trusted friend takes a long time. Taking ownership of and being faithful to our baptismal identity as God's beloved takes a lifetime.

• Christian baptism transforms our very identity: we become God's beloved in whom God is well pleased. While God freely gives us this gift of identity through the Holy Spirit, we must accept it and make it our own. This takes a lifetime of faithful living.

• Every choice we make on our Christian journey either deepens our identity as God's beloved or weakens it. We either respond to a person in need, or walk away. We either put in an honest day's work for an honest day's pay, or we steal time and money. We either take time for daily prayer, or neglect conversation time with God. We either strive to grow in understanding our faith, or remain content with inadequate formation. Who we are is God's beloved, that is, the Body of Christ. Our baptismal call is to become every day more fully who we are. Growing in our identity is our most important lifelong task.

Model Universal Prayer (Prayer of the Faithful)
Presider: Recognizing our baptismal identity as the beloved of God, in confidence we ask God for what we need.

Response:

Cantor:

That all members of the church grow in their identity as God's beloved daughters and sons . . . [pause]

That all peoples of the world come to a greater appreciation of God's immense love for them . . . [pause]

That all those in need receive comfort from knowing that they are the beloved of God . . . [pause]

That each of us be ever faithful to our baptism by choosing to do what is right and good, holy and pleasing to God . . . [pause]

Presider: O loving God, you name us your beloved daughters and sons: hear our prayers and fill us with your Spirit so we may be ever faithful to who we are and one day come to share the fullness of Life with you. We ask this through Christ our Lord. **Amen.**

COLLECT
Let us pray

Pause for silent prayer

Almighty ever-living God,
who, when Christ had been baptized in the River Jordan
and as the Holy Spirit descended upon him,
solemnly declared him your beloved Son,
grant that your children by adoption,
reborn of water and the Holy Spirit,
may always be well pleasing to you.
Through our Lord Jesus Christ, your Son,
who lives and reigns with you in the unity of the Holy Spirit,
one God, for ever and ever. **Amen.**

or:

O God, whose Only Begotten Son
has appeared in our very flesh,
grant, we pray, that we may be inwardly transformed
through him whom we recognize as outwardly like ourselves.
Who lives and reigns with you in the unity of the Holy Spirit,
one God, for ever and ever. **Amen.**

FIRST READING
Isa 55:1-11

Thus says the LORD:
All you who are thirsty,
    come to the water!
You who have no money,
    come, receive grain and eat;
come, without paying and without cost,
    drink wine and milk!
Why spend your money for what is not bread,
    your wages for what fails to satisfy?
Heed me, and you shall eat well,
    you shall delight in rich fare.
Come to me heedfully,
    listen, that you may have life.
I will renew with you the everlasting covenant,
    the benefits assured to David.
As I made him a witness to the peoples,
    a leader and commander of nations,
so shall you summon a nation you knew not,
    and nations that knew you not shall run to you,
because of the LORD, your God,
    the Holy One of Israel, who has glorified you.

Seek the LORD while he may be found,
    call him while he is near.
Let the scoundrel forsake his way,
    and the wicked man his thoughts;

let him turn to the LORD for mercy;
  to our God, who is generous in
    forgiving.
For my thoughts are not your thoughts,
  nor are your ways my ways, says the
    LORD.
As high as the heavens are above the earth
  so high are my ways above your ways
  and my thoughts above your thoughts.

For just as from the heavens
  the rain and snow come down
and do not return there
  till they have watered the earth,
  making it fertile and fruitful,
giving seed to the one who sows
  and bread to the one who eats,
so shall my word be
  that goes forth from my mouth;
my word shall not return to me void,
  but shall do my will,
  achieving the end for which I sent it.

RESPONSORIAL PSALM
Isa 12:2-3, 4bcd, 5-6

R/. (3) You will draw water joyfully from
the springs of salvation.

God indeed is my savior;
  I am confident and unafraid.
My strength and my courage is the LORD,
  and he has been my savior.
With joy you will draw water
  at the fountain of salvation.

R/. You will draw water joyfully from the
springs of salvation.

Give thanks to the LORD, acclaim his name;
  among the nations make known his
    deeds,
  proclaim how exalted is his name.

R/. You will draw water joyfully from the
springs of salvation.

Sing praise to the LORD for his glorious
    achievement;
  let this be known throughout all the
    earth.
Shout with exultation, O city of Zion,
  for great in your midst
  is the Holy One of Israel!

R/. You will draw water joyfully from the
springs of salvation.

SECOND READING
1 John 5:1-9

See Appendix A, p. 269.

Other readings may also be used.
See Appendix A, p. 269.

About Liturgy

Planning liturgy well: Notice that a number of choices for readings are possible for this feast: (1) the three readings that are assigned for L21ABC: Isa 42:1-4, 6-7; Ps 29:1-2, 3-4, 3, 9-10; Acts 10:34-38; and Matt 3:13-17; (2) using the above set of readings but substituting the Year B gospel (Mark 1:7-11); or (3) using all three readings proper for Year B, as the writing team has chosen for *Living Liturgy™*.

It is especially appropriate to use the Rite for the Blessing and Sprinkling of Water on this Sunday. This liturgical use of water is a reminder of our baptism and calls forth from us a renewed baptismal commitment. Moreover, our church entrances have holy water fonts into which we dip our fingers and make the sign of the cross as we come into church. Each time we gather for liturgy this gesture is a poignant reminder of our baptism and that through it we are plunged into the mystery of Christ's dying and rising, the mystery of the cross. Each time we recite the Creed on Sundays and solemnities we are reminded of our baptismal profession. This would be a good Sunday to choose the Apostles' Creed, which is closest in wording to the baptismal profession. It would also be appropriate to schedule baptisms on this Sunday at the eucharistic liturgy so that the entire parish community becomes more aware of their mutual responsibility for helping members grow in their baptismal commitment.

Environment for Ordinary Time: This feast of the Baptism of the Lord concludes the Christmas season, so Monday begins the first part of the season of Ordinary Time. It is tempting for the environment committee to leave the Christmas poinsettias in the sacred space since they tend to last a long time. However, since this flower is so closely associated with the Christmas season, it would be better to remove them. On Monday the space must clearly reflect that it is Ordinary Time.

About Liturgical Music

Music suggestions: Many songs about the baptism of Jesus exist in the repertoire. Alan Hommerding's "To Jordan Jesus Humbly Came" (W4, WC, WS) and Fred Pratt Green's "When Jesus Came to Jordan" (W4) are examples of texts set to strongly metered tunes that would fit the entrance procession. Both the length and the content of "When John Baptized by Jordan's River" (JS3, SS, W4, WC) and "When Jesus Comes to Be Baptized" (BB, JS3) make them more suitable for the preparation of the gifts. The tune of Adam M. L. Tice's "The Strong and Gentle Voice" (W4) makes this hymn also more appropriate for the preparation of the gifts.

Sylvia Dunstan's "Down Galilee's Slow Roadways" begins with "Down Galilee's slow roadways A stranger traveled on . . ." and ends with "We too have found a roadway; It led us to this place. We all have had to travel In search of hope and grace. But now beside this water Again a voice is heard, 'You are my own, my chosen, Beloved of your Lord.'" Set to LANCASHIRE, the hymn could be used for either the entrance or the preparation of the gifts. Set to Bob Moore's driving SATB choral arrangement (GIA octavo G-5502), this hymn would be an excellent choir prelude.

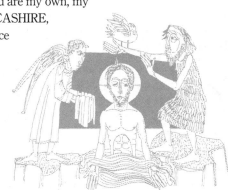

ORDINARY TIME I

SPIRITUALITY

GOSPEL ACCLAMATION
John 1:41, 17b

℟. Alleluia, alleluia.
We have found the Messiah:
Jesus Christ, who brings us truth and grace.
℟. Alleluia, alleluia.

Gospel

John 1:35-42; L65B

John was standing with two
of his disciples,
and as he watched Jesus
walk by, he said,
"Behold, the Lamb of
God."
The two disciples heard
what he said and
followed Jesus.
Jesus turned and saw them
following him and said
to them,
"What are you looking for?"
They said to him, "Rabbi"—which
translated means Teacher—,
"where are you staying?"
He said to them, "Come, and you will
see."
So they went and saw where Jesus was
staying,
and they stayed with him that day.
It was about four in the afternoon.
Andrew, the brother of Simon Peter,
was one of the two who heard John
and followed Jesus.
He first found his own brother Simon
and told him,
"We have found the Messiah"—which
is translated Christ—.
Then he brought him to Jesus.
Jesus looked at him and said,
"You are Simon the son of John;
you will be called Kephas"—which is
translated Peter.

Reflecting on the Gospel

So much of agriculture these days has been taken over by agribusiness. Family farms are being threatened and it is more and more difficult for the small farmer to compete with huge corporate farming enterprises. In spite of this shift in size and ownership of farms, farming still evokes in our minds and hearts images of lush fields, tidy gardens behind the farmhouse, and animals so well known by owners that they are given names. Daisy Duck is a beloved Disney cartoon character. Betsy is common as a cow's name. Shari Lewis's puppet Lamb Chop entertained children on TV for many years. Lambs are mentioned over two hundred times in the Bible. Shepherding was a common livelihood for the nomadic people of biblical times. They were used for their wool and meat. They were a staple of life. They were valuable and prized possessions, and so were also used in religious sacrifice. The gospel this Sunday names a very unique Lamb: the "Lamb of God." Lambs sacrificed for God are replaced by the "Lamb of God," a human-divine person whose sacrifice is once and for all.

This Sunday's gospel opens with the words, "John was standing with two of his disciples." These two disciples would have interpreted John the Baptist's cry, "Behold, the Lamb of God," within the Passover and temple tradition of sacrifice of lambs. What is startling about John's cry is that he uses this sacrificial reference not for a lamb, an animal, but for a human being who was walking by—Jesus. John is pointing to Jesus as the One who will be sacrificed. Little did they know at this point that the core of following Jesus is sacrifice—a total self-giving. Still, they followed him. As with all disciples, it took a time of rubbing shoulders with Jesus, hearing him teach and preach, observing his interactions with people, observing him pray, experiencing his resoluteness about his mission for them to begin to know Jesus, grasp his mission, and absorb the strength and courage to live his total self-giving life. Growing in total self-giving takes much time.

Self-giving is absolutely essential for anyone who claims to be a disciple of Jesus. None of us would choose the sacrifice that following Jesus requires. We are able to follow Jesus' example of total self-sacrifice only when we "Behold" him, when we keep our eyes focused on him and his Good News of salvation. We need to "stay" with Jesus, abide with him, never be parted from him in order for our self-giving to grow toward his total self-giving.

Living the Paschal Mystery

We cannot truly be disciples of Christ unless we, too, hear God's call and respond by transforming our lives, evidenced in the simple willingness to be obedient to God's will and take up the saving mission of Christ. This means more than keeping commandments or even of simply going to Mass on Sunday; it means that our whole lives are directed to being faithful in our allegiance to Christ and identifying with him so completely that his life is ours, his mission is ours, his total self-giving is ours.

Identifying with Christ and continuing his self-giving work of salvation make demands on us. Like Andrew in the gospel, we must boldly announce the Presence of Christ in our midst and bring others to Jesus. We do this best by living as he did: caring for others, bringing a healing touch, working at developing a deeper relationship with Christ through liturgy and prayer. The demand is surely there: become so intimate with Jesus that we do not waver in our love for him nor in our growing in his life-giving, total self-giving.

Focusing the Gospel

Key words and phrases: Behold, the Lamb of God; two disciples; followed Jesus

To the point: These two disciples would have interpreted John the Baptist's cry, "Behold, the Lamb of God," within the Passover and temple tradition of sacrifice of lambs. What is startling about John's cry is that he uses this sacrificial reference not for a lamb, but for a human being who was walking by—Jesus. John is pointing to Jesus as the One who will be sacrificed. Little did they know at this point that the core of following Jesus is sacrifice—a total self-giving. Still, they followed him.

Connecting the Gospel

to the first reading: Both the first reading and gospel are call-response narratives that challenge us to hear the voice of God, count the cost, and choose a faithful response.

to experience: While our response to God must always be total, it is not always immediate. John's disciples responded at once, but Samuel was called four times. God continues to call until we respond—and respond totally.

Connecting the Responsorial Psalm

to the readings: In Psalm 40, the one praying offers God thanksgiving for having been rescued from life-threatening danger. Having waited for God's help and not been disappointed, the person bursts into a "new song," praising God before all the world. But the psalmist also realizes it is not enough to offer God an external sacrifice of thanksgiving. What God seeks is the lifelong, all-consuming offering of a human heart willing to do God's will.

In these verses from Psalm 40, we express our willingness to do God's will with all our hearts. We choose, like Samuel, to keep listening until we recognize God's voice. We choose, like the disciples, to come close to Jesus so that we may know him better and follow him more fully. We choose, like Jesus the Lamb of God, to give our very selves so that others may have life. This choice will change our lives. Is this not what the journey of Ordinary Time is about?

to psalmist preparation: As you prepare to sing this Sunday's responsorial psalm, spend some time reflecting on why this psalm and these readings were selected for the Second Sunday in Ordinary Time. What is Ordinary Time calling you to do? to become? What are you as psalmist calling the assembly to do? to become?

**ASSEMBLY &
FAITH-SHARING GROUPS**
- I have heard God's call when . . . What God has called me to is . . .
- The cost of faithfully following Jesus in my life has been . . .
- My self-giving is still incomplete in these ways . . .

PRESIDERS
The manner in which I do my priestly ministry points to the Lamb of God in our midst when I . . .

DEACONS
My service to those in need is more challenging in its demand for total self-giving when . . .

HOSPITALITY MINISTERS
The manner of my greeting points those gathering for liturgy to the Presence of the Lamb of God when . . .

MUSIC MINISTERS
What and who helps me experience my music ministry as a call to self-giving is . . .

ALTAR MINISTERS
Acts of unobtrusive service help me be a faithful follower of Jesus in my daily living because . . .

LECTORS
When I practice Jesus' self-giving in my daily living, my proclamation sounds like . . .

**EXTRAORDINARY MINISTERS
OF HOLY COMMUNION**
My distributing Holy Communion helps me understand better that Mass is a sacrifice when . . .

Model Penitential Act

Presider: Just as Jesus called Andrew and Peter and the other disciples, he calls each of us to be his followers. As we begin this liturgy, we pause to ask ourselves how faithfully we have followed Jesus . . . [pause]

Lord Jesus, you are the Lamb of God whom we follow: Lord . . .

Christ Jesus, you are the Messiah who brings salvation: Christ . . .

Lord Jesus, you are the Teacher who forms us in discipleship: Lord . . .

Homily Points

• What kind of people immediately attract us? Blonds? Energetic? Intellectuals? Humorous? Honest? Trustworthy? Self-possessed? Humble? Wealthy? Powerful? What happens to our attraction as we get to know a person on a deeper level? Sometimes the attraction fades. At other times the attraction develops into an enduring bond. The two disciples in the gospel were so attracted to Jesus that they immediately followed him. What did they see in Jesus?

• When John the Baptist points out Jesus to his two disciples, they call Jesus "Rabbi." They see in Jesus knowledge, wisdom, authority. What they did not yet see is that Jesus is the "Lamb of God" who would sacrifice his own life for our salvation. Nor did they yet see that this sacrifice would also be asked of them as his followers.

• Our own journey of discipleship is a process of coming to know Jesus more fully, being more attracted to him, following him more faithfully even when the cost is great. What might that cost look like? We might have to walk away from the watercooler at work to avoid gossip. We might lose friends when we speak up for justice. We might be shunned by a social group when we live out our gospel values. In all these ways we unite ourselves more fully with the total self-giving of Jesus and grow in faithful discipleship.

Model Universal Prayer (Prayer of the Faithful)

Presider: Following Jesus as his disciples has its cost. Let us pray that we be given the strength to be faithful.

Response:

Lord,— hear our prayer.

Cantor:

we pray to the Lord,

That all members of the church remain faithful to Jesus even when the cost is great . . . [pause]

That all peoples of the world encounter God and come to salvation . . . [pause]

That the poor, the sick, and those in any need be helped by the self-giving of those who faithfully follow Jesus . . . [pause]

That all of us gathered here may grow in self-giving love . . . [pause]

Presider: O God, you call us to faithful discipleship and strengthen us to persevere: hear these our prayers and lead us to fullness of Life with you. We ask this through Christ our Lord. **Amen.**

COLLECT

Let us pray

Pause for silent prayer

Almighty ever-living God,
who govern all things,
both in heaven and on earth,
mercifully hear the pleading of your
    people
and bestow your peace on our times.
Through our Lord Jesus Christ, your Son,
who lives and reigns with you in the unity
    of the Holy Spirit,
one God, for ever and ever. **Amen.**

FIRST READING
1 Sam 3:3b-10, 19

Samuel was sleeping in the temple of the
    L ORD
    where the ark of God was.
The L ORD called to Samuel, who answered,
    "Here I am."
Samuel ran to Eli and said, "Here I am.
    You called me."
"I did not call you," Eli said. "Go back to
    sleep."
So he went back to sleep.
Again the L ORD called Samuel, who rose
    and went to Eli.
"Here I am," he said. "You called me."
But Eli answered, "I did not call you, my
    son. Go back to sleep."

At that time Samuel was not familiar with
    the L ORD,
    because the L ORD had not revealed
        anything to him as yet.
The L ORD called Samuel again, for the
    third time.
Getting up and going to Eli, he said, "Here
    I am. You called me."
Then Eli understood that the L ORD was
    calling the youth.
So he said to Samuel, "Go to sleep, and if
    you are called, reply,
    Speak, L ORD, for your servant is
        listening."
When Samuel went to sleep in his place,
    the L ORD came and revealed his
        presence,
    calling out as before, "Samuel, Samuel!"
Samuel answered, "Speak, for your
    servant is listening."

Samuel grew up, and the L ORD was with
    him,
    not permitting any word of his to be
        without effect.

RESPONSORIAL PSALM

Ps 40:2, 4, 7-8, 8-9, 10

R̸. (8a and 9a) Here am I, Lord; I come to do your will.

I have waited, waited for the LORD,
  and he stooped toward me and heard
    my cry.
And he put a new song into my mouth,
  a hymn to our God.

R̸. Here am I, Lord; I come to do your will.

Sacrifice or offering you wished not,
  but ears open to obedience you gave me.
Holocausts or sin-offerings you sought not;
  then said I, "Behold I come."

R̸. Here am I, Lord; I come to do your will.

"In the written scroll it is prescribed for
    me,
to do your will, O my God, is my delight,
  and your law is within my heart!"

R̸. Here am I, Lord; I come to do your will.

I announced your justice in the vast
    assembly;
  I did not restrain my lips, as you, O
    LORD, know.

R̸. Here am I, Lord; I come to do your will.

SECOND READING

1 Cor 6:13c-15a, 17-20

Brothers and sisters:
The body is not for immorality, but for the
    Lord,
  and the Lord is for the body;
  God raised the Lord and will also raise
    us by his power.

Do you not know that your bodies are
    members of Christ?
But whoever is joined to the Lord becomes
    one Spirit with him.
Avoid immorality.
Every other sin a person commits is
    outside the body,
  but the immoral person sins against his
    own body.
Do you not know that your body
  is a temple of the Holy Spirit within
    you,
  whom you have from God, and that you
    are not your own?
For you have been purchased at a price.
Therefore glorify God in your body.

About Liturgy

Ordinary Time: During Ordinary Time this year we proclaim the Good News according to Mark (Year B), and follow the gospel narrative from the call of the disciples at the beginning of Mark's gospel to confrontation with the cross to the joy of the resurrection near the end. Each Sunday liturgy brings us a piece of how salvation unfolds in the Gospel of Mark. What we can unfailingly expect during Ordinary Time—if we are faithful to our paschal mystery/gospel journey—is that God will transform us in some particular way during this particular year.

During all three years of the Lectionary cycle, however, the Second Sunday in Ordinary Time uses a gospel chosen from John rather than from the Synoptic Gospel assigned for the year. The reason for this is that the second Sunday "continues to center on the manifestation of the Lord, which is celebrated on the Solemnity of the Epiphany, through the traditional passage about the wedding feast at Cana [the gospel for Year C] and two other passages from the Gospel of John" (ILM no. 105).

The first period of Ordinary Time (from after the Christmas season until the beginning of Lent) focuses on the early events in Jesus' public life, especially the call of the disciples and the beginning of Jesus' public ministry. These weeks at the beginning of the new civil year might be a good time for each of us to assess how well we hear God's relentless call to be faithful followers of Jesus. Each of us can probably recall times when we have turned deaf ears to God; if we remember that God's call is relentless (see the first reading), then we might be encouraged to listen more carefully and sooner. God won't let go!

About Liturgical Music

Music suggestions: Two well-known songs that come immediately to mind for this Sunday are Dan Schutte's "Here I Am, Lord" and John Bell's "The Summons." Both are found in most resources and both could be sung during either the preparation of the gifts or the Communion procession. Michael Philip Ward's "Here I Am, Lord" (WC, WS) uses different words than the Schutte piece. Both text and melody are lovely and well-suited for use during Communion. Herbert O'Driscoll's text "Come and Journey with a Savior" (G3) expresses the many directions we must travel along the road of discipleship as we journey "inward," "outward," "upward," and "onward." This song would also be suitable during Communion. Delores Dufner's "The Baptist Bore Witness" (W4) would make an excellent recessional hymn. John the Baptist bore witness to Christ, "not only a shepherd but also a lamb." Now Christ "invites us, the Church here today, Baptized in the Spirit, to follow his way Not only in word but in love's daily deed, With justice and mercy for neighbor's in need."

SPIRITUALITY

GOSPEL ACCLAMATION
Mark 1:15

R⁊. Alleluia, alleluia.
The kingdom of God is at hand.
Repent and believe in the Gospel.
R⁊. Alleluia, alleluia.

Gospel   Mark 1:14-20; L68B

After John had been arrested,
   Jesus came to Galilee proclaiming the
      gospel of God:
   "This is the time of fulfillment.
The kingdom of God is at hand.
Repent, and believe in the gospel."

As he passed by the Sea of Galilee,
   he saw Simon and his brother Andrew
      casting their nets into the sea;
   they were fishermen.
Jesus said to them,
   "Come after me, and I will make you
      fishers of men."
Then they abandoned their nets and
   followed him.
He walked along a little farther
   and saw James, the son of Zebedee,
      and his brother John.
They too were in a boat mending their
   nets.
Then he called them.
So they left their father Zebedee in the
   boat
   along with the hired men and
      followed him.

Reflecting on the Gospel

The Innocence Project is an organization dedicated to proving the innocence of wrongfully convicted people through new and better DNA testing and other improved forensic methods. Each time we read or hear news about someone who has been proven innocent—sometimes after spending decades in prison maintaining his or her innocence—our heart goes out to the person. Prison is a bad enough life for the guilty; it would seem to us to be unbearable and impossible for the innocent. This Sunday's gospel begins with the words, "After John had been arrested." We know John was a holy and innocent man. He was arrested for speaking the truth. Jesus, too, would be arrested for speaking the truth. Both more than spoke the truth, however; they lived the truth of the Good News of salvation.

Anytime we speak the truth by the way we live we open ourselves to misunderstanding, conflict, and sometimes even arrest and death. We human beings do not like to be faced with the truth of our own inadequacies and the consequent need to constantly grow and improve ourselves. We hear in this gospel a call to "come after" Jesus. Following Jesus requires change, whether that be the radical one of leaving all to follow Jesus, or the more modest one of turning from the little everyday behaviors that cause us to focus on ourselves and our own needs rather than on Jesus and the needs of others. This means, of course, that this kind of change required for discipleship always has a cost.

John preached repentance, and was arrested in spite of his goodness and innocence. Jesus preached the Gospel and suffered and died in spite of his goodness and innocence. Hearing Jesus' call to discipleship and choosing to follow him faithfully literally assures us we will meet adversity and suffering, as did both John and Jesus. The surprise of the gospel is not that we will face adversity, however. The surprise is that in preaching repentance and changing our lives, "the time of fulfillment" is upon us. The change assures us of God's Presence.

This gospel (which begins this year's sequential reading from Mark) is a call-response episode similar to last Sunday's gospel from St. John. Here, however, the call comes within the context of Jesus' proclamation that now is "the time of fulfillment." "The kingdom of God is at hand" in Jesus who manifests God's abiding Presence, God's promise of forgiveness, God's unparalleled power to save. To enter into this "time of fulfillment," we must leave everything behind and answer Jesus' call to follow him.

Living the Paschal Mystery

The gospel portrays following Jesus in radical terms: turn from evil, leave all to follow Jesus. For most of us, this is not the kind of discipleship that following Jesus requires of us. Rather, to be faithful followers of Jesus we must change and be more Christlike in the little ways that are part of our everydays: turn to listen to someone rather than let our minds wander; root out whatever attitudes and behaviors most annoy those with whom we live; think only positive thoughts, especially about others. It's these little changes that probably actually cost us the most! It's also these little changes that help us grow into faithful disciples and that make evident that "the time of fulfillment" is now.

Focusing the Gospel

Key words and phrases: This is the time of fulfillment, The kingdom of God is at hand, Come after me, abandoned their nets, followed him

To the point: This gospel (which begins this year's sequential reading from Mark) is a call-response episode similar to last Sunday's gospel from St. John. Here, however, the call comes within the context of Jesus' proclamation that now is "the time of fulfillment." "The kingdom of God is at hand" in Jesus who manifests God's abiding Presence, God's promise of forgiveness, God's unparalleled power to save. To enter into this "time of fulfillment," we must leave everything behind and answer Jesus' call to follow him.

Connecting the Gospel

to the first reading: In both the first reading and gospel there is a call to repentance. Conversion of life is an ongoing requirement if we are to share in "the time of fulfillment" and faithfully follow Jesus.

to experience: Fulfillment is a natural human goal; we all seek relationship fulfillment, financial fulfillment, job fulfillment. The "time of fulfillment" Jesus proclaims in the gospel exceeds all our human expectations.

Connecting the Responsorial Psalm

to the readings: The Ninevites listen to Jonah's call to repentance and immediately reform their lives (first reading). The disciples hear Jesus' announcement of the kingdom of God and instantly abandon all to follow him (gospel). In Psalm 25 we pray for this same readiness to hear and to learn the ways of God. We acknowledge that the kingdom of God is at hand and ask for the grace to change our lives accordingly. Psalm 25, then, is a blueprint for our journey through Ordinary Time when God teaches and we learn the way of discipleship. May we sing it with confidence, courage, and commitment.

to psalmist preparation: As you sing these verses from Psalm 25, you become an icon before the assembly of response to God's call to conversion and discipleship. To help you prepare for this role, spend some time this week reflecting on these questions: Where in your life right now is God calling you to conversion? Through whom is God calling you? What does God wish to teach you?

**ASSEMBLY &
FAITH-SHARING GROUPS**
- I feel most fulfilled when . . . I experience Jesus' "time of fulfillment" when . . .
- What I must leave behind in order to follow Jesus more faithfully as a disciple is . . .
- For me, "the kingdom of God is at hand" when . . .

PRESIDERS
My life of prayer and ministry proclaims for my people "the time of fulfillment" when . . .

DEACONS
"The kingdom of God is at hand" when I serve in this way . . .

HOSPITALITY MINISTERS
In order for the people assembling for liturgy to hear Jesus' call to follow him, I need to greet them in these ways . . .

MUSIC MINISTERS
My manner of doing music enables members of the assembly to respond to Jesus' ongoing call to discipleship in these ways . . .

ALTAR MINISTERS
In order to serve faithfully at the altar, I must leave behind . . .

LECTORS
God's word is fulfilled in me when . . . then my proclamation sounds like . . .

**EXTRAORDINARY MINISTERS
OF HOLY COMMUNION**
Holy Communion is a "time of fulfillment" for me . . . for those coming to Holy Communion . . .

Model Penitential Act

Presider: In today's gospel Jesus calls disciples to follow him in his work of salvation. We pause at the beginning of this liturgy to reflect on Jesus' call to us and how well we have responded . . . [pause]

Lord Jesus, you announce that the kingdom of God is at hand: Lord . . .

Christ Jesus, you proclaim a "time of fulfillment": Christ . . .

Lord Jesus, you call us to repentance and belief: Lord . . .

Homily Points

• When someone yells "Stop!" we instantly freeze. When someone yells "Fore!" we instinctively duck. When someone yells "Fire!" we immediately run. All these exclamations carry a built-in urgency provoking an immediate and total response. When Jesus exclaims that this "is the time of fulfillment," we must hear him with the same urgency and respond with the same immediacy.

• This gospel is filled with a sense of urgency. John has been arrested. Persecution of those who speak truth has begun. The time is ripe for the proclamation of the "kingdom of God." The "time of fulfillment" is "at hand." This gospel portrays a Jesus urgently on the move, gathering coworkers to join him in his saving mission.

• We are challenged to respond with a sense of urgency and immediacy to Jesus. Do we have a sense of urgency about caring when we see someone in trouble? about loving when we notice someone excluded? about reconciling hurt? about eliminating, to the best of our ability, suffering in all its forms? Do we realize that every day is a "time of fulfillment," that every day brings the "kingdom of God" at hand? In our faithful responding, we become one with Jesus in his saving mission. Nothing is more urgent than this.

Model Universal Prayer (Prayer of the Faithful)

Presider: Jesus proclaimed that the "kingdom of God is at hand." Let us place our needs in the hand of our loving God so that all might savor God's goodness.

Response:

Lord,— hear our prayer.

Cantor:

we pray to the Lord,

For all members of the church, may they faithfully follow Jesus in all ways . . . [pause]

For all peoples of the world, may they hear the Good News of salvation and respond faithfully . . . [pause]

For the poor and the sick, may they be touched by the love of God through the faithful care and concern of others . . . [pause]

For all of us gathered here, may we faithfully respond with urgency and immediacy to the proclamation of God's reign at hand . . . [pause]

Presider: Gracious God, your Son calls us to share in his saving mission: hear these our prayers that we might respond faithfully and fully. We ask this through Christ our Lord. **Amen.**

COLLECT
Let us pray

Pause for silent prayer

Almighty ever-living God,
direct our actions according to your good
    pleasure,
that in the name of your beloved Son
we may abound in good works.
Through our Lord Jesus Christ, your Son,
who lives and reigns with you in the unity
    of the Holy Spirit,
one God, for ever and ever. **Amen.**

FIRST READING
Jonah 3:1-5, 10

The word of the LORD came to Jonah,
        saying:
    "Set out for the great city of Nineveh,
    and announce to it the message that I
        will tell you."
So Jonah made ready and went to Nineveh,
    according to the LORD's bidding.
Now Nineveh was an enormously large
        city;
    it took three days to go through it.
Jonah began his journey through the city,
    and had gone but a single day's walk
        announcing,
    "Forty days more and Nineveh shall be
        destroyed,"
    when the people of Nineveh believed
        God;
    they proclaimed a fast
    and all of them, great and small, put on
        sackcloth.

When God saw by their actions how they
        turned from their evil way,
    he repented of the evil that he had
        threatened to do to them;
    he did not carry it out.

RESPONSORIAL PSALM

Ps 25:4-5, 6-7, 8-9

R̂. (4a) Teach me your ways, O Lord.

Your ways, O Lord, make known to me;
  teach me your paths,
guide me in your truth and teach me,
  for you are God my savior.

R̂. Teach me your ways, O Lord.

Remember that your compassion, O Lord,
  and your love are from of old.
In your kindness remember me,
  because of your goodness, O Lord.

R̂. Teach me your ways, O Lord.

Good and upright is the Lord;
  thus he shows sinners the way.
He guides the humble to justice
  and teaches the humble his way.

R̂. Teach me your ways, O Lord.

SECOND READING

1 Cor 7:29-31

I tell you, brothers and sisters, the time is
  running out.
From now on, let those having wives act as
  not having them,
  those weeping as not weeping,
  those rejoicing as not rejoicing,
  those buying as not owning,
  those using the world as not using it
  fully.
For the world in its present form is
  passing away.

✠ CATECHESIS

About Liturgy

Proclamation and believability: This Sunday's readings point out the importance of the Liturgy of the Word and the Scriptures we hear proclaimed each Sunday. This means that the proclamation of the Scriptures must be believable. The best way for this to happen is for priests, deacons, and lectors to make a concerted effort to live the Scripture passage in as many practical ways in their daily life as they can the week before they proclaim it. In this way the believability of the proclamation comes from the conviction of their very lived experience of the Scriptures. For members of the assembly, this means that the Scriptures heard on Sunday aren't simply nice readings listened to then quickly forgotten, but words listened to so deeply that they make a difference in our lives. We hear these readings in order to be changed. We say it again: the readings ought not to be forgotten as soon as we're out of the church doors, but they ought to be carried over into the way we live. The Scriptures are a blueprint for our everyday Gospel living.

Fluidity in the liturgical year: At first glance the first reading and gospel might seem more appropriate for Lent than for a Sunday in Ordinary Time because they speak so strongly of repentance and fasting and penance. This challenges us to think about the liturgical year not in terms of discrete seasons with limited motifs, but as a fluidity in which the dying and rising of the paschal mystery keep showing up in different contexts. In this Sunday's readings the call to repentance comes within the context of the call to follow Jesus. During Lent we see a different context for repentance—preparation for or renewing our baptismal commitment and preparing to enter into the solemn Easter mysteries.

About Liturgical Music

Importance of the responsorial psalm refrain: This Sunday's responsorial psalm is an example of how the meaning of a psalm text is changed by its particular placement within the liturgical year. Psalm 25 is sung not only this Sunday but also on the First Sunday of Advent Year C, the First Sunday of Lent Year B, and the Twenty-Sixth Sunday in Ordinary Time Year A. It is also one of the common psalms which may be sung on all the Sundays of Advent. The refrain for each of these liturgies varies, however, to fit the particular season. There are also slight adjustments in the verses. These variations occur because the text of the psalm has been specifically chosen to fit the readings of the day. While we might be tempted to use the same refrain and verses for all of these liturgical celebrations, it is important to use the text given for the day because it helps us enter into this particular day, during this particular season, with these particular readings.

The refrain for this Sunday, "Teach me your ways, O Lord," invites us to consider the relationship between God's call and the necessity for conversion of life. In both the first reading and the gospel we see this relationship in action. In conjunction with the readings of the day, the responsorial psalm and its refrain tell us what Ordinary Time is all about: listening to and learning the ways of God, and opening ourselves to be forgiven and formed by the One who guides our ways.

SPIRITUALITY

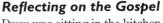

GOSPEL ACCLAMATION
Matt 4:16

R. Alleluia, alleluia.
The people who sit in darkness have
    seen a great light;
on those dwelling in a land
    overshadowed by death,
light has arisen.
R. Alleluia, alleluia.

Gospel

Mark 1:21-28; L71B

Then they came to
    Capernaum,
    and on the sabbath
        Jesus entered the
        synagogue and
        taught.
The people were
    astonished at his
    teaching,
    for he taught them as one having
        authority and not as the scribes.
In their synagogue was a man with an
    unclean spirit;
    he cried out, "What have you to do
        with us, Jesus of Nazareth?
Have you come to destroy us?
I know who you are—the Holy One of
    God!"
Jesus rebuked him and said,
    "Quiet! Come out of him!"
The unclean spirit convulsed him and
    with a loud cry came out of him.
All were amazed and asked one
    another,
    "What is this?
A new teaching with authority.
He commands even the unclean spirits
    and they obey him."
His fame spread everywhere
    throughout the whole region of
    Galilee.

Reflecting on the Gospel
Drew was sitting in the kitchen watching Mom finish icing and decorating a birthday cake for his older sister. His eyes were big and wanting through the whole process. Mom turned to the kitchen sink to wash up the baking dishes, and turned around when she heard a giggle. "Did you take some of the birthday cake icing?" she asked. "No, Mommy," Drew answered, despite the dead giveaway of the chocolate icing smudge on his lips. So Mom and Drew have a little chat about fibbing. Early on in life we are confronted with right from wrong, good from bad, holiness from evil. This gospel narrates the first of many dramatic confrontations between holiness and evil. Banishing evil is the work of salvation Jesus has been sent to do, and he does so with authority. He has this authority because he is "the Holy One of God." Holiness is "of God"; evil is everything that is opposed to God.

In the gospel, Jesus' "authority" is not perceived as a negative power over, as the ability to control others. Jesus' authority rests in the meaning of the word itself; from the Latin, *auctor*, "authority" refers to origin, originator. Jesus has authority not simply because he is "of God," but because he *is* God, the origin of all authority, goodness, and truth. Jesus' authority ushers forth from who he is: God, the originator of all life and holiness. Jesus' authority rests in his identity as the divine Son. The "new teaching with authority" about which the people are amazed is not the healing miracle in itself, but rather the display of God's face-to-face Presence mediated in Jesus. Jesus is the authority of holiness incarnate.

All of us must confront many battles waged between good and evil throughout our lives. As we grow older, the battles become much more serious than Drew's fib about eating some icing. We must face decisions between what destroys our relationship with God and others and what helps us grow in holiness. For us to destroy the evil that confronts us, we must be "of God," we must be holy. We, too, have this same authority to banish evil because, baptized into Christ, we are holy ones "of God." The authority of holiness is our baptismal birthright. It is God's Life given us that makes us holy; it is God's Life that makes us, too, "of God." Like Jesus, we must be the authority of holiness incarnate.

Living the Paschal Mystery
Jesus' authority rested in both his word and in his power and willingness to confront evil. The people in the synagogue were "astonished at his teaching" (his word) as well as his power over "an unclean spirit." Bringing forth healing, goodness, and life—the fruit of authority well exercised—is very much at the heart of the paschal mystery.

Paschal mystery living requires us to be so bold as Jesus in confronting whatever "demons" in us keep us from surrendering ourselves over to the growth and life to which God calls us. The call to die to self is more than idle talk. It is the ongoing demand in daily living to listen to God's word, know all that the Lord commands us, and embrace the life God offers. It is the ongoing demand in daily living to confront evil boldly and not let it win. In surrendering ourselves to God's will, in dying to self, we embrace our identity with "the Holy One of God" and are assured of the victory of new Life. Only by identifying with "the Holy One of God" can we speak and act with his authority. Truly, this is astonishing and amazing Good News.

Focusing the Gospel

Key words and phrases: one having authority, unclean spirit, Holy One of God, Come out of him

To the point: This gospel narrates the dramatic confrontation between holiness and evil. Banishing evil is the work of salvation Jesus has been sent to do, and he does so with authority. He has this authority because he is "the Holy One of God." We, too, have this same authority to banish evil because, baptized into Christ, we are holy ones "of God." The authority of holiness is our baptismal birthright.

Connecting the Gospel

to the first reading: True prophets can only speak the words God puts into their mouths. God is the source of their authority.

to experience: Authority is often used as an abuse of power over others. The kind of authority spoken of in this gospel is not an abuse of power over others, but a God-given empowerment for freeing others from evil.

Connecting the Responsorial Psalm

to the readings: These verses from Psalm 95 challenge us to hear the voice of God. In the first reading Moses and the prophets speak the words of God and do so in the recognizable voice of a fellow human being, a "kinsman." In the gospel, Jesus does the same—speaks the word of God in a human voice. But he does so with an authority far beyond anything the people have heard before. The words he speaks are a direct and victorious confrontation with the forces of evil which can possess the human heart.

But the psalm raises the question each of us faces in our struggle with faithful discipleship: will we surrender to this authority? The truth is that, despite how good the news Christ speaks, many elements in our hearts resist. The psalmist pleads with us to remain faithful in our listening to God, knowing full well how real is the possibility that we may choose otherwise. This psalm is a reality check; may we heed its message.

to psalmist preparation: Your singing of this psalm needs to come from a heart that hears the voice of God and responds. Just as God called the Israelites to be holy and faithful, so does God call you. What helps you hear and heed God's voice? What hinders you?

**ASSEMBLY &
FAITH-SHARING GROUPS**
- That Jesus is "the Holy One of God" says to me . . . That I am a holy one of God means to me . . .
- Jesus speaks to me with authority about . . . He gives me authority to . . .
- The evil within me that I must work to banish is . . . The evil in the world I must work to banish is . . .

PRESIDERS
What enables me to speak with the authority of holiness to the people is . . .

DEACONS
My service to those in need embodies true holiness when I . . .

HOSPITALITY MINISTERS
My greeting enables assembly members to appreciate that they are holy ones of God when I . . .

MUSIC MINISTERS
My birthright of holiness helps me banish the tendency to do music ministry out of self-interest when . . .

ALTAR MINISTERS
Holiness is my baptismal birthright, and so is serving. Remembering this helps me serve better in that . . .

LECTORS
I proclaim the word with the authority of holiness when . . .

**EXTRAORDINARY MINISTERS
OF HOLY COMMUNION**
My distributing the Body and Blood of Christ enables communicants to experience a holy God who calls them to holiness when I . . .

Model Penitential Act

Presider: In today's gospel, Jesus acts with the authority of holiness to banish an unclean spirit. As we prepare to celebrate this liturgy, let us call to mind our need for Jesus to banish the unclean spirits in our lives . . . [pause]

Lord Jesus, you are the Holy One of God: Lord . . .

Christ Jesus, you are God's authority made visible: Christ . . .

Lord Jesus, you are the Savior who teaches us how to be holy: Lord . . .

Homily Points

• Some argue that evil is pervasive and lurks right over our shoulder; others argue that evil is nonexistent. Rarely do we hear that holiness is pervasive, and yet it is. In fact, both evil and holiness exist, as this gospel demonstrates. Holiness is the greater authority. Holiness is our baptismal birthright.

• Jesus confronts evil head-on. Evil exists, but because of Jesus, "the Holy One of God," it does not triumph. The people in the synagogue were amazed and asked, "What is this?" It is a "new teaching" authenticated by Jesus' saving work of holiness that banishes evil.

• Like Jesus, we too must confront evil head-on. Like Jesus, we too are armed with God's holiness giving us the authority to banish evil. In this gospel banishing evil is dramatic and instant. In our daily lives the banishment of evil is more often less spectacular and more gradual. It is a lifelong process coming to fulfillment as we truly believe that we are holy and "of God."

Model Universal Prayer (Prayer of the Faithful)

Presider: God is holy and gives us a share in this holiness. Let us pray for our needs, confident that God hears the prayers of God's holy people.

Response:

Lord,——— hear our prayer.

Cantor:

we pray to the Lord,

For all leaders in the church, may they always speak and act with the truth and authority of Jesus . . . [pause]

For leaders of nations, may their authority bring life and holiness for all people . . . [pause]

For those who are sick and suffering, may they be comforted by God's holy people . . . [pause]

For all of us here, may we grow in our baptismal holiness and confront evil with authority and victory . . . [pause]

Presider: Good and gracious God, you call us to share in the holiness of who you are: hear our prayers that we may banish evil with the authority of holiness you have given us. We ask this through Christ our Lord. **Amen.**

COLLECT

Let us pray

Pause for silent prayer

Grant us, Lord our God,
that we may honor you with all our mind,
and love everyone in truth of heart.
Through our Lord Jesus Christ, your Son,
who lives and reigns with you in the unity
    of the Holy Spirit,
one God, for ever and ever. **Amen.**

FIRST READING

Deut 18:15-20

Moses spoke to all the people, saying:
  "A prophet like me will the LORD, your
      God, raise up for you
    from among your own kin;
    to him you shall listen.
This is exactly what you requested of the
     LORD, your God, at Horeb
    on the day of the assembly, when you
     said,
    'Let us not again hear the voice of the
     LORD, our God,
    nor see this great fire any more, lest we
     die.'
And the LORD said to me, 'This was well
    said.
I will raise up for them a prophet like you
    from among their kin,
    and will put my words into his mouth;
    he shall tell them all that I command
     him.
Whoever will not listen to my words
    which he speaks in my name,
    I myself will make him answer for it.
But if a prophet presumes to speak in my
    name
    an oracle that I have not commanded
     him to speak,
    or speaks in the name of other gods, he
     shall die.'"

RESPONSORIAL PSALM
Ps 95:1-2, 6-7, 7-9

℟. (8) If today you hear his voice, harden not your hearts.

Come, let us sing joyfully to the LORD;
let us acclaim the rock of our salvation.
Let us come into his presence with thanksgiving;
let us joyfully sing psalms to him.

℟. If today you hear his voice, harden not your hearts.

Come, let us bow down in worship;
let us kneel before the LORD who made us.
For he is our God,
and we are the people he shepherds, the flock he guides.

℟. If today you hear his voice, harden not your hearts.

Oh, that today you would hear his voice:
"Harden not your hearts as at Meribah,
as in the day of Massah in the desert,
where your fathers tempted me;
they tested me though they had seen my works."

℟. If today you hear his voice, harden not your hearts.

SECOND READING
1 Cor 7:32-35

Brothers and sisters:
I should like you to be free of anxieties.
An unmarried man is anxious about the things of the Lord,
how he may please the Lord.
But a married man is anxious about the things of the world,
how he may please his wife, and he is divided.
An unmarried woman or a virgin is anxious about the things of the Lord,
so that she may be holy in both body and spirit.
A married woman, on the other hand,
is anxious about the things of the world,
how she may please her husband.
I am telling you this for your own benefit,
not to impose a restraint upon you,
but for the sake of propriety
and adherence to the Lord without distraction.

CATECHESIS

About Liturgy

Liturgy as prophecy: Prophets were those persons chosen by God to announce anew the covenant, confronting the community with their choices to stray from God and calling them to renewed relationship with God and commitment to the covenantal terms. We usually think of John the Baptist as the last of the prophets. With the coming of Jesus, a new era of divine communication and relationship was opened up. But this does not mean that prophecy has ended. Just as with the people of old, sometimes we need a voice calling us to a renewed covenantal relationship with God. Liturgy itself has a prophetic thrust. Liturgy always reminds us of our baptismal covenant and calls us to deeper relationship with God, to a renewed commitment to live according to God's will.

Obviously, one way liturgy is prophetic is through the proclamation of Scriptures during the Liturgy of the Word. During this time we are continually reminded of God's abiding Presence and love, of the divine desire to be in intimate relationship with us. We hear in the Scriptures both challenge and encouragement as we journey deeper into our relationship with God. We hear in the Scriptures how to confront and overcome evil.

Another way liturgy is prophetic is through the universal prayer (prayer of the faithful). As we conclude our proclamation and reflection on Scripture, we turn our hearts to the church, world, those in need, and our own local community. As we pray for all these needs, we also nudge ourselves to face the systemic and personal causes of human suffering and commit ourselves to reach out to make our church and world a better place for everyone. There is a call to goodness in the universal prayer.

Yet another way the Sunday liturgy is prophetic is by hearing the proclamation of our Christian story in the eucharistic prayer and approaching God's table of abundance to be nourished on the heavenly food. By remembering God's great deeds for us and divine desire for salvation, we are invited to deeper commitment, remembering that our baptismal covenant has made us "kin," daughters and sons of God who are now conformed to the dying and rising of the beloved Son.

About Liturgical Music

Music suggestions: In Willard Jabusch's "The King of Glory" (found in most resources), we call one another to "open the gates" and let Christ enter. Like those in the synagogue who witness Jesus' authority over evil, we acknowledge that "in all of Galilee was never another" (verse 3). This well-known hymn would be an appropriate entrance song. Another suitable entrance song would be Bernadette Farrell's "Praise to You, O Christ, Our Savior" (found in many resources) in which we acclaim Jesus as the One whose power and authority leads us from darkness to light.

Thomas Troeger's "Silence! Frenzied, Unclean Spirit" (HG, W4) was written with this Sunday's gospel in mind. Verse 1 retells the dramatic event of Jesus, "God's healing, holy One," commanding the demon to leave the possessed man. Verses 2 and 3 express our prayer that Jesus do the same for us: "Silence, Lord, the unclean spirit, In our mind and in our heart. . . . Clear our thought and calm our feeling, Still the fractured, warring soul. By the power of your healing make us faithful, true, and whole." This hymn would make a good reflection on the gospel reading during the preparation of the gifts.

SPIRITUALITY

GOSPEL ACCLAMATION
Matt 8:17

R7. Alleluia, alleluia.
Christ took away our infirmities
and bore our diseases.
R7. Alleluia, alleluia.

Gospel   Mark 1:29-39; L74B

On leaving the synagogue
    Jesus entered the house of
        Simon and Andrew with
        James and John.
Simon's mother-in-law lay sick
    with a fever.
They immediately told him
    about her.
He approached, grasped her
    hand, and helped her up.
Then the fever left her and she
    waited on them.

When it was evening, after sunset,
    they brought to him all who were ill
        or possessed by demons.
The whole town was gathered at the
    door.
He cured many who were sick with
    various diseases,
    and he drove out many demons,
    not permitting them to speak because
        they knew him.

Rising very early before dawn, he left
    and went off to a deserted place,
        where he prayed.
Simon and those who were with him
    pursued him
    and on finding him said, "Everyone is
        looking for you."
He told them, "Let us go on to the
    nearby villages
    that I may preach there also.
For this purpose have I come."
So he went into their synagogues,
    preaching and driving out demons
        throughout the whole of Galilee.

Reflecting on the Gospel

The Learning Channel a few years back caused quite a controversy when they introduced *Here Comes Honey Boo Boo*. It was an instant hit. But the show was not without its controversy. Some thought this six-year-old beauty pageant sensation was adorable; others thought she was being exploited. Some thought what she was doing was innocent fun; others thought her dress and manner were hardly age-appropriate. As she grew in popularity, what is certain is that she loved the attention. We all love attention. In the gospel Simon says to Jesus, "Everyone is looking for you." Jesus is having great success healing many people and driving out demons. All who encounter him adore him. He is a rising star! People are paying great attention to him—"The whole town was gathered" at the door of Simon and Andrew's house. Jesus could have been a hit reality show!

Nonetheless, Jesus moves on to other villages. Personal idolization is not the purpose for which Jesus has come. His ministry is not about drawing attention to himself, but about preaching the Good News of salvation. Yet his ministry *is* about himself, for he *is* the Good News. His ministry is about reaching out to others and easing their burdens of life. And so he cures those brought to him who are "ill or possessed by demons." But his ministry is more than this.

Jesus never loses sight of why he came—to preach the Good News of salvation. His ministry is about helping others move beyond their immediate life concerns to reach for the Life he offers them. The healing is the medium for calling the people to a renewed relationship with God. In the midst of attention and adulation by the people for what he is doing, Jesus never loses sight of his mission to bring a deeper healing to everyone. Jesus never loses sight of his mission because he never loses sight of his Father. In the midst of his success, he goes "off to a deserted place, where he prayed." The source of Jesus' fidelity to his mission is his relationship with his Father.

Living the Paschal Mystery

Like those in the gospel who come to Jesus for healing, we all come to Jesus with expectations (after all, prayers of petition are the most common prayers we pray). The challenge is to move beyond our expectations to what Jesus really wants to give us—the Good News of salvation. Jesus' Presence to us today and his healing hand do not assure us that we will never suffer. Human life is full of suffering—physical, emotional, spiritual. The new life and hope Jesus brings by preaching the Good News assures us, however, of having the strength to keep the suffering in perspective. Jesus assures us that suffering belongs to this life, but this is not all there is to life. This is the Good News he preaches.

We need to allow Jesus' Presence to transform us so that our every breath is a proclamation of God's Good News, his saving mystery. Most of us won't go out to neighboring towns to preach. But we can smile a simple thank you to the tired cashier in the supermarket. We can bite our tongue rather than snap at the rambunctious children. We can do something thoughtful for someone when it is not expected. Like Jesus, we can be a living Gospel, the Good News in action. We are the Good News when we, like Jesus, take time in prayer to encounter him, grow in our love for him, draw strength from him.

Focusing the Gospel

Key words and phrases: cured many, drove out many demons, Everyone is looking for you, that I may preach, for this purpose have I come

To the point: In the gospel Simon says to Jesus, "Everyone is looking for you." Jesus is having great success healing many people and driving out demons. All who encounter him adore him. Nonetheless, Jesus moves on to other villages. Personal idolization is not the purpose for which Jesus has come. His ministry is not about drawing attention to himself, but about preaching the Good News of salvation. Yet his ministry *is* about himself, for he *is* the Good News.

Connecting the Gospel

to the first reading: Job's lament deepens our awareness of how much the human condition needs healing, and at this point in Job's miserable life he only sees "an end without hope." Jesus' ministry of preaching the Good News brings hope to all people by revealing that the present state of the human condition is not the end—salvation is.

to experience: We tend to limit the act of preaching to spoken words. Yet Jesus also preaches the Good News of salvation by acts of healing, exorcism, prayer, reaching out to all people. Indeed, Jesus is the Good News in action.

Connecting the Responsorial Psalm

to the readings: The first reading from Job painfully depicts the "drudgery," "restlessness," and "troubled nights" of the human condition. We hear these lines aware of the rest of Job's story: the destruction of his family, the loss of his property, his prolonged and painful illnesses, his degradation by friends and neighbors—all allowed by a God who seemed not to care. By contrast, the gospel reading reveals the truth about God's response to our condition: in the person of Jesus, God comes into human history preaching the Good News of salvation, healing illness, and driving out evil. This is clearly a God who does care.

In the responsorial psalm we proclaim that God heals the brokenhearted, binds the wounded, and sustains the lowly. We tell the world that into the midst of human suffering God comes with power and changes how things are. We become the Good News of salvation.

to psalmist preparation: How might you this week bring the Good News of salvation to someone who is brokenhearted, or discouraged, or restless, or without hope?

**ASSEMBLY &
FAITH-SHARING GROUPS**
- I look for Jesus in these places . . . I encounter Jesus when . . .
- Jesus is Good News for me because . . . I am Good News for others when . . .
- My life "preaches" Jesus' Presence and Good News when I . . .

PRESIDERS
My liturgical preaching goes beyond words in these ways . . .

DEACONS
Like Jesus, my service to those in need brings healing and salvation when . . .

HOSPITALITY MINISTERS
My greeting opens those gathering for liturgy to the Good News when . . .

MUSIC MINISTERS
My music ministry draws everyone to look for Jesus in these places . . .

ALTAR MINISTERS
My serving at the altar witnesses to my having encountered Jesus in my personal prayer when . . .

LECTORS
Like Jesus, I put the proclaimed word into action when I . . .

**EXTRAORDINARY MINISTERS
OF HOLY COMMUNION**
My acclamation "Body of Christ" or "Blood of Christ" preaches that . . .

CELEBRATION

Model Penitential Act

Presider: The purpose for which Jesus came among us was to preach the Good News and heal human suffering. Let us prepare to celebrate this liturgy by acknowledging times when we have failed to preach the Good News by our lives . . . [pause]

Lord Jesus, you heal those who come to you in need: Lord . . .

Christ Jesus, you are the Savior of the world: Christ . . .

Lord Jesus, you are the Good News of salvation: Lord . . .

Homily Points

• "Everyone is looking for you." For whom do people look today? Most often, the latest sports hero, rock or movie star, supermodel. Yet most often these people's personal lives leave little to admire. The challenge is to redirect for whom and for what we look.

• This gospel gives us clear direction. We look for Jesus whose way of living and relating is totally in accord with what he preached by word and action. He approached Simon's mother-in-law, grasped her hand, and helped her up; he cured the sick, drove out demons, prayed, went out to bring Good News to all people. Jesus did none of this to draw attention to himself, but instead to draw attention to God's work of salvation.

• God's work of salvation is the Good News. We ourselves become Good News when we look for Jesus in the goodness of others, during prayer, in choosing good over evil. We ourselves become Good News when we speak words of comfort to those who are suffering or grieving, encourage those in difficulties, take a stance for Gospel values. When, like Jesus, we make preaching the Good News through words and actions the purpose and pattern of our lives, others will say, "Everyone is looking for you."

Model Universal Prayer (Prayer of the Faithful)

Presider: God desires that we encounter the divine Son who is the Good News of salvation for us. And so with confidence we make our needs known.

Response:

Lord, hear our prayer.

Cantor:

we pray to the Lord,

That all members of the church preach in word and deed the Good News of salvation for all . . . [pause]

That all people hear and respond to the Good News of salvation . . . [pause]

That those sick in body, mind, or spirit be comforted and healed by those who bring the Good News . . . [pause]

That all of us gathered here become more fully the Good News through deeper encounters with Jesus . . . [pause]

Presider: Merciful God, you hear our prayers and answer all our needs: lead us to encounter your Son and to become with him your Good News of salvation. We ask this through Christ our Lord. **Amen.**

COLLECT

Let us pray

Pause for silent prayer

Keep your family safe, O Lord, with unfailing care,
that, relying solely on the hope of heavenly grace,
they may be defended always by your protection.
Through our Lord Jesus Christ, your Son, who lives and reigns with you in the unity of the Holy Spirit,
one God, for ever and ever. **Amen.**

FIRST READING

Job 7:1-4, 6-7

Job spoke, saying:
Is not man's life on earth a drudgery?
Are not his days those of hirelings?
He is a slave who longs for the shade,
a hireling who waits for his wages.
So I have been assigned months of misery,
and troubled nights have been allotted to me.
If in bed I say, "When shall I arise?"
then the night drags on;
I am filled with restlessness until the dawn.
My days are swifter than a weaver's shuttle;
they come to an end without hope.
Remember that my life is like the wind;
I shall not see happiness again.

RESPONSORIAL PSALM

Ps 147:1-2, 3-4, 5-6

R. (cf. 3a) Praise the Lord, who heals the brokenhearted.
or:
R. Alleluia.

Praise the Lord, for he is good;
sing praise to our God, for he is gracious;
it is fitting to praise him.
The Lord rebuilds Jerusalem;
the dispersed of Israel he gathers.

R. Praise the Lord, who heals the brokenhearted.
or:
R. Alleluia.

He heals the brokenhearted
   and binds up their wounds.
He tells the number of the stars;
   he calls each by name.

R̸. Praise the Lord, who heals the
brokenhearted.
   or:
R̸. Alleluia.

Great is our Lord and mighty in power;
   to his wisdom there is no limit.
The LORD sustains the lowly;
   the wicked he casts to the ground.

R̸. Praise the Lord, who heals the
brokenhearted.
   or:
R̸. Alleluia.

SECOND READING
1 Cor 9:16-19, 22-23

Brothers and sisters:
If I preach the gospel, this is no reason for
      me to boast,
   for an obligation has been imposed on
      me,
   and woe to me if I do not preach it!
If I do so willingly, I have a recompense,
   but if unwillingly, then I have been
      entrusted with a stewardship.
What then is my recompense?
That, when I preach,
   I offer the gospel free of charge
   so as not to make full use of my right in
      the gospel.

Although I am free in regard to all,
   I have made myself a slave to all
   so as to win over as many as possible.
To the weak I became weak, to win over
      the weak.
I have become all things to all, to save at
      least some.
All this I do for the sake of the gospel,
   so that I too may have a share in it.

✠ CATECHESIS

About Liturgy

The second reading during Ordinary Time: Usually during Ordinary Time the second reading does not fit with the first reading and gospel. The second reading during this season is a sequential reading of one of the New Testament letters. This is why during Ordinary Time little is said in *Living Liturgy*™ about the second reading.

   This Sunday is a happy coincidence in that the second reading reinforces the approach to the first reading and gospel taken in *Living Liturgy*™. Paul is emphasizing his (all Christians') role in preaching the Gospel, but this is no reason to boast. This is no reason to call attention to ourselves. Paul says we must become "all things to all, to save at least some" and find our own share in the Gospel we preach by the way we live the Good News.

Who may preach: With rare exception, for example, at Masses with children, current liturgical law limits preaching homilies during the eucharistic celebration to ordained ministers. This being said, it doesn't mean that all baptized Christians aren't called to preach the Gospel. In fact, we are, by the very way we live. And sometimes the preaching by the actions of our lives is far more eloquent and fruitful than words. And far more challenging. And far more rewarding.

About Liturgical Music

Music suggestions: An excellent entrance song would be "Your Hands, O Lord, in Days of Old" (WC, WS, W4) in which we speak of Jesus' healing power over the sick and suffering of his day and ask him to "be our mighty healer" today. A strong generic entrance hymn that would be particularly appropriate this Sunday is Delores Dufner's "Jesus Christ, by Faith Revealed" (WC, WS). In Bernadette Farrell's "Christ Be Our Light" (found in many resources), we call upon Christ to transform our troubled world where many are hungry, homeless, or despairing. We also ask Christ to make us servants who will work to make God's kingdom come. This song would be appropriate for either the entrance or the Communion procession. In the opening verse of Ruth Duck's "Healing River of the Spirit" (BB, G3, JS3), we beg God to "Bathe the wounds that living brings. Plunge our pain, our sins, our sadness Deep beneath your sacred springs." In the closing verse we ask God to "Make us channels of your pow'r" and "Guide our winding human course, Till we find our way together." Set to BEACH SPRING, this hymn would work well as the recessional song. Another good choice for the recessional would be Fred Kaan's "For the Healing of the Nations" (found in many resources).

FEBRUARY 8, 2015
FIFTH SUNDAY IN ORDINARY TIME

SPIRITUALITY

GOSPEL ACCLAMATION
Luke 7:16

℟. Alleluia, alleluia.
A great prophet has arisen in our midst,
God has visited his people.
℟. Alleluia, alleluia.

Gospel   Mark 1:40-45; L77B

A leper came to Jesus and
    kneeling down begged
    him and said,
  "If you wish, you can
    make me clean."
Moved with pity, he
    stretched out his hand,
  touched him, and said to
    him,
  "I do will it. Be made
    clean."
The leprosy left him
    immediately, and he was
    made clean.
Then, warning him sternly, he
    dismissed him at once.

He said to him, "See that you tell no
    one anything,
  but go, show yourself to the priest
  and offer for your cleansing what
    Moses prescribed;
  that will be proof for them."

The man went away and began to
    publicize the whole matter.
He spread the report abroad
  so that it was impossible for Jesus to
    enter a town openly.
He remained outside in deserted places,
  and people kept coming to him from
    everywhere.

Reflecting on the Gospel

Chronic or terminal diseases in those we love do more than frustrate us. They often leave us angry, edgy, tormented. With all our modern advances in medicine, why can't researchers and doctors overcome this disease, we ask. We wait interminably for promised breakthroughs, we hope desperately for a miracle, we pray nonstop for healing. Such experiences can help us empathize with the leper in today's gospel. For him no medical breakthrough awaits, no healing looms, no future dawns.

Lepers in biblical times were required to proclaim "unclean" and live in social and religious isolation from the community (see first reading). They lived painful lives, their only human contact being those in their same condition. Their only future was the relief of death. The leper in the gospel, excluded from the community and well aware of his miserable plight, understandably approached Jesus with caution ("If you wish") and humility ("kneeling down"). Jesus, however, has no doubt about his response, for his purpose in coming among us was to show the compassion of God for the outcast: "I do will it." Jesus' compassion gave the leper what he deeply wished— to be made clean, yes, but also once again to be restored to relations that were lost, to have a life other than one determined by pain, to have an opportunity for a different outlook on death. The leper's boldness in approaching Jesus changed his life in so many ways.

This healing account between a leper and Jesus dramatically unfolds in a conversation punctuated by concrete and very personal gestures. The leper comes to Jesus, kneels, and boldly begs for cleansing, gestures expressing his sense of unworthiness. Moved with pity, Jesus stretches out his hand and touches the leper, gestures revealing the leper's inherent dignity. Jesus heals more than the man's body. Encounter with Jesus and being healed always fashions a new relationship with him. Freed from pain and isolation, the leper can let his inherent dignity spill over into proclaiming the Good News of a new Presence, a new Awakening, a new Life.

Living the Paschal Mystery

Each of us has been touched by Jesus, healed of pain and suffering, been invited to grow into a deeper relationship with him. Our own inherent dignity is reinforced by Jesus' very personal compassion and care for each of us. We experience this compassion and care in our own moments of deep prayer as we turn to Jesus in our need. We experience Jesus' compassion and care in the helping hand of another, in the unexpected pat on the back for something we've done well, in a burst of energy we get from another noticing some good we've done. In these and many other ways, goodness abounds and relationships grow.

Paschal mystery living means taking up our cross daily and actually doing what Jesus did—willing the good of others. Doing so sometimes means risking isolation: being snubbed by coworkers, being laughed at by people who consider us religious fanatics, being ridiculed for giving of our time and possessions for the good of others. Such isolation because of paschal mystery living is not the loss it seems, however, for it gains us deeper community in the Body of Christ.

Focusing the Gospel

Key words and phrases: leper, Jesus, begged, touched, made clean

To the point: This healing account between a leper and Jesus dramatically unfolds in a conversation punctuated by concrete and very personal gestures. The leper comes to Jesus, kneels, and boldly begs for cleansing, gestures expressing his sense of unworthiness. Moved with pity, Jesus stretches out his hand and touches the leper, gestures revealing the leper's inherent dignity. Jesus heals more than the man's body. Encounter with Jesus and being healed always fashions a new relationship with him.

Connecting the Gospel

to the first reading: The first reading outlines the legal proscriptions impinging on someone with leprosy. Most importantly, they had to "dwell apart." In the gospel, both the leper and Jesus set aside the law: the leper approaches Jesus, Jesus touches the leper. Because of their willingness to go beyond the law, the leper is healed and restored to the community.

to experience: Some conversations have life-changing consequences, for example, that of a parent with a teen about his or her destructive behaviors, that of a spiritual director with a discouraged directee, that of a supervisor with a habitually late employee. With Christ, all conversations are life-changing.

Connecting the Responsorial Psalm

to the readings: Because the readings this Sunday move so quickly from the Old Testament notion of the uncleanness of leprosy to the responsorial psalm's confession of sin and guilt, we can be misled into thinking that serious illness and serious sin are interrelated. The point of the readings and psalm, however, is quite different. What ties the first reading, gospel, and psalm together is our willingness to admit our condition before God, be it ostracizing disease or sinful behavior, and God's readiness to heal and to forgive us. God will counter whatever debilities illness or sin create. We need but ask. May we, like this psalmist and this leper, turn to God with our "trouble" (psalm). And may we then tell everyone what happened when we did.

to psalmist preparation: To prepare to sing this psalm, reflect on a time when you experienced alienation from God and others. What caused this rift? Who or what helped you turn to God for healing? What did you learn from this experience about the mercy of God? How can you tell this story in your singing of this psalm?

ASSEMBLY & FAITH-SHARING GROUPS
- I come to Jesus, kneeling when . . . begging when . . . I leave Jesus . . .
- The healing for which I need to ask Jesus is . . . Jesus touches me and . . .
- My encounters with Jesus lead to new relationships when I . . .

PRESIDERS
The gestures I make while presiding are those of Jesus when I . . .

DEACONS
Like Jesus, I stretch out my hand in compassion to . . .

HOSPITALITY MINISTERS
My manner of welcoming people to the assembly reinforces their inherent dignity when I . . .

MUSIC MINISTERS
My manner of relating to other music ministers deepens our relationship and affects our music ministry in these ways . . .

ALTAR MINISTERS
My manner of serving at the altar reveals the dignity with which I regard myself in these ways . . .

LECTORS
When I have encountered Jesus during my preparation and deepened my relationship with him, my proclamation sounds like . . .

EXTRAORDINARY MINISTERS OF HOLY COMMUNION
When I see the inherent dignity of each person coming to receive Holy Communion, my ministry becomes . . .

Model Penitential Act

Presider: In today's gospel, Jesus does more than heal a leper. By stretching out his hand and touching him, Jesus restores his dignity as a person. As we prepare for this liturgy, we call to mind the times we have failed to treat others with dignity . . . [pause]

Lord Jesus, you heal those who come to you: Lord . . .

Christ Jesus, you are the joy of salvation: Christ . . .

Lord Jesus, you touch us and give us Life: Lord . . .

Homily Points

• Gestures speak volumes. Backhanding someone across the face says something very different from caressing the cheek. Slapping someone on the back in congratulations is different from punching a person in anger. A hand extended in friendship is the opposite of a hand withheld out of hostility. In all these cases, relationships are affected one way or another.

• The leper's gestures expressed courage and need, as well as a sense of unworthiness. Jesus' gestures expressed compassion, power, and reverence for the dignity of the leper. Any encounter with Jesus leaves us changed, exalted, and whole. Such encounter fashions a new relationship with him, with ourselves, and with others.

• We cannot contain the Good News of the changed relationship that comes from encounter with and being touched by Jesus. Like the leper, can we do anything less than "publicize the whole matter" as widely as possible? At the end of this gospel it is impossible for Jesus to enter any town openly. When we publicize the Good News of what Jesus has done to and for us, it becomes unnecessary for him to enter our town. He's already there, in us.

Model Universal Prayer (Prayer of the Faithful)

Presider: Just as Jesus touched the leper and healed him, so surely will God touch us and hear our prayers.

Response:

Lord,—— hear our prayer.

Cantor:

we pray to the Lord,

May all members of the church grow in their relationship with Jesus and touch others with his healing Presence . . . [pause]

May all people of the world have the Good News of God's healing and care preached to them . . . [pause]

May the sick be healed, the outcasts be welcomed, and those who feel unworthy have dignity restored to them . . . [pause]

May each of us here gathered publicly proclaim all that Jesus has done for us . . . [pause]

Presider: Almighty God, you sent your divine Son to heal us and proclaim the Good News of salvation: hear our prayers that we might come to the dignity of the fullness of Life you offer us. We ask this through Christ our Lord. **Amen.**

COLLECT

Let us pray

Pause for silent prayer

O God, who teach us that you abide
in hearts that are just and true,
grant that we may be so fashioned by your
    grace
as to become a dwelling pleasing to you.
Through our Lord Jesus Christ, your Son,
who lives and reigns with you in the unity
    of the Holy Spirit,
one God, for ever and ever. **Amen.**

FIRST READING

Lev 13:1-2, 44-46

The LORD said to Moses and Aaron,
    "If someone has on his skin a scab or
        pustule or blotch
    which appears to be the sore of leprosy,
    he shall be brought to Aaron, the priest,
    or to one of the priests among his
        descendants.
If the man is leprous and unclean,
    the priest shall declare him unclean
    by reason of the sore on his head.

"The one who bears the sore of leprosy
    shall keep his garments rent and his
        head bare,
    and shall muffle his beard;
    he shall cry out, 'Unclean, unclean!'
As long as the sore is on him he shall
        declare himself unclean,
    since he is in fact unclean.
He shall dwell apart, making his abode
        outside the camp."

RESPONSORIAL PSALM

Ps 32:1-2, 5, 11

R̸. (7) I turn to you, Lord, in time of trouble, and you fill me with the joy of salvation.

Blessed is he whose fault is taken away,
  whose sin is covered.
Blessed the man to whom the LORD
    imputes not guilt,
  in whose spirit there is no guile.

R̸. I turn to you, Lord, in time of trouble, and you fill me with the joy of salvation.

Then I acknowledged my sin to you,
  my guilt I covered not.
I said, "I confess my faults to the LORD,"
  and you took away the guilt of my sin.

R̸. I turn to you, Lord, in time of trouble, and you fill me with the joy of salvation.

Be glad in the LORD and rejoice, you just;
  exult, all you upright of heart.

R̸. I turn to you, Lord, in time of trouble, and you fill me with the joy of salvation.

SECOND READING

1 Cor 10:31–11:1

Brothers and sisters,
whether you eat or drink, or whatever you
    do,
  do everything for the glory of God.
Avoid giving offense, whether to the Jews
    or Greeks or the church of God,
  just as I try to please everyone in every
    way,
  not seeking my own benefit but that of
    the many,
  that they may be saved.
Be imitators of me, as I am of Christ.

About Liturgy

The role of hospitality ministers: Although it is every parish member's responsibility to make sure everyone feels included in both the liturgies and in the parish community, it is part of hospitality ministers' (including ushers and greeters) mandate as a "visible liturgical ministry" to model inclusiveness in the parish. Inadvertently, hospitality ministers (and other members of the assembly) can sometimes make others feel like religious and social "outcasts." Sometimes they are so busy catching up with friends coming into church that they miss an opportunity to say a welcome to the person they don't know. Sometimes they might miss an opportunity to help parents feel more at ease dealing with young children who are restless and noisy on a particular morning. Sometimes they miss an opportunity to be the first to comfort the person who might become sick during liturgy. Hospitality ministry is about inclusiveness, attending to the needs and comfort of others, and minimizing distractions and challenges so that members of the assembly can more easily surrender themselves to the transforming Presence and action of God.

Another consideration for the hospitality ministers that might be a reflection derived from this Sunday's gospel is that they are not simply welcoming people to a social gathering. Their welcome helps form the members of the assembly into the one Body of Christ. Their ministry is far more than a social welcome. The heart of it concerns helping the assembly become church made visible, gathered around the visible Head, Christ. This is why there can be no outcasts—we are all members of the one Body of Christ.

About Liturgical Music

Communion processional hymns: In the Communion procession we journey to the messianic banquet where we become one in the Body of Christ. Here there is food for all, love for all, healing for all. The text and style of the hymn we sing needs to express a sense of joyful completeness or fullness in the Lord which we share with the whole Body of Christ. The song needs to help us focus both on our oneness with one another and on the One in whom this oneness is made possible.

Music suggestions: The passages from the Gospel of Mark proclaimed during these particular weeks in Ordinary Time provide a series of stories in which Jesus heals those sick with diseases, possessed by demons, or paralyzed by sin. These gospel readings dramatize the mission of Jesus in concrete terms. Many of the songs suggested for last Sunday would be appropriate this Sunday and next. Also appropriate would be songs expressing our longing to be saved by Jesus. Examples include Deanna Light and Paul Tate's "Jesus, Hope of the World" (WC, WS) and Anne Quigley's "There Is a Longing" (BB, G3, JS3).

SEASON
OF LENT

✛ SPIRITUALITY

GOSPEL ACCLAMATION
See Ps 95:8

If today you hear his voice,
harden not your hearts.

Gospel   Matt 6:1-6, 16-18; L219

Jesus said to his disciples:
"Take care not to perform
   righteous deeds
   in order that people may see
      them;
   otherwise, you will have no
      recompense from your
      heavenly Father.
When you give alms,
   do not blow a trumpet before you,
   as the hypocrites do in the
      synagogues and in the streets
   to win the praise of others.
Amen, I say to you,
   they have received their reward.
But when you give alms,
   do not let your left hand know what your
      right is doing,
   so that your almsgiving may be secret.
And your Father who sees in secret will
   repay you.

"When you pray,
   do not be like the hypocrites,
   who love to stand and pray in the
      synagogues and on street corners
   so that others may see them.
Amen, I say to you,
   they have received their reward.
But when you pray, go to your inner room,
   close the door, and pray to your Father in
      secret.
And your Father who sees in secret will
   repay you.

"When you fast,
   do not look gloomy like the hypocrites.
They neglect their appearance,
   so that they may appear to others to be
      fasting.
Amen, I say to you, they have received their
      reward.
But when you fast,
   anoint your head and wash your face,
   so that you may not appear to be fasting,
   except to your Father who is hidden.
And your Father who sees what is hidden
   will repay you."

See Appendix A, p. 270, for other readings.

Reflecting on the Gospel

Even people who are not seemingly "religious" get into Lent. "Giving up" is as natural a part of Lent as eating candy is a part of Easter. Perhaps one reason why so many people do at least something by way of sacrifice during Lent is to remind self and others that we can always become better persons. This striving for being better has less to do with self-satisfaction and more to do with wanting to improve our relationships with each other. The opening line of the gospel mentions "righteous deeds." In a biblical context, "righteous deeds" are those which have to do with relationships; they are any acts which help us relate to others with the same care and goodness with which God relates to us. One is "righteous" when one is "right" with God and others, as expressed in our concrete behaviors.

On the surface, it's a little difficult not to get the point of this gospel: don't do spiritual acts—no matter how good and worthy they are—so that others see them and think well of us. Three times in this gospel Jesus tells us to do "righteous deeds" not to be noticed by others, but to be repaid by God. God's "repayment" is nothing less than a deepened relationship with God. In the first reading Joel admonishes us to "return to [God] with your whole heart." This is essentially a reminder of the work of Lent: to make God the center of our lives. The regard and praise of others is not what we seek, but a deeper love relationship with the God who is "gracious and merciful."

Thus our "righteous deeds"—our Lenten penances—are to be directed to forming a new habit of righteous relationships, not only with God, but also with each other. Ironically, penitential practices we have done "in secret" *will* be noticed by others—not for the deeds themselves, but for who, through these deeds, we have become. Our "righteous deeds" become noticed in our deepened relationships, relating to others in the same way God relates to us, by being more "gracious and merciful" (see first reading). Forming a habit of righteous relationships changes us. We become more like God. Saint Paul boldly states this in the second reading: "Be reconciled to God"—that is, be in right relationship with God—"so that we might become the righteousness of God in [Christ]." We *become* the very relationships we seek to deepen!

Living the Paschal Mystery

The ashes we receive in the form of a cross on our foreheads on this day remind us that the "now" mentioned in both the first and second readings imparts a real urgency about forming a habit of doing "righteous deeds." *Now* is the time. We cannot put off growing in our relationships with God and others.

One of the challenges of Ash Wednesday is to see this day as a *beginning* to Lent. It is well and good that so many people come to church on this day and resolve to do penance during Lent. The ashes we receive, however, are a sign that the call to penance and conversion lasts beyond a single day. The ashes are a reminder that conversion is ongoing, lasting even beyond our forty-day Lenten observance. Conversion is the effect of a habit of "righteous deeds."

Further, the ashes are a sign that penance is an essential part of paschal mystery living. This, because they remind us that dying is part of the human condition ("Remember . . . you are dust and to dust you will return") and the only way to share in risen Life is to embrace dying to self. Ash Wednesday and its special rite of signing the faithful with ashes is a singular call to die to ourselves—and that every day we wear ashes.

Focusing the Gospel

Key words and phrases: righteous deeds, that people may see, Father . . . will repay you

To the point: Three times in this gospel Jesus tells us to do "righteous deeds" not to be noticed by others, but to be repaid by God. This repayment is nothing less than the righteousness of a deepened relationship with God. Our "righteous deeds"—our Lenten penances—are to be directed to forming a new habit of righteous relationship. Ironically, what we have done "in secret" *will* be noticed by others—not for the deeds themselves, but for who, through these deeds, we have become.

Penitential Act

The blessing and distribution of ashes after the homily takes the place of the penitential act on Ash Wednesday.

Model Universal Prayer (Prayer of the Faithful)

Presider: As we begin our Lenten journey of conversion and growth in our relationship with God and others, we make our needs known to a Life-giving God.

Response:

Cantor:

That all Christians spend Lent seeking conversion of heart and growth in right relationships . . . [pause]

That all peoples everywhere rend their hearts that they may receive God's salvation . . . [pause]

That the poor may be lifted up by the Lenten almsgiving of this community of the faithful . . . [pause]

That each of us receive our ashes as a sign of our desire for ongoing conversion of life . . . [pause]

Presider: Merciful God, you hear the prayers of those who cry out to you: may our Lenten penance bring us closer to you and each other. We ask this through your Son, Jesus Christ our Lord. **Amen.**

FOR REFLECTION

- What in me most needs to be changed in order that I may grow into a deeper relationship with God is . . . The Lenten penance I must do to foster this conversion of life is . . .
- To persevere in my chosen Lenten penance and thus form a new habit of righteous living, I must . . .
- Who I hope to be at the end of Lent is . . .

Homily Points

- Why do we do what we do for penance during Lent? Often our Lenten penances are traditions that we practice without much thought, for example, giving up a favorite food, beverage, or TV program; taking up daily Mass or Stations of the Cross, or filling up the rice bowl. While these are worthy practices, Lent calls us to the more difficult work of relating our Lenten penance to conversion of life. What in us needs to change, to be converted, so that at the end of Lent we are better persons and have better relationships with God and others?

- Growth in our relationships requires the spiritual work that is at the core of conversion. Jesus warns us that this work needs to be done "in secret." Nonetheless, as we become more "righteous" in the eyes of God, this spiritual growth becomes evident in the way we relate to others. Inwardly transformed by our Lenten penances and God's grace, we become outwardly more patient, kind, understanding, loving, caring, just, merciful. Ironically, in this way what was done "in secret" does become public.

SPIRITUALITY

GOSPEL ACCLAMATION
Matt 4:4b

One does not live on bread alone,
but on every word that comes forth from the
    mouth of God.

Gospel

Mark 1:12-15; L23B

The Spirit drove Jesus out into the
    desert,
    and he remained in the desert for
        forty days, tempted by Satan.
He was among wild beasts,
    and the angels ministered to him.

After John had been arrested,
    Jesus came to Galilee proclaiming
        the gospel of God:
    "This is the time of fulfillment.
The kingdom of God is at hand.
Repent, and believe in the gospel."

Reflecting on the Gospel

How often do we make a remark we wish we could take back? How often do we regret not doing something we should have done? In both these cases and many more we regret choices we have made. Temptations to speak and act in certain ways force us to make choices, even if simply a choice to think before we speak or act. We would like to imagine that we can walk away from temptations and protect ourselves from having to make choices, especially when the temptation is serious and the choice difficult. But even walking away from temptation is a choice. We cannot avoid temptations in our lives. Nor can we avoid choices. Even Jesus had to face temptations, as this Sunday's gospel indicates. What we learn from him is how to make faithful choices in face of temptations. We also learn from him what effect our choices have on us and on others.

Mark's version of the temptation in the desert is short and to the point. He does not relay the details of Jesus' experience of temptation, but he does show its outcome: Jesus boldly enters Galilee proclaiming, "This is the time . . . Repent, and believe." Temptations always force us to make a choice. Jesus' choice is to take up his saving mission. What is our temptation? What is our choice? These are *the* questions of Lent. They are the questions those of us who are baptized into Christ (see second reading) must constantly ask if we wish to participate in his saving mission, proclaiming by the choices we make that the Gospel determines who we are and how we act.

Confronting temptation and overcoming the sinfulness that keeps us from righteous Christian living is a necessary first step for faithful baptismal living. We must turn from sinfulness before we can do our part to continue Jesus' mission. Since repentance, forgiveness, and belief are so central to Christian living, proclaiming the Gospel at least means that we turn from our sinful ways, forgive others, and express our belief by saying yes to God's will for us. None of these is easy to do, which is why proclaiming the Gospel is a lifelong mission. The most eloquent proclamation of the Gospel is the witness of the way we live. Ultimately, what we witness to is the "time of fulfillment" brought about by believing in and living the Gospel.

Living the Paschal Mystery

The first two readings this Sunday suggest that making good choices in face of temptation and the injunction to proclaim the Gospel are part of our baptismal response. In the baptismal waters we are plunged into the death of Christ to rise to the risen Life that renews the earth. Baptism is our entry into the death/resurrection mystery of Christ. We begin Lent by reminding ourselves that we are a baptized people; at the end of Lent we renew our baptismal promises at the Easter Vigil.

Our baptismal identity with Christ confers on us the same mission as Christ: to proclaim the "gospel of God." We know full well that we never will be rid of temptations and sinfulness. But this fact of the human condition ought not to keep us from taking up our baptismal mission to proclaim the Gospel. We proclaim the Gospel not because we are sinless, but because we have aligned ourselves with Christ. Our Lenten desert affords us the opportunity to examine how well we have aligned ourselves with Christ.

Focusing the Gospel

Key words and phrases: tempted by Satan, proclaiming the gospel of God

To the point: Mark's version of the temptation in the desert is short and to the point. He does not relay the details of Jesus' experience of temptation, but he does show its outcome: Jesus boldly enters Galilee proclaiming, "This is the time . . . Repent, and believe." Temptations always force us to make a choice. Jesus' choice is to take up his saving mission. What is our temptation? What is our choice?

Connecting the Gospel

to the second reading: Peter indicates in his letter that we are saved through baptism. In spite of our baptism into salvation, we are still tempted to be disobedient. Our choice must be to live our baptismal commitment and salvation.

to experience: Every moment of temptation is, in fact, a time of choice. Every moment of temptation is, then, a "time of fulfillment" and salvation offering us the opportunity to choose rightly who we want to be and how we want to live.

Connecting the Responsorial Psalm

to the readings: Lent is a "time of fulfillment" (gospel) during which we are called to renew our covenant relationship (first reading) with God. In Psalm 25 we ask God to teach us the ways of the covenant and to guide us in truth. We beg God to remember us with compassion and kindness and to offer us gentle correction and steady guidance. By singing Psalm 25 we choose, as did Jesus in the desert (gospel), to make our covenant relationship with God the guiding force of our lives. May this Lent lead us to deeper understanding of God's covenant with us and deeper commitment to its ways of "love and truth."

to psalmist preparation: In this responsorial psalm you reflect on the meaning of the covenant and ask to be led toward more faithful observance of its ways. How is God calling you this Lent to deepen your living of the covenant? How will you, like Jesus in the desert, struggle with this call? Who or what will help you say yes?

**ASSEMBLY &
FAITH-SHARING GROUPS**
- I am tempted when . . . to . . . The outcome is . . .
- When I am tempted, what helps me boldly choose the "gospel of God" is . . .
- What keeps me aware of participating in and furthering Jesus' saving mission is . . .

PRESIDERS
With Christ, I announce "the time of fulfillment" when I . . .

DEACONS
I am tempted to neglect my service ministry when . . . What helps me choose to serve faithfully is . . .

HOSPITALITY MINISTERS
My greeting helps people participate more fully in Christ's saving action in the liturgy when I . . .

MUSIC MINISTERS
When I am tempted to focus on myself during my music ministry, I . . . What helps me remain focused on Jesus and his saving mission is . . .

ALTAR MINISTERS
My serving at the altar helps me choose to live my baptismal covenant in these ways . . .

LECTORS
My proclamation of the word reflects my choice to live the "gospel of God" when I . . .

**EXTRAORDINARY MINISTERS
OF HOLY COMMUNION**
The manner in which I distribute Holy Communion strengthens the community's belief in the "gospel of God" when I . . .

Model Penitential Act

Presider: Today's gospel account invites us to go off to a deserted place to confront our temptations and to repent and believe the Gospel. We pause to repent of the times we have given in to temptation and failed to live the Gospel . . . [pause]

   Confiteor: I confess . . .

Homily Points

- "Don't tempt me!" We make this cry when we are faced with something we want, but know we shouldn't have or do. For example, when on a diet, we don't want to be offered candy. When yard work beckons, we don't want the neighbor inviting us to a ball game. We generally think of temptation as a negative. But temptation also has a positive side, for it offers us an opportunity to make a choice. In that choice we decide who we really want to be and how we really want to live.

- Jesus, tempted in the desert, decides who he wants to be and how he wants to live. He chooses to go to Galilee and proclaim the "gospel of God." Knowing "John had been arrested," Jesus was aware that there would be deadly consequences for his own choice. Nevertheless, he resolutely went ahead with his saving mission.

- Life experiences teach us to appraise choices before we make them. No matter how tempting the invitation to play golf, participating in Sunday Mass is a more life-giving choice. No matter how tempting gossip and judging another is, being kind and charitable is the right choice. In these and similar life experiences, what do we choose? The "gospel of God" teaches us just how serious our choices are. They decide who we really want to be and how we really want to live. They decide our salvation.

Model Universal Prayer (Prayer of the Faithful)

Presider: Let us ask God to strengthen us when we are tempted and guide us to make the choices leading to salvation.

Response:

Lord, hear our prayer.

Cantor:

we pray to the Lord,

That all members of the church face temptations with courage and make right choices leading to fullness of Life . . . [pause]

That leaders of nations govern in such a way that people are free to make right choices leading to fullness of life . . . [pause]

That those struggling to make right choices be guided by Gospel values . . . [pause]

That those elected for baptism at Easter be strengthened by the faithful witness of this community . . . [pause]

Presider: Merciful God, you sent your Son to guide us to salvation: hear our prayers that we might choose to follow him more faithfully and one day share the fullness of Life with him. We ask this through that same Son, Jesus Christ our Lord. **Amen.**

COLLECT

Let us pray

Pause for silent prayer

Grant, almighty God,
through the yearly observances of holy
   Lent,
that we may grow in understanding
of the riches hidden in Christ
and by worthy conduct pursue their
   effects.
Through our Lord Jesus Christ, your Son,
who lives and reigns with you in the unity
   of the Holy Spirit,
one God, for ever and ever. **Amen.**

FIRST READING

Gen 9:8-15

God said to Noah and to his sons with him:
"See, I am now establishing my covenant
   with you
   and your descendants after you
   and with every living creature that was
     with you:
   all the birds, and the various tame and
     wild animals
   that were with you and came out of the
     ark.
I will establish my covenant with you,
   that never again shall all bodily
     creatures be destroyed
   by the waters of a flood;
   there shall not be another flood to
     devastate the earth."
God added:
"This is the sign that I am giving for all
     ages to come,
of the covenant between me and you
and every living creature with you:
I set my bow in the clouds to serve as a
     sign
of the covenant between me and the earth.
When I bring clouds over the earth,
   and the bow appears in the clouds,
   I will recall the covenant I have made
     between me and you and all living
      beings,
   so that the waters shall never again
     become a flood
   to destroy all mortal beings."

RESPONSORIAL PSALM

Ps 25:4-5, 6-7, 8-9

R︎. (cf. 10) Your ways, O Lord, are love and truth to those who keep your covenant.

Your ways, O LORD, make known to me;
    teach me your paths,
guide me in your truth and teach me,
    for you are God my savior.

R︎. Your ways, O Lord, are love and truth to those who keep your covenant.

Remember that your compassion, O LORD,
    and your love are from of old.
In your kindness remember me,
    because of your goodness, O LORD.

R︎. Your ways, O Lord, are love and truth to those who keep your covenant.

Good and upright is the LORD,
    thus he shows sinners the way.
He guides the humble to justice,
    and he teaches the humble his way.

R︎. Your ways, O Lord, are love and truth to those who keep your covenant.

SECOND READING

1 Pet 3:18-22

Beloved:
Christ suffered for sins once,
    the righteous for the sake of the
        unrighteous,
    that he might lead you to God.
Put to death in the flesh,
    he was brought to life in the Spirit.
In it he also went to preach to the spirits
    in prison,
    who had once been disobedient
    while God patiently waited in the days
        of Noah
    during the building of the ark,
    in which a few persons, eight in all,
    were saved through water.
This prefigured baptism, which saves you
    now.
It is not a removal of dirt from the body
    but an appeal to God for a clear
        conscience,
    through the resurrection of Jesus Christ,
    who has gone into heaven
    and is at the right hand of God,
    with angels, authorities, and powers
        subject to him.

About Liturgy

Sacramental signs: The second reading assigned for this Sunday gives us a glimpse of how sacramental signs work. Peter says the water for baptism isn't about "a removal of dirt from the body but an appeal to God for a clear conscience." In other words, water is a sign used in baptism, but while its literal meaning (washing and sustaining life) does say something about what happens in the sacrament (wash us from sin and give us new life in God), the sacramental reality goes far beyond such a literal correspondence. Saint Augustine says it well: sacraments are visible signs of an invisible reality or grace.

One renewal effort in liturgy is to maximize the sacramental signs so that they can more fully speak of the grace they signify. For example, many churches now have baptismal fonts large enough for immersion in which an abundance of water can be used when baptizing. Another example: GIRM no. 321 states that the bread used at Mass ought to look like food and be large enough to be broken into pieces of which at least some are given to the faithful.

Since Lent is a period of Christian discipline, there are any number of ways we might practice maximizing the liturgical symbols we use. For example, we might pay particular attention so that our sign of the cross at the beginning of Mass be well formed and deliberate. When receiving Holy Communion we might intentionally and carefully place one hand within another, making a fitting and reverent "throne" on which to receive the Body of Christ. Even making a concerted effort to sing the service music and hymns at Mass (even if we don't have a very good voice) can be a witness to our desire for fuller participation in the sacramental signs.

About Liturgical Music

Music of the Lenten season: GIRM no. 313 provides us with directives concerning music during the seasons of Advent and Lent. During Advent, musical instruments should be used with moderation. During Lent, instruments should be used only to support the singing of the assembly. These directives are applications of the principle of progressive solemnity (STL, nos. 110–14). Some liturgical days and seasons call for musical exuberance, while other days and seasons call for musical restraint. Applying the principle of progressive solemnity allows the paschal mystery dynamic of the liturgical year—its built-in rhythm of not yet-already, of anticipation-celebration, of dying-rising—to have its formative effect upon us. This rhythm is no inconsequential thing, for it is the very rhythm which marks our identity as Body of Christ and our daily living as faithful members of the church.

SPIRITUALITY

GOSPEL ACCLAMATION

cf. Matt 17:5
From the shining cloud the Father's voice is
    heard:
This is my beloved Son, listen to him.

Gospel

Mark 9:2-10; L26B

Jesus took Peter, James, and John
    and led them up a high
        mountain apart by
        themselves.
And he was transfigured
    before them,
    and his clothes became
        dazzling white,
    such as no fuller on earth could
        bleach them.
Then Elijah appeared to them along
    with Moses,
    and they were conversing with Jesus.
Then Peter said to Jesus in reply,
    "Rabbi, it is good that we are here!
Let us make three tents:
    one for you, one for Moses, and one
        for Elijah."
He hardly knew what to say, they were
    so terrified.
Then a cloud came, casting a shadow
    over them;
    from the cloud came a voice,
    "This is my beloved Son. Listen to
        him."
Suddenly, looking around, they no
    longer saw anyone
    but Jesus alone with them.

As they were coming down from the
    mountain,
    he charged them not to relate what
        they had seen to anyone,
    except when the Son of Man had
        risen from the dead.
So they kept the matter to themselves,
    questioning what rising from the
        dead meant.

Reflecting on the Gospel

High mountains are a challenge to the adventuresome. They are just there, simply begging to be conquered. At 29,029 feet, Mount Everest is the highest mountain in the world. There were attempts already in the 1920s to reach the top, but they failed; yet climbers kept trying. In 1953 Edmund Hillary was the first person to put his foot on the summit. Many have followed his ascent since. No doubt for those who reach the top, there is a sense of conquering the world. Indeed, from that height the world lays at one's feet. No wonder in Scripture mountains were often locations where theophanies—manifestations of God—took place.

This gospel account tells of three theophanies and hints at two others.

On the mountain Peter, James, and John witness the first three theophanies: Jesus the transfigured One, Jesus the "beloved Son," Jesus the "Son of Man." As the transfigured One, Jesus reveals what is yet to come. As the "beloved Son," the Father reveals an intimate, divine relationship. As the "Son of Man," Jesus reveals that he is the new Israel (see Dan 7:13-14), the Messiah who would bring salvation. All three of these theophanies, these revelations of who Jesus is, point to something entirely new happening. But to embrace the new has its cost.

Coming "down from the mountain," Peter, James, and John would witness Jesus passing through death to the full revelation of what had been foreshadowed in his transfiguration: the theophany of his risen, glorified Body. This is a whole new Presence of the divine in our midst, a risen One who would never again face death. Finally, when Peter, James, and John choose dying to self, they are transfigured by Jesus' risen Life. *They* too become theophanies. So can *we*. But like Jesus and the apostles before us, our being transfigured by Jesus' risen Life has its cost, too. We can become a theophany of God only when we embrace Jesus' dying to self, his self-giving life of compassion, love, and mercy. We can become a theophany of God only when we surrender ourselves to the mystery of salvation, identify with Jesus, and live the Gospel he proclaimed as faithful members of his Body. We can be a theophany of God because we are the Body of Christ, the risen One.

Living the Paschal Mystery

Coming down from the high mountain of transfiguration, of theophany, the apostles questioned "what rising from the dead meant." Our whole Christian life is living this question. In the risen Christ, we are a theophany of God's desire for an intimate relationship with us. This relationship has its cost: we must learn to die to self so we can share in Jesus' transfigured glory.

When we make it a habit to key into the dying and rising of the paschal mystery, we begin to see its rhythm everywhere. In this Sunday's gospel the rhythm of dying and rising plays out between transfigured glory in the first part of the gospel and the allusion to Jesus' dying in the last part ("rising from the dead"). In our daily lives the paschal mystery might play out between work and leisure, between times with loved ones and times away, between success and failure, between doing something we would enjoy and doing something someone else would enjoy more. Our faithful dying to self is the way to share in Jesus' risen Life. Faithful dying to self is a way we are theophanies of God's Presence.

Focusing the Gospel

Key words and phrases: mountain, transfigured, beloved Son, Son of Man, risen from the dead

To the point: This gospel account tells of three theophanies and hints at two others. On the mountain Peter, James, and John witness the first three: Jesus the transfigured One, Jesus the "beloved Son," Jesus the "Son of Man." Coming "down from the mountain," they would witness Jesus passing through death to the full revelation of what had been foreshadowed in his transfiguration: the theophany of his risen, glorified Body. Finally, when Peter, James, and John choose dying to self, they are transfigured by Jesus' risen Life. *They* too become theophanies. So can *we*.

Connecting the Gospel

to the second reading: God "did not spare his own Son" but allowed him to be "handed over" to death; God also raised him from the dead to new Life. This same God will also give us new Life as we die to self in following the Son.

to experience: The notion of "theophany" seems so beyond us; who would expect to see God? Yet, we do: in a glorious sunset, in a newborn baby, in the Milky Way, in a selfless act, in the delight of a small child. God is seen in the traces of divine glory all around us.

Connecting the Responsorial Psalm

to the readings: Psalm 116 was a psalm of thanksgiving sung to God after being delivered from death: "I will walk before the Lord, in the land of the living" (psalm refrain). We can easily place its words on Abraham's lips after the voice from heaven stayed the knife he held over Isaac (first reading). We can hear its words on the lips of Christ who, having died for our sakes, was raised to new life (second reading). What does it mean for us to place these words on our lips on the Second Sunday of Lent? We sing this psalm knowing that what God desires for us is life, not death. We sing this psalm also knowing that to receive the fuller Life God wishes for us we must pass through whatever dying to self comes from listening to the call of God (first reading) and the voice of Jesus (gospel). Abraham listened and learned this. Peter, James, and John listened and learned this. Now is our time to listen and learn.

to psalmist preparation: To "walk before the Lord, in the land of the living" (psalm refrain) does not mean that you will never face death. On the contrary, the readings and gospel tell you just the opposite. Ask God this week for the grace you need to sing this psalm with the courage and the confidence it requires.

**ASSEMBLY &
FAITH-SHARING GROUPS**
- What impedes my ability to look for God is . . . What impedes my ability to see God is . . . When I see God, I . . .
- Dying to self means . . . requires . . . leads to . . .
- I am a theophany when I . . . Others who have been a theophany for me are . . .

PRESIDERS
The dying to self I resist in my ministry is . . . The transformation I experience when I do die to self is . . .

DEACONS
I am a theophany of God's compassion and care in my ministry when I . . .

HOSPITALITY MINISTERS
The manner of my greeting invites those gathering to die to self during liturgy when . . . during daily living when . . .

MUSIC MINISTERS
When I die to self, my music ministry becomes . . .

ALTAR MINISTERS
For my service at the altar to be truly a witness to the new Life of transfiguration, I must . . .

LECTORS
While preparing to proclaim God's word, the dying required of me is . . . the new Life I receive is . . .

**EXTRAORDINARY MINISTERS
OF HOLY COMMUNION**
I see the transfigured Christ in the faces of those coming to receive Holy Communion when I . . . This transforms me by . . .

Model Penitential Act

Presider: Jesus' transfiguration gives us a glimpse of the glory that awaits us when we, too, die to self for the sake of others. As we prepare to celebrate this liturgy, let us examine when we have put ourselves ahead of God and others and ask for God's mercy . . . [pause]

    Confiteor: I confess . . .

Homily Points

• The face of a newly engaged person shines with joy. The face of a child who has accomplished a difficult task glows with pride. The face of a person who has made a difficult choice to do what is right against all odds reflects peace. These are all visible expressions of transfiguration, although fleeting ones.

• The transfiguration the disciples witnessed on the "high mountain" was also fleeting: they came "down from the mountain." At the same time, this transfiguration foreshadowed the theophany of an eternal glory: Christ risen from the dead.

• Jesus' theophany of transfiguration and risen Life continues in us in the world today through our participation in the paschal mystery, the dying and rising mystery of Christ. This participation requires of us the same dying to self Jesus embraced. We must set aside our own agenda to pay more attention to the needs of others. We must be generous in recognizing and complimenting the good others do. We must be inclusive in accepting those who do not look or think like we do. These actions are fleeting, but they portend what is everlasting. Experiences of transfiguration help us see beyond what is here and now to what will be—our eternal share in Christ's risen Life.

Model Universal Prayer (Prayer of the Faithful)

Presider: God cares for, protects, and helps God's beloved ones. With confidence, let us pray to this God for our needs.

Response:

Lord, hear our prayer.

Cantor:

we pray to the Lord,

That all members of the church may faithfully die to self and share in Jesus' risen Life . . . [pause]

That leaders of nations may collaborate to transform the world into a community seeking salvation for all . . . [pause]

That the sick and the suffering may find hope for healing and strength in the transfigured Jesus . . . [pause]

That the Elect deepen their desire for the transformation that baptism will bring . . . [pause]

That our Lenten penance lead us to a share in Jesus' transfigured glory now and in the fullness to come . . . [pause]

Presider: Loving God, you clothed your Son Jesus in transfigured glory: grant these our prayers that one day we might also share fully in that same glory. We ask this through that same Son Jesus Christ our Lord. **Amen.**

COLLECT

Let us pray

Pause for silent prayer

O God, who have commanded us
to listen to your beloved Son,
be pleased, we pray,
to nourish us inwardly by your word,
that, with spiritual sight made pure,
we may rejoice to behold your glory.
Through our Lord Jesus Christ, your Son,
who lives and reigns with you in the unity
    of the Holy Spirit,
one God, for ever and ever. **Amen.**

FIRST READING
Gen 22:1-2, 9a, 10-13, 15-18

God put Abraham to the test.
He called to him, "Abraham!"
"Here I am!" he replied.
Then God said:
    "Take your son Isaac, your only one,
        whom you love,
    and go to the land of Moriah.
There you shall offer him up as a holocaust
    on a height that I will point out to you."

When they came to the place of which
    God had told him,
    Abraham built an altar there and
        arranged the wood on it.
Then he reached out and took the knife to
    slaughter his son.
But the LORD's messenger called to him
    from heaven,
    "Abraham, Abraham!"
"Here I am!" he answered.
"Do not lay your hand on the boy," said the
    messenger.
"Do not do the least thing to him.
I know now how devoted you are to God,
    since you did not withhold from me
        your own beloved son."
As Abraham looked about,
    he spied a ram caught by its horns in
        the thicket.
So he went and took the ram
    and offered it up as a holocaust in place
        of his son.

Again the LORD's messenger called to
    Abraham from heaven and said:
"I swear by myself, declares the LORD,
    that because you acted as you did
    in not withholding from me your
        beloved son,
I will bless you abundantly
    and make your descendants as countless
    as the stars of the sky and the sands of
        the seashore;

your descendants shall take possession
   of the gates of their enemies,
and in your descendants all the nations
   of the earth
      shall find blessing—
all this because you obeyed my
   command."

RESPONSORIAL PSALM

Ps 116:10, 15, 16-17, 18-19

R̸. (116:9) I will walk before the Lord, in
the land of the living.

I believed, even when I said,
   "I am greatly afflicted."
Precious in the eyes of the LORD
   is the death of his faithful ones.

R̸. I will walk before the Lord, in the land
of the living.

O LORD, I am your servant;
   I am your servant, the son of your
      handmaid;
   you have loosed my bonds.
To you will I offer sacrifice of
      thanksgiving,
   and I will call upon the name of the
      LORD.

R̸. I will walk before the Lord, in the land
of the living.

My vows to the LORD I will pay
   in the presence of all his people,
in the courts of the house of the LORD,
   in your midst, O Jerusalem.

R̸. I will walk before the Lord, in the land
of the living.

SECOND READING

Rom 8:31b-34

Brothers and sisters:
If God is for us, who can be against us?
He who did not spare his own Son
   but handed him over for us all,
   how will he not also give us everything
      else along with him?

Who will bring a charge against God's
      chosen ones?
   It is God who acquits us. Who will
      condemn?
Christ Jesus it is who died—or, rather, was
      raised—
   who also is at the right hand of God,
   who indeed intercedes for us.

About Liturgy

Lenten Sundays: There are many reminders during the Lenten Sunday Masses that we are observing a penitential season. The readings at the Sunday Masses bring to mind Lenten motifs and spur us on to fidelity in penance. Our Lenten Masses are less celebrative than even the Masses during Ordinary Time; for example, there is no *Gloria*, no alleluia, and less exuberant instrumentation. The penitential violet purple of the vestments and other appointments keep reminding us that we are in a penitential season, as well as does the simplicity of the environment and the lack of flowers.

This being said, the Sundays during Lent are not Lenten days at all. At a time when the symbolism of forty was heightened, the beginning of Lent was pushed back to the Wednesday before the first Sunday of Lent so there would be forty fasting days (hence, the period of Lent is actually longer than forty days). The Sundays of Lent are still days on which we celebrate the Lord's resurrection. Especially on this Second Sunday of Lent when we hear about the transfiguration of Jesus are we reminded that dying always leads to rising to new Life. In our very liturgical celebrations we see the paschal mystery rhythm. Lent is a time to practice the discipline of dying to self, yet we still have one day a week on which we always celebrate the new Life promised by Jesus' resurrection. What might be ways we can truly celebrate new Life even on Lenten Sundays, without getting out of the spirit of Lent?

About Liturgical Music

Music suggestions: Ricky Manalo's "Beyond the Days" (BB, JS3) is particularly appropriate for this day when we hear the story of Jesus' transfiguration. In the refrain we sing, "Beyond the days of hope and mystery we see a light of faith renewed, and in our longing we thirst for guidance to walk with you day by day." In verse 4 we pray, "On our Lenten path we see the dawn of a new day. Be our vision of hope; be the promise of our lives." The melody and the style of this piece make it suitable for the preparation of the gifts or the Communion procession. The text and style of Manalo's "Transfiguration" (BB, JS3) makes this piece suitable for the entrance procession. This song could be sung either as a through-composed setting for the entire assembly or as a verse-refrain piece led by cantor or choir.

A song well-suited for Communion this Sunday, as well as all the Sundays of Lent, is Bob Hurd's "Transfigure Us, O Lord" (BB, JS3). "'Tis Good, Lord, to Be Here," also titled "How Good, Lord, to Be Here" (found in most resources), would be a good text to sing as a hymn of praise after Communion, for it fits both the transfiguration story and the season of Lent. Part of "being here" is the transformation which takes place in us through the eucharistic action. But, as with the disciples in the gospel, we cannot remain on the mountain. We must return to the demands of daily living. The glimpse of glory given us in Jesus' transfiguration and the eucharistic banquet give us courage to move forward, for we can see what the future promises. Sylvia Dunstan's "Transform Us" (G3, LMGM2, SS, W4) would be a fitting recessional song. The text leads us from our encounter with the transfigured Jesus back to "those daily pathways" where we are to live as Christ's Body.

✠ SPIRITUALITY

GOSPEL ACCLAMATION
John 3:16

God so loved the world that he gave his only Son,
so that everyone who believes in him might have
eternal life.

Gospel John 2:13-25; L29B

Since the Passover of the Jews was near,
    Jesus went up to Jerusalem.
He found in the temple area those who
        sold oxen, sheep, and doves,
    as well as the money changers seated
        there.
He made a whip out of cords
    and drove them all out of the
        temple area, with the sheep
        and oxen,
    and spilled the coins of the money
        changers
    and overturned their tables,
    and to those who sold doves he said,
    "Take these out of here,
    and stop making my Father's house a
        marketplace."
His disciples recalled the words of Scripture,
    Zeal for your house will consume me.
At this the Jews answered and said to him,
    "What sign can you show us for doing this?"
Jesus answered and said to them,
    "Destroy this temple and in three days I
        will raise it up."
The Jews said,
    "This temple has been under construction
        for forty-six years,
    and you will raise it up in three days?"
But he was speaking about the temple of
    his body.
Therefore, when he was raised from the dead,
    his disciples remembered that he had
        said this,
    and they came to believe the Scripture
    and the word Jesus had spoken.

While he was in Jerusalem for the feast of
    Passover,
    many began to believe in his name
    when they saw the signs he was doing.
But Jesus would not trust himself to them
    because he knew them all,
    and did not need anyone to testify about
        human nature.
He himself understood it well.

*Year A readings may be used, see Appendix A,
pp. 271–273.*

Reflecting on the Gospel

Twice this gospel mentions the Passover—that event in Jewish history that marks Israel's passage from slavery to freedom. This is the founding, saving event that the Jewish people celebrate each year. Those who could came to Jerusalem to celebrate the feast. Jesus is there. On the feast. He goes to the temple. And becomes enraged. This is not a picture of Jesus we usually see. Something awfully important had to have been at stake.

The temple in Jerusalem was a sign to the Jews of God's Presence and saving works. This sign could be corrupted, however, by human beings who turn away from the temple's true purpose. Enraged, Jesus takes "a whip" and drives out of the temple area those who corrupt the sign. Then Jesus announces both a new temple (his own body) that could not be corrupted and a new sign ("raised from the dead") that would draw those who come to believe in him to a whole new reality. Even though the new temple of Jesus' body would be destroyed by death, in the end it was not. This temple would be an eternal sign of God's Presence and saving works and those who wish to share in Jesus' Life cannot lose sight of this sign.

God's Presence and saving works are not found in bricks and mortar, but in the risen Body of Christ. Now *we* are the new temple: the living sign of the new things God is doing for us. This living sign is no longer a place (a bricks and mortar temple), but a relationship of fidelity to a new temple (the risen Jesus).

The simple call of the gospel is to see the living signs of God's Presence in our midst. Unlike the signs the Jews asked to see in the gospel—signs which would justify Jesus' extraordinary action in the temple—we are to ask and look for different signs, ones which draw us into the deepest reality of what it means to be a disciple of Jesus. Jesus showed us the signs so clearly: he was crucified (see second reading) and then raised up. Just as surely as God raised up Jesus from the dead, so will we be raised up. The signs are there for us to see and believe. Oh, the jealousy and fidelity of the Divine (see first reading)! Yes, God can be trusted with our very lives.

Living the Paschal Mystery

Most of us get lost in the demands of our everyday living. We get up in the morning, spend our day working, prepare and clean up after meals, shop and clean, drive the kids to soccer practice, worry about them, and do countless other things before we fall into bed at the end of the day—usually totally exhausted. In the midst of all this it is pretty difficult to be single-minded about anything except the tasks at hand. This gospel strikingly challenges us to keep doing all these everyday tasks—but for the right reason: to continue to be living signs of Jesus' risen Presence within and among us.

Ultimately, we are to offer up the temple of our own bodies by dying to self and only in this way can we share in the new Life God offers us. This is our daily dying: not necessarily doing something different, but doing what is demanded of us out of love for God and the good of others. This is our daily rising: that we have kept our sight on God, have conformed ourselves more perfectly to Christ, and have believed the signs of God's Presence to us.

Focusing the Gospel

Key words and phrases: temple area, drove them all out, sign, temple of his body, raised from the dead, many began to believe

To the point: The temple in Jerusalem was a sign to the Jews of God's Presence and saving works. This sign could be corrupted, however, by human beings who turn away from the temple's true purpose. Enraged, Jesus takes "a whip" and drives out of the temple area those who corrupt the sign. Then Jesus announces both a new temple (his own body) that could not be corrupted and a new sign ("raised from the dead") that would draw those who come to believe in him to a whole new reality. God's Presence and saving works are not found in bricks and mortar, but in the risen Body of Christ. Now *we* are the new temple: the living sign of God's Presence and saving works.

Connecting the Gospel

to the second reading: The stumbling block for some becomes the building block for others. "Christ crucified" is the foundation of the new temple. This we proclaim by the way we live.

to experience: DNA is the building block of life. Jesus' paschal mystery (life, death, resurrection, and sending of the Spirit) is the building block of our redeemed life.

Connecting the Responsorial Psalm

to the readings: Psalm 19, from which this responsorial psalm is taken, has three sections. The first (vv. 2-7) describes the sun joyfully running its course from one end of heaven to the other. Nothing escapes its heat. The second (vv. 8-11) sings the praise of God's Law from which all good comes. The third (vv. 12-15) is an acknowledgment of sin, both unconscious and willful, with a plea that God keep the psalmist faithful.

Just as the sun gives light to the earth, so does God's Law give light to humankind. Both leave no corners in shadow. Yet, how easily humans fail to live in this light. In the temple Jesus, who understands "human nature" well, confronts this love of darkness with directness and force (gospel). He is "the power . . . and the wisdom of God" (second reading) bringing the light of God's judgment to bear upon human behavior. He is God's Law personified. By singing these verses from Psalm 19, we tell him that we hear his "words of everlasting life" (psalm refrain) and will heed them.

to psalmist preparation: Read and reflect on the entirety of Psalm 19 as you prepare to sing the portion of it assigned for this Sunday's responsorial psalm. The comparison of God's Law to the light of the sun and the honesty with which the psalmist prays to remain faithful to the Law reveal that the Law is not a list of things to do or not do, but the roadmap to a loving relationship with God and neighbor. How was Jesus faithful to this Law? How is he calling you to be faithful?

**ASSEMBLY &
FAITH-SHARING GROUPS**
- I am a living sign of the new temple when I . . . I corrupt the sign when I . . .
- Like Jesus, I become enraged by . . . What I do is . . .
- Jesus' being "raised from the dead" means to me . . . It affects me in that . . .

PRESIDERS
My zeal for God's house is evident to the assembly when . . .

DEACONS
My zeal for those in need strengthens them and lifts them up because . . .

HOSPITALITY MINISTERS
I greet those gathering for liturgy as the new temple of God's Presence when I . . .

MUSIC MINISTERS
My manner of leading music builds up the Body of Christ proclaiming "Christ crucified" when I . . .

ALTAR MINISTERS
My service ministry builds up . . .

LECTORS
No matter what Scripture I proclaim, the evident building block of my proclamation is "Christ crucified" when . . .

**EXTRAORDINARY MINISTERS
OF HOLY COMMUNION**
My manner of distributing Holy Communion reveals my reverence for the communicants as temples of God's Presence when I . . .

Model Penitential Act

Presider: In this Sunday's gospel we hear the account of Jesus cleansing the temple. As we prepare for this liturgy, let us reflect on what needs to be cleansed from the temple of our hearts . . . [pause]

> *Confiteor:* I confess . . .

Homily Points

- Constructing a new building is always challenging. Design details, funding concerns, building permits and codes, inspections are all time consuming and worrisome. Building up the community of the church as the living temple of God's Presence is even more challenging. Much more is at stake.

- In this gospel Jesus overturns more than money tables. He overturns the Jewish understanding of the temple from a building "under construction" to his own body. He overturns our understanding of death from the end of life to the beginning of new, risen Life. He overturns our very selves from an empty lot of unbelief to a beautiful edifice of believers. We are God's new construction and God overturns all challenges while building us into living signs of divine Presence and saving works.

- By overturning those aspects of our human nature given to pride, self-centeredness, anger, envy, jealousy, greed, God builds us into living signs of divine Presence and saving work. We become the new temple, the Body of Christ, given over to humility, compassion, forgiveness, healing, service, love. What is at stake is bringing to beautiful completion the construction of God's new temple.

Model Universal Prayer (Prayer of the Faithful)

Presider: God wishes to build us into more beautiful temples of divine Presence. Let us pray for our needs, that God's work may be brought to completion.

Response:

Cantor:

That all members of the Body of Christ may be living signs of God's Presence and saving works . . . [pause]

That all peoples of the world come to a deeper belief in God's saving works . . . [pause]

That those who are sick and suffering receive healing and care from those living as faithful disciples of Jesus . . . [pause]

That those preparing for the rites of initiation at Easter may grow in their commitment to follow the Gospel . . . [pause]

That all of us come to a deeper belief that God is drawing us to eternal Life in the heavenly temple of glory . . . [pause]

Presider: Gracious and loving God, you build us into your beautiful temple of divine Presence: hear these our prayers that we may be faithful in following your Son from death to Life. We ask this through that same Son, Jesus Christ our Savior. **Amen.**

COLLECT

Let us pray

Pause for silent prayer

O God, author of every mercy and of all
     goodness,
who in fasting, prayer and almsgiving
have shown us a remedy for sin,
look graciously on this confession of our
     lowliness,
that we, who are bowed down by our
     conscience,
may always be lifted up by your mercy.
Through our Lord Jesus Christ, your Son,
who lives and reigns with you in the unity
     of the Holy Spirit,
one God, for ever and ever. **Amen.**

FIRST READING

Exod 20:1-17

In those days, God delivered all these
     commandments:
     "I, the LORD, am your God,
who brought you out of the land of
     Egypt, that place of slavery.
You shall not have other gods besides me.
You shall not carve idols for yourselves
     in the shape of anything in the sky
          above
     or on the earth below or in the waters
          beneath the earth;
     you shall not bow down before them or
          worship them.
For I, the LORD, your God, am a jealous
     God,
     inflicting punishment for their fathers'
          wickedness
     on the children of those who hate me,
     down to the third and fourth generation;
     but bestowing mercy down to the
          thousandth generation
     on the children of those who love me
          and keep my commandments.

"You shall not take the name of the LORD,
     your God, in vain.
For the LORD will not leave unpunished
     the one who takes his name in vain.

"Remember to keep holy the sabbath day.
Six days you may labor and do all your
     work,
     but the seventh day is the sabbath of
          the LORD, your God.
No work may be done then either by you,
     or your son or daughter,
     or your male or female slave, or your
          beast,
     or by the alien who lives with you.

In six days the LORD made the heavens and
　　the earth,
　　the sea and all that is in them;
　　but on the seventh day he rested.
That is why the LORD has blessed the
　　sabbath day and made it holy.

"Honor your father and your mother,
　　that you may have a long life in the land
　　which the LORD, your God, is giving you.
You shall not kill.
You shall not commit adultery.
You shall not steal.
You shall not bear false witness against
　　your neighbor.
You shall not covet your neighbor's house.
You shall not covet your neighbor's wife,
　　nor his male or female slave, nor his ox
　　　or ass,
　　nor anything else that belongs to him."

or

Exod 20:1-3, 7-8, 12-17

In those days, God delivered all these
　　commandments:
　　"I, the LORD, am your God,
　　who brought you out of the land of
　　　Egypt, that place of slavery.
You shall not have other gods besides me.

"You shall not take the name of the LORD,
　　your God, in vain.
For the LORD will not leave unpunished
　　the one who takes his name in vain.

"Remember to keep holy the sabbath day.
Honor your father and your mother,
　　that you may have a long life in the land
　　which the LORD, your God, is giving you.
You shall not kill.
You shall not commit adultery.
You shall not steal.
You shall not bear false witness against
　　your neighbor.
You shall not covet your neighbor's house.
You shall not covet your neighbor's wife,
　　nor his male or female slave, nor his ox
　　　or ass,
　　nor anything else that belongs to him."

RESPONSORIAL PSALM
Ps 19:8, 9, 10, 11

SECOND READING
1 Cor 1:22-25

See Appendix A, p. 270.

About Liturgy

The Lenten Lectionary: There is perhaps no other portion of the Lectionary that has such strong paschal mystery motifs as the selections for Lent. Already on the first two Sundays of Lent the gospels—the temptation in the desert and the transfiguration—speak eloquently of dying and rising. In this Year B the gospels of the third to fifth Sundays of Lent (which we begin this Sunday) also focus on the dying and rising mystery which is clearly evident in the selections. Although Year B draws on Mark's gospel, we notice that all three of these Lenten Sunday gospels are from John. One of the earliest ways of keeping Lent (probably dating from the third century) was to read John's gospel through, culminating in the proclamation of John's passion on Good Friday. We see this pattern clearly this year.

Unlike other Sundays of the year, the first readings don't specifically relate to the gospels (although often there are converging themes). Instead, the first readings recount major salvation history events; these remind us that the paschal mystery is already foreshadowed in God's plan of salvation unfolding from the beginning of creation.

The second readings are the least related to each other but all of them speak of Christ's dying and rising and, therefore, are commentaries on the paschal mystery. As often occurs during the festal seasons, the second readings give us insight into the meaning of the season and feast that is being celebrated. To appreciate more fully the careful construction of the Lectionary, it is always helpful to see the readings in relation to each other and the season. This hermeneutic (way of interpreting) guides all our reflections in *Living Liturgy™*.

About Liturgical Music

Music suggestions: Written to accord with this Sunday's gospel reading, Herman Stuempfle's "You Strode within the Temple, Lord" (HG, W4) identifies the temple with Christ's body, with the human heart, and with the community of the church. This hymn would be effective at the entrance, the recessional, or during the preparation of the gifts. An excellent "old standby" appropriate for this Sunday would be Lucien Deiss's "Grant to Us, O Lord" (found in many resources). The verses speak of God recreating us by planting the Law deep within us and forgiving our failures. The song would work well as the entrance processional or the Communion song with choir or cantor singing the verses and assembly repeating the refrain. Also appropriate during Communion, or during the preparation of the gifts, would be David Haas's "Deep Within" (G3).

SPIRITUALITY

GOSPEL ACCLAMATION
John 3:16

God so loved the world that he gave his only Son,
so everyone who believes in him might have
eternal life.

Gospel

John 3:14-21; L32B

Jesus said to Nicodemus:
"Just as Moses lifted up the
serpent in the desert,
so must the Son of Man be lifted up,
so that everyone who believes in him
may have eternal life."

For God so loved the world that he gave
his only Son,
so that everyone who believes in him
might not perish
but might have eternal life.
For God did not send his Son into the
world to condemn the world,
but that the world might be saved
through him.
Whoever believes in him will not be
condemned,
but whoever does not believe has
already been condemned,
because he has not believed in the
name of the only Son of God.
And this is the verdict,
that the light came into the world,
but people preferred darkness to
light,
because their works were evil.
For everyone who does wicked things
hates the light
and does not come toward the light,
so that his works might not be
exposed.
But whoever lives the truth comes to
the light,
so that his works may be clearly seen
as done in God.

*Year A readings may be used, see Appendix A,
pp. 273–275.*

Reflecting on the Gospel

Being a defendant at a trial is no fun. Whether the crime is heinous like rape-murder, or not so serious like pickpocketing, the verdict is always anticipated with a greater or lesser amount of dread. The defendant's life and future is in the hands of those who make a judgment about the evidence. The defendant is no longer in control. The defendant is at the mercy of others.

There are two parts to this gospel, separated by the line "And this is the verdict." The first part concerns the evidence: God "gave his only Son" in whom we choose to believe or not. The second part gives the judgment: those are saved who believe in Jesus, live the truth, and come to the light. Those are condemned who do not believe in Jesus, prefer darkness, and do "wicked things." Our whole life is working out our own verdict. Thank God we are at the mercy of a gracious and forgiving God!

Jesus says clearly that believing "in the name of the only Son of God" is necessary if we are not to "be condemned" but be saved. What is this believing? Jesus makes this clear, as well: believing is coming "to the light" by living the truth. The light is the Jesus who was "lifted up." The words "believe" and "light" occur five times each in this gospel and the two words are not unrelated. The light (= Christ) enables us to see; in John's gospel, seeing is believing. Our coming to the light to see and believe is expressed in "works . . . done in God." God's work is this: to die to self so that we can be raised to new life. God demonstrates great love for us by giving the Son to be lifted up on the cross and then raised to eternal Life and glory. We demonstrate our great love for God by doing the work of God—dying and rising, conforming ourselves so completely to Christ that we cooperate in his very work of salvation. We need not fear the verdict of God's judgment at the end of our lives if we daily work at increasing the depth of our believing and conforming ourselves to Christ by living in his light.

Living the Paschal Mystery

The faith/belief mentioned in both the second reading and gospel allude to our self-surrender at baptism which begins a life lived as followers of Christ. Even more: at baptism we are plunged into Christ's death so that we might rise to new life with him (see Rom 6:5). This dying and rising mystery is the paschal mystery. Through it we are joined to Christ in his work of salvation.

The paradox of the paschal mystery is that what we abhor—the cross—becomes the instrument of redemption. God saves the Israelites from death but in the paschal mystery we must embrace death, for the only way to eternal Life is by dying to ourselves, by allowing ourselves to be lifted up like Christ. Our good works (reaching out to others, doing our daily tasks with love and care, acting justly and charitably, etc.), then, are our way of being "lifted up." This is how we are crucified, so that we might live.

This gospel, coming in the middle of Lent (this is traditionally called "*Laetare*" Sunday), is a reminder of what Lent is truly about and, indeed, what our whole Christian living is about. There are only three weeks of Lent left. Now is the time to renew our resolve to embrace dying to self so that we might truly rise with Christ in joy and Life on Easter.

Focusing the Gospel

Key words and phrases: God . . . gave his only Son, Whoever believes in him, whoever does not believe, verdict, preferred darkness, does wicked things, lives the truth, comes to the light

To the point: There are two parts to this gospel, separated by the line "And this is the verdict." The first part concerns the evidence: God "gave his only Son" in whom we choose to believe or not. The second part gives the judgment: those are saved who believe in Jesus, live the truth, and come to the light. Those are condemned who do not believe in Jesus, prefer darkness, and do "wicked things." Our whole life is working out our own verdict. Thank God we are at the mercy of a gracious and forgiving God!

Connecting the Gospel

to the second reading: The second reading makes clear that our very ability to believe in Jesus is "the gift of God." Being saved is a gift from God.

to experience: Most small children are afraid of the dark where the boogey-man dwells and bad things happen. This gospel tells us that adults also must be afraid of the "dark"—the "darkness" where people do "wicked things."

Connecting the Responsorial Psalm

to the readings: This Sunday's responsorial psalm is difficult to understand unless we see it in the context of Israel's exile in Babylon. The exile was devastating and the Israelites had brought it upon themselves through their unfaithfulness to the covenant (first reading). Psalm 137 echoes the bitterness of the exile and is a reflection upon the utter barrenness of that experience. It is also a plea that the Israelites never again forget what it means to be God's chosen people.

The second reading tells us that we, too, have been restored to life "even when we were dead in our transgressions." The only Son of God came not to condemn but to save us (gospel). And, just as the Israelites, we must make a choice: to believe, to walk toward the light, to live the truth. The psalm challenges us to remember the price of forgetting what God has given us by sending the Son.

to psalmist preparation: When have you been in exile from God and the community? What led you there? What did this exile feel like? How did God mercifully bring you back home?

**ASSEMBLY &
FAITH-SHARING GROUPS**
- I am prone to "prefer[ ] darkness" when . . . Who and what lead me back to the Light are . . .
- I come to deeper belief in Jesus through . . . I help others come to believe in Jesus by . . .
- Right now, the verdict on my life is . . .

PRESIDERS
My ministry most surely leads my people to truth and light when I . . .

DEACONS
My service lifts up Jesus for all to see when . . .

HOSPITALITY MINISTERS
I help those gathering for liturgy come to the light of Christ's Presence when I . . .

MUSIC MINISTERS
My music ministry draws the assembly to the truth of Jesus' saving mystery when . . .

ALTAR MINISTERS
God "gave his only Son" so that we might live in the light. I give . . .

LECTORS
My prayerful reading of Scripture and preparation for proclamation leads me to the light by . . .

**EXTRAORDINARY MINISTERS
OF HOLY COMMUNION**
My choosing to believe in Jesus is reflected in the way I minister Holy Communion in that . . .

Model Penitential Act

Presider: The gospel this Sunday challenges us to believe in Jesus and choose light over darkness. For the times when we have chosen the darkness of sin, let us ask for God's mercy and forgiveness . . . [pause]

    Confiteor: I confess . . .

Homily Points

- The word "verdict" derives from the Latin *dicere*, to speak, and *veritas*, truth. Those engaged in a trial by jury anxiously wait for the verdict, hoping it will be in their favor even if it is not actually the truth. The gospel tells us that a Life-giving verdict only comes to those who live the truth and come to the light.

- Jesus clearly says that believing "in the name of the only Son of God" is necessary if we are not to "be condemned." What is this believing? Jesus makes this clear, as well: coming "to the light" by living "the truth." Living "the truth" is the evidence that brings a favorable judgment. The verdict: "eternal life."

- It is really easy to fool ourselves about living "the truth" when actually we have chosen darkness. For example, we choose to engage in idle gossip, convincing ourselves that we need to be better informed about others. We know, however, we are living "the truth" when what we do stands up to the light of Christ and is consistent with "the truth" of gospel values. For example, we choose forgiveness rather than retaliation, we welcome the outsider rather than ignoring those not in our circle of friends, we choose words that uplift rather than those that hurt. This kind of living gives evidence of our believing in Jesus and leads us to the verdict we desire: "eternal life."

Model Universal Prayer (Prayer of the Faithful)

Presider: God is a just judge who desires that we have all good things and come to eternal Life. Let us pray for what we need.

Response:

    Lord, hear our prayer.

Cantor:

    we pray to the Lord,

For all members of the church, that they may walk in the truth of the Gospel and come to the light of Christ . . . [pause]

For all people of the world, that by believing in God's mercy and love they might have eternal Life . . . [pause]

For those struggling with darkness in their lives, that they may soon come to light and hope . . . [pause]

For all those preparing for the Easter sacraments, that they might come to greater belief in Jesus and commitment to his way of living . . . [pause]

For all of us here, that our belief in Jesus might be firm and our actions be true . . . [pause]

Presider: God of mercy and love, you call us out of darkness to eternal light: hear these our prayers that we might one day live forever with you and your Son Jesus Christ, together with the Holy Spirit, one God, for ever and ever. **Amen.**

COLLECT

Let us pray

Pause for silent prayer

O God, who through your Word
reconcile the human race to yourself in a
    wonderful way,
grant, we pray,
that with prompt devotion and eager faith
the Christian people may hasten
toward the solemn celebrations to come.
Through our Lord Jesus Christ, your Son,
who lives and reigns with you in the unity
    of the Holy Spirit,
one God, for ever and ever. **Amen.**

FIRST READING

2 Chr 36:14-16, 19-23

In those days, all the princes of Judah, the
    priests, and the people
  added infidelity to infidelity,
  practicing all the abominations of the
    nations
  and polluting the Lord's temple
  which he had consecrated in Jerusalem.

Early and often did the Lord, the God of
    their fathers,
  send his messengers to them,
  for he had compassion on his people
    and his dwelling place.
But they mocked the messengers of God,
  despised his warnings, and scoffed at
    his prophets,
  until the anger of the Lord against his
    people was so inflamed
  that there was no remedy.
Their enemies burnt the house of God,
  tore down the walls of Jerusalem,
  set all its palaces afire,
  and destroyed all its precious objects.
Those who escaped the sword were
    carried captive to Babylon,
  where they became servants of the king
    of the Chaldeans and his sons
  until the kingdom of the Persians came
    to power.
All this was to fulfill the word of the Lord
    spoken by Jeremiah:
  "Until the land has retrieved its lost
    sabbaths,
  during all the time it lies waste it shall
    have rest
  while seventy years are fulfilled."

In the first year of Cyrus, king of Persia,
    in order to fulfill the word of the Lᴏʀᴅ
        spoken by Jeremiah,
    the Lᴏʀᴅ inspired King Cyrus of Persia
    to issue this proclamation throughout
        his kingdom,
    both by word of mouth and in writing:
    "Thus says Cyrus, king of Persia:
    All the kingdoms of the earth
    the Lᴏʀᴅ, the God of heaven, has given
        to me,
    and he has also charged me to build him
        a house
    in Jerusalem, which is in Judah.
    Whoever, therefore, among you belongs to
        any part of his people,
    let him go up, and may his God be with
        him!"

RESPONSORIAL PSALM
Ps 137:1-2, 3, 4-5, 6

R̸. (6ab) Let my tongue be silenced, if I
ever forget you!

By the streams of Babylon
    we sat and wept
        when we remembered Zion.
On the aspens of that land
    we hung up our harps.

R̸. Let my tongue be silenced, if I ever
forget you!

For there our captors asked of us
    the lyrics of our songs,
and our despoilers urged us to be joyous:
    "Sing for us the songs of Zion!"

R̸. Let my tongue be silenced, if I ever
forget you!

How could we sing a song of the Lᴏʀᴅ
    in a foreign land?
If I forget you, Jerusalem,
    may my right hand be forgotten!

R̸. Let my tongue be silenced, if I ever
forget you!

May my tongue cleave to my palate
    if I remember you not,
if I place not Jerusalem
    ahead of my joy.

R̸. Let my tongue be silenced, if I ever
forget you!

SECOND READING
Eph 2:4-10

See Appendix A, p. 275.

About Liturgy

Best way to prepare for the liturgy: Because Scripture and the Lectionary are open to many interpretations, it is especially important that we reflect on the Scriptures before we come to Sunday Mass so we can be ready to hear God's word with all its depth and richness. The best preparation for the Liturgy of the Word is to read the Sunday Scriptures—especially the gospel—early during the week before and then to see how God's word begins to play itself out in our daily living. Let that word challenge us to live differently. Let that word invite us to new understanding. Let that word encourage us to die to ourselves every day so that we might more perfectly live the truth that only comes from God's light.

There is no substitution for preparing well for liturgy and the best preparation is by the way we live. A wonderful celebration of liturgy will be greatly aided by preparing well to hear the word on Sunday and by the kind of Christian living which evidences that we are consciously trying to live God's word in our everyday lives. This is when liturgy comes alive and is, indeed, a true celebration.

About Liturgical Music

Typology and Psalm 137: In biblical times it was common practice to hang Aeolian type harps on trees so that the wind could play them. Moreover, because prophetic trances were sometimes induced by playing on "lyres, tambourines, flutes and harps" (see 1 Sam 10:5), to "hang up the harp" was also a metaphor for the cessation of prophecy. Harps and prophecy were both associated with David, whom Scripture celebrates as a harpist and later Jewish tradition considers a prophet. In Christian typology, Jesus is not only the Star of David and from the house of David, he is also referred to as the harp of David. Thus, to hang the harp (Jesus) on the tree (cross) becomes a typology for the crucifixion. In its three-year cycle, the Lectionary uses Psalm 137 as the responsorial psalm only on this Sunday. Knowing the ancient typology associated with the harp adds to our appreciation of its meaning on this day.

Music suggestions: Herman Stuempfle's "Alone and Filled with Fear" (HG) tells a poetic version of the midnight encounter between Nicodemus and Jesus. We become Nicodemus saying to Jesus, "The Word you speak is filled With promise and with pain: 'There is no easy road to life; You must be born again.'" We become faithful disciples who find life by passing "from darkness into day." To be effective this text needs to be sung in its entirety, so it may work better at the preparation of the gifts than during the entrance procession. A good choice for Communion would be Marty Haugen's "For God So Loved the World" (G3), with cantor or choir singing the verses.

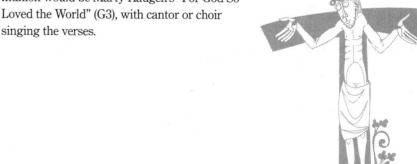

SPIRITUALITY

GOSPEL ACCLAMATION
Ps 84:5

Blessed are those who dwell in your house, O
   Lord;
they never cease to praise you.

Gospel   Luke 2:41-51a; L543

Each year Jesus' parents went to
      Jerusalem for the feast of
      Passover,
   and when he was twelve years
      old,
   they went up according to festival
      custom.
After they had completed its days, as
      they were returning,
   the boy Jesus remained behind
      in Jerusalem,
   but his parents did not know it.
Thinking that he was in the caravan,
   they journeyed for a day
   and looked for him among their relatives
      and acquaintances,
   but not finding him,
   they returned to Jerusalem to look for him.
After three days they found him in the
      temple,
   sitting in the midst of the teachers,
   listening to them and asking them
      questions,
   and all who heard him were astounded
   at his understanding and his answers.
When his parents saw him,
   they were astonished,
   and his mother said to him,
   "Son, why have you done this to us?
Your father and I have been looking for you
      with great anxiety."
And he said to them,
   "Why were you looking for me?
Did you not know that I must be in my
      Father's house?"
But they did not understand what he said to
      them.
He went down with them and came to
      Nazareth,
   and was obedient to them.

or Matt 1:16, 18-21, 24a in Appendix A, p. 276.

*See Appendix A, p. 276, for the other
   readings.*

84

Reflecting on the Gospel

Mary and Joseph are typical parents who spend time and undergo anxiety looking for a son they think is lost. Jesus, at twelve years old and growing into his adult responsibilities and mission, is where he knows he needs to be—in his "Father's house." But his time is not yet. Where he needs to be now is in the home of Mary and Joseph, "obedient to them." Working out God's plan of salvation for us includes discerning where we need to be. In this, Joseph is a model for us.

In all things Joseph was guided by God, responded to God's call, and was faithful to God's plan of salvation. He knew where he needed to be. This simple carpenter of Nazareth models for us what remaining in "my Father's house" really means: doing God's will in all things, both the great and the simple. No doubt many times Joseph was filled with wonder, awe, and not a little bit of confusion and consternation. After all, Jesus was no ordinary child—Mary did not conceive and give birth to him like an ordinary child; no ordinary child would remain three days apart from parents and, when found, be comfortably "listening . . . and asking . . . questions" of the teachers in the temple, seemingly unaware of the heartache he caused his parents. No, this is no ordinary child; neither is Joseph an ordinary father. Joseph was extraordinary because he always knew where he needed to be—open and listening for God's will for him.

It does not surprise us that the promises of God should come to fulfillment through such great figures as David (first reading) and Abraham (second reading). But the greatest of promises (the coming of the Savior, Jesus) is entrusted to the care of a simple man and woman who looked with great anxiety for their lost Son, found him, confronted him, and took him home where he was obedient to them. All these great people who came before us in faith knew that their response to God meant knowing where they needed to be at any given time. So, the question remains for us: Where do *we* need to be now?

Living the Paschal Mystery

Sometimes our expectations of ourselves with respect to our religious observances are great—especially during Lent. We begin with great fervor and take on demanding Lenten penance, usually only to fizzle out or continue the penance with a steadfast doggedness that borders on penance for the sake of penance and completing a task. This solemnity and St. Joseph remind us that God's promises come to fulfillment in our faithfulness to the everyday responsibilities that are ours. Holiness isn't simply a matter of doing great things; we grow into holiness by faithfulness to whatever God calls us, by knowing where God wants us to be at any given moment.

Beyond the infancy narratives in which Joseph is shown as one who cooperates perfectly with God's plans for salvation, the gospels say nothing else about him. It is precisely this "hidden life" that can be both model and encouragement for us in our everyday paschal mystery living. By responding to God and being a good husband to Mary and foster father to Jesus, Joseph fulfilled his vocation. Similarly, we fulfill our own vocations in the simple, everyday tasks. Paschal mystery living is about faithfulness in the little things as much as it is about dying on the cross. Both lead to risen Life. This is why we call Joseph "saint" and honor him on this day.

Focusing the Gospel

Key words and phrases: Jesus remained behind, parents . . . looked for him, great anxiety, my Father's house, obedient to them

To the point: Mary and Joseph are typical parents who spend time and undergo anxiety looking for a son they think is lost. Jesus, at twelve years old and growing into his adult responsibilities and mission, is where he knows he needs to be—in his "Father's house." But his time is not yet. Where he needs to be now is in the home of Mary and Joseph, "obedient to them." Where do we need to be now?

Model Penitential Act

Presider: St. Joseph is the model of fidelity to whatever God asked of him. Let us ask God for the grace to be faithful like Joseph, and for pardon for the times we have not been faithful . . . [pause]

Lord Jesus, you are Son of God and foster son of Joseph: Lord . . .

Christ Jesus, you now dwell in glory in your Father's house: Christ . . .

Lord Jesus, you were obedient to Joseph and Mary: Lord . . .

Model Universal Prayer (Prayer of the Faithful)

Presider: We now make our needs known to God, confident that they will be heard through the intercession of St. Joseph.

Response:

Cantor:

For the church, under the protection of St. Joseph . . . [pause]

For all peoples, called to fidelity to God's ways . . . [pause]

For the critically ill and dying, comforted by Joseph's fatherly care . . . [pause]

For all of us here, called to be obedient to God in all things . . . [pause]

Presider: Good and gracious God, you called Joseph to be the guardian and guide of your divine Son: hear these our prayers that we may be led by the Holy Spirit in Joseph's way of faithful living. We ask this through that same Son, Jesus Christ our Lord. **Amen.**

FOR REFLECTION

• In this gospel, Joseph's parental responsibilities and mission are . . . Where he needs to be is . . .

• My adult responsibilities and mission are . . . Where I need to be now is . . .

• Joseph teaches me that . . .

Homily Points

• The word "where" usually refers to a place. Where do we live? At home. Where do we work? At the factory. Where do we socialize? At the rec center. Where do we worship? At church. But also in our hearts. In our good acts. In our love. In our generosity. So "where" can also refer to who and how we are at a given moment. Where we need to be at every given moment is looking for Jesus.

• We naturally look for Jesus in certain expected places: in church, in prayer, in the Bible. But we must also look for him where we might least expect to find him. For example, we find Jesus in the suffering sick, in the homeless veteran, in the family members gathered around the dinner table. And where we find him is where we are meant to be now.

✠ SPIRITUALITY

GOSPEL ACCLAMATION
John 12:26

Whoever serves me must follow me, says the
    Lord;
and where I am, there also will my servant be.

Gospel

John 12:20-33; L35B

Some Greeks who had come to
    worship at the Passover Feast
came to Philip, who was from
    Bethsaida in Galilee,
and asked him, "Sir, we would
    like to see Jesus."
Philip went and told Andrew;
    then Andrew and Philip went
    and told Jesus.
Jesus answered them,
    "The hour has come for the Son
    of Man to be glorified.
Amen, amen, I say to you,
    unless a grain of wheat falls to the
    ground and dies,
    it remains just a grain of wheat;
    but if it dies, it produces much fruit.
Whoever loves his life loses it,
    and whoever hates his life in this
    world
    will preserve it for eternal life.
Whoever serves me must follow me,
    and where I am, there also will my
    servant be.
The Father will honor whoever serves
    me.

"I am troubled now. Yet what should I
    say?
'Father, save me from this hour'?
But it was for this purpose that I came
    to this hour.
Father, glorify your name."
Then a voice came from heaven,
    "I have glorified it and will glorify it
    again."

Continued in Appendix A, p. 277.
*Year A readings may be used, see Appendix A,
pp. 277–279.*

Reflecting on the Gospel

No pain, no gain. We often hear this proverb when faced with doing a difficult, demanding, even sometimes physically painful task. We forge ahead with the painful task because our desire for the end result is stronger than our impulse to avoid pain. A huge amount of medication costs are given over to relieving physical pain. Mental health professionals help us deal with emotional pain. Spiritual directors help us deal with spiritual pain. In this gospel Jesus speaks of different kinds of pain. There is the physical pain of his crucifixion, alluded to when he speaks of his being "lifted up from the earth." He also speaks of the pain of dying, of losing our life, of serving him by following him. In all this pain, the focus is not on the suffering, but on the fruits that come from being faithful. The dying grain "produces much fruit"; losing one's life now "preserves it for eternal life"; serving brings "honor." In all these examples, Jesus does not so much emphasize the pain, but the gain.

Jesus reveals his "hour . . . to be glorified" in surprisingly inglorious ways: dying grain, losing life, serving others. Jesus himself struggled with this: "I am troubled now." Who doesn't? When we focus only on the giving up and the giving over of our lives, however, we fail to take into account the glorification. We focus on the pain, but not on the gain.

By Jesus giving his life over for our salvation, glorification bursts forth. The Father is glorified in the very giving over of the Son. The Son is glorified in giving himself over to the cross. We are glorified in giving ourselves over to following Jesus to the cross. And this glorification is fullness of Life.

All three images in this gospel lead us to the basic truth of the mystery of salvation, the paschal mystery: by dying to self for the good of others we come to new life. Giving ourselves for the sake of others is never easy. Sometimes it even makes demands on us that seem impossible. Both the gospel and second reading make clear that Jesus did not want to suffer. Gospel: "I am troubled now . . . save me"; second reading: "he offered prayers and supplications with loud cries and tears" to his Father. We hear a similar plaintive cry when Jesus prays to his Father in the Garden of Gethsemane, asking his Father to save him from the cup of suffering he must drink. Jesus, however, taught us the most important lesson about the paschal mystery: death (self-giving) is the way—the only way—to fullness of Life. The dying itself is a gift and grace because it is a harbinger of new Life. Our glorification is *in* the very dying because in dying we fully identify with Jesus, who passed through death to risen Life. So will we.

Living the Paschal Mystery

Self-giving strengthens our fidelity as a servant-follower of Jesus. We must take up the habit of dying to self for the good of others. This defines what it means to be a faithful follower of Jesus. When we struggle with dying to self, we are in good company: Jesus himself was "troubled" (gospel) by this and cried out to be delivered from it (see second reading). We don't enter the paschal mystery as the dying and rising rhythm of our Christian living apart from Jesus. When we do take up the cross and die, not in the physical sense but by laying down our lives in service, we are able to see that the cross is the means of glory—for the Father, for Jesus, and for us. Our dying to self is hardly the pain of "no pain, no gain." It is the road to glorification.

Focusing the Gospel

Key words and phrases: hour . . . to be glorified, wheat . . . dies, loses, serves, troubled, lifted up from the earth

To the point: Jesus reveals his "hour . . . to be glorified" in surprisingly inglorious ways: dying grain, losing life, serving others. Jesus himself struggled with this: "I am troubled now." When we focus only on the giving up and the giving over of our lives, we fail to take into account the glorification. The Father is glorified in the very giving over of the Son. The Son is glorified in giving himself over to the cross. We are glorified in giving ourselves over to following Jesus to the cross. And this glorification is fullness of Life.

Connecting the Gospel

to the second reading: When we struggle with giving ourselves over to the cross, we are in good company: Jesus himself was "troubled" (gospel) by this and with "loud cries and tears" (second reading) prayed to be delivered from it.

to experience: The strongest human instinct is preservation of one's life. This gospel reveals, however, the only way truly to preserve our life is to lose it for the sake of others.

Connecting the Responsorial Psalm

to the readings: Often in the psalms, a person confronted with suffering claims innocence of any evildoing which could have caused the suffering (see Psalm 26, for example). In Psalm 51, however, the person praying readily acknowledges guilt. Moreover, the person begs not just to be forgiven but to be completely transformed. The very praying of Psalm 51, then, brings about a dying to self and a rising to new life.

In the first reading God offers us a new covenant, a new life, a new heart. In Psalm 51 we acknowledge our need for this transformation and ask God to do it. The good news is that our transformation has already been accomplished through Christ who freely chose death that he might bear the fruit of new life for us (first reading, gospel). When we sing Psalm 51 this Sunday, we open our hearts to receive what he has done for us. We acknowledge who we are—sinners in need of redemption—and receive who we have become because of him, a community filled with the joy of salvation (psalm).

to psalmist preparation: Singing these verses from Psalm 51 requires honesty about your own sinfulness and need for forgiveness. Arriving at such honesty is painful, but it is also a moment of resurrection, for it opens your heart to receive God's merciful forgiveness. Psalm 51 sings about the "ways" of God; your singing of Psalm 51 *is* the way to God.

ASSEMBLY & FAITH-SHARING GROUPS
- What troubles me about dying to self is . . . I resist it because . . . I am willing to die to self when . . .
- I am aware of serving Jesus in serving others when . . . This is easy for me when . . . This is difficult for me when . . .
- To be glorified is to . . .

PRESIDERS
My presiding calls me to die to self because . . . This dying opens the door to new life for me and the assembly in that . . .

DEACONS
My service is truly a dying to self when . . . The glorification I see is . . .

HOSPITALITY MINISTERS
The manner of my greeting helps others see the glory of Jesus and their own glory when . . .

MUSIC MINISTERS
When my music ministry glorifies God rather than myself, I . . . the assembly . . .

ALTAR MINISTERS
My service at church costs me . . . It glorifies God in that . . . The glorification I receive is . . .

LECTORS
Proclamation of God's word requires my dying to self in that . . .

EXTRAORDINARY MINISTERS OF HOLY COMMUNION
Some ways that I might manifest the Eucharist as both the suffering of the cross and the glory of the resurrection are . . .

Model Penitential Act

Presider: The gospel today calls us to be grains of wheat that die to bear fruit, to lose life to find new life, and to follow Jesus faithfully. Let us empty ourselves of anything that keeps us from dying to self and beg God's forgiveness and mercy for the times when we have failed . . . [pause]

  Confiteor: I confess . . .

Homily Points

- How much some athletes, rock and movie stars, politicians, even ourselves sacrifice to achieve glorification that is, in the end, short-lived. This sacrifice and glorification is self-serving. Jesus invites another kind of sacrifice and glorification that ultimately is also "self-serving," but in another way.

- Jesus teaches us that what leads to glorification is dying to self, losing our lives, serving him and others. He has shown us the way by being "lifted up from the earth." Unlike the self-serving and short-lived glorification fabricated by human beings, the glorification Jesus promises is "eternal life" given by God. Seeking this glorification is "self-serving" in a good way: we become who God created and intends us to be.

- Opportunities for dying to self, losing life for the sake of others, and serving Jesus in others are abundant; we need only to see them and respond. For example, parents giving time and energy to help their children grow; employees speaking the truth even when there is personal cost; neighbors responding to the needs of the poor. The glorification we receive for being other-centered is given to us even now in the joy that comes from deepened relationships, from seeing the relief and gratitude of others, from our own satisfaction for having acted like Jesus. In such faithful discipleship, we grow toward the ultimate glorification of eternal Life.

Model Universal Prayer (Prayer of the Faithful)

Presider: The God who calls us to life through death will give us the grace we need to be faithful. And so we pray.

Response:

Lord, hear our prayer.

Cantor:

we pray to the Lord,

That all members of the church may willingly die to self to bear fruit for the good of others . . . [pause]

That civil leaders faithfully model self-giving for the well-being of those they serve . . . [pause]

That those who are suffering or dying may be lifted up by the generous care and self-giving of others . . . [pause]

That those preparing for the Easter sacraments enter into the mystery of Jesus' dying and rising with expectation and joy . . . [pause]

That each of us continue our Lenten journey of dying to self, confident in Jesus' promise of glorification . . . [pause]

Presider: Merciful and loving God, you are glorified by those who follow your Son Jesus Christ into his dying and rising: hear these our prayers that we might come to our own glorification, the fullness of Life. We ask this through Christ our Lord. **Amen.**

COLLECT

Let us pray

Pause for silent prayer

By your help, we beseech you, Lord our
    God,
may we walk eagerly in that same charity
with which, out of love for the world,
your Son handed himself over to death.
Through our Lord Jesus Christ, your Son,
who lives and reigns with you in the unity
    of the Holy Spirit,
one God, for ever and ever. **Amen.**

FIRST READING

Jer 31:31-34

The days are coming, says the LORD,
    when I will make a new covenant with
        the house of Israel
    and the house of Judah.
It will not be like the covenant I made with
        their fathers
    the day I took them by the hand
    to lead them forth from the land of
        Egypt;
    for they broke my covenant,
    and I had to show myself their master,
        says the LORD.
But this is the covenant that I will make
    with the house of Israel after those
        days, says the LORD.
I will place my law within them and write
        it upon their hearts;
    I will be their God, and they shall be my
        people.
No longer will they have need to teach
        their friends and relatives
    how to know the LORD.
All, from least to greatest, shall know me,
        says the LORD,
    for I will forgive their evildoing and
        remember their sin no more.

CATECHESIS

RESPONSORIAL PSALM
Ps 51:3-4, 12-13, 14-15

R℣. (12a) Create a clean heart in me, O God.

Have mercy on me, O God, in your
    goodness;
  in the greatness of your compassion
    wipe out my offense.
Thoroughly wash me from my guilt
  and of my sin cleanse me.

R℣. Create a clean heart in me, O God.

A clean heart create for me, O God,
  and a steadfast spirit renew within me.
Cast me not out from your presence,
  and your Holy Spirit take not from me.

R℣. Create a clean heart in me, O God.

Give me back the joy of your salvation,
  and a willing spirit sustain in me.
I will teach transgressors your ways,
  and sinners shall return to you.

R℣. Create a clean heart in me, O God.

SECOND READING
Heb 5:7-9

In the days when Christ Jesus was in the
    flesh,
  he offered prayers and supplications
    with loud cries and tears
  to the one who was able to save him
    from death,
  and he was heard because of his
    reverence.
Son though he was, he learned obedience
    from what he suffered;
  and when he was made perfect,
  he became the source of eternal
    salvation for all who obey him.

About Liturgy

Lent, baptism, and covenant: The first reading from the prophet Jeremiah speaks of the covenant God made with the Israelites: "I will be their God, and they shall be my people." Lent is a time of the year when we especially join with those preparing for the Easter sacraments. Lent is a time for preparing for or renewing our baptismal covenant which makes us the new people of God—the Body of Christ.

We misunderstand covenant if we liken it to our notion of contract. When we enter into a contractual agreement with another the desire is to agree on as even terms as possible—maybe even one "putting it over" on the other and making a very good deal. God's covenants with us are never on even terms—God always gives more than we give. God made Israel the chosen people and gave them a land of plenty and in return all Israel had to do was obey the laws of God. In our baptismal covenant God makes us members of the Body of Christ by instilling in us the divine Life of the Spirit, and in return all we need to do is become a servant follower of Jesus.

Yet we know that we fail in keeping our covenant about as many times as Israel failed! If we constantly keep the terms of the baptismal covenant before us (which is why we renew our baptismal commitment at Easter), then perhaps we will allow the good terms of our covenant with God to entice us to give ourselves over to Gospel living. Lenten penance is to help us gain the discipline of dying to ourselves. Easter glory is a glimpse of what God ultimately has in store for those who keep the covenant by living the paschal mystery.

About Liturgical Music

Music suggestions: Thomas Troeger's "Before the Fruit Is Ripened by the Sun" (W4) uses the image of the seed which must die: "Before the fruit is ripened by the sun . . . A seed is dropped and buried in the soil . . . Before we gain the grace that comes through loss . . . We face with Christ the seed's renewing death." The pace and mood of this hymn would make it appropriate during the preparation of the gifts. Another fitting choice for the preparation of the gifts would be "Only This I Want" (BB, G3, JS3) in which we unite ourselves with Christ not only in bearing the cross but also in wearing his crown of glory. Lucien Deiss's "Grant to Us, O Lord" and David Haas's "Deep Within" bear repeating this Sunday, either during the preparation of the gifts or Communion. Bernadette Farrell's "Unless a Grain of Wheat" (found in most resources) would be another excellent choice for Communion, as would Lucien Deiss's "Keep in Mind" (found in most resources). A good choice for the recessional song would be "Take Up Your Cross" (found in most resources).

SPIRITUALITY

GOSPEL ACCLAMATION
John 1:14ab

The Word of God became flesh and made his
    dwelling among us;
and we saw his glory.

Gospel   Luke 1:26-38; L545

The angel Gabriel was sent from God
    to a town of Galilee called Nazareth,
    to a virgin betrothed to a man
        named Joseph,
    of the house of David,
    and the virgin's name was Mary.
And coming to her, he said,
    "Hail, full of grace! The Lord is with
        you."
But she was greatly troubled at what
        was said
    and pondered what sort of greeting
        this might be.
Then the angel said to her,
    "Do not be afraid, Mary,
    for you have found favor with God.
Behold, you will conceive in your womb and
        bear a son,
    and you shall name him Jesus.
He will be great and will be called Son of
        the Most High,
    and the Lord God will give him the throne
        of David his father,
    and he will rule over the house of Jacob
        forever,
    and of his Kingdom there will be no end."
But Mary said to the angel,
    "How can this be,
    since I have no relations with a man?"
And the angel said to her in reply,
    "The Holy Spirit will come upon you,
    and the power of the Most High will over-
        shadow you.
Therefore the child to be born
    will be called holy, the Son of God.
And behold, Elizabeth, your relative,
    has also conceived a son in her old age,
    and this is the sixth month for her who
        was called barren;
    for nothing will be impossible for God."
Mary said, "Behold, I am the handmaid of
        the Lord.
May it be done to me according to your word."
Then the angel departed from her.

See Appendix A, p. 280, for the other readings.

Reflecting on the Gospel

Lent is about turning our lives around, about turning away from whatever weakens our relationship with God and others toward what strengthens these relationships. In a real sense, Lent is about "futuring." We do penance, strive to mend our ways, become better persons now so that we open up new possibilities for living tomorrow, the next day, next year. The next life. Mary is a great model for "futuring."

"May it be done to me," says Mary to the angel Gabriel. What does she agree to have done? That she be overshadowed by the power of the Holy Spirit. That she bear a son, Jesus, who will be the "Son of God." That she give birth to One whose kingdom will have no end. Mary says yes to a future she does not yet fully know because she believes and trusts in a God for whom nothing is impossible. Gabriel's certainty about the incarnation is met by Mary's cooperation.

Yes, "nothing will be impossible for God." Not an angel coming to a simple maiden of the insignificant town of Nazareth. Not a virgin conceiving. Not the Holy Spirit and "power of the Most High" overshadowing Mary. Not a "child to be born" being "the Son of God." Not the barren and elderly Elizabeth's conception. Not Mary's yes to the mystery of the incarnation. Not our encounters with "the Most High." Not our bearing the Son of God within us through the indwelling of the Holy Spirit. Not our yes to all things God asks of us. Nothing will be impossible? Only if we say no.

Both Jesus and Mary said yes to the Father's will (see second reading and gospel). Such readiness to place self at the service of God's plan of salvation is the paschal mystery in action. Our Lenten practices of prayer, fasting, and charity are meant to lead us to this same gift of self. Lent is far more than a season of mere discipline. It is a time of conversion during which we enter more deeply into the paschal mystery announced at our baptism, modeled in our saying yes every day to God's call, and embraced for the sake of everlasting Life. Gabriel's annunciation of Jesus' conception in the womb of Mary is also the annunciation of our own yes which is an initiation into the paschal mystery and a share in God's plan of salvation. Saying no to God limits our own possibilities, limits our future, limits what God accomplishes through us. What happens to us and our future when we, in belief and trust, say yes to God? What happens to us when we allow Mary to be our model of "futuring"?

Living the Paschal Mystery

Mary's "May it be done to me according to your word" is the model for our own oblation of our very selves (see second reading), a self-emptying for the sake of the other that is one essential facet of our participation in the paschal mystery. The oblation of ourselves elevates the whole world to a share in divine Life. Since "nothing [is] impossible for God," we ought not to fear spending our lives as oblation by dying to ourselves for the sake of the other. Gabriel not only announces Jesus' conception in Mary's womb; in the course of salvation history Jesus' conception is the pledge of a new Life we all receive. All we must do is die to ourselves. Just as Jesus was destined for glory, so are we. Lent, Triduum, and Easter remind us that dying and rising are two facets of an incredible mystery: that God loves us so much as to offer us a share in divine Life. This is the future our yes promises: the fullness of Life.

Focusing the Gospel

Key words and phrases: you will conceive, nothing will be impossible for God, May it be done to me

To the point: "May it be done to me," says Mary to the angel. What does she agree to have done? That she be overshadowed by the power of the Holy Spirit. That she bear a son, Jesus, who will be the "Son of God." That she give birth to One whose kingdom will have no end. Mary says yes to a future she does not yet fully know because she believes and trusts in a God for whom nothing is impossible. What happens to us and our future when we, in belief and trust, say yes to God?

Model Penitential Act

Presider: In today's gospel for the solemnity of the Annunciation of the Lord Mary says yes to God's request that she become the mother of the Savior. Let us reflect on our own yes to God in our everyday living . . . [pause]

Lord Jesus, you are the Son of the Most High: Lord . . .

Christ Jesus, your reign is forever: Christ . . .

Lord Jesus, you were born of the Virgin Mary: Lord . . .

Model Universal Prayer (Prayer of the Faithful)

Presider: God sent the angel Gabriel to announce to Mary that she would conceive the Son of the Most High. Let us pray that we have the courage to say yes to God as did Mary.

Response:

Lord, hear our prayer.

Cantor:

we pray to the Lord,

That all members of the church, like Mary, say yes to God's call to cooperate in the divine plan of salvation . . . [pause]

That all people of the world say yes to the graciousness of God's Presence and salvation . . . [pause]

That the sick and the suffering say yes to trusting in God for whom nothing is impossible . . . [pause]

That each of us here say yes to a future of limitless possibilities for serving God and others . . . [pause]

Presider: O God, the power of your Spirit overshadowed Mary who said yes to becoming the mother of your divine Son. May we, like Mary, say yes to whatever you ask of us and come to fullness of Life for all eternity. We ask this through Jesus Christ our Lord. ***Amen.***

FOR REFLECTION
• Like Mary, I say yes to God when . . . Unlike Mary, I say no when . . .
• The impossible God has worked for me is . . . through me is . . . in me is . . .
• What happens to me and my future when I believe in, trust in, and say yes to God is . . .

Homily Points

• No, I can't do it! No, I don't have time for that! No, I won't deal with those people! No, you can't date that person! No, you can't have a raise! No, you can't live in your own home any longer. In all these situations, "no" limits possibilities, closes off futures, and shuts down creativity and imagination. "Yes," on the other hand, opens doors to new experiences, new relationships, new growth.

• The nature of "yes" is to open the future to possibilities; the nature of "no" is to control the future by closing off possibilities. Mary's yes opened her future and the future of the world to salvation. Our yes opens . . .

✚ SPIRITUALITY

GOSPEL ACCLAMATION
Phil 2:8-9

Christ became obedient to the point of death,
even death on a cross.
Because of this, God greatly exalted him
and bestowed on him the name which is above
    every name.

Gospel at the procession with palms

Mark 11:1-10; L37B (John 12:12-16 may also be
read.)

**When Jesus and his disciples drew near
    to Jerusalem,
  to Bethphage and Bethany at the Mount
      of Olives,
  he sent two of his disciples and said to
      them,
  "Go into the village opposite you,
  and immediately on entering it,
  you will find a colt tethered on which
      no one has ever sat.
Untie it and bring it here.
If anyone should say to you,
  'Why are you doing this?' reply,
  'The Master has need of it
  and will send it back here at once.'"
So they went off
  and found a colt tethered at a gate
    ・ outside on the street,
  and they untied it.**

Continued in Appendix A, p. 280.

Gospel at Mass   Mark 14:1–15:47; L38B
or Mark 15:1–39; L38B *in Appendix A,
pp. 281–284.*

Reflecting on the Gospel

Mark's passion account is filled with denial: Peter's, the apostles', Pilate's,
Jesus' accusers. But perhaps none is so imaginative as the denial of "a young
man" wearing a "linen cloth" who was following Jesus (see Mark 14:51-52). The
crowd who seized Jesus also seized him, but "he left the cloth behind and ran
off naked." How fast was that? He ran right out of his clothes, he was in such
a hurry to flee! This young man gives new meaning to the phrase, "I'm outta
here!" As we hear this passion proclaimed, what is our response?

In Mark's account of Jesus' passion, many persons respond to Jesus in
many different ways. A woman anoints him with perfumed oil, anticipating
his burial. At the Last Supper, Peter and the rest of the Twelve swear they will
never deny him. In Gethsemane, the apostles sleep. Judas betrays Jesus with a
kiss. In fear, a young man runs away naked (really fast!). During the trial, many
give false witness. Peter denies Jesus three times. Pilate hands him over to be
crucified. Soldiers mock him. Simon of Cyrene helps him carry the cross. Soldiers crucify him. The centurion proclaims Jesus to be the "Son of God." At the
crucifixion, many women remained present. Joseph of Arimathea buries Jesus.
During Jesus' last hours, only a few faithful people stand by Jesus. Most do not.
As we hear this passion proclaimed, where do we stand?

Mark paints a vivid picture of the sufferings of Jesus. At the same time his
passion account—and even his whole gospel—rises to a crescendo in the centurion's amazing proclamation of faith as he "stood facing" the crucified Jesus:
"Truly this man was the Son of God!" The One both hailed and derided as king
of the Jews, the One crucified, is finally revealed in his deepest identity as Son
of God. His mission is accomplished—in the shedding of his blood he gives
his blood as the new Fruit of the vine in which we all share each time we commemorate him. We might "roll a stone against the entrance of the tomb" where
he lay dead, but we cannot contain his true identity and mission. Our call as we
hear this passion account proclaimed and embrace more fully our baptismal
commitment is to stand with Jesus, to become so one with him that our denials
become fewer, our running from him becomes less quick, our faithfulness to following him and continuing his mission becomes stronger. Rather than denying
Jesus, we are called to stand with him.

Living the Paschal Mystery

The essence of discipleship is that we stand with Jesus and align our own identity with his, accept self-denial and self-giving, and in this way walk with him
to the cross. Disciples go wherever the Master goes.

Coming to understand who Jesus is, his mission, and how that relates to
us, his disciples, is no easy task; it takes a lifetime. Like Jesus, to be faithful
followers by taking up our cross means we will feel this to the depths of our
humanity: we will suffer, we will lose heart, we will cry out to God to take life's
miserable lot away from us. But also like Jesus, we have divine Life that gives
us the strength to carry our cross. It is divine Life pulsing within us—which
we first receive at our baptism—that raises up our humanity, enabling us to
be faithful disciples carrying our crosses, faithful disciples consistent with our
identity as Christians, as the Body of Christ. It is divine Life that strengthens
us to stand faithfully with Jesus.

Focusing the Passion Gospel
Key words and phrases: My God, my God, why have you forsaken me?

To the point: In Mark's account of Jesus' passion, many persons respond to Jesus in many different ways. A woman anoints him with perfumed oil, anticipating his burial. At the Last Supper, Peter and the rest of the Twelve swear they will never deny him. In Gethsemane, the apostles sleep. Judas betrays Jesus with a kiss. In fear, a young man runs away naked. During the trial, many give false witness. Peter denies Jesus three times. Pilate hands him over to be crucified. Soldiers mock him. Simon of Cyrene helps him carry the cross. Soldiers crucify him. The centurion proclaims Jesus to be the "Son of God." At the crucifixion, many women remained present. Joseph of Arimathea buries Jesus. During Jesus' last hours, only a few faithful people stand by Jesus. Most do not. As we hear this passion proclaimed, where do we stand?

Connecting the Gospel
to the first and second readings: Both of these readings speak of Jesus' subjugation. They also both reveal how the passion and crucifixion end in exaltation.

to experience: The media report so much violence that we can become inured to its horror. We can hear Jesus' passion account year after year and not let it affect us. But it must.

Connecting the Responsorial Psalm
to the readings: The Lectionary uses only a few verses of Psalm 22, and reading the whole psalm gives us a fuller understanding of why the church has traditionally used this psalm on Palm Sunday of the Lord's Passion. The psalm contains three thematic progressions. The first progression (vv. 12-17) is that of abandonment, first by God, then by fellow human beings, until finally the psalmist is surrounded by ravening animals. The second progression emerges simultaneously, but in the opposite direction. The distant God who has abandoned the psalmist (vv. 2-3) becomes an intimate God who has known us from birth (v. 11). The third progression (vv. 23-32) is a prayer of praise and thanksgiving into which an ever-widening circle is invited to participate: immediate family, the offspring of Jacob, all nations, generations yet unborn, all the ends of the earth, the afflicted, the poor, and even the dead. The praise is eschatological and cosmic. These thematic progressions transform our response to the proclamation of the passion. We are doing more than telling a story about abandonment and death, more than remembering the pain of Christ on the cross. We are joining Christ in his song of praise and thanksgiving. We are entering into the mystery of our salvation.

to psalmist preparation: The few verses of Psalm 22 used this Sunday offer only a glimpse of the psalm's depth and of its connection with the meaning of what the church celebrates during Holy Week. Spend some time this week praying the entirety of Psalm 22, and ask for the grace to enter fully with Jesus into the paschal mystery of death and resurrection, of God's absence and God's nearness, of suffering and praise.

**ASSEMBLY &
FAITH-SHARING GROUPS**
- I deny Jesus when . . . I betray Jesus when . . . I run away from Jesus when . . .
- I help Jesus carry the cross when . . .
- I stand by Jesus when . . .

PRESIDERS
My role of proclaiming the passion every year challenges me to . . .

DEACONS
When serving others, I proclaim my choice to stand by Jesus when I . . .

HOSPITALITY MINISTERS
My manner of greeting those assembling for liturgy invites them to enter into the mystery of Jesus' passion if I . . .

MUSIC MINISTERS
My music ministry is carrying a cross when . . . is exaltation when . . .

ALTAR MINISTERS
My serving at the altar shows how I respond to Jesus in that . . .

LECTORS
My proclamation reflects a life of standing by Jesus in that . . .

EXTRAORDINARY MINISTERS OF HOLY COMMUNION
My manner of distributing Holy Communion is a proclamation that Jesus is the "Son of God" when I . . .

Model Penitential Act *(only used at Masses with the simple entrance)*

Presider: As we begin this solemn week with this liturgy, we pause to reflect on our willingness to follow Jesus in times of glory, and our unwillingness to follow him when carrying the cross . . . [pause]

   Confiteor: I confess . . .

Homily Points

- What more is there to say in response to the proclamation of the passion than, "Where do you stand?"

- The proclamation challenges us to stand with Jesus, which always takes us to our own passion and crucifixion every day of our lives.

- As we embrace each day our own dying to self, we witness to others that we have truly chosen to stand with Jesus.

Model Universal Prayer (Prayer of the Faithful)

Presider: Let us pray that we have the courage to walk with Jesus to the cross.

Response:

Lord, hear our prayer.

Cantor:

we pray to the Lord,

That all members of the church walk with Jesus in his passion and so share abundantly in the new Life he offers . . . [pause]

That all peoples of the world come to salvation . . . [pause]

That those suffering pain and loss might find hope and consolation in the suffering Christ . . . [pause]

That each of us faithfully choose to stand by Jesus no matter the personal cost . . . [pause]

Presider: God of salvation, you sent your Son to bring us back to your loving embrace through his embrace of the cross: hear these our prayers that we might be strengthened to follow him faithfully along the journey through death to Life. We ask this through Christ our Lord. **Amen.**

COLLECT

Let us pray

Pause for silent prayer

Almighty ever-living God,
who as an example of humility for the
   human race to follow
caused our Savior to take flesh and submit
   to the Cross,
graciously grant that we may heed his
   lesson of patient suffering
and so merit a share in his Resurrection.
Who lives and reigns with you in the unity
   of the Holy Spirit,
one God, for ever and ever. **Amen.**

FIRST READING
Isa 50:4-7

The Lord GOD has given me
   a well-trained tongue,
that I might know how to speak to the
      weary
   a word that will rouse them.
Morning after morning
   he opens my ear that I may hear;
and I have not rebelled,
   have not turned back.
I gave my back to those who beat me,
   my cheeks to those who plucked my
      beard;
my face I did not shield
   from buffets and spitting.

The Lord GOD is my help,
   therefore I am not disgraced;
I have set my face like flint,
   knowing that I shall not be put to
      shame.

RESPONSORIAL PSALM
Ps 22:8-9, 17-18, 19-20, 23-24

℟. (2a) My God, my God, why have you abandoned me?

All who see me scoff at me;
   they mock me with parted lips, they
      wag their heads:
"He relied on the LORD; let him deliver him,
   let him rescue him, if he loves him."

℟. My God, my God, why have you abandoned me?

Indeed, many dogs surround me,
    a pack of evildoers closes in upon me;
they have pierced my hands and my feet;
    I can count all my bones.

R⁊. My God, my God, why have you
abandoned me?

They divide my garments among them,
    and for my vesture they cast lots.
But you, O Lord, be not far from me;
    O my help, hasten to aid me.

R⁊. My God, my God, why have you
abandoned me?

I will proclaim your name to my brethren;
    in the midst of the assembly I will
        praise you:
"You who fear the Lord, praise him;
    all you descendants of Jacob, give glory
        to him;
    revere him, all you descendants of
        Israel!"

R⁊. My God, my God, why have you
abandoned me?

SECOND READING
Phil 2:6-11

Christ Jesus, though he was in the form
    of God,
    did not regard equality with God
    something to be grasped.
Rather, he emptied himself,
    taking the form of a slave,
    coming in human likeness;
    and found human in appearance,
    he humbled himself,
    becoming obedient to the point of
        death,
    even death on a cross.
Because of this, God greatly exalted him
    and bestowed on him the name
    which is above every name,
    that at the name of Jesus
    every knee should bend,
    of those in heaven and on earth and
        under the earth,
    and every tongue confess that
Jesus Christ is Lord,
    to the glory of God the Father.

About Liturgy

Why choose John 12:12-16 as the gospel at the procession with palms?

Two choices are given for Year B for the gospel proclaimed before the procession with palms; it would be natural that the selection from Mark be used since this is the year we proclaim Mark. Yet we suggest that the Johannine selection be proclaimed because it clearly sets out the tension about Jesus' entry into Jerusalem: the crowd greets Jesus with the joyful accolades due to the one they perceive to be the messiah-king, but this entry into the City of David is not the moment of Jesus' glory. The "disciples did not understand" that Jesus' glory could only be achieved by suffering and death; death on the cross leads to the glory of risen Life.

This tension marks the vicissitudes of our own Christian living. We are willing to follow Jesus—but we would like it to be an easy road to glory. Contrary, Christian living is the hard work of proclaiming the Gospel by the way we live, a proclamation such that people can see us and, seeing how we live, proclaim, "Truly this person reveals the Son of God!" We cannot stress enough in our reflection and our preaching that this tension is a critical one, one that reminds us of the reality of the cross and its demand that we be faithful in standing with Jesus.

About Liturgical Music

Music and the paschal mystery: Perhaps more than any other week in the liturgical year, Holy Week makes evident the importance and power of the music we sing during the liturgy. The choir and music ministers will have put a great deal of extra time and effort into the music for these liturgies. Their intent, however, is not to entertain but to enable us to enter more deeply into the mystery we celebrate in ritual form: our participation with Christ in his death and resurrection. When we sing we actualize this very mystery as we die to ourselves to become one in heart and song with each other. May we sing during this Holy Week with full and conscious awareness of what we are doing.

Music suggestions: Songs in which we express our willingness to enter the passion with Christ and walk with him through Holy Week to the cross and resurrection include "Take up Your Cross," "When I Behold the Wondrous Cross" (both found in many resources), "Only This I Want" (BB, G3, JS3), and "Where He Leads Me" (LMGM2). Also appropriate this day would be songs referring directly to Jesus' death on the cross and its meaning for our salvation. Examples include "What Wondrous Love," "Were You There," "O Sacred Head Surrounded" (all found in most resources), and "Calvary" (LMGM2).

EASTER TRIDUUM

. . . we can never forsake Christ,
who suffered for the salvation
of the whole world . . .
For we worship this One as the Son of God,
but we love the martyrs
as disciples and imitators of the Lord,
deservedly so,
because of their unsurpassable devotion
to their own King and Teacher.
May it be also our lot
to be their companions
and fellow disciples!

—Martyrdom of Polycarp 17:2-3

Reflecting on the Triduum

Suffering: In our contemporary medical climate, pain is something that can reasonably be controlled with medication. Physical suffering is kept to a minimum if at all possible. We believe that suffering for the sake of suffering has no merit. Sometimes, however, we do endure suffering to achieve a perceived good. We, for example, get sore muscles while doing spring housecleaning or building up stamina to run a marathon. We ignore our own burning, tired eyes and get up to feed the newborn baby in the middle of the night. We endure the unpleasant side effects of chemotherapy in hopes of a cancer in remission or of a cure. Yes, sometimes we embrace suffering because the good we gain far outweighs the pain we endure. Suffering can teach us compassion and endurance; it can strengthen our wills to choose rightly; it helps us to realize how vulnerable and mortal we are. Suffering can teach us much.

Many of the passages speaking of suffering in the Old Testament equate it with the results of sin. For example, Job's three friends all think that his suffering has been caused by sin, insist that no human being is sinless, and that Job must admit his guilt and repent (Job 4; 8; 11). Jesus dispels this direct connection between suffering and sin; sometimes the innocent do suffer (John 9). Jesus himself is the Innocent One who suffers. He is scourged and crowned with thorns, spit upon and mocked, stripped and crucified. His suffering can teach us much.

We must be careful here. It is not the suffering in itself that is the focus of Jesus. He suffered because he was faithful to his Father's will, because he called people back to faithfulness to their covenant with God, because he never swerved from his message of salvation for all people. Jesus suffered because he did not put human laws above divine Law, angering some religious leaders. Jesus suffered because he loved. His suffering manifested his utter self-giving, his care and compassion, his righteousness and goodness. His suffering can teach us much.

From the earliest time the church has specially venerated those followers of Jesus who have suffered and died for the same reason Jesus did: utter fidelity, unshakable obedience to God's will. We call these holy and inspiring followers "martyrs," from the Greek word meaning "witness." By the way they live and die, martyrs witness to Jesus and his saving acts. The suffering and death of martyrs witnesses to—gives unsurpassed testimony to—their profession of faith in Christ. Martyrdom seals their total conformity to Christ. The martyrs, saints, and all of us who are faithful followers give meaning to suffering: through it we embrace Jesus and the meaning of his own passion—Life for all.

Living the Paschal Mystery

Jesus' life, suffering, death, and resurrection happened to him as historical events, but they also happen to all of us who claim to be his followers. These high holy days are a reminder and celebration of who we ourselves are and what our own lives are about: being faithful followers of Jesus Christ. Like Jesus, we empty ourselves for the good of others, we give over our wills for the other. Like the martyrs of long ago and our martyrs of today, we are called to be so faithful to Christ that nothing—even suffering and death—gets in the way of our imitating him. The issue, to repeat, is not the pain of suffering or even death. The issue is that we are to witness—be martyrs—to the risen Presence of Jesus among us, to his victory over death, and to the new Life he offers us. This is what we celebrate these days. Yes, indeed, Jesus' suffering can teach us much.

TRIDUUM

"Triduum" comes from two Latin words (*tres* and *dies*) which mean "a space of three days." But since we have four days with special names—Holy Thursday, Good Friday, Holy Saturday, and Easter Sunday— the "three" may be confusing to some.

The confusion is cleared up when we understand how the days are reckoned. On all high festival days the church counts a day in the same way as Jews count days and festivals; that is, from sundown to sundown. Thus, the Triduum consists of *three* twenty-four-hour periods that stretch over four calendar days.

Therefore, the Easter Triduum begins at sundown on Holy Thursday with the Mass of the Lord's Supper and concludes with Easter evening prayer at sundown on Easter Sunday; its high point is the celebration of the Easter Vigil (GNLYC no. 19).

SOLEMN PASCHAL FAST

According to the above calculation, Lent ends at sundown on Holy Thursday; thus, Holy Thursday itself is the last day of Lent. This doesn't mean that our fasting concludes on Holy Thursday, however; the church has traditionally kept a solemn forty-hour fast from the beginning of the Triduum until the fast is broken at Communion during the Easter Vigil.

SPIRITUALITY

GOSPEL ACCLAMATION
John 13:34

I give you a new commandment, says the Lord:
love one another as I have loved you.

Gospel John 13:1-15; L39ABC

Before the feast of Passover, Jesus
    knew that his hour had come
to pass from this world to the
    Father.
He loved his own in the world and
    he loved them to the end.
The devil had already induced
    Judas, son of Simon the
    Iscariot, to hand him over.
So, during supper,
    fully aware that the Father had
        put everything into his power
    and that he had come from God and was
        returning to God,
    he rose from supper and took off his
        outer garments.
He took a towel and tied it around his waist.
Then he poured water into a basin
    and began to wash the disciples' feet
    and dry them with the towel around his
        waist.
He came to Simon Peter, who said to him,
    "Master, are you going to wash my feet?"
Jesus answered and said to him,
    "What I am doing, you do not understand
        now,
    but you will understand later."
Peter said to him, "You will never wash my
    feet."
Jesus answered him,
    "Unless I wash you, you will have no
        inheritance with me."
Simon Peter said to him,
    "Master, then not only my feet, but my
        hands and head as well."
Jesus said to him,
    "Whoever has bathed has no need except
        to have his feet washed, for he is
        clean all over;
    so you are clean, but not all."
For he knew who would betray him;
    for this reason, he said, "Not all of you
        are clean."

Continued in Appendix A, p. 285.
See Appendix A, p. 285, for the other readings.

Reflecting on the Gospel and Living the Paschal Mystery
Key words and phrases from the gospel: knew that his hour had come,
loved them to the end, Judas . . . hand him over, Unless I wash you, a model to
follow

To the point: This night Jesus shows us how to redirect our lives by going beyond suffering to self-giving, and manifesting love in humble service. When we
celebrate Jesus' Supper in remembrance of him, we are redirect-
ing our lives to self-giving love and service of others.

To ponder and pray: Everything at the Supper pointed to a
wonderful time for all. There was a special festival time. There
was food. There was wine. There were gathered friends.
There was time for significant conversation. Yet this Supper
was like no other. This Supper included challenge, misunderstanding, betrayal. This banquet was the Lord's
Supper. It would be Jesus' last with his disciples before
his death. Did the disciples have a clue? Jesus certainly
did, for he "knew that his hour had come."

What must have been Jesus' emotions as he reclined with his disciples at this
hour? He knew that Judas would "hand him over." He knew Peter would betray
him. He knew most of the disciples would abandon him. What did the table
conversation sound like "during supper"? Was Jesus reserved? strained? What
suffering he must have endured this night even before the next day and his great
physical suffering! Did he look into Judas's eyes as he washed his feet? Did Peter's
misunderstanding about the meaning of the footwashing pierce his heart? Did he
wonder what all this time teaching the disciples and leading them had meant?

No matter the suffering, Jesus' focus was not on that. It was on his disciples
and his desire to help them understand what this night would mean. Jesus
"loved his own in the world, and he loved them to the end." Jesus never turned
his back on his disciples. So this night he taught them perhaps the biggest lesson of all. Or, rather, he coalesced all his previous teaching in this one grand
love feast and his actions during it.

First, he makes an everlasting sacrament out of self-giving. As we heard in
the second reading, he gave his body and blood for us. Jesus' self-giving continues into our own time; his love continues in his self-giving. When we "do this in
remembrance of" him (second reading), we not only receive his risen Body and
Blood for our nourishment, but we also challenge ourselves to participate in
this same act of self-giving, this same act of love. "For as often as [we] eat this
bread and drink the cup, [we] proclaim the death of the Lord until he comes"
(second reading). To proclaim, we must participate. To participate, we must
give ourselves over for others as did Jesus.

Second, Jesus gave us a profound witness to what self-giving love looks
like: he washed his disciples' feet. This act of humble service is our "model to
follow." We wash the feet of others when we love with the same kind of un-
reserved love as Jesus showed us. When we look beyond our own suffering to
the needs of others. When we look beyond misunderstanding and betrayal to
persons who are broken and need forgiveness, who need to be loved into new
life. This footwashing is more than a ritual act. It is a way of living and loving.
This sums up all Jesus taught. This sums up the meaning of the Supper. This
sums up the meaning of our continued participation in Jesus' self-giving. This
sums up this night. This sums up Jesus' whole life. So must it sum up ours.

Model Penitential Act

Presider: Tonight we begin the most solemn three days of our Christian year—the Easter Triduum. Tonight we remember Jesus' self-giving love in giving us his Body and Blood for nourishment. Tonight we remember his modeling for us how we are to give our lives in service. Let us prepare well to celebrate these great mysteries . . . [pause]

Lord Jesus, you love us to the end: Lord . . .

Christ Jesus, you give us your Body and Blood as heavenly food: Christ . . .

Lord Jesus, you model for us humble service: Lord . . .

Homily Points

- We all enjoy a festive meal together. It is a time when we eat more, take more time to enjoy one another's company, share from our hearts what is important to us, catch up on recent happenings, and simply rest in happiness and joy. Jesus' Last Supper with his disciples before he faced trial, suffering, and death included all these elements, but more. This Supper showed us how to overcome misunderstanding with self-giving, betrayal with love, formidable challenge with serving others.

- The focus of this Last Supper of Jesus with his disciples is a summary of all he had taught them. He donned a towel, took water and basin, and washed his disciples' feet. For Jesus the divine Teacher, no action is too humble and no serving lacks love. We remember Jesus not only through our participation in his Supper, but by witnessing to others the self-giving actions of loving and serving that he taught us.

- Serving others is love made visible. We do so in simple, everyday acts of kindness and compassion. We do so when we put aside our own interests to notice the needs of others and respond. We do so through witnessing to the gift of Self that Jesus gave us in the Holy Eucharist. This night challenges us to redirect our lives in the way Jesus taught us.

Model Universal Prayer (Prayer of the Faithful)

Presider: God loves us beyond compare and gives us every good thing. Let us pray that we receive God's gifts and use them for the good of others.

Response:

Lord, hear our prayer.

Cantor:

we pray to the Lord,

That all members of the church generously pour out their lives in service of others . . . [pause]

That all people know the redeeming love of God who desires for them a fruitful life . . . [pause]

That those suffering in mind, body, or spirit be lifted up by the self-giving love of the risen Jesus and those who follow him . . . [pause]

That all of us gathered here grow in our appreciation for the great gift of Self Jesus gives us in the Eucharist and its demand to serve others humbly and faithfully . . . [pause]

Presider: Gracious and ever-living God, you gave us your divine Son to show us the fullness of your divine love: hear our prayers so that, as we receive that love in all the good gifts you give us, we share our gifts with others through loving and serving. We ask this through Christ our Lord. **Amen.**

COLLECT

Let us pray

Pause for silent prayer

O God, who have called us to participate
in this most sacred Supper,
in which your Only Begotten Son,
when about to hand himself over to death,
entrusted to the Church a sacrifice new for
    all eternity,
the banquet of his love,
grant, we pray,
that we may draw from so great a mystery,
the fullness of charity and of life.
Through our Lord Jesus Christ, your Son,
who lives and reigns with you in the unity
    of the Holy Spirit,
one God, for ever and ever. **Amen.**

FOR REFLECTION

- Jesus has loved me to the end in these ways . . .
- I offer to others the self-giving, loving service Jesus modeled for me in these ways . . .
- The Eucharist means to me . . . It challenges me to . . .

SPIRITUALITY

GOSPEL ACCLAMATION
Phil 2:8-9

Christ became obedient to the point of death,
even death on a cross.
Because of this, God greatly exalted
     him
and bestowed on him the name which
     is above every other name.

Gospel   John 18:1–19:42; L40ABC

Jesus went out with his disciples across the
     Kidron valley
   to where there was a garden,
   into which he and his disciples entered.
Judas his betrayer also knew the place,
   because Jesus had often met there with
     his disciples.
So Judas got a band of soldiers and guards
   from the chief priests and the
     Pharisees
   and went there with lanterns, torches,
     and weapons.
Jesus, knowing everything that was going to
     happen to him,
   went out and said to them, "Whom are
     you looking for?"
They answered him, "Jesus the Nazorean."
He said to them, "I AM."
Judas his betrayer was also with them.
When he said to them, "I AM,"
   they turned away and fell to the ground.
So he again asked them,
   "Whom are you looking for?"
They said, "Jesus the Nazorean."
Jesus answered,
   "I told you that I AM.
So if you are looking for me, let these men
     go."
This was to fulfill what he had said,
   "I have not lost any of those you gave me."
Then Simon Peter, who had a sword, drew
     it,
   struck the high priest's slave, and cut off
     his right ear.
The slave's name was Malchus.
Jesus said to Peter,
   "Put your sword into its scabbard.
Shall I not drink the cup that the Father
     gave me?"

Continued in Appendix A, pp. 286–287.
See Appendix A, p. 288, for the other readings.

Reflecting on the Gospel and Living the Paschal Mystery

Key words and phrases from the gospel: Pilate; Then you are a king; Jesus; You say I am a king; I find no guilt in him; had him scourged, crown out of thorns; I find no guilt in him; became even more afraid; Pilate tried to release him; he handed him over to them; the King of the Jews; What I have written, I have written

To the point: John's passion account contrasts the two faces of Pilate with the single, resolute obedience of the King of the Jews. Who do we choose to be?

To ponder and pray: The late fifteenth-century morality play *Jedermann* ("Everyman") is still staged every year at the Salzburg Festival. It depicts God's summoning human beings to judgment, when their good and evil deeds are tallied. The issue is salvation and what everyone must do to attain it.

Pilate is *Jedermann*—"everyone." In John's passion account we see two sides of him and his struggle with good and evil. Pilate knows that Jesus is innocent; he repeatedly declares, "I find no guilt in him." He tries in several ways to release Jesus. He tries to get Jesus to admit that he is a king, which would at least give him a starting point for convicting Jesus of treason. Twice Pilate asks Jesus if he is a king; twice Jesus turns the question around on Pilate himself: "Jesus answered, 'You say I am a king.'" Jesus certainly does not condemn himself. But Pilate is afraid. He is weak. He believes that he has "power to release" Jesus and "power to crucify" him. But, in fact, he has no power because he does not have the conviction, strength, or courage to act on the truth that he knows in his heart. Pilate in the end handed Jesus over to his false accusers, who feared Jesus even more than Pilate did. We are often like Pilate. We, too, are *Jedermann*—"everyone." When faced with choices between good and evil, how often because of fear, weakness, lack of conviction do we, too, hand ourselves over to do what we know we ought not.

The other side of Pilate becomes apparent at the end of the passion narrative. Pilate had the inscription "Jesus the Nazarene, the King of the Jews" nailed to the cross of Jesus. Those bent on having Jesus die wanted no part of that; they asked Pilate to change it to read "he said, 'I am the King of the Jews.'" Here Pilate stands firm. Here he acts on his conviction. Here he shows that ultimately he was affected by his encounter with Jesus, for he answered, "What I have written, I have written." Sometimes, we too have the grace and strength to act on conviction, to stand for what is right, to declare truth boldly. In this we are like Pilate as well.

If we are like Pilate, then to become like Jesus is our hope. Jesus always did his Father's will. He always chose to do good. He always spoke and lived the truth. He accepted mockery and rejection rather than compromise the goodness he was. He accepted suffering and death as a climactic act of fidelity and love. He "handed over the spirit" in an awe-inspiring act of self-giving. Even after death, he poured forth "blood and water" from his side, foreshadowing our own baptismal entry into his mystery and our participation in his perpetual self-giving in the eucharistic sacrifice. On this "Good" Friday we are invited to choose good. We are invited to embrace Jesus' self-giving love. We are invited to become even more perfect members of his Body.

Homily Points

• Milquetoast. Wishy-washy. Coward. Two-faced. Wimp. Chicken. Yellow-bellied. We have a formidable vocabulary to describe persons who lack the courage or the ethical conviction to act with integrity. One way or another, most characters in this passion gospel could be so described. Except Jesus. He acts with utter integrity and truth, conviction and purpose.

• Judas betrays Jesus. Peter denies knowing Jesus. The Jewish leaders are intent on killing Jesus. Pilate lacks the courage to do what he knows is right. The soldiers scourge and mock Jesus. Only Jesus remains true to who he is: the divine One who submits completely to human suffering and death. He finishes his earthly life with submission, obedience, integrity. But this is not the end. Even in death he pours forth blood and water—signs of continued self-giving love. This is who Jesus is: self-giving love.

• On Good Friday we think of Jesus' suffering, his death, the end. But we also know this story does not end here. The complete story—Jesus' teaching and preaching, suffering and death, risen Life and promise of the Spirit—is what we seek to enter, seek to share, seek to become so we can also be persons of integrity and truth, conviction and purpose. Good Friday invites us to see beyond our own human frailty to the self-giving love Jesus enables us to embrace.

Suggestions for Music

The Good Friday liturgy does not *historicize* or reenact the past event of Jesus' crucifixion, but *ritualizes* our participation here-and-now in the mystery that the cross of Christ is the tree of life. The songs we sing this day need to lead us into this liturgical meaning rather than engage us in a devotional experience centered on details of Jesus' suffering and death.

Music during the adoration of the holy cross: What we honor in this procession is not the One crucified but the cross itself which embodies the mystery of Jesus—and our—redemptive triumph over sin and death. This procession is not one of sorrow or expiation, but one of gratitude, of triumph, and of quiet and confident acceptance (the very sentiments expressed in the closing verses of the responsorial psalm). The songs we sing during this procession need to speak about the mystery and triumph of the cross rather than about the details of Jesus' suffering and death. Examples include Jerome Siwek's "We Acclaim the Cross of Jesus" (WC, WS), Delores Dufner's "We Glory in the Cross" (SS, W4), and "O Cross of Christ, Immortal Tree" (WC).

Music during Holy Communion: The verses of Dan Schutte's "Glory in the Cross" (BB, JS3) assigned for Holy Thursday would be very appropriate for Communion on Good Friday (more appropriate to the liturgical meaning of this day, in fact, than the verses he gives for Good Friday). Verses 3 and 4 connect the mystery of the cross to the mystery of the Eucharist. Also appropriate for Communion is Schutte's "Only This I Want" (G3, JS3) in which we sing of our willingness to "bear his cross, so to wear the crown he wore." A third good choice is Fanny Crosby's "Jesus, Keep Me Near the Cross" (LMGM2) with its refrain, "In the cross, in the cross, Be my glory ever. Till my raptured soul shall find rest beyond the river."

COLLECT

Let us pray

Pause for silent prayer

Remember your mercies, O Lord,
and with your eternal protection sanctify
    your servants,
for whom Christ your Son,
by the shedding of his Blood,
established the Paschal Mystery.
Who lives and reigns for ever and ever.
Amen.

or:

O God, who by the Passion of Christ your
    Son, our Lord,
abolished the death inherited from ancient
    sin
by every succeeding generation,
grant that just as, being conformed to him,
we have borne by the law of nature
the image of the man of earth,
so by the sanctification of grace
we may bear the image of the Man of
    heaven.
Through Christ our Lord.
Amen.

FOR REFLECTION

• I am like Pilate when I . . . I resist being like Pilate when I . . .
• I find it easiest to imitate Jesus' self-giving love when . . . I find it most difficult when . . .
• What I am willing to endure so that truth and right prevail is . . .

SPIRITUALITY

Gospel

Mark 16:1-7; L41B

When the sabbath was over,
  Mary Magdalene, Mary, the
    mother of James, and
    Salome
  bought spices so that they
    might go and anoint
    him.
Very early when the sun had
    risen,
  on the first day of the
    week, they came to the
    tomb.
They were saying to one
    another,
  "Who will roll back the
    stone for us
  from the entrance to the
    tomb?"
When they looked up,
  they saw that the stone had been
    rolled back;
  it was very large.
On entering the tomb they saw a young
    man
  sitting on the right side, clothed in a
    white robe,
  and they were utterly amazed.
He said to them, "Do not be amazed!
You seek Jesus of Nazareth, the
    crucified.
He has been raised; he is not here.
Behold the place where they laid him.
But go and tell his disciples and Peter,
  'He is going before you to Galilee;
  there you will see him, as he told
    you.'"

Readings continued in Appendix A, pp. 289–294.

Reflecting on the Gospel and Living the Paschal Mystery

Key words and phrases from the gospel: Mary . . . Mary . . . Salome, anoint him, stone had been rolled back, utterly amazed, He has been raised, you will see him

To the point: No one can be prepared to encounter what the women in this gospel encountered. No one can be prepared to meet head-on the mystery of risen Life. The resurrection turns death into Life, sorrow into joy, empty hearts into ones longing for encounter. Like the women of long ago, we can only be "utterly amazed." We can only let our hearts ring out "Alleluia!"

To ponder and pray: Most cemeteries have signs posted regarding flowers, disposal of them, and other decorations for the grave sites. These regulations are not to hinder anyone from paying homage to their loved ones; rather, they are to make sure that the honor is appropriate, does not impinge on anyone else's loved ones, and that the cemetery is kept beautiful and in order. Most cemeteries are beautiful: green, orderly, quiet. They are peaceful places to be, even if some come with a heavy heart.

Mary and the other women came to Jesus' grave site to anoint him. No doubt they also wanted to make sure that nothing was disturbed. They wanted to make sure that the grave site of their beloved Jesus was beautiful. On the way they were concerned about the large stone that had been rolled in front of the entrance to seal off the tomb. How could they anoint Jesus if they could not enter the tomb? Even after Jesus' death and burial the women were filled with anguish, anxiety, suffering—and then "they were utterly amazed." Hope blossoms. Love swells. Faith erupts.

Hardly were they prepared for what they encountered: not a dead body to anoint, but a live "young man . . . clothed in a white robe" who declared to them, "He has been raised." They are told to go to Galilee and "there you will see him." Galilee is home for these women. The young man told them to go home. Be comfortable. Open themselves to an encounter like no other they had ever had or would ever have. We know what they found in Galilee: Jesus the risen One.

This night invites us to go home. To be at home. Be comfortable. Open ourselves to an encounter like no other we have ever had. We know what we also find in our midst: Jesus the risen One. Not in Galilee, but right here among us. This Jesus cannot be contained in a tomb. We do not visit a cemetery to encounter him. This Jesus has been raised from the dead and seeks us out, offers us new Life, prepares us to open ourselves to beauty, peace, and quiet like we have never before experienced.

No matter what we humans do that is unfaithful, our generous and merciful God is always faithful and invites us to salvation. All along God only desired for us life. "When the sun had risen," the Son rises. What an image! Concern for the weight of the stone at the entrance is allayed by seeing that it is already rolled back. What a sight! The women are greeted with the words, "Do not be amazed!" What words! How can we not be amazed? All the Scriptures had prepared us, but we could not quite imagine this zenith of God's plan of salvation: the One who was crucified is now raised to new Life. We are given a share of that Life at our baptism (see the epistle). Now is our time to see Jesus anew. To encounter him anew. To take up his saving mission anew. To have stones rolled back from closed hearts and open ourselves to the whole world. Life has dawned anew!

Homily Points

- When someone we love deeply dies, we feel sorrow, loss, heartache. Time might heal these initial grief feelings, but what never goes away is a sense of presence, of our loved one filling the empty spaces of our heart, of continued encounter. The women in the gospel did not find a body in the tomb; they found a living "young man . . . clothed in a white robe." The tomb was empty—but their hearts were full of hope and expectation.

- This tomb is empty—but really full. Instead of death, it is full of Life. The women's purpose for coming is forgotten. The spices are left behind. They must go. They must be witnesses of this mystery of risen Life to the "disciples and Peter." We must go. We must be witnesses of risen Life in our own daily living.

- Could the "young man . . . clothed in a white robe" be Jesus, but the good women were not yet ready to recognize him? The "young man" instructs them that they will see the risen One in Galilee. There was home—there they recognized Jesus amidst what was known to them, comfortable for them, where they would be at ease and most open to encountering a mystery never before known. Jesus, the crucified One, "has been raised." He lives! Now, in and through us. Are we ready for this encounter? for this mission? for this awesome mystery to be made known through us?

Model Universal Prayer (Prayer of the Faithful)

Presider: On this glorious night when the newly baptized join us for the first time in our priestly prayer for the church and world, let us confidently present our needs to God.

Response: Lord, hear our prayer.

Cantor: we pray to the Lord,

For the newly baptized and all members of the church, that we may be faithful to our baptismal dignity as sons and daughters of God . . . [pause]

For all peoples of the world, that they may find salvation, hope, and peace in the God who gives new life . . . [pause]

For those in need, that they might live a fulfilled life through the goodness and generosity of we who have encountered the risen Christ . . . [pause]

For all of us gathered here on this holy night, that we might be renewed in life by the joy we share . . . [pause]

Presider: God of life and salvation, you raised your divine Son up to new Life: help us to celebrate his resurrection with renewed life and joy, so that one day we might share everlasting Life with you. We ask this through your risen Son, Jesus Christ our Lord. **Amen.**

COLLECT

Let us pray

Pause for silent prayer

O God, who make this most sacred night
    radiant
with the glory of the Lord's Resurrection,
stir up in your Church a spirit of adoption,
so that, renewed in body and mind,
we may render you undivided service.
Through our Lord Jesus Christ, your Son,
who lives and reigns with you in the unity
    of the Holy Spirit,
one God, for ever and ever. **Amen.**

FOR REFLECTION

- I am like the women going to the tomb to anoint the dead Jesus when . . . I am utterly amazed at what I find when . . .
- My Easter joy spills over into witness to others of Jesus' Presence when . . .
- I encounter the risen Jesus and the Life he gives me enables me to . . .

SPIRITUALITY

GOSPEL ACCLAMATION
cf. 1 Cor 5:7b-8a

℞. Alleluia, alleluia.
Christ, our paschal lamb, has been sacrificed;
let us then feast with joy in the Lord.
℞. Alleluia, alleluia.

Gospel

John 20:1-9; L42ABC

On the first day of the week,
   Mary of Magdala came to
      the tomb early in the
         morning,
   while it was still dark,
   and saw the stone removed
      from the tomb.
So she ran and went to Simon Peter
   and to the other disciple whom Jesus
      loved, and told them,
   "They have taken the Lord from the
      tomb,
   and we don't know where they put him."
So Peter and the other disciple went out
   and came to the tomb.
They both ran, but the other disciple ran
   faster than Peter
   and arrived at the tomb first;
   he bent down and saw the burial cloths
      there, but did not go in.
When Simon Peter arrived after him,
   he went into the tomb and saw the
      burial cloths there,
   and the cloth that had covered his head,
   not with the burial cloths but rolled up
      in a separate place.
Then the other disciple also went in,
   the one who had arrived at the tomb
      first,
   and he saw and believed.
For they did not yet understand the
      Scripture
   that he had to rise from the dead.

or

Mark 16:1-7; L41B *in Appendix A, p. 295*

or, at an afternoon or evening Mass

Luke 24:13-35; L46 *in Appendix A, p. 295.*

See Appendix A, p. 296 for the other readings.

Reflecting on the Gospel and Living the Paschal Mystery

Key words and phrases from the gospel: Mary of Magdala came to the tomb, she ran, Peter and the other disciple . . . ran, believed, he had to rise from the dead

To the point: Good news is infectious. It spreads rapidly. It cannot be contained by tomb or stone or even unbelief. Mary and the disciples encountered an empty tomb. No one had "taken the Lord from the tomb"; he "had to rise from the dead." So the Scriptures said. So did they say when they themselves had encountered the risen Jesus. So must we say as we encounter the risen Jesus.

To ponder and pray: The little fellow was held tightly in his mother's arms during the first part of the Easter Sunday morning Mass. He might have been tired, or he might already have eaten too much of the Easter Bunny's chocolate. He was restless, energetic, looking all around. After the homily came the renewal of baptismal promises and sprinkling with the Easter water. Father used an evergreen branch and the water flew abundantly, some hitting the little fellow square in the face. At first he stopped short, startled. Then the most gorgeous and radiant smile burst over his face. He looked around at the other people being sprinkled. Soon, everyone around him couldn't help but smile. His radiance was infectious. This little fellow was wholly alive. This little fellow spread Easter joy.

The news of an empty tomb spread from Mary to Peter and the disciple. They ran—hope quickens us. They believed—faith urges us. They witnessed to the good news—good news cannot be contained. Good news is infectious. Good news brings radiance to tired, suffering, worn faces. Good news such as an empty tomb and soon an encounter with the risen One not only cannot be contained, it changes us. Like Mary and the disciples we become witnesses to Christ's risen Life. Our encounters with the risen One compel us to be witnesses, to spread Easter joy.

Easter Sunday is more than a celebration of the resurrection *of Jesus*. It is also an invitation to each of us to take our place in the long line of witnesses to encounters with him and his risen Life. Perhaps this is why we are so awed at the mystery: not just that Jesus was raised from the dead, but that God entrusts us with continuing Jesus' saving mission and with being witnesses to God's mighty deed of resurrection. It appears as though God trusts us a great deal. This trust is like the baptismal waters washing us anew, strengthening us to proclaim the unbelievable—that the tomb is empty; the crucified One is raised from the dead. Our encounters with the risen Jesus nudge us from unbelief to belief-acts. Our witnessing to his saving acts move us from our own comfort zones of life to radiating the joy of the risen One's dwelling within and among us.

We witness to Jesus' resurrection when we faithfully live our baptismal promises, witness to our belief that Jesus is alive and shares his risen Life with us. Believing is radiating the joy of our encounters with Christ, bringing others to encounter him, continuing Jesus' saving work. Believing is encountering emptiness in others and bringing them joy and hope. Believing is helping others move the large stones that block their growth and happiness. Believing is running to help those in need. Believing is turning our Easter Alleluias into good works that spread joy and hope and faith. Believing is Easter Alleluias lived every day.

Model Penitential Act

Presider: Today our Lenten penance gives way to the exuberant joy of celebrating Christ's resurrection. Let us resolve to witness by our lives to this new Life and ready ourselves to give God heartfelt thanks and praise during this celebration . . . [pause]

Lord Jesus, you were raised up to new Life by your Father: Lord . . .

Risen Christ, you conquered suffering and death: Christ . . .

Lord Jesus, you send us to witness to your risen Life: Lord . . .

Homily Points

- Deep grief can often paralyze a person. We can be numb. We seem to be in a trance. We become unaware of what is going on around us. We do not hear. We are blind. After Jesus' crucifixion, the disciples must have been paralyzed with grief, with dashed hopes, with utter anxiety about what to do next. How quickly an empty tomb shakes them out of their numbness and inaction and makes them *run*!

- Mary's first hint of the resurrection was of an empty tomb. She ran to Peter and "the other disciple whom Jesus loved" to tell them. Was her haste due to human anguish: "They have taken the Lord from the tomb"? The two disciples run to the tomb. Was their haste due to anguish or hope? When they saw the empty tomb, what did they believe? The gospel leaves open the answer to these questions. Belief in the resurrection takes time. It takes encounter with the risen One.

- We will not run to an empty tomb. Yet we believe in the resurrection. We believe because of the witness of disciples, beginning with those first ones who did see the empty tomb. Like them, we must *run*—to seek and encounter the risen One who enables us to witness to the new Life of resurrection.

Model Universal Prayer (Prayer of the Faithful)

Presider: In the joy and hope of the resurrection let us pray to our wondrous God for our needs.

Response:

Lord, hear our prayer.

Cantor:

we pray to the Lord,

That all members of the church radiate the joy of the good news of Jesus' risen Life . . . [pause]

That all peoples of the world come to see and believe in God's gift of salvation . . . [pause]

That those who are disheartened may find joy, those who are sick may find healing, those who are downtrodden may be lifted up . . . [pause]

That those initiated into the church this Easter diligently seek to encounter the risen One each day of their faith-filled lives . . . [pause]

That all of us here witness to the good news of Jesus' risen Life by the good works we do for others . . . [pause]

Presider: O saving God, you planned from the beginning of creation to shower us with life and light: hear these our prayers that one day we might enjoy everlasting Life with you and the risen Son, with the Holy Spirit, one God, for ever and ever. **Amen.**

COLLECT

Let us pray

Pause for silent prayer

O God, who on this day,
through your Only Begotten Son,
have conquered death
and unlocked for us the path to eternity,
grant, we pray, that we who keep
the solemnity of the Lord's Resurrection
may, through the renewal brought by your
    Spirit,
rise up in the light of life.
Through our Lord Jesus Christ, your Son,
who lives and reigns with you in the unity
    of the Holy Spirit,
one God, for ever and ever. **Amen.**

FOR REFLECTION

- I have "told" others about Jesus' risen Life in which I share by . . .
- What brings me the greatest joy and helps me come to greater belief in the new Life God offers me is . . .
- The radiant joy I have encountered through others is . . . The radiant joy I have brought to others is . . .

SEASON OF EASTER

SPIRITUALITY

GOSPEL ACCLAMATION
John 20:29

℟. Alleluia, alleluia.
You believe in me, Thomas, because you have
    seen me, says the Lord;
blessed are those who have not seen me, but still
    believe!
℟. Alleluia, alleluia.

Gospel   John 20:19-31; L44B

On the evening of that first day of the
    week,
    when the doors were locked, where the
        disciples were,
    for fear of the Jews,
    Jesus came and stood in their midst
    and said to them, "Peace be with you."
When he had said this, he showed them
    his hands and his side.
The disciples rejoiced when they saw the
    Lord.
Jesus said to them again, "Peace be with
    you.
As the Father has sent me, so I send you."
And when he had said this, he breathed
    on them and said to them,
    "Receive the Holy Spirit.
Whose sins you forgive are forgiven them,
    and whose sins you retain are retained."

Thomas, called Didymus, one of the
    Twelve,
    was not with them when Jesus came.
So the other disciples said to him, "We
    have seen the Lord."
But he said to them,
    "Unless I see the mark of the nails in
        his hands
    and put my finger into the nailmarks
    and put my hand into his side, I will not
        believe."

Now a week later his disciples were again
    inside
    and Thomas was with them.
Jesus came, although the doors were
    locked,
    and stood in their midst and said,
        "Peace be with you."

Continued in Appendix A, p. 297.

Continued in Appendix A, p. 297.

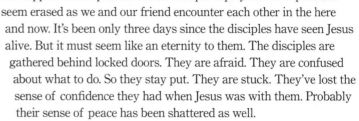

Reflecting on the Gospel

What happens when we meet a close friend whom we've not seen for a long time? We embrace the person warmly. We talk about shared past experiences. We share how our lives have changed. In the midst of this encounter is a deep sense of happiness and peace. Months and perhaps years of separation seem erased as we and our friend encounter each other in the here and now. It's been only three days since the disciples have seen Jesus alive. But it must seem like an eternity to them. The disciples are gathered behind locked doors. They are afraid. They are confused about what to do. So they stay put. They are stuck. They've lost the sense of confidence they had when Jesus was with them. Probably their sense of peace has been shattered as well.

On Easter evening, the risen Jesus appears and shows the disciples "his hands and his side." It is Jesus who makes the first, convincing move to enable the disciples to believe that he has truly risen from the dead. It is he who wants the disciples to see him, to regain their confidence and peace. To this end, he bestows upon them the gift of the Holy Spirit. With this gift, the disciples are able to rejoice, to believe that he is truly risen. But this Jesus is not just an old friend who has been absent for a time. The disciples have never before seen *this* Jesus. He bears the marks of suffering and death. Yet he is risen, never to die again. He has conquered death. For himself and for all of us.

Thomas is a convenient stand-in for all of us as we strive to deepen our belief in the risen Lord. Unlike Thomas, however, we do not literally "see" the risen Lord. Whether we see clearly like the gathered disciples, or only through doubting like Thomas, the risen Jesus is, nevertheless, always present in our midst removing all obstacles to belief. This is also how the risen Lord comes among us: in those in need, in those who reach out in self-giving to help those in need. Going from disbelief to belief is not a mental exercise. It is encountering the risen Lord in the people and circumstances around us. Believing is living faithfully the risen Life Jesus gives us.

Living the Paschal Mystery

Belief always goes beyond what we can prove, and often means we must go out on a limb. Belief in the risen Lord means that we die to self so that we can encounter the risen Jesus around us. This means, at times, that we ourselves might have "nail marks" from being wounded. Dying to self always runs a risk of being vulnerable. So it was with Jesus. Out of his vulnerability, love, and self-giving came risen Life! So it will be with us.

The challenge of this gospel is that we put aside our own fears and embrace belief, with all its consequences. Just as the risen Jesus was relentless in bringing the disciples from disbelief to belief, so is he with us. He is also just as relentless with us as he was with the disciples in bringing them to the cross. Even after his resurrection, Jesus always challenges us to both dying and rising. Having passed over from our Lenten discipline to Easter rejoicing doesn't mean that we can forget about the dying required for living the paschal mystery. Now, however, our "seeing" is heightened: we have experienced once again Easter joy, a glimpse and promise of the fullness of Life to come. This glimpse of the fullness of Life gives us the confidence to believe, to live the Life given us now, to embrace the risen Jesus.

Focusing the Gospel

Key words and phrases: in their midst, he showed them his hands and his side, peace, Holy Spirit, forgive, We have seen the Lord, come to believe

To the point: On Easter evening, the risen Jesus appears and shows the disciples "his hands and his side." It is Jesus who makes the first, convincing move to enable the disciples to believe that he has truly risen from the dead. Whether we see clearly like the disciples gathered around the risen Jesus, or only through doubting like Thomas, the risen Jesus is always present in our midst removing all obstacles to belief.

Connecting the Gospel

to the second reading: Loving one another and keeping God's commandments are visible ways we reveal that we believe Jesus is truly risen from the dead and we have seen him.

to experience: When people say "I believe you," they mean that they believe the fact we communicate. By contrast, when people say "I believe *in* you," they mean that they know us, trust our values, and can count on us. To believe in the resurrection is more than believing a *fact*. To believe in the risen Jesus is knowing, trusting, and counting on him.

Connecting the Responsorial Psalm

to the readings: Psalm 118 was a processional song in which the Israelites praised God for having saved them from destruction by an enemy. The psalm began with a call to worship and then continued as the people marched through Jerusalem to the temple. A soloist sang about facing death with confidence in God and a choir responded by singing about God's saving intervention. The rejected stone become the cornerstone may have referred to Israel itself, a puny nation considered easy to conquer by more powerful enemies. Or it may have referred to the stone of the temple, symbol of God, the rock of salvation.

Christian tradition applies the image to the risen Christ (Matt 21:42; Acts 4:11; 1 Pet 2:7). He is the foundation of our faith, the bedrock of our discipleship, the basis of our love for one another (second reading) and our care for the needy (first reading). He is the source of our victory over sin and death. In Psalm 118, we sing our joy and thanksgiving to the God who has made this happen.

to psalmist preparation: In this responsorial psalm you lead the assembly in praising God for the victory granted us in the risen Christ. Spend time this week giving God thanks. One way of doing this is to sing the psalm refrain as part of your personal prayer every day.

ASSEMBLY & FAITH-SHARING GROUPS

- The risen Jesus comes to me when . . . Obstacles that block my believing in his Presence include . . .
- What helps me grow in my belief in the risen Lord is . . . My belief needs to deepen because . . .
- Jesus removes obstacles that keep me from growing in my belief in his continued Presence by . . .

PRESIDERS

My moments of doubt have, like Thomas, led me to deeper faith by . . . Because of this, I am able to lead others to deeper faith when . . .

DEACONS

My service leads others to see the risen Jesus in their midst when . . .

HOSPITALITY MINISTERS

My welcome, care, and concern helps those gathering for liturgy to encounter the risen Jesus and believe in him more deeply when . . .

MUSIC MINISTERS

In my music ministry, I have encountered the Presence of the risen Jesus when . . . I have helped my fellow music ministers encounter this Presence by . . .

ALTAR MINISTERS

My believing in the risen Jesus helps me serve better because . . .

LECTORS

My prayerful preparation with the word leads me to a deeper belief in the risen Jesus when I . . .

EXTRAORDINARY MINISTERS OF HOLY COMMUNION

The way I express my belief in the risen Jesus in my daily living is carried over in how I distribute Holy Communion by . . .

Model Rite for the Blessing and Sprinkling of Water

Presider: Thomas doubted that Jesus had risen from the dead and only came to believe when he saw the risen Jesus. As we are sprinkled with this water reminding us of our baptism, may we come to deeper belief in his risen Presence among us . . . [pause]

   [continue with The Roman Missal, *Appendix II]*

Homily Points

• When do we go on the offense? When we feel threatened. When someone angers us. When we feel strongly about something. Jesus goes on the offense in this gospel, not because he is threatened or angry, but because he feels strongly about the disciples. He cares for them and wants them to know that he is risen from the dead, has not forsaken them, and wishes to remove any obstacles to their belief in him and following him.

• The disciples are locked in, afraid. The risen Jesus appears and removes the obstacles of their disbelief, their concern for their own safety, and their paralysis in response to his crucifixion. He removes these obstacles by bestowing peace upon them, giving them the Spirit, and empowering them to forgive. The disciples see the risen Jesus and are changed—they come to belief. When we see the risen Jesus, we also are changed—we come to deeper belief.

• The risen Jesus gives us everything we need to see him and believe in him. We respond to his Presence by being willing to change. We move from hardness of heart to forgiveness of those who have hurt us. We move from fear of losing the regard of others to embracing publicly Gospel values. We move from aloneness and discouragement to being loving and serving disciples. We reveal that we have seen the risen Jesus, have come to believe more deeply in him, and have changed.

Model Universal Prayer (Prayer of the Faithful)

Presider: Christ is risen and present among us. Let us ask for what we need to live as believing, faithful disciples.

Response:

Lord, hear our prayer.

Cantor:

we pray to the Lord,

That all members of the church come to deeper belief in the risen Jesus who dwells in us through the power of the Holy Spirit . . . [pause]

That all nations of the world grow in the lasting peace that is a gift of God . . . [pause]

That those who are poor and in need be supported by the care and concern of this believing community . . . [pause]

That those initiated into the church this Easter may continue to follow the risen Jesus with faith and freedom . . . [pause]

That all of us here gathered may rejoice in the risen Jesus, be changed by his Spirit, and receive new Life . . . [pause]

Presider: Gracious God, you raised your Son Jesus to risen Life and bring us to deeper belief in him: hear these our prayers that we might be faithful disciples making known his Presence and peace. We ask this through Jesus Christ our risen Lord. **Amen.**

COLLECT

Let us pray

Pause for silent prayer

God of everlasting mercy,
who in the very recurrence of the paschal
      feast
kindle the faith of the people you have
      made your own,
increase, we pray, the grace you have
      bestowed,
that all may grasp and rightly understand
in what font they have been washed,
by whose Spirit they have been reborn,
by whose Blood they have been redeemed.
Through our Lord Jesus Christ, your Son,
who lives and reigns with you in the unity
      of the Holy Spirit,
one God, for ever and ever. **Amen.**

FIRST READING

Acts 4:32-35

The community of believers was of one
      heart and mind,
   and no one claimed that any of his
         possessions was his own,
   but they had everything in common.
With great power the apostles bore
      witness
   to the resurrection of the Lord Jesus,
   and great favor was accorded them all.
There was no needy person among them,
   for those who owned property or houses
         would sell them,
   bring the proceeds of the sale,
   and put them at the feet of the apostles,
   and they were distributed to each
         according to need.

RESPONSORIAL PSALM

Ps 118:2-4, 13-15, 22-24

℟. (1) Give thanks to the Lord for he is
good, his love is everlasting.
   or:
℟. Alleluia.

Let the house of Israel say,
   "His mercy endures forever."
Let the house of Aaron say,
   "His mercy endures forever."
Let those who fear the LORD say,
   "His mercy endures forever."

℟. Give thanks to the Lord for he is good,
his love is everlasting.
   or:
℟. Alleluia.

I was hard pressed and was falling,
   but the LORD helped me.
My strength and my courage is the LORD,
   and he has been my savior.
The joyful shout of victory
   in the tents of the just.

R̸. Give thanks to the Lord for he is good,
his love is everlasting.
   or:
R̸. Alleluia.

The stone which the builders rejected
   has become the cornerstone.
By the LORD has this been done;
   it is wonderful in our eyes.
This is the day the LORD has made;
   let us be glad and rejoice in it.

R̸. Give thanks to the Lord for he is good,
his love is everlasting.
   or:
R̸. Alleluia.

SECOND READING
1 John 5:1-6

Beloved:
Everyone who believes that Jesus is the
      Christ is begotten by God,
   and everyone who loves the Father
   loves also the one begotten by him.
In this way we know that we love the
      children of God
   when we love God and obey his
      commandments.
For the love of God is this,
   that we keep his commandments.
And his commandments are not
      burdensome,
   for whoever is begotten by God
      conquers the world.
And the victory that conquers the world is
   our faith.
Who indeed is the victor over the world
   but the one who believes that Jesus is
      the Son of God?

This is the one who came through water
      and blood, Jesus Christ,
   not by water alone, but by water and
      blood.
The Spirit is the one that testifies,
   and the Spirit is truth.

About Liturgy

Easter octave: Two great festivals still retain an octave on the 1969 Revised General Roman Calendar: Christmas and Easter. For eight days we celebrate with great solemnity the joy of the festival; this is why, for example, we may sing the sequence every day during the octave of Easter and why no other celebration may take the place of these eight days.

Eight is an important symbolic number. The early Christians called Sunday the "eighth day." Since our week has seven days, "eighth day" referred to a day beyond the human reckoning of time—beyond time, belonging to the end times. Theologically, this refers to "eschatological" time when Jesus Christ will return in all his glory to gather everything back to God at the end and fullness of time. Thus, the Easter octave means more than simply going from one Sunday to the next; it heightens our expectation that the risen Life we celebrate is the same Life that we will one day share with the Trinity in everlasting glory.

Significance of the proclaimed word and the ministry of lector: The gospel for this Sunday makes clear that one way we come to belief is through the proclamation of the word. As caretakers of the word, lectors' ministry is intimately connected with the assembly's encountering the risen Christ and coming to belief. Before lectors can proclaim the word effectively so that Christ is encountered, they themselves must have encountered Christ in the word. Their proclamation must ring with their own belief so that the assembly is moved to respond, "My Lord and my God!" The way to come to this kind of proclamation is twofold: lectors must pray and reflect deeply and long on the word they will proclaim; lectors must live the word in their life so they know from their own experience of the word's challenges and blessings.

About Liturgical Music

A musical suggestion for singing Psalm 118: One way to highlight the structure of this psalm, and the festivity of the Easter season, would be to have the psalmist lead the first strophe as a litany with the assembly and/or choir responding on "His mercy endures forever," then sing the second strophe as a solo, then be joined on the third verse by the choir adding harmonizations.

Service music for the Easter season: Easter is the season when we need to sing our most festive, energetic, and musically embellished service music. Changing Mass settings in accord with the liturgical seasons helps us participate in the dynamic of the whole year. The interplay between festal seasons and Ordinary Time is one of the ways the liturgy enables us to recognize and enter into the dying and rising rhythm of the paschal mystery. It takes time to put seasonal service music in place in a parish, but doing so is important and worth the effort.

✚ SPIRITUALITY

GOSPEL ACCLAMATION
cf. Luke 24:32

℞. Alleluia, alleluia.
Lord Jesus, open the Scriptures to us;
make our hearts burn while you speak to us.
℞. Alleluia, alleluia.

Gospel   Luke 24:35-48; L47B

The two disciples recounted what had taken
    place on the way,
    and how Jesus was made known to them
    in the breaking of bread.

While they were still speaking about this,
    he stood in their midst and said to them,
    "Peace be with you."
But they were startled and terrified
    and thought that they were seeing a ghost.
Then he said to them, "Why are you troubled?
And why do questions arise in your hearts?
Look at my hands and my feet, that it is I
    myself.
Touch me and see, because a ghost does not
    have flesh and bones
    as you can see I have."
And as he said this,
    he showed them his hands and his feet.
While they were still incredulous for joy
    and were amazed,
    he asked them, "Have you anything here
    to eat?"
They gave him a piece of baked fish;
    he took it and ate it in front of them.

He said to them,
    "These are my words that I spoke to you
        while I was still with you,
    that everything written about me in the
        law of Moses
    and in the prophets and psalms must be
        fulfilled."
Then he opened their minds to understand
    the Scriptures.
And he said to them,
    "Thus it is written that the Christ would
        suffer
    and rise from the dead on the third day
    and that repentance, for the forgiveness
        of sins,
    would be preached in his name
    to all the nations, beginning from
        Jerusalem.
You are witnesses of these things."

Reflecting on the Gospel

Why think about sins and forgiveness during Easter time? What a bummer! Easter is a joyful time to celebrate new Life! It is thus surprising that repentance and forgiveness (acts we much more readily associate with Lent) figure so prominently in all three readings assigned to this Third Sunday of Easter. The readings suggest to us that we, unlike the disciples to whom Jesus appeared after the resurrection, cannot look at, touch, see with our own eyes this Jesus who was dead and now is risen to new Life. Yet Jesus gives us another, just as concrete, means to come to belief in the new Life of resurrection. Repentance and forgiveness are themselves encounters with the risen Jesus, an invitation to deeper belief, and an experience of our own coming to a share in Jesus' risen Life.

Jesus opened the minds of the disciples to grasp two things written in the Scriptures: that he "would suffer and rise from the dead," and that "repentance, for the forgiveness of sins, would be preached in his name to all the nations." Our repentance—conversion of life—turns us to the God who forgives and who fills us with the new Life of the resurrection. Ultimately, this risen Life within us empowers a way of living that witnesses to God's forgiveness of our sinfulness.

Our belief in the resurrection cannot be passive. Our belief in the risen Jesus is made visible when we "preach in his name" the kind of repentance leading to the new life of forgiveness. We encounter Jesus today when we repent of our sins and forgive others. Jesus "was made known" in the breaking of the bread and in repentance and forgiveness. Why is forgiveness so central to embracing Jesus' risen Life? Being forgiven by God for our offenses means that the weakened or destroyed relationship caused by sin is strengthened or restored. We become strong once again in the Life that God offers us. Forgiving others who have hurt us means that we are not controlled by their hurtful actions, a control that can lead to resentment, anger, hate. Forgiving another might not erase the hurt, but it does free us to live with compassion and joy. These are virtues of risen Life. This is risen Life: "You are forgiven." This is our witness to the resurrection: "I forgive you."

Living the Paschal Mystery

The resurrection claims us as witnesses not only to God's forgiveness of us, but also to our forgiveness of one another. Repentance—conversion of life—opens new opportunities to touch and see the risen Jesus. Repentance opens us to God's gift of forgiveness. Repentance opens us to the new Life of resurrection Jesus offers. Ultimately, the resurrection is a pledge of new Life for us and makes visible God's forgiveness of our sinfulness. Forgiveness is part of the reality of risen Life; it is the effect of death and resurrection.

Repentance and forgiveness do not belong simply to Lent—there, that's over for another year. Instead, they are very much a part of the Easter mystery. Forgiveness is the virtue that enables us not to allow past hurts to determine our decisions and actions in the here and now. Forgiveness opens up the space for creating together with the one forgiven a new future where we can "fall peacefully asleep" (responsorial psalm). Giving and receiving forgiveness is a resurrection activity. Walking and acting like a forgiven and forgiving people is how we make known the risen Jesus.

Focusing the Gospel

Key words and phrases: he opened their minds to understand the Scriptures; the Christ would suffer and rise from the dead; repentance, for the forgiveness of sins, would be preached in his name to all the nations

To the point: Jesus opened the minds of the disciples to grasp two things written in the Scriptures: that he "would suffer and rise from the dead," and that "repentance, for the forgiveness of sins, would be preached in his name to all the nations." Our repentance—conversion of life—turns us to the God who forgives and who fills us with the new Life of the resurrection. Ultimately, this risen Life within us empowers a way of living that witnesses to God's forgiveness of our sinfulness.

Connecting the Gospel

to the first two readings: Peter (first reading) and the First Letter of St. John (second reading) witness ways that the early communities obeyed Jesus' command in the gospel to preach repentance and forgiveness.

to experience: We usually think of repentance of wrongdoing and forgiveness as difficult and negative experiences. All three readings remind us that these are Life-giving actions leading us to deeper participation in the risen Life given us.

Connecting the Responsorial Psalm

to the readings: Psalm 4 is a lament begging God for mercy in a time of distress. The psalm promises God will hear this cry for help and transform distress into gladness, disturbance into peaceful sleep. Such a lament seems misplaced on the Third Sunday of Easter when we are well into our celebration of the mystery of the resurrection. But the readings and gospel place this psalm in an Easter context. The situation of distress in Psalm 4 is our sinfulness; what transforms our situation is God's saving forgiveness; what reveals both human sinfulness and divine forgiveness is the death and resurrection of Jesus. Most importantly, it is God's forgiveness that pervades and prevails. This, the risen Jesus commands us, is what we are to preach to every corner of the world.

to psalmist preparation: In the context of this Sunday's readings and gospel, you pray in this psalm for the transformation that comes through the forgiveness of sins. You pray knowing that God shines the divine Face of forgiveness upon us in the body of the risen Jesus. How might you turn to that Face? How might your face shine in response?

ASSEMBLY & FAITH-SHARING GROUPS
- What causes me to turn away from God in sinfulness is . . . What helps me return to God is . . .
- Examples of how I have experienced the new Life of the resurrection through repentance and forgiveness are . . .
- I witness to God's forgiveness of sinfulness when I . . .

PRESIDERS
I have helped another to repent and be forgiven when . . .

DEACONS
My service of others brings them the new Life of the resurrection when I . . .

HOSPITALITY MINISTERS
My greeting helps those gathering for liturgy to experience the Presence of the risen Jesus when . . .

MUSIC MINISTERS
As a music minister I need to seek forgiveness for . . . Seeking this forgiveness witnesses to the Presence of the risen Jesus by . . .

ALTAR MINISTERS
My serving at the altar is a fruitful expression of my repentance and forgiveness when . . .

LECTORS
My proclamation opens the minds of the assembly to understand the Scriptures when . . .

EXTRAORDINARY MINISTERS OF HOLY COMMUNION
The Eucharist has inspired and nourished me to be repentant and forgiving by . . .

Model Rite for the Blessing and Sprinkling of Water

Presider: The risen Jesus appears to the disciples and calls them to witness both to his resurrection and to God's offer of forgiveness. As we are sprinkled with this water that reminds us of our baptism, may we deepen our commitment to be Jesus' faithful followers and witnesses . . . [pause]

> [*continue with* The Roman Missal, *Appendix II*]

Homily Points

- To seek forgiveness of another requires that we admit wrongdoing. This is a difficult thing for us human beings to do. We would rather pretend—to ourselves and to the world—that we are "perfect," that we never hurt others. But, in fact, we do. In hurting others we harm our relationship with God and need to seek God's forgiveness.

- Why is forgiveness so central to the resurrection proclamation? Because seeking God's forgiveness is an admission of our own sinfulness, our need for conversion of life, and our belief in and desire for the new Life that Jesus' resurrection makes possible. Through seeking and receiving forgiveness—from God and others—we touch and see the Jesus who suffered and three days after death rose from the dead. We ourselves enter into an experience of resurrection.

- We experience the Presence of the risen Jesus when we rebuild a relationship broken by thoughtlessness or selfishness. When we repair damage done to another's reputation through idle gossip or malicious slander. When we counteract oppression and injustice by changing behaviors that hurt or diminish others. In all these examples, we witness to Jesus' new Life of the resurrection and open the door for God's continuing forgiveness.

Model Universal Prayer (Prayer of the Faithful)

Presider: The God who raised Jesus from the dead calls us to repentance and offers us the new Life of forgiveness. And so we pray.

Response:
Lord, hear our prayer.

Cantor:
we pray to the Lord,

That all members of the church be fonts of God's mercy and forgiveness . . . [pause]

That people of all nations hear God's call to repentance and celebrate the new life of forgiveness . . . [pause]

That those burdened by sin seek forgiveness and be freed by Jesus' offer of new Life . . . [pause]

That those newly initiated into the church may continue to grow in their relationship with the risen Jesus and with the God of mercy and forgiveness . . . [pause]

That each of us gathered here faithfully witness to the Presence of the risen Jesus and God's desire to forgive our wrongdoing . . . [pause]

Presider: Merciful God, you are quick to forgive and offer us the new Life of the resurrection: hear these our prayers that we may seek diligently conversion of life and come to know more deeply the risen Jesus. We ask this through the risen One, Jesus Christ our Lord. **Amen.**

COLLECT

Let us pray

Pause for silent prayer

May your people exult for ever, O God,
in renewed youthfulness of spirit,
so that, rejoicing now in the restored glory
    of our adoption,
we may look forward in confident hope
to the rejoicing of the day of resurrection.
Through our Lord Jesus Christ, your Son,
who lives and reigns with you in the unity
    of the Holy Spirit,
one God, for ever and ever. **Amen.**

FIRST READING

Acts 3:13-15, 17-19

Peter said to the people:
"The God of Abraham,
    the God of Isaac, and the God of Jacob,
    the God of our fathers, has glorified his
        servant Jesus,
    whom you handed over and denied in
        Pilate's presence
    when he had decided to release him.
You denied the Holy and Righteous One
    and asked that a murderer be released
        to you.
The author of life you put to death,
    but God raised him from the dead; of
        this we are witnesses.
Now I know, brothers,
    that you acted out of ignorance, just as
        your leaders did;
    but God has thus brought to fulfillment
    what he had announced beforehand
    through the mouth of all the prophets,
    that his Christ would suffer.
Repent, therefore, and be converted, that
    your sins may be wiped away."

RESPONSORIAL PSALM

Ps 4:2, 4, 7-8, 9

℟. (7a) Lord, let your face shine on us.
or:
℟. Alleluia.

When I call, answer me, O my just God,
    you who relieve me when I am in
        distress;
    have pity on me, and hear my prayer!

℟. Lord, let your face shine on us.
or:
℟. Alleluia.

Know that the LORD does wonders for his
    faithful one;
    the LORD will hear me when I call upon
        him.

℟. Lord, let your face shine on us.
or:
℟. Alleluia.

O LORD, let the light of your countenance
    shine upon us!
    You put gladness into my heart.

℟. Lord, let your face shine on us.
or:
℟. Alleluia.

As soon as I lie down, I fall peacefully
    asleep,
    for you alone, O LORD,
    bring security to my dwelling.

℟. Lord, let your face shine on us.
or:
℟. Alleluia.

SECOND READING

1 John 2:1-5a

My children, I am writing this to you
    so that you may not commit sin.
But if anyone does sin, we have an
    Advocate with the Father,
    Jesus Christ the righteous one.
He is expiation for our sins,
    and not for our sins only but for those of
        the whole world.
The way we may be sure that we know
    him is to keep
    his commandments.
Those who say, "I know him," but do not
    keep his commandments
    are liars, and the truth is not in them.
But whoever keeps his word,
    the love of God is truly perfected in him.

About Liturgy

Sacrament of penance: Much is being written in the Catholic press these days about the demise of the sacrament of penance—too few are making use of this sacrament of healing. Even participation in the typical twice-a-year (Advent and Lent) communal penance liturgies in our parishes is not always as robust as it could be. Perhaps part of the problem lies in a rather narrow understanding of this sacrament—that it is about acknowledging sins. This is true, but this is only one dimension of the sacrament. Far more important is that our seeking and receiving forgiveness, our firm resolve of repentance, and our doing some penance as an expression of our desire for conversion are all opportunities for encounters with the risen Christ.

Like all liturgy, the sacrament of penance makes present the paschal mystery. Perhaps we focus too much on the dying aspect of this mystery (confession of sins) and not enough on the rising (encounter with Christ and the restoration of our relationship with God). Like all sacraments, the Rite of Reconciliation includes a proclamation of the word, even when it is celebrated as private confession. Perhaps a good practice would be to reflect on some New Testament passage on forgiveness for a significant time before confession; perhaps this Sunday's gospel would be a good choice since it reminds us so well of the connection of forgiveness and risen Life.

About Liturgical Music

Music suggestions: Rae E. Whitney's "They Disbelieved for Joy" (W4) retells in hymn form the story of this Sunday's gospel and would be suitable during the preparation of the gifts. Hymns and songs calling us to celebrate the forgiveness we have been granted through the resurrection of Jesus would also be appropriate this Sunday. For example, in Brian Wren's "This Is a Day of New Beginnings" (G3, W4), we call one another to "step from the past, and leave behind our disappointment, guilt, and grieving" because "This is a day of new beginnings: our God is making all things new." W4 sets the text to RENDEZ A DIEU, which would be suitable during the preparation of the gifts. G3 uses a verse-refrain setting by Lori True which would work well during any of the processions (entrance, preparation of the gifts, Communion). For another example, in Christopher M. Idle's "If Christ Had Not Been Raised from Death" (W4) we sing that had Christ not been raised our sin and guilt would remain. But because Christ has risen "His Gospel meets a world of need—In Christ we are forgiv'n." This hymn would also be suitable during the preparation of the gifts.

✠ SPIRITUALITY

GOSPEL ACCLAMATION
John 10:14

R͞/. Alleluia, alleluia.
I am the good shepherd, says the Lord;
I know my sheep, and mine know me.
R͞/. Alleluia, alleluia.

Gospel

John 10:11-18; L50B

Jesus said:
  "I am the good shepherd.
A good shepherd lays down his
    life for the sheep.
A hired man, who is not a
    shepherd
  and whose sheep are not his
      own,
  sees a wolf coming and leaves the
      sheep and runs away,
  and the wolf catches and scatters
      them.
This is because he works for pay and
    has no concern for the sheep.
I am the good shepherd,
  and I know mine and mine know me,
  just as the Father knows me and I
      know the Father;
  and I will lay down my life for the
      sheep.
I have other sheep that do not belong to
    this fold.
These also I must lead, and they will
    hear my voice,
  and there will be one flock, one
      shepherd.
This is why the Father loves me,
  because I lay down my life in order to
      take it up again.
No one takes it from me, but I lay it
    down on my own.
I have power to lay it down, and power
    to take it up again.
This command I have received from my
    Father."

Reflecting on the Gospel

All children latch onto heroes. Perhaps they are characters with amazing powers they've seen on a TV program. Or maybe they are the characters in a video game. Sometimes they are a favorite aunt or uncle whom they admire. No matter who the hero, the child wants to imitate the actions, wear the clothes, talk like the hero. In this Sunday's gospel we are presented with a hero: the Good Shepherd. We are invited to imitate his actions: lay down our lives for others as he did.

In the gospel for this Sunday, Jesus proclaims that "I am the good shepherd" and "I know mine and mine know me." To know Jesus is to be one with him, the Good Shepherd. This means that we are not only sheep who hear our Good Shepherd's voice and come to know him, but we also are to become good shepherds ourselves. Transformed from sheep to shepherd, we take up the life our Good Shepherd has laid down. The good shepherd is concerned about, cares for, and protects the sheep even to the point of laying down the shepherd's life. Jesus requires of us disciples the same mission—to also lay down our lives (this phrase occurs five times in the gospel).

Shepherding, then, is serious and dangerous business! It means that we cannot run away from danger like the hired man, but we must meet danger head-on for the sake of God's beloved. Because of our baptism, we share in the new Life of Christ; our entry into this new Life is dying to ourselves—laying down our own lives. We are strengthened to lay down our lives for others when Jesus' voice is the guiding element in our daily living. By sorting through all the diverse voices we hear each day, and hearing in some of them the voice of Jesus, we know the fold to which we belong—"we are God's children now" (second reading). Hearing Jesus' voice, we know that "[t]here is no salvation through anyone else" (first reading). And we willingly lay down our own lives so that others can come to the same awesome truth: a share in Easter Life, the "love the Father has bestowed on us" (second reading).

Living the Paschal Mystery

Laying down our lives for the sake of others doesn't mean that we will be nailed to a cross. It does mean that we commit ourselves to "good deeds" (first reading) such as caring for the sick, forgiving those who wrong us (last Sunday's gospel), giving thanks and praise to God (responsorial psalm), loving others as God has loved us (second reading). These good deeds are the very "stuff" of our everyday living. We don't have to go out of our way to be good shepherds. We need only to relate as one filled with new Life in Christ to those who come our way.

Often it is easier to see the dying to self, the cost, of laying down our lives for the good of others than it is to see the new Life in which we share when our lives are patterned after that of our Good Shepherd. Easter joy reminds us that even in danger, even in dying to self, even in spending ourselves for a better life for others there is found great peace and happiness. This, because we know that in self-giving we are one with our Good Shepherd and the way of living he taught us. By dying to self we are much more open to hearing his voice calling us to himself, where there is always comfort and peace, strength and encouragement; where we know that we are never alone, but rest in the beloved arms of our Good Shepherd.

Focusing the Gospel

Key words and phrases: good shepherd, lays down his life, I know mine and mine know me, hear my voice, take it up again

To the point: In the gospel for this Sunday, Jesus proclaims that "I am the good shepherd" and "I know mine and mine know me." To know Jesus is to be one with him, the Good Shepherd. This means that we are not only sheep who hear our Good Shepherd's voice and come to know him, but we also are to become good shepherds ourselves. Transformed from sheep to shepherd, we take up the life our Good Shepherd has laid down.

Connecting the Gospel

to the second reading: More than beloved sheep, we are "God's children now." Because of this relationship, we already participate in the risen Life of Jesus, can like him be shepherds, and can like him know God.

to experience: Married couples who have faithfully lived together for years begin to pick up mannerisms from one another and use the same speech patterns. When we have been faithful followers of the Good Shepherd, we too take up his manner of acting and his way of speaking.

Connecting the Responsorial Psalm

to the readings: The readings and responsorial psalm for this Sunday present us with two very different images of Christ: cornerstone and good shepherd. One is an image of rock, the other of flesh and blood, and their juxtaposition deepens our understanding of who Jesus is for us. As cornerstone he stands as our foundation, the one upon whom we can build our lives. As shepherd he knows us intimately and loves us so fully that he lays down his life for us. Both images tell us we can count on Christ. There is no salvation through anyone else (first reading). He lays down his life for us on his own power (gospel). Rejection by other powers-that-be poses no ultimate threat to his mission of salvation (first reading, psalm). Christ is the one who never crumbles, the one who never flinches from the demands of saving us, the one who supports, the one who loves, the one on whom we stand, and the one whom we follow. Christ is the one for whom we give God thanks when we sing this psalm.

to psalmist preparation: As you prepare to sing this responsorial psalm, you might reflect on questions such as these: How is Christ the foundation of your life? How is Christ the Good Shepherd leading and supporting you? How is Christ faithful to you at all costs? How do you give Christ thanks?

ASSEMBLY & FAITH-SHARING GROUPS
- I experience Jesus as Good Shepherd when . . . I am a good shepherd for others when . . .
- I experience being one with Jesus most surely when I . . .
- I take up the life the Good Shepherd has laid down when . . . by . . . for . . .

PRESIDERS
I witness through my ministry that I am one with the Good Shepherd when I . . .

DEACONS
My service ministry indicates that I have heard and heeded the voice of the Good Shepherd when . . .

HOSPITALITY MINISTERS
My greeting prepares people to hear the voice of the Good Shepherd in the liturgy when . . .

MUSIC MINISTERS
My music ministry helps the assembly become one flock led by the Good Shepherd when I . . .

ALTAR MINISTERS
Often the voice of Jesus calls me through my service of the altar to . . .

LECTORS
The assembly hears the voice of the Good Shepherd through my proclamation when I . . .

EXTRAORDINARY MINISTERS OF HOLY COMMUNION
When I say "Body [Blood] of Christ" to communicants, I am the voice of the Good Shepherd when . . .

Model Rite for the Blessing and Sprinkling of Water

Presider: Dear friends, we ask God to bless this water as a reminder of our baptism through which we are empowered to hear the voice of Jesus the Good Shepherd. Let us pray that we may also be good shepherds, helping each other come to the fullness of Life . . . [pause]

 [continue with The Roman Missal, *Appendix II]*

Homily Points

• Getting to know who others are takes a great deal of time and commitment. We need to share life stories, we need to exchange visions and dreams, we need to empathize with each other's sufferings and joys. To know the Good Shepherd takes a lifetime of living the Gospel through which we come to live his life; share his vision; and enter into his suffering, death, and resurrection.

• By saying in the gospel, "I know mine and mine know me," Jesus acknowledges that a deep relationship is already in place between him and us. At the same time, he also affirms that he continues to lead us as we continue to hear his voice. Our relationship with Jesus isn't finished. It always grows deeper. It grows more sure. Only then can we be good shepherds, too.

• We are more apt to take up the life Jesus has laid down when we hear his voice challenge us to follow his lead more faithfully. What is the life he has laid down? A life of caring for and loving others, a life of listening and healing, a life of challenging and transforming. When we take up this kind of living, we, too, become good shepherds.

Model Universal Prayer (Prayer of the Faithful)

Presider: Called to hear and heed the voice of the Good Shepherd, we ask God for all we need to be faithful.

Response:

Lord, hear our prayer.

Cantor:

we pray to the Lord,

That all members of the church listen to the voice of the Good Shepherd calling them to follow him faithfully . . . [pause]

That all leaders of nations be good shepherds, caring for the welfare of their people . . . [pause]

That those who are suffering or downtrodden be lifted up by our living and acting like the Good Shepherd . . . [pause]

That the newly initiated witness to the joy of their new identity as members of the flock of the Good Shepherd . . . [pause]

That we here gathered take up the life of the Good Shepherd, leading others to Gospel living and caring for them with compassion . . . [pause]

Presider: Loving God, your Son is the Good Shepherd who leads us to fullness of Life: hear our prayers that we might hear his voice and take up his life faithfully. We ask this through Christ our Lord. **Amen.**

COLLECT

Let us pray

Pause for silent prayer

Almighty ever-living God,
lead us to a share in the joys of heaven,
so that the humble flock may reach
where the brave Shepherd has gone before.
Who lives and reigns with you in the unity
 of the Holy Spirit,
one God, for ever and ever. **Amen.**

FIRST READING

Acts 4:8-12

Peter, filled with the Holy Spirit, said:
 "Leaders of the people and elders:
 If we are being examined today
 about a good deed done to a cripple,
 namely, by what means he was saved,
 then all of you and all the people of
  Israel should know
 that it was in the name of Jesus Christ
  the Nazorean
 whom you crucified, whom God raised
  from the dead;
 in his name this man stands before you
  healed.
He is *the stone rejected by you, the builders,*
 which has become the cornerstone.
There is no salvation through anyone else,
 nor is there any other name under
  heaven
 given to the human race by which we
  are to be saved."

RESPONSORIAL PSALM

Ps 118:1, 8-9, 21-23, 26, 28, 29

R̸. (22) The stone rejected by the builders
has become the cornerstone.
 or:
R̸. Alleluia.

Give thanks to the LORD, for he is good,
 for his mercy endures forever.
It is better to take refuge in the LORD
 than to trust in man.
It is better to take refuge in the LORD
 than to trust in princes.

R̸. The stone rejected by the builders has
become the cornerstone.
 or:
R̸. Alleluia.

I will give thanks to you, for you have
    answered me
  and have been my savior.
The stone which the builders rejected
  has become the cornerstone.
By the LORD has this been done;
  it is wonderful in our eyes.

R⁊. The stone rejected by the builders has
become the cornerstone.
  or:
R⊽. Alleluia.

Blessed is he who comes in the name of
    the LORD;
  we bless you from the house of the
    LORD.
I will give thanks to you, for you have
    answered me
  and have been my savior.
Give thanks to the LORD, for he is good;
  for his kindness endures forever.

R⊽. The stone rejected by the builders has
become the cornerstone.
  or:
R⊽. Alleluia.

SECOND READING
1 John 3:1-2

Beloved:
See what love the Father has bestowed
    on us
  that we may be called the children of
    God.
Yet so we are.
The reason the world does not know us
  is that it did not know him.
Beloved, we are God's children now;
  what we shall be has not yet been
    revealed.
We do know that when it is revealed we
  shall be like him,
  for we shall see him as he is.

About Liturgy

The fifty-day Easter Lectionary: The gospels for the eight Sundays from Easter to Pentecost form a wonderfully cohesive progression from Jesus' resurrection to our taking up Jesus' mission to preach the gospel. There is movement from Jesus, the risen One, to ourselves as disciples who, set afire by the Spirit, continue his saving mission in our world today.

The gospels for the first three Sundays of Easter always feature appearance accounts of the risen Lord to the disciples. During this time we focus on Jesus who has passed through death to risen Life. We become convinced in our believing hearts that this Jesus is still present to us, has conquered death, is truly risen. Now, on this Fourth Sunday of Easter, we are invited to reflect on Jesus' great love and care for us and be assured that he will not abandon us. On Good Shepherd Sunday during this Year B, there is also a strong suggestion that we must take up Jesus' mission through our discipleship (especially pronounced in the other two readings). This notion of our taking up and continuing Jesus' mission moves us into the second half of the Easter season when the gospels explicitly focus on us as disciples. These last three Sunday gospels of Easter prepare us for the celebration of the descent of the Spirit at Pentecost, a Spirit who now dwells within us, conforms us to Christ, and strengthens us to take up his saving mission.

About Liturgical Music

Music suggestions: The refrain of Rory Cooney's "Heart of a Shepherd/El Corazon de un Buen Pastor" (G3; choral setting GIA G-6720) relates Jesus' shepherding care for us with our call to shepherd others: "If you love me, feed my lambs; Be my heart, my voice, my hands. If you love me, feed my sheep. And for my part, I give you the heart of a shepherd." Moreover, the piece weds old traditions with new by using Gelineau's classic setting of Psalm 23 for the verses. This would be a particularly fitting Communion song on this Good Shepherd Sunday.

The collective "I" of the psalms and of liturgical singing: Typical of many psalms, this Sunday's responsorial psalm is expressed for the most part in first-person singular. The psalms are a good example of texts where the use of the first-person singular is not individualistic, but communal. For the Israelites, the "I" of the psalms was always collective. Even when alone, an Israelite always prayed within the context of the communal identity of God's chosen people. Such collective understanding also characterizes our liturgical praying as the community of the church. Liturgical prayer is always a participation in our common identity as God's people. In these verses from Psalm 118, for example, it is *we* who give God thanks for having answered *us* by being *our* savior. We need to keep this collective understanding in mind in all our liturgical singing. Songs with "me" and "I" language that focus us on individualized, private prayer are not suitable for liturgy. Songs that, like the psalms, draw us to a collective understanding of "I" support liturgical prayer. The issue is not the use of "I" language, but whether this use draws our attention inward to private prayer or outward to shared identity and mission.

✝ SPIRITUALITY

GOSPEL ACCLAMATION
John 15:4a, 5b

R⁊. Alleluia, alleluia.
Remain in me as I remain in you, says the
Lord.
Whoever remains in me will bear much
fruit.
R⁊. Alleluia, alleluia.

Gospel

John 15:1-8; L53B

Jesus said to his disciples:
"I am the true vine, and my
Father is the vine grower.
He takes away every branch in me
that does not bear fruit,
and every one that does he prunes
so that it bears more fruit.
You are already pruned because of the
word that I spoke to you.
Remain in me, as I remain in you.
Just as a branch cannot bear fruit on
its own
unless it remains on the vine,
so neither can you unless you remain
in me.
I am the vine, you are the branches.
Whoever remains in me and I in him
will bear much fruit,
because without me you can do
nothing.
Anyone who does not remain in me
will be thrown out like a branch and
wither;
people will gather them and throw
them into a fire
and they will be burned.
If you remain in me and my words
remain in you,
ask for whatever you want and it will
be done for you.
By this is my Father glorified,
that you bear much fruit and become
my disciples."

Reflecting on the Gospel

A well-kept and appealing landscape takes many hours of work. Left without care, the shrubs become unkempt, the grass looks like hay, the flowers become leggy. Cutting back, cutting down, cutting away is what brings out the beauty of a landscape. This kind of work is more than a matter of simple tidiness. It shows that the people who live on the property care. In the gospel, Jesus metaphorically speaks of his Father's pruning us branches who are attached to the vine who is Jesus. God's care for us underlies the oft-repeated gospel words remain, fruit, vine, branch.

Just as God planted and tended the true vine Jesus, so does God tend us—prune us—so that we, too, might "bear much fruit." God prunes from us whatever does not give life, and nourishes within us whatever does. Our remaining in Jesus, our bearing fruit as disciples, our believing in the Son and keeping the commandments (see second reading) are all the work of the Father who tends with great care the risen Life we share with Jesus.

The pruning of which Jesus speaks in this gospel is simply a means to an end. The end is the bearing of much fruit. To this end, Jesus' word has a twofold purpose. On the one hand, his word is prophetic and prunes whatever drains life out of his disciples. On the other, his word is the very sap of life that enables disciples to remain in him and bear fruit. True discipleship is to "remain" in Jesus. Only then does his risen Life bloom in us for all to see.

The good fruit we bear when we remain in Jesus is witnessing to Gospel living, drawing others to the Life Jesus offers in the Holy Spirit, and glorifying the Father by the choices we make to live as Jesus taught us. True discipleship is about bearing this fruit. True discipleship, on the one hand, is very personal and at hand: we must remain in Jesus, grow in our relationship with him, and listen to his words and take them into our heart as a habit of living. On the other hand, true discipleship is very other-centered and broad: we must reach out to the whole world. The fruit we bear by remaining in Jesus is continuing his ministry of bringing salvation to all people. Oh, how sweet is this fruit!

Living the Paschal Mystery

In the first reading the disciples were afraid to relate to Saul because of his past reputation for persecuting Christians. Barnabas, a member of the community, took Paul under his wings and witnessed to the community on his behalf. In this way was Paul accepted so he could preach the word. Barnabas witnessed to how Paul was "pruned" by his encounter with the risen Jesus, an encounter so intense that he was "pruned" from his old zealous hatred of this new Jewish sect and became a disciple himself, one who "remained" in Jesus.

Part of our living the paschal mystery—its dying and rising—requires that we be willing to be pruned. We must allow God to tend us, so that we might rid ourselves of whatever gets in the way of our being a faithful disciple who not only proclaims the Gospel, but also lives it in "deed and truth." First of all, this means that we must witness to an intimate relationship with God. We do this through prayer and worship—both private and public acts of glorifying God. We also witness in "deed and truth" through how we relate to others. Taking someone troubled under our wing to help them is but one example of how we remain in Jesus through our caring for others.

Focusing the Gospel

Key words and phrases: I am the true vine, prunes, word that I spoke to you, remain in me, bear much fruit

To the point: The pruning of which Jesus speaks in this gospel is simply a means to an end. The end is the bearing of much fruit. To this end, Jesus' word has a twofold purpose. On the one hand, his word is prophetic and prunes whatever drains life out of his disciples. On the other, his word is the very sap of life that enables disciples to remain in him and bear fruit. True discipleship is to "remain" in Jesus. Only then does his risen Life bloom in us for all to see.

Connecting the Gospel

to the second reading: In the gospel, Jesus tells us that we remain in him and bear fruit through the power of his word abiding in us. In the second reading, John teaches that we remain in Jesus by believing in him and living his commandment of love. In the gospel, we remain in Jesus through the gift of his word. In the second reading, we remain in Jesus through our gift of believing and loving.

to experience: We tend to think that the word "remaining" implies being stagnant, staying put, not moving forward. Paradoxically, "remaining" in Jesus means growing, changing, and bearing fruit.

Connecting the Responsorial Psalm

to the readings: An Israelite facing trouble, danger, or death typically vowed to offer God a thanksgiving sacrifice and to proclaim God's saving deeds before the world if God would intervene to save. This is the meaning of the first line of this Sunday's responsorial psalm. What is the vow we fulfill as we sing these words this Sunday? Having been saved through the life, death, and resurrection of Jesus Christ, we vow to "remain" joined to him as a branch to the vine (gospel). We fulfill this vow by believing in him, by loving one another not only in word but also in deed (second reading). We fulfill this vow by letting Jesus' words run through our being as life-giving sap, and by allowing God to do whatever pruning is necessary that we may bear fruit (gospel). By fulfilling our vow, we draw all people, those living and those dead, even those not yet born, to worship and serve the God who saves (psalm).

to psalmist preparation: On Palm Sunday you sang parts of Psalm 22 as a lament. On this, the Fifth Sunday of Easter, you sing verses from Psalm 22 in which the cries of abandonment have been transformed into words of praise for the God who saves. What will help you move from one way of singing this psalm to another? What "pruning" might God need to do within you for this to happen?

**ASSEMBLY &
FAITH-SHARING GROUPS**
- I "remain" in Jesus when I . . .
- Jesus' word has pruned me in these ways . . . The pruning that yet needs to happen is . . .
- The fruit my discipleship has already borne is . . . New fruit that I sense is budding in me is . . .

PRESIDERS
I call the community to "remain in" Jesus by . . . The community helps me to "remain in" Jesus by . . .

DEACONS
I most surely bear Jesus' word of hope and compassion to those I serve when I . . .

HOSPITALITY MINISTERS
The manner of my welcome helps the assembly "remain in" Jesus when I . . .

MUSIC MINISTERS
My music ministry bears the fruit of deeper participation on the part of assembly when I . . .

ALTAR MINISTERS
The abundant fruit my service at the altar bears is . . .

LECTORS
My proclamation of the word bears fruit "in deed and truth" (second reading) when . . .

**EXTRAORDINARY MINISTERS
OF HOLY COMMUNION**
My ministry makes visible the unity of the Vine and the branches as I . . .

Model Rite for the Blessing and Sprinkling of Water

Presider: Dear friends, through baptism we become branches grafted onto the vine who is Christ. As we are sprinkled with this water, may we renew our commitment to remain in Christ . . . [pause]

> [continue with The Roman Missal, Appendix II]

Homily Points

• Those who tend vineyards regularly prune the grapevines of the suckers that drain the vines of life, yet do not produce any fruit. After the pruning, the vines look bare and lifeless. With sun, water, and the right time, however, they burst forth in new and healthy growth. Grapevines do not choose to be pruned in order to produce fruit. We, however, must make a choice to be pruned and produce fruit.

• Jesus' word is the life force that prunes disciples so that they may bear fruit. His word is revelation of himself, gift of his Spirit, and expression of his relationship with his Father and his disciples. To remain in the risen Jesus is to share in the power of his risen Life and to bear fruit. This is a choice we must make.

• Jesus' word prunes whatever in our life hinders us from choosing to remain fruitful branches on the Vine. Jesus' word comes to us through the proclamation of Scripture, to be sure. His word also comes to us in other ways: in the loving correction offered by another, in a gentle prod to make a good choice for our life, in a cry for help from someone in need. Responding to any word from the risen Jesus nurtures our growth and life, strengthens our relationship to the Vine, and enables us to produce visible fruit in our own lives. This fruit, in turn, may become Jesus' pruning word for another.

Model Universal Prayer (Prayer of the Faithful)

Presider: God is the faithful Vine-Grower who tends us lovingly. We can be confident that God hears our prayers.

Response:

Lord, hear our prayer.

Cantor:

we pray to the Lord,

That all members of the church heed Jesus' life-giving word and bear much fruit . . . [pause]

That all people of the world come to salvation by hearing and acting on God's word . . . [pause]

That the sick and the suffering receive the fruit of the compassionate love of this community . . . [pause]

That those initiated at Easter always remain in Christ, growing in love and truth . . . [pause]

That each of us remain in Jesus and obey his commands . . . [pause]

Presider: Gracious God, you carefully watch over us and help us to bear the fruit of your love: hear these our prayers that we might always remain in your risen Son. We pray through that same Son, Jesus Christ our Lord. **Amen.**

COLLECT

Let us pray

Pause for silent prayer

Almighty ever-living God,
constantly accomplish the Paschal
    Mystery within us,
that those you were pleased to make new
    in Holy Baptism
may, under your protective care, bear
    much fruit
and come to the joys of life eternal.
Through our Lord Jesus Christ, your Son,
who lives and reigns with you in the unity
    of the Holy Spirit,
one God, for ever and ever. **Amen.**

FIRST READING   Acts 9:26-31

When Saul arrived in Jerusalem he tried to
        join the disciples,
    but they were all afraid of him,
    not believing that he was a disciple.
Then Barnabas took charge of him and
        brought him to the apostles,
    and he reported to them how he had
        seen the Lord,
    and that he had spoken to him,
    and how in Damascus he had spoken
        out boldly in the name of Jesus.
He moved about freely with them in
        Jerusalem,
    and spoke out boldly in the name of the
        Lord.
He also spoke and debated with the
        Hellenists,
    but they tried to kill him.
And when the brothers learned of this,
    they took him down to Caesarea
    and sent him on his way to Tarsus.

The church throughout all Judea, Galilee,
        and Samaria was at peace.
It was being built up and walked in the
        fear of the Lord,
    and with the consolation of the Holy
        Spirit it grew in numbers.

RESPONSORIAL PSALM

Ps 22:26-27, 28, 30, 31-32

℟. (26a) I will praise you, Lord, in the assembly of your people.
    or:
℟. Alleluia.

I will fulfill my vows before those who fear
        the LORD.
    The lowly shall eat their fill;
they who seek the LORD shall praise him:
    "May your hearts live forever!"

℟. I will praise you, Lord, in the assembly of your people.
    or:
℟. Alleluia.

All the ends of the earth
   shall remember and turn to the LORD;
all the families of the nations
   shall bow down before him.

℟. I will praise you, Lord, in the assembly
of your people.
   or:
℟. Alleluia.

To him alone shall bow down
   all who sleep in the earth;
before him shall bend
   all who go down into the dust.

℟. I will praise you, Lord, in the assembly
of your people.
   or:
℟. Alleluia.

And to him my soul shall live;
   my descendants shall serve him.
Let the coming generation be told of the
      LORD
   that they may proclaim to a people yet
         to be born
   the justice he has shown.

℟. I will praise you, Lord, in the assembly
of your people.
   or:
℟. Alleluia.

SECOND READING
1 John 3:18-24

Children, let us love not in word or speech
   but in deed and truth.

Now this is how we shall know that we
      belong to the truth
   and reassure our hearts before him
   in whatever our hearts condemn,
   for God is greater than our hearts and
      knows everything.
Beloved, if our hearts do not condemn us,
   we have confidence in God
   and receive from him whatever we ask,
   because we keep his commandments
      and do what pleases him.
And his commandment is this:
   we should believe in the name of his
      Son, Jesus Christ,
   and love one another just as he
      commanded us.
Those who keep his commandments
   remain in him, and he in them,
   and the way we know that he remains
      in us
   is from the Spirit he gave us.

About Liturgy

Liturgy of the Word: One way to remain in the risen Christ is to allow God's words to remain in us, shape us, and help us bear fruit. This suggests that the Liturgy of the Word during Mass is more than just moral exhortation or a structural element of the liturgy that brings us to the Liturgy of the Eucharist. In the proclamation of the word we are being "pruned" so that we can remain in Christ. In the proclamation of the word we open ourselves to being shaped by Christ so that we can bear the fruit of making present God's reign in a world that is redeemed, but also torn by strife and selfishness. The proclamation of the word helps us hunger for the Bread of Life and Cup of Salvation that we receive during the Liturgy of the Eucharist, God's nourishment for our Life and fruitfulness.

   Clearly, good proclamation is essential if the Liturgy of the Word is to be taken into our hearts, made part of us, and lived each day. Proclamation is more than good reading—it implies that the lector has lived the word in his or her life (in "deed and truth"), is committed to its message, and allows the word to remain in him or her. Without this the word cannot be a living word nor can it change us so that we can be more fruitful.

About Liturgical Music

Music suggestions: The text of Thomas Troeger's "The Branch That Bends with Clustered Fruit" (HG) is drawn directly from this Sunday's gospel passage. Another hymn directly based on this gospel is John Bell's "I Am the Vine" (W4). Both hymns would work well as a reflection on the gospel during the preparation of the gifts. Songs directly connected to this Sunday's gospel and suitable for Communion include "We Have Been Told" and "Now We Remain" (both found in many resources), Steven Warner's "I Am the Vine" (WC, WS), and Delores Dufner's "Make Your Home in Me" (WC). Bob Hurd's Communion song "I Am the Way and the Truth and the Life" (BB) provides specific verses for the gospel reading from Year B. The verses given for Year C would also fit well on this Sunday. In John A. Dalles's "God, Bless Your Church with Strength!" (W4), we ask, "God, bless your Church with life! May all our branches thrive, Unblemished, wholesome, bearing fruit, Abundantly alive. From you, one Holy Vine, In freedom may we grow. Sustain us in our mission, Lord, Your life and peace to show." Both text and tune would make this hymn a strong recessional song.

SPIRITUALITY

GOSPEL ACCLAMATION
John 14:23

R︂. Alleluia, alleluia.
Whoever loves me will keep my word, says the
    Lord,
and my Father will love him and we will come
    to him.
R︂. Alleluia, alleluia.

Gospel

John 15:9-17; L56B

**Jesus said to his disciples:
"As the Father loves me, so I also
        love you.
Remain in my love.
If you keep my commandments,
        you will remain in my love,
    just as I have kept my
        Father's commandments
    and remain in his love.**

**"I have told you this so that my joy may
        be in you
    and your joy might be complete.
This is my commandment: love one
        another as I love you.
No one has greater love than this,
    to lay down one's life for one's
        friends.
You are my friends if you do what I
        command you.
I no longer call you slaves,
    because a slave does not know what
        his master is doing.
I have called you friends,
    because I have told you everything I
        have heard from my Father.
It was not you who chose me, but I who
        chose you
    and appointed you to go and bear
        fruit that will remain,
    so that whatever you ask the Father
        in my name he may give you.
This I command you: love one another."**

Reflecting on the Gospel

The gospel begins with God, not us. It describes in sweeping detail the unparalleled, intimate relationship to which the Father and Jesus invite us: chosen by them, given a share in their joy, called friends by them, told everything by them, appointed by them to bear fruit, and given whatever we ask in Jesus' name. In response, we are to incarnate this divine-human relationship in our relationships with each other: "love one another as I love you." God's love is so freely and lavishly given. In turn, we are to empty ourselves and give that love to those we meet. We are not to love on our terms; we are to love *as* Jesus has loved us. This love is demanding; this is the only love that brings us lasting joy.

Immediately after Jesus expresses the desire that his joy become complete in us, he commands us to "love one another." What is his joy? The deep resonance of risen Life that arises from being faithful to the Father's will. What is the love he commands? Laying "down one's life." Joy and love are the Easter mystery made visible. Love always brings us to Good Friday, because then we gaze upon the Jesus who lays down his life. This Jesus calls us to lay down our own life, to give ourselves over to the kind of self-giving life that brings Life to others. Joy always proclaims Easter Sunday, that day when Life burst forth from death. We who remain in Jesus' love and welcome his joy in us embody the Easter mystery, make visible God's saving events, witness to bearing the fruit of the Father's gift of Life.

What may sound like a convoluted gospel text using the word love way too many times (nine times!) boils down to something really quite simple: live the Easter mystery every day of our lives. The second reading and gospel help us understand how we are to bring our Easter living down to something concrete and measurable. God expressed divine love by sending the Son "as expiation for our sins" (second reading). Likewise, we express our love by "laying down" our lives (gospel). Love is no "pie-in-the-sky" feeling as our contemporary society might have us believe. Instead love is laying down one's life by caring for others, keeping God's commandments, treating everyone as friend. Jesus' love for us is the model: he sacrificed his life, so must we; he overcame death, so must we overcome our own reluctance to die to self for the good of others. Our joy can be complete only when we love as Jesus did.

Living the Paschal Mystery

The gospel command to "love one another" demands a different kind of love than is projected by the media and society in general. Our love for one another is to emulate Jesus' love—a love that is total, demanding, self-emptying, self-giving. Jesus doesn't ask us to do anything that he hasn't done first.

Yes, the command is simple: "love one another." The demand is imposing: lay down our lives. Keeping God's commandments is laying down our lives—we surrender our will to doing God's will and in this is the dying. Caring for and reaching out to others is laying down our lives—also a dying. Doing the little things every day not because we have to but because we see the other as the beloved of God is dying. We choose all these and other ways of dying because we know this is love and love is risen Life rising to kiss us with a share in divinity. And our joy is complete when we love in this way—as Jesus loves us.

Focusing the Gospel

Key words and phrases: kept my Father's commandments, my joy, your joy might be complete, love one another, lay down one's life

To the point: Immediately after Jesus expresses the desire that his joy become complete in us, he commands us to "love one another." What is his joy? The deep resonance of risen Life that arises from being faithful to the Father's will. What is the love he commands? Laying "down one's life." Joy and love are the Easter mystery made visible.

Connecting the Gospel

to the second reading: The joy we experience and the love we show do not originate with us. They are "revealed to us" (second reading) by God through whose Son we have risen Life.

to experience: Incidental happiness is commonly mistaken for joy; a fleeting feeling of attraction or desire is commonly mistaken for love. The gospel speaks of both joy and love and intimates they are abiding gifts of the Spirit that change who we are and how we live.

Connecting the Responsorial Psalm

to the readings: The full text of Psalm 98 uses the number seven as a literary device to communicate the fullness of God's eschatological plan of salvation. The psalm names God seven times, describes seven divine actions, lists seven divine attributes, and employs seven verbs of praise. The Lectionary uses verses from Psalm 98 for the Christmas Mass during the Day. By using further verses on this, the Sixth Sunday of Easter, the Lectionary is telling us that God's work of salvation begun with the birth of Jesus has come to completion in his resurrection. Already power is falling upon the Gentiles (first reading). John tells us this power is nothing less than God's love (second reading). It is now for us to tell the world (psalm refrain) by giving evidence of this divine power in our loving, joyful manner of living (gospel).

to psalmist preparation: In this responsorial psalm you express the joy of the church that God's saving power has been revealed to all peoples. How does your manner of living—at home, at work, on the street—reveal this joy?

**ASSEMBLY &
FAITH-SHARING GROUPS**
- I experience the joy of the risen Jesus when . . . He is completing his joy in me by . . .
- What helps me love others as Christ has commanded is . . .
- I find it most easy to lay down my life for others when . . . most difficult when . . .

PRESIDERS
The deep resonance of risen Life that I experience through my ministry is . . . This deepens my joy by . . .

DEACONS
My service brings the joy of the risen Jesus to those in need when I . . .

HOSPITALITY MINISTERS
My greeting opens those assembling for liturgy to the gifts of joy and love in that . . .

MUSIC MINISTERS
In my music ministry, the command to love others as Christ loves me is most challenging when . . . It is easiest when . . .

ALTAR MINISTERS
My joy is more evident when serving at the altar when I . . .

LECTORS
My proclamation of the word challenges the assembly to "love one another as I love you" when . . .

**EXTRAORDINARY MINISTERS
OF HOLY COMMUNION**
As a sacrament of love, Holy Communion helps me lay down my life for the good of others in that . . .

Model Rite for the Blessing and Sprinkling of Water

Presider: Dear friends, we ask God to bless this water as a reminder of our baptism through which we were given the gifts of Jesus' own joy and love. Let us renew our commitment to love one another as Jesus loves us and come to complete joy in him . . . [pause]
    [*continue with* The Roman Missal, *Appendix II*]

Homily Points

- From whom do we learn the real meaning of joy and love? From self-giving parents, from the serenity of those who suffer chronic pain, from patient teachers, from hospice caregivers, from those who are faithful to their life commitments, from someone who lives out of deep faith, from . . .

- Jesus is the master teacher of the real meaning of joy and love. He faithfully kept his Father's commandments, he loved unconditionally, he revealed his Father's plan of salvation, he appointed his followers to continue his saving mission and bear fruit, he laid down his life for us.

- The joy of Easter exhibits itself in the persistent, quiet ways we lay down our lives for others. We lay down our lives when we take time to have eye contact and really listen to another, when we spend time with the lonely or seemingly friendless, when we uncomplainingly pursue the mundane tasks of our daily living. In these and many other ways we reveal that we have learned the real meaning of joy and love. We reveal that we are living the Easter mystery.

Model Universal Prayer (Prayer of the Faithful)

Presider: In the joy and love of sharing in Jesus' risen Life, let us make known our needs to God.

Response:

Lord, hear our prayer.

Cantor:

we pray to the Lord,

For all members of the church, may their joy be complete and their love be sure . . . [pause]

For all leaders of the world, may they lay down their lives for the good of their people . . . [pause]

For those without joy and love in their lives, may they come to know the risen Jesus who calls them his friends . . . [pause]

For those newly initiated into the church, may they witness to the joy and love they have received from the risen Jesus . . . [pause]

For each of us here, may we grow in our faithfulness to the Father's will and share more perfectly in Jesus' risen Life . . . [pause]

Presider: Loving God, you sent your Son to live among us, love us to the end, and bring our joy to completion: hear these our prayers that we might enjoy fullness of risen Life with him. We ask this through Christ our Lord. **Amen.**

COLLECT
Let us pray
Pause for silent prayer

Grant, almighty God,
that we may celebrate with heartfelt
        devotion these days of joy,
which we keep in honor of the risen Lord,
and that what we relive in remembrance
we may always hold to in what we do.
Through our Lord Jesus Christ, your Son,
who lives and reigns with you in the unity
        of the Holy Spirit,
one God, for ever and ever. **Amen.**

FIRST READING
Acts 10:25-26, 34-35, 44-48

When Peter entered, Cornelius met him
        and, falling at his feet, paid him
        homage.
Peter, however, raised him up, saying,
        "Get up. I myself am also a human
        being."

Then Peter proceeded to speak and said,
        "In truth, I see that God shows no
        partiality.
Rather, in every nation whoever fears him
        and acts uprightly
        is acceptable to him."

While Peter was still speaking these
        things,
        the Holy Spirit fell upon all who were
        listening to the word.
The circumcised believers who had
        accompanied Peter
        were astounded that the gift of the Holy
        Spirit
        should have been poured out on the
        Gentiles also,
        for they could hear them speaking in
        tongues and glorifying God.
Then Peter responded,
        "Can anyone withhold the water for
        baptizing these people,
        who have received the Holy Spirit even
        as we have?"
He ordered them to be baptized in the
        name of Jesus Christ.

RESPONSORIAL PSALM

Ps 98:1, 2-3, 3-4

℞. (cf. 2b) The Lord has revealed to the nations his saving power.
or:
℞. Alleluia.

Sing to the LORD a new song,
  for he has done wondrous deeds;
his right hand has won victory for him,
  his holy arm.

℞. The Lord has revealed to the nations his saving power.
or:
℞. Alleluia.

The LORD has made his salvation known:
  in the sight of the nations he has
    revealed his justice.
He has remembered his kindness and his
    faithfulness
  toward the house of Israel.

℞. The Lord has revealed to the nations his saving power.
or:
℞. Alleluia.

All the ends of the earth have seen
  the salvation by our God.
Sing joyfully to the LORD, all you lands;
  break into song; sing praise.

℞. The Lord has revealed to the nations his saving power.
or:
℞. Alleluia.

SECOND READING

1 John 4:7-10

Beloved, let us love one another,
  because love is of God;
    everyone who loves is begotten by God
      and knows God.
Whoever is without love does not know
    God, for God is love.
In this way the love of God was revealed
    to us:
  God sent his only Son into the world
  so that we might have life through him.
In this is love:
  not that we have loved God, but that he
    loved us
  and sent his Son as expiation for our
    sins.

About Liturgy

Eucharist as love feast: The *Didache* (the "Teachings"), a church document probably originating from early in the second century, is divided into two parts. The first describes "two ways" of conducting oneself: do good and live, or do evil and die. The second part of this important document reports on early church services. Chapters 9 and 10 describe what today we call the Mass. Scholars are divided whether this really refers to a celebration of the Lord's Supper, or an *agape* (love) banquet. What is clear in both parts is that love and caring for one another are essential for how Christians are to conduct themselves and how Christians are to worship.

Eucharist is a celebration of a love feast from two directions. First, in the Eucharist God expresses divine love and care for us in giving us the Body and Blood of our Lord Jesus Christ for our nourishment and strength. Each celebration makes present Jesus' supreme act of self-giving to us. From our direction, Eucharist is not a private act. It is always the act of the whole church for the whole church, an expression of the community's unity in the Body of Christ which is made concrete in acts of charity and goodness, especially toward the less fortunate. At any number of places in the eucharistic celebration we are reminded of our bond of love and charity toward one another: in the times we ask for forgiveness for wrongdoing; in praying for the needs of the church, world, those in need, and for the local community during the universal prayer (prayer of the faithful); in presenting our gifts of bread and wine, of goods for the poor, of ourselves to be transformed; in the sign of peace where we embrace each other as members of Christ's Body, beloved of God and each other; in Holy Communion where we are fed at God's lavish messianic banquet table.

Eucharist is always a love feast, reminding us that our first responsibility as baptized members of the Body of Christ is to do as Jesus taught us: love one another as he has loved us.

Mother's Day: This Sunday is Mother's Day, and although we never focus our weekly celebration of the resurrection on this civil holiday, nevertheless it is always fitting to remind ourselves of how good mothers model so well for us the kind of self-giving love that Jesus invites. There may be another intention added to the prayer of the faithful, for example, "That all mothers nurture the children in their care and love unconditionally as Jesus loves us . . . [pause]." The Book of Blessings gives an "Order for the Blessing of Mothers on Mother's Day" (chapter 55).

About Liturgical Music

Music suggestions: James Quinn's "This Is My Will" (HG) is directly related to this Sunday's gospel passage, and would make a good reflection during the preparation of the gifts. Steve Janco's verse-refrain setting of the same text, "A New Commandment" (WC, WS), would be a fitting Communion song. Other good choices for this Sunday include "No Greater Love" (found in many resources); "Christians, Let Us Love One Another" (BB, JS3); "We Have Been Told" (found in many resources); Bob Dufford's "Love One Another" (BB, JS3); and any setting of "Ubi Caritas."

SPIRITUALITY

GOSPEL ACCLAMATION
Matt 28:19a, 20b

R⁊. Alleluia, alleluia.
Go and teach all nations, says the Lord;
I am with you always, until the end of
    the world.
R⁊. Alleluia, alleluia.

Gospel

Mark 16:15-20; L58B

Jesus said to his disciples:
    "Go into the whole
        world
    and proclaim the gospel
        to every creature.
Whoever believes and is
        baptized will be saved;
    whoever does not believe
        will be condemned.
These signs will accompany those who
        believe:
    in my name they will drive out
        demons,
    they will speak new languages.
They will pick up serpents with their
        hands,
    and if they drink any deadly thing, it
        will not harm them.
They will lay hands on the sick, and
        they will recover."

So then the Lord Jesus, after he spoke
        to them,
    was taken up into heaven
    and took his seat at the right hand of
        God.
But they went forth and preached
        everywhere,
    while the Lord worked with them
    and confirmed the word through
        accompanying signs.

Reflecting on the Gospel

When a very fine school principal retires, we might overhear one of the teachers say, "It will be difficult for the school board to fill her shoes." Or if a skilled and versatile worker dies of a heart attack, the boss might say, "It will be difficult to fill his shoes." Filling the shoes of someone beloved, someone uniquely qualified, someone highly professional can be pretty daunting. Personalities definitely play a part. So, it's not simply a matter of getting the work done; it's also a matter of how the work gets done, which raises the question of relationship. The better one relates to others, the more difficult it is to fill that person's shoes when he or she is gone. In this gospel, Jesus is taking his leave of the disciples. He commissions them to fill his shoes. My! Really?

The ascension marks the completion of Jesus' historical ministry and the beginning of our own commission to proclaim the Gospel. We are not forced to proclaim the Gospel, nor do we do this on our own authority. We undertake our mission "through the Holy Spirit" (first reading) and manifest the Holy Spirit through our mission. But always the mission is Christ's. At first this might seem an impossible commission: how can we expect to fill Jesus' shoes? On our own authority we cannot. In addition to his commission to "proclaim the gospel," Jesus also promised his disciples that signs would accompany their work attesting that Jesus remains with them.

What an awesome honor it is to be disciples of Christ—we fill his shoes! What meaning this accords the ascension—by returning to his rightful place at the hand of God, Jesus entrusts his mission to us. As the Jesus of history takes his leave of this world, it is clear that he intends his saving mission to continue. Seemingly without question, fear, or hesitation, the disciples "went forth." But they did not go forth alone: "the Lord worked with them." The mission, the work, and the signs are of the Lord Jesus. The disciples "who went forth and preached everywhere" were of the Lord Jesus. This relationship is the guarantee of Jesus' continued mission. So the gospel raises this question for disciples today: Are we of the Lord Jesus?

Living the Paschal Mystery

Before we even celebrate Pentecost we are already hearing about our taking up the mission of Christ. This mission describes our Christian living—preaching the Gospel. Ascension is a call to all the baptized, reminding us that baptism is far more than having original sin taken away; it is a receiving of the Spirit by which we are grafted onto the Body of Christ. Baptism is our Pentecost and it includes a mission. It initiates us into a way of life whereby we are of the Lord Jesus.

The gospel reminds us that the bearers of the Good News—those who continue Jesus' saving mission today—are *ordinary people*. This would seem to be an overwhelming and impossible task. How can we fill Jesus' shoes and continue the divine saving work? We can't, on our own. But Jesus assured us that he would work with us. Always, the mission is Christ's and we accomplish it by the strength and life of the Spirit who dwells in us who are baptized. It is the Spirit who works in us. This is why ordinary people can with enthusiasm, commitment, and love—and without question, fear, or hesitation—take up Jesus' saving mission.

Focusing the Gospel

Key words and phrases: proclaim the gospel, signs, they went forth, the Lord worked with them

To the point: As the Jesus of history takes his leave of this world, it is clear that he intends his saving mission to continue. Seemingly without question, fear, or hesitation, the disciples "went forth." But they did not go forth alone: "the Lord worked with them." The mission, the work, and the signs are of the Lord Jesus. The disciples "who went forth and preached everywhere" were of the Lord Jesus. So the gospel raises this question for disciples today: Are we of the Lord Jesus?

Connecting the Gospel

to the first reading: In the first reading, before he ascends into heaven, the risen Jesus promises those gathered that they would receive the power of the Holy Spirit. This Holy Spirit is the Presence of the risen Christ within them, ensuring that it is the Lord who works in, through, and with them as they preach the gospel.

to experience: We can easily let the spectacular signs mentioned in this gospel (driving out demons, speaking new languages, handling snakes, drinking any deadly thing, healing the sick) distract us from the saving work of proclaiming the message of the gospel with humility, gentleness, and bearing with one another (see second reading, Eph 4:1-7, 11-13).

Connecting the Responsorial Psalm

to the readings: The verses we sing from Psalm 47 for the solemnity of the Ascension are about more than the historical event of Jesus' being lifted up into the heavens. They are also a promise about our own ultimate victory over sin and death. Jesus' victory will be our victory, for the one who has commissioned us to proclaim the gospel (gospel) has also promised us the power to do so (first reading). Paul reminds us that each of us has been given the grace of Christ to carry out our particular part of the mission, and this is the "hope of our calling" (second reading). On dark days, then, when we do not know when the kingdom is to come (first reading), when we must wait patiently, remaining faithful to the daily virtues of Christian living (second reading), we can still shout, "God mounts his throne" (psalm refrain) and so do we!

to psalmist preparation: This responsorial psalm is not a memorial of a past event, but a celebration of a present reality. It is a declaration that the risen Christ is ascendant over sin and death, and that we, his Body on earth, will complete the mission he has given us. Victory is his, and victory is ours! Spend some time this week identifying where—in your life, in the church, in the world—you have seen this victory taking place.

ASSEMBLY & FAITH-SHARING GROUPS
- My life proclaims the Gospel when . . . One way I need to grow in living the Gospel is . . .
- One sign that the risen Lord is working in, through, and with me is . . .
- Signs that show I am of the Lord Jesus are . . .

PRESIDERS
What helps me realize that I act not on my own, but in, through, and with the risen Lord is . . .

DEACONS
My serving ministry proclaims in both word and action the saving work of the risen Lord when . . .

HOSPITALITY MINISTERS
My manner of greeting is a sign to others that I am ministering in, through, and with the Lord Jesus when I . . .

MUSIC MINISTERS
I am aware of the risen Lord working through me in my music ministry when . . .

ALTAR MINISTERS
My service at the altar truly proclaims the Gospel because . . .

LECTORS
My proclamation of the word leads the assembly to know that they are of the Lord Jesus when . . .

EXTRAORDINARY MINISTERS OF HOLY COMMUNION
My distribution of Holy Communion continues the mission of the Lord Jesus in that . . .

CELEBRATION

Model Rite for the Blessing and Sprinkling of Water

Presider: Dear friends, today we commemorate the risen Lord's ascension into heaven and his commissioning of the disciples to preach the Gospel. This water is a sign of our own baptism, when we, too, became Jesus' disciples and were commissioned to preach his Good News . . . [pause]

[continue with The Roman Missal, *Appendix II*]

Homily Points

• Team merchandise is big business. Jackets, hats, bumper stickers, license plates, pens, mugs all publicly proclaim that we "belong" to and support a particular team or school. How do we publicly proclaim that we are of the Lord Jesus?

• Jesus accompanied his words with signs of salvation (healing the sick, casting out demons, raising the dead). He continues today to speak and act through those who believe in him. Disciples do not spread the message of salvation on their own, but only in, through, and with the risen Jesus. Nor does the risen Jesus continue his saving mission alone. He continues it in, through, and with us.

• How do we publicly proclaim that we are of the Lord Jesus? We do so when, for example, we sit with someone sick and comfort them, when we help another know right from wrong, when we speak a word of hope to someone struggling with depression. These saving actions are signs that the Lord Jesus is working in, through, and with us.

Model Universal Prayer (Prayer of the Faithful)

Presider: Jesus commands the disciples to go into the whole world and proclaim the Gospel. Let us pray for ourselves and the world.

Response:

Cantor:

May all members of the church proclaim the Gospel in both word and action . . . [pause]

May all leaders of nations govern with humility and gentleness, with patience and love . . . [pause]

May those who are sick or suffering be healed by the gentle touch of this community . . . [pause]

May those newly initiated into the church be strengthened in their baptismal identity and commitment . . . [pause]

May each of us here remain faithful to the Lord Jesus and his saving mission that he has entrusted to us . . . [pause]

Presider: God of life, your risen Son now sits at your right hand in glory: hear these our prayers that we might faithfully continue his mission and make his Gospel known. We ask this through that same Son Jesus Christ. **Amen.**

COLLECT

Let us pray

Pause for silent prayer

Gladden us with holy joys, almighty God,
and make us rejoice with devout
    thanksgiving,
for the Ascension of Christ your Son
is our exaltation,
and, where the Head has gone before in
    glory,
the Body is called to follow in hope.
Through our Lord Jesus Christ, your Son,
who lives and reigns with you in the unity
    of the Holy Spirit,
one God, for ever and ever. **Amen.**

FIRST READING

Acts 1:1-11

In the first book, Theophilus,
    I dealt with all that Jesus did and taught
    until the day he was taken up,
    after giving instructions through the
        Holy Spirit
    to the apostles whom he had chosen.
He presented himself alive to them
    by many proofs after he had suffered,
    appearing to them during forty days
    and speaking about the kingdom of God.
While meeting with them,
    he enjoined them not to depart from
        Jerusalem,
    but to wait for "the promise of the
        Father
    about which you have heard me speak;
    for John baptized with water,
    but in a few days you will be baptized
        with the Holy Spirit."

When they had gathered together they
    asked him,
    "Lord, are you at this time going to
        restore the kingdom to Israel?"
He answered them, "It is not for you to
        know the times or seasons
    that the Father has established by his
        own authority.
But you will receive power when the Holy
        Spirit comes upon you,
    and you will be my witnesses in
        Jerusalem,
    throughout Judea and Samaria,
    and to the ends of the earth."
When he had said this, as they were
    looking on,
    he was lifted up, and a cloud took him
        from their sight.

While they were looking intently at the
   sky as he was going,
      suddenly two men dressed in white
      garments stood beside them.
They said, "Men of Galilee,
   why are you standing there looking at
      the sky?
This Jesus who has been taken up from
   you into heaven
      will return in the same way as you have
      seen him going into heaven."

RESPONSORIAL PSALM
Ps 47:2-3, 6-7, 8-9

R⁊. (6) God mounts his throne to shouts of
joy: a blare of trumpets for the Lord.
   or:
R⊽. Alleluia.

All you peoples, clap your hands,
   shout to God with cries of gladness,
for the LORD, the Most High, the awesome,
   is the great king over all the earth.

R⊽. God mounts his throne to shouts of joy:
a blare of trumpets for the Lord.
   or:
R⊽. Alleluia.

God mounts his throne amid shouts of joy;
   the LORD, amid trumpet blasts.
Sing praise to God, sing praise;
   sing praise to our king, sing praise.

R⊽. God mounts his throne to shouts of joy:
a blare of trumpets for the Lord.
   or:
R⊽. Alleluia.

For king of all the earth is God;
   sing hymns of praise.
God reigns over the nations,
   God sits upon his holy throne.

R⊽. God mounts his throne to shouts of joy:
a blare of trumpets for the Lord.
   or:
R⊽. Alleluia.

SECOND READING
Eph 1:17-23

or Eph 4:1-13

or Eph 4:1-7, 11-13

See Appendix A, p. 297.

About Liturgy

Celebrating Ascension on Sunday: Most dioceses have transferred the celebration of the Ascension to the Seventh Sunday of Easter. In addition to the obvious
pastoral reasons for this decision—more people will actually celebrate this important
mystery if it takes place on Sunday when people are used to coming to Mass—there
are also good theological reasons for this transfer of the festival from Thursday to
Sunday.

   The Synoptic Gospels present a different time frame for the Easter-Ascension-
Pentecost events than does John's gospel. Matthew, Mark, and Luke take a more historical approach: Jesus' ascension happened on the fortieth day after the resurrection
(John's gospel has Jesus ascending on Easter evening), with Pentecost being celebrated
on the fiftieth day. If the Ascension is transferred to Sunday, then Easter, Ascension,
and Pentecost are all celebrated on the same day of the week—Sunday, the Lord's Day.
The advantage of this is that it challenges a historical approach and helps us integrate
these events into a single mystery of salvation. Our annual celebration of the paschal
mystery is not a historical reenactment of those events of long ago, but a here-and-
now celebration of the reality of what it means to be baptized into Jesus' death and
resurrection, what it means for us to receive the Holy Spirit, and how we are to continue today Jesus' saving mission.

   If the celebration of the Ascension is transferred from Thursday to Sunday, then
the liturgy of the Seventh Sunday of Easter is omitted. The Lectionary does make a
rubrical note on the Sixth Sunday of Easter that when the Ascension is transferred,
the second reading and gospel from the Seventh Sunday may be proclaimed on the
Sixth Sunday. If some kind of a rotation between Sixth and Seventh Sunday readings
were observed, then the Seventh Sunday readings would be proclaimed, say, every
other year and not be lost.

About Liturgical Music

Music suggestions: Hymns celebrating the ascension of Christ are readily marked
in every hymnal. Especially suitable this year are ones which connect Christ's ascen-
dancy over heaven and earth with his continuing Presence among us, working within
and through us as his Body on earth. Steven Warner's "Christ Has No Body Now But
Yours" (G3, WC, WS; choral octavo WLP #007284), appealing both for its text and its
musical setting, does this perfectly and would be suitable during the preparation of the
gifts or Communion. Also suitable are songs speaking of our commission to continue
Christ's work, such as, "Go Make of All Disciples" (found in most resources); "Go, Be
Justice" (SS, WC, WS); "Go to the World" (found in
many resources); and "Lord, You Give the Great
Commission" (found in most resources). This last
is rather lengthy for use as a recessional and might
be better sung as an assembly hymn of praise
after Communion. The recessional could then be
accompanied by a rousing instrumental or choral
postlude. Finally, hymns celebrating Christ the
King, such as "Rejoice, the Lord Is King" and
"Crown Him with Many Crowns," would also
be appropriate for this solemnity.

✠ SPIRITUALITY

GOSPEL ACCLAMATION
cf. John 14:18

℟. Alleluia, alleluia.
I will not leave you orphans, says the Lord.
I will come back to you, and your hearts will
    rejoice.
℟. Alleluia, alleluia.

Gospel

John 17:11b-19; L60B

Lifting up his eyes to heaven,
    Jesus prayed, saying:
    "Holy Father, keep them in
        your name that you have
        given me,
    so that they may be one just
        as we are one.
When I was with them I protected them
    in your name that you gave me,
and I guarded them, and none of
    them was lost
except the son of destruction,
in order that the Scripture might be
    fulfilled.
But now I am coming to you.
I speak this in the world
    so that they may share my joy
        completely.
I gave them your word, and the world
    hated them,
    because they do not belong to the
        world
    any more than I belong to the world.
I do not ask that you take them out of
    the world
    but that you keep them from the evil
        one.
They do not belong to the world
    any more than I belong to the world.
Consecrate them in the truth. Your
    word is truth.
As you sent me into the world,
    so I sent them into the world.
And I consecrate myself for them,
    so that they also may be consecrated
        in truth."

Reflecting on the Gospel

Hate is an insidious and destructive emotion. It destroys relationships. It destroys nations. It destroys persons and families. Most of us recoil in face of hatred and avoid situations where we might be on the receiving end of it. Actions which precipitate hatred are those which cut to the core of persons and values.

In this gospel Jesus prays for the disciples whom he knows will take up his saving mission, and in some cases be hated for it. Jesus' mission is at the core of who we are and the Gospel values we embrace. His mission is to bring all people to wholeness and well-being. This necessarily means that people will be challenged to change, to let go, to surrender themselves more fully to doing God's will.

Jesus' prayer for his disciples at the Last Supper is very self-revealing. We can feel his anguish, love, and concern. He knows that if we speak the same words of truth that he spoke, the world will hate us, too. Jesus trusts that his disciples will take up his mission, and knows full well that we will face the same fate as he is facing—death. No wonder his prayer is so intense and personal!

Jesus is not naive about sending out disciples. His lengthy prayer for them (and us) recognizes that there will be resistance ("the world hated them") to the word of truth. Nevertheless, Jesus' prayer assures us that we are never alone. We are one with each other in the Body of Christ. And one with Christ, his Father, and their Spirit. In spite of the hard work of proclaiming the Gospel and meeting resistance, disciples experience joy because their relationship with God is secure.

Such confidence Jesus spawns in us by his prayer! This is our joy: to be so intimately loved, cared for, protected, guarded, and guided by Jesus—all for the sake of the world. Our relationship with God is secure because Jesus prays for us, makes us one with him, and promises that we will remain in him because of his gift of the Holy Spirit (see the second reading). With Jesus, hate can be turned to love. Thus does his saving mission continue.

Living the Paschal Mystery

All of the confidence and protection Jesus promises in his prayer rests on our surrendering to Jesus' discipleship—we must speak words of truth to a world that may or may not receive our words. The evangelist John's "world" is everything that is opposed to Jesus—yet God clearly loves the world because the Son was sent to redeem it. We may die because of the hatred the world has for the truth; but what life we find in God's love!

It doesn't take too many nights of watching the evening news to figure out that much of our world is opposed to Jesus and what he taught. Violence, crime of all kinds, selfishness, disrespect for life and property, hatred, abject greed—the list goes on and on of all the "wrongs" of our world. We may grow discouraged in our discipleship if we think that our deeds must make the nightly news and obviously turn our world around. Yet, this is not what Jesus asks of us.

Jesus asks that we do not "belong to the world" but to him. This means that in our ordinary daily living we act with the same protection and guardianship as Jesus extends to us. We do this by respecting life and property, by paying attention to the needs of those around us, by caring for ourselves. Doing the simple, everyday tasks well and relating to others with genuine love and joy is already an answer to Jesus' gospel prayer for us.

Focusing the Gospel

Key words and phrases: they may be one just as we are one, they may share my joy completely, the world hated them

To the point: Jesus is not naive about sending out disciples. His lengthy prayer for them (and us) recognizes that there will be resistance ("the world hated them") to the word of truth. Nevertheless, Jesus' prayer assures us that we are never alone. We are one with each other in the Body of Christ. And one with Christ, his Father, and their Spirit. In spite of the hard work of proclaiming the Gospel and meeting resistance, disciples experience joy because their relationship with God is secure.

Connecting the Gospel

to the second reading: The whole second reading is a complement to the gospel. It is a grand statement of assurance that we remain in God (gospel: "Father, keep them in your name") when we acknowledge Jesus as Savior and love one another as God loves us.

to experience: Our human response to resistance is to lash out or to run away. When meeting resistance in proclaiming the Gospel, we cannot do either, for fidelity to the mission entrusted to us by the Lord Jesus also means that we act like him by loving, forgiving, showing compassion, suffering, and overcoming obstacles.

Connecting the Responsorial Psalm

to the readings: The second reading for this Sunday assures us of God's love: "God is love, and whoever remains in love remains in God." The responsorial psalm describes this divine love which graces our lives as a kindness and mercy higher than the heavens and wider than the universe; in other words, as a love far beyond any we can ever imagine. In the gospel Jesus asks the Father to protect us. How well he knows from personal experience the demands discipleship will make upon us, the struggles we will face with the "world," the evil we will be called upon to confront. But he also knows from personal experience how much God's love will embrace us as we pursue the mission to which he has called us. Like the early disciples, we can take hold of this mission with decisiveness (first reading). We needn't hesitate, for the God who reigns in heaven (see psalm refrain) dwells in love within us (second reading).

to psalmist preparation: In this responsorial psalm you sing about a God enthroned in heaven whose power is made known on earth through the kindness and forgiveness he showers upon humankind. Christ sends you into the world to make God's kingdom known (gospel). How this week can you show God's kindness? How this week can you reveal God's forgiveness?

**ASSEMBLY &
FAITH-SHARING GROUPS**
- Knowing that Jesus prays for me, I . . .
- Some of the resistance I've met in being faithful to Jesus' mission is . . . Who/what has helped me overcome this resistance is . . .
- Knowing that I am one with Christ, his Father, and their Spirit helps me . . .

PRESIDERS
I pray for my parishioners and . . . I need their prayers when . . .

DEACONS
My service ministry assures those to whom I minister that they are united with God when I . . .

HOSPITALITY MINISTERS
My hospitality helps others come to know that God is always with them when . . .

MUSIC MINISTERS
A tension with the "world" I experience in my music ministry is . . . I sense God's presence helping me deal with this tension by . . .

ALTAR MINISTERS
My service at the altar proclaims that we are one with each other and God when I . . .

LECTORS
My proclamation strengthens the assembly to witness to the Gospel in their daily living when . . .

**EXTRAORDINARY MINISTERS
OF HOLY COMMUNION**
My distribution of Holy Communion is itself a prayer for unity when . . .

Model Rite for the Blessing and Sprinkling of Water

Presider: Dear friends, this water blessed and sprinkled is a reminder of our baptism which strengthens us to speak Christ's word of truth to the world. Let us pray that we are faithful to this mission . . . [pause]

   [*continue with* The Roman Missal, *Appendix II*]

Homily Points

- Keepsakes are mementos we treasure because of their association with important events or beloved persons. When the risen Jesus prays that the Father "keep them in your name," he is really praying that God keep us as God's keepsakes.

- Jesus' prayer for the disciples at the Last Supper reminds us that we truly are the beloved of God: God's "keepsakes" will be kept safe. This assurance gives us strength and courage to pursue the mission that has been made our keepsake.

- If we never experience resistance from others to our way of living, several questions are raised: Are we proclaiming the truth of the Gospel by the way we live? Are we living like we are truly God's "keepsakes"? Do we experience ourselves as God's "keepsakes"?

Model Universal Prayer (Prayer of the Faithful)

Presider: Let us pray that we may be faithful disciples even when God's word of truth is rejected and hated.

Response:

Lord, hear our prayer.

Cantor:

we pray to the Lord,

That all members of the church proclaim the Gospel with vision and courage . . . [pause]

That all peoples be protected and guarded from harm . . . [pause]

That those persecuted or imprisoned for the sake of the Gospel find courage and strength . . . [pause]

That the newly initiated into the church remain always in God's name and share the joy of the risen Lord . . . [pause]

That each of us be the prayer and strength of Jesus to each other . . . [pause]

Presider: Loving God, you guard and protect those who are one with your risen Son Jesus Christ: hear these our prayers that we might be consecrated in truth and one day have everlasting joy with you. We ask this through Christ our Lord. **Amen.**

COLLECT

Let us pray

Pause for silent prayer

Graciously hear our supplications, O Lord,
so that we, who believe that the Savior of
   the human race
is with you in your glory,
may experience, as he promised,
until the end of the world,
his abiding presence among us.
Who lives and reigns with you in the unity
   of the Holy Spirit,
one God, for ever and ever. **Amen.**

FIRST READING

Acts 1:15-17, 20a, 20c-26

Peter stood up in the midst of the brothers
   —there was a group of about one
      hundred and twenty persons
   in the one place—.
He said, "My brothers,
   the Scripture had to be fulfilled
   which the Holy Spirit spoke beforehand
   through the mouth of David, concerning
      Judas,
   who was the guide for those who
      arrested Jesus.
He was numbered among us
   and was allotted a share in this ministry.

"For it is written in the Book of Psalms:
   May another take his office.

"Therefore, it is necessary that one of the
   men
   who accompanied us the whole time
   the Lord Jesus came and went among us,
   beginning from the baptism of John
   until the day on which he was taken up
      from us,
   become with us a witness to his
      resurrection."
So they proposed two, Judas called
   Barsabbas,
   who was also known as Justus, and
      Matthias.
Then they prayed,
   "You, Lord, who know the hearts of all,
   show which one of these two you have
      chosen
   to take the place in this apostolic
      ministry
   from which Judas turned away to go to
      his own place."
Then they gave lots to them, and the lot
   fell upon Matthias,
   and he was counted with the eleven
      apostles.

Change in
Relationship

Jesus / ordered

Woman / Husband

Community

Reia / Jesus / Community

CATECHESIS

RESPONSORIAL PSALM

Ps 103:1-2, 11-12, 19-20

℟. (19a) The Lord has set his throne in heaven.
or:
℟. Alleluia.

Bless the LORD, O my soul;
  and all my being, bless his holy name.
Bless the LORD, O my soul,
  and forget not all his benefits.

℟. The Lord has set his throne in heaven.
or:
℟. Alleluia.

For as the heavens are high above the
    earth,
  so surpassing is his kindness toward
     those who fear him.
As far as the east is from the west,
  so far has he put our transgressions
     from us.

℟. The Lord has set his throne in heaven.
or:
℟. Alleluia.

The LORD has established his throne in
    heaven,
  and his kingdom rules over all.
Bless the LORD, all you his angels,
  you mighty in strength, who do his
    bidding.

℟. The Lord has set his throne in heaven.
or:
℟. Alleluia.

SECOND READING

1 John 4:11-16

Beloved, if God so loved us,
  we also must love one another.
No one has ever seen God.
Yet, if we love one another, God remains
    in us,
  and his love is brought to perfection in
    us.

This is how we know that we remain in
    him and he in us,
  that he has given us of his Spirit.
Moreover, we have seen and testify
  that the Father sent his Son as savior of
    the world.
Whoever acknowledges that Jesus is the
    Son of God,
  God remains in him and he in God.
We have come to know and to believe in
    the love God has for us.

God is love, and whoever remains in love
  remains in God and God in him.

About Liturgy

Historicizing salvation events: We tend to think linearly through the liturgical year, beginning with anticipation of Jesus' birth during Advent; his birth and epiphany during Christmas; beginnings of his public ministry during the first part of Ordinary Time; suffering, death, and resurrection during Lent and Easter; ascension and Pentecost leading to the second part of Ordinary Time. The Lectionary often seems to encourage a historicizing interpretation and this Sunday is a good example. Last Thursday was the celebration of the ascension (in some dioceses in the United States) and so the gospel makes temporal sense when it has Jesus saying, "I am coming to you"; the first reading records an event that also occurs after the ascension.

The point is that liturgy isn't a celebration of historical events (even though they are sometimes put to us in that way); rather, liturgy is the celebration of saving events. This isn't to deny the fact of those historical events, but it is to underscore that liturgy breaks us out of a temporal time frame and helps us focus on God's saving events happening at all times for all peoples.

About Liturgical Music

Music suggestions: Good choices for processional songs this Sunday would be ones expressing the challenge our mission brings but also the hope we have because of Christ's remaining Presence with us. For example, "Alleluia! Sing to Jesus" (found in most resources) could be sung for the entrance, the preparation of the gifts, or the recessional. "Lord of the Dance/I Danced in the Morning" (found in most resources), in which the risen Christ calls us to dance with him "wherever you may be," would be delightful during the preparation of the gifts or as a post-Communion song of praise. The strong imagery of "We Know That Christ Is Raised" (SS, WC, W3) identifies us as the risen Body of Christ. The thought of each verse is continued and completed by succeeding verses. For example, verses 3-4 state, "The Spirit's power stirs the Church of God . . . As Christ's new body takes on flesh and blood. The universe restored and whole will sing." Combined with the powerful tune ENGELBERG this hymn would be excellent for either the entrance procession or a hymn of praise after Communion. Brian Wren's "Christ Is Risen! Shout Hosanna!" (found in many resources) would also make an excellent entrance song, especially because of the lines "Break the bread of new creation Where the world is still in pain. Tell its grim, demonic chorus: 'Christ is risen! Get you gone!'" If the given tune is unfamiliar, another strong melody such as HYFRYDOL or BEACH SPRING or ABBOT'S LEIGH could be substituted. Desmond Tutu's "Goodness Is Stronger Than Evil" (G3, W4, LMGM2) would be a particularly strong recessional song, sending us out with a shout of confidence in our victory over evil and darkness because of "him who loved us." Another strong recessional song would be Kenneth W. Louis's "Go Ye Therefore" (LMGM2) with its repeated assurance, "Don't be afraid!"

MAY 17, 2015

SEVENTH SUNDAY OF EASTER
or CELEBRATION OF ASCENSION

SPIRITUALITY

GOSPEL ACCLAMATION

℟. Alleluia, alleluia.
Come, Holy Spirit, fill the hearts of your faithful
and kindle in them the fire of your love.
℟. Alleluia, alleluia.

Gospel   John 20:19-23; L63B

On the evening of that first day of the
     week,
  when the doors were locked, where
     the disciples were,
  for fear of the Jews,
  Jesus came and stood in their midst
  and said to them, "Peace be with you."
When he had said this, he showed them
     his hands and his side.
The disciples rejoiced when they saw
     the Lord.
Jesus said to them again, "Peace be with you.
As the Father has sent me, so I send you."
And when he had said this, he breathed on
     them and said to them,
  "Receive the Holy Spirit.
Whose sins you forgive are forgiven them,
  and whose sins you retain are retained."

or John 15:26-27; 16:12-15

Jesus said to his disciples:
  "When the Advocate comes whom I will
     send you from the Father,
  the Spirit of truth that proceeds from the
     Father,
  he will testify to me.
And you also testify,
  because you have been with me from the
     beginning.
"I have much more to tell you, but you
     cannot bear it now.
But when he comes, the Spirit of truth,
  he will guide you to all truth.
He will not speak on his own,
  but he will speak what he hears,
  and will declare to you the things that are
     coming.
He will glorify me,
  because he will take from what is mine
     and declare it to you.
Everything that the Father has is mine;
  for this reason I told you that he will take
     from what is mine
  and declare it to you."

Reflecting on the Gospel

We celebrate this Sunday a wondrous and unprecedented gift of God—"the Spirit of truth" given to us. This Spirit of truth God gives is relational. This Spirit of truth changes us—through the Spirit we share a common identity as the Body of Christ and take up a common mission to proclaim the Gospel by the sheer goodness of our lives. The Spirit enables us to live with one another in a new way: with

"love, joy, peace, patience, kindness, generosity," etc. (second reading). The Spirit propels us to engage with the world in a new way: we "testify" (gospel) to the "mighty acts of God" (first reading) through the very way that we live. The truth God gives transforms us and, through us, transforms the world.

According to this gospel, both the Spirit and the disciples testify to Jesus. What is this testimony? It is the revelation that Jesus is of the Father, is the divine Son. Furthermore, this gospel says that the Spirit glorifies Jesus by testifying. So then do we. What is this glory? It is Jesus himself who is the visible Presence of the Father. Like the Spirit of truth, when we testify we also glorify.

This Pentecost commemoration does not simply recall a past event, but celebrates what God is doing within us now. In baptism each of us received the Spirit; that is our Pentecost. The Spirit is not something we have, is not a possession. The Spirit dwells within us as divine Life, enabling us to be faithful and true disciples. The Spirit is given for the sake of mission: to proclaim the gospel ("you also testify"), to be molded as disciples ("the Spirit . . . will guide you to all truth"), and, ultimately, to worship ("glorify me"). The indwelling of the Spirit is a continual Pentecost so that everyone can hear of the "mighty acts of God" (first reading) and thus bring glory to God.

Living the Paschal Mystery

Our daily living is to "testify" to the Spirit of truth who dwells within us. We often think of "truth" in terms of "truths"—dogmas to believe. The gospel leads us to something far more dynamic, relational. The Spirit who dwells in each of us enfleshes within us the "mighty acts of God." Truth is being faithful to the identity and mission offered us. Truth is what is of God.

If we are to be living icons of the Spirit of truth dwelling within us, then the good choices we make daily testify to this divine indwelling. Simply put, Pentecost invites us to act like God! Although our testimony is not about ourselves—it is about the risen Jesus as the Son of God present among us and bringing us to salvation—in one respect it truly is about ourselves. Through the indwelling Spirit we are made members of the Body of Christ. We are living icons of the Spirit of truth, and living icons of the risen Jesus who dwells within and among us.

If we are to exude the fruits of the Spirit (see second reading), we must be willing to die to ourselves. We cannot love another if we do not give of ourselves to others. We cannot have joy if we are turned in on ourselves. We cannot have peace if we are distracted by getting and doing only what we want. We cannot have patience if we do not respect the dignity of others. We cannot have gentleness if we do not see the need in others. We cannot have self-control if we don't put the good of others first. We cannot have any of these fruits if we do not live the wondrous mystery of the Spirit dwelling within us. Come, Holy Spirit!

Focusing the Gospel

Key words and phrases: Spirit of truth . . . will testify to me, you also testify, will glorify me, Everything that the Father has is mine

To the point: According to this gospel, both the Spirit and the disciples testify to Jesus. What is this testimony? The revelation that Jesus is of the Father, is the divine Son. Furthermore, this gospel says that the Spirit glorifies Jesus by testifying. So then do we. What is this glory? Jesus himself who is the visible Presence of the Father. Like the Spirit of truth, when we testify we also glorify.

Connecting the Gospel

to the second reading from Galatians 5:16-25: Having received the Spirit, we are confronted with a choice: to "live by the Spirit" or to live by what is opposed to the Spirit. When we "live by the Spirit," we testify to the truth and give glory to the risen Lord. When we live by what is opposed to the Spirit, we . . .

to experience: Testimonial dinners are held to extol an honoree for some achievement. The one giving testimony usually shares firsthand knowledge of the honoree which helps the other dinner guests come to know this person. Our testifying to the risen Jesus must arise from firsthand knowledge of him which helps others encounter him.

Connecting the Responsorial Psalm

to the readings: In Psalm 104 we beg God to send the Spirit of renewal upon the earth. This Spirit will enable us to receive the truth of God and give testimony to Christ. This Spirit will bear in us the fruits of "love, joy, peace, patience, kindness," and much more (second reading). The Spirit, then, renews the earth by first transforming us. Moreover, the Spirit enables us to communicate the good news of salvation in whatever tongue is necessary for people to hear and understand (first reading). What we pray for in this responsorial psalm, then, is not extraneous to our very selves. Nor is it minuscule in scope. We are asking that the Spirit re-create us so that, through us, the Spirit may re-create the earth (psalm).

to psalmist preparation: As you sing the responsorial psalm for Pentecost, you celebrate the Spirit's wonderful deeds and renewing energies. But you also pray for your own transformation. The renewal of the earth begins within you. Where has the Spirit been leading you to grow in "love, joy, peace, patience, kindness, generosity, faithfulness, gentleness, [and] self-control" (second reading)? Are you willing to allow the Spirit to continue transforming you?

**ASSEMBLY &
FAITH-SHARING GROUPS**
- The testimony I give of the risen Jesus is . . .
- I glorify the risen Jesus when . . .
- The Spirit of truth leads me to . . .

PRESIDERS
My ministry shines forth the glory of the risen Jesus when I . . .

DEACONS
My service builds up the community in the Spirit when I . . .

HOSPITALITY MINISTERS
My greeting makes visible the fruits of the Spirit (see the second reading) when . . .

MUSIC MINISTERS
My music ministry glorifies the risen Jesus when I . . .

ALTAR MINISTERS
The manner of my serving at the altar reveals . . .

LECTORS
I know my preparation for and proclamation of the word are both Spirit-filled when . . .

**EXTRAORDINARY MINISTERS
OF HOLY COMMUNION**
Every time I distribute Holy Communion, I celebrate Pentecost in that . . .

Model Rite for the Blessing and Sprinkling of Water

Presider: Dear friends, we ask God to bless this water as a reminder of the gift of the Spirit given us at baptism. Let us celebrate with great joy and pray to live faithfully the life to which the Spirit calls us . . . [pause]

 [continue with The Roman Missal, *Appendix II]*

Homily Points

- Selected persons testify before congregational committees to the competency and integrity of persons nominated for government positions. Court witnesses testify to the innocence or guilt of defendants. These testimonies are not about the ones testifying. Disciples testify to the truth of who Jesus is. Their testimony is not about themselves.

- On this Pentecost Sunday we celebrate the giving of the Holy Spirit by the risen Jesus to his disciples. This Spirit testifies to Jesus and so do we. This Spirit glorifies Jesus. And so do we. Our giving Jesus glory adds nothing to his greatness. It does, however, reveal our relationship to Jesus.

- We first receive the Holy Spirit at baptism. This initiates an intimate relationship with the risen Lord, his Father, in the Holy Spirit. Growing in our relationship, we learn to testify to the truth of Jesus' saving deeds, becoming more faithful disciples. We testify to Jesus not only through words, but also through our whole manner of living. Like the Spirit of truth given us, when we testify we also glorify. Glorifying the Father, Son, and Holy Spirit describes the very life of a disciple.

Model Universal Prayer (Prayer of the Faithful)

Presider: The Spirit of truth has been given us so that we testify to the risen Jesus. Let us pray that we may be faithful.

Response:

Cantor:

That all members of the church respond faithfully to the enlivening Presence of the Spirit dwelling within them . . . [pause]

That all peoples share in the fullness of salvation . . . [pause]

That those in need be lifted up by the love and care of this community in whom the Spirit dwells . . . [pause]

That those initiated into the church continue to testify to the risen Jesus and bring him glory . . . [pause]

That the Spirit guide each of us to proclaim the Gospel in word and deed with sincerity and truth . . . [pause]

Presider: Gracious God, you send your Spirit to be with us and to guide us in all things: hear these our prayers that we might testify to the risen Jesus by our lives and come to share in his eternal glory. We ask this through Christ our Lord. **Amen.**

COLLECT

Let us pray

Pause for silent prayer

O God, who by the mystery of today's
 great feast
sanctify your whole Church in every
 people and nation,
pour out, we pray, the gifts of the Holy
 Spirit
across the face of the earth
and, with the divine grace that was at work
when the Gospel was first proclaimed,
fill now once more the hearts of believers.
Through our Lord Jesus Christ, your Son,
who lives and reigns with you in the unity
 of the Holy Spirit,
one God, for ever and ever. **Amen.**

FIRST READING

Acts 2:1-11

When the time for Pentecost was fulfilled,
 they were all in one place together.
And suddenly there came from the sky
 a noise like a strong driving wind,
 and it filled the entire house in which
  they were.
Then there appeared to them tongues as
 of fire,
 which parted and came to rest on each
  one of them.
And they were all filled with the Holy Spirit
 and began to speak in different tongues,
 as the Spirit enabled them to proclaim.

Now there were devout Jews from every
 nation under heaven
 staying in Jerusalem.
At this sound, they gathered in a large
 crowd,
 but they were confused
 because each one heard them speaking
  in his own language.
They were astounded, and in amazement
 they asked,
 "Are not all these people who are
  speaking Galileans?
Then how does each of us hear them in
 his native language?
We are Parthians, Medes, and Elamites,
 inhabitants of Mesopotamia, Judea and
  Cappadocia,
 Pontus and Asia, Phrygia and Pamphylia,
 Egypt and the districts of Libya near
  Cyrene,
 as well as travelers from Rome,
 both Jews and converts to Judaism,
 Cretans and Arabs,
 yet we hear them speaking in our own
  tongues
of the mighty acts of God."

RESPONSORIAL PSALM

Ps 104:1, 24, 29-30, 31, 34

R̶⁊. (cf. 30) Lord, send out your Spirit, and renew the face of the earth.
or:
R̶⁊. Alleluia.

Bless the LORD, O my soul!
   O LORD, my God, you are great indeed!
How manifold are your works, O LORD!
   The earth is full of your creatures.

R̶⁊. Lord, send out your Spirit, and renew the face of the earth.
or:
R̶⁊. Alleluia.

If you take away their breath, they perish
   and return to their dust.
When you send forth your spirit, they are created,
   and you renew the face of the earth.

R̶⁊. Lord, send out your Spirit, and renew the face of the earth.
or:
R̶⁊. Alleluia.

May the glory of the LORD endure forever;
   may the LORD be glad in his works!
Pleasing to him be my theme;
   I will be glad in the LORD.

R̶⁊. Lord, send out your Spirit, and renew the face of the earth.
or:
R̶⁊. Alleluia.

SECOND READING

1 Cor 12:3b-7, 12-13

or

Gal 5:16-25

SEQUENCE

See Appendix A, p. 298.

About Liturgy

Pentecost sequence: The Pentecost sequence is a remarkably beautiful composition attributed to the late-twelfth, early-thirteenth century archbishop of Canterbury Stephen Langton. This composition beautifully captures a wide range of actions of the Spirit: the One who brings light, is the source of goods for the poor and all of us, is the comforter, is sweet refreshment, is solace, is healer, is strength, is guide, is source of joy. It would be well to spend some time meditating on all these actions of the Spirit. Moreover, if these actions are attributed to the Spirit, then because of the gift of the Spirit's indwelling we, too, are to live and act in this way.

Optional readings: In addition to the Year A readings (permitted to be used any year), the revised Lectionary has given us an optional set of readings for each of the three years of the Lectionary cycle for Pentecost, and this year we have opted to reflect on those proper for Year B in *Living Liturgy*™. These new choices of readings not only provide us with exposure to more Scripture texts, but they also offer fresh avenues for exploring the insights and meaning of this solemnity.

Memorial Day: Monday is Memorial Day and many parishioners will be celebrating liturgy or attending other memorial services. It would not be appropriate to use patriotic songs either Sunday or Monday at the liturgies because the music at liturgy has its own requirements that are dictated by the liturgy and liturgical year. An intention could be added at the universal prayer (prayer of the faithful) for either Sunday or Monday that might read: That those who have given their lives in defense of the values of our country may enjoy the peace of eternal Life . . . [pause].

About Liturgical Music

The Pentecost sequence: The sequences developed during the Middle Ages as extensions of the Alleluia verse. They were chanted meditations on the word of God. Historically, the sequence was sung after the Alleluia verse before the final Alleluia. In 1974, the sequence was moved to after the last Alleluia. In either position, the sequence acted as a continuation of the Alleluia verse, allowing for a more solemn and extensive procession with the *Book of the Gospels.*

STL, no. 166, indicates the sequence text given in the Lectionary is to be sung; however, a metrical paraphrase that has been given ecclesiastical approval may also be used. STL further states that the sequence may be sung by all present, or in alternation between the assembly and choir or cantor, or by choir or cantor alone. The sequence is to be sung before the Alleluia (GIRM, no. 64). The people remain seated and stand when the Alleluia is begun.

Today only four sequences remain in liturgical use. *Victimae paschali laudes* is required on Easter. *Veni, Sancte Spiritus* is required on Pentecost for the Mass during the Day (when the Mass during the Day replaces the Vigil Mass of Pentecost, the sequence is to be sung). *Lauda, Sion, Salvatorem* is optional for the Most Holy Body and Blood. *Stabat mater dolorosa* is optional for Our Lady of Sorrows.

ORDINARY TIME II

✛ SPIRITUALITY

℟. Alleluia, alleluia.
Glory to the Father, the Son, and the Holy Spirit;
to God who is, who was, and who is to come.
℟. Alleluia, alleluia.

Gospel

Matt 28:16-20; L165B

**The eleven disciples went to Galilee,
to the mountain to which Jesus had
ordered them.
When they all saw him, they
worshiped, but they doubted.
Then Jesus approached and said to
them,
"All power in heaven and on earth
has been given to me.
Go, therefore, and make disciples of all
nations,
baptizing them in the name of the
Father,
and of the Son, and of the Holy
Spirit,
teaching them to observe all that I
have commanded you.
And behold, I am with you always, until
the end of the age."**

Reflecting on the Gospel

Military officers are commissioned; they are given specific authority to carry out the duties of their rank. Sales personnel might earn a commission; they are given a percentage of a sale over and above their regular salary. Etymologically, the word "commission" means to be "sent with." So, someone commissioned might be sent forth with authority and reaps the rewards of a task well done. This year the gospel for this Sunday concludes with what is sometimes called the "Great Commission." No other gospel so explicitly refers to the three Persons of the Most Holy Trinity. We hear the very words of the baptismal formula we use today, and no doubt this gospel passage reflects the baptismal practice of the Matthean community some decades after the historical events of Jesus' life, death, resurrection, and ascension. The disciples are sent forth to "all nations" with the authority of Jesus and they reap the rewards of being faithful to Jesus' command and having Jesus always with them.

In this gospel passage for the solemnity of the Most Holy Trinity, Jesus commands the disciples to baptize "in the name of the Father, and of the Son, and of the Holy Spirit." Jesus reveals his undivided, divine relationship with the Father when he declares, "All power in heaven and on earth has been given to me." Baptism professes our faith in the Holy Trinity and celebrates our insertion into the intimate, relational life of Father, Son, and Holy Spirit.

The depth and intimacy of God's relationship with us leads to our own identity—"we are children of God" and "heirs of God and joint heirs with Christ" (second reading). As children and heirs, we share in the identity of Christ and, therefore, of God (compare 2 Peter 1:4: "share in the divine nature," NABRE). Moreover, we participate in God's saving work because we share in the power and mission of Christ (gospel) through the Spirit (see second reading). To share in divine identity is to share in divine doing—we, too, are to do mighty deeds (see the first reading). To be formed into the identity of Christ, therefore, is to be formed into his mission.

The gospel rather succinctly and clearly lays out the mission with which Jesus charged the disciples (and us) before he ascended into heaven: make disciples, baptize in the name of the Trinity, teach, and observe "all that [Jesus] has commanded." Jesus can entrust this mission to us because we share in his identity through the power of the Spirit. This identity is the fruit of our fidelity. Has anything more wondrous or greater happened before?

Living the Paschal Mystery

Liturgy does for us what the Deuteronomy texts (first reading) did for Israel of old: helps us remember God's mighty deeds and enter into a covenantal relationship with the Divine. Liturgy calls us together to ask, "Who is this God?"

Knowing God isn't something we can find out in the abstract; knowing God is sought and expressed in our own doing—in taking up Christ's mission and living our own privileged identity as daughters and sons of God "until the end of the age." Without doing as Jesus did, we cannot answer "Who is God?" This doing is nothing less than to "suffer with" Christ (second reading), which means a constant dying to self. By our own self-emptying are we filled with the divine identity, are faithful to our own baptismal identity, and continue the mission with which Jesus has entrusted us.

Focusing the Gospel

Key words and phrases: All power in heaven and on earth has been given to me; Go . . . baptizing them in the name of the Father, and of the Son, and of the Holy Spirit

To the point: In this gospel passage for the solemnity of the Most Holy Trinity, Jesus commands the disciples to baptize "in the name of the Father, and of the Son, and of the Holy Spirit." Jesus reveals his undivided, divine relationship with the Father when he declares, "All power in heaven and on earth has been given to me." Baptism professes our faith in the Holy Trinity and celebrates our insertion into the intimate, relational life of Father, Son, and Holy Spirit.

Connecting the Gospel

to the second reading: By calling us children and heirs of God, Paul affirms our intimate relationship with God. This is the relationship into which we are initiated by being baptized "in the name of the Father, and of the Son, and of the Holy Spirit."

to experience: There are intangible realities in everyday living that we know such as love, happiness, joy, peace, sorrow. We experience these intangibles through their effects and our feelings. The Trinity is the mystery of God we behold and embrace. The effect of this triune God in our lives is our very Life.

Connecting the Responsorial Psalm

to the readings: The readings for Trinity Sunday reveal God's desire to relate to human beings with unimaginable intimacy. God takes Israel as "a nation for himself" (first reading). God adopts us as children (second reading). Jesus promises us his personal presence "until the end" (gospel). God chooses us human beings to participate in the intimate personal relationship which is the very core of the divine nature. "Did anything so great ever happen before?" (first reading). The mystery of the Trinity may be beyond our comprehension, but the desire of the Trinity's heart has been revealed to us continually throughout salvation history. The Trinity of divine Persons loves us and has chosen us as its own (psalm refrain). Blessed are we!

to psalmist preparation: As you sing this responsorial psalm refrain, remember that you yourself have been chosen to be God's own. How does this awareness affect your sense of yourself? Remember also that God desires to draw all people into the embrace of the Trinity. How does this awareness affect your sense of others?

ASSEMBLY & FAITH-SHARING GROUPS

- For me, the Trinity touches my life when . . .
- The Trinity influences how I relate to others by . . .
- My baptismal commitment means to me . . .

PRESIDERS

My presiding helps the assembly to see themselves as God's sons and daughters when . . .

DEACONS

My care of those in need incarnates the intimate, relational life of the Trinity by . . .

HOSPITALITY MINISTERS

My greeting helps the gathering assembly see themselves as a trinitarian community when . . .

MUSIC MINISTERS

What helps me do my music ministry "in the name of" the Trinity is . . .

ALTAR MINISTERS

The unobtrusiveness of my ministry reflects the hidden life of the Trinity because . . .

LECTORS

Recalling my baptismal commitment as I prepare to lector affects my proclamation in that . . .

EXTRAORDINARY MINISTERS OF HOLY COMMUNION

Jesus' promise, "I am with you always," is fulfilled in me when . . .

Model Penitential Act

Presider: We honor today the Most Holy Trinity in whose name we have been baptized. Let us prepare for this liturgy by calling to mind the times we have not been faithful to our baptismal commitment . . . [pause]

> Lord Jesus, you are the divine Son of God: Lord . . .
>
> Christ Jesus, you sit at the right hand of the Father: Christ . . .
>
> Lord Jesus, you send your Spirit to be with your church: Lord . . .

Homily Points

• Being born into a family is a birthright. Growing in relationship with family members, accepting their values, sacrificing for their good is a constant choice. While a birth family can be rejected, the reality of being born into a given family cannot be changed. Baptism is our birth into the Trinity and the family of the church. It is our choice to accept or reject this baptismal birthright.

• Jesus commissions his disciples to baptize in the name of the Trinity. Belonging to the Trinity is our baptismal birthright. It is God's unparalleled gift to us to be invited into the intimate, relational life of Father, Son, and Holy Spirit. It is our choice to accept or reject this gift.

• We accept our baptismal family when we, for example, gather with other members of the church for liturgy, share ourselves and our goods with those less fortunate than us, forgive those who hurt us, help others grow in their love of God. We reject our baptismal family when we turn against another, destroy another's reputation with idle gossip, do not take time for prayer, put ourselves first. God gives us all the help we need to choose to live our baptismal birthright into the intimate Life of the Most Holy Trinity. Do we choose it?

Model Universal Prayer (Prayer of the Faithful)

Presider: Our triune God loves us and cares for us. Let us make known our needs to this God of mystery and wonder.

Response:

Lord, hear our prayer.

Cantor:

we pray to the Lord,

That all members of the church choose to live their baptismal commitment with love and courage . . . [pause]

That all peoples of the world may come to salvation . . . [pause]

That the outcast and the stranger be embraced as family by this community of care and concern . . . [pause]

That each of us deepen our relationship with the triune God by growing in our relationships with each other . . . [pause]

Presider: Holy God, you are present to your people in your mighty deeds and dwell within us by your grace: hear these our prayers that we might one day enjoy fullness of Life with you. We ask this in Christ and through the Holy Spirit, one God, for ever and ever. **Amen.**

COLLECT

Let us pray

Pause for silent prayer

God our Father, who by sending into the world
the Word of truth and the Spirit of sanctification
made known to the human race your wondrous mystery,
grant us, we pray, that in professing the true faith,
we may acknowledge the Trinity of eternal glory
and adore your Unity, powerful in majesty.
Through our Lord Jesus Christ, your Son,
who lives and reigns with you in the unity of the Holy Spirit,
one God, for ever and ever. **Amen.**

FIRST READING

Deut 4:32-34, 39-40

Moses said to the people:
> "Ask now of the days of old, before your time,
> ever since God created man upon the earth;
> ask from one end of the sky to the other:
> Did anything so great ever happen before?
> Was it ever heard of?
> Did a people ever hear the voice of God speaking from the midst of fire, as you did, and live?
> Or did any god venture to go and take a nation for himself
> from the midst of another nation,
> by testings, by signs and wonders, by war,
> with strong hand and outstretched arm,
> and by great terrors,
> all of which the LORD, your God,
> did for you in Egypt before your very eyes?
> This is why you must now know,
> and fix in your heart, that the LORD is God
> in the heavens above and on earth below,
> and that there is no other.
> You must keep his statutes and commandments that I enjoin on you today,
> that you and your children after you may prosper,
> and that you may have long life on the land
> which the LORD, your God, is giving you forever."

RESPONSORIAL PSALM
Ps 33:4-5, 6, 9, 18-19, 20, 22

R̶}. (12b) Blessed the people the Lord has chosen to be his own.

Upright is the word of the LORD,
   and all his works are trustworthy.
He loves justice and right;
   of the kindness of the LORD the earth
      is full.

R̶}. Blessed the people the Lord has chosen to be his own.

By the word of the LORD the heavens were
      made;
   by the breath of his mouth all their
      host.
For he spoke, and it was made;
   he commanded, and it stood forth.

R̶}. Blessed the people the Lord has chosen to be his own.

See, the eyes of the LORD are upon those
      who fear him,
   upon those who hope for his kindness,
to deliver them from death
   and preserve them in spite of famine.

R̶}. Blessed the people the Lord has chosen to be his own.

Our soul waits for the LORD,
   who is our help and our shield.
May your kindness, O LORD, be upon us
   who have put our hope in you.

R̶}. Blessed the people the Lord has chosen to be his own.

SECOND READING
Rom 8:14-17

Brothers and sisters:
Those who are led by the Spirit of God are
      sons of God.
For you did not receive a spirit of slavery
      to fall back into fear,
   but you received a Spirit of adoption,
      through whom we cry, "Abba, Father!"
The Spirit himself bears witness with our
      spirit
   that we are children of God,
   and if children, then heirs,
   heirs of God and joint heirs with Christ,
   if only we suffer with him
   so that we may also be glorified with
      him.

About Liturgy

Return to Ordinary Time: It might be tempting to think of this Sunday as a continuation of the festive Easter season, since this solemnity comes immediately after Pentecost. After all, this is just one more high festival in a whole string of them. It seems like we have been celebrating resurrection and new Life for a long time, and we have—for a full fifty days. It is good to remind ourselves at this point in the liturgical year that we resumed Ordinary Time on the Monday after Pentecost, so Trinity Sunday is a solemnity during Ordinary Time. It is now that we consciously take up Jesus' paschal mission and live what we have been celebrating. All good things come to an end and we must get on with our life. So it is with Easter. The constant celebration has come to an end. Now we must live what the celebration means.

About Liturgical Music

Music suggestions: We have many tried-and-true hymns to the Trinity, such as "Sing Praise to Our Creator" and "All Hailed Adored Trinity." Today we are also blessed with an abundance of additional hymns—some new, some newly available— offering us fresh insight into this divine mystery. Here are some examples:

Brian Wren's "How Wonderful the Three-in-One" (G3, SS, W4, WC) names the persons of the Trinity as "Creation's Lover"; the "Lover's own Beloved"; their "Equal Friend"; and calls them "our hope's beginning, way and end."

Delores Dufner's "O Dawn of All Creation" (LMGM2, W4) ends with "Transcendent Mystery: You dwell where none can follow, In worlds beyond our own, Yet all who seek may find you In flesh and blood and bone."

Mary Louise Bringle's "The Play of the Godhead" (G3, W4) expresses our participation in the internal dance of the Trinity: "In God's gracious image of coequal parts, We gather as dancers, uniting our hearts. Men, women, and children, and all living things, We join in the round of bright nature that rings With rapture and rhythm: Creation now sings!"

Richard Leach captures the same image in his "Come, Join the Dance of Trinity" (W4). The opening verse sings, "Come, join the dance of Trinity, Before all worlds begun, the interweaving of the Three, The Father, Spirit, Son. The universe of space and time did not arise by chance, But as the Three, in love and hope, Made room within their dance."

Genevieve Glen's "Farther Than the Farthest Sun" (BB) begins with these words: "Farther than the farthest sun, Nearer than our breath and thought, Uncreated Three-in-One, Heartbeat of the world you wrought, God unknowable but known, Let us worship you alone!"

"Stand Up, Friends" (G3), another by Brian Wren, sings of the dignity and freedom we have been granted by the Persons of the Trinity. The energetic refrain is "Stand up friends! Hold your heads high! Freedom is our song! Alleluia! Freedom is our song! Alleluia!"

MAY 31, 2015
THE SOLEMNITY OF
THE MOST HOLY TRINITY

SPIRITUALITY

R∕. Alleluia, alleluia.
I am the living bread that came down from heaven,
says the Lord; / whoever eats this bread
    will live forever.
R∕. Alleluia, alleluia.

Gospel   Mark 14:12-16, 22-26;
L168B

On the first day of the Feast of
    Unleavened Bread,
  when they sacrificed the
    Passover lamb,
  Jesus' disciples said to him,
  "Where do you want us to go
  and prepare for you to eat the
    Passover?"
He sent two of his disciples and said to
    them,
  "Go into the city and a man will meet you,
  carrying a jar of water.
Follow him.
Wherever he enters, say to the master of
    the house,
  'The Teacher says, "Where is my guest
    room
  where I may eat the Passover with my
    disciples?"'
Then he will show you a large upper room
    furnished and ready.
Make the preparations for us there."
The disciples then went off, entered the city,
  and found it just as he had told them;
  and they prepared the Passover.

While they were eating,
  he took bread, said the blessing,
  broke it, gave it to them, and said,
  "Take it; this is my body."
Then he took a cup, gave thanks, and gave
    it to them,
  and they all drank from it.
He said to them,
  "This is my blood of the covenant,
  which will be shed for many.
Amen, I say to you,
  I shall not drink again the fruit of the vine
  until the day when I drink it new in the
    kingdom of God."
Then, after singing a hymn,
  they went out to the Mount of Olives.

Reflecting on the Gospel

This Sunday's feast is a "repeat" of what we celebrated just a few weeks ago on Holy Thursday. Jesus does something entirely new and unimaginably significant: he gives himself—his very Body and Blood—to us as our heavenly Food. This is the mystery we celebrate on Holy Thursday and this Sunday. This gospel, however, gives us a different context and some different details that move us deeper into the mystery.

How confidently does Jesus send his disciples "into the city" to prepare for their celebration of Passover! How wondrously does God provide for the unfolding of salvation! The identifying sign for the man of the house where they would have this meal with Jesus was "a jar of water." Our own identifying sign as disciples is the waters of baptism, marking us as belonging to Christ and his mystery. The room where Jesus would celebrate the Passover with his disciples is described as a "guest room." Guest rooms are not where we are at home—they are transition rooms, temporary quarters, gifts of another's generosity. We are always "guests" in God's accommodations. We are to stay only temporarily, to move on from one place to another, from one person to another to witness to God's mighty deeds of salvation. God's gifts to us are not so we can settle in, stay put, become inert. God's gifts always impel us to move on, to spread the Good News, to "pass over" into someone new.

Jesus wants to "eat the Passover with [his] disciples." This annual festival celebrates the Jewish people "passing over" from lives of slavery and drudgery in Egypt to lives of freedom and abundance in the Promised Land. This meal portends another passover—Jesus' own passing over from suffering and death to risen Life. Through our baptism we enter into Jesus' mystery of dying and rising. And yet another passover: our passing over from old self to new self, from life of sin to life of grace. Each Eucharist, each time we eat and drink the Body and Blood of Christ, we embrace anew our passing over to new Life in Christ.

Each celebration of the Eucharist is a passover for us. It celebrates our plunging ever more deeply into the paschal mystery, into Jesus' passing from death to risen Life. It celebrates our embrace of the new identity baptism first bestows on us and Eucharist celebrates and nourishes: that we ourselves are members of the Body of Christ. As Jesus continually gives himself to us in the mystery of his Body and Blood, so does Eucharist call us to the same self-giving.

Living the Paschal Mystery

The covenant God made with Israel and sealed through the sprinkling of the sacrificial animal blood was a relationship with God in which they were to hear God's word and keep his commandments. Now, rather than being sprinkled "with the blood of goats and calves" (second reading), we drink the Blood of the risen Lord and by that action seal our new covenant with God. We are still to hear God's word and keep his commandments, like of old, but now something else is added: we ourselves are to take up God's redemptive work as we conform ourselves more perfectly to Christ and continue his self-giving ministry.

Our everyday living is preparation for sharing in the Eucharist and receiving eternal Life. We sprinkle among the people with whom we live and work little acts of self-giving, sealing our relationship with them and with God. This is how we "worship the living God" (second reading): by self-giving.

Focusing the Gospel

Key words and phrases: sacrificed the Passover lamb, I may eat the Passover, my disciples, this is my body, This is my blood

To the point: Jesus wants to "eat the Passover with [his] disciples." This annual festival celebrates the Jewish people "passing over" from lives of slavery and drudgery in Egypt to lives of freedom and abundance in the Promised Land. This meal portends another passover—Jesus' own passing over from suffering and death to risen Life. And yet another passover: our passing over from old self to new self, from life of sin to life of grace. Each Eucharist, each time we eat and drink the Body and Blood of Christ, we embrace anew our passing over to new Life in Christ.

Connecting the Gospel

to the second reading: Christ is our "high priest" who mediates through his Blood our passing over "from dead works to worship the living God," our passing over from "transgressions" to "eternal inheritance."

to experience: We firmly believe in the transformation ("passing over") of bread and wine into the risen Christ's Body and Blood. Do we *live* the transformation ("passing over") that also takes place in us when we eat Christ's Body and drink his Blood?

Connecting the Responsorial Psalm

to the readings: What does it mean for us to "take the cup of salvation" (psalm refrain)? For a Hebrew this phrase meant taking a cup of wine and pouring it out as a libation in thanksgiving for some saving deed on God's part. On this solemnity we sing this refrain with added meaning. The cup of salvation that is poured out is Christ's Blood, his very life given for our salvation (second reading). We take up this cup not to pour it out, however, but to drink it (gospel) so that our blood, transformed into Christ's, may be poured out for others. The libation we make in thanksgiving for God's saving deeds in Christ is to tip over the cup of our own hearts in self-sacrificing love. How precious is such death in God's eyes (psalm). How challenging on our part! May we sing this refrain aware of what we are saying.

to psalmist preparation: In these verses from Psalm 116, you thank God for the gift of redemption in Christ. You also promise to become God's faithful servant. You promise to "take [up] the cup of salvation" in the same way Christ does: as your own blood to be poured out for others. Where in your life at this moment are you being called to pour out your blood? How will God help you?

**ASSEMBLY &
FAITH-SHARING GROUPS**
- Jesus' passing over from death to risen Life is exemplified in my daily living by . . .
- As a disciple of the risen Christ, what happens to me when I "eat the Passover" with him is . . .
- The "passing over" that happens to me when I eat and drink the risen Christ's Body and Blood is . . .

PRESIDERS
Every eucharistic celebration, I lead and encourage the people to enter anew into the "passing over" from sinfulness to new Life when I . . .

DEACONS
When serving others, I "pass over" from . . . to . . .

HOSPITALITY MINISTERS
The manner of my greeting readies those gathering for liturgy to celebrate Jesus' death and resurrection when I . . .

MUSIC MINISTERS
Music making helps me "pass over" from . . . to . . .

ALTAR MINISTERS
My service helps people grasp the deepest meaning of the eucharistic celebration in that . . .

LECTORS
Preparing the word deepens my participation in the Eucharist by . . . The Eucharist deepens my "passing over" anew to a life of living the Word by . . .

**EXTRAORDINARY MINISTERS
OF HOLY COMMUNION**
My distributing the Body and Blood of Christ is carried forth in the way I live when I . . .

Model Penitential Act

Presider: Today we celebrate Jesus' gift to us of his Body and Blood for our strength and nourishment. Let us prepare for this liturgy by asking God's mercy for the times we have not lived up to the promise of this gift . . . [pause]

Lord Jesus, you are the Body given for our salvation: Lord . . .

Christ Jesus, you are the Blood poured out for us: Christ . . .

Lord Jesus, you are the strength and nourishment we need on our journey to eternal Life: Lord . . .

Homily Points

• Transitions—"pass overs"—regularly occur in our lives. Some of these "pass overs" are unexpected, for example, a sudden death, an unforeseen pregnancy, a job loss. Other "pass overs" are expected, for example, from single to married life, from adolescence to adulthood, a planned move from job to job or city to city. Every "pass over," whether expected or not, leads from one way of being to another. How much more so with the "passing over" that inherently belongs to every eucharistic celebration.

• For us, the feast of Unleavened Bread is fulfilled in the feast of the Body and Blood of the risen Christ. Ordinary bread becomes the Bread of everlasting Life. Through the words and self-giving of Jesus, bread "passes over" from one way of being to another. And we who consume this Bread and drink this Wine also "pass over" from one way of being to another. In every eucharistic celebration, we continually "eat" our own "pass over."

• Every eucharistic celebration challenges us to "pass over" more deeply from being hearers of the word to doers of the word, from rugged individuals to the community of the church, from self-centered to self-giving persons. To eat the Body and drink the Blood of the risen Christ is to surrender ourselves to these and other "pass overs." This, because the Eucharist transforms us into the very One we eat and drink. We pass over from one way of being to Another.

Model Universal Prayer (Prayer of the Faithful)

Presider: The gift of the risen Christ's Body and Blood for our nourishment and strength gives us courage to pray for our own needs, and the needs of the church and the whole world.

Response:

Lord, hear our prayer.

Cantor:

we pray to the Lord,

That all members of the church may live the new Life given them in receiving the Body and Blood of the risen Christ . . . [pause]

That all people of the world come to the unity and peace for which Jesus prayed at the Last Supper . . . [pause]

That those without food and drink receive sufficient nourishment to live healthy and strong lives . . . [pause]

That each of us proclaim through just deeds and worthy lives the mystery of our being transformed by the gift of the Eucharist . . . [pause]

Presider: Gracious God, your Son has given us his Body and Blood for our nourishment and strength: may we grow in his likeness and be faithful to his saving ministry. We ask this through Jesus Christ our Lord. **Amen.**

COLLECT

Let us pray

Pause for silent prayer

O God, who in this wonderful Sacrament have left us a memorial of your Passion, grant us, we pray, so to revere the sacred mysteries of your Body and Blood that we may always experience in ourselves the fruits of your redemption. Who live and reign with God the Father in the unity of the Holy Spirit, one God, for ever and ever. **Amen.**

FIRST READING

Exod 24:3-8

When Moses came to the people
　and related all the words and ordinances
　　of the LORD,
　they all answered with one voice,
　"We will do everything that the LORD
　　has told us."
Moses then wrote down all the words of
　the LORD and,
　rising early the next day,
　he erected at the foot of the mountain
　　an altar
　and twelve pillars for the twelve tribes
　　of Israel.
Then, having sent certain young men of
　the Israelites
　to offer holocausts and sacrifice young
　　bulls
　as peace offerings to the LORD,
Moses took half of the blood and put it
　　in large bowls;
　the other half he splashed on the altar.
Taking the book of the covenant, he read
　it aloud to the people,
　who answered, "All that the LORD has
　　said, we will heed and do."
Then he took the blood and sprinkled it on
　the people, saying,
　"This is the blood of the covenant
　that the LORD has made with you
　in accordance with all these words of
　　his."

CATECHESIS

RESPONSORIAL PSALM

Ps 116:12-13, 15-16, 17-18

℟. (13) I will take the cup of salvation, and call on the name of the Lord.
or:
℟. Alleluia.

How shall I make a return to the LORD
   for all the good he has done for me?
The cup of salvation I will take up,
   and I will call upon the name of the
      LORD.
℟. I will take the cup of salvation, and call on the name of the Lord.
or:
℟. Alleluia.

Precious in the eyes of the LORD
   is the death of his faithful ones.
I am your servant, the son of your
   handmaid;
   you have loosed my bonds.
℟. I will take the cup of salvation, and call on the name of the Lord.
or:
℟. Alleluia.

To you will I offer sacrifice of
      thanksgiving,
   and I will call upon the name of the
      LORD.
My vows to the LORD I will pay
   in the presence of all his people.
℟. I will take the cup of salvation, and call on the name of the Lord.
or:
℟. Alleluia.

SECOND READING

Heb 9:11-15

OPTIONAL SEQUENCE

See Appendix A, p. 299.

About Liturgy

Preparing for and appreciating the mystery: The General Instruction of the Roman Missal provides that there be a brief period of silence or hymn of praise after Communion (see GIRM nos. 88 and 164). Thus the ritual action itself encourages us to spend some time reflecting on and praising God for the gracious and wondrous gift of the Body and Blood of Christ. Even if we faithfully do this every Mass, we know that we cannot begin to have sufficient time to reflect on the depths of the mystery or to give sufficient thanks for it. For this reason it is always appropriate to spend some other devotional time before the Blessed Sacrament. Our time of adoration and thanksgiving, however, must always flow from the action of the Eucharist itself and lead us to witness more clearly in our lives the self-giving of Jesus. This great Gift always—during Mass and at times of adoration—leads us to identify our lives more closely with Christ. We are reminded, then, that this Gift has its cost: we, too, are to give ourselves for others. Anything less than this is to rob the mystery of its greatest depth—the fact that we eat and drink Christ's true Body and Blood and become what we eat so that we can be the self-giving Christ for others.

Since we naturally take sufficient preparation time for significant events in our lives, it would seem that this would also be part of our weekly celebration of Eucharist. Perhaps because it is a weekly event, far too many of us take little or no time to prepare for this most important event of our week. The church gives us ways to prepare: every Friday is a day of penance on which we fast, pray, and do acts of charity to prepare ourselves spiritually for the Gift we receive on Sunday. Every act of self-giving for the good of others is also preparation for celebrating Eucharist. Reading the Scriptures ahead of time so we can better hear God's word proclaimed is another way to prepare. Dressing in something other than everyday or work clothes is another way we prepare ourselves and also witness to others the importance of Eucharist in our lives.

About Liturgical Music

The song during Communion: This solemnity offers a good opportunity to reflect on the purpose of the music we sing during Communion. GIRM states that the purpose of the Communion song is to express our union through the union of our voices, to communicate our joy as we gather for the eucharistic banquet, and to emphasize the communal nature of the Communion procession (no. 86). GIRM also indicates that the song is to begin when the presider gives himself Communion and is to last until everyone in the assembly has received. One implication of these directives is that we are to be attentive to one another as we receive Holy Communion. The song we sing is meant to lead us both to Christ and to all the others to whom we are being united through his Body and Blood.

STL indicates that communal singing of the people is "preeminent" during the Communion procession (no. 189). Addressing what kinds of songs are suitable for Communion, STL guides us to look for texts with themes of joy, wonder, unity, gratitude, praise; or texts that reflect themes from the gospel reading of the day; or songs that support the liturgical action of eating and drinking the Body and Blood of Christ (no. 191).

JUNE 7, 2015

THE SOLEMNITY OF THE MOST HOLY BODY AND BLOOD OF CHRIST

SPIRITUALITY

GOSPEL ACCLAMATION
Matt 11:29ab

R7. Alleluia, alleluia.
Take my yoke upon you, says the Lord;
and learn from me, for I am meek and humble
  of heart.
R7. Alleluia, alleluia.

or

1 John 4:10b

R7. Alleluia, alleluia.
God first loved us
and sent his Son as expiation for our sins.
R7. Alleluia, alleluia.

Gospel John 19:31-37; L171B

Since it was preparation day,
  in order that the bodies might not
    remain on the cross on the
    sabbath,
  for the sabbath day of that week
    was a solemn one,
  the Jews asked Pilate that their legs
    be broken
  and they be taken down.
So the soldiers came and broke the legs
  of the first
  and then of the other one who was
    crucified with Jesus.
But when they came to Jesus and saw
  that he was already dead,
  they did not break his legs,
  but one soldier thrust his lance into his
    side,
  and immediately blood and water
    flowed out.
An eyewitness has testified, and his
    testimony is true;
  he knows that he is speaking the truth,
  so that you also may come to believe.
For this happened so that the Scripture
    passage might be fulfilled:
  Not a bone of it will be broken.
And again another passage says:
  *They will look upon him whom they
    have pierced.*

See Appendix A, p. 300, for the other readings.

Reflecting on the Gospel

The human heart is a physical organ—it pumps blood that carries oxygen and nutrients throughout our body. Even its placement in the human body—close to the middle of the chest cavity—suggests that the heart is central to us. At one time the heart's pumping or not was the decisive factor for determining life or death. And although brain waves have taken over that crucial determination, the brain has never caught the human imagination like the heart. We don't have familiar metaphors for the brain. But we have loads of them for the heart: heavy heart, broken heart, hard heart, sweet heart, heart of gold, heart of a lion, have a heart, home is where the heart is. And on and on. Behind these metaphors is human emotion: concern, sadness, selfishness, love, generosity, courage, empathy. But of all these emotions and many more, the heart has become most surely a symbol of love. This feast honoring the Most Sacred Heart of Jesus is a festival of love.

This solemnity celebrates the overflowing love of the Sacred Heart of Jesus for the people he came to save. Jesus' overflowing love from the cross makes concrete the overwhelming divine tender love of the Father. The first reading from the prophet Hosea tells eloquently and tenderly of God's great love for the people Israel in spite of their constant infidelity—God loved, called, taught, enveloped Israel with divine "bands of love," fed, and healed. The second reading declares that this same love is poured forth into our hearts, so that we "may be filled with all the fullness of God." It concludes that the "breadth and length and height and depth" of the love of Christ surpasses everything and anything we can know.

God's tender love is no passive love, no intellectual love, no cheap love. Nor is it a metaphoric love. God's love is real. It is concrete. It is pervasive. God's is a love extending from the beginning of creation through Israel's infidelity and through our own infidelity to the end of time so that "the plan of the mystery hidden from ages past . . . might now be made known through the church" and "accomplished in Christ Jesus our Lord" (second reading)—God's remarkable plan for our salvation. God has taken the greatest of care to ensure that we have life, even to the point of sacrificing the divine Son whose heart was "filled with all the fullness of God" and overflows to fill our own hearts. Ultimately what we celebrate this day is fullness. We celebrate not death but Life. We celebrate self-giving beyond compare. We celebrate love. God's love. Jesus' love. Our love.

Living the Paschal Mystery

The Sacred Heart of Jesus has been a popular devotion; the traditional Litany of the Sacred Heart contains language that reminds us of the real demand of discipleship: "Heart of Jesus, abode of justice and love . . . of Whose fullness we have all received . . . patient and most merciful . . . obedient unto death . . . our life and resurrection." We have received fullness of life from God through the death and resurrection of Jesus; now we must be abodes of justice and love, patient and more merciful, obedient even unto death. Although this solemnity speaks of God's great tenderness in loving us, even this has its demand. It is God's tenderness that encourages us to give ourselves so that others might receive the fullness of life through us. We can do this because God loved us first.

Focusing the Gospel

Key words and phrases: Jesus . . . already dead, flowed out, may come to believe

To the point: This solemnity celebrates the overflowing love of the Sacred Heart of Jesus for the people he came to save. Jesus' overflowing love from the cross makes concrete the overwhelming divine tender love of the Father (see first reading). The second reading declares that this same love is poured forth into our hearts, so that we "may be filled with all the fullness of God."

Model Penitential Act

Presider: On this solemnity of the Most Sacred Heart of Jesus, we celebrate God's great love for us and the gift of life we receive through the sacrifice of the divine Son. As we prepare to celebrate the sacrifice at this Eucharist, let us open our hearts to the divine love given us . . . [pause]

Lord Jesus, you died on the cross for our salvation: Lord . . .

Christ Jesus, the blood and water of sacramental life flowed from your side: Christ . . .

Lord Jesus, your love draws us to belief: Lord . . .

Model Universal Prayer (Prayer of the Faithful)

Presider: Assured of God's great and tender love, we do not hesitate to ask for what we need.

Response:

Cantor:

That the Sacred Heart's self-giving love be manifested through the community of the church . . . [pause]

That Jesus' pouring out his life come to fulfillment in the salvation of all people . . . [pause]

That the Sacred Heart's gift of love be a beacon of hope for those in any need . . . [pause]

That the overwhelming love of the Sacred Heart motivate us to love our brothers and sisters by our own self-giving . . . [pause]

Presider: Loving God, you have cared for us from the moment we came into being: hear these our prayers that we may one day enjoy the fullness of your everlasting Life. We ask this through the Sacred Heart of your divine Son Jesus Christ our Lord. **Amen.**

COLLECT

Let us pray

Pause for silent prayer

Grant, we pray, almighty God,
that we, who glory in the Heart of your
 beloved Son
and recall the wonders of his love for us,
may be made worthy to receive
an overflowing measure of grace
from that fount of heavenly gifts.
Through our Lord Jesus Christ, your Son,
who lives and reigns with you in the unity
 of the Holy Spirit,
one God, for ever and ever. **Amen.**

Or:

O God, who in the Heart of your Son,
wounded by our sins,
bestow on us in mercy
the boundless treasures of your love,
grant, we pray,
that, in paying him the homage of our
 devotion,
we may also offer worthy reparation.
Through our Lord Jesus Christ, your Son,
who lives and reigns with you in the unity
 of the Holy Spirit,
one God, for ever and ever. **Amen.**

FOR REFLECTION

• For me the image of the heart of Jesus reveals divine love in these ways . . .
• I have encountered the love of Jesus in . . . through . . . by . . .
• The fullness of God filling me is . . . Because of this, I am able to . . .

Homily Points

• Fulfillment is a strong human drive. Fundamental to fulfillment is love. But no human love we give or receive is as deep, all-encompassing, life-giving as the love of God. The Sacred Heart of Jesus is a visceral symbol of that divine love. Our ultimate fulfillment is found only in God.
• Filled "with all the fullness of God," we are enabled to share this same love with others. When we lend a sympathetic heart to someone who is struggling, when we offer a listening heart to someone who is lonely, when we share a joyful heart with a friend, we are sharing God's love, God's fullness.

✠ SPIRITUALITY

GOSPEL ACCLAMATION

℟. Alleluia, alleluia.
The seed is the word of God, Christ is the sower.
All who come to him will live forever.
℟. Alleluia, alleluia.

Gospel

Mark 4:26-34; L92B

Jesus said to the crowds:
   "This is how it is with the
         kingdom of God;
   it is as if a man were to
         scatter seed on the land
   and would sleep and rise
         night and day
   and through it all the seed
         would sprout and grow,
   he knows not how.
Of its own accord the land yields fruit,
   first the blade, then the ear, then the
         full grain in the ear.
And when the grain is ripe, he wields
         the sickle at once,
   for the harvest has come."

He said,
   "To what shall we compare the
         kingdom of God,
   or what parable can we use for it?
It is like a mustard seed that, when it is
         sown in the ground,
   is the smallest of all the seeds on the
         earth.
But once it is sown, it springs up and
         becomes the largest of plants
   and puts forth large branches,
   so that the birds of the sky can dwell
         in its shade."
With many such parables
   he spoke the word to them as they
         were able to understand it.
Without parables he did not speak to
         them,
   but to his own disciples he explained
         everything in private.

Reflecting on the Gospel

No modern farmer would do what the first parable of this gospel relates. Seeds are not "scatter[ed] . . . on the land" but carefully placed in precise rows. The farmer does not "sleep and rise night and day" without any regard for what has been planted. Instead, the farmer knows that of "its own accord the land" may not yield what the farmer needs to cover costs and make a living. So the farmer fertilizes, irrigates, spreads weed killer and pesticides, checks weather reports, and prays a lot! Farming has become big business and an exacting science. But, ultimately, the farmer knows that neither nature alone nor human effort can guarantee a desired agricultural outcome. In Jesus' time husbandry was still the largest of human occupations. It is no wonder Jesus draws so many parables from what would have been very familiar to his listeners. In the end, however, seeds planted, growing, and yielding a harvest remains a mystery somewhat under our control, but largely still a mystery to which we must yield. We know that a fruitful harvest is, ultimately, a gift.

In this gospel both the land and the mustard seed actualize their potential—they do what by nature they are created to do. At least in the ideal circumstances of parables. A parable is meant to take us beyond the literal. These two are used by Jesus to help us grasp what is surely a mystery: the "kingdom of God." This kingdom is not a place or space. It is not something we can discover or conquer. Instead, these parables invite us to be who we are and allow God's kingdom to conquer us. These parables call us to surrender to God's word and action within us, to cooperate with God in bringing about a world filled with abundance and promise. These parables challenge us to make the kingdom of God a visible reality shaping our daily living.

The "kingdom of God" is visible when we, like the land and mustard seed, actualize our own potential and do what we are called to do as Jesus' disciples. What are we to do? Hear God's word, nurture it in the fertile soil of our hearts, and let it sprout good works. In other words, God's kingdom is visible in us when we surrender ourselves to God's ways, when we hear God's will for us, when we live in a way consistent with who God created us to be and how God intends us to do. In this way we become living parables doing what God created us to do and being who God created us to be. In the end we ourselves are God's abundant harvest. And perhaps this is the greatest mystery of all.

Living the Paschal Mystery

If we are to be God's abundant harvest, then our first task for living the Gospel and paschal mystery is to hear God's word. In that divine word we receive God's direction for our lives, hear God's will, and determine how we are to live God's mystery of salvation. The word is like the mustard seed that is planted in us. We nurture it with caring acts, help it to grow by watering it with the tears of our self-giving, weed it by rooting out all in us that is opposed to God's desires for us. Each good or not so good choice we make each day affects the growth of the mustard seed-word that God plants deep within us.

It is never enough to merely *hear* God's word. We must always let that word inform the actions we undertake. Understanding God's word is a matter of standing up for Gospel values, standing under those who need support and encouragement, standing for Jesus and his invitation to live as he did.

Called / Sent

= Do as Jesus

Preach, Heal, Feed, Care

For

= New Evangelization

= Pope Francis'.

STORE
milk
toothpaste

LAUNDRY

yard

school

Focusing the Gospel

Key words and phrases: kingdom of God, land yields fruit, mustard seed
. . . sown . . . largest of plants, his own disciples, parables

To the point: Both the land and the mustard seed actualize their potential—
they do what by nature they are created to do. The "kingdom of God" is visible
when we, like the land and mustard seed, actualize our own potential and do
what we are called to do as Jesus' disciples. What are we to do? Hear God's
word, nurture it in the fertile soil of our hearts, and let it sprout good works. In
this way we become living parables doing what God created us to do.

Connecting the Gospel

to the first reading: The work of giving life and growth is God's. In the first
reading, God takes a "tender shoot" from a tree, plants it, and it grows and
bears fruit. In the gospel Jesus speaks divine words to his disciples so that they
might "sprout and grow" the kingdom of God.

to experience: Many grade school teachers have students plant a seed in a
little cup of soil. The children are so excited to watch the seed sprout and grow.
They run each day to see the progress. What growth does God see in us when
the divine word is preached and we take it in?

Connecting the Responsorial Psalm

to the readings: The first reading reminds us it is not our efforts which assure salvation, but God's. The context of the reading is the destruction of Israel by Babylon. Into their despair Ezekiel speaks words of hope: God will take
from this destroyed people "a tender shoot" and will replant it "on the mountain
heights of Israel." Nothing will stop God from doing this.

Jesus tells us that because of God's steadfast and attentive care even the
smallest seed becomes a large plant (gospel). Such growth occurs without our
intervention, while we sleep (gospel), because God has designed things so. The
good news for us is that we are the tender shoots transplanted by God, the seed
scattered by God for silent growth, the trees planted in the house of the Lord to
"bear fruit even in old age" (psalm). The kingdom of God will come to fruition
in us and in the world. We have God's very Self on whom to hang this hope. Let
us give God thanks!

to psalmist preparation: In the midst of destruction and despair, God
replants the tender shoot of life (first reading). In the silent hours of our night-
time sleep, God pursues the growth of the kingdom (gospel). What seeds of
growth is God planting in you? What tender shoots is God nurturing? How this
week can you thank God for this?

**ASSEMBLY &
FAITH-SHARING GROUPS**
- The potential I see in myself is . . . The potential God sees in me is . . .
- I nurture God's word in my heart by . . . the fruit this bears for others is . . .
- I make the kingdom of God visible when I . . .

PRESIDERS
When I nurture God's word in my heart, my preaching becomes . . . my living becomes . . .

DEACONS
My serving others is a living parable of God's kingdom in these ways . . .

HOSPITALITY MINISTERS
The manner of my greeting helps the as-sembly members do what God created them to do when I . . .

MUSIC MINISTERS
My music making is a preaching of God's word when I . . .

ALTAR MINISTERS
Through my serving ministry I grow in my ability to hear God's word and act on it in these ways . . .

LECTORS
When I truly hear and understand God's word in my heart, my proclamation be-comes . . .

**EXTRAORDINARY MINISTERS
OF HOLY COMMUNION**
My ministry of distributing the Body and Blood of the risen Jesus nurtures my own growth and potential in these ways . . .

Model Penitential Act

Presider: The kingdom of God grows and bears fruit when we hear God's word and nurture it in our hearts. As we begin this liturgy, we pause to seek God's mercy for the times we have not listened to God's word and responded in our lives . . . [pause]

> Lord Jesus, you are the Word made flesh: Lord . . .
>
> Christ Jesus, you are the fullness of Life: Christ . . .
>
> Lord Jesus, you came to announce the kingdom of God: Lord . . .

Homily Points

- Our experience teaches us that seeds planted do not always produce a harvest. Weather patterns, soil conditions, and human labor are determinate factors. The growth of the kingdom of God, however, is assured because it rests on the power and promise of God: "As I, the LORD, have spoken, so will I do" (first reading).

- Jesus teaches in these parables that what is planted grows of its own accord following natural laws. This we understand from experience. The growth of the kingdom of God is assured because of Jesus' word and the law of the Spirit. We do not always understand this, however. We come to understand only when we truly hear Jesus' word and make it our way of living—that is, by growing and bearing fruit.

- The kingdom of God starts small—with each of us—but when we allow ourselves to grow in God's life, the kingdom becomes all-encompassing. As the community of the church, we are able to respond to the needs of the entire world. As a parish community, we are able to reach out with help and goods to our cities and neighborhoods. As individuals, we are able to embrace enemies as well as friends, strangers as well as family, those in need as well as those with plenty. In these ways we become living parables doing what God created us to do.

Model Universal Prayer (Prayer of the Faithful)

Presider: God entrusts to us the work of furthering the growth of the kingdom. Let us pray that God's kingdom grow and bear fruit among us.

Response:

Lord,—— hear our prayer.

Cantor:

we pray to the Lord,

That all members of the church may truly hear Jesus' words, take them into their hearts, and produce fruit by living them . . . [pause]

That all people may live in God's kingdom and come to salvation . . . [pause]

That those discouraged by lack of growth or by failure to flourish may be re-created by Jesus' words of hope and promise . . . [pause]

That members of this faith community may be living parables of the presence of God's kingdom . . . [pause]

Presider: Lord of life and abundance, you nurture in us the ability to hear the words of your divine Son: hear these our prayers and be with us as we strive to live in your kingdom. We ask this through Jesus Christ our Lord. **Amen.**

COLLECT

Let us pray

Pause for silent prayer

O God, strength of those who hope in you,
graciously hear our pleas,
and, since without you mortal frailty can
    do nothing,
grant us always the help of your grace,
that in following your commands
we may please you by our resolve and our
    deeds.
Through our Lord Jesus Christ, your Son,
who lives and reigns with you in the unity
    of the Holy Spirit,
one God, for ever and ever. **Amen.**

FIRST READING

Ezek 17:22-24

Thus says the Lord GOD:
  I, too, will take from the crest of the
      cedar,
    from its topmost branches tear off a
       tender shoot,
  and plant it on a high and lofty
      mountain;
    on the mountain heights of Israel I
       will plant it.
  It shall put forth branches and bear
      fruit,
    and become a majestic cedar.
  Birds of every kind shall dwell beneath
      it,
    every winged thing in the shade of its
       boughs.
  And all the trees of the field shall know
      that I, the LORD,
  bring low the high tree,
    lift high the lowly tree,
  wither up the green tree,
    and make the withered tree bloom.
  As I, the LORD, have spoken, so will I do.

RESPONSORIAL PSALM
Ps 92:2-3, 13-14, 15-16

℟. (cf. 2a) Lord, it is good to give thanks to you.

It is good to give thanks to the LORD,
  to sing praise to your name, Most High,
to proclaim your kindness at dawn
  and your faithfulness throughout the
    night.

℟. Lord, it is good to give thanks to you.

The just one shall flourish like the palm
    tree,
  like a cedar of Lebanon shall he grow.
They that are planted in the house of the
    LORD
  shall flourish in the courts of our God.

℟. Lord, it is good to give thanks to you.

They shall bear fruit even in old age;
  vigorous and sturdy shall they be,
declaring how just is the LORD,
  my rock, in whom there is no wrong.

℟. Lord, it is good to give thanks to you.

SECOND READING
2 Cor 5:6-10

Brothers and sisters:
We are always courageous,
  although we know that while we are at
      home in the body
  we are away from the Lord,
  for we walk by faith, not by sight.
Yet we are courageous,
  and we would rather leave the body and
      go home to the Lord.
Therefore, we aspire to please him,
  whether we are at home or away.
For we must all appear before the
      judgment seat of Christ,
  so that each may receive recompense,
  according to what he did in the body,
      whether good or evil.

About Liturgy

Human labor: Each year on the first Monday of September (coming up in about six weeks) we celebrate the civil holiday Labor Day. More than an excuse for a day off from work, it is fitting that at least once a year we pause as a nation to pray for the safety of all laborers, pray that all receive just wages and benefits, pray in gratitude for the work of others who make our own lives more wholesome and comfortable. It is also a good day to remember that work is not drudgery; it is an opportunity to cooperate with God in bringing about God's kingdom.

We can look at work in a negative way, as a "necessary evil." After Adam and Eve sinned in the Garden, God expelled them from Paradise and said they would now toil and sweat to produce food (see Gen 3:17-19) that was once freely given to them. But it is more helpful to look at work in a positive way: God worked to create and redeem us, and by this showed us that work has an inherent dignity. Through our choice to contribute to a ministry in the parish we help build up the Body of Christ as we share our gifts with our sisters and brothers in Christ. Our reaching out to do good for others is work that makes God present in new and ever creating ways. The work of cooperating in Jesus' saving ministry raises up our labors to being an imitation of the divine action making present God's reign of peace and justice, abundance and life, mercy and forgiveness.

About Liturgical Music

Service music for Ordinary Time: As we return to Sundays in Ordinary Time, it is once again important to begin singing a set of service music which fits this season. It might be well to have two sets in place, one to use from now through the Twenty-Third Sunday in Ordinary Time, the other to begin singing on the Twenty-Fourth Sunday when the gospel readings turn us more intently toward Jesus'—and our—journey to Jerusalem and the cross.

Music suggestions: In "What Shall We Say God's Realm Is Like" (HG), John A. Dalles puts Jesus' parable of the mustard seed into musical form. This hymn could be sung at the entrance, or during the preparation of the gifts. Delores Dufner's "The Reign of God" (G3, W4) draws on several parables using seed and farming as metaphors for the reign of God. Verse 5 speaks of the mustard seed in this Sunday's gospel. This hymn would be suitable during the preparation of the gifts. Delores Dufner's "Sing a New Church" (found in many resources) would also work for the entrance song. Verse 3 particularly resonates with themes from this Sunday's readings: "Trust the goodness of creation; Trust the Spirit strong within. Dare to dream the vision promised, Sprung from seed of what has been." "For the Fruits of All Creation" (found in many resources) sings not just about the harvests of the earth that silently grow while we are sleeping, but also about the "harvests of the Spirit" growing quietly within us. This hymn would work well either during the preparation of the gifts or as the recessional song. Although not precisely related, "Seed, Scattered and Sown" (BB, JS3) does bear a thematic connection to this Sunday's gospel and would make a fitting song during Communion.

✢ SPIRITUALITY

GOSPEL ACCLAMATION
Luke 7:16

R⁊. Alleluia, alleluia.
A great prophet has risen in our midst,
God has visited his people.
R⁊. Alleluia, alleluia.

Gospel

Mark 4:35-41; L95B

On that day, as evening drew on, Jesus said to his disciples:
  "Let us cross to the other side."
Leaving the crowd, they took Jesus with them in the boat just as he was.
And other boats were with him.
A violent squall came up and waves were breaking over the boat,
  so that it was already filling up.
Jesus was in the stern, asleep on a cushion.
They woke him and said to him,
  "Teacher, do you not care that we are perishing?"
He woke up,
  rebuked the wind, and said to the sea, "Quiet! Be still!"
The wind ceased and there was great calm.
Then he asked them, "Why are you terrified?
Do you not yet have faith?"
They were filled with great awe and said to one another,
  "Who then is this whom even wind and sea obey?"

Reflecting on the Gospel

Little children hide under their bedcovers; dogs howl; adults cringe. Violent storms frighten us, even if we are told by a weather report that the storm is too far away to cause serious damage to us. With the changing weather patterns we've been having, all too many people have found themselves in the middle of violent storms with their consequent loss of lives and property. For good reason we have a healthy respect for storms that are breaking around us. So we can readily identify with the disciples' fear of the "violent squall" reported in this Sunday's gospel—even more so since the disciples are in a boat out on a sea. Violent "waves were breaking over the boat." The boat was "already filling up." Drowning seems a real possibility. The disciples are understandably frightened. Jesus, however, is comfortably asleep "on a cushion," seemingly oblivious to the violence around him.

At the end of a day of preaching and healing, Jesus was no doubt tired. The disciples took him in the boat "just as he was." So, Jesus fell fast asleep. When a "violent squall" arose, the disciples thought that Jesus didn't care that they were "perishing." But Jesus did care; he came precisely to save humanity from perishing. The boat was filling up with water from the waves, while the disciples' hearts were empty of the depth of faith needed to be calm, to be still, to know that Jesus surely does care for them. The disciples' faith is weak because the disciples do not yet know who Jesus is and why he came.

The response that welled up in the disciples after Jesus calmed the storm was one of "great awe" which led them to ask about Jesus' identity. And here is the crunch of the gospel: only God has power over nature. When Jesus asked faith of the disciples, he was asking them to grow in their relationship to him as more than a "Teacher." He was revealing further that he was the long-expected Messiah, the Son of God (which is revealed later in Mark's gospel). When Jesus asked faith of the disciples, then, he was not asking faith in him as their Teacher and leader. He was asking them to have faith and trust in him as the divine One with power to save.

After Jesus commanded the sea to be quiet, "there was great calm." We might surmise that a similar calm washed over the disciples—that their "great awe" brought them to humble silence before this Teacher who had such extraordinary power. Calm comes out of trust. And thus is diverted the real "storm" at sea. The disciples' faith was tested, and this became an occasion for them to grow in faith and in knowing who Jesus is. So it is with us. The "storms" of our own lives become occasions for us to grow in faith and trust that God is ever present to us, calming whatever threatens us, bringing us to a deeper relationship with the God who cares for us. We have an advantage over the disciples in that boat on a stormy sea: we know who Jesus is. But nevertheless we must still ask the critical question: how strong is *our* faith?

Living the Paschal Mystery

Faith cannot be separated from Jesus who is the reason for our faith. To deepen our faith, then, is to deepen our grasp of who Jesus is for us. We constantly seek to encounter him in others, through good works, by caring for those in need—and in all these ways we grow in our understanding of who Jesus is. Whatever "storms" come our way in life, if we have a deep relationship with Jesus and have faith, we know we will weather them.

Focusing the Gospel

Key words and phrases: just as he was, violent squall, do you not care that we are perishing, Do you not yet have faith, Who then is this

To the point: At the end of a day of preaching and healing, Jesus was no doubt tired. The disciples took him in the boat "just as he was." So, Jesus fell fast asleep. When a "violent squall" arose, the disciples thought that Jesus didn't care that they were "perishing." But Jesus did care; he came precisely to save humanity from perishing. The disciples' faith is weak because the disciples do not yet know who Jesus is and why he came. We, however, do. So how strong is *our* faith?

Connecting the Gospel

to the first reading: The first reading describes a theophany: God speaks to Job in the midst of a storm and assures him of divine power over creation. The gospel, too, describes a theophany; Jesus speaks to the disciples in the midst of a "violent squall" and calls them to deeper faith by exercising divine power over nature.

to experience: Our seabeds are littered with ships that have gone down in violent storms. Storms at sea, despite modern weather technology and ship design, are still incredibly dangerous. So even today we can fully connect to the disciples' fear of perishing. We can also fully connect to their lack of understanding about who Jesus is and why he came.

Connecting the Responsorial Psalm

to the readings: Psalm 107 as a whole relates the story of God's continual intervention to save Israel from distress and terror. The psalm conveys these terrors through vivid images of thirst experienced in the desert, fear felt in face of primordial darkness, agony suffered because of fatal illness, and perils undergone on the sea. In every situation Israel called upon God and was saved.

The verses we sing this Sunday invite us to have the same faith in God as did Israel. When dangers and disasters mark our journey of discipleship, we needn't be surprised or terrified. Such traumas are inevitable, but so is the intervention of the One whom wind and sea obey (first reading, gospel). The psalm assures us that our all-powerful God will calm not only these "storms" but also our overwhelmed hearts. The psalm reminds us God's saving love is steadfast and everlasting (refrain).

to psalmist preparation: It is important that you not let the concrete imagery of this responsorial psalm sidetrack you from its real meaning. The storm is but a metaphor: you are not singing about dangers at sea but about the ongoing reality of faithful discipleship. How does this metaphor shed light on your own experience of discipleship? How does it strengthen your trust in the God who saves?

**ASSEMBLY &
FAITH-SHARING GROUPS**
- The "violent squall" in life of which I am most fearful is . . .
- A "violent squall" which tested my faith in Jesus was . . . It also strengthened my faith in that . . .
- For me, Jesus is . . .

PRESIDERS
In my ministry I calm the storms in others' lives when . . .

DEACONS
My serving others makes visible Jesus' care for them in the midst of stress whenever I . . .

HOSPITALITY MINISTERS
My hospitality has a calming effect when . . . for . . .

MUSIC MINISTERS
One of the "squalls" that keeps coming up in my music ministry is . . . I experience Jesus calming this squall by . . .

ALTAR MINISTERS
My serving has helped me come to know more fully who Jesus is by . . .

LECTORS
My ongoing reflection on God's word has deepened my faith in Jesus by . . .

**EXTRAORDINARY MINISTERS
OF HOLY COMMUNION**
Distributing Holy Communion deepens my understanding of who Jesus is and why he came when I . . .

✠ CELEBRATION

Model Penitential Act

Presider: In the gospel today Jesus calms the storm at sea and leads the disciples to greater faith in who he is. As we prepare to celebrate this liturgy, let us open ourselves to Jesus revealing himself and his saving power to us during this celebration . . . [pause]

Lord Jesus, you are the divine Son who comes in power: Lord . . .

Christ Jesus, you save us from perishing: Christ . . .

Lord Jesus, you call us to faith in you: Lord . . .

Homily Points

- We live most of our days on the surface; we tend to take things at face value. It often takes a "storm" to shake us up and make us delve deeper into who we are and where we are going on life's journey. So, too, does the "violent squall" in this gospel story challenge the disciples to move from their surface understanding of who Jesus is to the deeper faith in him that discipleship demands.

- Disciples take Jesus into their boat "just as he was." How was he? Very tired and very human; he fell asleep. But also divine and very powerful; he calmed the storm. Jesus, for his part, took the disciples just as they were—still not fully understanding who he was. In this story of the storm at sea Jesus reveals just who he was and leads the disciples to become more fully who they could be—disciples with deeper faith in him.

- Like the disciples, we must learn to leave the crowd and take Jesus with us in our "boat"—on our life's journey. When violent squalls come up, waves break over our boat, frightening us. Jesus can seem asleep until we cry out to him. As with the disciples in the gospel story, so it is with us: in the storms of our life, Jesus quiets us and teaches us to "Be still" and come to deeper faith in him.

Model Universal Prayer (Prayer of the Faithful)

Presider: The God who has power over all creation and sent the Son for our salvation will give us all we need to grow more deeply in faith. And so we pray.

Response:

Lord, hear our prayer.

Cantor:

we pray to the Lord,

That each member of the church come to deeper faith in Jesus and his saving work . . . [pause]

That all people of the world face the storms in life with confidence in God's saving power . . . [pause]

That those overwhelmed by danger or disaster find courage in Jesus' abiding Presence and power . . . [pause]

That members of this faith community accept one another as we are and lead one another to grow more deeply into who Jesus calls us to be . . . [pause]

Presider: Almighty God, you still the storms of our lives and call us to deeper faith in your divine Son: hear these our prayers that one day we might enjoy everlasting peace with you. We ask this through Christ our Lord. **Amen.**

COLLECT

Let us pray

Pause for silent prayer

Grant, O Lord,
that we may always revere and love your
holy name,
for you never deprive of your guidance
those you set firm on the foundation of
your love.
Through our Lord Jesus Christ, your Son,
who lives and reigns with you in the unity
of the Holy Spirit,
one God, for ever and ever. **Amen.**

FIRST READING

Job 38:1, 8-11

The Lord addressed Job out of the storm
and said:
Who shut within doors the sea,
when it burst forth from the womb;
when I made the clouds its garment
and thick darkness its swaddling bands?
When I set limits for it
and fastened the bar of its door,
and said: Thus far shall you come but no
farther,
and here shall your proud waves be
stilled!

RESPONSORIAL PSALM

Ps 107:23-24, 25-26, 28-29, 30-31

℟. (1b) Give thanks to the Lord, his love is
everlasting.
or:
℟. Alleluia.

They who sailed the sea in ships,
trading on the deep waters,
these saw the works of the LORD
and his wonders in the abyss.

℟. Give thanks to the Lord, his love is
everlasting.
or:
℟. Alleluia.

His command raised up a storm wind
which tossed its waves on high.
They mounted up to heaven; they sank to
the depths;
their hearts melted away in their plight.

℟. Give thanks to the Lord, his love is
everlasting.
or:
℟. Alleluia.

They cried to the LORD in their distress;
from their straits he rescued them,
he hushed the storm to a gentle breeze,
and the billows of the sea were stilled.

R℣. Give thanks to the Lord, his love is everlasting.
or:
R℣. Alleluia.

They rejoiced that they were calmed,
and he brought them to their desired haven.
Let them give thanks to the LORD for his kindness
and his wondrous deeds to the children of men.

R℣. Give thanks to the Lord, his love is everlasting.
or:
R℣. Alleluia.

SECOND READING
2 Cor 5:14-17

Brothers and sisters:
The love of Christ impels us,
once we have come to the conviction that one died for all;
therefore, all have died.
He indeed died for all,
so that those who live might no longer live for themselves
but for him who for their sake died and was raised.

Consequently, from now on we regard no one according to the flesh;
even if we once knew Christ according to the flesh,
yet now we know him so no longer.
So whoever is in Christ is a new creation:
the old things have passed away;
behold, new things have come.

About Liturgy

Why not celebrate Father's Day? Many important days occur throughout the year and we may be struck by the fact that most of these are not included on the liturgical calendar. It isn't that the church wants to ignore important days such as this Sunday, Father's Day, or birthdays, or most national holidays. These are important times for us and to say they are not part of our religious lives is to split ourselves in two—spiritual selves and everyday get-on-with-our-business selves. To help us understand why we seem to ignore so much at our liturgies, we must keep in mind what liturgy is really all about. The church keeps the liturgy for celebrating what is absolutely central to us Christians—the paschal mystery, events that mark it, and saints who have lived it and now share in everlasting glory.

Nevertheless, although these kinds of holidays do not have a place on our liturgical calendar, we don't have to ignore them altogether. Liturgy always encompasses the whole person, which means that there are ways to incorporate these days into our liturgical celebrations. It is always good to pray when marking these other celebrations, and so it would be appropriate to add a fifth intercession this Sunday for fathers; for example, "For all fathers to grow in their relationship with Jesus and teach their children of his goodness and care . . ." The *Book of Blessings* in chapter 56 provides other sample intercessions and a prayer over the people that may be used before the blessing of the people during the concluding rite.

About Liturgical Music

Music suggestions: Thomas Troeger's "The Sails Were Spilling Wind" (HG) moves from Jesus calming the storm at sea (verses 1-3) to Jesus taming hate and fear in the world (verses 4-6). Verse 3 ends with the disciples marveling "that Jesus could command and make the sea obey." Verse 6 ends by praying that through our words and deeds "Christ's own voice be heard, Until the world obeys." This hymn follows a verse refrain format; choir or cantor(s) could sing the verses, with the assembly joining in on the refrain, as well as verse 6.

Sylvia Dunstan's "The Storm Is Strong" (W4) retells this Sunday's gospel story and would be a good hymn to sing during the preparation of the gifts. "Be Still, My Soul" (BB, JS3, LMGM2) would be a marvelous prayer response to the gospel reading during the preparation of the gifts, as would "It Is Well with My Soul" (LMGM2), and the Taizé setting of St. Teresa of Jesus' prayer "Nada Te Turbe/Nothing Can Trouble" (G3, W4). The African American "Be Still, God Will Fight Your Battles" (LMGM2) would be an energetic recessional song, as would the Quaker hymn "How Can I Keep from Singing" (found in most resources), and "Though the Mountains May Fall" (BB, G3, JS3).

SPIRITUALITY

GOSPEL ACCLAMATION
cf. Luke 1:76

R̸. Alleluia, alleluia.
You, child, will be called prophet of the Most High,
for you will go before the Lord to prepare his way.
R̸. Alleluia, alleluia.

Gospel

Luke 1:57-66, 80; L587

When the time arrived for Elizabeth to have her child
   she gave birth to a son.
Her neighbors and relatives heard
   that the Lord had shown his
      great mercy toward her,
   and they rejoiced with her.
When they came on the eighth
      day to circumcise the child,
   they were going to call him
      Zechariah after his father,
   but his mother said in reply,
"No. He will be called John."
But they answered her,
   "There is no one among your
      relatives who has this name."
So they made signs, asking his father
   what he wished him to be called.
He asked for a tablet and wrote, "John
   is his name,"
   and all were amazed.
Immediately his mouth was opened, his
   tongue freed,
   and he spoke blessing God.
Then fear came upon all their neighbors,
   and all these matters were discussed
   throughout the hill country of Judea.
All who heard these things took them
   to heart, saying,
"What, then, will this child be?"
For surely the hand of the Lord was with
   him.
The child grew and became strong in
   spirit,
   and he was in the desert until the
      day
   of his manifestation to Israel.

*See Appendix A, p. 301, for the other
   readings.*

Reflecting on the Gospel

Elizabeth and Zechariah's obedience to the angel's choice of a name for this child is more than a decision about a name. The neighbors and relatives expected that "they were going to call him Zechariah after his father." By naming him according to the instruction of Gabriel when he appeared to Zechariah in the temple, John's parents already announced that this child was not theirs (not "after his father"). Thus the naming already equates John's identity with his mission to herald the coming of the Messiah: "formed . . . as [God's] servant from the womb" (first reading), John announced the "one . . . coming after" (second reading) him who was the "word of salvation" that was sent. Like his parents, John was obedient to the mission for which he was born; he was utterly faithful to God's plan of salvation.

John evoked amazement from others as a baby and as an adult carrying on the mission given him. "What, then, will this child be?" John "grew and became strong in spirit," he prepared himself for his public ministry by dwelling in the desert alone, he was humble in face of his Savior cousin, he spoke boldly the truth, and he was beheaded.

John's birth came about because "the Lord had shown his great mercy." Faithful to his death, John the Baptist is celebrated today as the prophet who announced the new reign of God. John fulfilled his mission to herald the coming of the Messiah who was God's most gracious gift of all. "What, then, will this child be?" John is remembered as one who said, "I am not worthy to unfasten the sandals of [the Savior's] feet" (second reading), and yet through him God showed his glory (see first reading). His mission was accomplished; the Word of salvation was heralded. John now lives forever in God's eternal glory.

As David carried out God's will (see second reading), so did Elizabeth and Zechariah when they named their newborn son John as the angel commanded. John, too, carried out God's will when he heralded the coming of "a savior, Jesus" (second reading). So do we carry out God's will when we herald the presence of Jesus, call others to repentance as did John, and faithfully bear the name bestowed on us by our baptism: Christ. Identified with Christ at baptism and carrying his name, we are most ourselves when we are obedient as Christ, preach the Good News of salvation, and remain faithful to the paschal journey of passing through death to new Life.

Living the Paschal Mystery

None of us had such striking incidents surround our conception and birth as did John; we didn't grow up in a desert wearing strange clothes and eating weird food. We are just simple, ordinary folks who, nevertheless, are also called to herald the Word of salvation in our midst, a Word whose name we bear because of our baptism. We make known Christ's risen Presence and carry forth his saving work in simple ways: by a truthful word, a courageous word, a humble word. Like John, we are called to die to self so that Christ might be announced to the world. We celebrate on this day John's identity and mission— which is ours, too: we are named Christ for the world, called to be faithful to God and to announce the reign of salvation. We are faithful to our name when we are obedient to God's way of life and holiness. Saint John the Baptist is our witness and model.

Focusing the Gospel

Key words and phrases: He will be called John, John is his name, manifestation

To the point: As David carried out God's will (see second reading), so did Elizabeth and Zechariah when they named their newborn son John as the angel commanded. John, too, carried out God's will when he heralded the coming of "a savior, Jesus" (second reading). So do we carry out God's will when we herald the presence of Jesus, call others to repentance as did John, and faithfully bear the name bestowed on us by our baptism: Christ.

Model Penitential Act

Presider: Today we celebrate the birth of John the Baptist, the prophet sent to herald the coming of Jesus our Savior. Let us prepare ourselves to hear God's word and celebrate these mysteries . . . [pause]

Lord Jesus, you are a Light to the nations: Lord . . .

Christ Jesus, you are the Savior of the world: Christ . . .

Lord Jesus, you are the Messiah heralded by John the Baptist: Lord . . .

Model Universal Prayer (Prayer of the Faithful)

Presider: God graciously sent the divine Son to be our Savior. Let us make our needs known that we may receive the salvation offered us.

Response:

Lord, hear our prayer.

Cantor:

we pray to the Lord,

That all members of the church may herald the presence of the Savior in our day and time . . . [pause]

That world leaders may announce by their deeds a time of peace and prosperity . . . [pause]

That all newborn infants may grow in grace and become strong in spirit . . . [pause]

That each of us may bless God in all we do and willingly pay the price of obedience to God's will . . . [pause]

Presider: Saving God, you bring us to salvation: hear these our prayers, help us to rejoice on this festival of the birth of John the Baptist, and one day be with you in eternal glory. We ask this through Jesus Christ our Lord. **Amen.**

COLLECT

Let us pray

Pause for silent prayer

O God, who raised up Saint John the Baptist to make ready a nation fit for Christ the Lord, give your people, we pray, the grace of spiritual joys and direct the hearts of all the faithful into the way of salvation and peace. Through our Lord Jesus Christ, your Son, who lives and reigns with you in the unity of the Holy Spirit, one God, for ever and ever. **Amen.**

FOR REFLECTION

- Like Elizabeth and Zechariah, I am obedient to God's will for me when . . .
- Like John the Baptist, I herald the Presence of the Savior and call myself and others to repentance in that . . .
- I live up to my name "Christ" when I . . .

Homily Points

- How time-bound the story of salvation is! "When the time had arrived" John the Baptist was born. "On the eighth day" he was named. As an adult he waited in the desert "until the day of his manifestation." How amazing that it is through these very time-bound events that God unbinds the human community from the chains of sin and death. God enters human time to unleash the power of salvation. We respond by living in our time as messengers of salvation faithful to God's will.

- When we do God's will, like Zechariah, our mouth will be opened, our tongue freed, and we will speak "blessing God." John faithfully does God's will—and pays the price. We also will have a price to pay when we do God's will, but the gift of Life given us when we are faithful far outweighs whatever price we pay. Because of this gift of Life and salvation, we glory in the name Christ and bless God at all times.

SPIRITUALITY

GOSPEL ACCLAMATION
cf. 2 Tim 1:10

R̸. Alleluia, alleluia.
Our Savior Jesus Christ destroyed death
and brought life to light through the Gospel.
R̸. Alleluia, alleluia.

Gospel Mark 5:21-43; L98B

When Jesus had crossed again in the
     boat
  to the other side,
  a large crowd gathered around
     him, and he stayed close
     to the sea.
One of the synagogue officials,
     named Jairus, came forward.
Seeing him he fell at his feet and pleaded
     earnestly with him, saying,
  "My daughter is at the point of death.
Please, come lay your hands on her
  that she may get well and live."
He went off with him,
  and a large crowd followed him and
     pressed upon him.

There was a woman afflicted with
     hemorrhages for twelve years.
She had suffered greatly at the hands of
     many doctors
  and had spent all that she had.
Yet she was not helped but only grew
     worse.
She had heard about Jesus and came up
     behind him in the crowd
  and touched his cloak.
She said, "If I but touch his clothes, I
     shall be cured."
Immediately her flow of blood dried up.
She felt in her body that she was healed
  of her affliction.
Jesus, aware at once that power had gone
     out from him,
  turned around in the crowd and asked,
     "Who has touched my clothes?"

Continued in Appendix A, p. 302.

or Mark 5:21-24, 35b-43, *in Appendix A,
p. 302.*

Reflecting on the Gospel

Who among us, when seriously ill, does not chase after every means possible—both medicinally and spiritually—to be healed? We avoid sickness because it limits, diminishes, discourages us. In this Sunday's gospel a woman has had an illness for twelve years and Jairus's twelve-year-old daughter is dead. We would expect the woman and Jairus to go to any length to overcome their tragedies. And they do. Both Jairus and the "woman afflicted with hemorrhages" have faith that Jesus would heal. What, really, is their faith? Simply in Jesus' power to heal? Even to raise from the dead? This they and the crowd would know from hearsay or other encounters with Jesus. However, the faith that saves is not based on physical miracles. Nor is the faith that saves merely an intellectual consent to revelation. The faith that saves is an act of coming to Jesus.

Faith in who Jesus is and what he can do brings us to act. Jairus approaches Jesus directly, kneels before him, and asks for healing for his daughter. The "woman afflicted with hemorrhages" dares not approach Jesus directly; she simply wishes to "touch his clothes" to be cured. In both cases their faith gave them the courage to approach Jesus and raised their expectation that he had the power to heal. Our faith, too, gives us courage and expectation. What do we do with it? Our first challenge is to come to Jesus with open hearts.

Both healing events in the long form of this Sunday's gospel disclose great faith and trust in Jesus on behalf of the petitioners. On the other hand, the disciples were critical of Jesus, and the crowd gathered in Jairus's house ridiculed him until the raising of the child to life left them "utterly astounded." The faith of Jairus and the woman stand in opposition to the hardheaded realism of the disciples and the crowd. Coming to Jesus and encountering him always changes experience, situations, expectations. It is precisely Jairus's and the woman's faith that a new situation with a different outcome would be ushered in by the presence of Jesus that opened the door to the new Life Jesus offered. These humble petitioners make visible the faith to which the disciples, the crowd, and we are called. They teach us that faith is an act of seeking Jesus.

The crowd is "utterly astounded" after Jesus raises Jairus's daughter back to life. The miracle cued them into the new situation. The challenge of this gospel is that we must see a new situation in all of life's circumstances, precisely because Jesus is present and so absolutely nothing is the same. The challenge is to see the little "miracles" that happen every day in our lives simply because God has as much care for us as Jesus had care for Jairus's daughter and the woman. God always can bring something new out of the ordinary, out of pain, out of even death. The Good News of Jesus' life and mission is that suffering and death are not hopeless situations, but out of them come life. All we need is faith and trust in Jesus. All we need to do is come to him.

Living the Paschal Mystery

It is hard to develop a spirituality that is open to the constant in-breaking of God's life, to the constant Presence of the risen Jesus to us. Our own faith must grow in a way that enables us to see God present and at work in all circumstances of our lives. Even something so ordinary and simple as getting over a cold and feeling good again is a sign of God's Presence which brings us a healing touch. By recognizing these signs of God's Presence we are able to see new possibilities, have new expectations, and hear Jesus' command, "Go in peace."

Focusing the Gospel

Key words and phrases: Jairus, came forward; She . . . came up behind him; your faith has saved you; just have faith

To the point: Faith in who Jesus is and what he can do brings us to act. Jairus approaches Jesus directly, kneels before him, and asks for healing for his daughter. The "woman afflicted with hemorrhages" dares not approach Jesus directly; she simply wishes to "touch his clothes" to be cured. In both cases their faith gave them the courage to approach Jesus and raised their expectation that he had the power to heal. Our faith, too, gives us courage and expectation. What do we do with it?

Connecting the Gospel

to the first reading: Wisdom reminds us that we are made in God's image. Jesus' healing re-creates us in the wholeness and well-being that God intends for us.

to experience: When faced with something we really don't want to do, we often drag our feet about getting going. When excited about something, the excitement itself is motivation to act. This gospel raises the issue about whether our faith is deep enough to motivate us to act.

Connecting the Responsorial Psalm

to the readings: The Sunday Lectionary uses Psalm 30 four times (Easter Vigil 4, Third Sunday of Easter C, Tenth Sunday in Ordinary Time C, and Thirteenth Sunday in Ordinary Time B) and each time the readings deal with our need to be delivered from death. Even though God has made all things for life (first reading), we nonetheless experience death coming toward us over and over, in many guises. We find ourselves caught in the middle of a cosmic struggle between the force of life and the force of death. The good news, as the gospel so concretely dramatizes, is that Christ holds the ultimate power in this struggle. By singing these verses from Psalm 30, we acknowledge what oftentimes only our faith can see: that death with its contingent weeping and mourning is not the end of the story—life is. It is no wonder that we can sing with such confidence.

to psalmist preparation: When you sing this psalm, you embody the confidence of the entire Body of Christ that God saves from death, even when the whole world groans under its threat. Pray this week for those who are facing death in any form—physical, mental, emotional. Pray that you become a vessel of hope for them.

ASSEMBLY & FAITH-SHARING GROUPS
- Those who live a deep faith life and through their example call me to grow in my faith are . . .
- I struggle with faith when . . .
- Because of my faith, my expectations are . . . My faith moves me to act in these ways . . .

PRESIDERS
My ministry deepens my faith when . . . challenges my faith when . . .

DEACONS
My service brings new courage and expectations to those I serve when I . . .

HOSPITALITY MINISTERS
My hospitality ministry helps those coming to liturgy to encounter Jesus in these ways . . .

MUSIC MINISTERS
Whenever the task of music ministry becomes burdensome to me, I need to come to Jesus and . . .

ALTAR MINISTERS
My serving at the altar increases my faith and helps me encounter Jesus when . . .

LECTORS
God's word leads me to act on my faith in these ways . . .

EXTRAORDINARY MINISTERS OF HOLY COMMUNION
When I see the communicants as those who want healing and new Life from Jesus, my ministry becomes . . .

Model Penitential Act

Presider: In this Sunday's gospel, because of their faith Jesus heals a woman and raises Jairus's daughter from the dead. As we prepare to celebrate this liturgy, let us ask for God's mercy for those times when we failed to act on our faith . . . [pause]

> Lord Jesus, you heal those who come to you in faith: Lord . . .
>
> Christ Jesus, you are the divine Son who has all power over sickness and death: Christ . . .
>
> Lord Jesus, you give us faith and courage: Lord . . .

Homily Points

- Who, when they are seriously ill, doesn't beg God to heal them? Illness diminishes us and forces us to face our own vulnerability and mortality. We naturally shrink from it. Knowing full well the human condition, Jesus made healing an important aspect of his saving ministry. But his healing work required faith on the part of those in need. Indeed, Jesus often specifically commends ill persons for their faith, as in this Sunday's gospel.

- In the midst of "a large crowd gathered around" Jesus, Jairus kneels humbly at his feet and the "woman afflicted with hemorrhages" quietly touches his cloak. Both individuals act out of faith. In response, Jesus heals. We learn from these healing accounts how important it is to have faith, to approach Jesus with courage and expectation, and to receive the gift of healing and the deeper faith he offers.

- Faith is a gift of God. We nurture it and allow it to deepen within us. But when we come in faith to God for healing, why does it not always happen according to our prayer and expectation? Our prayer for healing is always answered; our expectation is not always met. Simply coming to Jesus is already a healing. So let us come in faith.

Model Universal Prayer (Prayer of the Faithful)

Presider: Let us bring our needs to the God who calls us to deeper faith and new life.

Response:

Lord, hear our prayer.

Cantor:

we pray to the Lord,

That all members of the church may continue to grow in faith that leads to action . . . [pause]

That all people may come to the wholeness and well-being God intends for us . . . [pause]

That the sick and the suffering be strengthened and healed . . . [pause]

That all members of this community approach Jesus often with courage and expectation . . . [pause]

Presider: Gracious God, you sent your divine Son to heal us of all that keeps us from you: hear our prayers that our faith may increase and one day we may share everlasting Life with you. We ask this through Christ our Lord. **Amen.**

COLLECT

Let us pray

Pause for silent prayer

O God, who through the grace of adoption
chose us to be children of light,
grant, we pray,
that we may not be wrapped in the
    darkness of error
but always be seen to stand in the bright
    light of truth.
Through our Lord Jesus Christ, your Son,
who lives and reigns with you in the unity
    of the Holy Spirit,
one God, for ever and ever. **Amen.**

FIRST READING

Wis 1:13-15; 2:23-24

God did not make death,
    nor does he rejoice in the destruction of
        the living.
For he fashioned all things that they might
        have being;
    and the creatures of the world are
        wholesome,
and there is not a destructive drug among
        them
    nor any domain of the netherworld on
        earth,
    for justice is undying.
For God formed man to be imperishable;
    the image of his own nature he made
        him.
But by the envy of the devil, death entered
    the world,
    and they who belong to his company
        experience it.

RESPONSORIAL PSALM
Ps 30:2, 4, 5-6, 11, 12, 13

R⁒. (2a) I will praise you, Lord, for you have rescued me.

I will extol you, O Lord, for you drew me clear
    and did not let my enemies rejoice over me.
O Lord, you brought me up from the netherworld;
    you preserved me from among those going down into the pit.

R⁒. I will praise you, Lord, for you have rescued me.

Sing praise to the Lord, you his faithful ones,
    and give thanks to his holy name.
For his anger lasts but a moment;
    a lifetime, his good will.
At nightfall, weeping enters in,
    but with the dawn, rejoicing.

R⁒. I will praise you, Lord, for you have rescued me.

Hear, O Lord, and have pity on me;
    O Lord, be my helper.
You changed my mourning into dancing;
    O Lord, my God, forever will I give you thanks.

R⁒. I will praise you, Lord, for you have rescued me.

SECOND READING
2 Cor 8:7, 9, 13-15

Brothers and sisters:
As you excel in every respect, in faith, discourse,
    knowledge, all earnestness, and in the love we have for you,
    may you excel in this gracious act also.

For you know the gracious act of our Lord Jesus Christ,
    that though he was rich, for your sake he became poor,
    so that by his poverty you might become rich.
Not that others should have relief while you are burdened,
    but that as a matter of equality
    your abundance at the present time should supply their needs,
    so that their abundance may also supply your needs,
    that there may be equality.
As it is written:
    Whoever had much did not have more,
    and whoever had little did not have less.

✠ CATECHESIS

About Liturgy

Liturgical expectations, people, and situations: Liturgy always challenges us to examine our expectations of God, the faith community, and ourselves. If we come looking for what liturgy is not supposed to do, we tend to go away disappointed, often lashing out at the people who work hard to help liturgy unfold gracefully and prayerfully.

Primarily liturgy is about enacting in our present situation and lives the dying and rising mystery of Christ. In the here and now we celebrate the mystery into which we were plunged at baptism and which defines our daily living. As members of the Body of Christ, we are to live with the self-giving care, compassion, and openness to new life that Jesus demonstrated in his life. This is not always easy, especially when we want to make liturgy something very personal which satisfies our own prayer, aesthetic, and relational needs. Liturgy, then, calls us to come to each celebration as if for the first time. It calls us to drop our preconceived notions and expectations—derived from countless liturgical experiences—and be open to each celebration as a new encounter with God and each other. The satisfaction of liturgy must come much less from our own personal needs and taste and much more from our surrendering ourselves to God's action within each of us and within the community as a whole.

If we form ourselves in an attitude that each liturgy is new, then we have prepared ourselves for whatever surprises God may have in store for us. Liturgy is rarely an emotional high, nor should it be. But it is always an opportunity to encounter God and each other in faith, celebrating what is defining for us: the life, death, and resurrection of Jesus Christ and our participation in that saving mystery.

About Liturgical Music

Music suggestions: Songs about Jesus' power over sickness and death and our need to have faith in him would be appropriate this Sunday. "Your Hands, O Lord, in Days of Old" (W4, WC, WS) would make a strong entrance song. "Healer of Our Every Ill" (G3, W4, WC, WS) would be suitable for either the preparation of the gifts or Communion. John Bell's "We Cannot Measure How You Heal" (G3, W4) expresses the confident trust we hold in Jesus' healing power and care for us. This hymn would be appropriate for the preparation of the gifts or as a choral prelude (SATB arrangement GIA, G-6128). Janet Vogt's "Age to Age" (BB, JS3; SATB arrangement OCP 10900) invites us to trust in the Lord's care. The verses are best led by cantor or choir; the refrain is our response. Verse 4 in particular captures the content of this Sunday's gospel: "Lord, let my faith in you be revealed. Only say the word and I shall be healed." This lovely and engaging piece would work well during the Communion procession. "Jesus, Heal Us" (G3) and "You Are Mine" (found in many resources), both by David Haas, would work well during the preparation of the gifts or Communion. "Precious Lord, Take My Hand" (found in many resources) sings of faith in God's care and protection, and would fit either the preparation of the gifts or Communion. Other good choices for Communion are Scott Soper's "You Are the Healing" (BB) and M. D. Ridge's "The Lord Is My Hope" (BB).

SPIRITUALITY

Gospel   Matt 16:13-19; L591

When Jesus went into the region of
    Caesarea Philippi
    he asked his disciples,
    "Who do people say that the
        Son of Man is?"
They replied, "Some say John the
    Baptist, others Elijah,
    still others Jeremiah or one of
        the prophets."
He said to them, "But who do you
    say that I am?"
Simon Peter said in reply,
    "You are the Christ, the Son of the liv-
        ing God."
Jesus said to him in reply, "Blessed are
    you, Simon son of Jonah.
For flesh and blood has not revealed this
    to you, but my heavenly Father.
And so I say to you, you are Peter,
    and upon this rock I will build my
        Church,
    and the gates of the netherworld shall
        not prevail against it.
I will give you the keys to the Kingdom of
    heaven.
Whatever you bind on earth shall be
    bound in heaven;
    and whatever you loose on earth shall
        be loosed in heaven."

See Appendix A, p. 303, for the other readings.

FIRST READING
Acts 12:1-11

RESPONSORIAL PSALM
Ps 34:2-3, 4-5, 6-7, 8-9

SECOND READING
2 Tim 4:6-8, 17-18

Reflecting on the Gospel

It is too easy to write off great saints such as Peter and Paul as beyond what
we ourselves can reach. Yet, both of these founding apostles had to grow in
their knowledge of Jesus and what encounter with him called them to be. Both
Peter and Paul underwent great changes in their lives. Neither began as a rock,
a pillar of the church. Simon, a simple fisherman and one who doubted and denied Jesus, only gradually becomes Peter, the outspoken leader of the apostles
and the one who announces clearly Jesus' identity as the Christ. Saul, a devout Pharisee who persecuted Christians (Acts 9 and 22), only gradually becomes Paul the evangelizer of the Gentiles (see second reading). With both
of these great apostles, encounter with the risen Christ changed
who they were and what their life was about. Both Peter
and Paul are revered in the church because of their
unique relationship with Jesus. Both revealed in word
and action that they knew Jesus to be "the Christ, the Son
of the living God."

These two great apostles call us to willingness to
change, a change that can only come from encounters with
Jesus. This is how we come to encounter Jesus: in the very
willingness to change, to identify with him more, to grow in
our own identity as his disciples who continue his mission.

Our answer to the identity question Jesus asks cannot be based
only on what we have heard about him or on the witness or authority of others,
as was the first answer of some of the disciples in the gospel. Jesus' question is
a *personal* one that each of us must, like Peter, answer from the depths of who
we have come to know Jesus to be *for us*. Not just a celebration honoring these
two apostles, this solemnity is also a celebration of the church—the believing
community which continually professes before the world who Jesus is. We, too,
are rocks upon which the church is built and the missionaries through whom
"the proclamation [of Christ] might be completed" (second reading).

To recognize and proclaim Jesus' identity requires a response: total conformity to "Christ, the Son of the living God." We can speak of the church being
built upon these two great apostles because of their total conformity to Christ.
Both the identity and mission of the church are the same: to be Christ. This is
the rock upon which the church is built: utter conformity and fidelity to being
the Body of Christ. This is the challenge of this festival for us.

Living the Paschal Mystery

We ourselves are called to change in the same way as Peter and Paul—not
simply a change in form that is external but a change in being that conforms
us completely to Christ, so much so that we continue his saving mission in all
we do. This is the challenge of this solemnity honoring the two great apostles
Peter and Paul: totally conform to Christ. The netherworld cannot prevail
against those who carry the identity of the Body of Christ. Like Peter and Paul,
this conformity promises us that "the crown of righteousness awaits" us, too.
Unlike Peter and Paul, most of us won't suffer and die a martyr's death. But
like Peter and Paul, we are all called to put Christ first in our lives. We are all
called to change. We are all called to encounter Jesus and follow his call. This
means that sometimes we may have to make choices that make us unpopular at
home or in the workplace. This is the cost of faithful conformity to Christ.

Focusing the Gospel

Key words and phrases: But who do you say that I am?, You are the Christ, rock . . . church

To the point: Jesus' question, "who do you say that I am?" is a *personal* one each of us must, like Peter and Paul, answer from the depths of who we have come to know Jesus to be *for us*. Not just a celebration honoring these two apostles, this solemnity is also a celebration of the church—the believing community which continually professes before the world who Jesus is.

Model Penitential Act

Presider: God raised up two great apostles, Peter and Paul, to be pillars of his church and models of faithful discipleship. As we begin our celebration, let us pray for the strength to walk in the footsteps of Peter and Paul . . . [pause]

> Lord Jesus, you are the Christ, the Son of the living God: Lord . . .
> Christ Jesus, you named Peter, the rock upon which you built your church: Christ . . .
> Lord Jesus, you called Paul, the apostle to the nations: Lord . . .

Model Universal Prayer (Prayer of the Faithful)

Presider: We pray for the strength to conform our lives totally to Christ and to be faithful witnesses of the Gospel.

Response:

Lord, hear our prayer.

Cantor:

we pray to the Lord,

That all members of the church profess in word and action that Jesus is the Christ, the Son of God . . . [pause]

That all peoples may hear God call them to live good and fruitful lives . . . [pause]

That those imprisoned or persecuted for spreading the faith be restored to their communities . . . [pause]

That all of us faithfully bring the message of the Gospel to all we meet by the way we live our lives in conformity to Christ . . . [pause]

Presider: O living God, you raised up for us Peter and Paul as models of faith and discipleship: hear these our prayers that one day we might join them in sharing your everlasting glory. We ask this through Christ our Lord. **Amen.**

FOR REFLECTION
- Jesus poses the question of his identity to me when . . . My answer is . . .
- Others have revealed to me who Jesus is by . . .
- This celebration of Peter and Paul helps me understand that the church is . . .

Homily Points

- Both Peter and Paul are honored on this festival because of their unique relationship with Jesus. In word and in action both revealed that they knew who Jesus was for themselves personally and for the mission of the church: "the Christ, the Son of the living God."

- Peter and Paul were both called by Jesus to be his apostles. So are we, through baptism, called by him to be members of the community of the church sent to profess who Jesus is for the world. We do so by living Gospel values, such as treating others with respect and dignity, forgiving others who hurt us, loving beyond minimums, reaching out with help to the poor and those in need, touching with a healing presence those who are sick. In these and many other ways of living the Gospel, Jesus hears us answering his question, who am I?

SPIRITUALITY

GOSPEL ACCLAMATION
cf. Luke 4:18

R⁊. Alleluia, alleluia.
The Spirit of the Lord is upon me,
for he sent me to bring glad tidings to the poor.
R⁊. Alleluia, alleluia.

Gospel

Mark 6:1-6; L101B

**Jesus departed from there
and came to his native
place, accompanied by
his disciples.
When the sabbath came he
began to teach in the
synagogue,
and many who
heard him were
astonished.
They said, "Where did
this man get all this?
What kind of wisdom has been given
him?
What mighty deeds are wrought by his
hands!
Is he not the carpenter, the son of
Mary,
and the brother of James and Joses
and Judas and Simon?
And are not his sisters here with us?"
And they took offense at him.
Jesus said to them,
"A prophet is not without honor
except in his native place
and among his own kin and in his
own house."
So he was not able to perform any
mighty deed there,
apart from curing a few sick people
by laying his hands on them.
He was amazed at their lack of faith.**

Reflecting on the Gospel

We are always surprised—sometimes even shocked—when someone acts out of character. A shy, quiet person might speak out forcefully, publicly against an injustice. A reserved, serious person might some night be the life of a party. A person without higher education reveals eloquence, insight, and brilliance on a challenging topic. Persons acting out of character shake up the expectations that limit our responses to others. Shockingly, in this Sunday's gospel Jesus encounters resistance and rejection "among his own kin and in his own house." This, because Jesus' words and deeds went beyond his neighbors' understanding of who he was ("the carpenter"). Jesus was acting way out of character for them.

The limited expectations of those in Jesus' "native place" blocked their ability to see in faith who Jesus really was. In response to Jesus' teaching and wisdom, mighty deeds and healings, "they took offense." Their limited expectations limited Jesus' own ability to show that a new in-breaking of God was among them. This gospel challenges us to examine the limits of our own expectations about who Jesus is and what he can do for us. It challenges us to examine our own expectations of others and allow them the space to be who God is helping them become.

God continually offers us what we need for salvation, but we often resist it. Our receptivity is key for hearing God's word and receiving the salvation God offers. The rejected prophet has no power to influence the behavior of the people (see first reading); Jesus is unable to work miracles for those who do not believe in him. God always offers everything we need to come to salvation; it is for us to recognize and receive it. Our very receptivity to God's Presence and gifts is an act of faith, and this is decisive for whether we receive God's ultimate gift of eternal Life. On the other hand, our rebellion, obstinacy, lack of faith (revealed in this gospel as rejection) keep us from recognizing God's Presence and works in our midst, keep us from recognizing Jesus.

The shock of the gospel is the weight that our faith or lack of faith has. God never pushes salvation on us; it is a faithful gift, but one freely given and only asking of us a free response. Jesus "was not able" to perform miracles in his hometown because of the townspeople's lack of faith. Shockingly, God never quits on us or abandons us; it is we who choose to resist or have faith. It is we who choose . . . is Jesus able to perform any mighty deed or not?

Living the Paschal Mystery

Our own "mighty deeds" which bring forth faith in others lie in our doing our daily tasks the best we can, accepting others for who they are, being patient with others' responses to us. We may not do the "mighty deed" of healing the sick, but we can surely visit them and bring a word of hope. We might not all be theologians, but we can speak from our hearts the conviction of God's word in Scripture which we've heard over and over again at Mass and in private prayer.

We are anointed prophets in baptism. We receive the wisdom of the Holy Spirit. We are empowered to do the mightiest of mighty deeds: be the Body of Christ, bringing Christ's risen Presence to our broken world. What will people say of us? We will shock them into taking a second look at who we are only when we live as Jesus did—giving ourselves for others.

Focusing the Gospel

Key words and phrases: came to his native place, wisdom, mighty deeds, took offense at him, lack of faith

To the point: The limited expectations of those in Jesus' "native place" blocked their ability to see in faith who Jesus really was. In response to Jesus' teaching and wisdom, mighty deeds and healings, "they took offense." Their limited expectations limited Jesus' own ability to show that a new in-breaking of God was among them. This gospel challenges us to examine the limits of our own expectations about who Jesus is and what he can do for us.

Connecting the Gospel

to the first reading: In spite of our rejection, rebellion, nonreceptivity, God persists in sending "a prophet . . . among" us (first reading) to teach us and call us to faithfulness.

to experience: We find it easier to confine encounters with God to amazing places or events (for example, apparitions). But God's normative manner of coming to us is in the ordinary circumstances of our daily lives ("native place") and in the human beings closest to us ("among his own kin and in his own house").

Connecting the Responsorial Psalm

to the readings: What is the mercy for which we plead in this responsorial psalm refrain? Are we prophets like Jesus and Ezekiel who need God's support to remain faithful to our mission despite intense opposition from those closest to us (gospel, first reading)? Or are we the ones who reject the words of Jesus because we refuse to recognize who he is (gospel)? Chances are, the answer is sometimes one and sometimes the other. The good news is that in either case God hears our cry for mercy and responds. Because of God's response, we can do whatever is necessary, be it to remain faithful servants of God (psalm), or to open our eyes to see Jesus more clearly. We have only to fix our eyes in the right direction.

to psalmist preparation: Whether you speak the word of God or hear that word spoken by another, you need to keep your eyes fixed firmly on God. Only by doing this can you be faithful to your mission as psalmist. What helps you remain faithful? What helps you keep your eyes focused on God?

**ASSEMBLY &
FAITH-SHARING GROUPS**

- Someone who opens me to the wisdom of God is . . . Someone who brings me the healing of God is . . .
- I tend to limit my expectations of what Jesus does for me when . . . does for others when . . .
- I have experienced a new in-breaking of God in my life at these times . . .

PRESIDERS

My priestly ministry helps others be receptive to the Presence and "mighty deeds" of the risen Jesus when . . .

DEACONS

My serving others is truly a faith-filled response to Jesus acting through me when . . .

HOSPITALITY MINISTERS

My ministry to those gathering for liturgy increases their ability to hear Jesus' teaching and experience Jesus' "mighty deeds" by . . .

MUSIC MINISTERS

I encounter the risen Jesus in the familiarity of my fellow music ministers when I . . .

ALTAR MINISTERS

I have been astonished and surprised to experience the risen Jesus through the mundane, lowly business of service when . . .

LECTORS

My manner of proclaiming the Scripture moves beyond the familiar to something astonishing and powerful when . . .

**EXTRAORDINARY MINISTERS
OF HOLY COMMUNION**

My distributing Holy Communion challenges me to recognize Jesus among my "own kin" and "in [my] own house" because . . .

Model Penitential Act

Presider: The gospel today describes the rejection of Jesus by those most familiar with him—his kin and neighbors. Let us ask God's mercy for the times we have rejected Jesus . . . [pause]

Lord Jesus, you are among us as one kin to us: Lord . . .

Christ Jesus, you dwell in eternal glory in your Father's house: Christ . . .

Lord Jesus, you offer us words of wisdom and acts of healing: Lord . . .

Homily Points

- Who does Jesus think he is? Does he think he's better than we are? We folks from Nazareth merely see him as the carpenter—he's just one of us. We don't have prophetic wisdom. We don't perform mighty deeds. And Jesus shouldn't either. Yet even for us folks today, how often is a saving intervention from God right in front of us and we refuse to recognize it because it is too ordinary?

- Many who heard Jesus teach in the synagogue were astonished and offended. They could not tolerate such wisdom from someone whose origins they thought they knew. Jesus, in turn, was "angered" at their lack of faith. What is it they were unable to believe? That God comes with mighty deeds and healing through persons we know, in ways familiar to us.

- God's interventions to bring us salvation are always extraordinary, but most often come in ordinary and familiar circumstances. For example, a neighbor brings some homemade soup to us when we are sick; parents share their faith with their children; someone notices we are having a rough day and takes time to sit and listen to us. Ordinary people acting in such ordinary ways reveal to us who Jesus is—the mighty Savior still present to us and among us.

Model Universal Prayer (Prayer of the Faithful)

Presider: God cares for us through familiar people and circumstances. We are encouraged to make our needs known to this God who is always present to us.

Response:

Lord, hear our prayer.

Cantor:

we pray to the Lord,

For all members of the church, may their faith be deepened through encounters with the risen Jesus in the familiar and ordinary . . . [pause]

For all world leaders, may they govern with wisdom and justice . . . [pause]

For the sick and the suffering, may they be strengthened and healed by the Presence of the risen Jesus through the care and concern of this community . . . [pause]

For each of us here, may the actions of our ordinary, familiar lives reveal the Presence of the risen Jesus in all we do . . . [pause]

Presider: O God who continue to work mighty deeds, you are present to us in the ordinary circumstances of our lives: hear these our prayers that we might always recognize Christ among us. We pray through that same Jesus Christ our Lord. **Amen.**

COLLECT

Let us pray

Pause for silent prayer

O God, who in the abasement of your Son
have raised up a fallen world,
fill your faithful with holy joy,
for on those you have rescued from slavery
   to sin
you bestow eternal gladness.
Through our Lord Jesus Christ, your Son,
who lives and reigns with you in the unity
   of the Holy Spirit,
one God, for ever and ever. **Amen.**

FIRST READING

Ezek 2:2-5

As the LORD spoke to me, the spirit entered
   into me
   and set me on my feet,
   and I heard the one who was speaking
      say to me:
   Son of man, I am sending you to the
      Israelites,
   rebels who have rebelled against me;
   they and their ancestors have revolted
      against me to this very day.
Hard of face and obstinate of heart
   are they to whom I am sending you.
But you shall say to them: Thus says the
   Lord GOD!
And whether they heed or resist—for they
   are a rebellious house—
   they shall know that a prophet has been
      among them.

RESPONSORIAL PSALM

Ps 123:1-2, 2, 3-4

℟. (2cd) Our eyes are fixed on the Lord, pleading for his mercy.

To you I lift up my eyes
    who are enthroned in heaven—
as the eyes of servants
    are on the hands of their masters.

℟. Our eyes are fixed on the Lord, pleading for his mercy.

As the eyes of a maid
    are on the hands of her mistress,
so are our eyes on the LORD, our God,
    till he have pity on us.

℟. Our eyes are fixed on the Lord, pleading for his mercy.

Have pity on us, O LORD, have pity on us,
    for we are more than sated with
        contempt;
our souls are more than sated
    with the mockery of the arrogant,
    with the contempt of the proud.

℟. Our eyes are fixed on the Lord, pleading for his mercy.

SECOND READING

2 Cor 12:7-10

Brothers and sisters:
That I, Paul, might not become too elated,
    because of the abundance of the
        revelations,
    a thorn in the flesh was given to me, an
        angel of Satan,
    to beat me, to keep me from being too
        elated.
Three times I begged the Lord about this,
    that it might leave me,
    but he said to me, "My grace is
        sufficient for you,
    for power is made perfect in weakness."
I will rather boast most gladly of my
        weaknesses,
    in order that the power of Christ may
        dwell with me.
Therefore, I am content with weaknesses,
        insults,
    hardships, persecutions, and
        constraints,
    for the sake of Christ;
    for when I am weak, then I am strong.

About Liturgy

Gospel and Creed: Each Sunday at Mass we hear the gospel proclaimed and profess our faith. Perhaps there is a challenge this Sunday in the readings to connect these two—gospel and creedal statement. In the proclamation of the gospel we hear of Jesus' mighty deeds; as we proclaim what Jesus does we learn more about who he was. Jesus' deeds are a window into who Jesus is. More than a carpenter, he was a prophet speaking the word of God on our behalf and showing us how we must live in order for God's reign to come. It is as response to this gospel proclamation of Christ in our midst that we profess our faith.

The challenge is always to make the Creed more than a superficial recitation of some tenets of our faith. The assent of our belief is expressed in how we live. As we recite the Creed, we might think back to what has just been proclaimed in the gospel on a particular Sunday. Then "I believe" means that we commit ourselves to doing in our everyday lives what Jesus was doing in the gospel. This is why the Creed is included every Sunday: so that we might publicly profess that we are the Body of Christ and will act this week as Jesus shows us in the gospel.

July 4th: July 4th occurred on Saturday, and (if there is a morning Mass) it would be pastorally good to celebrate liturgy on that day (there is a votive Mass for celebrating Independence Day in the U.S. *Roman Missal*). If there is only an evening Mass, the Mass for the Fourteenth Sunday in Ordinary Time is used. But it would be appropriate at the Saturday evening and Sunday Masses to include an intention for the good of the country. Here is a model: For the people of the United States, may we embrace the religious principles upon which our nation is built and work for justice and freedom, peace and abundance for all peoples . . . [pause]

About Liturgical Music

Singing the Holy, Holy, Holy: The eucharistic prayer is the "center and high point" of the whole Mass. The presider addresses this prayer "in the name of the entire community to God the Father through Jesus Christ in the Holy Spirit." All present join themselves with Christ in confessing the saving deeds of God and offering themselves in sacrifice. Because of its importance, we are to listen to this prayer with "reverence and in silence" (GIRM, no. 78).

There are, however, three moments when we participate in the eucharistic prayer with song: the Holy, Holy, Holy; the Mystery of Faith; and the Great Amen. The first of these acclamations of faith is the longest. The Holy, Holy, Holy is based on a text taken from the Jewish morning synagogue service: "Holy, holy, holy is the LORD of hosts; / the whole earth is full of his glory" (Isa 6:3, NABRE). The book of Revelation describes the four living creatures who surround God's throne praying in similar fashion: "Holy, holy, holy is the Lord God almighty, / who was, and who is, and who is to come" (Rev 4:8, NABRE). Every time we sing this acclamation, then, we unite with believers past, present, and future in acclaiming the sovereignty of God over all creation and over all time. We acclaim that heaven, earth, and history are in God's hands.

JULY 5, 2015
FOURTEENTH SUNDAY
IN ORDINARY TIME

SPIRITUALITY

GOSPEL ACCLAMATION
cf. Eph 1:17-18

R̥. Alleluia, alleluia.
May the Father of our Lord Jesus Christ
enlighten the eyes of our hearts,
that we may know what is the hope that
belongs to our call.
R̥. Alleluia, alleluia.

Gospel

Mark 6:7-13; L104B

**Jesus summoned the Twelve
and began to send them
out two by two
and gave them authority
over unclean spirits.
He instructed them to take
nothing for the journey
but a walking stick—
no food, no sack, no money
in their belts.
They were, however, to wear
sandals
but not a second tunic.
He said to them,
"Wherever you enter a house, stay
there until you leave.
Whatever place does not welcome you
or listen to you,
leave there and shake the dust off
your feet
in testimony against them."
So they went off and preached
repentance.
The Twelve drove out many demons,
and they anointed with oil many who
were sick and cured them.**

Reflecting on the Gospel

Hospital ERs are typically very, very busy. Waits for those who are not critically ill or possibly facing death can be very long. One development that has relieved ER overload is the emergence of urgent care facilities all over our cities. These are for after-hours, nonappointment kinds of health care needs. The operative word is "urgent"; the needed care cannot wait until the physician office opens in the morning. Something needs to be done *now*. Few things in our life carry the natural sense of urgency that serious, unexpected health care issues generate. In this gospel Jesus sends the Twelve out on mission, and the way he does so indicates that there is an urgency about this sending forth.

"Jesus *summoned* the Twelve." "Summoned" is a significant word here. This is a call that cannot be ignored because the mission is so urgent: to preach repentance. The mission is so urgent that the Twelve are not even to burden themselves with seeming necessities of life. The mission is so urgent that the Twelve are not even to stay with those who do not receive them or listen to them. The mission is so urgent that the Twelve are given Jesus' own authority to expel demons and cure illnesses. Jesus sends the Twelve off to preach repentance. The mission is so urgent because what is at stake is our relationship with God and each other. Repentance heals the wounds that separate; repentance overflows into forgiveness; repentance changes our behavior; repentance is basic to growth in our covenantal fidelity; repentance makes us whole again.

It is an awesome thought that Jesus entrusts his mission to us. We cannot ignore Jesus' command performance to preach repentance. The mission of Jesus is so urgent that he must use others to reach out to all people at all times to bring them salvation. But the only way we can be successful is to make sure that our mission is, indeed, that of Jesus. Who Jesus is, disciples are—prophets sent on a mission (see the first reading). With our own power and talent, we can do little; with a deep relationship with Jesus and the realization that we continue his saving work, we can do much.

Living the Paschal Mystery

The practical instructions of Jesus to his Twelve would not serve us well today; it would be irresponsible to divest ourselves of all our possessions. At the same time this gospel does invite us to examine what it is that hinders us from fulfilling the mission on which Jesus sends all of us because of our baptism and the covenantal relationship it establishes between God and us and others and us. Each of us is a disciple who is sent. What distracts us from this urgent mission?

For most of us the greatest distractions probably don't come from our possessions, but from our interior emotions and attitudes. We don't like rejection—so it is difficult to preach an unpopular Gospel with its demands for righteousness and love. We don't like the risk of being unsuccessful—so it is easier to live our religion by saying prayers rather than by ceaseless self-giving. We don't like pushing our own faith to its limits—so it is easier to be more concerned with right doctrine than with right living. In spite of our excuses and human weakness, Jesus is clear: "Go . . . to my people" (first reading). We must keep moving forward with his urgent mission. We must faithfully preach repentance, because that is how our relationships are healed and grow strong.

Focusing the Gospel

Key words and phrases: Jesus summoned the Twelve, gave them authority over unclean spirits, take nothing, leave there, preached repentance

To the point: "Jesus *summoned* the Twelve." "Summoned" is a significant word here. This is a call that cannot be ignored because the mission is so urgent: to preach repentance. The mission is so urgent that the Twelve are not even to burden themselves with seeming necessities of life. The mission is so urgent that the Twelve are not even to stay with those who do not receive them or listen to them. The mission is so urgent that the Twelve are given Jesus' own authority to expel demons and cure illnesses. The mission is so urgent that . . .

Connecting the Gospel

to the first reading: As with Jesus summoning the Twelve in the gospel, God summoned Amos to "prophesy to my people Israel." As with the Twelve, the mission of Amos was urgent.

to experience: When we receive a phone call and the voice of the caller sounds urgent, we respond immediately. We intently listen and then decisively act. Jesus' summons of the Twelve is such a "phone call."

Connecting the Responsorial Psalm

to the readings: God sent Amos on a mission to prophesy to "the people Israel" (first reading). Jesus sent the Twelve on a mission to preach repentance (gospel). Neither Amos nor the Twelve chose this mission. The call to be prophet, the mission to preach, and the power to confront evil and cure disease come not from ourselves but from God. In these verses from Psalm 85, we pray to hear and see what we are to preach and do. We promise to hear God proclaiming peace, and see God bringing together kindness and truth, justice and peace. We also announce the good news that despite the opposition and rejection we will face (first reading and gospel), God will bring the mission to completion. We can count on it.

to psalmist preparation: Do you hear what God is proclaiming in the world? Do you see what God is doing? How does your singing of this responsorial psalm proclaim that you do, indeed, hear and see what God is doing for human salvation? How does your daily living proclaim it?

**ASSEMBLY &
FAITH-SHARING GROUPS**
- I am summoned by Jesus to . . . The mission is so urgent that . . .
- Traveling light because of discipleship gives me freedom to . . . is difficult for me when . . .
- The authority of Jesus that I have is . . . I act out of this authority when . . .

PRESIDERS
I convey the urgency of Jesus' mission when I . . .

DEACONS
To serve with Jesus' authority feels like . . . looks like . . .

HOSPITALITY MINISTERS
The manner of my greeting helps those who gather for liturgy to shed their extra baggage to take up Jesus' mission when . . .

MUSIC MINISTERS
What I feel is urgent for me as a music minister is . . . What Jesus teaches is urgent about my ministry is . . .

ALTAR MINISTERS
My ministry has many "urgent" things about it, and this is related to the overall mission of Jesus in that . . .

LECTORS
As I prepare to proclaim the Scriptures, I hear Jesus summon me to . . .

**EXTRAORDINARY MINISTERS
OF HOLY COMMUNION**
My ministry of distributing the Body (Blood) of the risen Jesus summons me to . . .

CELEBRATION

Model Penitential Act

Presider: Jesus summons the Twelve to go out on the urgent mission of preaching repentance. As we prepare for this liturgy, let us consider the times we have not heeded Jesus' summons to continue his mission in our own lives and ask for his mercy . . . [pause]

Lord Jesus, you call all people to repentance: Lord . . .

Christ Jesus, you continue your saving mission through your disciples: Christ . . .

Lord Jesus, you shower mercy on those who turn to you: Lord . . .

Homily Points

- A subpoena summons us to court. A principal summons a student to the office. Parents summon a wayward child to a family conference. Summons such as these do not admit of being ignored, carry grave importance, and tend to put us on edge. Their urgency is already the message: something's up. What was up when Jesus summoned the Twelve in this gospel passage?

- What was up was the salvation of the world. What was up was the call to repentance. What was up was the healing of humanity. Nothing—neither life necessities nor rejection—can keep us from faithfully hearing and responding to Jesus' summons to preach repentance. The summons is urgent because the mission is urgent.

- This gospel poses two challenges for us: first, that we hear Jesus' summons; second, that we grasp its urgency. We hear Jesus' summons through his word in the gospels, the cry of those in need, the desire of those wishing to grow in their faith. We grasp the urgency of the summons when we respond without counting personal cost, actively seek ways to preach repentance, consistently shape our everyday living in accord with the demands of the Gospel. What is at stake is the salvation of the world. The summons is urgent because the mission is urgent.

Model Universal Prayer (Prayer of the Faithful)

Presider: Jesus summons each of us to continue his saving mission. We turn to God to help us respond faithfully.

Response:

Lord, hear our prayer.

Cantor:

we pray to the Lord,

That all members of the church may hear Jesus' summons to continue his saving mission . . . [pause]

That all peoples of the world may come to salvation through the faithful ministry of others . . . [pause]

That the sick and the suffering may be lifted up by those who respond to Jesus' summons to care for those in need . . . [pause]

That all of us gathered here may be bold in living the Gospel call to repentance . . . [pause]

Presider: Loving God, your divine Son summons us to preach repentance: hear these our prayers that we might be strengthened for this urgent mission which you entrust to us. We ask this through Christ our Lord. **Amen.**

Let us pray

Pause for silent prayer

O God, who show the light of your truth
to those who go astray,
so that they may return to the right path,
give all who for the faith they profess
are accounted Christians
the grace to reject whatever is contrary to
the name of Christ
and to strive after all that does it honor.
Through our Lord Jesus Christ, your Son,
who lives and reigns with you in the unity
of the Holy Spirit,
one God, for ever and ever. **Amen.**

FIRST READING
Amos 7:12-15

Amaziah, priest of Bethel, said to Amos,
"Off with you, visionary, flee to the land
of Judah!
There earn your bread by prophesying,
but never again prophesy in Bethel;
for it is the king's sanctuary and a royal
temple."
Amos answered Amaziah, "I was no
prophet,
nor have I belonged to a company of
prophets;
I was a shepherd and a dresser of
sycamores.
The LORD took me from following the
flock, and said to me,
Go, prophesy to my people Israel."

RESPONSORIAL PSALM
Ps 85:9-10, 11-12, 13-14

R̂. (8) Lord, let us see your kindness, and
grant us your salvation.

I will hear what God proclaims;
the LORD—for he proclaims peace.
Near indeed is his salvation to those who
fear him,
glory dwelling in our land.

R̂. Lord, let us see your kindness, and
grant us your salvation.

Kindness and truth shall meet;
justice and peace shall kiss.
Truth shall spring out of the earth,
and justice shall look down from
heaven.

R̂. Lord, let us see your kindness, and
grant us your salvation.

The LORD himself will give his benefits;
   our land shall yield its increase.
Justice shall walk before him,
   and prepare the way of his steps.

R̸. Lord, let us see your kindness, and
grant us your salvation.

SECOND READING

Eph 1:3-14

Blessed be the God and Father of our Lord
      Jesus Christ,
   who has blessed us in Christ
   with every spiritual blessing in the
      heavens,
   as he chose us in him, before the
      foundation of the world,
   to be holy and without blemish before
      him.
In love he destined us for adoption to
      himself through Jesus Christ,
   in accord with the favor of his will,
   for the praise of the glory of his grace
   that he granted us in the beloved.
In him we have redemption by his blood,
   the forgiveness of transgressions,
   in accord with the riches of his grace
      that he lavished upon us.
In all wisdom and insight, he has made
      known to us
   the mystery of his will in accord with
      his favor
   that he set forth in him as a plan for the
      fullness of times,
   to sum up all things in Christ, in heaven
      and on earth.

In him we were also chosen,
   destined in accord with the purpose of
      the One
   who accomplishes all things according
      to the intention of his will,
   so that we might exist for the praise of
      his glory,
   we who first hoped in Christ.
In him you also, who have heard the word
      of truth,
   the gospel of your salvation, and have
      believed in him,
   were sealed with the promised Holy
      Spirit,
   which is the first installment of our
      inheritance
   toward redemption as God's possession,
      to the praise of his glory.

or Eph 1:3-10

See Appendix A, p. 304.

About Liturgy

Second reading during Ordinary Time: Since the second reading during
Ordinary Time is not chosen to accord with the gospel and first reading but is a semi-
continuous reading from one of the letters of the New Testament, we suggest that the
short form (when given a choice, such as on this Sunday) be proclaimed. This is not to
say that all of Sacred Scripture isn't important, for surely it is. It does remind us that
the centerpiece of the Liturgy of the Word is the gospel and that the first reading and
responsorial psalm are specifically chosen to relate to it. During the festal seasons even
the second reading accords with the rest of the Liturgy of the Word, and it is often a
theological commentary on the feast or season. During those seasons it would be appropriate to read the long form of the second reading if there is a choice.

   This Sunday we begin reading from the letter to the Ephesians and will complete it on
the Twenty-First Sunday in Ordinary Time. This letter stresses the unity of the church
and the Body of Christ (see chapters 1 and 2) as well as the church's mission to the world
and the gifts given to fulfill this mission (see chapters 3 and 4). It is a good letter to begin
reading on this Sunday when the gospel relates Jesus' sending of the apostles on their
mission. The letter to the Ephesians is not without its admonitions to right living, either
(see chapters 5 and 6). This letter is a good blueprint for Ordinary Time: the church sent
on mission living rightly. This characterizes our journey with Christ.

About Liturgical Music

Singing the Mystery of Faith: The current *Roman Missal* not only changed the
name of this element of the eucharistic prayer from "Memorial Acclamation" to "Mystery of Faith," but also gave us these revised texts:

   We proclaim your Death, O Lord, / and profess your Resurrection / until you come
   again.
   When we eat this Bread and drink this Cup, / we proclaim your Death, O Lord, /
   until you come again.
   Save us, Savior of the world, / for by your Cross and Resurrection / you have set
   us free.

   Prior to these changes the most common text sung in the United States for the Mystery of Faith was a fourth form, "Christ has died, Christ is risen, Christ will come again."
Popular as it was, this text presented us with two problems. First, because this text was
sung only in the United States, it separated us from the rest of the
universal church. Second, because this text was not direct
address to the person of Christ, but a didactic statement, it
changed the nature of the acclamation. The importance of directly addressing the risen Christ when
we sing this acclamation cannot be overstated.
By using direct address, we acknowledge that he
is truly present among us, leading our praying of the
eucharistic prayer. We acknowledge that he is alive even
though he died, and that he will come again in glory. We
become the Body addressing the Head, who in his very
person brings the mystery of salvation to fulfillment in
us and in the world. When we sing the Mystery of Faith,
then, we address the person of Christ as the living mystery
present among us and leading us to salvation.

✝ SPIRITUALITY

GOSPEL ACCLAMATION
John 10:27

R♭. Alleluia, alleluia.
My sheep hear my voice, says the Lord;
I know them, and they follow me.
R♭. Alleluia, alleluia.

Gospel

Mark 6:30-34; L107B

The apostles
    gathered
        together with
        Jesus
    and reported all they
        had done and
        taught.
He said to them,
    "Come away by
        yourselves to a
        deserted place
        and rest a while."
People were coming and
    going in great numbers,
    and they had no opportunity even to
    eat.
So they went off in the boat by
    themselves to a deserted place.
People saw them leaving and many
    came to know about it.
They hastened there on foot from all
    the towns
    and arrived at the place before them.

When he disembarked and saw the vast
    crowd,
    his heart was moved with pity for
        them,
    for they were like sheep without a
        shepherd;
    and he began to teach them many
        things.

Reflecting on the Gospel

When we are overwhelmed by life, often it is because the needs crashing down upon us are far greater than the time, energy, and know-how we have to meet them. It seems like we never get to the point when all our needs are over and done with. One need is met, another crops up. We can easily identify with the needs presented in this Sunday's gospel: the weary disciples need rest; the persistent crowd needs to be where Jesus is.

This gospel follows last week's when Jesus sent the Twelve to preach repentance and gave them authority to overcome demons. Noticeably absent in this Sunday's gospel is any mention of healing that the disciples had done. Instead, Jesus' pity for the crowd arises from their need to be led by Jesus; they "were like sheep without a shepherd." This need was so great that even Jesus' seeking a "deserted place" for him and the disciples to rest did not keep the people from hastening to him. Jesus discerned the differing needs of the weary disciples and the persistent crowd, and responded to each accordingly. The crowd won! Jesus interrupted his rest to tend to their needs. So did Jesus win! He shepherded them beyond their need for healing to teach them what they needed to learn about the saving mission he came to fulfill.

Jesus, the true shepherd of God, always responds to the needs of others. How does Jesus respond when the apostles return from their mission and report to him? He invites them to come away and rest. How does Jesus respond when the crowd persists in hastening to him? He teaches them. In fact, he shepherds both the apostles and the crowd. Jesus shepherds everyone toward fuller life through both the re-creating power of rest and the transforming possibilities of new teaching. Jesus is ever the caring shepherd. Jeremiah reproved the shepherds who misled God's people and scattered them (see the first reading); Jesus is the divine shepherd who both knows the needs of others and responds to them. Jesus never misleads. By his own good example, Jesus teaches that responding to others' needs, fostering caring relationships, and teaching the Good News are at the heart of bringing his mission to completion.

Living the Paschal Mystery

We all need to go off to a "deserted place" occasionally to "rest a while." Whether this means taking some time alone each day to pray and rest in God, making Sunday truly a day of rest, or setting aside a few days a year to make a retreat, all of us need time to regain our strength so we can take up our own shepherding tasks. If the mission overwhelms us, we are unable to persevere. If the mission overwhelms us, we are at risk of losing sight of the mission itself. We even run the risk of becoming the misleading prophets against whom Jeremiah warned.

Achieving a balanced rhythm between the work of discipleship and the need to rest from weariness can be no easy task in itself. Like Jesus, we are called to shepherd—to care, teach, heal, listen, etc. At the same time, we must know when it is time for us to renew ourselves, to allow Jesus to shepherd and teach us, to balance our work of sharing the Gospel with rest, with time to replenish our spirit and energy. Self-giving and rest are two parallel poles to the dying and rising dynamic of the paschal mystery. Too much dying can crush us. Too much rest can lull us into being uncaring shepherds. The mission calls us to a balanced rhythm.

Focusing the Gospel

Key words and phrases: apostles . . . reported, Come away . . . and rest, They hastened there, shepherd, teach them many things

To the point: How does Jesus respond when the apostles return from their mission and report to him? He invites them to come away and rest. How does Jesus respond when the crowd persists in hastening to him? He teaches them. In fact, he shepherds both the apostles and the crowd. Jesus shepherds everyone toward fuller life through both the re-creating power of rest and the transforming possibilities of new teaching.

Connecting the Gospel

to the first reading: Jeremiah warns against misleading shepherds. Jesus never misleads us, but always teaches what we need to "dwell in security."

to experience: How relieved we are when we are in need and someone recognizes and responds to us! We know when we need rest. We do not always know when we need to be taught. Jesus knows when we need both and always responds.

Connecting the Responsorial Psalm

to the readings: Psalm 23, perhaps the best known and most loved of all the psalms, uses two images for God: shepherd and host. Both images communicate how God cares for, protects, nurtures, and feeds us. In Jeremiah when the appointed leaders fail to care, God intervenes and promises to send new shepherds (first reading). In the gospel when the disciples are exhausted and the crowd lost and leaderless, Jesus responds to both groups with care and compassion. Jesus reveals himself to be the new shepherd promised by God.

We might ask as we sing this psalm whether we are the crowd in need of care and direction or the disciples in need of rest. If we look deeply enough we will see that the answer is "both" and that Jesus pays heed to us in either case. May we rest in him from the labors of discipleship; may we learn from him all that we need for salvation.

to psalmist preparation: According to Psalm 23, God will leave you wanting for nothing. Do you believe this? Do you tell God your wants and needs? What is it that you want? What is it that you need?

ASSEMBLY & FAITH-SHARING GROUPS
- I need Jesus to shepherd me to . . .
- I hasten to Jesus when . . .
- I experience the fuller life to which Jesus is shepherding me when . . .

PRESIDERS
As pastor, I am able to shepherd my people better when . . .

DEACONS
My serving others teaches them that . . .

HOSPITALITY MINISTERS
My greeting helps those who gather open themselves to be taught by Jesus during liturgy that . . .

MUSIC MINISTERS
My music ministry helps those who have gathered become a community with one Shepherd when . . .

ALTAR MINISTERS
My serving at the altar is about responding to needs and so I . . .

LECTORS
God's word shepherds me by . . . From this I learn . . .

EXTRAORDINARY MINISTERS OF HOLY COMMUNION
I experience my ministry of distributing Holy Communion as responding to communicants' needs in that . . .

Model Penitential Act

Presider: Jesus is the caring Shepherd who teaches us and gives us rest. Let us reflect on the times we have not responded to Jesus and ask for his mercy . . . [pause]

Lord Jesus, you are the One in whom we find our rest: Lord . . .

Christ Jesus, you are the Shepherd who cares for your people: Christ . . .

Lord Jesus, you are the One who teaches us to live the Gospel: Lord . . .

Homily Points

• On a farm, the animals, crops, and weather determine the rhythm of the farm family. In a hospital, the needs of the sick determine the rhythm of the medical staff. In fact, much of our life is determined by a rhythm of being and acting, of needs and responding. In our baptismal lives, Jesus is the one who determines the rhythm of how we work and make known the Gospel, how we rest and re-create ourselves, how we learn and grow in the saving ways he teaches us. Jesus shepherds us in living these rhythms well.

• In the gospel Jesus shepherds both the apostles who need rest and the crowd who needs teaching. Jesus shepherds us in both rest and teaching. The rest Jesus provides re-creates us to have energy for continuing his mission. The Good News Jesus teaches opens us to the transforming possibilities of his abundant life given to us.

• We accept Jesus' gift of rest when we, for example, keep Sunday as a day of rest, take time to rest in him through prayer, rest with family and friends over a leisurely meal. We put into practice the Good News Jesus teaches when forgiving another leads to a restored relationship, when helping another brings joy to us, when teaching others brings life and insight to us. Jesus is surely our Shepherd who leads us to life and helps life flow from us.

Model Universal Prayer (Prayer of the Faithful)

Presider: We pray now to our caring God who sent the divine Son to shepherd us to fullness of Life.

Response:

Lord, hear our prayer.

Cantor:

we pray to the Lord,

That the church always be a haven of rest for those weary in body and spirit . . . [pause]

That nations find creative ways to feed their hungry and care for their downtrodden . . . [pause]

That those weary from life's burdens be shepherded to a fuller life through the care of this community . . . [pause]

That each of us listen to what the Shepherd teaches and learn to follow his way of living and loving . . . [pause]

Presider: Shepherd God, you grant rest to the weary and respond to the needs of those who come to you: hear these our prayers that one day we may enjoy eternal rest with you. We ask this through Christ our Lord. **Amen.**

Let us pray

Pause for silent prayer

Show favor, O Lord, to your servants
and mercifully increase the gifts of your
grace,
that, made fervent in hope, faith and
charity,
they may be ever watchful in keeping your
commands.
Through our Lord Jesus Christ, your Son,
who lives and reigns with you in the unity
of the Holy Spirit,
one God, for ever and ever. **Amen.**

FIRST READING
Jer 23:1-6

Woe to the shepherds
    who mislead and scatter the flock of my
        pasture,
    says the Lord.
Therefore, thus says the Lord, the God of
    Israel,
    against the shepherds who shepherd my
        people:
    You have scattered my sheep and driven
        them away.
You have not cared for them,
    but I will take care to punish your evil
        deeds.
I myself will gather the remnant of my
    flock
    from all the lands to which I have driven
        them
    and bring them back to their meadow;
    there they shall increase and multiply.
I will appoint shepherds for them who will
    shepherd them
    so that they need no longer fear and
        tremble;
    and none shall be missing, says the
        Lord.

Behold, the days are coming, says the
    Lord,
    when I will raise up a righteous shoot
        to David;
as king he shall reign and govern wisely,
    he shall do what is just and right in the
        land.
In his days Judah shall be saved,
    Israel shall dwell in security.
This is the name they give him:
    "The Lord our justice."

RESPONSORIAL PSALM

Ps 23:1-3, 3-4, 5, 6

R⁄. (1) The Lord is my shepherd; there is nothing I shall want.

The LORD is my shepherd; I shall not want.
  In verdant pastures he gives me repose;
beside restful waters he leads me;
  he refreshes my soul.

R⁄. The Lord is my shepherd; there is nothing I shall want.

He guides me in right paths
  for his name's sake.
Even though I walk in the dark valley
  I fear no evil; for you are at my side
with your rod and your staff
  that give me courage.

R⁄. The Lord is my shepherd; there is nothing I shall want.

You spread the table before me
  in the sight of my foes;
you anoint my head with oil;
  my cup overflows.

R⁄. The Lord is my shepherd; there is nothing I shall want.

Only goodness and kindness follow me
  all the days of my life;
and I shall dwell in the house of the LORD
  for years to come.

R⁄. The Lord is my shepherd; there is nothing I shall want.

SECOND READING

Eph 2:13-18

Brothers and sisters:
In Christ Jesus you who once were far off
  have become near by the blood of
    Christ.

For he is our peace, he who made both one
  and broke down the dividing wall of
    enmity, through his flesh,
  abolishing the law with its
    commandments and legal claims,
  that he might create in himself one new
    person in place of the two,
  thus establishing peace,
  and might reconcile both with God,
  in one body, through the cross,
  putting that enmity to death by it.
He came and preached peace to you who
    were far off
  and peace to those who were near,
  for through him we both have access in
    one Spirit to the Father.

About Liturgy

Sunday—a day of rest: The emperor Constantine in the fourth century made Sunday a day of rest for all the people of the realm. It was a day when fasting and kneeling were forbidden, but also a day given over to acts of mercy and kindness. Sunday as a day of celebration and rest has given Christians time for enjoyment of and appreciation for God's gifts and for redeemed life in all its human dimensions. Sunday rest is more than merely abstaining from productive work; the rest encourages the realization of the work of God's redeeming power which frees us. Sunday rest reminds us that all we have is really a gift from a provident and generous God, that the fruitful work of our hands is sharing in God's creative power.

Unfortunately, for all too many Christians, Sunday is as busy a day as any other. Stores are all open so the numbers of people who must work have increased dramatically. It takes constant effort and a great deal of planning and commitment to make Sunday a special day. But, like the message of this Sunday's gospel, there must be a balance in our lives between productive work and rest, between weekdays and Sunday. Changing the rhythm of our week so that Sunday is truly a day of rest—marked by quality time for God and family—has its built-in rewards. We find not only a better balance in our lives, but find our God as well.

About Liturgical Music

Singing the Great Amen: The Great Amen is our resounding "So be it!" to the story of salvation retold in the eucharistic prayer. Between the fourth and eighth centuries the Great Amen was considered the epitome of the assembly's participation in their baptismal priesthood. This belief was so strong, in fact, that some argued rebaptism was not necessary for persons seeking entrance into the church from a heretical sect—participation in the eucharistic prayer and its Great Amen was proof enough of their identity in Christ.

In all three of the eucharistic prayer acclamations we assent to the mystery of salvation. We acclaim God sovereign over all creation and all history (Holy, Holy, Holy). We acclaim the death, resurrection, and final coming of Christ as the mystery of our faith and foundation of our lives (Mystery of Faith). We acclaim our union with Christ in his priesthood as we participate in his offering of himself for the life of the world (Great Amen). We acclaim who God is, who Christ is, and who we, the community of the church, are. No wonder the church lists these acclamations among the most important elements to be sung in the Mass (GIRM, no. 40; STL, no. 115a).

✚ SPIRITUALITY

GOSPEL ACCLAMATION
Luke 7:16

R̸. Alleluia, alleluia.
A great prophet has risen in our
    midst.
God has visited his people.
R̸. Alleluia, alleluia.

Gospel

John 6:1-15; L110B

Jesus went across the
    Sea of Galilee.
A large crowd followed him,
    because they saw the signs he was
        performing on the sick.
Jesus went up on the mountain,
    and there he sat down with his disciples.
The Jewish feast of Passover was near.
When Jesus raised his eyes
    and saw that a large crowd was coming
        to him,
    he said to Philip,
    "Where can we buy enough food for
        them to eat?"
He said this to test him,
    because he himself knew what he was
        going to do.
Philip answered him,
    "Two hundred days' wages worth of
        food would not be enough
    for each of them to have a little."
One of his disciples,
    Andrew, the brother of Simon Peter,
        said to him,
    "There is a boy here who has five barley
        loaves and two fish;
    but what good are these for so many?"
Jesus said, "Have the people recline."
Now there was a great deal of grass in that
    place.
So the men reclined, about five thousand in
    number.
Then Jesus took the loaves, gave
    thanks,
    and distributed them to those who
        were reclining,
    and also as much of the fish as they
        wanted.

Continued in Appendix A, p. 304.

Reflecting on the Gospel

Let's let a miracle be a miracle! Jesus tested Philip, who failed the test because he fixated on calculating the amount of food needed to feed the hungry crowd and its cost. He couldn't even imagine another way. Jesus, however, "knew what he was going to do"—he gave the crowd "as much . . . as they wanted." Amazingly, the miracle of giving them "as much . . . as they wanted" was still less than the other miracle Jesus gave them: "the sign" of the fullness of messianic Life. So much Life—even "twelve wicker baskets" more than they wanted. Calculate that!

The abundance in this multiplication account points to an eschatological sign of risen Life. The multiplication of the loaves points to a time of fulfillment when God's plan for redemption is finally realized. Even the context of this gospel passage points to a time of fulfillment: it is Passover—Israel's annual celebration of God's mighty deeds on their behalf. The wondrous and impressive sign that Jesus works on this occasion—feeding five thousand with five loaves—points beyond taking care of the hunger of the "large crowd." Rather, Jesus' sign points to a time when God's mighty deeds come to fulfillment—a time when all people are abundantly filled and every need is met.

The question about having food to feed the crowd is put to two particular apostles (Philip and Andrew) who traditionally are considered to be ministers to the Gentiles ("Jesus went across the Sea of Galilee" = to Gentile territory); in the messianic reign even the Gentiles will share in the abundance and be saved. The bread is specified as barley, the grain used by the poor; in the messianic reign the poor will also share in God's abundance. Twelve baskets of bread fragments were gathered up after all had their fill; the leftovers and the number twelve point to the new Israel in its eschatological perfection.

Jesus' unprecedented miracle of abundance doesn't warrant his being made an earthly king, in spite of the crowd's understandable enthusiasm; rather, "he withdrew . . . alone" so that the miracle of abundance points to the establishment of a new kingdom, a new Israel. Jesus supersedes both the apostles' and the crowd's expectations of God's reign: with little he feeds many and thus reveals that he is not an earthly king but, ironically, Jesus is a king. Jesus himself is an eschatological sign of abundance—of God's lavish Presence.

Living the Paschal Mystery

This gospel account is far more than an interesting story about a miracle and abundance; it primes us to ponder the great mystery of Jesus himself as the Bread of Life (which we will hear about on subsequent Sundays) and his self-giving that enables us to share in it. The challenge for us is far more than believing in Jesus' power to multiply loaves and fishes; the challenge is recognizing Jesus' self-giving as a sign of fulfillment and promise of eschatological glory that we share even now. We Christians are to see our lives through the lens of God's lavish abundance. Do we?

It is too easy to think of God's lavish abundance primarily (maybe exclusively?) in terms of the Eucharist we share each Sunday. Indeed, this is a mighty act of God on our behalf, and Eucharist always is an eschatological sign of God's abundance and a time of future fulfillment. However, we ought not to let this lull us into missing other signs of God's abundance: the abundance of family and friends, steady job, support and care of others. God's abundance is all around us. Calculate that!

Focusing the Gospel

Key words and phrases: said this to test him, knew what he was going to do, Two hundred days' wages, as much . . . as they wanted, twelve wicker baskets with fragments

To the point: Let's let a miracle be a miracle! Jesus tested Philip, who failed the test because he fixated on calculating the amount of food needed to feed the hungry crowd and its cost. Jesus "knew what he was going to do"—he gave the crowd "as much . . . as they wanted." Amazingly, the miracle of giving them "as much . . . as they wanted" was still less than the other miracle Jesus gave them: "the sign" of the fullness of messianic Life. So much Life—even "twelve wicker baskets" more than they wanted. Calculate that!

Connecting the Gospel

to the first reading: In the first reading Elisha miraculously uses twenty loaves to feed one hundred people with "some left over." In the gospel Jesus uses only five loaves to feed five thousand with "twelve wicker baskets" left over. No one could be prepared for the superabundance of God's Gift that Jesus brings—the fullness of messianic Life.

to experience: In our society abundance is usually a sign of inheritance, hard work, or lucky investments. In the first reading and gospel this Sunday, abundance is a sign of God's free gift.

Connecting the Responsorial Psalm

to the readings: Elisha feeds a hundred people with "twenty barley loaves" and has "some left over" (first reading). Jesus feeds five thousand with "five barley loaves and two fish," and has twelve baskets left over (gospel). In Jesus, God's gift of abundant, overflowing, everlasting Life comes to fulfillment. In him every human need will be met (see psalm refrain), not only for the twelve tribes of Israel, but for all nations. What we need and what Jesus gives us, however, is more than bread. What we need and what Jesus gives us is Bread that will never diminish, his very self given for our salvation. In Jesus, God satisfies "the desire of every living thing" (psalm) for fullness of Life. It is this we believe, and this for which we "look hopefully" (psalm).

to psalmist preparation: This responsorial psalm promises that God will feed all who hunger. What human beings truly hunger for, however, is not passing satisfactions, but messianic Life which lasts forever. This is the gift God gives in the person of Jesus (gospel). How do you "look hopefully" for this Gift? Where do you find it?

ASSEMBLY & FAITH-SHARING GROUPS
- I tend to calculate and fixate on amounts of God's gifts to me when . . .
- God has given me "as much . . . as [I] wanted" when . . . God gives me even more than I could possibly want when . . .
- I experience the fullness of the "twelve wicker baskets" of fragments left over when . . .

PRESIDERS
What frustrates me about not being able to meet every need is . . . Jesus helps me with this frustration by . . .

DEACONS
My serving is a sign of "twelve wicker baskets" of fragments left over when . . .

HOSPITALITY MINISTERS
My hospitality opens people to recognize God's abundance given to them when . . .

MUSIC MINISTERS
Jesus helps me feed the assembly through my music ministry by . . . He feeds me by . . .

ALTAR MINISTERS
In light of Jesus' example of abundance left over, the true spirit of Christian service for me is . . .

LECTORS
I have been filled "as much . . . as [I] wanted" by God's word when . . .

EXTRAORDINARY MINISTERS OF HOLY COMMUNION
I become most aware of Holy Communion being "the sign" of the fullness of messianic Life when . . .

CELEBRATION

Model Penitential Act

Presider: Jesus feeds the five thousand with a few loaves and fishes. As we prepare to be fed on Word and sacrament, let us ask for God's mercy for the times we have not been grateful for the abundance of God's gifts to us . . . [pause]

Lord Jesus, you are the fullness of God's providential care: Lord . . .
Christ Jesus, you are the fullness of divine Life given to us: Christ . . .
Lord Jesus, you are the fullness of all that we seek: Lord . . .

Homily Points

- Wow! These Fourth of July fireworks went far beyond what we expected! Wow! The birth of our first child overwhelmed us far beyond what we anticipated! Wow! What we are learning about the immensity of the universe goes far beyond what we can imagine! Wow! God's abundant gift of the fullness of messianic Life goes far, far, far beyond . . .

- Philip miscalculates when he tries to calculate the cost of feeding the hungry crowd. He has no inkling of what Jesus intends to do. Who can? The gift of the fullness of messianic Life is beyond calculation, beyond expectation, beyond imagination. Yet, this is precisely Jesus' Gift to us.

- What a newborn baby will become as he or she grows into adulthood unfolds over many years. Even at the moment of death, the mystery of life continues to unfold. The Life God unceasingly offers us is "the sign" of fullness to come, of incalculable mystery, of Gift so far beyond imagining that we spend this life and all of eternity growing into it. For the fullness of Life is nothing less than the very Life of God.

Model Universal Prayer (Prayer of the Faithful)

Presider: God unceasingly invites us into the mystery of the fullness of Life. Let us make our needs known to this gracious God.

Response:

Cantor:

That all members of the church enter more deeply into the mystery of the fullness of Life God offers us . . . [pause]

That all people be able to share in the fullness and goodness of life leading to salvation . . . [pause]

That those who are hungry may be filled through God's grace and this community's generosity . . . [pause]

That each of us here becomes a sign of God's abundant Life . . . [pause]

Presider: Gracious God, you sent your divine Son to be your gift of Life to us: hear our prayers that we receive this Gift with joy and one day come to share the fullness of Life with you for ever. We ask this through Christ our Lord. **Amen.**

Let us pray

Pause for silent prayer

O God, protector of those who hope in you,
without whom nothing has firm foundation, nothing is holy,
bestow in abundance your mercy upon us
and grant that, with you as our ruler and guide,
we may use the good things that pass
in such a way as to hold fast even now
to those that ever endure.
Through our Lord Jesus Christ, your Son,
who lives and reigns with you in the unity of the Holy Spirit,
one God, for ever and ever. **Amen.**

FIRST READING
2 Kgs 4:42-44

A man came from Baal-shalishah bringing to Elisha, the man of God,
twenty barley loaves made from the firstfruits,
and fresh grain in the ear.
Elisha said, "Give it to the people to eat."
But his servant objected,
"How can I set this before a hundred people?"
Elisha insisted, "Give it to the people to eat.
For thus says the LORD,
'They shall eat and there shall be some left over.'"
And when they had eaten, there was some left over,
as the LORD had said.

RESPONSORIAL PSALM

Ps 145:10-11, 15-16, 17-18

℟. (cf. 16) The hand of the Lord feeds us; he answers all our needs.

Let all your works give you thanks, O
     LORD,
   and let your faithful ones bless you.
Let them discourse of the glory of your
     kingdom
   and speak of your might.

℟. The hand of the Lord feeds us; he answers all our needs.

The eyes of all look hopefully to you,
   and you give them their food in due
     season;
you open your hand
   and satisfy the desire of every living
     thing.

℟. The hand of the Lord feeds us; he answers all our needs.

The LORD is just in all his ways
   and holy in all his works.
The LORD is near to all who call upon him,
   to all who call upon him in truth.

℟. The hand of the Lord feeds us; he answers all our needs.

SECOND READING

Eph 4:1-6

Brothers and sisters:
I, a prisoner for the Lord,
     urge you to live in a manner worthy of
         the call you have received,
     with all humility and gentleness, with
         patience,
     bearing with one another through love,
     striving to preserve the unity of the
         spirit through the bond of peace:
     one body and one Spirit,
     as you were also called to the one hope
         of your call;
     one Lord, one faith, one baptism;
     one God and Father of all,
     who is over all and through all and in
         all.

About Liturgy

John 6—the Bread of Life discourse: John's gospel is read extensively during the festal seasons, but there is no block of Sundays during these high celebration times when the beautiful Bread of Life discourse from John's sixth chapter could be included without breaking it up. Those who compiled the Lectionary made the decision to include extensive portions of this sixth chapter from John's gospel on five consecutive Sundays during Year B as a theological commentary on the multiplication of the loaves and, by extension, on the Eucharist. It is inserted in Mark's gospel just at the point of Mark's multiplication account (which is omitted in order to proclaim the multiplication account from John's gospel).

This decision reminds us that the Lectionary is not a Bible, but is a liturgical book with its own purpose. Since, further, the Lectionary is a liturgical book used primarily during the celebration of Eucharist, it should come as no surprise to us that the intent is precisely to draw our attention to the mystery of the Eucharist.

In Reflecting on the Gospel we mentioned a number of indicators in the text that the passage is eschatological, that is, refers to the final fulfillment at the end times. The gospel for this Sunday also includes indicators that the passage is eucharistic. For example, Jesus gives thanks; the Greek term used here is *eucharistēsas*, the word, of course, from which we derive our term Eucharist. Further, unlike the account in Mark, in the Johannine account Jesus *himself* distributes the bread to the hungry crowd, pointing to himself as the Bread of Life. Finally, the Passover and eschatological contexts remind us that Eucharist is a sacrament related to the end times and our share in Christ's risen Life.

About Liturgical Music

Singing the Communion song, part 1: The proclamation of Jesus' Bread of Life discourse we begin this Sunday offers us a good opportunity to reflect on the purpose of the Communion song. According to GIRM (no. 86), the Communion song has three purposes: (1) to express the communicants' unity by means of the unity of their voices, (2) to express "gladness of heart," and (3) to make the communal nature of the Communion procession more evident. This week we reflect on the first purpose.

GIRM indicates the Communion song is an outward expression of our inward unity in Christ. This means the song is itself sacramental. It both celebrates our communion and assists it to happen. It is never to be lightly omitted, either by the liturgy planners or by an individual member of the assembly who chooses not to sing. For music planners, this means choosing Communion songs the assembly is able to sing easily and well. For us as assembly members, this means choosing to enter into the communal singing even when the hymn is a little unfamiliar to us, or perhaps not to our liking. It means adding our singular voice, no matter what we think about its quality, to the communal voice of the community. It means entering into the Communion procession with full hearts, and letting the singing transform our private prayer into the shared prayer of the Body of Christ.

✦ SPIRITUALITY

GOSPEL ACCLAMATION
Matt 4:4b

℟. Alleluia, alleluia.
One does not live on bread alone, but by
    every
word that comes forth from the mouth of
    God.
℟. Alleluia, alleluia.

Gospel

John 6:24-35; L113B

**When the crowd saw that neither
    Jesus nor his disciples were
    there,
    they themselves got into boats
    and came to Capernaum looking
        for Jesus.
And when they found him across
        the sea they said to him,
    "Rabbi, when did you get here?"
Jesus answered them and said,
    "Amen, amen, I say to you,
    you are looking for me not because
        you saw signs
    but because you ate the loaves and
        were filled.
Do not work for food that perishes
    but for the food that endures for
        eternal life,
    which the Son of Man will give you.
For on him the Father, God, has set his
        seal."
So they said to him,
    "What can we do to accomplish the
        works of God?"
Jesus answered and said to them,
    "This is the work of God, that you
        believe in the one he sent."
So they said to him,
    "What sign can you do, that we may
        see and believe in you?
What can you do?
Our ancestors ate manna in the desert,
        as it is written:
    He gave them bread from heaven to
        eat."**

Continued in Appendix A, p. 304.

Reflecting on the Gospel

Every now and then we hear talk about developing a pill that would contain all the nourishment we would need. Take the pill and our food supply for the day is finished. The lure of such a pill would be that there would be no more hunger, we wouldn't worry so much about the weather's impact on agriculture, we would be freed from cooking and cleaning up. We hear about such a pill, but most of us react quite negatively, even after considering its benefits. We know that there is so much more to nourishment than simply giving the body what it needs to be an efficient living "machine." Eating includes being satisfied, engaging in a social event, choosing a variety of interesting tastes. In this Sunday's gospel, the crowd is seeking Jesus. They have been fed with the bread and fish abundantly provided by Jesus (last Sunday's gospel about the multiplication of the loaves). They want more. What they were not prepared for was that the bread Jesus offers is so much more than food that satisfies their immediate hunger; it is so much more than a "pill" that takes care of nourishment needs.

The bread the crowd seeks is perishable. They eat this bread but become hungry again—they must keep procuring this bread. The bread Jesus offers is eternal. Those who eat this bread will never hunger again. They cannot procure this bread because it is the Father's gift: the "true bread from heaven" that is Jesus himself. There is a tension—a grave misunderstanding—between what the crowd seeks and what Jesus offers. What do we seek?

Do we seek only nourishment? Or do we seek the Bread only God can give—Bread that is abundant and Life-giving? God's abundance is a sign of messianic times, of God's reign being established, of eternal Life. Our sharing in this abundance is already a sharing in the fullness of Life to come. The "bread of God . . . which comes down from heaven . . . gives life to the world." We consume the bread from heaven so that the mystery of Life may consume us, drawing us to eternal Life.

Living the Paschal Mystery

What we need to receive Eucharist fruitfully is a personal relationship with Jesus. This "bread from heaven" is ultimately a person, Jesus Christ. If Jesus is the bread from heaven given for us and we are the Body of Christ, then we must conclude that we ourselves are to be bread from heaven that fosters eternal Life for others. As God has "set his seal" on Jesus, so through baptism and confirmation has God "set his seal" on us. Jesus gives himself as bread from heaven; we give ourselves to others as bread from heaven when we live our baptismal commitment by doing the ordinary things of every day as Jesus would—with care, compassion, love, generosity, patience.

The very person of Jesus is *everything* for which we long. Jesus is the deep well of what's beyond our immediate satisfaction, the deep well that brings us face to face with our longing and dissatisfaction. Just as the crowd followed Jesus across the lake, looking for him to satisfy them, so must we follow Jesus as faithful disciples. We look for him in our everyday lives—in the people and circumstances around us. Looking for him, we can faithfully bring that divine Presence to others. The bread God offers us is the abiding Presence of Jesus among us, always reaching out to satisfy us with what is imperishable, what endures forever: eternal Life.

Focusing the Gospel

Key words and phrases: food that perishes, food that endures, Father gives you the true bread, I am the bread of life

To the point: The bread the crowd seeks is perishable. They eat this bread but become hungry again—they must keep procuring this bread. The bread Jesus offers is eternal. Those who eat this bread will never hunger again. They cannot procure this bread because it is the Father's gift: the "true bread from heaven" that is Jesus himself. There is a tension—a grave misunderstanding— between what the crowd seeks and what Jesus offers. What do we seek?

Connecting the Gospel

to the first reading: In the first reading, the Israelites grumble about being hungry and look to their past experience in Egypt where they had their "fill of bread." In the gospel Jesus is calling the crowd to look beyond being filled with bread that perishes to an everlasting bread—Jesus himself who is "the bread of life."

to experience: Bread is the staff of life. For healthy living, we need to eat from the basic food groups every day—including bread, carbohydrates. Even more so, Jesus is the staff of life. For a healthy Christian life, we need to nurture every day our relationship with Jesus, "the bread of life."

Connecting the Responsorial Psalm

to the readings: Psalm 78 retells the history of God's continual interventions to save Israel, and Israel's constant failure to remember what God has done for them and to remain faithful. The psalmist reminds the people this is their story and calls them to be faithful. The verses we sing this Sunday tell of God providing manna to support the Israelites on their desert journey. The first strophe sings about passing on the story of God's "glorious deeds" to generations yet to come. The third strophe sings about the end of the journey when God delivered the people to the "holy land" prepared for them.

The Lectionary uses these verses from Psalm 78 to remind us that this story is also ours. God continually acts to save us. Like the Israelites, we can see and believe or we can grumble (first reading). God sends us Jesus, the Bread of Life, to nourish us on our journey into eternal Life (gospel). Will we eat and be faithful, or eat and forget? The responsorial psalm challenges us to eat, remember, and remain faithful.

to psalmist preparation: The bread from heaven you sing about in this psalm is the person of Jesus given to us so that we may have fullness of Life. In your singing you call the community to believe in this gift and remain faithful to the relationship it establishes. How is Jesus giving you bread from heaven every day? How do you remain faithful?

ASSEMBLY & FAITH-SHARING GROUPS
- What I most seek in my daily living is . . . What most satisfies is . . .
- The tension (perhaps even misunderstanding) I feel about Jesus as the "bread of life" is . . .
- I encounter Jesus as the "bread of life" when . . .

PRESIDERS
My ministry calls me to be the "bread of life" for others in that . . .

DEACONS
My ministry of service satisfies these hungers in others . . .

HOSPITALITY MINISTERS
My greeting of those who gather for Eucharist invites them to nurture their relationship with Jesus, the Bread of Life, when I . . .

MUSIC MINISTERS
The bread of my music making that nourishes the faith of the assembly is . . .

ALTAR MINISTERS
Preparing the table from which the community receives the Bread of Life nourishes me in that . . .

LECTORS
The Word of Life I proclaim becomes the Bread of Life when . . .

EXTRAORDINARY MINISTERS OF HOLY COMMUNION
Distributing the Bread of Life to the community nourishes my own daily living by . . .

Model Penitential Act

Presider: Jesus is the Bread of Life, given to us as our everlasting Food. We pray during this Eucharist to come to a deeper relationship with Jesus and ask forgiveness for the times we have not responded to his gift of himself . . . [pause]

Lord Jesus, you are the true Bread from heaven: Lord . . .

Christ Jesus, you are the Bread that brings everlasting Life: Christ . . .

Lord Jesus, you are the Bread that satisfies all hunger: Lord . . .

Homily Points

- We seek success, but often misunderstand its allure. We seek happiness, but often misunderstand its source. We seek love, but often misunderstand its cost. We seek Jesus, but often misunderstand where we find him, how he nourishes us, who he really is.

- When we realize through an encounter with Jesus what it is he desires to give us— bread that lasts—we ask him to "give us this bread always." But, like the crowd in this gospel, we do not always fully understand what Jesus is actually giving us—not bread but his very Self. This Gift is the work of God; our work is to receive this Gift.

- We grow in our understanding of Jesus as the Bread of Life by counting the many ways he nourishes us. He nourishes us through the witness of people who are remarkably self-giving, by the kind word or smile of a stranger, by the challenge to grow that comes from a true friend, by the calming presence of a beloved family member, through our own quiet moments of prayer. In all of these examples we receive life from another. This life is Jesus' gift of Self. This Life is what we ultimately seek.

Model Universal Prayer (Prayer of the Faithful)

Presider: God gives the gift of Jesus to be the Bread of Life nourishing and sustaining us. And so we pray.

Response:

Lord, hear our prayer.

Cantor:

we pray to the Lord,

That all members of the church come to a deeper understanding of Jesus' gift of himself to us as the Bread of Life . . . [pause]

That all peoples of the world be nourished as they seek fuller life . . . [pause]

That those who lack the basic necessities of life receive from those who have been given the Bread of Life . . . [pause]

That all of us here seek Jesus with all our hearts and make known to others his gift of Presence and nourishment . . . [pause]

Presider: God of blessings, you send bread from heaven so that we might have eternal Life: give us this bread always. We ask this through the Bread of Life, Jesus Christ our Lord. **Amen.**

COLLECT

Let us pray

Pause for silent prayer

Draw near to your servants, O Lord,
and answer their prayers with unceasing kindness,
that, for those who glory in you as their Creator and guide,
you may restore what you have created
and keep safe what you have restored.
Through our Lord Jesus Christ, your Son,
who lives and reigns with you in the unity of the Holy Spirit,
one God, for ever and ever. **Amen.**

FIRST READING

Exod 16:2-4, 12-15

The whole Israelite community grumbled against Moses and Aaron.
The Israelites said to them,
"Would that we had died at the Lord's hand in the land of Egypt,
as we sat by our fleshpots and ate our fill of bread!
But you had to lead us into this desert to make the whole community die of famine!"

Then the Lord said to Moses,
"I will now rain down bread from heaven for you.
Each day the people are to go out and gather their daily portion;
thus will I test them,
to see whether they follow my instructions or not.

"I have heard the grumbling of the Israelites.
Tell them: In the evening twilight you shall eat flesh,
and in the morning you shall have your fill of bread,
so that you may know that I, the Lord, am your God."

In the evening quail came up and covered the camp.
In the morning a dew lay all about the camp,
and when the dew evaporated, there on the surface of the desert
were fine flakes like hoarfrost on the ground.
On seeing it, the Israelites asked one another, "What is this?"
for they did not know what it was.
But Moses told them,
"This is the bread that the Lord has given you to eat."

RESPONSORIAL PSALM

Ps 78:3-4, 23-24, 25, 54

℟. (24b) The Lord gave them bread from heaven.

What we have heard and know,
   and what our fathers have declared to
      us,
we will declare to the generation to come
   the glorious deeds of the LORD and his
      strength
   and the wonders that he wrought.

℟. The Lord gave them bread from heaven.

He commanded the skies above
   and opened the doors of heaven;
he rained manna upon them for food
   and gave them heavenly bread.

℟. The Lord gave them bread from heaven.

Man ate the bread of angels,
   food he sent them in abundance.
And he brought them to his holy land,
   to the mountains his right hand had
      won.

℟. The Lord gave them bread from heaven.

SECOND READING

Eph 4:17, 20-24

Brothers and sisters:
I declare and testify in the Lord
   that you must no longer live as the
      Gentiles do,
   in the futility of their minds;
   that is not how you learned Christ,
   assuming that you have heard of him
      and were taught in him,
   as truth is in Jesus,
   that you should put away the old self of
      your former way of life,
   corrupted through deceitful desires,
   and be renewed in the spirit of your
      minds,
   and put on the new self,
   created in God's way in righteousness
      and holiness of truth.

About Liturgy

Eucharist, believing, and action: Believing in the Eucharist is more than believing in the Real Presence. Or, to put it another way, believing in the Real Presence—the Eucharist is truly the Body and Blood of Christ—demands something of us. Eucharist nourishes us, transforms us into being more perfectly members of the Body of Christ, so that we might live this holy mystery more effectively in our daily lives. As St. Augustine said in his famous Sermon 272, "If you are the Body of Christ and members of it, then it is that mystery which is placed on the Lord's table: you receive the mystery, which is to say the Body of Christ, your very self. You answer Amen to who you are and in the answer embrace yourself. You hear Body of Christ and answer Amen. Be a member of Christ's Body, that your Amen will be true."

Believing itself is an action—a commitment to a relationship. To say we believe in Jesus as the Bread of Life and to say Amen to the Body and Blood we receive at Communion is to make a commitment: that we live who we are, the Body of Christ. The only way our Amen to the Body and Blood of Christ can be true is for each of us to be Christ in our everyday actions. This is a tall order! On our own we could not do it. But Jesus himself is our strength and helps us say our Amen.

About Liturgical Music

Singing the Communion song, part 2: GIRM (no. 86) indicates the second purpose of the Communion song is to show our gladness of heart as we receive Communion. The Communion song expresses the joy we experience in being called to the messianic table to feast on the Body and Blood of Christ. It expresses the joy we experience in being drawn beyond our individual selves to become the one Body of Christ. Appropriate Communion hymns express praise, thanksgiving, joy in being fed and filled, gratitude for being healed and forgiven, gladness in being one in Christ, etc.

This purpose is especially important to keep in mind during the festal seasons when we often sing a seasonal song during Communion. Songs of expectation during Advent, nativity carols during Christmas season, hymns filled with alleluias during Easter season easily accord with expressing our joy of heart at approaching the banquet of eternal Life. Even during Lent, songs we sing during Communion that express sorrow or penitence carry an undercurrent of joy, for it is at the table of the Lord that we are fully forgiven, reconciled to God and one another, and made whole.

AUGUST 2, 2015
EIGHTEENTH SUNDAY IN ORDINARY TIME

✠ SPIRITUALITY

GOSPEL ACCLAMATION
John 6:51

℞. Alleluia, alleluia.
I am the living bread that came down
    from heaven, says the Lord;
whoever eats this bread will live
    forever.
℞. Alleluia, alleluia.

Gospel

John 6:41-51; L116B

The Jews murmured about
    Jesus because he said,
  "I am the bread that came
      down from heaven,"
  and they said,
  "Is this not Jesus, the son of
      Joseph?
Do we not know his father and
    mother?
Then how can he say,
  'I have come down from heaven'?"
Jesus answered and said to them,
  "Stop murmuring among yourselves.
No one can come to me unless the
    Father who sent me draw him,
  and I will raise him on the last day.
It is written in the prophets:
  They shall all be taught by God.
Everyone who listens to my Father and
    learns from him comes to me.
Not that anyone has seen the Father
    except the one who is from God;
  he has seen the Father.
Amen, amen, I say to you,
  whoever believes has eternal life.
I am the bread of life.
Your ancestors ate the manna in the
    desert, but they died;
  this is the bread that comes down
      from heaven
  so that one may eat it and not die.
I am the living bread that came down
    from heaven;
  whoever eats this bread will live
      forever;
  and the bread that I will give is my
      flesh for the life of the world."

Reflecting on the Gospel

"Murmur" is an interesting word; in English, grammatically, we call it an "onomatopoeia," that is, a word that sounds like what it means. It is a low, sustained sound—background noise, a hum, a subdued grumble. It comes from the Latin which is exactly the same word: *murmur*. In Latin, however, to murmur is to make a big noise, to roar. The Latin is probably closer to the crowd's response, in this gospel, to Jesus' declaration that he is "the bread that came down from heaven." The Jews were murmuring because of their limited perception of who Jesus is; after all, "Is this not . . . the son of Joseph?" Their murmur was probably not a subdued grumble, but a crowd-sized noise.

"The Jews murmured" because they could not get beyond their limited perception of who they thought Jesus was to the mystery about himself he reveals: "I am the bread of life," the Bread "come down from heaven," the Bread to whom we must come, the Bread who gives us a share in his "eternal life," the Bread in whom we must believe, the Bread who gives Self "for the life of the world." Jesus persists in revealing himself as the Bread sent by God to nourish the crowd (and us) for the journey to eternal Life. Jesus gives his life so that we might have new Life: "the bread that I will give is my flesh for the life of the world." The surprise of the gospel is that Jesus himself, as the "bread . . . from heaven," is both the promise and fulfillment of the eternal Life for which we long. Jesus declares himself to be "the living bread" and when we share in this Bread we "will live forever." Such mystery! Who can believe it? Who can afford not to believe it?

The ultimate act of God's persistence in bringing us to new and eternal Life is to send the Son who gives his life for us. And herein is another new revelation in the text: the bread of heaven isn't without its cost. For Jesus, the cost is the cross ("the bread that I will give is my flesh for the life of the world"). The bread of life is the bread of self-sacrifice. Here is the real source of the murmuring (the shouting!): to eat the bread of Life is to eat the bread of suffering. To encounter Jesus by eating the bread of Life is to take upon ourselves Jesus' life of self-giving. This is why the gospel is so difficult, why the Jews are really murmuring: we, too, must die in order to live forever.

Living the Paschal Mystery

In the mystery of Christ we are reminded that life and death always go together. If we wish to live, we must be willing to die to ourselves. Lest we get too discouraged, we must always remember that the paschal mystery is a rhythm of dying and rising. We are able to embrace dying to self because, through Jesus, we know that in the very dying is new life. Jesus has gone before us and taught us that death brings life. The rhythm of the paschal mystery enables us to identify with Jesus in this great mystery of dying and eternity. Cross leads to resurrection. Dying leads to eternal Life.

God's persistence in bringing us Life is a gift, indeed. But the gift invites more than our own openness to receive it. To receive God's gift of Life—Jesus as living bread—is to pledge ourselves also to bring that Life of God to others. We are not "come down from heaven"; we have our feet planted firmly on this good earth, giving our own "flesh for the life of the world" through the good we do every day for others.

Focusing the Gospel

Key words and phrases: I am the bread of life, come down from heaven, come to me, whoever believes has eternal life, my flesh for the life of the world

To the point: "The Jews murmured" because they could not get beyond their limited perception of who they thought Jesus was to the mystery about himself he reveals: "I am the bread of life,"

the Bread "come down from heaven,"

the Bread to whom we must come

the Bread who gives us a share in his "eternal life,"

the Bread in whom we must believe,

the Bread who gives Self "for the life of the world."

Such mystery! Who can believe it? Who can afford not to believe it?

Connecting the Gospel

to the first reading: In the first reading, the bread given to Elijah strengthened him to reach his goal—the mountain of God. In the gospel, the bread Jesus gives us—his very self—*is* the goal in whom we have eternal Life.

to experience: Most of us get caught up in good mystery stories. We can't wait to get to the end to resolve the mystery. The mystery of Jesus as "the bread of life" does not have an end, cannot be resolved. This mystery is forever. And we get caught up in it by believing.

Connecting the Responsorial Psalm

to the readings: In the beginning of the first reading, Elijah is resistant to God. He is tired of life and wants to die. Even after his first feeding by an angel, he wants only to continue sleeping. But God will not leave him to either his despair or his exhaustion. God sends more food to strengthen Elijah so that he may complete his walk to the mountain.

The food God sent was not just physical bread, however. What God sent was the grace to believe and respond. In the gospel reading Jesus tells his challengers that those who have "learned from" the Father will know whom they are encountering when they meet Jesus. Those who have "tasted and seen the goodness of the Lord" (psalm) will recognize Jesus and come to him. They will hunger for what they have acquired a taste. As we sing this responsorial psalm, may we who have already been fed by God hunger for more and come gladly to receive the More which is offered.

to psalmist preparation: In every verse of this responsorial psalm you address the assembly. You sing about your experience of God's goodness and invite them to respond to God with your confidence and joy. Who in your life has led you to "taste and see" God's goodness? What leads you to hunger for more?

**ASSEMBLY &
FAITH-SHARING GROUPS**

- The depth of the mystery of who Jesus reveals himself to be moves me to . . .
- I murmur about the mystery of who Jesus is when he challenges me to . . .
- When I come to Jesus, "the bread of life," what happens is . . .

PRESIDERS

My ministry helps the assembly come to Jesus when I . . .

DEACONS

Like Jesus, I give myself "for the life of the world" and . . .

HOSPITALITY MINISTERS

My greeting opens people to come to Jesus when I . . .

MUSIC MINISTERS

When, like Elijah in the first reading, I am exhausted by the demands of music ministry, Jesus feeds me by . . .

ALTAR MINISTERS

My serving at the altar is like bread "come down from heaven" when . . .

LECTORS

My manner of proclaiming the word reveals that I have come to Jesus and believe in him when I . . .

**EXTRAORDINARY MINISTERS
OF HOLY COMMUNION**

Like the angel ministering to Elijah in the first reading, I nourish people for their journey to eternal Life in these ways . . .

Model Penitential Act

Presider: God desires eternal Life for us and sends the Son as Bread from heaven to nourish and strengthen us. Let us prepare ourselves for this liturgy by thanking God for this great Gift . . . [pause]

> Lord Jesus, you are the Bread of Life: Lord . . .
>
> Christ Jesus, you are the promise of eternal Life: Christ . . .
>
> Lord Jesus, you give your flesh for the life of the world: Lord . . .

Homily Points

- How often do we spend a great amount of time thinking about what gift to give a loved one for Christmas, birthday, or anniversary! How often is it not true that the only gift a loved one really desires is the gift of ourselves expressed in the giving of time, attention, and presence! Jesus' gift of himself as "the bread of life" is a gift of eternal Life, boundless care, and abiding Presence.

- In this gospel Jesus teaches us the mystery of who he is as "the bread of life." He is the One who gives himself to us as a pledge of eternal Life, who draws us to himself, who gives himself so that we might live. The mystery of his being the "bread of life" goes beyond all human expectation because the mystery reveals a divine giving of a divine Self.

- Jesus gives himself to us as "the bread of life." We must respond to this gift by believing and living it. To believe the mystery is, in fact, to live it. We believe and live the mystery when we give ourselves for the life of others, such as giving time to those who are lonely, giving food to those who are hungry, giving forgiveness to those who have hurt us, giving attention to those who are discouraged, giving patience to those who annoy us. Believing and living the mystery of "the bread of life" means that we, like Jesus, give, give, give . . .

Model Universal Prayer (Prayer of the Faithful)

Presider: The God who sends down from heaven the Bread of Life surely hears our prayers and grants our needs. And so we pray.

Response:

Lord, hear our prayer.

Cantor:

we pray to the Lord,

For all members of the church, may they believe ever more firmly and live ever more fully the mystery of Jesus who gives himself to us as the Bread of Life . . . [pause]

For all peoples of the world, may they learn what God teaches and come to salvation . . . [pause]

For those who are sick or suffering, may they come to Jesus and receive his life-giving care . . . [pause]

For each of us here, may we learn from Jesus how to give ourselves more fully for the life of the world . . . [pause]

Presider: Gracious God, you send your divine Son down from heaven to be our Bread of Life: grant these our prayers, deepen our faith in him, and bring us to eternal Life. We ask this through Jesus Christ our Lord. **Amen.**

COLLECT

Let us pray

Pause for silent prayer

Almighty ever-living God,
whom, taught by the Holy Spirit,
we dare to call our Father,
bring, we pray, to perfection in our hearts
the spirit of adoption as your sons and
daughters,
that we may merit to enter into the
inheritance
which you have promised.
Through our Lord Jesus Christ, your Son,
who lives and reigns with you in the unity
of the Holy Spirit,
one God, for ever and ever. **Amen.**

FIRST READING

1 Kgs 19:4-8

Elijah went a day's journey into the desert,
    until he came to a broom tree and sat
        beneath it.
He prayed for death, saying:
    "This is enough, O Lᴏʀᴅ!
Take my life, for I am no better than my
        fathers."
He lay down and fell asleep under the
        broom tree,
    but then an angel touched him and
        ordered him to get up and eat.
Elijah looked and there at his head was a
        hearth cake
    and a jug of water.
After he ate and drank, he lay down again,
    but the angel of the Lᴏʀᴅ came back a
        second time,
    touched him, and ordered,
    "Get up and eat, else the journey will be
        too long for you!"
He got up, ate, and drank;
    then strengthened by that food,
    he walked forty days and forty nights
        to the mountain of God, Horeb.

RESPONSORIAL PSALM

Ps 34:2-3, 4-5, 6-7, 8-9

R̸. (9a) Taste and see the goodness of the Lord.

I will bless the LORD at all times;
   his praise shall be ever in my mouth.
Let my soul glory in the LORD;
   the lowly will hear me and be glad.

R̸. Taste and see the goodness of the Lord.

Glorify the LORD with me,
   let us together extol his name.
I sought the LORD, and he answered me
   and delivered me from all my fears.

R̸. Taste and see the goodness of the Lord.

Look to him that you may be radiant with
    joy,
   and your faces may not blush with
     shame.
When the afflicted man called out, the
   LORD heard,
   and from all his distress he saved him.

R̸. Taste and see the goodness of the Lord.

The angel of the LORD encamps
   around those who fear him and delivers
    them.
Taste and see how good the LORD is;
   blessed the man who takes refuge in
    him.

R̸. Taste and see the goodness of the Lord.

SECOND READING

Eph 4:30–5:2

Brothers and sisters:
Do not grieve the Holy Spirit of God,
   with which you were sealed for the day
    of redemption.
All bitterness, fury, anger, shouting, and
    reviling
   must be removed from you, along with
    all malice.
And be kind to one another,
    compassionate,
   forgiving one another as God has
    forgiven you in Christ.

So be imitators of God, as beloved
    children, and live in love,
   as Christ loved us and handed himself
    over for us
   as a sacrificial offering to God for a
    fragrant aroma.

About Liturgy

Eucharist, cross, and sacrifice: Eucharist and cross go together because, in the Christian mystery, dying and rising go together. There has been a long-standing tradition in the church to use the image of sacrifice in relation to Eucharist. One aspect of sacrifice surely refers to Jesus' physical death on the cross. Another aspect is that Jesus' death embodies his total giving of himself, holding back nothing. The shedding of his blood is the pouring out of his life for us. Eucharist, as well, is a total and perpetual giving of himself to us for our strength and nourishment. When we celebrate Eucharist, then, we are really not reenacting Calvary and the Last Supper, as if we are engaging in a religious drama. No, the eucharistic celebration enacts in the present moment the continual gift of Jesus' self-giving. The cross and the Last Supper are once-and-for-all unrepeatable historical events. Jesus' acts of self-giving are an ongoing outpouring of his love for us. But there is more.

Our sharing in Eucharist is the concrete manifestation of our encounter with Christ and our participation in his mystery. Eating and drinking Christ's Body and Blood transforms us more perfectly into being the Body of Christ. This means that we ourselves are better equipped to embrace the dying to self that is an essential prerequisite for rising to eternal Life. We must embrace the cross of self-giving each time we share in the Bread of eternal Life. This is the power of the mystery: to transform us into believers committed to self-surrender.

About Liturgical Music

Singing the Communion song, part 3: The third purpose of the Communion song is to highlight the communal nature of the Communion procession (GIRM, no. 86). This purpose is two-pronged. On the one hand, the song is to direct our attention outward toward communal celebration rather than inward toward private prayer. This means that songs which speak of adoration of the Blessed Sacrament (songs proper to Benediction and to times of eucharistic adoration) are not appropriate during the Communion rite at Mass. Suitable songs have texts which speak of our being brought together as the one Body of Christ, as the community of the church, and/or of our mission to be the Body of Christ in the world.

Secondly, the song needs to support our procession to and from the eucharistic table. The procession is itself symbolic of what is taking place: all of us—the able and the lame, the ready and the not-so-ready, the healed and those in need of healing—march together to the messianic table to celebrate the fullness of our redemption in Christ as one Body. Our singing is a way that we engage our hearts with our bodies in this important processional movement. And it is a way that we keep ourselves engaged with the whole Body of Christ even after we have concluded our individual movement to and from the table. More than any other activity at this moment in the Mass, our singing together is perhaps the one which most effectively draws us out of our separate worlds into our shared identity as the Body of Christ.

✠ SPIRITUALITY

℟. Alleluia, alleluia.
Mary is taken up to heaven;
a chorus of angels exults.
℟. Alleluia, alleluia.

Gospel   Luke 1:39-56; L622

Mary set out
    and traveled to the hill
        country in haste
to a town of Judah,
    where she entered the house
        of Zechariah
and greeted Elizabeth.
When Elizabeth heard Mary's
        greeting,
    the infant leaped in her womb,
    and Elizabeth, filled with the Holy Spirit,
    cried out in a loud voice and said,
    "Blessed are you among women,
    and blessed is the fruit of your womb.
And how does this happen to me,
    that the mother of my Lord should
        come to me?
For at the moment the sound of your
        greeting reached my ears,
    the infant in my womb leaped for joy.
Blessed are you who believed
    that what was spoken to you by the Lord
    would be fulfilled."

And Mary said:

"My soul proclaims the greatness of
        the Lord;
    my spirit rejoices in God my Savior
    for he has looked with favor on his
        lowly servant.
From this day all generations will call
        me blessed:
    the Almighty has done great things
        for me,
    and holy is his Name.
He has mercy on those who fear him
    in every generation.
He has shown the strength of his arm,
    and has scattered the proud in their
        conceit.

Continued in Appendix A, p. 305.
See Appendix A, p. 305, for the other readings.

Reflecting on the Gospel

Journeys that we plan have a beginning and an end. We leave, reach our destination, do what we journeyed to do, then return home. Journeys we plan are like circles—we come back home from where we began. This gospel's context is a planned journey. "Mary set out." However, her journey extended far beyond traveling to Elizabeth to help her in her need. Its duration was actually Mary's lifelong journey of praising God, of allowing God to do great things through her, of showing how God is turning upside down the order of things, of being an instrument for God to keep the divine promise of salvation.

Scriptures do not give us very much information about Mary, but from what little is revealed, we do get glimpses of what her lifelong journey was like. She conceived and gave birth to the Son of God, the One who even in her womb caused the unborn John the Baptist to leap "for joy" in Elizabeth's womb. She searched for the twelve-year-old Jesus until she found him in the temple, in his Father's house. She was with her Son during his public ministry. She stood beneath the cross. It seems as though much of her lifelong journey was one of sorrow. Still, her *Magnificat* is marked by an attitude of praise, awe, wonder at the things God is doing for her and all of humanity.

This day we celebrate the completion of Mary's journey, when she "returned to her home," being taken body and soul into heaven to be forever with her Lord whom she bore in her womb. Mary's journey comes full circle—she began life united with God for she was conceived without sin, in perfect holiness. She concludes life by being united with God.

Mary is blessed because she said yes to God's invitation to place herself at the disposal of the divine will. Mary is blessed because her body gave life to the Word incarnate. This is why we believe that her body is assumed into heaven: hers was a uniquely blessed body. Mary had the singular privilege of nourishing the Lord with her body. Body and soul, she was assumed into heaven to enjoy eternal Life with the divine Word, her Son. Because she said yes. Not just once to Gabriel. Not just to Elizabeth's need. But she said yes to God throughout her lifelong journey, a yes that rings out through the centuries into our own hearts, reminding us that our own lifelong journey must be like hers: responding to God with our yes, with our praise, with our awe and wonder at the great things God is doing through us. When our life journey parallels Mary's journey of fidelity, then we, too, come "home."

Living the Paschal Mystery

Our own yes to God must be so strong that self-giving defines our own lifelong journey as it did Mary's. Sometimes self-giving is seen in only a negative, death-dealing sense. And self-giving does involve a dying to self. The gospel for this festival reminds us that there is joy in self-giving as well. The joy that comes from seeing the suffering of another lightened, or a smile brought to the face of someone who is lonely, or the peace of little ones tucked safely into bed for the night is an incarnation in our midst of self-giving. Our self-giving unfolds in the simple events of our days that embody our own yes to God, which in turn overflows into our own *Magnificat*. Self-giving defines the lifelong journey that brings us "home" to be with Mary and her divine Son forever.

Focusing the Gospel
Key words and phrases: Mary set out, returned to her home

To the point: "Mary set out." Her journey extended far beyond traveling to Elizabeth to help her in her need. Its duration was actually Mary's lifelong journey of praising God, of allowing God to do great things through her, of showing how God is turning upside down the order of things, of being an instrument for God to keep the divine promise of salvation. This day we celebrate the completion of Mary's journey, when she "returned to her home," being taken body and soul into heaven to be forever with her Lord whom she bore in her womb.

Model Penitential Act
Presider: We celebrate today the dogma that Mary was taken into heaven body and soul to enjoy eternal Life with her divine Son. As we prepare to celebrate these sacred mysteries, let us ask for God's mercy for the times when we have not been faithful as Mary was faithful . . . [pause]

Lord Jesus, you became incarnate in the womb of Mary your mother: Lord . . .

Christ Jesus, you raised up Mary your mother to be with you in eternal glory: Christ . . .

Lord Jesus, you are the Savior in whom Mary your mother rejoiced: Lord . . .

Model Universal Prayer (Prayer of the Faithful)
Presider: God of salvation, your divine Son became incarnate in the womb of Mary our mother. Hear our prayers that one day we might be with them forever in eternal Life.

Response:

Lord, hear our prayer.

Cantor:

we pray to the Lord,

That all members of the church imitate Mary's fidelity to God's will and praise of God's greatness . . . [pause]

That all people of the world come to the salvation God so graciously promises . . . [pause]

That the lowly be lifted up, the hungry receive their fill, and all generations receive God's mercy . . . [pause]

That each of us, like Mary, faithfully travel the path of life toward our true home with God . . . [pause]

Presider: God of our Savior, you entrusted Mary to be the mother of your Son and brought her to share in your eternal glory: hear these our prayers that one day we might share that same glory. We ask this through Christ our Lord. **Amen.**

FOR REFLECTION
• My life journey is calling me to set out to . . . for . . .
• God does great things through me when I . . .
• My life gives praise to God when I . . . This leads me "home" when . . .

Homily Points
• Any journey beyond a half hour is interminable to small children. "Are we there yet?" A lifelong journey is totally outside of their experience. Yet, from birth on, we all are on a lifelong journey, like Mary, that returns us to our true "home." Along the way, like Mary, we are called to be faithful travelers.

• Like Mary, our journey of faithfulness must include praising God, being open to God's doing great things through us, turning right side up what in our world is out of order, being witnesses of the divine promise of salvation. Our journey will, at times, seem tiring, tedious, and interminable. But we will one day arrive "home" with Mary and her divine Son for all eternity. At this time all of us can ask, "Are we there yet?" And the answer will be, "Yes."

✠ SPIRITUALITY

℞. Alleluia, alleluia.
Whoever eats my flesh and drinks my blood
remains in me and I in him, says the Lord.
℞. Alleluia, alleluia.

Gospel   John 6:51-58; L119B

Jesus said to the crowds:
"I am the living
    bread that
    came down
    from heaven;
whoever eats this
    bread will live
    forever;
and the bread that I
    will give
is my flesh for the
    life of the world."

The Jews quarreled among themselves,
    saying,
"How can this man give us his flesh to
    eat?"
Jesus said to them,
"Amen, amen, I say to you,
unless you eat the flesh of the Son of
    Man and drink his blood,
you do not have life within you.
Whoever eats my flesh and drinks my
    blood
has eternal life,
and I will raise him on the last day.
For my flesh is true food,
    and my blood is true drink.
Whoever eats my flesh and drinks my
    blood
remains in me and I in him.
Just as the living Father sent me
and I have life because of the Father,
so also the one who feeds on me
will have life because of me.
This is the bread that came down from
    heaven.
Unlike your ancestors who ate and still
    died,
whoever eats this bread will live
    forever."

Reflecting on the Gospel

Little children quarrel over sharing toys, who gets to sit next to Nana at a holiday dinner, who gets to choose the TV channel. This is a normal part of the growing up process, of how they grow in self-esteem, of how they learn to live peacefully with others. But when adults quarrel, we are uncomfortable. Adult quarrels are different from childhood misunderstandings or disagreements. Quarrels are usually marked by anger, selfishness, stubbornness. The "quarrel" of the Jews in this gospel is neither a misunderstanding nor disagreement. Jesus' teaching and their quarrel go to the heart of issues held dear to their Jewish tradition: dietary laws and blood taboos. To follow Jesus is to let go of tradition and enter a whole new way of living and believing. The key to delving into the reason for the "quarrel" of the Jews in this gospel is the absolute singularity of the incarnation and the resurrection. They could not accept that Jesus was divine. After the resurrection, they could not grasp the meaning of Jesus' being raised from the dead. Without this understanding, they could not accept eating Jesus' flesh and blood. They could not understand that partaking in the divine, risen One is the way to "eternal life."

Who is "this man"? This question underlies the quarrel the Jews in this gospel are having "among themselves." Jesus declares that he is "living bread" sent by his "living Father"; he shares divine Life with the Father. In Jesus divine Life has been incarnated in human flesh. When we eat his flesh and drink his blood, we partake in this same divine Life. And so, like God, we will "live forever." And so, like the risen Christ, we will be the Presence of God incarnated in human flesh. What a mystery! Its depth challenges us no less than the Jews of Jesus' time. We, too, are faced with the question, Who is "this man"?

Not only the Jewish people of Jesus' time who encountered him and heard his teaching about his being the "living bread" struggled with who Jesus is; so do we. We spend our lives encountering Jesus in many different ways and grappling with the mystery of who he is and what he did for us. The mystery of life and death is at the heart of what Jesus was teaching about his being the "living bread" given for us. The mystery of life and death is at the heart of Eucharist, present to us on the altar of sacrifice during Mass and on the altars of sacrifice of our daily living as we give ourselves over for the good of others. In this giving we learn who Jesus is.

Living the Paschal Mystery

Jesus' invitation to eat and drink his flesh and blood is an invitation to enter into his own mystery of self-giving dying and rising. Eucharist is self-giving. We can be self-giving like Jesus because by eating his flesh and drinking his blood we become more perfectly the Body of Christ. This is why we can "remain" in Jesus—we are transformed by what we eat. Our relationship to Jesus, then, becomes a relationship of indwelling, of divine Life. This is why Eucharist is a promise of eternal Life: because we already have divine Life within us.

Eucharist is both gift given and an invitation to live as Jesus did. The mystery of the Eucharist strengthens us for our daily dying and rising, our daily giving of ourselves for the sake of others so that we all might share more abundantly in divine Life. By our daily living as Jesus did we delve deeper into who he is, and begin to answer that question for ourselves. Surely, this is a life-long process of encounters with the One who ever so patiently teaches us who he is. Indeed, who is "this man"?

Focusing the Gospel

Key words and phrases: living bread, this man, unless you eat the flesh
. . . and drink his blood, living Father sent me, live forever

To the point: Who is "this man"? This question underlies the quarrel the Jews
in this gospel are having "among themselves." Jesus declares that he is "living
bread" sent by his "living Father"; he shares divine Life with the Father. When
we eat his flesh and drink his blood, we partake in this same divine Life. And
so, like God, we will "live forever." And so, like the risen Christ, we will be the
Presence of God incarnated in human flesh. What a mystery! Its depth challenges us no less than the Jews of Jesus' time. We, too, are faced with the question, Who is "this man"?

Connecting the Gospel

to the first reading: At this point in John's Bread of Life discourse, our banquet table is finally set. Not, however, with meat and wine (see first reading),
but with the very Body and Blood of Jesus.

to experience: A venerable Catholic tradition is eucharistic adoration. This
private time before the Blessed Sacrament helps us answer the ongoing question, Who is "this man"? It also helps us come to a deeper appreciation of what
a divine Gift the Eucharist is.

Connecting the Responsorial Psalm

to the readings: Many who hear Jesus proclaim himself the Bread of Life
reject what he is saying (gospel). They simply cannot understand such radical
revelation. Nor can we if we merely put our heads to it. Belief does not come
from rational explanation, however. Rather, as the words from Wisdom and
from Psalm 34 reveal, belief comes through experience. All we need to do is
simply "come and eat" (first reading), "taste and see" (psalm).

   The Lectionary repeats the psalm used last Sunday and will do so again
next week. In her wisdom the church knows that what we need to believe is to
experience over and over the life-giving nourishment that is Jesus. The more we
taste of Jesus the more we will know who he is. And so, let us "Taste and see"
and know his goodness!

to psalmist preparation: As you prepare to call others in this responsorial
psalm to feast on the goodness of God, you might take some time to reflect on
who first called you to the table of the Lord. Who calls you now to keep coming? Who witnesses for you that feasting again and again on the Body and
Blood of Christ will transform your life?

**ASSEMBLY &
FAITH-SHARING GROUPS**
- For me, Jesus is . . . I am his risen Pres-
  ence for others when . . .
- What and who have helped me grow in
  my understanding of the Eucharist are
  . . . I help others grow in their under-
  standing of Eucharist by . . .
- To partake in divine Life means to me . . .

PRESIDERS
My presiding at the Eucharist helps me
live the Eucharist in daily life by . . . My
daily living Eucharist helps me be a better
presider when . . .

DEACONS
Like Christ, I am the living Presence of God
for those I serve when I . . .

HOSPITALITY MINISTERS
My greeting those who gather for Eucharist
helps them and me partake more consciously
in the mystery of the Body and Blood of
Christ when I . . .

MUSIC MINISTERS
My manner of doing music ministry reveals
how I have answered the question, Who is
"this man"?

ALTAR MINISTERS
My serving at the altar leads me more
deeply into the eucharistic mystery when
I . . .

LECTORS
My proclamation helps the assembly connect the table of the word with the table of
the Eucharist when . . .

**EXTRAORDINARY MINISTERS
OF HOLY COMMUNION**
My manner of distributing Holy Communion reveals to communicants how I understand the eucharistic mystery in that . . .

Model Penitential Act

Presider: Jesus invites us in the gospel today to eat his Body and drink his Blood that we may have Life. Let us prepare ourselves to participate in this great mystery . . . [pause]

 Lord Jesus, your Body and Blood nourish us for our journey to eternal Life: Lord . . .
 Christ Jesus, you are the living Bread come down from heaven: Christ . . .
 Lord Jesus, you are the resurrection and the Life: Lord . . .

Homily Points

- Eating is necessary for life. Do we eat to live, or live to eat? With respect to the Eucharist, the answer to this question—both parts of it—is yes. Eating and drinking the risen Christ's Body and Blood gives us a share *now* in divine Life: we eat to live. Further, we must daily deepen our hunger for this divine Food that leads to *eternal* Life: therefore, in a real sense, we live to eat.

- Jesus makes clear in this gospel that he is giving himself—his very flesh and blood—to us as our "living bread." This "living bread" nourishes us now for our life in the risen Christ, and it also nourishes us on our journey toward Life everlasting. Jesus always *invites* us to his banquet table; it is ours to *choose* to take, eat and drink, and live this mystery.

- It is easy to choose to take part in the Communion procession at Mass—to take and eat and drink. It is the more difficult choice to *live* the mystery in which we have participated. This is daily living: to choose to nourish others who are hungry both physically and spiritually, to choose to invite others into deeper relationship with ourselves and the risen Christ, to choose to take time to savor the mystery with which God in Christ has blessed us. In this kind of daily living we answer for ourselves and for others the central question of this gospel: Who is "this man"?

Model Universal Prayer (Prayer of the Faithful)

Presider: We place our needs before God, mindful that God nourishes us and strengthens us with the living Bread come down from heaven.

Response:

Cantor:

That all members of the church raise grateful hearts in praise for the gift of Eucharist . . . [pause]

That all nations enjoy the peace that anticipates everlasting Life . . . [pause]

That those who are hungry either physically or spiritually be fed through our generosity and presence . . . [pause]

That all of us nourished by the Eucharist come to a deeper appreciation for who the risen Christ is for us and who we are for him . . . [pause]

Presider: O wondrous God, you give us the gift of your Son's Body and Blood: hear these our prayers and bring us to the fullness of eternal Life. We ask this through Jesus Christ our Lord. **Amen.**

COLLECT

Let us pray

Pause for silent prayer

O God, who have prepared for those who
 love you
good things which no eye can see,
fill our hearts, we pray, with the warmth
 of your love,
so that, loving you in all things and above
 all things,
we may attain your promises,
which surpass every human desire.
Through our Lord Jesus Christ, your Son,
who lives and reigns with you in the unity
 of the Holy Spirit,
one God, for ever and ever. **Amen.**

FIRST READING

Prov 9:1-6

Wisdom has built her house,
 she has set up her seven columns;
she has dressed her meat, mixed her wine,
 yes, she has spread her table.
She has sent out her maidens; she calls
 from the heights out over the city:
"Let whoever is simple turn in here;
 To the one who lacks understanding,
  she says,
Come, eat of my food,
 and drink of the wine I have mixed!
Forsake foolishness that you may live;
 advance in the way of understanding."

RESPONSORIAL PSALM
Ps 34:2-3, 4-5, 6-7

℟. (9a) Taste and see the goodness of the Lord.

I will bless the LORD at all times;
    his praise shall be ever in my mouth.
Let my soul glory in the LORD;
    the lowly will hear me and be glad.

℟. Taste and see the goodness of the Lord.

Glorify the LORD with me,
    let us together extol his name.
I sought the LORD, and he answered me
    and delivered me from all my fears.

℟. Taste and see the goodness of the Lord.

Look to him that you may be radiant with
        joy,
    and your faces may not blush with
        shame.
When the poor one called out, the LORD
        heard,
    and from all his distress he saved him.

℟. Taste and see the goodness of the Lord.

SECOND READING
Eph 5:15-20

Brothers and sisters:
Watch carefully how you live,
    not as foolish persons but as wise,
    making the most of the opportunity,
    because the days are evil.
Therefore, do not continue in ignorance,
    but try to understand what is the will of
        the Lord.
And do not get drunk on wine, in which
        lies debauchery,
    but be filled with the Spirit,
    addressing one another in psalms and
        hymns and spiritual songs,
    singing and playing to the Lord in your
        hearts,
    giving thanks always and for
        everything
in the name of our Lord Jesus Christ to
        God the Father.

About Liturgy

Mass, Communion, Eucharist: We know that one of our seven sacraments is Eucharist. We also know that it is the third and final of our initiation sacraments (baptism makes us members of the Body of Christ, confirmation seals us through the Holy Spirit in our new identity, Eucharist nourishes us on our life's journey). But if we would survey members of the liturgical assembly about what "Eucharist" means, we would probably get various answers, chief among them being Mass, Holy Communion, or Christ's real Body and Blood. All of these are correct, of course, but a few remarks might bring greater clarity.

Mass (the name is derived from the Latin dismissal, *Ite, missa est*) is the ritual action we gather to celebrate at least every Sunday and for some people, almost every day. We call it a "ritual action" because its structure is something that has come down to us through the tradition of the church and, for the most part, is a sequence of repeated actions; we are familiar with how it unfolds. Mass is broader than Holy Communion which is one ritual element of Mass, the time during which we process to the altar (the symbol in the sacred space of the risen Christ and his messianic banquet) to receive the Body and Blood of Christ. The term "Eucharist" includes both Mass and Holy Communion, but it has an even broader meaning. As we have been reflecting on these gospels from John 6, Eucharist includes our giving thanks to God for these wondrous gifts, a thanksgiving that is concretized by our emulating Christ's life of self-giving. Eucharist, then, goes beyond the walls of the church building and characterizes our lives as Christians. The greatest thanks we can give God for this marvelous Gift is to give of ourselves to others to build up the Body of Christ.

About Liturgical Music

Singing a song after Communion: One of the most misunderstood musical options in the Mass is the song after Communion. According to GIRM (no. 88), once the distribution of Holy Communion is completed the assembly may spend some time in silent prayer or "a Psalm or other canticle of praise or a hymn may also be sung by the whole congregation." This may surprise those accustomed to listening to a "Communion meditation" sung after Communion by a soloist or the choir. But GIRM indicates this song, when used, is to be a hymn of praise rather than a meditation. Moreover, it is to be sung by everyone present. In other words, this song has a liturgical function rather than a devotional one. Its purpose is to express our communal gratitude at having been fed at the table of the Lord and united with Christ and one another through his Body and Blood.

GIRM (no. 86) indicates the Communion song is to begin when the priest gives himself Communion, and is to continue until all the faithful have received. When the congregation is going to sing a hymn of praise after Communion, however, the Communion song itself should be concluded in a "timely manner" that allows people to settle in before singing again. GIRM says nothing about posture during the song after Communion, but its nature as a hymn of praise suggests that standing to sing it would be most appropriate.

SPIRITUALITY

℟. Alleluia, alleluia.
Your words, Lord, are Spirit and life;
you have the words of everlasting life.
℟. Alleluia, alleluia.

Gospel

John 6:60-69; L122B

Many of Jesus' disciples who
    were listening said,
  "This saying is hard; who can
    accept it?"
Since Jesus knew that
    his disciples were
    murmuring about this,
  he said to them, "Does this
    shock you?
What if you were to see the Son
    of Man ascending
  to where he was before?
It is the spirit that gives life,
  while the flesh is of no avail.
The words I have spoken to you are
    Spirit and life.
But there are some of you who do not
    believe."
Jesus knew from the beginning the
    ones who would not believe
  and the one who would betray him.
And he said,
  "For this reason I have told you that
    no one can come to me
  unless it is granted him by my Father."

As a result of this,
  many of his disciples returned to
    their former way of life
  and no longer accompanied him.
Jesus then said to the Twelve, "Do you
    also want to leave?"
Simon Peter answered him, "Master, to
    whom shall we go?
You have the words of eternal life.
We have come to believe
  and are convinced that you are the
    Holy One of God."

Reflecting on the Gospel

We love to have choices between two goods—that way we cannot lose. The disciples in this gospel are faced with a choice. This choice, however, is not between two goods. It is a choice between life and death. Just as Joshua sets before the Israelites a choice ("decide today whom you will serve") so, too, does Jesus set before us a choice ("Do you also want to leave?"). Staying with Jesus is a choice for "eternal life." It cannot be a half-hearted choice. It is a choice that must be backed up by who we are and the way we choose to live.

Jesus' teaching about the Eucharist is the fulcrum upon which this choice rests, for it is the Eucharist which draws together our relationship with Jesus as well as with one another in lives of self-giving. And this is what makes choosing to follow Jesus so difficult: the demand of discipleship is that we embrace *all* of Jesus' way of living—we embrace the goodness of who he is and the demands of self-giving living as he did. On our own, we could not even make such a demanding and all-encompassing choice. But Jesus also reminds us that we are not alone; the Spirit is given us as well and enables us to make the choice to which Jesus calls us.

Thus the choice Jesus sets before the disciples in this gospel is deeper than simply "Do you also want to leave?" Jesus is inviting them to come to believe in who he is ("the Holy One of God" given as Bread from heaven) and what he offers (his own Body and Blood for eternal Life). Believing, however, is not mere verbal assent. It must become the lived conviction of choosing to stay with and in the risen Christ. Choosing to stay with Jesus is a way of living modeled on Jesus' own way of self-giving living.

Choosing Jesus and his teaching requires letting go of what we know of God and allowing God to act in a whole new way toward us. Israel's expectations of God and who the Messiah would be blocked the way for some to see God acting in a new way and offering a whole new way of relating to us. Never before had Israel heard of a God who becomes incarnate and dwells among the people. Never before had God demanded so much of the people—to give one's life for others. To share in Jesus' Body and Blood demands of us this same kind of self-giving. The gift transforms us and in this it makes harsh demands on us, for we become like the Master and can expect to have done to us what the Master had done to him. Choosing to follow Jesus and accept his gift of Self to us is a challenge to see beyond the sacrifice of self-giving and continual dying for the sake of others to the Life that comes from this self-sacrifice. It is always good to remember that Jesus is the Bread of Life. Self-giving always leads to new life and this is why we are able to make the choice to stay with the Master—he has "the words of eternal life."

Living the Paschal Mystery

"It is the spirit that gives life." The Holy Spirit dwells within us and is the source of our life in the risen Christ and of our commitment to follow Jesus wholeheartedly. Without the Spirit we would not be able to shoulder the demands of discipleship, and we would return to our "former way of life." The Spirit enables us to enter into the rhythm of paschal mystery living—of dying and rising, of self-giving and the Life of the indwelling Spirit. Constant vigilance and openness to the Spirit within nudges any halfhearted response to a wholehearted one to choose Jesus and the way of living to which he invites us.

Focusing the Gospel

Key words and phrases: Do you also want to leave?, eternal life, come to believe and are convinced, Holy One of God

To the point: The choice Jesus sets before the disciples in this gospel is deeper than "Do you also want to leave?" Jesus is inviting them to come to believe in who he is ("the Holy One of God" given as Bread from heaven) and what he offers (his own Body and Blood for eternal Life). Believing, however, is not mere verbal assent. It must become the lived conviction of choosing to stay with and in the risen Christ.

Connecting the Gospel

to the first reading: Just as Joshua sets before the Israelites a choice ("decide today whom you will serve") so, too, does Jesus set before us a choice to believe in him. Jesus' teaching about the Eucharist is the fulcrum upon which our choice rests.

to experience: It is easier to live out of habit and routine than to see our participation in the Eucharist as a continual choice which carries consequences for our life now and for Life forever.

Connecting the Responsorial Psalm

to the readings: For the third Sunday in a row we sing "Taste and see the goodness of the Lord" (psalm refrain). In the context of this week's first reading and gospel, however, we see that to taste and see the goodness of God requires a choice and that this choice will affect the entire direction of our lives. While all the Israelites confronted by Joshua chose to maintain their allegiance to God, many of Jesus' disciples walked away from him, unable to believe. This Sunday's readings ask us to make our choice. Will we, like Peter, profess that we have tasted the Lord and found him good? Will we allow what we have tasted to transform us and our way of living?

to psalmist preparation: The Lectionary gives you the opportunity this week to really mean what you say: for the third time you sing, "Taste and see the goodness of the Lord." To whom do you sing this? For whom do you sing it? How does your way of living offer those you encounter a taste of the goodness of God?

**ASSEMBLY &
FAITH-SHARING GROUPS**

- The daily choices I make that point to my belief in Jesus as the "Holy One of God" are . . .
- My eating and drinking the Body and Blood of Christ deepens my conviction about how I should live as a follower of the risen Christ in these ways . . .
- My belief is borne out in lived conviction when I . . .

PRESIDERS
The manner of my presiding helps the assembly encounter the risen Christ, the "Holy One of God," when I . . .

DEACONS
My ministry of service makes visible the conviction of my belief in that . . .

HOSPITALITY MINISTERS
My manner of greeting reveals my choice to remain faithful to Jesus in that . . .

MUSIC MINISTERS
My music ministry deepens my belief in the risen Christ and my participation in the Eucharist by . . .

ALTAR MINISTERS
My choice to be a believer in the risen Christ is evident in my service at the altar when I . . .

LECTORS
My proclamation of the word reveals whom I have chosen to serve when . . .

**EXTRAORDINARY MINISTERS
OF HOLY COMMUNION**
My ministry is to distribute Holy Communion, but it is also . . .

Model Penitential Act

Presider: Today's gospel concludes our reading of John's Bread of Life discourse. Jesus invites us to stay with him or leave, to believe in him or not. As we prepare to celebrate this liturgy, let us reflect on the choices we have made . . . [pause]

Lord Jesus, you are the Holy One of God: Lord . . .

Christ Jesus, you are both Son of God and Son of Man: Christ . . .

Lord Jesus, you are the Bread from heaven given to us: Lord . . .

Homily Points

- The more serious the choice, the more far-reaching are its consequences. For example, the simple choice of whether or not to go out to eat has rather limited consequences: for budget, for diet, for companionship. The more serious choice, for example, of being faithful to our responsibilities in life has far-reaching consequences: for ensuring the well-being of others, for modeling honesty and justice, for maintaining wholesome relationships. The most serious choice we make in life is to believe in the risen Christ as our Bread of Life and to bear this out by the way we live.

- Jesus confronts his hearers with a most serious choice: to stay with him or leave, to believe in him or not. The consequences of this choice are as far-reaching as possible: encountering the "Holy One of God," being given "Spirit and life," receiving "eternal life." Every time we choose to eat the Body and drink the Blood of the risen Christ, we witness to our choice to stay with Jesus and believe in him. We can make this choice because, in the Eucharist, Jesus has chosen to stay with us, believe in us, and give himself to us.

- We must show others that we have chosen to stay with Jesus and believe in him beyond our participation in the eucharistic celebration and receiving him in Holy Communion. We do this, for example, by looking on the face of others we encounter each day as the face of Christ, by confronting others with the consequences of their choices, by giving ourselves to others in need as Jesus gives himself to us. The way we live is already a choice to stay or go, believe or not.

Model Universal Prayer (Prayer of the Faithful)

Presider: Let us pray that we might make the choice always to be faithful followers of Jesus who is the Bread of Life.

Response:

Lord, hear our prayer.

Cantor:

we pray to the Lord,

That all members of the church choose to live as members of the Body of Christ nourished by the Bread from heaven . . . [pause]

That the people of the world choose to live in a way that witnesses to their openness to the Spirit's guidance . . . [pause]

That those who are struggling with serious choices for their daily living be guided by the Spirit and come to peace . . . [pause]

That we here gathered choose to live the Eucharist as a concrete expression of our believing in the risen Jesus . . . [pause]

Presider: Gracious God, your divine Son is Bread from heaven who nourishes us to be faithful followers. Hear these our prayers and bring us to the eternal Life he promises to those who believe. We ask this through that same Jesus Christ our Lord. **Amen.**

COLLECT

Let us pray

Pause for silent prayer

O God, who cause the minds of the faithful
to unite in a single purpose,
grant your people to love what you
    command
and to desire what you promise,
that, amid the uncertainties of this world,
our hearts may be fixed on that place
where true gladness is found.
Through our Lord Jesus Christ, your Son,
who lives and reigns with you in the unity
    of the Holy Spirit,
one God, for ever and ever. **Amen.**

FIRST READING

Josh 24:1-2a, 15-17, 18b

Joshua gathered together all the tribes of
    Israel at Shechem,
    summoning their elders, their leaders,
    their judges, and their officers.
When they stood in ranks before God,
    Joshua addressed all the people:
    "If it does not please you to serve the
      Lord,
    decide today whom you will serve,
    the gods your fathers served beyond the
      River
    or the gods of the Amorites in whose
      country you are now dwelling.
As for me and my household, we will
    serve the Lord."

But the people answered,
    "Far be it from us to forsake the Lord
    for the service of other gods.
For it was the Lord, our God,
    who brought us and our fathers up out
      of the land of Egypt,
    out of a state of slavery.
He performed those great miracles before
      our very eyes
    and protected us along our entire journey
    and among the peoples through whom
      we passed.
Therefore we also will serve the Lord, for
    he is our God."

RESPONSORIAL PSALM

Ps 34:2-3, 16-17, 18-19, 20-21

℟. (9a) Taste and see the goodness of the Lord.

I will bless the Lord at all times;
    his praise shall be ever in my mouth.
Let my soul glory in the Lord;
    the lowly will hear me and be glad.

℟. Taste and see the goodness of the Lord.

The LORD has eyes for the just,
and ears for their cry.
The LORD confronts the evildoers,
to destroy remembrance of them from
the earth.

RJ. Taste and see the goodness of the Lord.

When the just cry out, the LORD hears them,
and from all their distress he rescues
them.
The LORD is close to the brokenhearted;
and those who are crushed in spirit he
saves.

RJ. Taste and see the goodness of the Lord.

Many are the troubles of the just one,
but out of them all the LORD delivers him;
he watches over all his bones;
not one of them shall be broken.

RJ. Taste and see the goodness of the Lord.

SECOND READING
Eph 5:21-32

Brothers and sisters:
Be subordinate to one another out of
reverence for Christ.
Wives should be subordinate to their
husbands as to the Lord.
For the husband is head of his wife
just as Christ is head of the church,
he himself the savior of the body.
As the church is subordinate to Christ,
so wives should be subordinate to their
husbands in everything.
Husbands, love your wives,
even as Christ loved the church
and handed himself over for her to
sanctify her,
cleansing her by the bath of water with
the word,
that he might present to himself the
church in splendor,
without spot or wrinkle or any such thing,
that she might be holy and without
blemish.
So also husbands should love their wives
as their own bodies.
He who loves his wife loves himself.
For no one hates his own flesh
but rather nourishes and cherishes it,
even as Christ does the church,
because we are members of his body.
*For this reason a man shall leave his father
and his mother
and be joined to his wife,
and the two shall become one flesh.*
This is a great mystery,
but I speak in reference to Christ and
the church.

or Eph 5:2a, 25-32 in Appendix A, p. 306.

About Liturgy

Eucharist—doctrine and response: For all too many Christians Eucharist is a matter primarily of believing in the right teachings. Right doctrine is important—we believe that the substance of the bread and wine truly are changed into the substance of the Body and Blood of Christ. (This is what "transubstantiation" means: substance is changed.) We aren't just saying Jesus' Body and Blood are given to us for our nourishment; the change in substance is real. At the same time that we struggle with right doctrine, we are also faced with a choice every time we go to Holy Communion: to become more perfectly the Body of Christ and to live as Jesus did. Eucharist always demands a self-giving response. Eucharist draws forth from us belief and conviction.

Whether our believing in Jesus' Body and Blood stops at the level of doctrine or is carried over into our living is measured by how much over time we (and others) can actually see a difference in our lives. Are we becoming more charitable, more just, more holy? Is this measurable in our everyday actions—for example, do we say fewer unkind words, are we more aware of others' needs, are we happier individuals? Eucharist must make a difference in our lives.

We often hear that we are a eucharistic church, that Eucharist defines who we are. What this means in a nutshell is that we are a self-giving people, concerned always for the good of others. The Eucharist is a great gift; the gift is received not only when we eat and drink Jesus' Body and Blood, but also when we live the self-giving this gift demands. Eucharist changes us, changes our church, and changes our world. But only when we truly live who we become in Jesus—"the Holy One of God."

About Liturgical Music

Music suggestions: This Sunday concludes our proclamation of the Bread of Life discourse from the Gospel of John, when Jesus confronts us with the questions, Do you believe in who I am, and will you follow me? Particularly appropriate Communion songs would be ones that speak of our choice to believe and follow. For example, in the refrain of Scott Soper's "Lord, to Whom Shall We Go" (BB), we join in Peter's response: "Lord, to whom shall we go? . . . You alone have the words of lasting life." In verse 3 we identify Jesus as the way, the truth, and the life; in verse 4, we call him the "First and Last, Alpha and Omega . . . the Christ, the Beginning and the End!" Another example is "Bread of Life from Heaven/Pan de Vida Eterna" (G3, SS, W4). Verse 5 reads, "Dwell in the One who now dwells in you; Make your home in the life-giving Word. Know only Christ, Holy One of God, and believe in the truth you have heard." A third example is "This Is My Body" (WC, WS), in which we sing, "I am the Way and Truth and Life, come Follow me, believe and live."

At other points in the Mass, Herman Stuempfle's "To Whom, Lord, Shall We Go" (W4) would make an excellent reflective response during the preparation of the gifts, and "I Have Decided to Follow Jesus" (LMGM2) would make an appropriate and energetic recessional song.

SPIRITUALITY

GOSPEL ACCLAMATION
James 1:18

R̸. Alleluia, alleluia.
The Father willed to give us birth by the word
    of truth
that we may be a kind of firstfruits of
    his creatures.
R̸. Alleluia, alleluia.

Gospel

Mark 7:1-8, 14-15, 21-23; L125B

**When the Pharisees with
    some scribes who had
    come from Jerusalem
    gathered around Jesus,
    they observed that some of
        his disciples ate their
        meals
    with unclean, that is, unwashed,
        hands.
—For the Pharisees and, in fact, all Jews,
    do not eat without carefully washing
        their hands,
    keeping the tradition of the elders.
And on coming from the marketplace
    they do not eat without purifying
        themselves.
And there are many other things that
    they have traditionally observed,
    the purification of cups and jugs and
        kettles and beds.—
So the Pharisees and scribes
    questioned him,
    "Why do your disciples not follow the
        tradition of the elders
    but instead eat a meal with unclean
        hands?"
He responded,
    "Well did Isaiah prophesy about you
        hypocrites, as it is written:
    *This people honors me with their
        lips,
        but their hearts are far from me;
    in vain do they worship me,
        teaching as doctrines human
        precepts.***

Continued in Appendix A, p. 306.

Reflecting on the Gospel

Some cities have installed red lights and speed cameras at intersections. Generally, people hate them. They generate far more traffic tickets than the police can issue. In spite of the negative reaction, over and over again these cameras have proven their worth: they force people to keep the law and they prevent harm from accidents that all too frequently happen at particularly busy and dangerous intersections. Yes, we hate the cameras because they cost those who disobey the law money. Yes, we also tolerate them because they save injury and lives. Ultimately, traffic laws are not about the city coffers, but about good order and eliminating accidents. This gospel is about laws, too. In their goal to be acceptable before God, some Pharisees and scribes became caught up in mere human traditions. Jesus contrasts God's just laws that free us for deeper relationships with God and each other with mere human traditions that bind and harm relationships.

In the gospel it appears that "the Pharisees with some scribes" are judging Jesus and his disciples for how they fail to keep the Jewish traditions. In fact, Jesus is passing judgment on the Pharisees and scribes by facing them with their own self-righteousness. The Pharisees fixate on keeping human traditions; Jesus frees people from rigid adherence to human traditions and redirects them to authentic living of God's commandments. At stake is right covenantal relationship with God and others in the community. Law is about right relationships, not about self-righteousness.

One can keep the letter of the law and miss entirely the point of the law—moral living is a sign of covenantal relationship with God. Israel's taking possession of the land (see first reading) is a realization of salvation—God delivered them from their enemies as a sign that God is faithful to the covenant that God made with Israel. Israel, in turn, is to observe God's commands. But these "wise and intelligent people" don't merely keep the commandments; they know that the commandments are a sign of their faithful covenantal relationship with God. When our hearts are turned to God, we have life. This is what is at stake. God's Life is what unbinds us and gives us the ultimate freedom.

Living the Paschal Mystery

It's easier to clean the pots and pans than to clean one's heart! The Pharisees are concerned with washing hands; Jesus is concerned about washing feet! Law is not given to be kept for its own sake; law is given for the good of the people. Any traditions to which we adhere must be for the sake of the purpose of God's commandments: to live in right relationship with God and each other.

What traditions do we blindly cling to? Perhaps it is enough for us just to go to Mass on Sunday; after all, this is what most of us grew up doing; this is what Catholics do. Or perhaps we cling to rote prayers that we learned as a child rather than stretch our relationship with God to find new prayer expressions. We need to look at the way we live, and this will tell us whether we have hearts truly turned toward God in a healthy and life-giving relationship. Purity of heart is expressed in righteous living—self-giving for the sake of others that deepens our relationships. This is how we have life. This is how commandments free us.

Focusing the Gospel

Key words and phrases: Pharisees and scribes questioned him, He responded, You disregard God's commandment but cling to human tradition, Hear me . . . and understand

To the point: In the gospel it appears that "the Pharisees with some scribes" are judging Jesus. In fact, Jesus is passing judgment on the Pharisees and scribes by facing them with their own self-righteousness. The Pharisees fixate on keeping human traditions; Jesus frees people from rigid adherence to human traditions and redirects them to authentic living of God's commandments. At stake is right covenantal relationship with God and others in the community. Law is about right relationships, not about self-righteousness.

Connecting the Gospel

to the first reading: God gives us commandments so we "may live." The purpose of keeping the law is not a matter of blind obedience, but is a matter of relationship, of growing closer to the Lord God who has first come "so close" to us.

to experience: Fixating on anything leads quickly to broken relationships and untold harm. This is no less true of laws and traditions. Jesus judges and warns against such fixations because he knows the consequences: strained and/or broken relationships with God and others.

Connecting the Responsorial Psalm

to the readings: Psalm 15 was a liturgical psalm used when the Israelites ritually renewed their covenant with God. The psalm began by asking, "Lord, who may abide in your tent?" then answered by describing a person who treats others with justice. The mark of fidelity to the covenant, then, was acting justly toward one's neighbor.

In the first reading Moses commands the people to be faithful to all the statutes and decrees given them by God because the Law was a sign of God's closeness to them and was a guide to justice. When the Pharisees and scribes confront Jesus about the failure of his disciples to keep the ritual laws of washing before eating, they are not concerned with either closeness to God or justice but with undermining the authority of Jesus (gospel). Jesus responds by challenging their infidelity and calling them to the deep conversion of heart which is at the core of the Law. Psalm 15 invites us to listen to the words of Jesus by taking God's Law to heart and living lives of justice and truth. In singing it we are choosing to be persons near to our God (first reading) and near to our neighbor.

to psalmist preparation: This psalm challenges you by making the manner of your relating to other human beings the benchmark of your fidelity to God. Do you act with the truth, justice, and love described in the psalm? When do you struggle to act this way? When do you find it easy? How does Christ help you?

ASSEMBLY & FAITH-SHARING GROUPS

- The "human tradition[s]" on which I am fixated are . . . This affects my relationship with God and others in that . . .
- I tend to judge others about how they live when . . . Jesus judges me and I learn that . . .
- Keeping God's commandments helps me to be in right relationships in these ways . . .

PRESIDERS

When I fixate on the rubrics, my presiding looks like . . . When I focus on liturgy as prayer, my presiding becomes . . .

DEACONS

The manner in which I serve others helps them and me grow in having hearts focused on God when . . .

HOSPITALITY MINISTERS

My manner of practicing hospitality builds right relationships when I . . .

MUSIC MINISTERS

I find mere human observance shaping my music ministry when . . . What helps me refocus on God is . . .

ALTAR MINISTERS

My ministry calls me to focus on the "pots and kettles." What helps me put this in perspective is . . .

LECTORS

What keeps my proclamation from being mere lip service is . . . It originates from a heart near the Lord when . . .

EXTRAORDINARY MINISTERS OF HOLY COMMUNION

My manner of distributing Holy Communion fosters deeper relationships with the risen Christ and with each other in that . . .

✝ CELEBRATION

Model Penitential Act

Presider: In the gospel today, Jesus invites us to reflect on how and why we keep human and divine commandments. Let us ask God's mercy for the times we have not been faithful to the spirit of the law . . . [pause]

Lord Jesus, you are the way, the truth, and the life: Lord . . .

Christ Jesus, you call us to hear and understand your Father's commandments: Christ . . .

Lord Jesus, you draw us close to the God who is close to us: Lord . . .

Homily Points

- Every social grouping—families, schools, cities, various organizations, nations—has rules or laws. The purpose of these rules or laws is not to bind people to rigid behaviors, but to facilitate the relationships that bind them to one another as a social grouping. So it is with God's commandments and our relationship to God and each other.

- In this gospel Jesus faces the Pharisees and some scribes with how they use human traditions to oppress the community of God's people. In effect they have put themselves above God, upsetting the relationships that God's commandments are meant to preserve and deepen. Jesus turns their judgment about him and his disciples back on them. He teaches that no human tradition can supplant God's commandments.

- Good laws never oppress, but always promote the common good. God's commandments never oppress, but always promote right relationships with God and others. To illustrate this principle: each of the Ten Commandments has an important value at its heart. For example, the fifth commandment not only prohibits killing another, but demands respect for all of life. The first commandment directs us not only to keep Sunday holy, but to keep God at the center of our lives every day. Commandments always take us beyond the letter to the spirit, beyond minimal obedience to the conscious surrender of our heart to God and others.

Model Universal Prayer (Prayer of the Faithful)

Presider: God's commandments free us to deepen our relationships with God and each other. Let us pray that we be obedient to what God asks of us.

Response:

Lord, hear our prayer.

Cantor:

we pray to the Lord,

That all members of the church keep God's commandments in such a way as to draw closer to God and each other . . . [pause]

That all nations establish and keep laws that promote right relationships and the good of all . . . [pause]

That those justly imprisoned for breaking the law may repent and come closer to God . . . [pause]

That each of us come to a deeper appreciation for God's law and embrace living it wholeheartedly . . . [pause]

Presider: All-powerful God, you gave your people commandments to guide them to right relationship with you and each other: hear these our prayers that our hearts may always be turned to you so that one day we might enjoy everlasting Life. We ask this through Christ our Lord. **Amen.**

206

COLLECT
Let us pray

Pause for silent prayer

God of might, giver of every good gift,
put into our hearts the love of your name,
so that, by deepening our sense of
reverence,
you may nurture in us what is good
and, by your watchful care,
keep safe what you have nurtured.
Through our Lord Jesus Christ, your Son,
who lives and reigns with you in the unity
of the Holy Spirit,
one God, for ever and ever. **Amen.**

FIRST READING
Deut 4:1-2, 6-8

Moses said to the people:
"Now, Israel, hear the statutes and
decrees
which I am teaching you to observe,
that you may live, and may enter in and
take possession of the land
which the LORD, the God of your fathers,
is giving you.
In your observance of the commandments
of the LORD, your God,
which I enjoin upon you,
you shall not add to what I command
you nor subtract from it.
Observe them carefully,
for thus will you give evidence
of your wisdom and intelligence to the
nations,
who will hear of all these statutes and
say,
'This great nation is truly a wise and
intelligent people.'
For what great nation is there
that has gods so close to it as the LORD,
our God, is to us
whenever we call upon him?
Or what great nation has statutes and
decrees
that are as just as this whole law
which I am setting before you today?"

RESPONSORIAL PSALM

Ps 15:2-3, 3-4, 4-5

R͛. (1a) The one who does justice will live in the presence of the Lord.

Whoever walks blamelessly and does justice;
  who thinks the truth in his heart
  and slanders not with his tongue.

R͛. The one who does justice will live in the presence of the Lord.

Who harms not his fellow man,
  nor takes up a reproach against his neighbor;
by whom the reprobate is despised,
  while he honors those who fear the LORD.

R͛. The one who does justice will live in the presence of the Lord.

Who lends not his money at usury
  and accepts no bribe against the innocent.
Whoever does these things
  shall never be disturbed.

R͛. The one who does justice will live in the presence of the Lord.

SECOND READING

Jas 1:17-18, 21b-22, 27

Dearest brothers and sisters:
All good giving and every perfect gift is from above,
  coming down from the Father of lights,
  with whom there is no alteration or shadow caused by change.
He willed to give us birth by the word of truth
  that we may be a kind of firstfruits of his creatures.

Humbly welcome the word that has been planted in you
  and is able to save your souls.

Be doers of the word and not hearers only, deluding yourselves.

Religion that is pure and undefiled before God and the Father is this:
  to care for orphans and widows in their affliction
  and to keep oneself unstained by the world.

About Liturgy

Second reading fits this Sunday: By happy coincidence the second reading corresponds nicely with the gospel—it gives the counterpart behaviors for the list of sins with which the gospel selection concludes. It points us in the direction of forming right relationships. This would be a good Sunday to spend some time reflecting on the second reading.

Liturgy and life: The gospel's inclusion of the quotation from Isaiah (29:13) is a strong reminder for us of the necessity of an inherent relationship between liturgy and life. The prophets often sounded the warning that worship without right living is not acceptable to God (for example, Micah 6:6-8 and Amos 5:21-24). Our Christian liturgy, however, demands more of us than simply doing just deeds. Our liturgy forms us into a just people so that our good deeds come from within us. Both liturgy and life are rooted in the paschal mystery with its demand to die to self so that we can rise to new life. This isn't something we can do occasionally—it is a way of life.

What is at stake in this way of life is a relationship with God evidenced in keeping God's commandments. Obedience goes way beyond blind obedience—it is really about coming closer to the Lord God. Paying attention to the Presence of God dwelling within us and then living out of this intimate relationship with the Divine is what brings us to the good way of living described in the second reading.

About Liturgical Music

Music suggestions: Thomas Troeger's "As a Chalice Cast of Gold" (HG, W4), composed to coincide with this gospel reading, addresses our need to be saved "from the soothing sin of the empty cultic deed" and calls us to say an internal "Amen" to our gestures of worship. This hymn would be appropriate for either the entrance procession or the preparation of the gifts. Another good choice for the entrance procession would be Gail Coon's "Renew Us" (BB). Lucien Deiss's "Grant to Us, O Lord" (W4, WC, WS) reminds us of our need for ongoing conversion of heart and could be sung for the entrance, the preparation of the gifts, or Communion. David Haas's "Deep Within" (G3) also calls us to renewal of heart and would work well during the preparation of the gifts, as would Rory Cooney's "Change Our Hearts" (G3). Another suitable song for the preparation of the gifts would be the spiritual "Lord, I Want to Be a Christian" (LMGM2). Two songs which would send us on our way reminded to live the justice to which God's Law calls us are "What Does the Lord Require?" (W4) and "Go, Be Justice" (SS, WC, WS).

SPIRITUALITY

R͑. Alleluia, alleluia.
Jesus proclaimed the Gospel of the kingdom
and cured every disease among the people.
R͑. Alleluia, alleluia.

Gospel

Mark 7:31-37; L128B

**Again Jesus left the
district of Tyre
and went by way of
Sidon to the Sea of
Galilee,
into the district of the
Decapolis.
And people brought to
him a deaf man
who had a speech
impediment
and begged him to lay
his hand on him.
He took him off by himself away from
the crowd.
He put his finger into the man's ears
and, spitting, touched his tongue;
then he looked up to heaven and
groaned, and said to him,
"Ephphatha!"—that is, "Be
opened!"—
And immediately the man's ears were
opened,
his speech impediment was removed,
and he spoke plainly.
He ordered them not to tell anyone.
But the more he ordered them not to,
the more they proclaimed it.
They were exceedingly astonished and
they said,
"He has done all things well.
He makes the deaf hear and the mute
speak."**

Reflecting on the Gospel

In this gospel Jesus opens the ears and loosens the tongue of the deaf-mute. Both he and the crowd cannot contain themselves, but proclaim what Jesus has done. What has Jesus really done? Healed the man? Yes, but more. Jesus has revealed that he is far more than a miracle worker, as fascinating and wonderful as that may be. Understood only as an external sign, however, the miracle falls short of the reality. The miracles Jesus performs reveal his own divine power, his own compassion for the human condition, his own mission. Jesus cares for each of us, cares enough to reach out and touch us! What must be proclaimed is not the sign itself, but that to which it points: God's Presence bringing salvation (see first reading). Faced with this revelation, no one can keep silent. The Word grants the power of word.

We surmise that something very profound must have happened between Jesus and the deaf man even before the miracle that brought the deaf and mute man to an intensified insight about Jesus. Jesus must have communicated something to him that resonated deep within the man's very being and changed him. This is why he could not help but proclaim the miracle—his encounter with Jesus changed him. He was able to see beyond the miracle to the wholeness (salvation) Jesus offered him.

The crowd recognized that Jesus is the fulfillment of Isaiah's prophecy (see first reading) when they say, "He has done all things well. He makes the deaf hear and the mute speak." Jesus' miracle points beyond himself as a miracle worker to himself as the One who has come to save us. The miracles are a sign of salvation—God's new Life is breaking in on humanity and changing who we are and giving us a whole new insight into our relationship with God. We now see God's mighty deeds, know Jesus is our savior, and proclaim God's salvation. This Good News cannot be contained.

Jesus is very personal with the man he heals: he touches his ears and tongue; he prays to his Father ("looked up to heaven") with a groan, as if his whole being were involved. How much Jesus wishes to touch us, heal us, encounter us! Like the healed man and crowd in the gospel, we cannot keep quiet, either. Encounter with Jesus leads to our proclaiming his nearness, his care, his healing. We are never alone. We only need to open ourselves to Jesus' touch. We only need to open ourselves to the Word who grants us all power to proclaim his nearness to the whole world.

Living the Paschal Mystery

In terms of Christian discipleship, we must come to know Jesus before we can proclaim who he is. Looking to mighty deeds that we think may be unfolding around us today—reports of miracles, etc.—is not where this gospel leads us. Rather, the gospel leads us to see Christ in the little things around us—the caring touch, the encouraging smile, the unexpected friendly phone call—and interpret these as evidence of God's Presence and salvation. We ought to be "astonished" today by the many manifestations of God's Presence in and through the people around us. We ought to be astonished at how God uses us as instruments to proclaim the Good News of salvation. We ought to be so keyed into Jesus' Presence that we, too, cannot contain ourselves, but must proclaim God's mighty deeds to anyone who has ears to hear.

Focusing the Gospel

Key words and phrases: deaf man who had a speech impediment, Be opened, he spoke plainly, they proclaimed it

To the point: In this gospel Jesus opens the ears and loosens the tongue of the deaf-mute. Both he and the crowd cannot contain themselves, but proclaim what Jesus has done. What has Jesus really done? Healed the man? Yes, but more: he has revealed his own divine power, his own compassion for the human condition, his own mission. Faced with this revelation, no one can keep silent. The Word grants the power of word.

Connecting the Gospel

to the first reading: There's more to this gospel than the healing miracle because there's more to Jesus than being a miracle worker—he is the fulfillment of Isaiah's prophecy ("the ears of the deaf be cleared . . . the tongue of the mute will sing"). This event discloses Jesus as savior: "Here is your God . . . he comes to save you."

to experience: What makes us tongue-tied? Intimidation, awe, mystification, fear, or shock. What loosens our tongues? Conviction, newfound courage, necessity, pressure, or renewed compassion for others. When we are tongue-tied about proclaiming who Jesus is, it is the Word himself who loosens our tongues.

Connecting the Responsorial Psalm

to the readings: Psalm 146 is the first of five psalms that form the conclusion to the Hebrew Psalter. These psalms shout Alleluia to God who, throughout human history, has continually saved us, transforming impairment to wholeness, injustice to right, and suffering to joy. The reading from Isaiah proclaims God's promise to do these very things. The gospel shows these promises fully realized in the person of Jesus.

Unlike the psalmist, however, who repeatedly commands us to shout praise for God's saving deeds (psalm refrain), Jesus commands the crowd to keep quiet about the miracle they have witnessed. In these contradictory commands, both the psalmist and Jesus want the same thing—that we see beneath the physical miracles to the deeper reality of God's gift of salvation. We are called to do more than merely shout about wonderworking. We are called to recognize salvation in our midst, and to tell the world by the way we live. This is our praise, this is our Alleluia!

to psalmist preparation: In this psalm you proclaim the many concrete ways God grants salvation to the suffering and the downtrodden. You offer hope to all those in the midst of such intense suffering that salvation seems impossible. You praise God for sending salvation in human form: Jesus (gospel). You sing praise to God and hope to the people. How do you need to prepare yourself to proclaim this word of salvation?

**ASSEMBLY &
FAITH-SHARING GROUPS**
- I have been tongue-tied and silent when . . . Jesus, the Word, has given me courage to proclaim . . .
- I have experienced Jesus' divine power and compassion coursing through me when . . .
- I am compelled to proclaim Jesus' mission to . . .

PRESIDERS
The Word has granted me the power to proclaim the word in these ways . . .

DEACONS
My service to those in need is a proclamation of the compassion of the Word when . . .

HOSPITALITY MINISTERS
The words I use to greet those who are gathering for liturgy proclaim that . . .

MUSIC MINISTERS
My music making enables the assembly to open their ears and loosen their tongues to proclaim the Word when . . .

ALTAR MINISTERS
My ministry seems wordless, but it proclaims . . .

LECTORS
What I proclaim is . . .

**EXTRAORDINARY MINISTERS
OF HOLY COMMUNION**
When I say the words "Body of Christ" or "Blood of Christ," I am proclaiming . . .

Model Penitential Act

Presider: In today's gospel Jesus heals the deaf man with a speech impediment. As we prepare to celebrate this liturgy, let us ask Jesus to open our ears to hear his word, our tongues to proclaim his praise, our hearts to receive his mercy . . . [pause]

Lord Jesus, you are the Word made flesh who dwells among us: Lord . . .

Christ Jesus, you are the Savior of the world: Christ . . .

Lord Jesus, you are ever the compassionate Son of God who brings us healing: Lord . . .

Homily Points

- People don't keep good news to themselves. Fingers fly tapping out text messages. Conversation around the proverbial watercooler gets louder. In this gospel Jesus orders the crowd to keep quiet about the healing. He's got to be kidding! Contain good news? Not possible!

- This whole gospel is essentially about relationship and communication. Jesus establishes a unique relationship with the deaf-mute man when he reaches out to him with a healing touch. In this gesture, he has opened this man to a deeper relationship with himself as the Christ, as the One who saves. Healed, the man "spoke plainly" and the crowd proclaimed widely.

- What do we communicate about our relationship with the person of Jesus? Do we speak "plainly" about him, for example, to those who are suffering or in sorrow? to those who need to hear words of forgiveness? to those who need to be challenged to grow deeper in their relationship with Jesus? In all this, through word and act, we are proclaiming good news. When we truly encounter and hear the Word, our tongues cannot refrain from proclaiming him widely. Contain such Good News? Not possible!

Model Universal Prayer (Prayer of the Faithful)

Presider: Our God speaks to us, heals us, and saves us. Let us make our needs known to such a caring God.

Response:

Lord, hear our prayer.

Cantor:

we pray to the Lord,

That all members of the church grow in their relationship with Jesus and widely proclaim his Good News . . . [pause]

That all leaders of nations be instruments of God's healing touch bringing well-being to all . . . [pause]

That those who are hurting physically, mentally, or spiritually be healed by the power of Jesus . . . [pause]

That all of us here continue Jesus' saving ministry in both word and action . . . [pause]

Presider: Lord our God, you heal and draw us to yourself by your tender care: hear these our prayers and open our eyes and ears to receive the Good News proclaimed by your divine Son. Who lives and reigns for ever and ever. **Amen.**

COLLECT
Let us pray

Pause for silent prayer

O God, by whom we are redeemed and
     receive adoption,
look graciously upon your beloved sons
     and daughters,
that those who believe in Christ
may receive true freedom
and an everlasting inheritance.
Through our Lord Jesus Christ, your Son,
who lives and reigns with you in the unity
     of the Holy Spirit,
one God, for ever and ever. **Amen.**

FIRST READING
Isa 35:4-7a

Thus says the Lord:
     Say to those whose hearts are
          frightened:
          Be strong, fear not!
     Here is your God,
          he comes with vindication;
     with divine recompense
          he comes to save you.
     Then will the eyes of the blind be
          opened,
          the ears of the deaf be cleared;
     then will the lame leap like a stag,
          then the tongue of the mute will sing.
     Streams will burst forth in the desert,
          and rivers in the steppe.
     The burning sands will become pools,
          and the thirsty ground, springs of
               water.

RESPONSORIAL PSALM
Ps 146:6-7, 8-9, 9-10

℟. (1b) Praise the Lord, my soul!
  or:
℟. Alleluia.

The God of Jacob keeps faith forever,
  secures justice for the oppressed,
  gives food to the hungry.
The LORD sets captives free.

℟. Praise the Lord, my soul!
  or:
℟. Alleluia.

The LORD gives sight to the blind;
  the LORD raises up those who were
    bowed down.
The LORD loves the just;
  the LORD protects strangers.

℟. Praise the Lord, my soul!
  or:
℟. Alleluia.

The fatherless and the widow the LORD
    sustains,
  but the way of the wicked he thwarts.
The LORD shall reign forever;
  your God, O Zion, through all
    generations.
Alleluia.

℟. Praise the Lord, my soul!
  or:
℟. Alleluia.

SECOND READING
Jas 2:1-5

My brothers and sisters, show no
    partiality
  as you adhere to the faith in our
    glorious Lord Jesus Christ.
For if a man with gold rings and fine
    clothes
  comes into your assembly,
  and a poor person in shabby clothes
    also comes in,
  and you pay attention to the one
    wearing the fine clothes
  and say, "Sit here, please,"
  while you say to the poor one, "Stand
    there," or "Sit at my feet,"
  have you not made distinctions among
    yourselves
  and become judges with evil designs?

Listen, my beloved brothers and sisters.
Did not God choose those who are poor in
    the world
  to be rich in faith and heirs of the
    kingdom
  that he promised to those who love him?

About Liturgy

Labor Day: This is Labor Day weekend, and it would be appropriate to add a fifth intention at the universal prayer (prayer of the faithful). For example, "That all laborers, by the quality of their work, proclaim God's care and love for all people."

Lectors, assembly, and proclamation of the word: Proclamation involves more than just speaking and hearing. True proclamation demands a commitment of self on the part of both lector and assembly that is evident in the way one lives. This is why being a lector is much more than being a good reader. One might read flawlessly, but the word would not necessarily be proclamation. True proclamation comes from the lived experience of the lector (the individual has already lived God's word during the week before proclamation) and rings so true that it moves the assembly to live the word as well. In other words, proclamation demands something of the proclaimer and something of the hearer. If either is lacking, then the proclamation is lacking.

Good proclamation requires living what we might call a "spirituality of the word." This means that one isn't a lector just on the Sunday when one proclaims, but is a lector every moment of every day. It also means that the assembly is called to live the word proclaimed as well. Proclamation of God's word becomes a way of life that is evident in the way one speaks in ordinary daily living (kind, uplifting words; no profanity; encouragement and challenge; etc.). A spirituality of the word would also be characterized by one who spends extra time with God's word—the Bible or Lectionary—perhaps reading a few verses each day and keeping them in mind while one goes about the day. In this way God's word becomes so familiar as to become the very words of the individual.

About Liturgical Music

Music suggestions: The healing of the deaf-mute in this Sunday's gospel is a sign of Jesus' power to open up all the ways human beings are closed off to fullness of Life. Jesus is God's Presence bringing salvation. Our response is to be human presence proclaiming in word and deed that this salvation has come.

In James Quinn's "Word of God, Come Down on Earth" (W4, WC), we address Jesus as the "Word that caused blind eyes to see" and ask him to "Speak and heal our mortal blindness; Deaf we are: our healer be; Loose our tongues to tell your kindness." This hymn would work very well as the entrance song. Another good choice for the entrance procession would be "Your Hands, O Lord, in Days of Old" (W4, WC, WS), in which we sing of the healing miracles Jesus worked long ago and beg that he continue to use his saving power today "In ev'ry street, in ev'ry home, In ev'ry troubled friend." In Scott Soper's "You Are the Healing" (BB), we sing "Jesus, you are the healing . . . you are the freedom . . . you are the power . . . you are the resurrection . . . come show us how to live." This song would work well during the preparation of the gifts. In Jesse Manibusan's "Open My Eyes" (BB, G3, JS3), we beg Jesus to "Open my eyes . . . to see your face"; "Open my ears . . . to hear your voice"; "Open my heart . . . to love like you." This piece could be sung as a prayerful meditation on the gospel during the preparation of the gifts, with choir or cantor singing the bridge between verses 3 and 4. Verse 1 of Delores Dufner's "A Year of God's Favor" (HG, W4) speaks of Christ bringing "Recov'ry of sense to the deaf and the blind, Full healing for spirit, for body and mind." In verse 3, we pray that God's saving word in Christ be fulfilled today "in our loving, our work, and our play, . . . in justice, in mercy and peace, In joyful thanksgiving and praise without cease." This hymn would make an excellent recessional song.

SEPTEMBER 6, 2015
TWENTY-THIRD SUNDAY
IN ORDINARY TIME

SPIRITUALITY

GOSPEL ACCLAMATION
Gal 6:14

R7. Alleluia, alleluia.
May I never boast except in the cross of our
    Lord
through which the world has been crucified to
    me and I to the world.
R7. Alleluia, alleluia.

Gospel   Mark 8:27-35; L131B

Jesus and his disciples set out
    for the villages of Caesarea
        Philippi.
Along the way he asked his disciples,
    "Who do people say that I am?"
They said in reply,
    "John the Baptist, others Elijah,
        still others one of the
            prophets."
And he asked them,
    "But who do you say that I am?"
Peter said to him in reply,
    "You are the Christ."
Then he warned them not to tell anyone
    about him.

He began to teach them
    that the Son of Man must suffer greatly
    and be rejected by the elders, the chief
        priests, and the scribes,
    and be killed, and rise after three days.
He spoke this openly.
Then Peter took him aside and began to
    rebuke him.
At this he turned around and, looking at
    his disciples,
    rebuked Peter and said, "Get behind
        me, Satan.
You are thinking not as God does, but as
    human beings do."

He summoned the crowd with his
    disciples and said to them,
    "Whoever wishes to come after me
        must deny himself,
    take up his cross, and follow me.
For whoever wishes to save his life will
    lose it,
    but whoever loses his life for my sake
    and that of the gospel will save it."

Reflecting on the Gospel

Self-identity is a big deal in our society. Knowing who we are enables us to journey forward through life with confidence, a sense of direction and purpose, an accurate assessment of our capabilities as well as weaknesses. In this gospel, Jesus' question to his disciples, "Who do people say that I am?" was not about his seeking his own self-awareness. It was a question put to the disciples that would *reveal to them* more deeply who he was and why he came among them. In Peter's response, "You are the Christ," we meet a high point in Mark's gospel account. We are invited to struggle more deeply with who Jesus is. We are invited to prepare ourselves for what faithful discipleship entails.

Yes, Peter acknowledges that Jesus is "the Christ," but misses the deeper point. From Jewish tradition Peter has a preconceived notion of who Jesus is and also of who "the Christ" would be—as the "anointed one," the Messiah, he would be a great king (kings of Israel were anointed), overthrow Roman domination, and restore the powerful Israel of old. But this is not "the Christ" who Jesus came to be. Jesus' self-awareness is revealed ever so fully: he is "the Christ" who will "suffer greatly," "be rejected," and "be killed." Jesus also makes something else explicit—disciples must also "take up [their] cross" if they are to follow Jesus. The disciples are hardly prepared for understanding Jesus' identity as "the Christ"; they are even less prepared to grasp the demands of following him.

Jesus is called "the Christ"—Peter is called Satan. Salvation confronts human resistance. Peter had a certain image, belief, expectation of what "the Christ" was to be, to do. Suffering, rejection, and being killed had nothing to do with Peter's Christ. But they have everything to do with the Christ of God. Without a right understanding of "the Christ," we cannot, with him, rise to new Life. Alone, the demands of discipleship would be impossible, the struggle beyond us. But with God as our help, we can begin to think as God does, not as humans. And how does God think? Not in terms of beatings, buffets, pain, ridicule, or even death. God thinks in terms of life and love. God thinks in terms of salvation. God only wills for us what is good for us and what brings us to new Life. We take up our own cross daily because this is the way to a share in risen Life.

Living the Paschal Mystery

This gospel makes explicit the parameters of discipleship: self-denial, bearing hardship. It makes equally explicit why in the world anyone would follow Jesus: because this is the way to have Life. Herein is a clear gospel presentation of the paschal mystery: it means death and new Life, it means making a choice, it means that we, too, must embrace this way of living if we are to receive the gift of salvation Jesus offers.

It is no small coincidence that this gospel begins with the question of Jesus' identity and then ends with the cost of discipleship. Identity and discipleship are inextricably related because who we are, our own self-awareness, shapes how we follow. Our identity through baptism is that of Body of Christ; by being united with him in identity, we are also united with him in his life, death, *and* resurrection. Unlike him, we will not die on a cross. Like him, we are called to be followers who give themselves for the good of others.

Focusing the Gospel

Key words and phrases: You are the Christ, suffer greatly, rejected, be killed, rise after three days, Satan, Whoever wishes to come after me

To the point: Jesus is called "the Christ"—Peter is called Satan. Salvation confronts human resistance. Peter had a certain image, belief, expectation of what "the Christ" was to be, to do. Suffering, rejection, and being killed had nothing to do with Peter's Christ. But they have everything to do with the Christ of God. Without a right understanding of "the Christ," we cannot, with him, rise to new Life.

Connecting the Gospel

to the first reading: Jesus does not ask his followers to undergo anything he himself has not undergone. He "gave his back to those who beat" him, and he was not shielded "from buffets and spitting." He was killed by those who rejected him. But he was also raised from the dead. So, too, will his followers be.

to experience: We naturally shun or put off what is distasteful, difficult, or painful. Yet, we often endure these very things because they are the way to growth, greater well-being, and new life.

Connecting the Responsorial Psalm

to the readings: Psalm 116 was a song of thanksgiving prayed by an individual while offering a sacrifice in gratitude for God's deliverance from grave danger. On this Sunday when both the first reading and gospel place the necessity of death before us, this psalm is our statement of profound confidence in God's ultimate Presence and protection. The suffering servant of Isaiah faces persecution without "turn[ing] back" (first reading). Jesus begins to teach that the cost of following him is the cross (gospel). If we remain faithful to discipleship, then, we are indeed in grave danger. But we can face the danger because we know, like the psalmist, that no danger—even death—is greater than God's desire to give us life. As we walk with Jesus toward our death, then, we walk straight "before the Lord, in[to] the land of the living" (psalm refrain).

to psalmist preparation: To sing this psalm well you must combine confidence in God's protection with willingness to take up the cross. How in your life does the one feed the other?

**ASSEMBLY &
FAITH-SHARING GROUPS**
- When I think in human terms, I resist "the Christ" in that . . . For me "the Christ" is . . .
- Jesus' call to carry the cross means that I must . . .
- Times when I have embraced the necessity of losing my life to experience new life have been . . .

PRESIDERS
I model how to follow faithfully "the Christ" when I serve in these ways . . .

DEACONS
My image, belief, expectation about my serving ministry is . . . The Christ teaches me that . . .

HOSPITALITY MINISTERS
My manner of greeting those gathering for liturgy opens them to encounter "the Christ" when I . . .

MUSIC MINISTERS
The struggles I have met in being faithful to music ministry have brought me new life by . . .

ALTAR MINISTERS
My serving models one way to deny self in following Christ when I . . .

LECTORS
My proclamation brings hope and strength to those who struggle with taking up their cross when . . .

**EXTRAORDINARY MINISTERS
OF HOLY COMMUNION**
My ministry has everything to do with "the Christ" of God in that . . .

Model Penitential Act

Presider: In today's gospel Jesus makes known that he is "the Christ" who will suffer, die, and rise. Let us prepare ourselves to hear his words and his call to follow him through death to new Life . . . [pause]

Lord Jesus, you are the Christ who suffered and died for our salvation: Lord . . .

Christ Jesus, you were raised to new Life: Christ . . .

Lord Jesus, you call us to take up the cross and follow you: Lord . . .

Homily Points

- Getting to know someone progresses through phases. We begin with knowing name, address, job. Continuing the relationship, we progress to knowing values, extended family, accomplishments. Coming to know another more fully sometimes entails letting go of previous assumptions and expectations. As Peter (and all the disciples) come to know Jesus more fully, they must let go of their prior assumptions and expectations of who "the Christ" is.

- In response to Peter's revelation of who Jesus is—"the Christ"—Jesus reveals the right understanding of what it means to be "the Christ": "suffer greatly," "be rejected," "be killed," "rise after three days." Peter strongly rebukes Jesus for saying that "the Christ" would suffer and die. He totally misses that Jesus would be raised to new Life. Yet this is exactly what happens.

- The resurrection gives meaning to suffering, rejection, and death. We grow in being faithful followers of Jesus as we come to know him better, learn that suffering and death are not ends in themselves, and experience the new Life Jesus promises. Coming to know Jesus more deeply leads to knowing more fully who we are—followers of Jesus for whom the way of "the Christ" becomes our very way of living.

Model Universal Prayer (Prayer of the Faithful)

Presider: We pray to God who sent "the Christ" for our salvation, making known our needs.

Response:

Lord, hear our prayer.

Cantor:

we pray to the Lord,

That all members of the church remain faithful in following Jesus even when the cost seems great . . . [pause]

That the expectations of world leaders be rooted in the just needs of their people . . . [pause]

That those whose cross of suffering seems unbearable be strengthened by the support and care of this Christian community and God's grace . . . [pause]

That all of us here grow in knowing Jesus better and making his way of life our way of living . . . [pause]

Presider: Loving God, you sent your Son to be "the Christ" and our Savior: hear our prayers, be with us always as we follow him faithfully, and lead us to eternal Life. We ask this through Christ our Lord. **Amen.**

COLLECT

Let us pray

Pause for silent prayer

Look upon us, O God,
Creator and ruler of all things,
and, that we may feel the working of your
    mercy,
grant that we may serve you with all our
    heart.
Through our Lord Jesus Christ, your Son,
who lives and reigns with you in the unity
    of the Holy Spirit,
one God, for ever and ever. **Amen.**

FIRST READING

Isa 50:4c-9a

The Lord GOD opens my ear that I may
    hear;
and I have not rebelled,
    have not turned back.
I gave my back to those who beat me,
    my cheeks to those who plucked my
    beard;
my face I did not shield
    from buffets and spitting.

The Lord GOD is my help,
    therefore I am not disgraced;
I have set my face like flint,
    knowing that I shall not be put to
    shame.
He is near who upholds my right;
    if anyone wishes to oppose me,
    let us appear together.
Who disputes my right?
    Let that man confront me.
See, the Lord GOD is my help;
    who will prove me wrong?

RESPONSORIAL PSALM

Ps 116:1-2, 3-4, 5-6, 8-9

R̷. (9) I will walk before the Lord, in the
land of the living.
    or:
R̷. Alleluia.

I love the LORD because he has heard
    my voice in supplication,
because he has inclined his ear to me
    the day I called.

R̷. I will walk before the Lord, in the land
of the living.
    or:
R̷. Alleluia.

The cords of death encompassed me;
    the snares of the netherworld seized
        upon me;
    I fell into distress and sorrow,
and I called upon the name of the LORD,
    "O LORD, save my life!"

R̸. I will walk before the Lord, in the land
of the living.
    or:
R̸. Alleluia.

Gracious is the LORD and just;
    yes, our God is merciful.
The LORD keeps the little ones;
    I was brought low, and he saved me.

R̸. I will walk before the Lord, in the land
of the living.
    or:
R̸. Alleluia.

For he has freed my soul from death,
    my eyes from tears, my feet from
        stumbling.
I shall walk before the LORD
    in the land of the living.

R̸. I will walk before the Lord, in the land
of the living.
    or:
R̸. Alleluia.

SECOND READING
Jas 2:14-18

What good is it, my brothers and sisters,
    if someone says he has faith but does
        not have works?
Can that faith save him?
If a brother or sister has nothing to wear
    and has no food for the day,
    and one of you says to them,
      "Go in peace, keep warm, and eat well,"
    but you do not give them the necessities
        of the body,
    what good is it?
So also faith of itself,
    if it does not have works, is dead.

Indeed someone might say,
    "You have faith and I have works."
Demonstrate your faith to me without
    works,
    and I will demonstrate my faith to you
      from my works.

About Liturgy

Turning point: This gospel selection from Mark 8 is one of this gospel's two structural climaxes. The other occurs in chapter 15, when the centurion at the foot of the cross exclaims, "Truly this man was the Son of God!" (verse 39). In both instances Jesus' identity is revealed in the context of his suffering and death. These climaxes highlight the overall thrust of Mark's gospel with its focus on Jesus' identity and the demands of discipleship.

This Sunday might also mark something of a turning point in our own journey through the liturgical year (notice the change in music for the universal prayer or prayer of the faithful). We are into mid-September, a time when the new school year has begun, vacations are over, the feel of fall is beginning to creep in (in the northern states), and we have a sense of "hunkering down." However well we have paid attention or however much we have learned through our journey through Mark's gospel during Ordinary Time of this Year B, it is never too late to ask ourselves two questions: Have we encountered Jesus and learned more of who he is for us? Have we learned better how to shoulder the cost of discipleship, discovered new ways to be faithful, and recognized that in the very dying—in conforming ourselves to Jesus in our own style of self-giving—we are already rising to new Life?

About Liturgical Music

Change of service music: This Sunday marks a turning point in the tenor of the first reading and gospel from now until the close of the liturgical year. Setting his "face like flint" (first reading), Jesus begins his resolute journey to Jerusalem, where he will face his passion and death and then be raised to new Life (gospel). He makes explicit to his disciples that they, too, must lose their lives if they wish to save them. One way to mark this turning point is to change the service music the community has been singing. Switch to one of the other Ordinary Time settings the parish has in its repertoire and to a different gospel acclamation. (In line with this *Living Liturgy*™ has changed the musical setting for the intercessions [see facing page].) Making this change helps the people grasp the significance of this day in the liturgical year as a turning point, not only for Jesus and disciples, but for themselves as well.

Music suggestions: Carl Daw's "Let Kings and Prophets Shield Their Name" (HG, W4) applies the story of this Sunday's gospel to us. In verse 3 we sing, "Give us, O God, the grace to know the limits of our certainty: Help us, like Peter, to declare The still-unfolding mystery Of One who reigns though sacrificed, Our Lamb and Shepherd, Jesus Christ." This hymn would work well during the preparation of the gifts. In E. W. Blandy's "Where He Leads Me" (LMGM2), we promise to go with Jesus "through the garden" and "through the judgment" because we know he will give us "grace and glory." This hymn could be sung during the preparation of the gifts, or as a communal song after Communion.

Another effective choice for the preparation of the gifts would be Dan Schutte's "Only This I Want" (BB, G3, JS3). An excellent choice for Communion would be Dan Schutte's "Glory in the Cross" (BB, JS3). This song was written to be sung over the three days of the Triduum. On this Sunday, combine verses from the Holy Thursday section calling us to make the journey to the cross with verses from the Easter section singing of the victory of the resurrection. "I Have Decided to Follow Jesus" (LMGM2), with its repeated "No turning back, no turning back!" would make a fitting recessional song.

✠ SPIRITUALITY

GOSPEL ACCLAMATION
cf. 2 Thess 2:14

R/. Alleluia, alleluia.
God has called us through the Gospel
to possess the glory of our Lord Jesus Christ.
R/. Alleluia, alleluia.

Gospel

Mark 9:30-37; L134B

Jesus and his disciples left from
   there and began a journey
   through Galilee,
but he did not wish anyone to
   know about it.
He was teaching his disciples and
   telling them,
   "The Son of Man is to be handed
      over to men
   and they will kill him,
   and three days after his death the
      Son of Man will rise."
But they did not understand the
   saying,
   and they were afraid to question him.

They came to Capernaum and, once
   inside the house,
he began to ask them,
   "What were you arguing about on the
      way?"
But they remained silent.
They had been discussing among
   themselves on the way
who was the greatest.
Then he sat down, called the Twelve,
   and said to them,
   "If anyone wishes to be first,
   he shall be the last of all and the
      servant of all."
Taking a child, he placed it in their
   midst,
and putting his arms around it, he
   said to them,
   "Whoever receives one child such as
      this in my name, receives me;
   and whoever receives me,
   receives not me but the One who sent
      me."

Reflecting on the Gospel

Jesus is so patient with the disciples. Having asked them the question about his own identity, he teaches them about what "the Christ" really means. But the disciples don't get it. In this Sunday's gospel Jesus for a second time predicts his passion and death. The disciples still don't get it! The "wicked" in the first reading try the patience of the "just one." It seems as though the disciples in the gospel are also trying the patience of the "just one."

We humans test God and each other all the time; our transgressions are all too evident in the world around us. It is as though we are like those wicked folks in the first reading—we push and push to see how far we can go. Undaunted, God does "take care of" us, but not in the way we think. God did not spare the Son from "revilement and torture"; God delivered him by raising him from death. The same is true for Jesus' disciples. We will be tested and God will care for us, too. But along the way we can expect others to revile us, too. Being a disciple means that we will be obnoxious to some people (those for whom transgression is a way of life). This is the risk of discipleship.

Jesus uses the model of a little child to illustrate his point. Children are innocent and without pretensions. They naturally embody what "least of all" means. This also illustrates to what extent the disciple is to become the "servant of all" by receiving even the "least of all." The total self-emptying that enables one to receive the "least of all" describes the disciple. This is how we receive Jesus—by receiving the least. No one is insignificant. Everyone is worth dying for.

The scandal of this gospel is that Jesus, the leader and teacher of the disciples, will be reduced to the least when he is handed over and dies. How do the disciples react to this scandalous teaching? They argue among themselves about who is the greatest! Jesus rightly reduces them to silence. The disciples do not understand greatest and least, first and last, servant of all. They do not understand that Jesus' own death is a call to die to self, to choose to become the greatest by being the least. Confronted with this saving mystery, we ought to all be reduced to silence—but now for the right reason.

Living the Paschal Mystery

How and when does Jesus reduce us to silence? This is a good question that each of us ought to ponder seriously and at length. We are reduced to silence when Jesus teaches us what we do not want to hear because we will need to change our way of life. Being least and servant of all goes against the grain of all of us. Yet, this is the only way to share in Jesus' risen Life.

No wonder Jesus focused his time on the journey to Jerusalem on his disciples—this teaching is so hard to hear! No wonder the disciples do not understand—this teaching is so hard to accept! We are no different from the disciples. How often do we fail to come to Jesus to question him so that we can understand the cost of discipleship? How often do we fail to take time to be with him in silence, to listen to him? We are afraid to question Jesus about discipleship when we choose the easy way which is not discipleship: when we ignore the plea of others for help; when we only spend time with people in our own inner circle; when we harbor racial, sexual, or religious prejudices; when we . . .

Focusing the Gospel

Key words and phrases: teaching his disciples, handed over, death, arguing, silent, greatest, servant of all

To the point: The scandal of this gospel is that Jesus, the leader and teacher of the disciples, will be reduced to the least when he is handed over and dies. How do the disciples react to this scandalous teaching? They argue among themselves about who is the greatest! Jesus rightly reduces them to silence. The disciples do not understand greatest and least, first and last, servant of all. They do not understand that Jesus' own death is a call to die to self, to choose to become the greatest by being the least. Confronted with this saving mystery, we ought to all be reduced to silence—but now for the right reason.

Connecting the Gospel

to the first reading: In the first reading, the wicked test God by making "the just one" undergo revilement and torture. Jesus, "the just one," also undergoes revilement, torture, and death, and proves that "God will take care of him" when he is raised from the dead.

to experience: The "me first" way of acting began in the Garden of Eden with Adam and Eve's disobedience and continues to our own time. When Jesus teaches we are to be least and servant of all, he is calling us to become who God originally created us to be.

Connecting the Responsorial Psalm

to the readings: This responsorial psalm is a cry of confidence in face of certain death. In the first reading the wicked plot "a shameful death" for one whose righteous manner of living is an affront to their unrighteous ways. In the gospel Jesus warns the disciples that this same end is in store for him. But he promises also that on the third day he will rise. Like the psalmist, Jesus knows that God will uphold his life. We, too, can bear the consequences of discipleship because we believe that even in death God will uphold us. Such confidence does not come from intellectual conviction, but from personal intimacy with God. When we sing this psalm we are not merely whistling in the dark. We are professing faith in a saving God whose very name we know (psalm).

to psalmist preparation: Any normal person would rather avoid the death which fidelity to discipleship makes inevitable. How can singing this psalm give you courage? How in singing it can you give other disciples courage?

ASSEMBLY & FAITH-SHARING GROUPS
- I find myself clamoring for status when . . . At these times Jesus challenges me to be servant by . . .
- I am the least when . . . I am the greatest when . . .
- I am reduced to silence when . . .

PRESIDERS
My ordained ministry constantly calls me to die to self and this is a burden to me when . . . Dying to self brings joy to me when . . .

DEACONS
In Jesus' name I embrace the least among us when . . . I am the one Jesus embraces when . . .

HOSPITALITY MINISTERS
The way I greet others lifts them up and . . .

MUSIC MINISTERS
Whenever I find myself vying with other music ministers over status, what helps me die to self and choose to be least and servant of all is . . .

ALTAR MINISTERS
My ministry draws me to be the "servant of all" which leads me to . . .

LECTORS
When I take time to be silent as I prepare for proclamation, God's word to the assembly sounds like . . .

EXTRAORDINARY MINISTERS OF HOLY COMMUNION
Distributing the Body (Blood) of Christ requires my dying to self in that . . .

Model Penitential Act

Presider: Jesus teaches the disciples in today's gospel about who they ought to be: servants of all. Let us ask God's mercy for the times we have put ourselves before others . . . [pause]

Lord Jesus, you teach us that the last shall be first: Lord . . .
Christ Jesus, you conquered death by being raised to new Life: Christ . . .
Lord Jesus, you came among us as the Suffering Servant: Lord . . .

Homily Points

• People camp out for days to be the first to get tickets to a rock concert, to purchase the latest techno gadget, to crash the doors to stores on Black Friday. How quickly whatever is gained from these efforts to be first passes! Jesus teaches in this gospel that what endures is to be last—to be servant of all.

• The lesson Jesus teaches in this gospel is so important that he takes the disciples off by themselves. Yet, for all his effort, they do not understand. It takes a lifetime of discipleship to come to a deeper, life-giving appreciation for what dying to self means, for what being servant of all entails, for where choosing to be least leads. This lifetime of effort opens onto an eternity of Life.

• First and last are not positions in line, but ways to be oriented toward one another. We become first in relation to others not by shouldering our way past them, but by being last through serving them. We serve in simple, everyday ways: holding a door open, smiling at someone, listening instead of always being the one talking. How quickly these small gestures of dying to self for others pass, yet they have lasting merit now and for the Life to come.

Model Universal Prayer (Prayer of the Faithful)

Presider: Jesus instructs us to become servants of all. Let us pray to God for the strength to die to ourselves to bring life to others.

Response:

Cantor:

That all members of the church conform themselves more perfectly to Christ, the servant of all . . . [pause]

That all people come to salvation through choosing to put the good of others before personal gain . . . [pause]

That the least among us be lifted up by the selfless service of others . . . [pause]

That we here gathered faithfully choose to die to self and bring life to others . . . [pause]

Presider: O God, you sent your Son to teach us how to be servants of all: hear these our prayers that we might one day take our place with you in the fullness of Life. We ask this through Christ our Lord. **Amen.**

COLLECT
Let us pray

Pause for silent prayer

O God, who founded all the commands of
   your sacred Law
upon love of you and of our neighbor,
grant that, by keeping your precepts,
we may merit to attain eternal life.
Through our Lord Jesus Christ, your Son,
who lives and reigns with you in the unity
   of the Holy Spirit,
one God, for ever and ever. **Amen.**

FIRST READING
Wis 2:12, 17-20

The wicked say:
   Let us beset the just one, because he is
      obnoxious to us;
      he sets himself against our doings,
   reproaches us for transgressions of the
      law
      and charges us with violations of our
         training.
   Let us see whether his words be true;
      let us find out what will happen to
         him.
   For if the just one be the son of God,
      God will defend him
      and deliver him from the hand of his
         foes.
   With revilement and torture let us put
      the just one to the test
      that we may have proof of his
         gentleness
      and try his patience.
   Let us condemn him to a shameful
      death;
      for according to his own words, God
         will take care of him.

RESPONSORIAL PSALM

Ps 54:3-4, 5, 6-8

℟. (6b) The Lord upholds my life.

O God, by your name save me,
  and by your might defend my cause.
O God, hear my prayer;
  hearken to the words of my mouth.

℟. The Lord upholds my life.

For the haughty have risen up against me,
  the ruthless seek my life;
  they set not God before their eyes.

℟. The Lord upholds my life.

Behold, God is my helper;
  the Lord sustains my life.
Freely will I offer you sacrifice;
  I will praise your name, O Lord, for its
    goodness.

℟. The Lord upholds my life.

SECOND READING

Jas 3:16–4:3

Beloved:
Where jealousy and selfish ambition exist,
  there is disorder and every foul practice.
But the wisdom from above is first of all
    pure,
  then peaceable, gentle, compliant,
  full of mercy and good fruits,
  without inconstancy or insincerity.
And the fruit of righteousness is sown in
    peace
  for those who cultivate peace.

Where do the wars
  and where do the conflicts among you
    come from?
Is it not from your passions
  that make war within your members?
You covet but do not possess.
You kill and envy but you cannot obtain;
  you fight and wage war.
You do not possess because you do not
    ask.
You ask but do not receive,
  because you ask wrongly, to spend it on
    your passions.

About Liturgy

Communion and greatness: In this Sunday's gospel the disciples are arguing about "who was the greatest" and Jesus teaches them that true discipleship consists in becoming "the last of all." The dynamic is from greatest to least. It is interesting that in the Communion rite exactly the opposite dynamic happens: we go from least to greatest.

At the invitation of the presider to begin the Communion procession ("Behold the Lamb of God . . . Blessed are those called to the supper of the Lamb") we respond with "Lord, I am not worthy . . ." Before coming to the messianic table to participate in the Lord's feast we declare that we are the least among God's people. Then we come to the table and share in the feast and, indeed, become the greatest because we eat the Body and Blood and become what we eat—the Body of Christ.

The biblical source for this familiar liturgical text is Matthew 8:8, where the Capernaum centurion approaches Jesus and asks him to heal his servant. When Jesus answers that he will come, the servant replies, "Lord, I am not worthy to have you enter under my roof; only say the word" (NABRE). Jesus' word is a substitution for the visit—Lord, don't come; you only have to give the word. At Communion these words are an invitation to Jesus to visit us, now in the most wondrous gift of his Body and Blood. In addition to a confession of humility, these words we utter just before Communion are also an expression of confidence that our Lord will come to us—to nourish us, heal us, strengthen us, save us, and transform us.

About Liturgical Music

Music suggestions: In Albert J. Bayly's "Lord, Whose Love in Humble Service" (found in most resources), we ask Christ who "Bore the weight of human need" on the cross to help us see that the "height and depth of greatness" is found in "faithful service." This hymn would function well for the entrance procession. Another excellent choice for the entrance song is Fred Pratt Green's "The Church of Christ in Every Age" (found in most resources). The hymn calls us to accept that "We have no mission but to serve In full obedience to our Lord." In Herman Stuempfle's "Lord, Help Us Walk Your Servant Way" (HG, SS, W4), we ask Christ to enable us to "walk your servant way . . . And bending low, forgetting self, Each serve the other's need." This lovely hymn would be effective during the preparation of the gifts. Each hymn resource uses a different tune for this text; an additional option would be to sing it to the melody of "Where Charity and Love Prevail" (CHRISTIAN LOVE). In "The Servant Song" (found in most resources) we ask permission to be servant to one another. The final verse speaks of the "harmony" we will share in heaven because, having chosen servanthood, we will know "Of Christ's love and agony." This would be a lovely song during the preparation of the gifts, or the choir could sing it as a prelude using, for example, the David Haas setting (GIA G-4995) or the arrangement by Francis Patrick O'Brien (GIA G-5451). Finally, "Make Us True Servants" (SS, WC, WS) would be a good recessional song, sending us out the door ready to put this gospel into action.

✠ SPIRITUALITY

GOSPEL ACCLAMATION
cf. John 17:17b, 17a

℟. Alleluia, alleluia.
Your word, O Lord, is truth;
consecrate us in the truth.
℟. Alleluia, alleluia.

Gospel Mark 9:38-43, 45, 47-48;
L137B

At that time, John said to
    Jesus,
    "Teacher, we saw someone
        driving out demons in
        your name,
    and we tried to prevent him
        because he does not
        follow us."
Jesus replied, "Do not
    prevent him.
There is no one who performs a mighty
    deed in my name
    who can at the same time speak ill of me.
For whoever is not against us is for us.
Anyone who gives you a cup of water to drink
    because you belong to Christ,
    amen, I say to you, will surely not lose his
        reward.

"Whoever causes one of these little ones who
    believe in me to sin,
    it would be better for him if a great
        millstone
    were put around his neck
    and he were thrown into the sea.
If your hand causes you to sin, cut it off.
It is better for you to enter into life maimed
    than with two hands to go into Gehenna,
    into the unquenchable fire.
And if your foot causes you to sin, cut it off.
It is better for you to enter into life crippled
    than with two feet to be thrown into
        Gehenna.
And if your eye causes you to sin, pluck it out.
Better for you to enter into the kingdom of
    God with one eye
    than with two eyes to be thrown into
        Gehenna,
    where 'their worm does not die, and the
        fire is not quenched.'"

Reflecting on the Gospel

Magnets attract. The stronger the magnet, the stronger the attraction. Some large magnets are so powerful that it takes a great deal of muscle power to pull the magnet off the metal. Like attracts like. The more the convergences of ideas, values, and interests, the stronger the attraction. Jesus was a strong magnet who attracted disciples to him, disciples who acted in "his name," who assumed his values. This gospel also shows others who were attracted to Jesus, those acting with Jesus' power who were not among Jesus' band of disciples. In this gospel Jesus illustrates two opposing ways to be his disciple: someone who does not seemingly follow Jesus, but does good; someone who follows Jesus, but sins. The issue goes beyond who is with or against Jesus—it goes to *what* is against Jesus. Those who follow Jesus must live as he did, no matter what the cost. Their attraction to him must be like a strong magnet: they adhere to his values, act in his name, do good for others as he did.

Focused completely on his saving mission to bring about the kingdom of God, Jesus directly confronts human pettiness and sinfulness. He uses graphic examples to demand that disciples turn from whatever is inconsistent with acting in his name, with continuing his mission. Any behavior which causes us to sin or to lead others into sin must be cut off. Part of a disciple's work is to take on Jesus' values, Jesus' goodness. Being a disciple demands radical choices about how we live and relate to others. It means being as completely focused on Jesus' saving mission as he was. It means that acting in his name is exactly that: doing as he would do. And Jesus never sinned.

Discipleship is decided by our *behavior* rather than by our being identified with a particular group or not. What is crucial to discipleship is how we act. Jesus uses extreme terms to tell us that we must turn from whatever is inconsistent with acting in his name. Any behavior which causes us to sin or to lead others into sin must be cut off. We are to root out the cause of sin in us at all costs—root out whatever is not consistent with our attraction to who Jesus is. What is at stake is "enter[ing] into the kingdom of God," entering into fullness of Life. Any attitude which limits the Presence and power of the Spirit must also be cut off (see first reading). Being a disciple demands radical choices about how we live and relate to others. Being a disciple demands that we make radical choices about how we adhere to Jesus, act in his name, and draw others to him as well.

Living the Paschal Mystery

Through our baptismal anointing we truly are prophets (see first reading); all of us are commissioned to speak and do deeds in the Lord's name. Thus baptism is more than initiation into a group—it is the transformation of ourselves into disciples of Christ who follow the Teacher by faithful service "in [his] name." Faithful service is not expressed in occasional good deeds, but in ongoing patterns of unselfish, life-giving behaviors. Faithful service is expressed in making our own the values and mission that attract us to Jesus in the first place.

As a follower of Christ, discipleship means doing something so great as volunteering for one of the liturgical ministries or so simple as taking the garbage out without being asked. It means that our words and actions are consistent with Jesus' Gospel values. It means that we are ruthless about choosing to cut out behaviors inconsistent with Jesus' values and gentle about choosing to do the works of the Teacher.

Focusing the Gospel

Key words and phrases: in my name, causes you to sin, cut it off, kingdom of God

To the point: Focused completely on his saving mission to bring about the kingdom of God, Jesus directly confronts human pettiness and sinfulness. He uses graphic examples to demand that disciples turn from whatever is inconsistent with acting in his name, with continuing his mission. Any behavior which causes us to sin or to lead others into sin must be cut off. Being a disciple demands radical choices about how we live and relate to others. It means being as completely focused on Jesus' saving mission as he was.

Connecting the Gospel

to the first reading: Jesus is the new Moses. Moses of old taught that anyone upon whom God's spirit rests can prophesy. Jesus teaches that anyone who speaks and acts in his name belongs to him ("whoever is not against us is for us").

to experience: The more focused we are on achieving a specific goal, the less influence distractions have on our energy and attention. The challenge of discipleship is to make Jesus and his saving mission so much the focus of our lives that no distraction sways us.

Connecting the Responsorial Psalm

to the readings: The Law of the Lord brings us refreshment, wisdom, and joy (psalm). But even the most faithful adherent can fall prey to petty jealousies (first reading and gospel). And so it is not surprising in this psalm that while we praise the purity and perfection of the Law, we also ask God to protect us from the gamut of infidelities—ranging from "unknown faults" to "wanton sin"—which can rule our hearts. How fortunate we are to have God's Law which acts as guide and safeguard, protecting us from more dire measures we might otherwise need to take to enter the kingdom of heaven (gospel). For as Jesus points out in no uncertain terms, we must allow nothing to stand in the way of our entrance into eternal Life (gospel). Thank God for the Law which keeps us on the path of what is "perfect," "trustworthy," "pure," and "true."

to psalmist preparation: As you prepare to sing this Sunday's responsorial psalm, you might reflect on questions such as these: What does the Law of God ask of you? What wisdom have you gained because of your obedience to it? What sacrifices has such obedience required? What joys have resulted?

**ASSEMBLY &
FAITH-SHARING GROUPS**
- The human pettiness and sinfulness I need to confront is . . .
- I find myself distracted from Jesus and his mission when . . . by . . . Jesus calls me to refocus by . . .
- What I need to "cut . . . off" in order to be a more faithful disciple is . . . What I need to "add in" is . . .

PRESIDERS
The radical choices in my ministry I must continually make in order to act in Jesus' name are . . .

DEACONS
The radical choices I must continually make in order to serve "these little ones" are . . .

HOSPITALITY MINISTERS
In order to be inclusive in my welcoming those gathering for liturgy I must . . .

MUSIC MINISTERS
My music ministry helps me focus more clearly on Jesus and his saving mission when I . . .

ALTAR MINISTERS
My serving at the altar witnesses to my commitment to Jesus and his saving mission in that . . .

LECTORS
The manner in which I proclaim God's word reveals that I "belong to Christ" in these ways . . .

**EXTRAORDINARY MINISTERS
OF HOLY COMMUNION**
When I am completely focused on my ministry and what it means, I . . .

Model Penitential Act

Presider: Discipleship calls us to make radical choices about how we live as followers of Jesus. We ask God's pardon for the times we have failed and for the strength to be faithful disciples . . . [pause]

    Lord Jesus, you are the divine Teacher: Lord . . .

    Christ Jesus, you are the Way to eternal Life: Christ . . .

    Lord Jesus, you call disciples to act in your name: Lord . . .

Homily Points

- We act in another's name in many different circumstances, for example, as ambassadors, those with power of attorney, parents until a child is of legal age. When we act in another's name, we are not acting as ourselves, but as the other. We are not serving our own needs or interests, but the other's. So it is with those who act in Jesus' name.

- What does it mean to act in Jesus' name? What is done in his name, even by those who seemingly are not disciples, continues his saving mission. Jesus is not concerned about who "belong" or not, but rather about whether what they do is consistent with his saving mission. Whoever places serving Jesus and his saving mission above serving their own needs and interests is a true disciple.

- Faithfully acting in Jesus' name requires radical choices on our part. For example, choosing to be a full, conscious, active participant in liturgy; choosing to follow Gospel values rather than merely follow the crowd; choosing to follow God's call to ordained ministry or religious life. While these and many other radical choices are never easy, when we remain focused on Jesus and his saving mission, we cooperate with him in bringing about the kingdom of God. These choices are life-giving for us and others ("will surely not lose his reward").

Model Universal Prayer (Prayer of the Faithful)

Presider: We pray now that we may be faithful followers of Jesus the Teacher.

Response:

Lord,   hear   our   prayer.

Cantor:

we   pray   to   the   Lord,

That all members of the church be faithful disciples who act in Jesus' name in serving others . . . [pause]

That all peoples be freed from sin and come to eternal Life . . . [pause]

That the poor and the lowly have their fill of the good things of God, strengthening them to act in Jesus' name . . . [pause]

That all of us here support one another in making the radical choices that faithful discipleship demands . . . [pause]

Presider: Good and gracious God, you are merciful to the sinner and kind to those who follow your Son: hear these our prayers that we might one day enjoy with you eternal Life. We ask this through that same Son, Jesus Christ our Lord. **Amen.**

COLLECT

Let us pray

Pause for silent prayer

O God, who manifest your almighty power
above all by pardoning and showing
    mercy,
bestow, we pray, your grace abundantly
    upon us
and make those hastening to attain your
    promises
heirs to the treasures of heaven.
Through our Lord Jesus Christ, your Son,
who lives and reigns with you in the unity
    of the Holy Spirit,
one God, for ever and ever. **Amen.**

FIRST READING

Num 11:25-29

The LORD came down in the cloud and
    spoke to Moses.
Taking some of the spirit that was on
    Moses,
    the LORD bestowed it on the seventy
      elders;
    and as the spirit came to rest on them,
      they prophesied.

Now two men, one named Eldad and the
    other Medad,
    were not in the gathering but had been
      left in the camp.
They too had been on the list, but had not
    gone out to the tent;
    yet the spirit came to rest on them also,
    and they prophesied in the camp.
So, when a young man quickly told Moses,
    "Eldad and Medad are prophesying in
      the camp,"
    Joshua, son of Nun, who from his youth
      had been Moses' aide, said,
    "Moses, my lord, stop them."
But Moses answered him,
    "Are you jealous for my sake?
Would that all the people of the LORD were
    prophets!
Would that the LORD might bestow his
    spirit on them all!"

RESPONSORIAL PSALM

Ps 19:8, 10, 12-13, 14

℟. (9a) The precepts of the Lord give joy
to the heart.

The law of the LORD is perfect,
    refreshing the soul;
    the decree of the LORD is trustworthy,
      giving wisdom to the simple.

℟. The precepts of the Lord give joy to the
heart.

The fear of the LORD is pure,
enduring forever;
the ordinances of the LORD are true,
all of them just.

R℣. The precepts of the Lord give joy to the heart.

Though your servant is careful of them,
very diligent in keeping them,
yet who can detect failings?
Cleanse me from my unknown faults!

R℣. The precepts of the Lord give joy to the heart.

From wanton sin especially, restrain your servant;
let it not rule over me.
Then shall I be blameless and innocent
of serious sin.

R℣. The precepts of the Lord give joy to the heart.

SECOND READING
Jas 5:1-6

Come now, you rich, weep and wail over
your impending miseries.
Your wealth has rotted away, your clothes
have become moth-eaten,
your gold and silver have corroded,
and that corrosion will be a testimony
against you;
it will devour your flesh like a fire.
You have stored up treasure for the last
days.
Behold, the wages you withheld from the
workers
who harvested your fields are crying
aloud;
and the cries of the harvesters
have reached the ears of the Lord of
hosts.
You have lived on earth in luxury and
pleasure;
you have fattened your hearts for the
day of slaughter.
You have condemned;
you have murdered the righteous one;
he offers you no resistance.

✝ CATECHESIS

About Liturgy

Penitential Act: If we could go back in time and be present at a Mass celebrated during the first few centuries of the church (say, up until Charlemagne during the ninth century), one of the things that would strike us is that the Mass had much more lengthy intercessory prayer than it has today. In these earlier periods the beginning of the Mass included an extended list of petitions which culminated in the collect. The collect "collected together" in a general formula all the prayers that had just been prayed.

In those earlier centuries the *Kyrie* (Lord, have mercy) belonged to the genre of intercessory prayer. It was used at the hours of the Divine Office as well as at Mass. At this time the "Lord, have mercy" was a response to petitions (called "tropes") that were most often presented in the form of a litany; the list of petitions would vary, of course, but usually included prayers for the whole church, clergy, rulers, the people, the sick, benefactors, the poor, and peace. Eventually in some churches the *Kyrie* stood alone and was simply repeated a number of times—anywhere from three to forty! Another development is that the tropes became an embellishment of the invocation (Lord or Christ). It is this latter form that is used in the models in *The Roman Missal, Third Edition* for the form of the penitential act that we use in *Living Liturgy*™. The *Kyrie* litany "is a chant by which the faithful acclaim the Lord and implore his mercy" (GIRM no. 52).

The important point to remember is that the beginning of Mass is a time for prayer. This is the time when we dispose ourselves toward God so that God's actions can take root in us and change us, so that our behaviors are more consistent with the vision and values of Jesus.

About Liturgical Music

Music suggestions: Jesus challenges us in this Sunday's gospel to let nothing stand in the way of our allegiance to him. "The Kingdom of God" (G3, W4, WC) would be a strong choice for the entrance hymn. The text sings about the kingdom as "justice and joy," "mercy and grace," "challenge and choice," "the gift and the goal." The first reading challenges us to let nothing stand in the way of the working of the Holy Spirit. "O Breathe on Me, O Breath of God" (found in most resources) would be a good choice during the preparation of the gifts. In this hymn we ask God's Spirit to take over every part of our heart until God's will becomes our will. Hymns in which we pray that Christ be all-in-all in our lives include "Christ Be Beside Me" (BB, JS3, WC, WS); "Christ Before Us" (BB, JS3); "Christ, Be Near at Either Hand" (WC, WS); "Christ Be in Your Senses" (G3, W4); and "Be Thou My Vision" (BB, JS3, SS). Any of these songs would be appropriate during the preparation of the gifts. Fred Pratt Green's "When Jesus Came Preaching the Kingdom of God" (W4) would make an excellent recessional song, with its final words: "So let none of us swerve from our mission to serve, That has made us his Church from the start: May Jesus, the Light of the World, send us out In the strength of the humble of heart."

SPIRITUALITY

GOSPEL ACCLAMATION
1 John 4:12

R⁊. Alleluia, alleluia.
If we love one another, God remains in us
and his love is brought to perfection in us.
R⁊. Alleluia, alleluia.

Gospel

Mark 10:2-16; L140B

The Pharisees approached
 Jesus and asked,
 "Is it lawful for a
  husband to divorce
  his wife?"
They were testing him.
He said to them in reply,
 "What did Moses com-
  mand you?"
They replied,
 "Moses permitted a hus-
  band to write a bill
  of divorce
 and dismiss her."
But Jesus told them,
 "Because of the hardness of your
  hearts
 he wrote you this commandment.
But from the beginning of creation,
 God made them male and female.
*For this reason a man shall leave his
  father and mother*
 and be joined to his wife,
 and the two shall become one flesh.
So they are no longer two but one flesh.
Therefore what God has joined together,
 no human being must separate."
In the house the disciples again questioned Jesus about this.
He said to them,
 "Whoever divorces his wife and marries another
 commits adultery against her;
 and if she divorces her husband and
  marries another,
  she commits adultery."

Continued in Appendix A, p. 307.

or Mark 10:2-12, in Appendix A, p. 307.

Reflecting on the Gospel

The longer form of this Sunday's gospel unfolds in two interrelated situations. The Pharisees approach Jesus to test him about his stance concerning marriage and divorce; the disciples rebuke the people for bringing their children to Jesus. In both situations, God's intentions for human relationships are being thwarted. In both situations, Jesus upholds human relationships as fundamental to embracing the kingdom of God. In both situations, faithful ones are embraced and blessed by God. In this gospel Jesus exposes the hardness of the Pharisees' hearts. This challenges us to look deep within our own hearts.

The context for this gospel is confrontation ("They were testing him," "the disciples rebuked them") and the content is about divorce ("Is it lawful for a husband to divorce his wife?"). But digging deeper into the text, we find that the reverberating message of the gospel is about hardness of hearts: "Because of the hardness of your hearts [Moses] wrote you this commandment." The Pharisees show "hardness of . . . hearts" by putting the law of Moses (which allows divorce) ahead of the plan of God ("what God has joined together, no human being must separate"). Even the disciples show "hardness of . . . hearts" in rebuking the children. The plan of God, as revealed in creation (see first reading), is the blueprint for creation's completion. "[H]ardness of . . . hearts" cuts us off from the blueprint. Jesus always challenges human traditions when they diverge from action hindering our entering fully the life and blessing God offers us.

The world in which the Creator blessed marriage is the world before sin. The world in which Jesus and the Pharisees debate divorce is a world in which sin abounds, and so one must be directed by laws. One purpose of law is to delineate clear parameters for making right choices. This is necessary in a world where sin and hard hearts cloud people's judgment and sometimes lead them to make selfish choices rather than self-giving choices. The Pharisees ask about a point of the law and Jesus answers by pointing to God's intention. This gospel presents the tension between God's plan and sin, between the divine ideal and concessions to human weakness. Marriage is not an absolute in itself—being faithful to kingdom ideals is.

In the deepest recesses of our hearts, we all desire to live in union with one another as God intends. The gospel intimates that the kingdom of God belongs to those who yield "hardness of . . . hearts" to the open embrace Jesus models. Just as the gospel moves from shortsighted confrontation over Mosaic laws of divorce to Jesus' tender embrace of little children, so must our lives move from our own shortsightedness to the wide embrace of God's ultimate plan—hearts turned toward God and each other in relationships that are holy.

Living the Paschal Mystery

God's design for all of creation is that it be harmonious and whole. Paradoxically, it's the rhythm of the paschal mystery—between dying and rising—that keeps us harmonious and whole. Dying to self means that our own selfish interests are not put ahead of the good of another—which promotes harmony. The new Life that always comes from self-giving is a sign of wholeness. Always what stands in the way of harmony and wholeness is hardness of heart—our own or another's. The challenge is in the example of Jesus: embrace and bless even the little ones.

Focusing the Gospel

Key words and phrases: testing him, hardness of your hearts, rebuked them, come to me, kingdom of God belongs to such as these

To the point: The longer form of this Sunday's gospel unfolds in two interrelated situations. The Pharisees approach Jesus to test him about his stance concerning marriage and divorce; the disciples rebuke the people for bringing their children to Jesus. In both situations, God's intentions for human relationships are being thwarted. In both situations, Jesus upholds human relationships as fundamental to embracing the kingdom of God. In both situations, faithful ones are embraced and blessed by God.

Connecting the Gospel

to the first reading: The greatest deterrent to our living in union with one another in healthy and Godlike human relationships is our own "hardness of . . . hearts."

to experience: In human history, divorce has always been problematic. The Pharisees tested Jesus, which is to say they used a thorny issue to nail him. Jesus moves them from a specific theological debate to the larger perspective of the ways of God's kingdom.

Connecting the Responsorial Psalm

to the readings: Because of its patriarchal imagery, Psalm 128 is a difficult one for us to pray. Understanding its original purpose, however, places the psalm in a broader context than the specifics of patriarchal family structure, and sheds light on its aptness for this Sunday's Liturgy of the Word. Psalm 128 was a song of ascents, one of a sequential set (Pss 120–34) scholars believe the Israelites sang as they traveled up to Jerusalem to celebrate their major feasts. Psalm 128 was perhaps a blessing sung over the people as they began their journey back home. The psalm is about the blessings which fidelity to "walk[ing] in [God's] ways" brings. The image of the happy family projected by the psalm was the symbol par excellence of Israel's covenant relationship with God. The blessings described—fruitfulness, fulfillment, prosperity, and peace—were extended to all of the Hebrew people. Thus Psalm 128 is not so much about the blessings of marriage as it is about the blessings of a way of life faithful to the ways of God. We can sing it this Sunday, then, as a prayer for one another that our relationships in the church, in our families, and in our world truly be marked by such fidelity to God and such blessings.

to psalmist preparation: The refrain to this responsorial psalm is a prayer of blessing over the people. Spend some time praying this week for members of your parish and for the whole church. Pray that they know the blessings of fulfillment and peace which come from walking in the ways of God. Then, as you travel to church this Sunday, consider praying the psalm as your own song of ascent.

**ASSEMBLY &
FAITH-SHARING GROUPS**
- What helps me grow in healthy relationships is . . . I struggle in my relationships with others when . . .
- I am hard of heart when . . . What softens my heart is . . .
- I experience the tender embrace and blessing of Jesus when . . .

PRESIDERS
When presiding at liturgy and inviting the people to pray, my gesture embraces them in that . . .

DEACONS
My serving others is Jesus' tender embrace of them when . . .

HOSPITALITY MINISTERS
My greeting enables those gathering for liturgy to open themselves to Jesus' embrace and blessing when I . . .

MUSIC MINISTERS
My music making embraces the assembly in that . . . they are then able to . . .

ALTAR MINISTERS
My serving at the altar is my way of embracing Jesus when I . . .

LECTORS
When I allow God to embrace and bless me during my proclamation, the people see and hear . . .

**EXTRAORDINARY MINISTERS
OF HOLY COMMUNION**
- Receiving and distributing Holy Communion is both an embrace by and blessing of God in that . . .

✚ CELEBRATION

Model Penitential Act

Presider: The Pharisees in today's gospel show hardness of heart when they test Jesus. Let us begin this liturgy by examining our own heart and ask for the healing embrace of Jesus . . . [pause]

Lord Jesus, you gather us to yourself: Lord . . .

Christ Jesus, you are the Word made flesh of our Creator-God: Christ . . .

Lord Jesus, you embrace us and bless us: Lord . . .

Homily Points

• Children quickly learn that good behavior is rewarded. How much they love the tight embrace of a parent when they have done the right thing! In this embrace they experience the blessing of human relationships. As children grow spiritually, they learn the blessed embrace of divine-human relationship. God's divine Law is their guide in all relationships.

• In testing Jesus by pitting Moses' commands against the original Law of God, the Pharisees harden their hearts to the divine-human relationship that the Law and covenant establish. Jesus demonstrates this divine-human relationship when he calls the children to come to him and embraces and blesses them. God's intention "from the beginning of creation" is that we live our relationships with each other with the openness and trust of children.

• Growing in healthy human relationships is demanding, requires a great deal of give-and-take, and calls for openness to self and other. God's embrace and blessing of each of us fosters these healthy human relationships. We experience God's embrace and blessing, for example, during prayer, when we forgive another, as we delight in another's goodness. Growing in life-giving divine and faithful human relationships is the concrete expression of our accepting the kingdom of God "like a child."

Model Universal Prayer (Prayer of the Faithful)

Presider: From the very beginning of creation, we are called to union with God and each other. Let us pray that our relationships be faithful and strong.

Response:

Cantor:

For all members of the church, may they continue to grow in openness to Jesus' embrace and blessing . . . [pause]

For all people who govern, may the laws they enact always promote God's plan for creation . . . [pause]

For the lowly, the downtrodden, and the disadvantaged, may they be embraced by us and be given new hope for life . . . [pause]

For all of us here gathered, may we grow stronger in our relationships with each other and witness to the presence of the kingdom of God . . . [pause]

Presider: Compassionate God, you embrace us and bless us: hear these our prayers that we might enjoy everlasting union with you and your Son, Jesus Christ our Lord. **Amen.**

COLLECT

Let us pray

Pause for silent prayer

Almighty ever-living God,
who in the abundance of your kindness
surpass the merits and the desires of those
    who entreat you,
pour out your mercy upon us
to pardon what conscience dreads
and to give what prayer does not dare to
    ask.
Through our Lord Jesus Christ, your Son,
who lives and reigns with you in the unity
    of the Holy Spirit,
one God, for ever and ever. **Amen.**

FIRST READING

Gen 2:18-24

The LORD God said: "It is not good for the
    man to be alone.
I will make a suitable partner for him."
So the LORD God formed out of the ground
    various wild animals and various birds
        of the air,
    and he brought them to the man to see
        what he would call them;
    whatever the man called each of them
        would be its name.
The man gave names to all the cattle,
    all the birds of the air, and all wild
        animals;
    but none proved to be the suitable
        partner for the man.

So the LORD God cast a deep sleep on the
    man,
    and while he was asleep,
    he took out one of his ribs and closed
        up its place with flesh.
The LORD God then built up into a woman
    the rib
    that he had taken from the man.
When he brought her to the man, the man
    said:
    "This one, at last, is bone of my bones
        and flesh of my flesh;
    this one shall be called 'woman,' for
        out of 'her man' this one has been
        taken."
That is why a man leaves his father and
    mother
    and clings to his wife,
    and the two of them become one flesh.

RESPONSORIAL PSALM
Ps 128:1-2, 3, 4-5, 6

℟. (cf. 5) May the Lord bless us all the days of our lives.

Blessed are you who fear the LORD,
    who walk in his ways!
For you shall eat the fruit of your
        handiwork;
    blessed shall you be, and favored.

℟. May the Lord bless us all the days of our lives.

Your wife shall be like a fruitful vine
    in the recesses of your home;
your children like olive plants
    around your table.

℟. May the Lord bless us all the days of our lives.

Behold, thus is the man blessed
    who fears the LORD.
The LORD bless you from Zion:
    may you see the prosperity of Jerusalem
    all the days of your life.

℟. May the Lord bless us all the days of our lives.

May you see your children's children.
    Peace be upon Israel!

℟. May the Lord bless us all the days of our lives.

SECOND READING
Heb 2:9-11

Brothers and sisters:
He "for a little while" was made "lower
    than the angels,"
    that by the grace of God he might taste
        death for everyone.

For it was fitting that he,
    for whom and through whom all things
        exist,
    in bringing many children to glory,
    should make the leader to their
        salvation perfect through suffering.
He who consecrates and those who are
    being consecrated
    all have one origin.
Therefore, he is not ashamed to call them
    "brothers."

About Liturgy

Lectionary hermeneutic: "Hermeneutic" is a word which means "interpretation." The phrase "Lectionary hermeneutic" means that when the compilers of the Lectionary chose the particular passages for a given day, they had a particular interpretation in mind. The various choices are themselves a kind of interpretation of Sacred Scripture. Thus, the Lectionary isn't just a shortened Bible; it has a built-in interpretive stance that has to do with the unfolding of the liturgical year. Sometimes a particular combination of readings might even lead us to interpret a passage of Scripture in a slightly different way from its context in the Bible. Liturgy is the context for the Lectionary and that celebration provides the interpretive clue. This Sunday's selection of readings is a good case in point.

The second creation account in Genesis which describes the relationship between husband and wife ("and the two of them become one flesh"), the responsorial psalm which speaks of family blessings, and the question the Pharisees in the gospel put to Jesus about divorce would all tend to lead us to focus this Sunday on the relationship of husband and wife, on marriage and divorce, and this is certainly one interpretive direction to take. When we take into account the last verses of the gospel (which is why choosing the longer form of the gospel changes how one might approach the Scriptures for this Sunday) and where we are in Mark's gospel, other interpretive stances emerge, such as delving into the ramifications of "hardness of . . . hearts" and how the kingdom of God is built on right relationships with God and each other.

About Liturgical Music

Music suggestions: In Timothy Rees's "God Is Love" (BB, JS3), we sing about the all-embracing love of God. Set to the strong tune ABBOT'S LEIGH, this hymn would make an excellent entrance song. James Marchionda's "Let the Children Come to Me" (WC) is based on this Sunday's gospel reading and would make an excellent reflection during the preparation of the gifts. Rory Cooney's "Let the Children Come" (WC, WS) is also drawn from this gospel. Its verse-refrain and call-response structure would lend itself to the Communion procession. Another good choice for Communion would be Michael Joncas's "God Is Love" (BB, JS3). In verse 2 we sing, "Therefore, as now we gather into one, let discord find no place, nor hatred rule our hearts. Let evil deeds and bitter words now cease, that Christ stay in our midst and dwell with us forever."

OCTOBER 4, 2015
TWENTY-SEVENTH SUNDAY IN ORDINARY TIME

TWENTY-EIGHTH SUNDAY IN ORDINARY TIME

SPIRITUALITY

GOSPEL ACCLAMATION
Matt 5:3

℟. Alleluia, alleluia.
Blessed are the poor in spirit,
for theirs is the kingdom of heaven.
℟. Alleluia, alleluia.

Gospel   Mark 10:17-30; L143B

As Jesus was setting out on a
    journey, a man ran up,
    knelt down before him, and
    asked him,
    "Good teacher, what must I do
    to inherit eternal life?"
Jesus answered him, "Why do
    you call me good?
No one is good but God alone.
You know the commandments:
    You shall not kill;
    you shall not commit
        adultery;
    you shall not steal;
    you shall not bear false witness;
    you shall not defraud;
    honor your father and your mother."
He replied and said to him,
    "Teacher, all of these I have observed
        from my youth."
Jesus, looking at him, loved him and said to
    him,
    "You are lacking in one thing.
Go, sell what you have, and give to the poor
    and you will have treasure in heaven;
        then come, follow me."
At that statement his face fell,
    and he went away sad, for he had many
        possessions.

Jesus looked around and said to his disciples,
    "How hard it is for those who have wealth
        to enter the kingdom of God!"
The disciples were amazed at his words.
So Jesus again said to them in reply,
    "Children, how hard it is to enter the
        kingdom of God!

Continued in Appendix A, p. 307.

or Mark 10:17-27, in Appendix A, p. 307.

Reflecting on the Gospel

Who of us wouldn't want to be the man in the gospel who approaches Jesus with the question about what he must "do to inherit eternal life"? Jesus does more than affirm his faithful living of the commandments: "looking at him," Jesus "loved him." Wouldn't we all want that look? Wouldn't we all want to have such concrete affirmation that Jesus loves us? Then again, maybe we wouldn't want to be that man. Jesus clearly tells him the cost of following him: he must give up everything. The man "went away sad." Are we not also sometimes sad at the demands of being faithful followers of Jesus? What does it mean to give up everything?

The man must have had an inkling that keeping the commandments was not enough, or else he never would have approached Jesus with his question about how to inherit eternal Life. In spite of his faithfulness in keeping God's commandments and his being loved by Jesus, the man nevertheless had a divided heart: "he went away sad, for he had many possessions." The man needed to turn his focus from earthly life to eternal Life, from possessions (and, yes, even God's commandments) to single-heartedly following Jesus to salvation. Where is our heart? Are we overjoyed at Jesus' glance of love, or are we sad because it is too much?

Giving our all to follow Jesus doesn't mean that we literally sell everything; we all have family and social obligations that make having things a necessity. Jesus is saying that we can't let possessions (or anything else, for that matter) divide our hearts. Too often possessions possess us; we must let go so only God possesses us. Riches are a stumbling block to following Jesus when they command our attention so that we are not turned toward doing right—which is what following Jesus means.

The man in the gospel turned away from Jesus because he couldn't let go. It's not impossible to enter the kingdom of God because "all things are possible for God." But it is hard to enter the kingdom of God because too often our hearts are divided—we want to let go and follow Jesus at the same time we want to hang onto our possessions and, indeed, even to their commanding our attention and focus of life. Divided hearts just won't do. We can't have everything we want and give all to follow Jesus at the same time. The very hard demands of following Jesus include not swerving from what is central to us—allowing ourselves to be possessed by Jesus fully and completely so that we receive the hundredfold promised those who are faithful: "eternal life."

Living the Paschal Mystery

The "rich man" who couldn't "give up" his wealth was not ready to follow Jesus. After all, following Jesus leads to the cross—where everything is given up! Following Jesus goes beyond keeping the commandments to paschal living. This means that "giving up" is more than dispossessing ourselves of what we have. It means that we make our very lives available—this is what following Jesus truly entails. Jesus' teaching about giving up everything is very hard and demanding, but this is the only way to receive a hundredfold now and in eternal Life. This is another description of discipleship, of paschal living: "giving up" is dying, receiving a hundredfold now is experienced in terms of already sharing in the glory of eternal Life. Now this is topsy-turvy: by giving up all, we gain everything!

228

Focusing the Gospel

Key words and phrases: what must I do, inherit eternal life, follow me, went away sad, had many possessions

To the point: The man must have had an inkling that keeping the commandments was not enough, or else he never would have approached Jesus with his question about how to inherit eternal Life. In spite of his faithfulness in keeping God's commandments and his being loved by Jesus, the man nevertheless had a divided heart: "he went away sad, for he had many possessions." The man needed to turn his focus from earthly life to eternal Life, from possessions (and, yes, even God's commandments) to single-heartedly following Jesus to salvation. Where is our heart?

Connecting the Gospel

to the first reading: Jesus is the wisdom of God—no riches or possessions compare to him. When we choose to follow him, all good things come to us.

to experience: It is a human tendency to do the minimum—just enough to get by. According to Jesus, keeping the commandments is the minimum; faithfully following him requires much more.

Connecting the Responsorial Psalm

to the readings: In different words, both the young man and the disciples ask the same question in this Sunday's gospel: "How can we be saved?" Jesus answers that salvation comes only through dispossessing self of all that stands in the way of making God the complete focus of one's life. The teaching is hard—the young man walks away from it and the disciples question their ability to live it.

To all who ask, God offers the wisdom to see both the reward offered (first reading, psalm, gospel) and the price required (first reading, gospel). The price is nothing less than our giving everything; the reward is nothing less than our receiving fullness of Life. But we must choose to pay the price. In the psalm refrain we ask God to fill us with the divine love we need to make this choice. God granted such love to the author of the first reading, and Jesus offered it to the young man in the gospel. This Sunday we ask for this love, and know it will be given to us.

to psalmist preparation: In singing this Sunday's responsorial psalm, you make a dangerous request: you ask God for the "wisdom of heart" which will lead to deeper discipleship. You are, in a sense, the young man in the gospel reading. You are also the disciples who struggle with Jesus' answer. Are you willing to make the request?

**ASSEMBLY &
FAITH-SHARING GROUPS**
- My heart is divided when . . .
- I find it hardest to follow Jesus when . . .
- What I have given up to follow Jesus is
  . . . What I have yet to give up is . . .

PRESIDERS
What I must give up in order to be a better presider is . . . What I receive is . . .

DEACONS
What I must give up in order to better serve those in need is . . . What I receive from them is . . .

HOSPITALITY MINISTERS
When I have a divided heart in following Jesus, my greeting sounds like . . . When my heart is focused on Jesus, my greeting is . . .

MUSIC MINISTERS
One thing more Jesus is asking of me in my music ministry is . . .

ALTAR MINISTERS
I am able to go beyond the minimum requirements of my ministry when I . . . This leads me to . . .

LECTORS
When I prepare for my ministry with a single-hearted attentiveness, my proclamation becomes . . .

**EXTRAORDINARY MINISTERS
OF HOLY COMMUNION**
As Jesus looked upon the man in the gospel with love, I look upon each communicant with love when I . . . and they . . .

✚ CELEBRATION

Model Penitential Act

Presider: The man in the gospel kept all God's commandments, but he was not able to do the one thing more Jesus asked of him. As we prepare for this liturgy, let us ask God's mercy for the times we have not done what Jesus asks of us . . . [pause]

Lord Jesus, you are the good Teacher who shows us the way to eternal Life: Lord . . .

Christ Jesus, you are the Savior who gave your all for us: Christ . . .

Lord Jesus, you love us and call us to follow you: Lord . . .

Homily Points

• Ignorance is bliss! The man eagerly approached Jesus, oblivious to how challenging the encounter would become. Jesus' reply to the man's question about what he must do to inherit eternal Life changed his eagerness to sadness. Yes, ignorance is bliss. But is it?

• This gospel could be interpreted as saying that we must dispossess ourselves of everything we have. In today's world, this is not really possible. Possessions in themselves are not a stumbling block to following Jesus. The issue is whether we are willing to let go and single-heartedly follow him. Nothing should take precedence in our lives over following Jesus and inheriting eternal Life—not possessions, family, property, or even the bliss of ignorance.

• We ought to be careful about putting a question to Jesus if we are not ready to hear his answer! If we approach Jesus and ask him what more we need to do to gain eternal Life, he will tell us in no uncertain terms. Will we hold back from Jesus lest he tell us the "one thing" yet lacking in our lives? Do we choose the bliss of ignorance? Or the joy of hearing Jesus invite us to follow him and inherit eternal Life?

Model Universal Prayer (Prayer of the Faithful)

Presider: Those who faithfully follow Jesus have been promised an inheritance of eternal Life. We ask God for the grace to be faithful.

Response:

Cantor:

For all baptized followers of Jesus, may they choose faithful discipleship above any earthly possession . . . [pause]

For all peoples of the world, may they keep God's commandments and live in justice and harmony . . . [pause]

For all those who are sick or suffering, may they be comforted by those who faithfully follow Jesus . . . [pause]

For each of us here, may we follow Jesus with undivided hearts . . . [pause]

Presider: Good and gracious God, you provide us with all things and keep us in your loving care: hear these our prayers that one day we might enjoy the inheritance of your eternal Life. We ask this through Christ our Lord. **Amen.**

COLLECT

Let us pray

Pause for silent prayer

May your grace, O Lord, we pray, at all times go before us and follow after and make us always determined to carry out good works. Through our Lord Jesus Christ, your Son, who lives and reigns with you in the unity of the Holy Spirit, one God, for ever and ever. **Amen.**

FIRST READING

Wis 7:7-11

I prayed, and prudence was given me;
 I pleaded, and the spirit of wisdom
  came to me.
I preferred her to scepter and throne,
and deemed riches nothing in comparison
  with her,
 nor did I liken any priceless gem to her;
because all gold, in view of her, is a little
  sand,
 and before her, silver is to be accounted
  mire.
Beyond health and comeliness I loved her,
and I chose to have her rather than the
  light,
 because the splendor of her never yields
  to sleep.
Yet all good things together came to me in
  her company,
 and countless riches at her hands.

RESPONSORIAL PSALM

Ps 90:12-13, 14-15, 16-17

R⁊. (14) Fill us with your love, O Lord, and we will sing for joy!

Teach us to number our days aright,
that we may gain wisdom of heart.
Return, O LORD! How long?
Have pity on your servants!

R⁊. Fill us with your love, O Lord, and we will sing for joy!

Fill us at daybreak with your kindness,
that we may shout for joy and gladness
all our days.
Make us glad, for the days when you
afflicted us,
for the years when we saw evil.

R⁊. Fill us with your love, O Lord, and we will sing for joy!

Let your work be seen by your servants
and your glory by their children;
and may the gracious care of the Lord our
God be ours;
prosper the work of our hands for us!
Prosper the work of our hands!

R⁊. Fill us with your love, O Lord, and we will sing for joy!

SECOND READING

Heb 4:12-13

Brothers and sisters:
Indeed the word of God is living and
effective,
sharper than any two-edged sword,
penetrating even between soul and
spirit, joints and marrow,
and able to discern reflections and
thoughts of the heart.
No creature is concealed from him,
but everything is naked and exposed to
the eyes of him
to whom we must render an account.

About Liturgy

Presentation of the gifts: The entire eucharistic liturgy is an invitation to empty ourselves, to dispossess ourselves of anything that stands in the way of our being transformed more perfectly into the Body of Christ. One concrete symbol of this dispossession takes place at the presentation of the gifts. This procession is more than a practical way to get the bread and wine on the altar; if this were the case, they could simply be placed there by an altar minister after the universal prayer (prayer of the faithful; which, for simplicity, is often what happens during a weekday Mass).

The procession with the bread and wine is symbolic of our own journey from this life to eternal Life when we will stand at the messianic banquet "in the age to come." The bread and wine are also symbolic of ourselves; just as the bread and wine are substantially changed into the real Body and Blood of Christ, so are we transformed into more perfect members of that Body. Finally, when the gifts of the community include food, necessities, and money for the poor, this is wonderfully symbolic of our willingness to "give to the poor" and puts Jesus' invitation to follow him into visible practice. It is a concrete way for us to show our willingness not to be possessed by our riches, not to have divided hearts, but to give of ourselves, emptying ourselves to better follow Jesus with undivided hearts. Therefore, the presentation of the gifts is symbolic of our own desire for dispossession—for having the undivided heart needed to follow Jesus.

About Liturgical Music

Music suggestions: Jesus asks us in this Sunday's gospel to give our entire selves to following him. In "Is Your All on the Altar" (LMGM2), we challenge one another to make this total gift. In "Give Me a Clean Heart" (LMGM2), we ask God to "fix my heart so that I may be used by you." In "Completely Yes" (LMGM2), we sing "Yes, Lord! Yes, Lord! From the bottom of my heart to the depths of my soul. Yes, Lord! Completely yes!" The first song would make an excellent response to the gospel reading during the preparation of the gifts. The second would make a moving prayer during Communion. The third would make a wonderful recessional song as we leave the liturgy ready to serve Christ fully and wholly in our daily living.

In "The Love of the Lord" (G3, W4), we sing that riches, wealth, honors, all that we cherish are worthless "in the light of the love of the Lord." This song would work well during either the preparation of the gifts or Communion. In "Only This I Want" (BB, G3, JS3, W4) we acknowledge "All but this is loss, worthless refuse to me, for to gain the Lord is to gain all I need." This song would be appropriate during either the preparation of the gifts or Communion.

SPIRITUALITY

GOSPEL ACCLAMATION
Mark 10:45

R̦. Alleluia, alleluia.
The Son of Man came to serve
and to give his life as a ransom for many.
R̦. Alleluia, alleluia.

Gospel   Mark 10:35-45; L146B

James and John, the sons of
    Zebedee, came to Jesus and
    said to him,
"Teacher, we want you to do for us
    whatever we ask of you."
He replied, "What do you wish
    me to do for you?"
They answered him, "Grant that
    in your glory
we may sit one at your right
    and the other at your left."
Jesus said to them, "You do not know what
    you are asking.
Can you drink the cup that I drink
    or be baptized with the baptism with
        which I am baptized?"
They said to him, "We can."
Jesus said to them, "The cup that I drink,
    you will drink,
and with the baptism with which I am
    baptized, you will be baptized;
but to sit at my right or at my left is not
    mine to give
but is for those for whom it has been
    prepared."
When the ten heard this, they became
    indignant at James and John.
Jesus summoned them and said to them,
"You know that those who are recognized
    as rulers over the Gentiles
lord it over them,
and their great ones make their authority
    over them felt.
But it shall not be so among you.
Rather, whoever wishes to be great among
    you will be your servant;
whoever wishes to be first among you will
    be the slave of all.
For the Son of Man did not come to be served
    but to serve and to give his life as a
        ransom for many."

or Mark 10:42-45

See Appendix A, p. 308.

Reflecting on the Gospel

Hard lessons take a long time to learn. Some lessons take an entire lifetime. Children learn quickly not to touch the hot stove burner. It takes them a bit longer to learn that applying themselves in school will reap future rewards. It takes them a lifetime to learn what it means to be a responsible person contributing to church and society. This Sunday's gospel begins with apostles seeking glory; they had yet to learn what being a follower of Jesus truly entails. There is more demand to being disciples than would appear, and finally facing that true glory is not found where we usually seek it. We receive true glory when we finally give up pursuing it and instead follow Jesus and the demanding life he offers.

Why did the apostles follow Jesus? This gospel suggests they had reward on their minds: the glory of sitting at the right and left of Jesus in positions of honor. It took the apostles a long time to learn that the real reward of following Jesus would be to "drink the cup" and "be baptized" with his baptism. His baptism was his lifelong choice to do the will of the Father no matter what the cost. The cost would be humbly serving others to the point even of giving his life "for many." As Jesus' followers, we can choose no less. Like the apostles, it takes us no less time to learn this.

This gospel includes the third prediction of the passion in Mark's gospel, but it does more than predict Jesus' passion and the consequences of being Jesus' disciples. It points to and challenges the basic human tendency to seek fleeting glory. There is nothing in this life that can bring us lasting glory—the eternal Life that has been prepared for us and in which we already share—except self-giving for the sake of others, a self-giving that conforms us more closely to Jesus' own self-identity as the suffering servant. Jesus' baptism was an entry into his willingness to suffer and die for our salvation, and then be raised up on the third day to risen Life. Thus a share in Jesus' glory ultimately means that we faithfully live our own baptism into Jesus' suffering and death and thus identify with Jesus and his saving work. It also means that, faithfully following him in serving others, we will share in his risen Life—now and in the age to come.

Jesus responds to the apostles' request for a share in his glory by saying that discipleship isn't about raw power ("lord it over them," "make their authority felt"). Discipleship is about servanthood, even when it entails suffering and giving one's life (see first reading). The only way to glory is by self-emptying, serving, giving one's life. The apostles weren't ready for this—they abandoned Jesus at his passion and death. Are we ready to follow? Are we ready to choose our baptism into his suffering and death?

Living the Paschal Mystery

Much of our serving others is simply part of our everyday circumstances, for example, parents taking care of their children or a worker cooperating with others on a team job. Being the servant of all isn't always something extra or big; most of the time it is simply doing our everyday tasks generously and with integrity while keeping in mind that others are the Body of Christ and to serve them is to serve Christ. If we can do these everyday tasks with loving care, then when something big comes along we won't deny Jesus like the apostles, but will say "we can." And mean it, knowing full well the demands that identity with Christ entails.

Focusing the Gospel

Key words and phrases: glory, drink the cup, be baptized, to serve and give his life

To the point: Why did the apostles follow Jesus? This gospel suggests they had reward on their minds: the glory of sitting at the right and left of Jesus in positions of honor. It took the apostles a long time to learn that the real reward of following Jesus would be to "drink the cup" and "be baptized" with his baptism. His baptism was his lifelong choice to do the will of the Father no matter what the cost. The cost would be humbly serving others to the point even of giving his life "for many." As Jesus' followers, we can choose no less. Like the apostles, it takes us no less time to learn this.

Connecting the Gospel

to the first reading: This selection is also read as part of the first reading on Good Friday, thus pointing us to Jesus' passion and death. James and John desire glory. Jesus reveals the stark requirement for sharing in his glory: drink his cup of suffering, be baptized into his death.

to experience: Like James and John, how readily we say "we can" to a commitment which promises glory and appears easy. Jesus, however, hides none of the fine print—our "we can" to him commits us to serving others, no matter the cost.

Connecting the Responsorial Psalm

to the readings: Over and over in the refrain of this responsorial psalm we beg God for mercy. On the one hand, we need God's mercy because of our persistent failure to understand the servant demands of discipleship (gospel). On the other, we need God's mercy once we have accepted these demands, for they require that we die to self (first reading, gospel). Our call as disciples is to serve as Christ served to the point of laying down our lives for the sake of others. We must "drink the cup" Christ offers. While we waver in our response—hoping to gain the glory promised without paying its price—God remains steadfast toward us at all times, in every situation, to the ends of the earth (psalm). God will deliver those who "drink the cup" Jesus drinks. In this we can "place our trust" (psalm refrain).

to psalmist preparation: In the first strophe of this responsorial psalm you tell people about the trustworthiness of God. In the second you invite them to place their hope in God who delivers from death. In the third you speak for them as you voice their surrender to God in hope and trust. How will you communicate these shifts in the psalm? How have you experienced these shifts in your own faith journey?

**ASSEMBLY &
FAITH-SHARING GROUPS**
- The glory I often discover myself seeking is . . . The glory Jesus invites me to seek is . . .
- The "cup" Jesus asks me to drink is . . . When I drink of this cup, I . . .
- I am being baptized into . . .

PRESIDERS
I help the members of the assembly make the lifelong choice baptism requires when I . . .

DEACONS
Everything about my ministry witnesses to the call to "drink the cup" of the Lord in that . . .

HOSPITALITY MINISTERS
The manner of my greeting helps the gathering assembly to learn anew the cost of following Jesus when I . . .

MUSIC MINISTERS
I find myself using my music ministry as an avenue to personal glory when . . . Who/what calls me back to a ministry of service is . . .

ALTAR MINISTERS
My serving at the altar is an expression of my ongoing baptismal living when I . . .

LECTORS
My preparation of the word leads me to serve others in my daily living when . . .

**EXTRAORDINARY MINISTERS
OF HOLY COMMUNION**
The "cup that I drink" and offer to others during my ministry demands that I live in service of others in that . . .

Model Penitential Act

Presider: In today's gospel Jesus teaches us that our glory lies in serving others. Let us prepare to celebrate this liturgy by asking the Lord Jesus to forgive us for the times we have sought glory for ourselves in other ways . . . [pause]

    Lord Jesus, you are the Savior who gave your life for us: Lord . . .

    Christ Jesus, you sit at the right hand of the Father in glory: Christ . . .

    Lord Jesus, you are the cup of salvation we drink: Lord . . .

Homily Points

- Glory is so attractive! Who doesn't want to be wealthy and famous? Who doesn't want a shelf lined with trophies and awards? The attraction of glory spurs us to greater achievement. This is especially true of our baptismal life in the risen Christ. What glory attracts us? What do we aspire to achieve to share in this glory?

- "Do whatever we ask of you," James and John demand of Jesus. But they have it backwards. They should have said, "Lord, what do you ask of us?" Are we willing to ask Jesus this question? If so, it will mean redefining our understanding of glory. It will mean shaping our life around choosing to serve others rather than be served. It will mean drinking the cup of suffering and undergoing the baptism of Jesus' passion, death, and resurrection. Can we do this?

- What spurs us to faithful baptismal, Gospel living is the attraction of sharing in Jesus' glory. Increasing this attraction increases our willingness to drink Jesus' cup of suffering through serving others. We do this, for example, when we live a joy-filled life in face of prolonged illness; see the good in others despite their hurtful actions; take time to reach out to the lonely, the outcast, the needy. Can we do this? Will we do this?

Model Universal Prayer (Prayer of the Faithful)

Presider: Let us confidently approach God's throne of glory and present our needs.

Response:

Lord, hear our prayer.

Cantor:

we pray to the Lord,

For the church, the Body of Christ called to be servant of all . . . [pause]

For world leaders, called to serve the common good of all . . . [pause]

For those suffering and dying, called to be united with Christ in glory . . . [pause]

For all of us here, called to embrace Jesus' life of self-giving . . . [pause]

Presider: Almighty and ever-living God, you hear the prayers of your humble servants: grant our needs that one day we might share in your eternal glory. We ask this through Christ our Lord. **Amen.**

COLLECT

Let us pray

Pause for silent prayer

Almighty ever-living God,
grant that we may always conform our
    will to yours
and serve your majesty in sincerity of
    heart.
Through our Lord Jesus Christ, your Son,
who lives and reigns with you in the unity
    of the Holy Spirit,
one God, for ever and ever. **Amen.**

FIRST READING

Isa 53:10-11

The LORD was pleased
    to crush him in infirmity.

If he gives his life as an offering for sin,
    he shall see his descendants in a long
        life,
    and the will of the LORD shall be
        accomplished through him.

Because of his affliction
    he shall see the light in fullness of days;
through his suffering, my servant shall
        justify many,
    and their guilt he shall bear.

RESPONSORIAL PSALM

Ps 33:4-5, 18-19, 20, 22

R̸. (22) Lord, let your mercy be on us, as we place our trust in you.

Upright is the word of the LORD,
    and all his works are trustworthy.
He loves justice and right;
    of the kindness of the LORD the earth
        is full.

R̸. Lord, let your mercy be on us, as we place our trust in you.

See, the eyes of the LORD are upon those
        who fear him,
    upon those who hope for his kindness,
to deliver them from death
    and preserve them in spite of famine.

R̸. Lord, let your mercy be on us, as we place our trust in you.

Our soul waits for the LORD,
    who is our help and our shield.
May your kindness, O LORD, be upon us
    who have put our hope in you.

R̸. Lord, let your mercy be on us, as we place our trust in you.

SECOND READING

Heb 4:14-16

Brothers and sisters:
Since we have a great high priest who has
        passed through the heavens,
    Jesus, the Son of God,
    let us hold fast to our confession.
For we do not have a high priest
    who is unable to sympathize with our
        weaknesses,
    but one who has similarly been tested in
        every way,
    yet without sin.
So let us confidently approach the throne
        of grace
    to receive mercy and to find grace for
        timely help.

✢ CATECHESIS

About Liturgy

Parish ministry and servanthood: Every Sunday at Mass we see any number of men, women, and children selflessly give of themselves by means of the various liturgical ministries—presiders, deacons, hospitality ministers, music ministers, altar ministers (including servers, sacristans, janitors, environment committee members), lectors, extraordinary ministers of Holy Communion. These are quite visible to all those who come to Sunday Mass. Additionally, there are many other parish ministers (e.g., members of the pastoral council, education board, etc.) who, generally, work behind the scenes. Yet when we add all these numbers together, sad to say, the persons actively ministering in a parish remain a rather small percentage of the whole parish census. Two points might be worth our reflection time.

First, the parish ministries express real servanthood. Many people sacrifice much of themselves in order to minister in their parishes and this is truly part of what Jesus asks when we are to be the servant of all. If we truly believe that the parish is really the people, then being serious about our commitment to follow Christ means that our service begins with our own parish community.

Second, we ought to encourage and thank one another for this faithful commitment of service. One time someone mentioned that she had given selflessly for twenty-three years to her parish and no one had ever come up to her and said "thank you." This is a sad commentary on how much we take for granted! Perhaps our greatest expression of servanthood is to recognize and thank those who selflessly model for us what serving all really means.

This being said, we must always remember that the primary locus for our self-emptying is in serving the world, neighborhood, home. The primary role of the church is to serve the world and be a sign of God's reign in our midst.

About Liturgical Music

Singing the Lamb of God: The plea for God's mercy which the assembly sings in this Sunday's responsorial psalm refrain makes sense in light of the first reading and gospel's reminder that discipleship means dying with Christ so that others might live. The Lamb of God we sing every Eucharist at the fraction rite makes the same kind of sense. This litany is not filler music to cover the time it takes for the eucharistic ministers to gather around the altar and receive Communion. Rather it is a litany we sing to accompany the presider's action of breaking the consecrated bread and preparing it for distribution. It is a litany we sing as a final act of preparing ourselves for what we are about to do: eat this bread and drink this cup.

This bread is Christ's Body, this wine his Blood given for the world. We who consume this bread become Christ's Body meant to be broken so that the world may eat. We who drink this wine become his Blood meant to be poured out so that others may live. The Lamb of God is a litany of petition that Christ have mercy on us for what we are about to undertake. Do we realize why we are singing these words at this moment? Do our presiders break the bread with deliberation? Do we watch it with awareness and attention? Does the style and tempo of the Lamb of God we sing fit the awesomeness of what we are doing at this moment in the liturgy?

OCTOBER 18, 2015
TWENTY-NINTH SUNDAY IN ORDINARY TIME

SPIRITUALITY

GOSPEL ACCLAMATION
cf. 2 Tim 1:10

R̸. Alleluia, alleluia.
Our Savior Jesus Christ destroyed death
and brought life to light through the Gospel.
R̸. Alleluia, alleluia.

Gospel

Mark 10:46-52; L149B

**As Jesus was leaving Jericho with
his disciples and a sizable
crowd,
Bartimaeus, a blind man, the
son of Timaeus,
sat by the roadside begging.
On hearing that it was Jesus of
Nazareth,
he began to cry out and say,
"Jesus, son of David, have pity
on me."
And many rebuked him, telling
him to be silent.
But he kept calling out all the more,
"Son of David, have pity on me."
Jesus stopped and said, "Call him."
So they called the blind man, saying to
him,
"Take courage; get up, Jesus is
calling you."
He threw aside his cloak, sprang up,
and came to Jesus.
Jesus said to him in reply, "What do
you want me to do for you?"
The blind man replied to him, "Master,
I want to see."
Jesus told him, "Go your way; your
faith has saved you."
Immediately he received his sight
and followed him on the way.**

Reflecting on the Gospel

This gospel is filled with movement, energy, drive. The verbs describing Bartimaeus's actions in this gospel say everything about faith, encountering Jesus, and choosing to follow him. Each verb, each action word says so much beyond itself.

He cried out: Bartimaeus sought Jesus' attention. He hoped for what—a few coins? Maybe. But probably more. He called Jesus the "Son of David," a messianic reference. He no doubt recognized Jesus for more than simply an itinerant preacher. For Bartimaeus, Jesus was the one who could save him—from his blindness? Yes, but much more.

He kept calling: Bartimaeus was persistent. He did not let a crowd's rebuke keep him from calling out again. He knew what he wanted. He was going to encounter Jesus and present himself. He had trust that Jesus would "have pity" on him.

He threw aside his cloak: Did Bartimaeus think he wouldn't need it anymore? More likely, the cloak would get in his way, slow down his effort to get to Jesus. Bartimaeus is a man on a mission! He knows what he wants, he knows how to get it, he knows who will grant it.

He sprang up and came to Jesus: Bartimaeus is decisive; he doesn't amble, tarry, or hesitate. He leaps to encounter Jesus. Without this personal approach, personal relationship, personal engagement Bartimaeus remains simply a beggar. With an encounter with Jesus, he becomes so much more.

He stated his request: In such simple words does Bartimaeus bare his heart to Jesus: "Master, I want to see." The Greek text is *Rabbouni*—teacher. Bartimaeus comes to Jesus for more than sight—he wants Jesus the Teacher to grant him insight.

He received his sight: Now able to see, Bartimaeus could well go independently on his merry way. After all, Jesus even tells him to "Go your way." If all Bartimaeus received was physical sight, that is probably what he would have done. However, Bartimaeus received more than sight: "your faith has saved you." Saved him from begging? Saved him from himself? Saved for . . . ?

He followed Jesus: Having encountered Jesus, Bartimaeus could not go his own way. His encounter with Jesus formed a bond, a relationship with Jesus that Bartimaeus chose not to weaken but instead to deepen. Instead of going his own way, he chose to go Jesus' way.

Such need, such urgency, such conviction did Bartimaeus have! These verbs describe Bartimaeus's faith-in-action, his deepening relationship with Jesus. Faith is the insight and cause of action. So must it be for us.

Living the Paschal Mystery

Without persistence in prayer and seeking encounters with Jesus, it will be impossible for us to follow him faithfully. Encounters with Jesus in prayer keep our relationship to him growing, keep our relationship with him healthy and strong. The paschal mystery rhythm of dying and rising plays itself out in many ways—this Sunday in a rhythm of faith and action. In practical, everyday terms this means that at times we are *doing* our faith—reaching out to those around us in need. At other times we are *being* our faith—taking time to savor our relationship with God.

Focusing the Gospel

Key words and phrases: blind man, sat by the roadside begging, Jesus . . . have pity on me, your faith has saved you, followed him

To the point: The verbs describing Bartimaeus's actions in this gospel say everything about faith, encountering Jesus, and choosing to follow him. He cried out, kept calling, threw aside his cloak, sprang up and came to Jesus, stated his request, received his sight, followed Jesus. Such need, such urgency, such conviction! These verbs describe Bartimaeus's faith-in-action, his deepening relationship with Jesus. Faith is the insight and cause of action. So must it be for us.

Connecting the Gospel

to the first reading: Using many images of healing, the first reading describes the salvation ultimately given by Jesus to Bartimaeus and to us: deliverance, homecoming, consolation, guidance, life-giving water, and level roads where no one stumbles.

to experience: How energetic and persistent we can be when we clearly know what we want and need! How true this is of Bartimaeus in this gospel!

Connecting the Responsorial Psalm

to the readings: In the gospel Jesus is on a journey, leaving Jericho on his way to Jerusalem. Bartimaeus is on a journey, moving from blindness to sight, from encounter with Jesus to faith, from going his own way to walking the way of Jesus. Psalm 126 depicts a dramatic moment in Israel's journey of faith toward the God who had formed them as a people. The psalm describes their return from exile in Babylon to their homeland. At first they do not see clearly. They think they are "dreaming." But faith opens their eyes to see the "great things" (psalm refrain) God is doing for them: delivering them, gathering them home, leading them to fullness of life (see first reading). Salvation is not a dream, but real.

Psalm 126 describes our faith journey as well. Like Bartimaeus, we cry out to Jesus to heal our clouded vision. Jesus responds, and we see him as salvation made real in our midst. How can we not, like Bartimaeus, follow in his footsteps?

to psalmist preparation: One of the "great things" God does (psalm refrain) is grant you faith to see Jesus as Savior and grace to follow him wherever he leads. Can you accept the weeping this "great thing" will bring? Do you believe this weeping will be turned into joy?

ASSEMBLY & FAITH-SHARING GROUPS
- I am like Bartimaeus when . . .
- When I cry out in prayer, I ask for . . . Jesus answers me by . . .
- Faith is the insight and cause of my actions when . . .

PRESIDERS
As presider I lead the assembly to call out to Jesus and follow him more faithfully by . . .

DEACONS
My service helps those in need to encounter Jesus and deepen their faith by . . .

HOSPITALITY MINISTERS
The manner of my greeting helps those who are gathering for liturgy come to Jesus in these ways . . .

MUSIC MINISTERS
My music making is a way I cry out to Jesus in faith in that . . .

ALTAR MINISTERS
I encounter Jesus during my service at the altar most surely when . . .

LECTORS
My faith-filled insight into God's word deepens the assembly's faith when I . . .

EXTRAORDINARY MINISTERS OF HOLY COMMUNION
My distributing Holy Communion is my faith-in-action when I . . .

Model Penitential Act

Presider: In the gospel today Bartimaeus the blind beggar cries out in faith to Jesus. As we prepare for this liturgy, let us ask for God's mercy for the times we have lacked the faith to cry out to Jesus . . . [pause]

Lord Jesus, you are the Son of David: Lord . . .

Christ Jesus, you are the One who heals: Christ . . .

Lord Jesus, you answer our every cry: Lord . . .

Homily Points

- We spring into action when what we need seems at hand. Bartimaeus springs into action—he cries out his need and comes to Jesus. These actions spring from faith that Jesus is the "son of David," from belief that Jesus has the power to grant every request. Indeed, does anyone approach Jesus except out of boldness born of need and faith in him?

- Bartimaeus has faith. Faith that Jesus will hear him, faith that Jesus is the Son of David who has power, faith that Jesus will have pity on him, faith that Jesus will heal him. Bartimaeus's faith was rewarded, but even more than he thought he needed. Jesus also assures him of being saved. Bartimaeus's actions are the manifestation of his faith. Jesus' actions are a manifestation of his saving power in response to another's faith.

- The blind Bartimaeus knows exactly his position in relation to the community: off to the side and begging. He also knows his position in relation to Jesus: crying out, springing up, following. His position in relation to the community arises from his need; his position in relation to Jesus arises from his faith. Indeed, does anyone approach Jesus except out of boldness born of need and faith in him?

Model Universal Prayer (Prayer of the Faithful)

Presider: God hears the prayers of those who cry in faith for their needs. With courage we make our needs known.

Response:

Cantor:

For all members of the church, may their faith draw them confidently to Jesus . . . [pause]

For the people of all nations, may they boldly seek salvation . . . [pause]

For the sick and the suffering, may they trust in Jesus' healing power to save . . . [pause]

For each of us gathered here, may we persist in prayer and come to a deeper relationship with Jesus . . . [pause]

Presider: Gracious God, you hear the prayers of those who cry out to you: in our need may we have confidence that our prayers are heard and answered. Through Christ our Lord. *Amen.*

COLLECT

Let us pray

Pause for silent prayer

Almighty ever-living God,
increase our faith, hope and charity,
and make us love what you command,
so that we may merit what you promise.
Through our Lord Jesus Christ, your Son,
who lives and reigns with you in the unity
      of the Holy Spirit,
one God, for ever and ever. **Amen.**

FIRST READING
Jer 31:7-9

Thus says the LORD:
Shout with joy for Jacob,
      exult at the head of the nations;
      proclaim your praise and say:
The LORD has delivered his people,
      the remnant of Israel.
Behold, I will bring them back
      from the land of the north;
I will gather them from the ends of the
            world,
      with the blind and the lame in their
            midst,
the mothers and those with child;
      they shall return as an immense throng.
They departed in tears,
      but I will console them and guide them;
I will lead them to brooks of water,
      on a level road, so that none shall
            stumble.
For I am a father to Israel,
      Ephraim is my firstborn.

RESPONSORIAL PSALM
Ps 126:1-2, 2-3, 4-5, 6

R̸. (3) The Lord has done great things for us; we are filled with joy.

When the LORD brought back the captives of Zion,
      we were like men dreaming.
Then our mouth was filled with laughter,
      and our tongue with rejoicing.

R̸. The Lord has done great things for us; we are filled with joy.

Then they said among the nations,
 "The Lord has done great things for
 them."
The Lord has done great things for us;
 we are glad indeed.

R/. The Lord has done great things for us;
we are filled with joy.

Restore our fortunes, O Lord,
 like the torrents in the southern desert.
Those that sow in tears
 shall reap rejoicing.

R/. The Lord has done great things for us;
we are filled with joy.

Although they go forth weeping,
 carrying the seed to be sown,
they shall come back rejoicing,
 carrying their sheaves.

R/. The Lord has done great things for us;
we are filled with joy.

SECOND READING
Heb 5:1-6

Brothers and sisters:
Every high priest is taken from among
 men
 and made their representative before
 God,
 to offer gifts and sacrifices for sins.
He is able to deal patiently with the
 ignorant and erring,
 for he himself is beset by weakness
 and so, for this reason, must make sin
 offerings for himself
 as well as for the people.
No one takes this honor upon himself
 but only when called by God,
 just as Aaron was.
In the same way,
 it was not Christ who glorified himself
 in becoming high priest,
 but rather the one who said to him:
 *You are my son: this day I have
 begotten you;*
 just as he says in another place:
 *You are a priest forever according to
 the order of Melchizedek.*

CATECHESIS

About Liturgy

Petitions during liturgy: By now all of us are familiar with having petitions at Mass, especially in the form of the universal prayer (prayer of the faithful). We are familiar with crying out to God out of our need. This is an ancient custom, and in the early history of the church petitions abounded in several places during the liturgy, sometimes becoming quite lengthy (even running to several pages of text). We remarked on the Twenty-Sixth Sunday in Ordinary Time in the catechesis on the act of penitence that originally one form of the *Kyrie* included a litany of petitions to which the "Lord, have mercy" was a common response. We still have petitions in our eucharistic prayers for both the living and the dead. One interesting form of petitions is called "diptychs" which are lists of individuals mentioned right in the liturgy—surely martyrs, but we think some were even living benefactors. An example of this still remaining in our contemporary liturgy is the list of men and women martyrs that are part of Eucharistic Prayer I. Also, we pray by name for our pope and bishop, and then mention all the clergy and faithful.

Some people have grumbled about the constant petitions during Mass, especially that there seems to be so much repetition—we are praying for the same things all the time. One response to this attitude is to consider the blind man in this gospel: God might not seem to hear all our prayers, but persistence reminds us of how utterly dependent upon God we are.

A good practice during the universal prayer (prayer of the faithful) is to have a pause of reasonable length after the announcement of each intention (the model suggested in *Living Liturgy*™). This pause allows time for personal prayer, for making the general intentions very much our own prayer. In this way even general intercessions which seem similar or repetitious can take on individuality and freshness.

About Liturgical Music

Music suggestions: Herman Stuempfle's "A Blind Man Sat beside the Road" (HG, W4) retells the story in this Sunday's gospel. The final verse makes this our story: "Our blindness cries for vision bright, Our poverty for grace. O Lord, have mercy now on us; to us reveal your face." This hymn would make an excellent reflection on the gospel during the preparation of the gifts. Another good choice for the preparation of the gifts would be "Jesus, Lead the Way" (G3, W4) in which we sing about Jesus as our light and ask him to lead us on the way of salvation until the "course is o'er." A third possibility during the preparation of the gifts would be Greg Hayakawa's "I Am the Light of the World" (BB, JS3). Appropriate choices for Communion include any setting of Psalm 27 in which we sing about Christ as our light and salvation, for example, Suzanne Toolan's "Jesus Christ, Inner Light" (BB) with its refrain, "Jesus Christ, inner light, let not our own darkness conquer us. Jesus Christ, inner light, enable us to welcome your love"; Jesse Manibusan's "Open My Eyes" (BB, JS3); and Kathleen Thomerson's "I Want to Walk as a Child of the Light" (found in most resources). Examples of fitting choices for the recessional song include Doris M. Akers's powerful "Lead Me, Guide Me" (found in most resources), and "We Walk by Faith" (found in most resources), set either to Marty Haugen's tune or set to ST. ANNE.

SPIRITUALITY

GOSPEL ACCLAMATION
Matt 11:28

R7. Alleluia, alleluia.
Come to me, all you who labor and are burdened,
and I will give you rest, says the Lord.
R7. Alleluia, alleluia.

Gospel

Matt 5:1-12a; L667

When Jesus saw the crowds, he
        went up the mountain,
    and after he had sat down, his
        disciples came to him.
He began to teach them, saying:

    "Blessed are the poor in spirit,
        for theirs is the Kingdom of
            heaven.
    Blessed are they who mourn,
        for they will be comforted.
    Blessed are the meek,
        for they will inherit the land.
    Blessed are they who hunger and thirst
        for righteousness,
        for they will be satisfied.
    Blessed are the merciful,
        for they will be shown mercy.
    Blessed are the clean of heart,
        for they will see God.
    Blessed are the peacemakers,
        for they will be called children of God.
    Blessed are they who are persecuted
        for the sake of righteousness,
        for theirs is the Kingdom of heaven.
    Blessed are you when they insult you
        and persecute you
        and utter every kind of evil against
            you falsely because of me.
    Rejoice and be glad,
        for your reward will be great in
            heaven."

Reflecting on the Gospel

Mountains are majestic. They awe us. They inspire us. They draw us. Mountains are ever changing in our beholding—sunrise and sunset bathe them in different lights and colors; winter and summer clothe them in different array; storms and wind wrap them in tremor. No wonder in biblical imagery mountaintops are places of theophany—places where God reveals the divine Self to human beings. The sublime majesty of mountains draws us to the ineffable majesty of the God who creates, who blesses, who draws to Self those who are drawn to seek the One who is good beyond all measure, is holy beyond all reckoning, is caring beyond all imagining.

It is no accident that the Gospel of Matthew has Jesus go "up the mountain," traditionally a place associated with divine encounter, to teach the Beatitudes to his disciples. The Beatitudes reveal the very Being of God ("Blessed," holy), God's care for God's beloved people ("poor in spirit," "those who mourn," etc.), God's intent for faithful ones ("theirs is the kingdom of heaven"). The Beatitudes reveal the mind and heart of God. Those who have encountered God and lived the Beatitudes have the same mind and heart. We call them "saints." There is a countless multitude of saints in heaven, "wearing white robes and holding palm branches in their hands" (first reading), endlessly singing God's praises. There is a countless multitude of saints here among us who "are God's children now" (second reading) who have embraced the beatific, Godlike way of living. While this feast day primarily honors the saints who have gone before us, we cannot forget ourselves on this day. They have gone where we hope to go.

There are many ways to be blessed. One of the attractions of honoring saints is that they offer a great deal of variety and richness of life for us to emulate. No matter what situation in life we find ourselves or what difficulty we face, some Saint offers us a model for perseverance in our blessedness and the assurance of care. This solemnity reminds us that our life of blessedness rests on an intimate relationship with God and each other expressed through enduring bonds of mutual care, mercy, humility, and self-giving.

Living the Paschal Mystery

We often think of the saints as out-of-this-world holy people who are far beyond our own experience or sense of our own goodness. When we pray the Litany of All Saints (for example, before the baptisms during the Easter Vigil) we ask the intercession of very many saints who lived centuries ago in a very different time and culture. They seem far away. This solemnity reminds us that at one time they were ordinary people just like us, living ordinary lives in faithfulness to Gospel values.

This festival is one of encouragement—God doesn't judge us only on our weaknesses but on our persevering in a willingness to live as God's blessed children. The simple, everyday things we do well wash us in the blood of the Lamb (see first reading). Our smile is a saintly one. Our gesture of kindness is an expression of blessedness. Our humility is Godlike. Others' holy gestures toward us are reminders that there is glory awaiting us. To each of us who embraces our blessedness: ours "is the kingdom of heaven."

Focusing the Gospel

Key words and phrases: went up the mountain, teach them, Blessed, kingdom of heaven

To the point: It is no accident that the Gospel of Matthew has Jesus go "up the mountain," traditionally a place associated with divine encounter, to teach the Beatitudes to his disciples. The Beatitudes reveal the very Being of God ("Blessed," holy), God's care for God's beloved people ("poor in spirit," "those who mourn," etc.), God's intent for faithful ones ("theirs is the kingdom of heaven"). The Beatitudes reveal the mind and heart of God. Those who have encountered God and lived the Beatitudes have the same mind and heart. We call them "saints."

Connecting the Gospel

to the first reading: The "kingdom of heaven" given to those who are faithful is not a place, but the community of those who rejoice in eternal encounter with God, engage in heavenly worship, and raise an unending chorus of blessing and glory unto God.

to experience: While the news media is filled with the actions of those who seem godless, in fact we all know many people who live with the mind and heart of God. We all know "saints."

Connecting the Responsorial Psalm

to the readings: Psalm 24 was a psalm of ascent sung as the Israelites journeyed to the temple for festival. As they approached the entrance, a designated person asked, "Who can ascend the mountain of the LORD? or who may stand in his holy place?" A temple representative then answered, "One whose hands are sinless, whose heart is clean, who desires not what is vain." The response functioned as an examination of fidelity to the covenant. After questioning those at the doorway, the temple attendant would declare, "this is the people . . . that seeks the face of the God of Jacob" and allow them entrance.

On this solemnity we honor all those who stand in the presence of God because they have been faithful to the covenant mediated through Christ. These are the ones who have been poor in spirit, who have hungered for righteousness, who have shown mercy. These holy ones now see God "as he is" and know they are "like him" (second reading). These are the blessed ones who have crossed the threshold into the fullness of light. We stand at the door and sing their praises.

to psalmist preparation: In this psalm refrain you sing about all the holy ones in heaven who now see God face-to-face. You also sing about all the holy ones still on earth who long to see God's face. What are you saying to God about them? What are you saying to them about God?

**ASSEMBLY &
FAITH-SHARING GROUPS**
- I encounter God and learn the divine mind and heart when . . .
- The most challenging Beatitude for me is . . . The most encouraging Beatitude for me is . . .
- Persons who inspire me to saintly living are . . .

PRESIDERS
My ministry encourages the assembly to seek the intent of God for their lives when . . .

DEACONS
My service ministry witnesses to how I embrace the Beatitudes in that . . .

HOSPITALITY MINISTERS
When I look upon those gathering for liturgy as the blessed, my manner of greeting them becomes . . .

MUSIC MINISTERS
My ministry joins the singing of this assembly with the singing of the heavenly choir (see first reading) when . . .

ALTAR MINISTERS
My serving at the altar is my "mountain" where I encounter God when . . .

LECTORS
My proclamation of the word reveals God's mind and heart in that . . .

**EXTRAORDINARY MINISTERS
OF HOLY COMMUNION**
What helps me recognize the holiness of those who come for Holy Communion is . . .

✠ CELEBRATION

Model Penitential Act

Presider: On this solemnity we honor the saints who have been faithful to Gospel living. As we prepare for this liturgy, let us ask for God's mercy for the times we have been unfaithful . . . [pause]

Lord Jesus, you are the holy One of God: Lord . . .

Christ Jesus, you are the Lamb who receives blessing and glory, wisdom and thanksgiving, honor, power, and might: Christ . . .

Lord Jesus, you are the joy of all saints: Lord . . .

Homily Points

- We human beings have always honored our departed loved ones. Ancestors' pictures adorn our walls. Buildings are named after long-deceased benefactors. Accomplishments are marked with obelisks or monuments. It is not surprising, then, that from earliest times the church has also desired to honor the saints.

- Jesus "saw the crowds," but left the crowds behind to teach the Beatitudes to the disciples. The beatific life, however, is not meant only for the disciples, but for everyone. The Beatitudes are characteristic of a holy, Gospel way of living. The heart of discipleship is to live in such a way that all know themselves to be blessed, to be holy, to be saints. This is surely a radical way of living. What makes it possible is that we are not alone. We are all members of the communion of All Saints.

- The saints we honor this day are not "up there," but "in here"—in our minds and hearts. They model for us how to live the Gospel faithfully in concrete, everyday ways. They preached the Gospel in word and action: they cared for their families, they served the least among us, they forgave enemies, they sought justice and peace, they showed mercy, they suffered persecution all for the sake of Jesus. The saints witness for us heroic virtue, unwavering fidelity, simplicity of life, great humility, and outstanding charity. We must also witness to this saintly way of living for others.

Model Universal Prayer (Prayer of the Faithful)

Presider: God is holy, and calls us to be holy. Let us pray to hear this call.

Response:

Lord, hear our prayer.

Cantor:

we pray to the Lord,

That all members of the church have the mind and heart of God and live holy lives . . . [pause]

That all peoples of the world share in the blessings of creation . . . [pause]

That those who are poor, oppressed, in mourning, or persecuted be strengthened by God's promise of blessedness . . . [pause]

That each of us here gathered more faithfully model our lives after that of the saints who have gone before us . . . [pause]

Presider: Loving God, you raise up holy men and women in every age to offer hope and encouragement to your beloved people: hear these our prayers that one day we might join with them in eternal joy with you. We ask this through our Lord Jesus Christ. **Amen**.

COLLECT

Let us pray

Pause for silent prayer

Almighty ever-living God,
by whose gift we venerate in one celebration
the merits of all the Saints,
bestow on us, we pray,
through the prayers of so many intercessors,
an abundance of the reconciliation with you
for which we earnestly long.
Through our Lord Jesus Christ, your Son,
who lives and reigns with you in the unity of
    the Holy Spirit,
one God, for ever and ever. **Amen.**

FIRST READING
Rev 7:2-4, 9-14

I, John, saw another angel come up from
    the East,
    holding the seal of the living God.
He cried out in a loud voice to the four angels
    who were given power to damage the
        land and the sea,
    "Do not damage the land or the sea or
        the trees
    until we put the seal on the foreheads of
        the servants of our God."
I heard the number of those who had been
    marked with the seal,
    one hundred and forty-four thousand
        marked
    from every tribe of the children of Israel.

After this I had a vision of a great
    multitude,
    which no one could count,
    from every nation, race, people, and
        tongue.
They stood before the throne and before
    the Lamb,
    wearing white robes and holding palm
        branches in their hands.
They cried out in a loud voice:

    "Salvation comes from our God,
        who is seated on the throne,
    and from the Lamb."

All the angels stood around the throne
    and around the elders and the four
        living creatures.
They prostrated themselves before the
    throne,
    worshiped God, and exclaimed:

    "Amen. Blessing and glory, wisdom and
        thanksgiving,
        honor, power, and might
        be to our God forever and ever. Amen."

Then one of the elders spoke up and said
    to me,

"Who are these wearing white robes,
and where did they come from?"
I said to him, "My lord, you are the one
who knows."
He said to me,
"These are the ones who have survived
the time of great distress;
they have washed their robes
and made them white in the Blood of
the Lamb."

RESPONSORIAL PSALM
Ps 24:1bc-2, 3-4ab, 5-6

R̸. (cf. 6) Lord, this is the people that longs
to see your face.

The LORD's are the earth and its fullness;
the world and those who dwell in it.
For he founded it upon the seas
and established it upon the rivers.

R̸. Lord, this is the people that longs to see
your face.

Who can ascend the mountain of the
LORD?
or who may stand in his holy place?
One whose hands are sinless, whose heart
is clean,
who desires not what is vain.

R̸. Lord, this is the people that longs to see
your face.

He shall receive a blessing from the LORD,
a reward from God his savior.
Such is the race that seeks him,
that seeks the face of the God of Jacob.

R̸. Lord, this is the people that longs to see
your face.

SECOND READING
1 John 3:1-3

Beloved:
See what love the Father has bestowed
on us
that we may be called the children of
God.
Yet so we are.
The reason the world does not know us
is that it did not know him.
Beloved, we are God's children now;
what we shall be has not yet been
revealed.
We do know that when it is revealed we
shall be like him,
for we shall see him as he is.
Everyone who has this hope based on him
makes himself pure,
as he is pure.

About Liturgy

Origin of the festival of All Saints: The earliest cult of the saints focused on the martyrs, those who courageously gave their life out of commitment to Christ. From at least the fourth century the Eastern church had a festival honoring all the saints who have departed; in Rome in the fifth century the pagan Pantheon was consecrated as a church honoring Mary and the martyrs. By the eighth century the cult of the saints is extended beyond the martyrs to honor others who lived selfless, faithful Christian lives. At this time there is the first indication that the festival was fixed on November 1 in the West.

This festival is not primarily about remembering the faithful departed (we do that on November 2). It is about honoring those who have been faithful disciples of Jesus, those who model for us Gospel living, those who inspire us to be likewise faithful.

The communion of saints: There are numerous references in the New Testament of addressing the early Christians as "saints." Most of Paul's salutations at the beginning of his letters address "God's beloved . . . who are called to be saints" (Rom 1:7; NRSV). In the Apostles' Creed we profess belief in "the communion of saints." This article of our faith comes immediately after our profession of belief in the Holy Spirit, and before our profession of belief in the resurrection of the body and everlasting life. The communion of saints cannot be doctrinally separated from the Holy Spirit's work of binding us into a church, whereby we are members of the Body of Christ, nor from Christ's promise and our hope that we will receive a share in his risen Life. Our union with one another in Christ through the Spirit is one of intimacy with our triune God and with one another—one another both living and dead. We saints on earth are united with the saints in heaven in Christ's one Body, forever giving God glory and praise.

About Liturgical Music

Music suggestions: We might sing a number of well-known songs on this day, such as "For All the Saints," "Ye Watchers and Ye Holy Ones," and "Blest Are They." Less well known but also worth singing are Bob Hurd's "With All the Saints" (BB, JS3), Alan Hommerding's "We Sing of the Saints" (WC), and Jeremy Young's "We Shall Rise Again" (G3, LMGM2). Each verse of Hurd's verse-refrain piece would work well during Communion. Hommerding's would be fitting during the preparation of the gifts. The verse specified for this solemnity reads, "There are many saints whom we don't know by name, For God works through people who never find fame. But, gathered together, they now sing God's might, With martyrs and prophets, in heavenly light." Young's verse-refrain song would also work during Communion, with choir or cantor singing the verses. The final verse reads, "At the door there to greet us, martyrs, angels and saints, And our fam'ly and loved ones, ev'ryone freed from their chains. We shall feel their acceptance, and the joy of new life. We shall join in the gathering, reunited in God's love!"

✠ SPIRITUALITY

GOSPEL ACCLAMATION
See John 6:40

This is the will of my Father, says the Lord,
that everyone who sees the Son and believes in
     him
may have eternal life.

Gospel

John 6:37-40; L668

Jesus said to the crowds:
"Everything that the Father gives
     me will come to me,
     and I will not reject anyone who
          comes to me,
     because I came down from heaven
          not to do my own will
     but the will of the one who sent
          me.
And this is the will of the one
     who sent me,
     that I should not lose
          anything of what he gave
          me,
     but that I should raise it on
          the last day.
For this is the will of my Father,
     that everyone who sees the Son and
          believes in him
     may have eternal life,
     and I shall raise him on the last day."

See Appendix A, p. 308, for the other readings.

FIRST READING
Dan 12:1-3; L1011.7

RESPONSORIAL PSALM
Ps 27:1, 4, 7, 8b, 9a, 13-14; L1013.3

SECOND READING
Rom 6:3-9; L1014.3

*or any other readings from L668 or any readings
from the Masses for the Dead (L1011–1015)*

Reflecting on the Gospel

We generally think of God's will as meaning what God wants *us* to do—obey God's laws. In this gospel God's will means what *God* wants to do—raise us up to have eternal Life. This day we celebrate the hope we have for our faithful departed, because of God's gracious will for each of us. The amazing assurance of this gospel is a clear statement of what God *wills* for us: God *wills* that we all be saved ("this is the will of my father . . . everyone . . . may have eternal life") and this has already been accomplished in Christ (see second reading). God our Father extends divine generosity and love toward us in Christ for the wildest wish possible: that we "have eternal life" and are raised up with Christ "on the last day." Christ assures us that this is the will of the Father for us.

Yes, indeed, here is the good news: God *wills* that we all be saved (gospel). Here is more good news: our salvation has already been accomplished in Christ through whom we are dead to sin and alive with new life (see second reading). Our share in new and eternal Life rests wholly on our identity with Christ and our firm belief in him. Because of Christ, those who have been faithful will not disappear into darkness but will shine brightly forever (see first reading).

This feast day reminds us that God is faithful to God's promise to save and that the victory of salvation is possible for all. We begin our lives by belonging to the Father who wills that not one of us be lost. God's will that we gain everlasting Life is so strong that God sent the only-begotten Son to unite with us in our weak humanity so that we can be raised to a share in divine Life. But temptations abound; we make choices selfishly to serve ourselves rather than gracefully serve others and do the will of God. Truly, there is a choice to be made in face of God's will for our salvation.

This festival honoring all the faithful departed also reminds us that victory is possible. On November 1 we celebrated the solemnity of All Saints. This November 2 commemoration of all the faithful departed is not a totally different feast. The souls in purgatory are like all of us weak human creatures; they have sinned. But they also have already won the victory; they have believed in the Son and are not lost. All that remains is the satisfaction for their weak moments and righting their relationships with God and others in the Body of Christ. The souls in purgatory are not lost; they have won their victory. We pray for them as brothers and sisters in Christ, in the communion of saints.

Living the Paschal Mystery

In the immediacy of our everyday lives we don't see how our specific choices to be faithful disciples are related to how we spend eternity. This festival in general and the gospel in particular remind us that we must believe in Christ. Belief, however, is not something passive. It is the right living which evidences our commitment to live our baptismal plunge into Christ's death and resurrection. This is the only way to new and eternal Life.

Each choice we make to believe in Christ and live as faithful disciples—no matter how small and seemingly insignificant the choice or action might be—truly does take us either closer to God and each other or farther away. The gospel invites us to think of our everyday choices as having consequences—eternal Life.

Focusing the Gospel
Key words and phrases: the will of my Father, have eternal life, I shall raise . . . on the last day

To the point: We generally think of God's will as meaning what God wants *us* to do—obey God's laws. In this gospel God's will means what *God* wants to do—raise us up to have eternal Life. This day we celebrate the hope we have for our faithful departed, because of God's gracious will for each of us.

Model Penitential Act
Presider: Today we commemorate the faithfulness of the souls in purgatory and pray that they might come to the fullness of risen Life. We pause to open ourselves to the great mystery of God's mercy . . . [pause]

    Lord Jesus, you came that not one of God's beloved be lost: Lord . . .

    Christ Jesus, you will raise the faithful to eternal Life: Christ . . .

    Lord Jesus, you fulfill the Father's will for our salvation: Lord . . .

Model Universal Prayer (Prayer of the Faithful)
Presider: We make our needs known to the God of mercy who wills that all be raised to eternal Life.

Response:

Lord, hear our prayer.

Cantor:

we pray to the Lord,

That all members of the church stand firm in the hope that the poor souls will receive eternal Life . . . [pause]

That all peoples of the world come to the fullness of Life God wills for them . . . [pause]

That those mourning the loss of a loved one find hope and consolation in God's promise of eternal Life . . . [pause]

That each of us here may discern God's will for us and be faithful to the Gospel . . . [pause]

Presider: Merciful God, you will that all people enter into eternal Life with you: hear these our prayers for ourselves and our beloved faithful departed and give us hope in the fullness of Life to come. We ask this through your Son, Jesus Christ our Lord. **Amen.**

COLLECT (from the first Mass)
Let us pray

Pause for silent prayer

Listen kindly to our prayers, O Lord,
and, as our faith in your Son,
raised from the dead, is deepened,
so may our hope of resurrection for your
    departed servants
also find new strength.
Through our Lord Jesus Christ, your Son,
who lives and reigns with you in the unity
    of the Holy Spirit,
one God, for ever and ever. **Amen.**

FOR REFLECTION
- What God wants me to do is . . . What God wants to do for me is . . .
- My will is in conformity with God's will for all to have eternal Life when . . .
- This feast day gives me hope for all those who have died in that . . . It gives me hope for . . .

Homily Points
- From early on in life, we tend to exert our own wills. Sometimes insisting on our own will has destructive consequences, for example, when we hurt another. Sometimes insisting on our own will is life-giving, for example, when we do good for another. God's will for us is always directed to the giving of life.

- This feast day is not about death but about life, not about sorrow but about hope. Our hope rests in the will of God, in the divine Savior who came to reveal that will to us, in the saints who have gone before us and have already received the fullness of Life. The souls in purgatory, whom we remember this day, are already saved and have already received God's mercy. After their purification, they will have the fullness of Life. This is God's gracious will.

✠ SPIRITUALITY

GOSPEL ACCLAMATION
Matt 5:3

R̸. Alleluia, alleluia.
Blessed are the poor in spirit,
for theirs is the kingdom of heaven.
R̸. Alleluia, alleluia.

Gospel

Mark 12:38-44; L155B

In the course of his teaching Jesus
said to the crowds,
"Beware of the scribes, who like
to go around in long robes
and accept greetings in the
marketplaces,
seats of honor in synagogues,
and places of honor at
banquets.
They devour the houses of
widows and, as a pretext
recite lengthy prayers.
They will receive a very severe
condemnation."

He sat down opposite the treasury
and observed how the crowd put
money into the treasury.
Many rich people put in large sums.
A poor widow also came and put in two
small coins worth a few cents.
Calling his disciples to himself, he said
to them,
"Amen, I say to you, this poor widow
put in more
than all the other contributors to the
treasury.
For they have all contributed from their
surplus wealth,
but she, from her poverty, has
contributed all she had,
her whole livelihood."

or Mark 12:41-44

See Appendix A, p. 309.

Reflecting on the Gospel

In this Sunday's gospel Jesus is observing how people of his time were making donations to the treasury. The score is clear—scribes: 0; widow: 1! But another layer of interpretation might be opened up besides considering who wins or who loses, who is miserly or who is generous, who is hypocritical or who is honest. This gospel is really a metaphor for true discipleship, a central theme in the Gospel of Mark. What does it mean to be a disciple of Jesus? Jesus tells us when he contrasts the behavior of the self-important and insincere scribes with the action of a poor and seemingly insignificant widow.

Jesus teaches the crowds to beware of the hypocrisy of the scribes who know God's word and law, yet seek places of honor and hurt those whom the law demands they protect—the widows. Jesus condemns them severely. "Calling his disciples to himself," he teaches them that they are not to do like the scribes. They are instead to do like the widow in the temple who gives all she has. True disciples give all they have, their whole livelihood—not goods, but *themselves*. The *amount* of what we have and give is really not important at all in the long run. What is important is how we regard and care for others; how we fulfill our responsibilities in the community; how we embrace the unlimited possibilities of deeper relationships, new riches, everlasting Life.

Without calculating the cost to herself, the widow gave "all she had," not out of her surplus. Disciples, too, give all they have without counting the cost, calculating self-gain, or seeking attention. The amazing thing about faithful discipleship is that God provides us with astonishing surplus: protection, talents, blessings. The "whole livelihood" disciples give is their very selves; disciples give of what God has already given them. Ultimately, discipleship is about good stewardship of who we are.

Similar to the surplus of meaning in the gospel, the first reading is really about more than a widow who risks the last bit of her flour and oil to respond to Elijah's need. Elijah rewards her obedience and generous hospitality—out of her need—with an abundance of flour and oil, enough to feed herself and her son for a whole year. The story depicts the hundredfold God returns to those who are so exceptionally generous. Paradoxically, by being generous to others we open ourselves to God's unbounded generosity toward us. Such is the hundredfold of those who are faithful disciples. Disciples give their all, and in turn receive what our generous God offers: "salvation to those who eagerly await him" (second reading).

Living the Paschal Mystery

We learn how to be good disciples from others who follow Jesus faithfully, who contribute to the good of all out of the surplus with which God has blessed them. The gospel holds up the poor widow as a model for the total self-giving of the true disciple. We need but look around us to find strong models for true discipleship. Nor is it a matter of these disciple-models giving large sums of money. Giving a bit of time each week for the good of another, participating in at least some parish activities beyond going to Mass and contributing to the collection basket, signing up when volunteers are needed are all ways of contributing a little, which makes a huge difference in overall parish life and community life. Even "something" can be our "all." So, are we true disciples?

Focusing the Gospel

Key words and phrases: teaching . . . the crowds, Beware of the scribes, severe condemnation, Calling his disciples, widow, contributed all she had, her whole livelihood

To the point: Jesus teaches the crowds to beware of the hypocrisy of the scribes who know God's word and law, yet seek places of honor and hurt those whom the law demands they protect—the widows. Jesus condemns them severely. "Calling his disciples to himself," he teaches them that they are not to do like the scribes. They are instead to do like the widow in the temple who gives all she has. True disciples give all they have, their whole livelihood—not goods, but *themselves*. So, are we true disciples?

Connecting the Gospel

to the first reading: Like the widow in the gospel who gives all she has, the widow of Zarephath gives the last bit of what she has for the man of God. The widow in the gospel does not go unnoticed by Jesus; the widow of Zarephath does not go unrewarded by God.

to experience: The law of survival tells us to watch out for ourselves first. The law of the Gospel tells us to give of ourselves first. Which law do we live by?

Connecting the Responsorial Psalm

to the readings: Psalm 146 tells of how God cares without fail for those in need—the hungry, the disabled, the bowed down, the widowed. We sang these verses from Psalm 146 on the Twenty-Third Sunday in Ordinary Time when Jesus cured a deaf-mute brought to him by the crowd. This Sunday we catch a glimpse of two widows who have lost almost everything yet willingly give to God the little they have left. God rewards the first with abundant sustenance; Jesus identifies the second as the model for all discipleship. If we are to be fully committed disciples we must give all we have for the sake of the kingdom. Nothing can be held back. When we find ourselves left with nothing because of the kingdom, we needn't fear, for we will have staked our security on a God who holds nothing back in return (psalm).

to psalmist preparation: This responsorial psalm needs to be sung with confidence in God's providence and protection. But unless you give all that you have—your whole heart—you will never discover what God is giving you in return. What do you hold back? What would give you the courage to hand it over?

**ASSEMBLY &
FAITH-SHARING GROUPS**
- I act like the scribes when I . . . I act like the widow when I . . .
- For me, discipleship means . . . I become a true disciple when I . . .
- As a disciple I have given . . . I have yet to give . . .

PRESIDERS
As presider I model for the assembly what it means to give all even when I feel I have little to give when . . .

DEACONS
I am most able to give myself to those whom I serve when . . .

HOSPITALITY MINISTERS
Like Jesus, my role as a hospitality minister is to recognize those who seem insignificant. I find this difficult when . . . I find this easy when . . .

MUSIC MINISTERS
I hold myself back in my music ministry when . . . What helps me give my all is . . .

ALTAR MINISTERS
The "all" I give each time I minister at the altar is . . .

LECTORS
As I prepare for proclamation, Jesus teaches me . . .

**EXTRAORDINARY MINISTERS
OF HOLY COMMUNION**
At every eucharistic celebration, Jesus gives fully of himself to us, and so my response is to give . . .

Model Penitential Act

Presider: The gospel today tells about the poor widow who gave two small coins to the temple treasury. As we prepare to celebrate this liturgy, let us look into our hearts and see what we are prepared to give to the Lord Jesus . . . [pause]

Lord Jesus, you gave your all for our salvation: Lord . . .

Christ Jesus, you are the fullness of Life we seek: Christ . . .

Lord Jesus, you are the Teacher who calls us to discipleship: Lord . . .

Homily Points

• Teachers, employers, civil officials, etc., are leaders from whom we expect integrity. When they seek personal gain instead of fulfilling the responsibility and expectations of their positions, we become disillusioned, disheartened, and even angry. Instead of giving self, they serve self.

• The scribes were responsible for transmitting the Jewish faith. They copied the scrolls and taught the word and law of God. However, they often did not live what they taught. They served themselves instead of giving themselves. Jesus calls his disciples to him and instructs them on how to become new "scribes" who authentically transmit and teach the faith that Jesus reveals and fulfills. As with the widow in the gospel, disciples are to give their all—their very selves.

• Now we are Jesus' disciples, we are the new "scribes" called to authentically transmit and teach what Jesus reveals and fulfills. We are to *live* Gospel values. This is the primary way we teach. We teach, for example, when our loving is self-giving; when we care for the downtrodden; when we persist in reaching out to anyone in need even when we seemingly have little to give. Instead of serving self, we give self—our all.

Model Universal Prayer (Prayer of the Faithful)

Presider: Knowing that we need God's help to be true disciples, let us pray for strength and make our needs known.

Response:

Lord,   hear   our   prayer.

Cantor:

we pray   to   the Lord,

That all members of the church be generous in giving self to God and others wholeheartedly . . . [pause]

That leaders of nations may serve those they govern with integrity and authentic self-giving . . . [pause]

That those who need or seek models of integrity look to Jesus' true disciples for direction for their lives . . . [pause]

That all members of our community continue to learn from Jesus and grow in true discipleship . . . [pause]

Presider: Gracious God, your divine Son calls disciples and teaches them the meaning of giving self for others: hear these our prayers and strengthen us to follow what Jesus teaches. We ask this through that same Jesus Christ our Lord. **Amen.**

COLLECT

Let us pray

Pause for silent prayer

Almighty and merciful God,
graciously keep from us all adversity,
so that, unhindered in mind and body
    alike,
we may pursue in freedom of heart
the things that are yours.
Through our Lord Jesus Christ, your Son,
who lives and reigns with you in the unity
    of the Holy Spirit,
one God, for ever and ever. **Amen.**

FIRST READING

1 Kgs 17:10-16

In those days, Elijah the prophet went to
    Zarephath.
As he arrived at the entrance of the city,
    a widow was gathering sticks there; he
    called out to her,
    "Please bring me a small cupful of
    water to drink."
She left to get it, and he called out after
    her,
    "Please bring along a bit of bread."
She answered, "As the LORD, your God,
    lives,
    I have nothing baked; there is only a
    handful of flour in my jar
and a little oil in my jug.
Just now I was collecting a couple of
    sticks,
    to go in and prepare something for
    myself and my son;
    when we have eaten it, we shall die."
Elijah said to her, "Do not be afraid.
Go and do as you propose.
But first make me a little cake and bring
    it to me.
Then you can prepare something for
    yourself and your son.
For the LORD, the God of Israel, says,
    'The jar of flour shall not go empty,
    nor the jug of oil run dry,
    until the day when the LORD sends rain
    upon the earth.'"
She left and did as Elijah had said.
She was able to eat for a year, and he and
    her son as well;
    the jar of flour did not go empty,
    nor the jug of oil run dry,
    as the LORD had foretold through Elijah.

RESPONSORIAL PSALM
Ps 146:7, 8-9, 9-10

℟. (1b) Praise the Lord, my soul!
or:
℟. Alleluia.

The LORD keeps faith forever,
secures justice for the oppressed,
gives food to the hungry.
The LORD sets captives free.

℟. Praise the Lord, my soul!
or:
℟. Alleluia.

The LORD gives sight to the blind;
the LORD raises up those who were bowed down.
The LORD loves the just;
the LORD protects strangers.

℟. Praise the Lord, my soul!
or:
℟. Alleluia.

The fatherless and the widow he sustains,
but the way of the wicked he thwarts.
The LORD shall reign forever;
your God, O Zion, through all generations. Alleluia.

℟. Praise the Lord, my soul!
or:
℟. Alleluia.

SECOND READING
Heb 9:24-28

Christ did not enter into a sanctuary made by hands,
a copy of the true one, but heaven itself,
that he might now appear before God on our behalf.
Not that he might offer himself repeatedly,
as the high priest enters each year into the sanctuary
with blood that is not his own;
if that were so, he would have had to suffer repeatedly
from the foundation of the world.
But now once for all he has appeared at the end of the ages
to take away sin by his sacrifice.
Just as it is appointed that human beings die once,
and after this the judgment, so also Christ,
offered once to take away the sins of many,
will appear a second time, not to take away sin
but to bring salvation to those who eagerly await him.

CATECHESIS

About Liturgy

Discipleship and intercession for the dead: We have recently celebrated All Souls' Day, and we customarily keep all of November as a month when we remember the dead. Rather than our remembrance of the dead becoming just a rote or mechanical practice, we might consciously place our prayers for the dead in the larger context of true discipleship. Praying for the dead beyond our own loved ones is an act of discipleship because it evidences our connection with each other as members of the Body of Christ and our continued care and concern for one another.

Traditionally the church prays for the faithful departed each night at the intercessions during Evening Prayer and this is structurally where this intention belongs. Since most of our parishioners do not regularly celebrate Liturgy of the Hours, this presents a pastoral problem—when do we as a community pray for the dead? Many parishes include an intention for those who have died as part of the universal prayer (prayer of the faithful) at Sunday Mass. Although there is nothing "wrong" with this, it might be kept in mind that this practice is by way of exception and pastoral sensitivity rather than tradition. The principle here is that as a Christian community we do pray together for the faithful departed. Perhaps a good pastoral compromise might be to include at Sunday Mass an intention for the deceased only when someone in the parish has died during that week. A model might be "That N. and all the faithful departed enjoy everlasting Life, standing with Jesus at the messianic banquet . . . [pause]."

About Liturgical Music

Music suggestions: Herman Stuempfle's "The Temple Rang with Golden Coins" (HG, W4) is based on this Sunday's gospel story of the widow's mite. Stuempfle connects the widow's offering of all she had with Christ's self-offering on the cross: "At last he brought his offering And laid it on a tree; There gave himself, his life, his love For all humanity" (v. 4). The hymn would be effective during preparation of the gifts. "I Surrender All" and "Is Your All on the Altar" (both in LMGM2) address the call to give our all to God. The first sings peacefully about the self-gift already given. The second asks repeatedly, "Is your all on the altar of sacrifice laid? Your heart does the Spirit control? You can only be blest, and have peace and sweet rest, as you yield him your body and soul." Either would be appropriate for the preparation of the gifts or for Communion.

NOVEMBER 8, 2015

THIRTY-SECOND SUNDAY IN ORDINARY TIME

SPIRITUALITY

GOSPEL ACCLAMATION
Luke 21:36

R⁊. Alleluia, alleluia.
Be vigilant at all times
and pray that you have the strength to
stand before the Son of Man.
R⁊. Alleluia, alleluia.

Gospel

Mark 13:24-32; L158B

**Jesus said to his disciples:
"In those days after that
tribulation
the sun will be darkened,
and the moon will not give its
light,
and the stars will be falling from
the sky,
and the powers in the heavens
will be shaken.**

**"And then they will see 'the Son of
Man coming in the clouds'
with great power and glory,
and then he will send out the angels
and gather his elect from the four
winds,
from the end of the earth to the end
of the sky.**

**"Learn a lesson from the fig tree.
When its branch becomes tender and
sprouts leaves,
you know that summer is near.
In the same way, when you see these
things happening,
know that he is near, at the gates.
Amen, I say to you,
this generation will not pass away
until all these things have taken
place.
Heaven and earth will pass away,
but my words will not pass away.**

**"But of that day or hour, no one knows,
neither the angels in heaven, nor the
Son, but only the Father."**

Reflecting on the Gospel

At this time when we near the end of another liturgical year, the Lectionary includes gospels about the end times that call for us to look far into the future. These gospels inevitably paint a dark and dismal picture of calamity and doom, and so we often dismiss them. The apocalyptic (the word "apocalyptic" comes from the Greek which means to "uncover" or "reveal") imagery of this Sunday's gospel ("sun will be darkened," "moon will not give its light," "stars will be falling from the sky," and "powers in the heavens will be shaken") is no exception. We are tempted to ask, "When, Lord?" Jesus' answer, "no one knows," ought to bring us to pay more attention to the present. Now is an opportune time for the in-breaking of Christ. Now is what counts. The future is now.

We think of Jesus' Second Coming as a future event. In fact, the darkening of the sun and moon and stars is already happening in the trials and tribulations that not only beset the first disciples, but also are part of our own lives. Jesus promises that all these things will happen. He further promises that he is "near, at the gates." This gospel is about the ultimate victory over darkness that belongs to those who are faithful. That victory is now. The future is now.

What ought to startle us into sober reality is that we know the end will come. Like the gospel, Daniel's vision describes in the first reading "a time unsurpassed in distress." Also like the gospel, his vision reveals the victory of those "written in the book" who are the elect, those who have been faithful. We have all the means at hand to face darkness and evil with confidence, assured that one day we "shall live forever." The future holds no fear for us; rather than fear, we anticipate our future with joyful expectation, because the one we await is within and among us now. The future is now.

In previous gospel passages, Jesus' teaching about future events dealt with his impending suffering, death, and resurrection. Jesus predicted several times the coming end of his earthly life, which was not too far into the future. The disciples could not hear what Jesus was teaching; they could not envision a future such as Jesus predicted. In this gospel, too, he teaches about the future; however, this time his words deal with an unknown, distant future, with cosmic events, which his final coming in power to overcome darkness, and with his drawing the elect into the light of his final glory. Jesus uses the image of the greening of "the fig tree" when summer is near as a sign that "he is near." Summer is a time of life, growth, fruitfulness. Those who hear and heed his words are in the greening of their lives; they choose for themselves life, growth, fruitfulness. For them, the future is now.

Living the Paschal Mystery

Just as big calamities are not what the future is really about, neither are big deeds what our present is about. Our present is about doing the little things well, and we know how we "lead the many to justice" (first reading): by listening to Jesus' words. Jesus has already given us all we need to have our names "written in the book." We just need to live like he did: with compassion and understanding, wisdom and care, love and hope.

Focusing the Gospel

Key words and phrases: darkened, powers in the heavens will be shaken, Son of Man coming, fig tree . . . sprouts, summer is near, he is near

To the point: In previous gospel passages, Jesus' teaching about future events dealt with his impending suffering, death, and resurrection. In this gospel, too, he teaches about the future; however, this time his words deal with cosmic events, his final coming in power to overcome darkness, and his drawing the elect into the light of his final glory. Jesus uses the image of the greening of "the fig tree" when summer is near as a sign that "he is near." Those who hear and heed his words are in the greening of their lives. For them, the future is now.

Connecting the Gospel

to the first reading: The gospel refers to the demise of the cosmos; Daniel's vision describes "a time unsurpassed in distress." Those "written in the book" of Daniel's vision are the elect whom the Son of Man will gather at the end of time.

to experience: The end of the world is a prediction taken as literal and immediate by some or dismissed as a joke by others. For still others, it is of no concern at all. Jesus teaches that "no one knows" when the end will happen, yet its very prediction should bring the end of time and his final coming to an immediacy that shapes how we choose to live now.

Connecting the Responsorial Psalm

to the readings: There will come a time of tribulation and great suffering when the world as we know it will end and certainties will be shattered (first reading, gospel). But Christ assures us that this collapse of things will be no more than the announcement of his coming (gospel) when he will send his angels to gather the elect (gospel)—those who have lived by wisdom and justice (first reading)—into Life everlasting. No one knows the moment of his coming (gospel), but the readings and psalm promise life-giving judgment for those who have been faithful.

The readings—as well as Jesus' life—reveal that faithful discipleship will not protect us from catastrophe, suffering, and death. Ironically it will lead us directly to them. But we have Jesus' word as our surety (gospel) and God's promise as our hope (psalm). As we continue to walk with Jesus toward Jerusalem, we pray today that we maintain our focus on God who is our "path" and our "inheritance" (psalm).

to psalmist preparation: As you prepare to sing this responsorial psalm, ask yourself if you really believe that God is your inheritance. What hope does this give you for the future? What strength for the present?

ASSEMBLY & FAITH-SHARING GROUPS
- I think about the end of the world when . . . I ought to think about the end of the world when . . .
- The darkness that Jesus' coming dispels in my life is . . . I need the Light to shine on . . .
- The words of Jesus that speak to me most clearly now are . . . They bring life to me in that . . .

PRESIDERS
Jesus' image of the greening of "the fig tree" challenges the way I minister in that . . .

DEACONS
My service ministry reveals that Jesus is near when I . . .

HOSPITALITY MINISTERS
My openhearted hospitality gathers people "from the end of the earth to the end of the sky" to the nearness of Jesus in that . . .

MUSIC MINISTERS
My music ministry announces that Jesus is near when I . . .

ALTAR MINISTERS
My serving at the altar announces that Jesus is near when I . . .

LECTORS
The manner of my proclamation indicates that Jesus' teaching has taken hold in me and the way I live when I . . .

EXTRAORDINARY MINISTERS OF HOLY COMMUNION
My manner of distributing Holy Communion indicates that the future coming of Jesus is now when I . . .

✠ CELEBRATION

Model Penitential Act

Presider: Today's gospel speaks of the tribulations accompanying Jesus' Second Coming; it also assures us of his nearness now. As we prepare to celebrate this liturgy, let us ask God's mercy for the times we have not been attentive to Jesus' nearness . . . [pause]

Lord Jesus, your words will not pass away: Lord . . .

Christ Jesus, you will come in glory at the end of time: Christ . . .

Lord Jesus, you are the hope and salvation of all people: Lord . . .

Homily Points

- After a hard, cold, difficult winter, how welcome is the greening of late spring into early summer! The rhythms of nature affect us, capture us, direct us. Even when we do not pay conscious attention to them, we are drawn into their changes. In nature, beginning and ending are blurred in the ever-repeated pattern of death and life. What seems to be an end is, in fact, a beginning.

- In this gospel Jesus predicts the end of the old, created world; he also announces the beginning of a new world order. This new world order is the reign of God: darkness giving way to light, dormancy giving way to new growth and life. The words of Jesus in this gospel communicate hope for those who may hear only the destruction and darkness this gospel foretells: when our world is falling apart, he is breaking in. He is eternal Light. He is always near.

- We must remain focused on Jesus, and when we do so the end times hold no fear for us. We remain focused on Jesus, for example, when we continue to study and pray over his words; when we remain faithful to the dying and rising rhythm of life; when we see his face in the goodness of others, in the surprise of an unexpected gift, in those we encounter each day. Immersed in the now, we find him always near. In his nearness, the new world order dawns anew each day.

Model Universal Prayer (Prayer of the Faithful)

Presider: God sends the Son as our hope and strength who is always near. And so we pray with confidence for our needs.

Response:

Lord, hear our prayer.

Cantor:

we pray to the Lord,

For all members of the church to focus on the nearness of Jesus and come to deeper Life in him . . . [pause]

For all peoples of the world to come to salvation . . . [pause]

For all those in any need to encounter the nearness of Jesus who brings comfort and care . . . [pause]

For all of us here gathered to welcome new beginnings and possibilities that come in everyday encounters with others . . . [pause]

Presider: God of heaven and earth, you gather all people into your loving care: hear these our prayers, bring us to newness of life now, and keep us faithful unto Life everlasting. We ask this through your Son, Jesus Christ our Lord. **Amen.**

COLLECT

Let us pray

Pause for silent prayer

Grant us, we pray, O Lord our God,
the constant gladness of being devoted
    to you,
for it is full and lasting happiness
to serve with constancy
the author of all that is good.
Through our Lord Jesus Christ, your Son,
who lives and reigns with you in the unity
    of the Holy Spirit,
one God, for ever and ever. **Amen.**

FIRST READING

Dan 12:1-3

In those days, I, Daniel,
    heard this word of the Lord:
"At that time there shall arise
    Michael, the great prince,
    guardian of your people;
it shall be a time unsurpassed in distress
    since nations began until that time.
At that time your people shall escape,
    everyone who is found written in the
    book.

"Many of those who sleep in the dust of
    the earth shall awake;
some shall live forever,
others shall be an everlasting horror
    and disgrace.

"But the wise shall shine brightly
    like the splendor of the firmament,
and those who lead the many to justice
    shall be like the stars forever."

RESPONSORIAL PSALM

Ps 16:5, 8, 9-10, 11

℟. (1) You are my inheritance, O Lord!

O LORD, my allotted portion and my cup,
    you it is who hold fast my lot.
I set the LORD ever before me;
    with him at my right hand I shall not be
        disturbed.

℟. You are my inheritance, O Lord!

Therefore my heart is glad and my soul
    rejoices,
    my body, too, abides in confidence;
because you will not abandon my soul to
    the netherworld,
    nor will you suffer your faithful one to
        undergo corruption.

℟. You are my inheritance, O Lord!

You will show me the path to life,
    fullness of joys in your presence,
    the delights at your right hand forever.

℟. You are my inheritance, O Lord!

SECOND READING

Heb 10:11-14, 18

Brothers and sisters:
Every priest stands daily at his ministry,
    offering frequently those same sacrifices
        that can never take away sins.
But this one offered one sacrifice for sins,
    and took his seat forever at the right
        hand of God;
    now he waits until his enemies are made
        his footstool.
For by one offering
    he has made perfect forever those who
        are being consecrated.

Where there is forgiveness of these,
    there is no longer offering for sin.

About Liturgy

Parousia and eschatology: "Parousia" is a technical theological term that refers to Jesus' Second Coming. This Sunday's gospel only mentions the great cosmic events that will accompany his return. Additionally, when Christ comes at the end of time there will be the general judgment (see Matt 25) and general resurrection. If this Second Coming would be all there is at the end times, then perhaps there could be reason for fear. However, the Parousia isn't all there is—it ushers in the final age of fulfillment. This time of fulfillment is theologically referred to as the "eschatological times." This strange term comes from two Greek words meaning the study of finality or end times. Eschatology, then, marks the point (not to be understood chronologically) in time when God's reign will be finally and fully established.

It is easy to put these future events out of our heads; most of us (when we think of them at all, usually only on these last Sundays of the liturgical year) think of the end times as way off in the future. Contrary, in the very early church they thought that Christ would return immediately and so they lived their lives in a most radical way— sharing all things in common, devoting themselves to prayer, etc. (see, for example, Acts 2:42-47 and Acts 4:32-35). One of the challenges of these future events is that we, too, learn to live in the present as faithful disciples, making Christ's saving Presence known in our world. We are to live in expectation, not in fear.

About Liturgical Music

Music suggestions: Timothy Dudley-Smith's "From the Father's Throne on High" (W4) speaks of Christ's return "to rule and reign" and would be a suitable entrance hymn. Dudley-Smith's "When the Lord in Glory Comes" (W4) identifies the voice and face of Christ as what will be most important when the end times come. The setting by Bob Moore can be sung responsorially with cantor(s) and choir leading and the assembly joining in on the repeats of the final phrase. This piece would be effective during the preparation of the gifts. The well-known Quaker hymn "How Can I Keep from Singing" (found in most resources) speaks of our hope in the midst of tumult and tribulation because we know "love is Lord of heaven and earth." This hymn would work during the preparation of the gifts or as a choral prelude using, for example, Paul Gibson's arrangement (OCP #9202). Andraé Crouch's "Soon and Very Soon" (found in most resources) would make an excellent recessional song, letting us sing our "Hallelujah!" as we prepare for Christ's return in glory.

SPIRITUALITY

GOSPEL ACCLAMATION
Mark 11:9, 10

R⁄. Alleluia, alleluia.
Blessed is he who comes in the name of the
    Lord!
Blessed is the kingdom of our father David that
    is to come!
R⁄. Alleluia, alleluia.

Gospel

John 18:33b-37; L161B

Pilate said to Jesus,
  "Are you the King
    of the Jews?"
Jesus answered, "Do
  you say this on
  your own
  or have others told
    you about me?"
Pilate answered, "I am
  not a Jew, am I?
Your own nation and the
  chief priests handed
  you over to me.
What have you done?"
Jesus answered, "My kingdom does not
  belong to this world.
If my kingdom did belong to this world,
  my attendants would be fighting
  to keep me from being handed over
    to the Jews.
But as it is, my kingdom is not here."
So Pilate said to him, "Then you are a
  king?"
Jesus answered, "You say I am a king.
For this I was born and for this I came
  into the world,
  to testify to the truth.
Everyone who belongs to the truth
  listens to my voice."

Reflecting on the Gospel

On this last Sunday of the liturgical year we honor the victory of Christ over suffering and death, over evil and infidelity, over this world and all its lures. In this conversation Pilate questions Jesus about his identity ("Are you the King of the Jews?") and about why he is on trial ("What have you done?"). What unfolds is a conversation about two very different worlds. That of Pilate and the chief priests, in which fighting, falsehood, and obstinacy predominate. That of Jesus, in which life, truth, and openness prevail. Yes, Jesus is a King—but of a kingdom different from Herod's. What he has done is reveal a kingdom that "does not belong to this world," but is meant to transform it. From evil to goodness. From sinfulness to salvation. From death to life.

We clearly see that Jesus' kingdom is not of this world. Christ's kingdom is not a spatial place ("does not belong to this world"), but an interior identity defined by our relationship to Christ the King. This Sunday we celebrate a King whose Presence and power we have already experienced: Christ, whose kingdom is not territory but virtue, not power but service, not wealth but grace. This King has loved us with his very life.

"My kingdom does not belong to this world." Where is Jesus' kingdom? It exists wherever people embody Jesus' manner of acting and relating ("belongs to the truth"), wherever the Spirit of Jesus is the rule of life. We enter into Jesus' kingdom whenever we listen to his voice and proclaim him "the Alpha and the Omega" (second reading) of all that is. The liturgical year culminates with a summary statement of the identity of Jesus—"Christ the King." As Christ, he is worthy of our worship. As King, he is deserving of our service. As we celebrate this enthronement of Christ in glory (compare first reading), we also look forward to his victory in us when we are "freed . . . from our sins" and "made . . . into a kingdom" (second reading).

Thus this solemnity invites us to renew our commitment to serve him with all our hearts. It invites us to renew our self-giving stance as disciples who follow our King. In our self-giving we are transformed, and as we are transformed so is the world because he has made us into a kingdom (second reading). The surprise of this day is that we are God's kingdom already. We already share in his victory for we are "freed from our sins."

At the end of this liturgical year we are invited by the liturgy once again to fall in love with our King who has won for us eternal Life. "[T]o him be glory and power forever and ever. Amen" (second reading).

Living the Paschal Mystery

Self-giving service is a small price to pay for our share in this eternal glory. Living the paschal mystery means that we don't count the cost, but always find strength, hope, encouragement in the glimpse of final victory that we are repeatedly given throughout the liturgical year. Living the paschal mystery means that we see the victorious Christ even in the everyday trials and difficulties that we face. Living the paschal mystery means that we are ever faithful to the rhythm of dying and rising as it unfolds in our everyday prayer, work, and leisure. Living the paschal mystery means that we are "priests" (that is, mediators) for those whom we meet—that we are the Body of Christ leading others to holier lives and happier commitment. If someone should then ask us, "What have you done?" (see gospel) our answer would come quickly and surely—we have served our King. We have loved our King. In doing so, we have shared in the greatest wealth possible—his kingdom where all is glory.

Focusing the Gospel

Key words and phrases: Are you the King of the Jews?, What have you done?, My kingdom does not belong to this world, belongs to the truth, listens to my voice

To the point: In this conversation Pilate questions Jesus about his identity ("Are you the King of the Jews?") and about why he is on trial ("What have you done?"). What unfolds is a conversation about two very different worlds. That of Pilate and the chief priests, in which fighting, falsehood, and obstinacy predominate. That of Jesus, in which life, truth, and openness prevail. Yes, Jesus is a King—but of a kingdom different from Herod's. What he has done is reveal a kingdom that "does not belong to this world," but is meant to transform it. From evil to goodness. From sinfulness to salvation. From death to life.

Connecting the Gospel

to the first and second readings: As we celebrate this enthronement of Christ in glory as the "Son of man [who] received dominion, glory, and kingship" (first reading), we also look forward to his victory in us when we are "freed . . . from our sins" and "made . . . into a kingdom" (second reading).

to experience: We have a limited understanding of kings today, and when we think about them, it tends to be from history and/or memory rather than from our immediate experience. This Sunday we celebrate a King whose Presence and power we have experienced: Christ, whose kingdom is not territory but virtue, not power but service, not wealth but grace.

Connecting the Responsorial Psalm

to the readings: The whole of Psalm 93 depicts the cosmic conflict between the forces of evil and the power of God. The Hebrews pictured the world as a platform balanced on the chaotic waters of the sea. The surging waters constantly threatened to overwhelm the earth, and would have done so were it not for the stabilizing hand of God who "made the world firm, not to be moved" (psalm). There was no doubt in the minds of the Israelites that God held ultimate power over all the forces threatening their life and well-being.

We sing these verses from Psalm 93 to celebrate the victory of Christ over sin and death. Throughout the weeks of Ordinary Time we have listened to his voice and obeyed his call to discipleship. We have walked with him to Jerusalem and the cross. This Sunday we celebrate the glory that awaits us beyond the cross. We proclaim to the world that "The Lord is King . . . robed in majesty" (psalm) and that we are his kingdom (second reading), not to be moved (psalm).

to psalmist preparation: The conviction with which you will sing this psalm will be directly related to the faithfulness with which you have walked this year's journey through Ordinary Time. Take time this week to thank Christ for showing you the way and for strengthening you when you felt weak and weary. Take time also to thank Christ for the many other faithful disciples who have walked with you.

**ASSEMBLY &
FAITH-SHARING GROUPS**
- I live in Pilate's world when I . . . I live in Jesus' kingdom when I . . .
- Who/what helps me listen to Jesus' voice is . . .
- The truth of Jesus' kingdom that transforms my world is . . .

PRESIDERS
My way of being a servant priest invites my people to be better servants of Christ the King when . . .

DEACONS
My serving makes visible Christ's kingdom when I . . .

HOSPITALITY MINISTERS
My manner of welcoming members of the assembly helps them become more conscious of their dignity as servants of Christ the King when . . .

MUSIC MINISTERS
My manner of doing music ministry reveals Christ's kingdom in that . . .

ALTAR MINISTERS
My ministry of service exemplifies the spirit of Christ's kingdom by . . .

LECTORS
My awareness of belonging "to the truth" helps me proclaim better the word of God because . . .

**EXTRAORDINARY MINISTERS
OF HOLY COMMUNION**
My manner of distributing Holy Communion helps people experience more fully their coming to the banquet of the Messiah-King when . . .

CELEBRATION

Model Penitential Act

Presider: Today we acclaim Christ as our King. Let us look into our hearts and see how Christ is enthroned there . . . [pause]

> Lord Jesus, your kingdom is not of this world: Lord . . .
>
> Christ Jesus, you are King of the universe: Christ . . .
>
> Lord Jesus, you receive all dominion and glory and service: Lord . . .

Homily Points

- Realistically, we all live in both the world of Pilate and that of Jesus. We have one foot in the world of fighting, falsehood, and obstinacy and the other foot in the world of life, truth, and openness. We spend all our lives getting both feet into one world or the other. Which world do we choose?

- Jesus is on trial before Pilate. The stakes are high—the verdict is life or death. Yet Jesus and Pilate seem to quibble over words about worlds. Does Jesus look like a king? No. Does Jesus act like a king? No. Does Jesus say he is a king? Not really, even though he admits, "My kingdom does not belong to this world." Born a babe in meager surroundings, yet he was born "to testify to the truth." A King, indeed!

- Jesus "was born" and "came into the world" to establish his kingdom over the ruling forces of the world. Jesus is our King—our model, our head. He embodies the fullest expression of what God intends for human beings: "testify to the truth," belong "to the truth," and listen and heed Jesus' voice. Jesus makes clear what his kingdom is. Do we hear him? Do we follow him?

Model Universal Prayer (Prayer of the Faithful)

Presider: God intends for human beings to belong to the kingdom of God with Christ as the King. Let us pray that we be good servants of this King.

Response:

Lord, hear our prayer.

Cantor:

we pray to the Lord,

That Christ's reign be visible through the loving service of all members of the church . . . [pause]

That Christ's reign be visible through all peoples' commitment to truth, justice, and peace . . . [pause]

That Christ's reign be visible through our active concern for the suffering, for the poor, for those who are imprisoned or persecuted . . . [pause]

That Christ's reign be visible in our daily choices to be faithful to his kingdom rather than to the kingdom of the world . . . [pause]

Presider: Father all-powerful, God of love, you raised your Son to risen Life and seated him at your right hand in glory where he reigns as King for ever: hear these our prayers and help us to be faithful in our service of him. We ask this in the name of Jesus Christ the King now and for ever. **Amen.**

COLLECT

Let us pray

Pause for silent prayer

Almighty ever-living God,
whose will is to restore all things
in your beloved Son, the King of the
    universe,
grant, we pray,
that the whole creation, set free from
    slavery,
may render your majesty service
and ceaselessly proclaim your praise.
Through our Lord Jesus Christ, your Son,
who lives and reigns with you in the unity
    of the Holy Spirit,
one God, for ever and ever. **Amen.**

FIRST READING

Dan 7:13-14

As the visions during the night continued,
    I saw
  one like a Son of man coming,
    on the clouds of heaven;
  when he reached the Ancient One
    and was presented before him,
  the one like a Son of man received
    dominion, glory, and kingship;
  all peoples, nations, and languages
    serve him.
His dominion is an everlasting dominion
    that shall not be taken away,
  his kingship shall not be destroyed.

RESPONSORIAL PSALM
Ps 93:1, 1-2, 5

R⁊. (1a) The Lord is king; he is robed in majesty.

The LORD is king, in splendor robed;
   robed is the LORD and girt about with
      strength.

R⁊. The Lord is king; he is robed in majesty.

And he has made the world firm,
   not to be moved.
Your throne stands firm from of old;
   from everlasting you are, O LORD.

R⁊. The Lord is king; he is robed in majesty.

Your decrees are worthy of trust indeed;
   holiness befits your house,
   O LORD, for length of days.

R⁊. The Lord is king; he is robed in majesty.

SECOND READING
Rev 1:5-8

Jesus Christ is the faithful witness,
   the firstborn of the dead and ruler of
      the kings of the earth.
To him who loves us and has freed us from
      our sins by his blood,
   who has made us into a kingdom,
      priests for his God and Father,
   to him be glory and power forever and
      ever. Amen.

Behold, he is coming amid the clouds,
   and every eye will see him,
   even those who pierced him.
All the peoples of the earth will lament
      him.
   Yes. Amen.

"I am the Alpha and the Omega," says the
   Lord God,
   "the one who is and who was and who
      is to come, the almighty."

About Liturgy

Celebration: Just as Lent opens onto Easter, if we have patiently worked our way through Ordinary Time—and, indeed, through the whole of this past liturgical year—when we come to this solemnity we are ready for a jubilant celebration. The fruits of our labors will be consistent with the extent of our labors. If our liturgical year has been rather lackadaisical, then these high festivals probably won't move us. We will depend on the environment and the music to carry us rather than on the inner strength that comes from watching ourselves be transformed ever more perfectly into the Body of Christ during this past year.

Liturgical celebration has little to do with "whoop-dee-do" and much to do with self-emptying. Our greatest joy and celebration come not from what we do but from the deep experience of what God has done in us. We need to be careful that we don't cloud the real meaning of these high festivals with externals that actually keep us from the deepest and most satisfying feasting. Celebration is really the play between surrender and encounter in which we are transformed. Anything less than this gets in the way of our being God's Presence, God's reign in this redeemed world.

About Liturgical Music

Music suggestions: Closing the journey of Ordinary Time, this solemnity is like a second Easter. We would want to use our most festive service music (for example, the Easter season set). We might use an SATB setting of the responsorial psalm. We might do a full gospel procession with an extended Alleluia. We might use "Lift High the Cross" (most appropriate this year when the gospel reading is taken from the passion of John) for the entrance procession and add brass. Or we might sing Richard Hilbert's majestic Easter hymn "Festival Canticle: Worthy Is Christ." During a quieter moment such as the preparation of the gifts or Communion, we might sing the Christmas hymn "Of the Father's Love Begotten." Singing about the babe born on Christmas who now reigns as Alpha and Omega of all time and history will bring the liturgical year full circle.

Assessing another year of music ministry: This solemnity bringing the liturgical year to a close is an opportunity to evaluate how well the music ministry has enabled people to enter more fully into the paschal mystery of Christ. How have the cantors and choir members grown in faithful discipleship through the doing of music ministry? How has the music sung this year led assembly members to give themselves over to God's work of transformation? The criterion for answering these questions will not be whether people have stomped their feet and clapped their hands during the music, but whether the music has led them to surrender themselves more fully to the dying and rising mystery of Christ whose Body they are.

SPIRITUALITY

GOSPEL ACCLAMATION
1 Thess 5:18

R̕. Alleluia, alleluia.
In all circumstances, give thanks,
for this is the will of God for you in Christ Jesus.
R̕. Alleluia, alleluia.

Gospel   Luke 17:11-19; L947.6

As Jesus continued his
   journey to Jerusalem,
   he traveled through Samaria and Galilee.
As he was entering a vil-
   lage, ten lepers met
   him.
They stood at a distance
   from him and raised
   their voices, saying,
   "Jesus, Master! Have
   pity on us!"
And when he saw them, he said,
   "Go show yourselves to the priests."
As they were going they were cleansed.
And one of them, realizing he had been
   healed,
   returned, glorifying God in a loud voice;
   and he fell at the feet of Jesus and
   thanked him.
He was a Samaritan.
Jesus said in reply,
   "Ten were cleansed, were they not?
Where are the other nine?
Has none but this foreigner returned to
   give thanks to God?"
Then he said to him, "Stand up and go;
   your faith has saved you."

See Appendix A, p. 309, for the other readings.

FIRST READING
Sir 50:22-24; L943.2

RESPONSORIAL PSALM
Ps 138:1-2a, 2bc-3, 4-5; L945.3

SECOND READING
1 Cor 1:3-9; L944.1

*Additional reading choices may be found in the
Lectionary for Mass, vol. IV, "In Thanksgiving to
God," nos. 943–947.*

Reflecting on the Gospel

Some of our high festivals have been transferred to Sunday so that more people can celebrate them, for example, Epiphany, the Body and Blood of Christ, and Ascension. Most people—because of work schedules and family commitments—find it difficult to be at church during the week. Isn't it interesting, however, how filled our churches are on this civic holiday, Thanksgiving Day? There is no "obligation" to celebrate Mass, yet our liturgy is full. We do not need a day of "obligation" to remind us that God is the source of all our blessings. Yes, it's very appropriate to observe Thanksgiving Day with a eucharistic celebration—with the supreme act of thanksgiving.

As the first reading from Sirach reminds us, we bless God because God "has done wondrous things on earth." The second reading picks up on the same theme: we "continually thank" God "because of the favor he has bestowed on [us] in Christ Jesus." It is natural for us to have grateful hearts, especially as we become more and more aware that all we have has been given to us in one way or another. Gratitude reminds us that we are ever dependent on others, especially God. This gospel is about gratitude, but about so much more.

The lepers address Jesus as "Master." When they asked that he have pity on them, for what really were they asking? Perhaps simply that he pause, recognize them, and say a few kind words. Perhaps only for a little dignity and respect. Or perhaps to teach them as he taught others (as lepers they could not have come close enough to hear Jesus). As outcasts the lepers could not have come near the crowds. Even to call out to Jesus was bold. To come near? Not possible! What does Jesus do? He responds to the lepers' cry, and in that simple kindness he closes the wide gap between outcast and community. Jesus, the Master, teaches a most profound lesson, not with words but with deed: he heals them. However, only one understood the lesson—only one returned "to give thanks to God." Only one learned who Jesus was: the God who saves.

Living the Paschal Mystery

What is the difference between the one who returned to thank Jesus and the nine who didn't? All ten were cured. All ten received the gift of healing from Jesus. All ten were outcasts but now restored with dignity to the community. Only one, though, went beyond the joy all ten must have felt in being healed; only one transcended self and returned to thank the Giver of the gift. This leper's self-awareness was not self-centered; his self-awareness of having been healed prompted him to forget self and give thanks for the gift of healing that came from outside of himself.

Thanksgiving Day is a national time for giving thanks for all the abundance with which our nation has been blessed. Like the leper, though, we must transcend ourselves and express our gratitude in concrete acts of generous thanksgiving. More than going to church (as important as that is), we also express our gratitude by reaching out to those less fortunate than ourselves, to those who don't seem to share in the abundance of our nation in the same way. Genuine gratitude calls us to die to ourselves by giving of our own abundance so that others may share in God's gracious gifts, receiving life more abundantly themselves. Thankfulness is more than words—it is actions expressed in loving service of others, bestowing dignity on the outcasts, giving to others as God has given to us.

Focusing the Gospel

Key words and phrases: Master, Have pity on us, they were cleansed, returned to give thanks to God, your faith has saved you

To the point: The lepers address Jesus as "Master." When they asked that he have pity on them, for what really were they asking? Perhaps simply that he pause, recognize them, and say a few kind words. Or perhaps to teach them as he taught others (as lepers they could not have come close enough to the crowds to hear Jesus). What does Jesus do? He teaches a most profound lesson, not with words but with deed: he heals them. However, only one understood the lesson—only one returned "to give thanks to God." Only one learned who Jesus was: the God who saves.

Model Penitential Act

Presider: We gather today as a nation to give thanks to God for the many blessings bestowed upon us. We gather today as church to give thanks to God for salvation, our most precious gift . . . [pause]

Lord Jesus, you heal those who come to you in faith: Lord . . .

Christ Jesus, you are worthy of all worship and thanksgiving: Christ . . .

Lord Jesus, you are the Savior of the world: Lord . . .

Model Universal Prayer (Prayer of the Faithful)

Presider: The God who has blessed us with all good things, will continue to give us what we need. And so we pray with hearts filled with gratitude and confidence.

Response:

Lord, hear our prayer.

Cantor:

we pray to the Lord,

That all members of the church always and everywhere give thanks for God's abundant graciousness . . . [pause]

That nations share the abundance of God's wondrous creation so that all peoples have what they need . . . [pause]

That all those in need of healing seek Jesus and receive his blessings . . . [pause]

That each of us raise our hearts in thanksgiving for the blessings of faith and salvation . . . [pause]

Presider: Gracious God, you have given us all good things: hear these our prayers, that in sharing our prosperity with others all may know your goodness and blessings. We ask this through the intercession of your most gracious Gift to us of all, Jesus Christ our Lord. **Amen.**

FOR REFLECTION
- What Jesus teaches me about what I need from him is . . .
- I take time to give God thanks when . . . for . . . because . . .
- Every Thanksgiving Day I . . .

Homily Points

- On this day of national thanksgiving, we are grateful to God for the many blessings showered upon our nation, our families, and ourselves. While this is primarily a civic holiday, we also thank God on this day for the gift of faith, for the community of the church, and for salvation. God is the source of all these blessings. God is the One who saves.

- We are thankful that Jesus, the Son of God, has come to us with salvation. Thankful that to gain our salvation he steadfastly journeyed to Jerusalem. Thankful that on this very journey he worked wonders of healing. Thankful that on our own journey through life he continues to lead us to salvation and to heal us of anything which impedes our movement forward. Thankful we have been given the faith that saves.

Readings *(continued)*

The Immaculate Conception of the Blessed Virgin Mary, *December 8, 2014*

Gospel (cont.)
Luke 1:26-38; L689

But Mary said to the angel,
"How can this be,
since I have no relations with a man?"
And the angel said to her in reply,
"The Holy Spirit will come upon you,
and the power of the Most High will overshadow you.
Therefore the child to be born
will be called holy, the Son of God.
And behold, Elizabeth, your relative,
has also conceived a son in her old age,
and this is the sixth month for her who was called barren;
for nothing will be impossible for God."
Mary said, "Behold, I am the handmaid of the Lord.
May it be done to me according to your word."
Then the angel departed from her.

FIRST READING
Gen 3:9-15, 20

After the man, Adam, had eaten of the tree,
the LORD God called to the man and asked
him, "Where are you?"
He answered, "I heard you in the garden;
but I was afraid, because I was naked,
so I hid myself."
Then he asked, "Who told you that you were
naked?
You have eaten, then,
from the tree of which I had forbidden you
to eat!"
The man replied, "The woman whom you put
here with me—
she gave me fruit from the tree, and so I
ate it."
The LORD God then asked the woman,
"Why did you do such a thing?"
The woman answered, "The serpent tricked
me into it, so I ate it."

Then the LORD God said to the serpent:
"Because you have done this, you shall be
banned
from all the animals
and from all the wild creatures;
on your belly shall you crawl,
and dirt shall you eat
all the days of your life.
I will put enmity between you and the
woman,
and between your offspring and hers;
he will strike at your head,
while you strike at his heel."

The man called his wife Eve,
because she became the mother of all the
living.

RESPONSORIAL PSALM
Ps 98:1, 2-3, 3-4

R℟. (1a) Sing to the Lord a new song, for he has
done marvelous deeds.

Sing to the LORD a new song,
for he has done wondrous deeds;
His right hand has won victory for him,
his holy arm.

R℟. Sing to the Lord a new song, for he has
done marvelous deeds.

The LORD has made his salvation known:
in the sight of the nations he has revealed
his justice.
He has remembered his kindness and his
faithfulness
toward the house of Israel.

R℟. Sing to the Lord a new song, for he has
done marvelous deeds.

All the ends of the earth have seen
the salvation by our God.
Sing joyfully to the LORD, all you lands;
break into song; sing praise.

R℟. Sing to the Lord a new song, for he has
done marvelous deeds.

SECOND READING
Eph 1:3-6, 11-12

Brothers and sisters:
Blessed be the God and Father of our Lord
Jesus Christ,
who has blessed us in Christ
with every spiritual blessing in the
heavens,
as he chose us in him, before the foundation
of the world,
to be holy and without blemish before him.
In love he destined us for adoption to himself
through Jesus Christ,
in accord with the favor of his will,
for the praise of the glory of his grace
that he granted us in the beloved.

In him we were also chosen,
destined in accord with the purpose of the
One
who accomplishes all things according to the
intention of his will,
so that we might exist for the praise of his
glory,
we who first hoped in Christ.

Gospel (cont.)
Matt 1:1-25; L13ABC

David became the father of Solomon,
    whose mother had been the wife of Uriah.
Solomon became the father of Rehoboam,
    Rehoboam the father of Abijah,
    Abijah the father of Asaph.
Asaph became the father of Jehoshaphat,
    Jehoshaphat the father of Joram,
    Joram the father of Uzziah.
Uzziah became the father of Jotham,
    Jotham the father of Ahaz,
    Ahaz the father of Hezekiah.
Hezekiah became the father of Manasseh,
    Manasseh the father of Amos,
    Amos the father of Josiah.
Josiah became the father of Jechoniah and his brothers
    at the time of the Babylonian exile.

After the Babylonian exile,
    Jechoniah became the father of Shealtiel,
    Shealtiel the father of Zerubbabel,
    Zerubbabel the father of Abiud.
Abiud became the father of Eliakim,
    Eliakim the father of Azor,
    Azor the father of Zadok.
Zadok became the father of Achim,
    Achim the father of Eliud,
    Eliud the father of Eleazar.
Eleazar became the father of Matthan,
    Matthan the father of Jacob,
    Jacob the father of Joseph, the husband of Mary.
Of her was born Jesus who is called the Christ.

Thus the total number of generations
    from Abraham to David
    is fourteen generations;
    from David to the Babylonian exile,
    fourteen generations;
    from the Babylonian exile to the Christ,
    fourteen generations.

Now this is how the birth of Jesus Christ came about.
When his mother Mary was betrothed to Joseph,
    but before they lived together,
    she was found with child through the Holy Spirit.
Joseph her husband, since he was a righteous man,
    yet unwilling to expose her to shame,
    decided to divorce her quietly.
Such was his intention when, behold,

the angel of the Lord appeared to him in a dream and said,
    "Joseph, son of David,
    do not be afraid to take Mary your wife into your home.
For it is through the Holy Spirit
    that this child has been conceived in her.
She will bear a son and you are to name him Jesus,
    because he will save his people from their sins."
All this took place to fulfill
    what the Lord had said through the prophet:
        Behold, the virgin shall conceive and bear a son,
          and they shall name him Emmanuel,
    which means "God is with us."
When Joseph awoke,
    he did as the angel of the Lord had commanded him
    and took his wife into his home.
He had no relations with her until she bore a son,
    and he named him Jesus.

or Matt 1:18-25

This is how the birth of Jesus Christ came about.
When his mother Mary was betrothed to Joseph,
    but before they lived together,
    she was found with child through the Holy Spirit.
Joseph her husband, since he was a righteous man,
    yet unwilling to expose her to shame,
    decided to divorce her quietly.
Such was his intention when, behold,
    the angel of the Lord appeared to him in a dream and said,
    "Joseph, son of David,
    do not be afraid to take Mary your wife into your home.
For it is through the Holy Spirit
    that this child has been conceived in her.
She will bear a son and you are to name him Jesus,
    because he will save his people from their sins."
All this took place to fulfill
    what the Lord had said through the prophet:
        Behold, the virgin shall conceive and bear a son,
          and they shall name him Emmanuel,
    which means "God is with us."
When Joseph awoke,
    he did as the angel of the Lord had commanded him
    and took his wife into his home.
He had no relations with her until she bore a son,
    and he named him Jesus.

The Nativity of the Lord, *December 25, 2014 (Vigil Mass)*

FIRST READING
Isa 62:1-5

For Zion's sake I will not be silent,
  for Jerusalem's sake I will not be quiet,
until her vindication shines forth like the dawn
  and her victory like a burning torch.

Nations shall behold your vindication,
  and all the kings your glory;
you shall be called by a new name
  pronounced by the mouth of the LORD.
You shall be a glorious crown in the hand of
  the LORD,
  a royal diadem held by your God.
No more shall people call you "Forsaken,"
  or your land "Desolate,"
but you shall be called "My Delight,"
  and your land "Espoused."
For the LORD delights in you
  and makes your land his spouse.
As a young man marries a virgin,
  your Builder shall marry you;
and as a bridegroom rejoices in his bride
  so shall your God rejoice in you.

RESPONSORIAL PSALM
Ps 89:4-5, 16-17, 27, 29

R̸. (2a) Forever I will sing the goodness of the Lord.

I have made a covenant with my chosen one,
  I have sworn to David my servant:
forever will I confirm your posterity
  and establish your throne for all
    generations.

R̸. Forever I will sing the goodness of the Lord.

Blessed the people who know the joyful shout;
  in the light of your countenance, O LORD,
    they walk.
At your name they rejoice all the day,
  and through your justice they are exalted.

R̸. Forever I will sing the goodness of the Lord.

He shall say of me, "You are my father,
  my God, the rock, my savior."
Forever I will maintain my kindness toward
  him,
  and my covenant with him stands firm.

R̸. Forever I will sing the goodness of the Lord.

SECOND READING
Acts 13:16-17, 22-25

When Paul reached Antioch in Pisidia and
    entered the synagogue,
  he stood up, motioned with his hand, and
    said,
    "Fellow Israelites and you others who are
      God-fearing, listen.
The God of this people Israel chose our
    ancestors
  and exalted the people during their sojourn
    in the land of Egypt.
With uplifted arm he led them out of it.
Then he removed Saul and raised up David
    as king;
  of him he testified,
  'I have found David, son of Jesse, a man
    after my own heart;
  he will carry out my every wish.'
From this man's descendants God, according
    to his promise,
  has brought to Israel a savior, Jesus.
John heralded his coming by proclaiming a
    baptism of repentance
  to all the people of Israel;
  and as John was completing his course, he
    would say,
  'What do you suppose that I am? I am not he.
Behold, one is coming after me;
  I am not worthy to unfasten the sandals of
    his feet.'"

The Nativity of the Lord, *December 25, 2014 (Mass at Midnight)*

Gospel (cont.)
Luke 2:1-14; L14ABC

Now there were shepherds in that region living in the fields
  and keeping the night watch over their flock.
The angel of the Lord appeared to them
  and the glory of the Lord shone around them,
  and they were struck with great fear.
The angel said to them,
  "Do not be afraid;
  for behold, I proclaim to you good news of great joy
  that will be for all the people.
For today in the city of David
  a savior has been born for you who is Christ and Lord.
And this will be a sign for you:
  you will find an infant wrapped in swaddling clothes
  and lying in a manger."
And suddenly there was a multitude of the heavenly host with the
    angel,
  praising God and saying:
    "Glory to God in the highest
        and on earth peace to those on whom his favor rests."

The Nativity of the Lord, *December 25, 2014 (Mass at Midnight)*

FIRST READING
Isa 9:1-6

The people who walked in darkness
    have seen a great light;
upon those who dwelt in the land of gloom
    a light has shone.
You have brought them abundant joy
    and great rejoicing,
as they rejoice before you as at the harvest,
    as people make merry when dividing
        spoils.
For the yoke that burdened them,
    the pole on their shoulder,
and the rod of their taskmaster
    you have smashed, as on the day of Midian.
For every boot that tramped in battle,
    every cloak rolled in blood,
    will be burned as fuel for flames.
For a child is born to us, a son is given us;
    upon his shoulder dominion rests.
They name him Wonder-Counselor, God-Hero,
    Father-Forever, Prince of Peace.
His dominion is vast
    and forever peaceful,
from David's throne, and over his kingdom,
    which he confirms and sustains
by judgment and justice,
    both now and forever.
The zeal of the LORD of hosts will do this!

RESPONSORIAL PSALM
Ps 96:1-2, 2-3, 11-12, 13

R. (Luke 2:11) Today is born our Savior,
Christ the Lord.

Sing to the LORD a new song;
    sing to the LORD, all you lands.
Sing to the LORD; bless his name.

R. Today is born our Savior, Christ the Lord.

Announce his salvation, day after day.
    Tell his glory among the nations;
among all peoples, his wondrous deeds.

R. Today is born our Savior, Christ the Lord.

Let the heavens be glad and the earth rejoice;
    let the sea and what fills it resound;
    let the plains be joyful and all that is in
        them!
Then shall all the trees of the forest exult.

R. Today is born our Savior, Christ the Lord.

They shall exult before the LORD, for he
        comes;
    for he comes to rule the earth.
He shall rule the world with justice
    and the peoples with his constancy.

R. Today is born our Savior, Christ the Lord.

SECOND READING
Titus 2:11-14

Beloved:
The grace of God has appeared, saving all
    and training us to reject godless ways and
        worldly desires
    and to live temperately, justly, and devoutly
        in this age,
    as we await the blessed hope,
    the appearance of the glory of our great
        God
    and savior Jesus Christ,
    who gave himself for us to deliver us from
        all lawlessness
    and to cleanse for himself a people as his
        own,
    eager to do what is good.

The Nativity of the Lord, *December 25, 2014 (Mass at Dawn)*

FIRST READING
Isa 62:11-12

See, the LORD proclaims
    to the ends of the earth:
say to daughter Zion,
    your savior comes!
Here is his reward with him,
    his recompense before him.
They shall be called the holy people,
    the redeemed of the LORD,
and you shall be called "Frequented,"
    a city that is not forsaken.

RESPONSORIAL PSALM
Ps 97:1, 6, 11-12

R. A light will shine on us this day: the Lord
is born for us.

The LORD is king; let the earth rejoice;
    let the many isles be glad.
The heavens proclaim his justice,
    and all peoples see his glory.

R. A light will shine on us this day: the Lord
is born for us.

Light dawns for the just;
    and gladness, for the upright of heart.
Be glad in the LORD, you just,
    and give thanks to his holy name.

R. A light will shine on us this day: the Lord
is born for us.

SECOND READING
Titus 3:4-7

Beloved:
When the kindness and generous love
    of God our savior appeared,
not because of any righteous deeds we had
        done
    but because of his mercy,
he saved us through the bath of rebirth
    and renewal by the Holy Spirit,
whom he richly poured out on us
    through Jesus Christ our savior,
so that we might be justified by his grace
    and become heirs in hope of eternal life.

Gospel (cont.)

John 1:1-18; L16ABC

The true light, which enlightens everyone,
    was coming into the world.

He was in the world,
    and the world came to be through him,
    but the world did not know him.
He came to what was his own,
    but his own people did not accept him.

But to those who did accept him
    he gave power to become children of God,
    to those who believe in his name,
    who were born not by natural generation
    nor by human choice nor by a man's decision
    but of God.

And the Word became flesh
    and made his dwelling among us,
    and we saw his glory,
    the glory as of the Father's only Son,
    full of grace and truth.

John testified to him and cried out, saying,
    "This was he of whom I said,
    'The one who is coming after me ranks ahead of me
    because he existed before me.'"
From his fullness we have all received,
    grace in place of grace,
    because while the law was given through Moses,
    grace and truth came through Jesus Christ.
No one has ever seen God.
The only Son, God, who is at the Father's side,
    has revealed him.

or John 1:1-5, 9-14

In the beginning was the Word,
    and the Word was with God,
    and the Word was God.
He was in the beginning with God.
All things came to be through him,
    and without him nothing came to be.
What came to be through him was life,
    and this life was the light of the human race;
the light shines in the darkness,
    and the darkness has not overcome it.
The true light, which enlightens everyone,
    was coming into the world.

He was in the world,
    and the world came to be through him,
    but the world did not know him.
He came to what was his own,
    but his own people did not accept him.

But to those who did accept him
    he gave power to become children of God,
    to those who believe in his name,
    who were born not by natural generation
    nor by human choice nor by a man's decision
    but of God.

And the Word became flesh
    and made his dwelling among us,
    and we saw his glory,
    the glory as of the Father's only Son,
    full of grace and truth.

FIRST READING

Isa 52:7-10

How beautiful upon the mountains
    are the feet of him who brings glad tidings,
announcing peace, bearing good news,
    announcing salvation, and saying to Zion,
    "Your God is King!"

Hark! Your sentinels raise a cry,
    together they shout for joy,
for they see directly, before their eyes,
    the LORD restoring Zion.
Break out together in song,
    O ruins of Jerusalem!
For the LORD comforts his people,
    he redeems Jerusalem.
The LORD has bared his holy arm
    in the sight of all the nations;
all the ends of the earth will behold
    the salvation of our God.

RESPONSORIAL PSALM

Ps 98:1, 2-3, 3-4, 5-6

℟. (3c) All the ends of the earth have seen the saving power of God.

Sing to the LORD a new song,
    for he has done wondrous deeds;
his right hand has won victory for him,
    his holy arm.

℟. All the ends of the earth have seen the saving power of God.

The LORD has made his salvation known:
    in the sight of the nations he has revealed
        his justice.
He has remembered his kindness and his
    faithfulness
    toward the house of Israel.

℟. All the ends of the earth have seen the saving power of God.

All the ends of the earth have seen
    the salvation by our God.
Sing joyfully to the LORD, all you lands;
    break into song; sing praise.

℟. All the ends of the earth have seen the saving power of God.

Sing praise to the LORD with the harp,
    with the harp and melodious song.
With trumpets and the sound of the horn
    sing joyfully before the King, the LORD.

℟. All the ends of the earth have seen the saving power of God.

The Nativity of the Lord, *December 25, 2014 (Mass during the Day)*

SECOND READING
Heb 1:1-6

Brothers and sisters:
In times past, God spoke in partial and
    various ways
  to our ancestors through the prophets;
  in these last days, he has spoken to us
      through the Son,
  whom he made heir of all things
  and through whom he created the universe,
  who is the refulgence of his glory, the very
      imprint of his being,
    and who sustains all things by his
      mighty word.
  When he had accomplished purification
    from sins,

he took his seat at the right hand of the
    Majesty on high,
  as far superior to the angels
  as the name he has inherited is more
      excellent than theirs.

For to which of the angels did God ever say:
  *You are my son; this day I have begotten
      you?*
Or again:
  *I will be a father to him, and he shall be a
      son to me?*
And again, when he leads the firstborn into
    the world, he says:
  Let all the angels of God worship him.

The Holy Family of Jesus, Mary, and Joseph, *December 28, 2014*

Gospel (cont.)
Luke 2:22-40; L17B

  "Now, Master, you may let your servant go
    in peace, according to your word,
  for my eyes have seen your salvation,
    which you prepared in sight of all the peoples,
  a light for revelation to the Gentiles,
    and glory for your people Israel."
The child's father and mother were amazed at what was said about
    him;
  and Simeon blessed them and said to Mary his mother,
  "Behold, this child is destined
  for the fall and rise of many in Israel,
  and to be a sign that will be contradicted
  —and you yourself a sword will pierce—
  so that the thoughts of many hearts may be revealed."
There was also a prophetess, Anna,
  the daughter of Phanuel, of the tribe of Asher.
She was advanced in years,
  having lived seven years with her husband after her marriage,
  and then as a widow until she was eighty-four.
She never left the temple,
  but worshiped night and day with fasting and prayer.
And coming forward at that very time,
  she gave thanks to God and spoke about the child
  to all who were awaiting the redemption of Jerusalem.

When they had fulfilled all the prescriptions
  of the law of the Lord,
  they returned to Galilee,
  to their own town of Nazareth.
The child grew and became strong, filled with wisdom;
  and the favor of God was upon him.

or

Luke 2:22, 39-40

When the days were completed for their purification
    according to the law of Moses,
  the parents of Jesus took him up to Jerusalem
  to present him to the Lord.

When they had fulfilled all the prescriptions
  of the law of the Lord,
  they returned to Galilee,
  to their own town of Nazareth.
The child grew and became strong, filled with wisdom;
  and the favor of God was upon him.

SECOND READING (cont.)
Heb 11:8, 11-12, 17-19

By faith Abraham, when put to the test, offered up Isaac,
  and he who had received the promises was ready to offer
      his only son,
  of whom it was said,
  "Through Isaac descendants shall bear your name."
He reasoned that God was able to raise even from the dead,
  and he received Isaac back as a symbol.

FIRST READING

Sir 3:2-6, 12-14

God sets a father in honor over his children;
a mother's authority he confirms over her
sons.
Whoever honors his father atones for sins,
and preserves himself from them.
When he prays, he is heard;
he stores up riches who reveres his mother.
Whoever honors his father is gladdened by
children,
and, when he prays, is heard.
Whoever reveres his father will live a long life;
he who obeys his father brings comfort to
his mother.

My son, take care of your father when he is
old;
grieve him not as long as he lives.
Even if his mind fail, be considerate of him;
revile him not all the days of his life;
kindness to a father will not be forgotten,
firmly planted against the debt of your sins
—a house raised in justice to you.

RESPONSORIAL PSALM

Ps 128:1-2, 3, 4-5

R̷. (cf. 1) Blessed are those who fear the Lord
and walk in his ways.

Blessed is everyone who fears the Lord,
who walks in his ways!
For you shall eat the fruit of your handiwork;
blessed shall you be, and favored.

R̷. Blessed are those who fear the Lord and
walk in his ways.

Your wife shall be like a fruitful vine
in the recesses of your home;
your children like olive plants
around your table.

R̷. Blessed are those who fear the Lord and
walk in his ways.

Behold, thus is the man blessed
who fears the Lord.
The Lord bless you from Zion:
may you see the prosperity of Jerusalem
all the days of your life.

R̷. Blessed are those who fear the Lord and
walk in his ways.

SECOND READING

Col 3:12-21

Brothers and sisters:
Put on, as God's chosen ones, holy and beloved,
heartfelt compassion, kindness, humility,
gentleness, and patience,
bearing with one another and forgiving one
another,
if one has a grievance against another;
as the Lord has forgiven you, so must you
also do.
And over all these put on love,
that is, the bond of perfection.
And let the peace of Christ control your
hearts,
the peace into which you were also called in
one body.
And be thankful.
Let the word of Christ dwell in you richly,
as in all wisdom you teach and admonish
one another,
singing psalms, hymns, and spiritual songs
with gratitude in your hearts to God.
And whatever you do, in word or in deed,
do everything in the name of the Lord Jesus,
giving thanks to God the Father through
him.

Wives, be subordinate to your husbands,
as is proper in the Lord.
Husbands, love your wives,
and avoid any bitterness toward them.
Children, obey your parents in everything,
for this is pleasing to the Lord.
Fathers, do not provoke your children,
so they may not become discouraged.

or

Col 3:12-17

Brothers and sisters:
Put on, as God's chosen ones, holy and beloved,
heartfelt compassion, kindness, humility,
gentleness, and patience,
bearing with one another and forgiving one
another,
if one has a grievance against another;
as the Lord has forgiven you, so must you
also do.
And over all these put on love,
that is, the bond of perfection.
And let the peace of Christ control your hearts,
the peace into which you were also called in
one body.
And be thankful.
Let the word of Christ dwell in you richly,
as in all wisdom you teach and admonish
one another,
singing psalms, hymns, and spiritual songs
with gratitude in your hearts to God.
And whatever you do, in word or in deed,
do everything in the name of the Lord Jesus,
giving thanks to God the Father through him.

Solemnity of Mary, the Holy Mother of God, *January 1, 2015*

FIRST READING
Num 6:22-27

The LORD said to Moses:
"Speak to Aaron and his sons and tell them:
This is how you shall bless the Israelites.
Say to them:
The LORD bless you and keep you!
The LORD let his face shine upon
you, and be gracious to you!
The LORD look upon you kindly and
give you peace!
So shall they invoke my name upon the
Israelites,
and I will bless them."

RESPONSORIAL PSALM
Ps 67:2-3, 5, 6, 8

℟. (2a) May God bless us in his mercy.

May God have pity on us and bless us;
may he let his face shine upon us.
So may your way be known upon earth;
among all nations, your salvation.

℟. May God bless us in his mercy.

May the nations be glad and exult
because you rule the peoples in equity;
the nations on the earth you guide.

℟. May God bless us in his mercy.

May the peoples praise you, O God;
may all the peoples praise you!
May God bless us,
and may all the ends of the earth fear him!

℟. May God bless us in his mercy.

SECOND READING
Gal 4:4-7

Brothers and sisters:
When the fullness of time had come, God sent
his Son,
born of a woman, born under the law,
to ransom those under the law,
so that we might receive adoption as sons.
As proof that you are sons,
God sent the Spirit of his Son into our
hearts,
crying out, "Abba, Father!"
So you are no longer a slave but a son,
and if a son then also an heir, through God.

The Epiphany of the Lord, *January 4, 2015*

Gospel (cont.)
Matt 2:1-12; L20ABC

And behold, the star that they had seen at its rising preceded them,
until it came and stopped over the place where the child was.
They were overjoyed at seeing the star,
and on entering the house
they saw the child with Mary his mother.
They prostrated themselves and did him homage.
Then they opened their treasures
and offered him gifts of gold, frankincense, and myrrh.
And having been warned in a dream not to return to Herod,
they departed for their country by another way.

SECOND READING

1 John 5:1-9

Beloved:
Everyone who believes that Jesus is the Christ
    is begotten by God,
  and everyone who loves the Father
  loves also the one begotten by him.
In this way we know that we love the children
    of God
  when we love God and obey his
    commandments.
For the love of God is this,
  that we keep his commandments.
And his commandments are not burdensome,
  for whoever is begotten by God conquers
    the world.
And the victory that conquers the world is
  our faith.
Who indeed is the victor over the world
  but the one who believes that Jesus is the
    Son of God?

This is the one who came through water and
  blood, Jesus Christ,
  not by water alone, but by water and
    blood.
The Spirit is the one who testifies,
  and the Spirit is truth.
So there are three that testify,
  the Spirit, the water, and the blood,
  and the three are of one accord.
If we accept human testimony,
  the testimony of God is surely greater.
Now the testimony of God is this,
  that he has testified on behalf of his Son.

FIRST READING

Isa 42:1-4, 6-7

Thus says the LORD:
Here is my servant whom I uphold,
  my chosen one with whom I am pleased,
upon whom I have put my spirit;
  he shall bring forth justice to the nations,
not crying out, not shouting,
  not making his voice heard in the street.
A bruised reed he shall not break,
  and a smoldering wick he shall not quench,
until he establishes justice on the earth;
  the coastlands will wait for his teaching.

I, the LORD, have called you for the victory of
  justice,
  I have grasped you by the hand;
I formed you, and set you
  as a covenant of the people,
  a light for the nations,
to open the eyes of the blind,
  to bring out prisoners from confinement,
  and from the dungeon, those who live in
    darkness.

RESPONSORIAL PSALM

Ps 29:1-2, 3-4, 3, 9-10

R̸. (11b) The Lord will bless his people with
peace.

Give to the LORD, you sons of God,
  give to the LORD glory and praise,
give to the LORD the glory due his name;
  adore the LORD in holy attire.

R̸. The Lord will bless his people with peace.

The voice of the LORD is over the waters,
  the LORD, over vast waters.
The voice of the LORD is mighty;
  the voice of the LORD is majestic.

R̸. The Lord will bless his people with peace.

The God of glory thunders,
  and in his temple all say, "Glory!"
The LORD is enthroned above the flood;
  the LORD is enthroned as king forever.

R̸. The Lord will bless his people with peace.

SECOND READING

Acts 10:34-38

Peter proceeded to speak to those gathered
  in the house of Cornelius, saying:
  "In truth, I see that God shows no
    partiality.
Rather, in every nation whoever fears him
  and acts uprightly
  is acceptable to him.
You know the word that he sent to the
  Israelites
  as he proclaimed peace through Jesus
    Christ, who is Lord of all,
  what has happened all over Judea,
  beginning in Galilee after the baptism
  that John preached,
  how God anointed Jesus of Nazareth
  with the Holy Spirit and power.
He went about doing good
  and healing all those oppressed by the
    devil,
  for God was with him."

Ash Wednesday, *February 18, 2015*

FIRST READING
Joel 2:12-18

Even now, says the LORD,
　　return to me with your whole heart,
　　with fasting, and weeping, and mourning;
Rend your hearts, not your garments,
　　and return to the LORD, your God.
For gracious and merciful is he,
　　slow to anger, rich in kindness,
　　and relenting in punishment.
Perhaps he will again relent
　　and leave behind him a blessing,
Offerings and libations
　　for the LORD, your God.

Blow the trumpet in Zion!
　　proclaim a fast,
　　call an assembly;
Gather the people,
　　notify the congregation;
Assemble the elders,
　　gather the children
　　and the infants at the breast;
Let the bridegroom quit his room
　　and the bride her chamber.
Between the porch and the altar
　　let the priests, the ministers of the LORD,
　　　　weep,
And say, "Spare, O LORD, your people,
　　and make not your heritage a reproach,
　　with the nations ruling over them!
Why should they say among the peoples,
　　'Where is their God?'"

Then the LORD was stirred to concern for his
　　land
　　and took pity on his people.

RESPONSORIAL PSALM
Ps 51:3-4, 5-6ab, 12-13, 14, and 17

R̷. (see 3a) Be merciful, O Lord, for we have
sinned.

Have mercy on me, O God, in your goodness;
　　in the greatness of your compassion wipe
　　　　out my offense.
Thoroughly wash me from my guilt
　　and of my sin cleanse me.

R̷. Be merciful, O Lord, for we have sinned.

For I acknowledge my offense,
　　and my sin is before me always:
"Against you only have I sinned,
　　and done what is evil in your sight."

R̷. Be merciful, O Lord, for we have sinned.

A clean heart create for me, O God,
　　and a steadfast spirit renew within me.
Cast me not out from your presence,
　　and your Holy Spirit take not from me.

R̷. Be merciful, O Lord, for we have sinned.

Give me back the joy of your salvation,
　　and a willing spirit sustain in me.
O Lord, open my lips,
　　and my mouth shall proclaim your praise.

R̷. Be merciful, O Lord, for we have sinned.

SECOND READING
2 Cor 5:20–6:2

Brothers and sisters:
We are ambassadors for Christ,
　　as if God were appealing through us.
We implore you on behalf of Christ,
　　be reconciled to God.
For our sake he made him to be sin who did
　　not know sin,
　　so that we might become the righteousness
　　　　of God in him.

Working together, then,
　　we appeal to you not to receive the grace of
　　　　God in vain.
For he says:

In an acceptable time I heard you,
　　and on the day of salvation I helped you.

Behold, now is a very acceptable time;
　　behold, now is the day of salvation.

Third Sunday of Lent, *March 8, 2015*

RESPONSORIAL PSALM
Ps 19:8, 9, 10, 11

R̷. (John 6:68c) Lord, you have the words of
everlasting life.

The law of the LORD is perfect,
　　refreshing the soul;
the decree of the LORD is trustworthy,
　　giving wisdom to the simple.

R̷. Lord, you have the words of everlasting life.

The precepts of the LORD are right,
　　rejoicing the heart;
the command of the LORD is clear,
　　enlightening the eye.

R̷. Lord, you have the words of everlasting life.

The fear of the LORD is pure,
　　enduring forever;
the ordinances of the LORD are true,
　　all of them just.

R̷. Lord, you have the words of everlasting life.

They are more precious than gold,
　　than a heap of purest gold;
sweeter also than syrup
　　or honey from the comb.

R̷. Lord, you have the words of everlasting life.

SECOND READING
1 Cor 1:22-25

Brothers and sisters:
Jews demand signs and Greeks look for
　　wisdom,
　　but we proclaim Christ crucified,
　　a stumbling block to Jews and foolishness
　　　　to Gentiles,
　　but to those who are called, Jews and
　　　　Greeks alike,
　　Christ the power of God and the wisdom
　　　　of God.
For the foolishness of God is wiser than
　　human wisdom,
　　and the weakness of God is stronger than
　　　　human strength.

Gospel

John 4:5-42; L28A

Jesus came to a town of Samaria called Sychar,
    near the plot of land that Jacob had given to his son Joseph.
Jacob's well was there.
Jesus, tired from his journey, sat down there at the well.
It was about noon.

A woman of Samaria came to draw water.
Jesus said to her,
    "Give me a drink."
His disciples had gone into the town to buy food.
The Samaritan woman said to him,
    "How can you, a Jew, ask me, a Samaritan woman, for a drink?"
—For Jews use nothing in common with Samaritans.—
Jesus answered and said to her,
    "If you knew the gift of God
    and who is saying to you, 'Give me a drink,'
    you would have asked him
    and he would have given you living water."
The woman said to him,
    "Sir, you do not even have a bucket and the cistern is deep;
    where then can you get this living water?
Are you greater than our father Jacob,
    who gave us this cistern and drank from it himself
    with his children and his flocks?"
Jesus answered and said to her,
    "Everyone who drinks this water will be thirsty again;
    but whoever drinks the water I shall give will never thirst;
    the water I shall give will become in him
    a spring of water welling up to eternal life."
The woman said to him,
    "Sir, give me this water, so that I may not be thirsty
    or have to keep coming here to draw water."

Jesus said to her,
    "Go call your husband and come back."
The woman answered and said to him,
    "I do not have a husband."
Jesus answered her,
    "You are right in saying, 'I do not have a husband.'
For you have had five husbands,
    and the one you have now is not your husband.
What you have said is true."
The woman said to him,
    "Sir, I can see that you are a prophet.
Our ancestors worshiped on this mountain;
    but you people say that the place to worship is in Jerusalem."
Jesus said to her,
    "Believe me, woman, the hour is coming
    when you will worship the Father
    neither on this mountain nor in Jerusalem.
You people worship what you do not understand;
    we worship what we understand,
    because salvation is from the Jews.
But the hour is coming, and is now here,

when true worshipers will worship the Father in Spirit and truth;
    and indeed the Father seeks such people to worship him.
God is Spirit, and those who worship him
    must worship in Spirit and truth."
The woman said to him,
    "I know that the Messiah is coming, the one called the Christ;
    when he comes, he will tell us everything."
Jesus said to her,
    "I am he, the one speaking with you."

At that moment his disciples returned,
    and were amazed that he was talking with a woman,
    but still no one said, "What are you looking for?"
    or "Why are you talking with her?"
The woman left her water jar
    and went into the town and said to the people,
    "Come see a man who told me everything I have done.
Could he possibly be the Christ?"
They went out of the town and came to him.
Meanwhile, the disciples urged him, "Rabbi, eat."
But he said to them,
    "I have food to eat of which you do not know."
So the disciples said to one another,
    "Could someone have brought him something to eat?"
Jesus said to them,
    "My food is to do the will of the one who sent me
    and to finish his work.
Do you not say, 'In four months the harvest will be here'?
I tell you, look up and see the fields ripe for the harvest.
The reaper is already receiving payment
    and gathering crops for eternal life,
    so that the sower and reaper can rejoice together.
For here the saying is verified that 'One sows and another reaps.'
I sent you to reap what you have not worked for;
    others have done the work,
    and you are sharing the fruits of their work."

Many of the Samaritans of that town began to believe in him
    because of the word of the woman who testified,
    "He told me everything I have done."
When the Samaritans came to him,
    they invited him to stay with them;
    and he stayed there two days.
Many more began to believe in him because of his word,
    and they said to the woman,
    "We no longer believe because of your word;
    for we have heard for ourselves,
    and we know that this is truly the savior of the world."

their own encounter w Jesus!

271

Gospel

John 4:5-15, 19b-26, 39a, 40-42; L28A

Jesus came to a town of Samaria called Sychar,
    near the plot of land that Jacob had given to his son Joseph.
Jacob's well was there.
Jesus, tired from his journey, sat down there at the well.
It was about noon.

A woman of Samaria came to draw water.
Jesus said to her,
    "Give me a drink."
His disciples had gone into the town to buy food.
The Samaritan woman said to him,
    "How can you, a Jew, ask me, a Samaritan woman, for a drink?"
—For Jews use nothing in common with Samaritans.—
Jesus answered and said to her,
    "If you knew the gift of God
    and who is saying to you, 'Give me a drink,'
    you would have asked him
    and he would have given you living water."
The woman said to him,
    "Sir, you do not even have a bucket and the cistern is deep;
    where then can you get this living water?
Are you greater than our father Jacob,
    who gave us this cistern and drank from it himself
    with his children and his flocks?"
Jesus answered and said to her,
    "Everyone who drinks this water will be thirsty again;
    but whoever drinks the water I shall give will never thirst;
    the water I shall give will become in him
    a spring of water welling up to eternal life."
The woman said to him,
    "Sir, give me this water, so that I may not be thirsty
    or have to keep coming here to draw water.

"I can see that you are a prophet.
Our ancestors worshiped on this mountain;
    but you people say that the place to worship is in Jerusalem."
Jesus said to her,
    "Believe me, woman, the hour is coming
    when you will worship the Father
    neither on this mountain nor in Jerusalem.
You people worship what you do not understand;
    we worship what we understand,
    because salvation is from the Jews.
But the hour is coming, and is now here,
    when true worshipers will worship the Father in Spirit and truth;
    and indeed the Father seeks such people to worship him.
God is Spirit, and those who worship him
    must worship in Spirit and truth."
The woman said to him,
    "I know that the Messiah is coming, the one called the Christ;
    when he comes, he will tell us everything."
Jesus said to her,
    "I am he, the one speaking with you."

Many of the Samaritans of that town began to believe in him.
When the Samaritans came to him,
    they invited him to stay with them;
    and he stayed there two days.
Many more began to believe in him because of his word,
    and they said to the woman,
    "We no longer believe because of your word;
    for we have heard for ourselves,
    and we know that this is truly the savior of the world."

Third Sunday of Lent, March 8, 2015

FIRST READING
Exod 17:3-7

In those days, in their thirst for water,
  the people grumbled against Moses,
  saying, "Why did you ever make us leave
    Egypt?
Was it just to have us die here of thirst
  with our children and our livestock?"
So Moses cried out to the LORD,
  "What shall I do with this people?
A little more and they will stone me!"
The LORD answered Moses,
  "Go over there in front of the people,
  along with some of the elders of Israel,
  holding in your hand, as you go,
  the staff with which you struck the river.
I will be standing there in front of you on the
    rock in Horeb.
Strike the rock, and the water will flow from it
  for the people to drink."
This Moses did, in the presence of the elders
  of Israel.
The place was called Massah and Meribah,
  because the Israelites quarreled there
  and tested the LORD, saying,
  "Is the LORD in our midst or not?"

RESPONSORIAL PSALM
Ps 95:1-2, 6-7, 8-9

R℣. (8) If today you hear his voice, harden not
your hearts.

Come, let us sing joyfully to the LORD;
  let us acclaim the Rock of our salvation.
Let us come into his presence with
    thanksgiving;
  let us joyfully sing psalms to him.

R℣. If today you hear his voice, harden not
your hearts.

Come, let us bow down in worship;
  let us kneel before the LORD who made us.
For he is our God,
  and we are the people he shepherds, the
    flock he guides.

R℣. If today you hear his voice, harden not
your hearts.

Oh, that today you would hear his voice:
  "Harden not your hearts as at Meribah,
  as in the day of Massah in the desert,
Where your fathers tempted me;
  they tested me though they had seen my
    works."

R℣. If today you hear his voice, harden not
your hearts.

SECOND READING
Rom 5:1-2, 5-8

Brothers and sisters:
Since we have been justified by faith,
  we have peace with God through our Lord
    Jesus Christ,
  through whom we have gained access by
    faith
  to this grace in which we stand,
  and we boast in hope of the glory of God.

And hope does not disappoint,
  because the love of God has been poured
    out into our hearts
  through the Holy Spirit who has been given
    to us.
For Christ, while we were still helpless,
  died at the appointed time for the ungodly.
Indeed, only with difficulty does one die for a
    just person,
  though perhaps for a good person one
    might even find courage to die.
But God proves his love for us
  in that while we were still sinners Christ
    died for us.

Fourth Sunday of Lent, March 15, 2015

Gospel
John 9:1, 6-9, 13-17, 34-38; L31A

As Jesus passed by he saw a man blind from birth.
He spat on the ground and made clay with the saliva,
  and smeared the clay on his eyes, and said to him,
  "Go wash in the Pool of Siloam"—which means Sent—.
So he went and washed, and came back able to see.

His neighbors and those who had seen him earlier as a beggar said,
  "Isn't this the one who used to sit and beg?"
Some said, "It is,"
  but others said, "No, he just looks like him."
He said, "I am."

They brought the one who was once blind to the Pharisees.
Now Jesus had made clay and opened his eyes on a sabbath.
So then the Pharisees also asked him how he was able to see.
He said to them,
  "He put clay on my eyes, and I washed, and now I can see."
So some of the Pharisees said,
  "This man is not from God,
  because he does not keep the sabbath."
But others said,
  "How can a sinful man do such signs?"
And there was a division among them.

So they said to the blind man again,
  "What do you have to say about him,
  since he opened your eyes?"
He said, "He is a prophet."

They answered and said to him,
  "You were born totally in sin,
  and are you trying to teach us?"
Then they threw him out.

When Jesus heard that they had thrown him out,
  he found him and said, "Do you believe in the Son of Man?"
He answered and said,
  "Who is he, sir, that I may believe in him?"
Jesus said to him,
  "You have seen him,
  and the one speaking with you is he."
He said,
  "I do believe, Lord," and he worshiped him.

Gospel

John 9:1-41; L31A

As Jesus passed by he saw a man blind from birth.
His disciples asked him,
    "Rabbi, who sinned, this man or his parents,
    that he was born blind?"
Jesus answered,
    "Neither he nor his parents sinned;
    it is so that the works of God might be made visible through him.
We have to do the works of the one who sent me while it is day.
Night is coming when no one can work.
While I am in the world, I am the light of the world."
When he had said this, he spat on the ground
    and made clay with the saliva,
    and smeared the clay on his eyes, and said to him,
    "Go wash in the Pool of Siloam"—which means Sent—.
So he went and washed, and came back able to see.

His neighbors and those who had seen him earlier as a beggar said,
    "Isn't this the one who used to sit and beg?"
Some said, "It is,"
    but others said, "No, he just looks like him."
He said, "I am."
So they said to him, "How were your eyes opened?"
He replied,
    "The man called Jesus made clay and anointed my eyes
    and told me, 'Go to Siloam and wash.'
So I went there and washed and was able to see."
And they said to him, "Where is he?"
He said, "I don't know."

They brought the one who was once blind to the Pharisees.
Now Jesus had made clay and opened his eyes on a sabbath.
So then the Pharisees also asked him how he was able to see.
He said to them,
    "He put clay on my eyes, and I washed, and now I can see."
So some of the Pharisees said,
    "This man is not from God,
    because he does not keep the sabbath."
But others said,
    "How can a sinful man do such signs?"
And there was a division among them.
So they said to the blind man again,
    "What do you have to say about him,
    since he opened your eyes?"
He said, "He is a prophet."

Now the Jews did not believe
    that he had been blind and gained his sight
    until they summoned the parents of the one who had gained his
        sight.
They asked them,
    "Is this your son, who you say was born blind?
How does he now see?"
His parents answered and said,
    "We know that this is our son and that he was born blind.
We do not know how he sees now,
    nor do we know who opened his eyes.
Ask him, he is of age;
    he can speak for himself."
His parents said this because they were afraid of the Jews,

for the Jews had already agreed
    that if anyone acknowledged him as the Christ,
    he would be expelled from the synagogue.
For this reason his parents said,
    "He is of age; question him."

So a second time they called the man who had been blind
    and said to him, "Give God the praise!
We know that this man is a sinner."
He replied,
    "If he is a sinner, I do not know.
One thing I do know is that I was blind and now I see."
So they said to him,
    "What did he do to you?
    How did he open your eyes?"
He answered them,
    "I told you already and you did not listen.
Why do you want to hear it again?
Do you want to become his disciples, too?"
They ridiculed him and said,
    "You are that man's disciple;
    we are disciples of Moses!
We know that God spoke to Moses,
    but we do not know where this one is from."
The man answered and said to them,
    "This is what is so amazing,
    that you do not know where he is from, yet he opened my eyes.
We know that God does not listen to sinners,
    but if one is devout and does his will, he listens to him.
It is unheard of that anyone ever opened the eyes of a person born
        blind.
If this man were not from God,
    he would not be able to do anything."
They answered and said to him,
    "You were born totally in sin,
    and are you trying to teach us?"
Then they threw him out.

When Jesus heard that they had thrown him out,
    he found him and said, "Do you believe in the Son of Man?"
He answered and said,
    "Who is he, sir, that I may believe in him?"
Jesus said to him,
    "You have seen him,
    and the one speaking with you is he."
He said,
    "I do believe, Lord," and he worshiped him.
Then Jesus said,
    "I came into this world for judgment,
    so that those who do not see might see,
    and those who do see might become blind."

Some of the Pharisees who were with him heard this
    and said to him, "Surely we are not also blind, are we?"
Jesus said to them,
    "If you were blind, you would have no sin;
    but now you are saying, 'We see,' so your sin remains."

SECOND READING
Eph 2:4-10

Brothers and sisters:
God, who is rich in mercy,
    because of the great love he had for us,
    even when we were dead in our
        transgressions,
    brought us to life with Christ—by grace
        you have been saved—,
    raised us up with him,
    and seated us with him in the heavens in
        Christ Jesus,
    that in the ages to come
    he might show the immeasurable riches of
        his grace
    in his kindness to us in Christ Jesus.
For by grace you have been saved through
    faith,
    and this is not from you; it is the gift of
        God;
    it is not from works, so no one may boast.
For we are his handiwork, created in Christ
    Jesus for the good works
    that God has prepared in advance,
    that we should live in them.

The readings for Year A may also be used:

FIRST READING
1 Sam 16:1b, 6-7, 10-13a

The LORD said to Samuel:
    "Fill your horn with oil, and be on your
        way.
I am sending you to Jesse of Bethlehem,
    for I have chosen my king from among his
        sons."

As Jesse and his sons came to the sacrifice,
    Samuel looked at Eliab and thought,
    "Surely the LORD's anointed is here before
        him."
But the LORD said to Samuel:
    "Do not judge from his appearance or from
        his lofty stature,
    because I have rejected him.
Not as man sees does God see,
    because man sees the appearance
    but the LORD looks into the heart."
In the same way Jesse presented seven sons
    before Samuel,
    but Samuel said to Jesse,
    "The LORD has not chosen any one of
        these."
Then Samuel asked Jesse,
    "Are these all the sons you have?"
Jesse replied,
    "There is still the youngest, who is tending
        the sheep."
Samuel said to Jesse,
    "Send for him;
    we will not begin the sacrificial banquet
        until he arrives here."
Jesse sent and had the young man brought to
    them.
He was ruddy, a youth handsome to behold
    and making a splendid appearance.
The LORD said,
    "There—anoint him, for this is the one!"
Then Samuel, with the horn of oil in hand,
    anointed David in the presence of his
        brothers;
    and from that day on, the spirit of the LORD
        rushed upon David.

RESPONSORIAL PSALM
Ps 23:1-3a, 3b-4, 5, 6

R̶/. (1) The Lord is my shepherd; there is nothing I shall want.

The LORD is my shepherd; I shall not want.
    In verdant pastures he gives me repose;
beside restful waters he leads me;
    he refreshes my soul.

R̶/. The Lord is my shepherd; there is nothing
I shall want.

He guides me in right paths
    for his name's sake.
Even though I walk in the dark valley
    I fear no evil; for you are at my side
with your rod and your staff
    that give me courage.

R̶/. The Lord is my shepherd; there is nothing
I shall want.

You spread the table before me
    in the sight of my foes;
you anoint my head with oil;
    my cup overflows.

R̶/. The Lord is my shepherd; there is nothing
I shall want.

Only goodness and kindness follow me
    all the days of my life;
and I shall dwell in the house of the LORD
    for years to come.

R̶/. The Lord is my shepherd; there is nothing
I shall want.

SECOND READING
Eph 5:8-14

Brothers and sisters:
You were once darkness,
    but now you are light in the Lord.
Live as children of light,
    for light produces every kind of goodness
    and righteousness and truth.
Try to learn what is pleasing to the Lord.
Take no part in the fruitless works of
    darkness;
    rather expose them, for it is shameful even
        to mention
    the things done by them in secret;
    but everything exposed by the light
        becomes visible,
    for everything that becomes visible is light.
Therefore, it says:
    "Awake, O sleeper,
    and arise from the dead,
    and Christ will give you light."

Gospel
Matt 1:16, 18-21, 24a; L543

Jacob was the father of Joseph, the husband of Mary.
Of her was born Jesus who is called the Christ.

Now this is how the birth of Jesus Christ came about.
When his mother Mary was betrothed to Joseph,
   but before they lived together,
   she was found with child through the Holy Spirit.
Joseph her husband, since he was a righteous man,
   yet unwilling to expose her to shame,
   decided to divorce her quietly.
Such was his intention when, behold,
   the angel of the Lord appeared to him in a dream and said,
   "Joseph, son of David,
   do not be afraid to take Mary your wife into your home.
For it is through the Holy Spirit
   that this child has been conceived in her.
She will bear a son and you are to name him Jesus,
   because he will save his people from their sins."
When Joseph awoke,
   he did as the angel of the Lord had commanded him
   and took his wife into his home.

FIRST READING
2 Sam 7:4-5a, 12-14a, 16

The LORD spoke to Nathan and said:
"Go, tell my servant David,
   'When your time comes and you rest with
      your ancestors,
   I will raise up your heir after you, sprung
      from your loins,
   and I will make his kingdom firm.
It is he who shall build a house for my name.
And I will make his royal throne firm forever.
I will be a father to him,
   and he shall be a son to me.
Your house and your kingdom shall endure
      forever before me;
   your throne shall stand firm forever.'"

RESPONSORIAL PSALM
Ps 89:2-3, 4-5, 27 and 29

R̶̸. (37) The son of David will live forever.

The promises of the LORD I will sing forever,
   through all generations my mouth will
      proclaim your faithfulness,
For you have said, "My kindness is
     established forever";
   in heaven you have confirmed your
     faithfulness.

R̶̸. The son of David will live forever.

"I have made a covenant with my chosen one;
   I have sworn to David my servant:
Forever will I confirm your posterity
   and establish your throne for all
     generations."

R̶̸. The son of David will live forever.

"He shall say of me, 'You are my father,
   my God, the Rock, my savior.'
Forever I will maintain my kindness toward
     him,
   and my covenant with him stands firm."

R̶̸. The son of David will live forever.

SECOND READING
Rom 4:13, 16-18, 22

Brothers and sisters:
It was not through the law
   that the promise was made to Abraham
     and his descendants
   that he would inherit the world,
   but through the righteousness that comes
     from faith.
For this reason, it depends on faith,
   so that it may be a gift,
   and the promise may be guaranteed to all
     his descendants,
   not to those who only adhere to the law
   but to those who follow the faith of Abraham,
   who is the father of all of us, as it is written,
   I have made you father of many nations.
He is our father in the sight of God,
   in whom he believed, who gives life to the
     dead
   and calls into being what does not exist.
He believed, hoping against hope,
   that he would become *the father of many*
     nations,
   according to what was said, *Thus shall*
     your descendants be.
That is why *it was credited to him as*
   righteousness.

Gospel (cont.)

John 12:20-33; L35B

The crowd there heard it and said it was thunder;
   but others said, "An angel has spoken to him."
Jesus answered and said,
   "This voice did not come for my sake but for yours.
Now is the time of judgment on this world;
   now the ruler of this world will be driven out.
And when I am lifted up from the earth,
   I will draw everyone to myself."
He said this indicating the kind of death he would die.

FIRST READING

Ezek 37:12-14

Thus says the Lord GOD:
   O my people, I will open your graves
   and have you rise from them,
   and bring you back to the land of Israel.
Then you shall know that I am the LORD,
   when I open your graves and have you rise
      from them,
   O my people!
I will put my spirit in you that you may live,
   and I will settle you upon your land;
   thus you shall know that I am the LORD.
I have promised, and I will do it, says the
   LORD.

RESPONSORIAL PSALM

Ps 130:1-2, 3-4, 5-6, 7-8

℞. (7) With the Lord there is mercy and fullness of redemption.

Out of the depths I cry to you, O LORD;
   LORD, hear my voice!
Let your ears be attentive
   to my voice in supplication.

℞. With the Lord there is mercy and fullness of redemption.

If you, O LORD, mark iniquities,
   LORD, who can stand?
But with you is forgiveness,
   that you may be revered.

℞. With the Lord there is mercy and fullness of redemption.

I trust in the LORD;
   my soul trusts in his word.
More than sentinels wait for the dawn,
   let Israel wait for the LORD.

℞. With the Lord there is mercy and fullness of redemption.

For with the LORD is kindness
   and with him is plenteous redemption;
and he will redeem Israel
   from all their iniquities.

℞. With the Lord there is mercy and fullness of redemption.

SECOND READING

Rom 8:8-11

Brothers and sisters:
Those who are in the flesh cannot please God.
But you are not in the flesh;
   on the contrary, you are in the spirit,
   if only the Spirit of God dwells in you.
Whoever does not have the Spirit of Christ
   does not belong to him.
But if Christ is in you,
   although the body is dead because of sin,
   the spirit is alive because of righteousness.
If the Spirit of the One who raised Jesus from
   the dead dwells in you,
   the One who raised Christ from the dead
   will give life to your mortal bodies also,
   through his Spirit dwelling in you.

Gospel
John 11:1-45; L34A

Now a man was ill, Lazarus from Bethany,
   the village of Mary and her sister Martha.
Mary was the one who had anointed the Lord with perfumed oil
   and dried his feet with her hair;
   it was her brother Lazarus who was ill.
So the sisters sent word to Jesus saying,
   "Master, the one you love is ill."
When Jesus heard this he said,
   "This illness is not to end in death,
   but is for the glory of God,
   that the Son of God may be glorified through it."
Now Jesus loved Martha and her sister and Lazarus.
So when he heard that he was ill,
   he remained for two days in the place where he was.
Then after this he said to his disciples,
   "Let us go back to Judea."
The disciples said to him,
   "Rabbi, the Jews were just trying to stone you,
   and you want to go back there?"
Jesus answered,
   "Are there not twelve hours in a day?
If one walks during the day, he does not stumble,
   because he sees the light of this world.
But if one walks at night, he stumbles,
   because the light is not in him."
He said this, and then told them,
   "Our friend Lazarus is asleep,
   but I am going to awaken him."
So the disciples said to him,
   "Master, if he is asleep, he will be saved."
But Jesus was talking about his death,
   while they thought that he meant ordinary sleep.
So then Jesus said to them clearly,
   "Lazarus has died.
And I am glad for you that I was not there,
   that you may believe.
Let us go to him."
So Thomas, called Didymus, said to his fellow disciples,
   "Let us also go to die with him."

When Jesus arrived, he found that Lazarus
   had already been in the tomb for four days.
Now Bethany was near Jerusalem, only about two miles away.
And many of the Jews had come to Martha and Mary
   to comfort them about their brother.
When Martha heard that Jesus was coming,
   she went to meet him;
   but Mary sat at home.
Martha said to Jesus,
   "Lord, if you had been here,
   my brother would not have died.
But even now I know that whatever you ask of God,
   God will give you."
Jesus said to her,
   "Your brother will rise."
Martha said to him,
   "I know he will rise,
   in the resurrection on the last day."
Jesus told her,

"I am the resurrection and the life;
   whoever believes in me, even if he dies, will live,
   and everyone who lives and believes in me will never die.
Do you believe this?"
She said to him, "Yes, Lord.
I have come to believe that you are the Christ, the Son of God,
   the one who is coming into the world."

When she had said this,
   she went and called her sister Mary secretly, saying,
   "The teacher is here and is asking for you."
As soon as she heard this,
   she rose quickly and went to him.
For Jesus had not yet come into the village,
   but was still where Martha had met him.
So when the Jews who were with her in the house comforting her
   saw Mary get up quickly and go out,
   they followed her,
   presuming that she was going to the tomb to weep there.
When Mary came to where Jesus was and saw him,
   she fell at his feet and said to him,
   "Lord, if you had been here,
   my brother would not have died."
When Jesus saw her weeping and the Jews who had come with her
    weeping,
   he became perturbed and deeply troubled, and said,
   "Where have you laid him?"
They said to him, "Sir, come and see."
And Jesus wept.
So the Jews said, "See how he loved him."
But some of them said,
   "Could not the one who opened the eyes of the blind man
   have done something so that this man would not have died?"

So Jesus, perturbed again, came to the tomb.
It was a cave, and a stone lay across it.
Jesus said, "Take away the stone."
Martha, the dead man's sister, said to him,
   "Lord, by now there will be a stench;
   he has been dead for four days."
Jesus said to her,
   "Did I not tell you that if you believe
   you will see the glory of God?"
So they took away the stone.
And Jesus raised his eyes and said,
   "Father, I thank you for hearing me.
I know that you always hear me;
   but because of the crowd here I have said this,
   that they may believe that you sent me."
And when he had said this,
   he cried out in a loud voice,
   "Lazarus, come out!"
The dead man came out,
   tied hand and foot with burial bands,
   and his face was wrapped in a cloth.
So Jesus said to them,
   "Untie him and let him go."

Now many of the Jews who had come to Mary
   and seen what he had done began to believe in him.

Gospel

John 11:3-7, 17, 20-27, 33b-45; L34A

The sisters of Lazarus sent word to Jesus saying,
"Master, the one you love is ill."
When Jesus heard this he said,
"This illness is not to end in death,
but is for the glory of God,
that the Son of God may be glorified through it."
Now Jesus loved Martha and her sister and Lazarus.
So when he heard that he was ill,
he remained for two days in the place where he was.
Then after this he said to his disciples,
"Let us go back to Judea."

When Jesus arrived, he found that Lazarus
had already been in the tomb for four days.
When Martha heard that Jesus was coming,
she went to meet him;
but Mary sat at home.
Martha said to Jesus,
"Lord, if you had been here,
my brother would not have died.
But even now I know that whatever you ask of God,
God will give you."
Jesus said to her,
"Your brother will rise."
Martha said,
"I know he will rise,
in the resurrection on the last day."
Jesus told her,
"I am the resurrection and the life;
whoever believes in me, even if he dies, will live,
and everyone who lives and believes in me will never die.
Do you believe this?"
She said to him, "Yes, Lord.
I have come to believe that you are the Christ, the Son of God,
the one who is coming into the world."

He became perturbed and deeply troubled, and said,
"Where have you laid him?"
They said to him, "Sir, come and see."
And Jesus wept.
So the Jews said, "See how he loved him."
But some of them said,
"Could not the one who opened the eyes of the blind man
have done something so that this man would not have died?"

So Jesus, perturbed again, came to the tomb.
It was a cave, and a stone lay across it.
Jesus said, "Take away the stone."
Martha, the dead man's sister, said to him,
"Lord, by now there will be a stench;
he has been dead for four days."
Jesus said to her,
"Did I not tell you that if you believe
you will see the glory of God?"
So they took away the stone.
And Jesus raised his eyes and said,
"Father, I thank you for hearing me.
I know that you always hear me;
but because of the crowd here I have said this,
that they may believe that you sent me."
And when he had said this,
he cried out in a loud voice,
"Lazarus, come out!"
The dead man came out,
tied hand and foot with burial bands,
and his face was wrapped in a cloth.
So Jesus said to them,
"Untie him and let him go."

Now many of the Jews who had come to Mary
and seen what he had done began to believe in him.

The Annunciation of the Lord, *March 25, 2015*

FIRST READING
Isa 7:10-14; 8:10

The LORD spoke to Ahaz, saying:
Ask for a sign from the LORD, your God;
    let it be deep as the nether world, or high
      as the sky!
But Ahaz answered,
    "I will not ask! I will not tempt the LORD!"
Then Isaiah said:
    Listen, O house of David!
Is it not enough for you to weary people,
    must you also weary my God?
Therefore the Lord himself will give you this
    sign:
    the virgin shall be with child, and bear a
      son,
    and shall name him Emmanuel,
    which means "God is with us!"

RESPONSORIAL PSALM
Ps 40:7-8a, 8b-9, 10, 11

R?. (8a and 9a) Here I am, Lord; I come to do
your will.

Sacrifice or offering you wished not,
    but ears open to obedience you gave me.
Holocausts and sin-offerings you sought not;
    then said I, "Behold, I come."

R?. Here I am, Lord; I come to do your will.

"In the written scroll it is prescribed for me,
To do your will, O God, is my delight,
    and your law is within my heart!"

R?. Here I am, Lord; I come to do your will.

I announced your justice in the vast assembly;
    I did not restrain my lips, as you, O LORD,
    know.

R?. Here I am, Lord; I come to do your will.

Your justice I kept not hid within my heart;
    your faithfulness and your salvation I have
    spoken of;
I have made no secret of your kindness and
    your truth
    in the vast assembly.

R?. Here I am, Lord; I come to do your will.

SECOND READING
Heb 10:4-10

Brothers and sisters:
It is impossible that the blood of bulls and
    goats
    takes away sins.
For this reason, when Christ came into the
    world, he said:

    "Sacrifice and offering you did not desire,
      but a body you prepared for me;
    in holocausts and sin offerings you took no
      delight.
    Then I said, 'As is written of me in the scroll,
    behold, I come to do your will, O God.'"

First Christ says, "Sacrifices and offerings,
    holocausts and sin offerings,
    you neither desired nor delighted in."
These are offered according to the law.
Then he says, "Behold, I come to do your will."
He takes away the first to establish the
    second.
By this "will," we have been consecrated
    through the offering of the body of Jesus
    Christ once for all.

Palm Sunday of the Passion of the Lord, *March 29, 2015*

Gospel at the Procession with Palms (cont.)
Mark 11:1-10; L37B

Some of the bystanders said to them,
    "What are you doing, untying the colt?"
They answered them just as Jesus had told them to,
    and they permitted them to do it.
So they brought the colt to Jesus
    and put their cloaks over it.
And he sat on it.
Many people spread their cloaks on the road,
    and others spread leafy branches
    that they had cut from the fields.

Those preceding him as well as those following kept crying out:
    "Hosanna!
      Blessed is he who comes in the name of the Lord!
      Blessed is the kingdom of our father David that is to come!
    Hosanna in the highest!"

Gospel at Mass
Mark 14:1–15:47; L38B

The Passover and the Feast of Unleavened Bread
    were to take place in two days' time.
So the chief priests and the scribes were seeking a way
    to arrest him by treachery and put him to death.
They said, "Not during the festival,
    for fear that there may be a riot among the people."

When he was in Bethany reclining at table
    in the house of Simon the leper,
    a woman came with an alabaster jar of perfumed oil,
    costly genuine spikenard.
She broke the alabaster jar and poured it on his head.
There were some who were indignant.
"Why has there been this waste of perfumed oil?
It could have been sold for more than three hundred days' wages
    and the money given to the poor."
They were infuriated with her.
Jesus said, "Let her alone.
Why do you make trouble for her?
She has done a good thing for me.
The poor you will always have with you,
    and whenever you wish you can do good to them,
    but you will not always have me.
She has done what she could.
She has anticipated anointing my body for burial.
Amen, I say to you,
    wherever the gospel is proclaimed to the whole world,
    what she has done will be told in memory of her."

Then Judas Iscariot, one of the Twelve,
    went off to the chief priests to hand him over to them.
When they heard him they were pleased and promised to pay him
    money.
Then he looked for an opportunity to hand him over.

On the first day of the Feast of Unleavened Bread,
    when they sacrificed the Passover lamb,
    his disciples said to him,
    "Where do you want us to go
    and prepare for you to eat the Passover?"
He sent two of his disciples and said to them,
    "Go into the city and a man will meet you,
    carrying a jar of water.
Follow him.
Wherever he enters, say to the master of the house,
    'The Teacher says, "Where is my guest room
    where I may eat the Passover with my disciples?"'
Then he will show you a large upper room furnished and ready.
Make the preparations for us there."
The disciples then went off, entered the city,
    and found it just as he had told them;
    and they prepared the Passover.

When it was evening, he came with the Twelve.
And as they reclined at table and were eating, Jesus said,
    "Amen, I say to you, one of you will betray me,
    one who is eating with me."
They began to be distressed and to say to him, one by one,
    "Surely it is not I?"

He said to them,
    "One of the Twelve, the one who dips with me into the dish.
For the Son of Man indeed goes, as it is written of him,
    but woe to that man by whom the Son of Man is betrayed.
It would be better for that man if he had never been born."

While they were eating,
    he took bread, said the blessing,
    broke it, and gave it to them, and said,
    "Take it; this is my body."
Then he took a cup, gave thanks, and gave it to them,
    and they all drank from it.
He said to them,
    "This is my blood of the covenant,
    which will be shed for many.
Amen, I say to you,
    I shall not drink again the fruit of the vine
    until the day when I drink it new in the kingdom of God."
Then, after singing a hymn,
    they went out to the Mount of Olives.

Then Jesus said to them,
    "All of you will have your faith shaken, for it is written:
     I will strike the shepherd,
       and the sheep will be dispersed.
But after I have been raised up,
    I shall go before you to Galilee."
Peter said to him,
    "Even though all should have their faith shaken,
    mine will not be."
Then Jesus said to him,
    "Amen, I say to you,
    this very night before the cock crows twice
    you will deny me three times."
But he vehemently replied,
    "Even though I should have to die with you,
    I will not deny you."
And they all spoke similarly.

Then they came to a place named Gethsemane,
    and he said to his disciples,
    "Sit here while I pray."
He took with him Peter, James, and John,
    and began to be troubled and distressed.
Then he said to them, "My soul is sorrowful even to death.
Remain here and keep watch."
He advanced a little and fell to the ground and prayed
    that if it were possible the hour might pass by him;
    he said, "Abba, Father, all things are possible to you.
Take this cup away from me,
    but not what I will but what you will."
When he returned he found them asleep.
He said to Peter, "Simon, are you asleep?
Could you not keep watch for one hour?
Watch and pray that you may not undergo the test.
The spirit is willing but the flesh is weak."
Withdrawing again, he prayed, saying the same thing.
Then he returned once more and found them asleep,
    for they could not keep their eyes open
    and did not know what to answer him.

He returned a third time and said to them,
  "Are you still sleeping and taking your rest?
It is enough. The hour has come.
Behold, the Son of Man is to be handed over to sinners.
Get up, let us go.
See, my betrayer is at hand."

Then, while he was still speaking,
  Judas, one of the Twelve, arrived,
  accompanied by a crowd with swords and clubs
  who had come from the chief priests,
  the scribes, and the elders.
His betrayer had arranged a signal with them, saying,
  "The man I shall kiss is the one;
  arrest him and lead him away securely."
He came and immediately went over to him and said,
  "Rabbi." And he kissed him.
At this they laid hands on him and arrested him.
One of the bystanders drew his sword,
  struck the high priest's servant, and cut off his ear.
Jesus said to them in reply,
  "Have you come out as against a robber,
  with swords and clubs, to seize me?
Day after day I was with you teaching in the temple area,
  yet you did not arrest me;
  but that the Scriptures may be fulfilled."
And they all left him and fled.
Now a young man followed him
  wearing nothing but a linen cloth about his body.
They seized him,
  but he left the cloth behind and ran off naked.

They led Jesus away to the high priest,
  and all the chief priests and the elders and the scribes came together.
Peter followed him at a distance into the high priest's courtyard
  and was seated with the guards, warming himself at the fire.
The chief priests and the entire Sanhedrin
  kept trying to obtain testimony against Jesus
  in order to put him to death, but they found none.
Many gave false witness against him,
  but their testimony did not agree.
Some took the stand and testified falsely against him,
  alleging, "We heard him say,
  'I will destroy this temple made with hands
  and within three days I will build another
  not made with hands.'"
Even so their testimony did not agree.
The high priest rose before the assembly and questioned Jesus,
  saying, "Have you no answer?
What are these men testifying against you?"
But he was silent and answered nothing.
Again the high priest asked him and said to him,
  "Are you the Christ, the son of the Blessed One?"
Then Jesus answered, "I am;
  and 'you will see the Son of Man
    seated at the right hand of the Power
    and coming with the clouds of heaven.'"
At that the high priest tore his garments and said,
  "What further need have we of witnesses?
You have heard the blasphemy.
What do you think?"
They all condemned him as deserving to die.

Some began to spit on him.
They blindfolded him and struck him and said to him, "Prophesy!"
And the guards greeted him with blows.

While Peter was below in the courtyard,
  one of the high priest's maids came along.
Seeing Peter warming himself,
  she looked intently at him and said,
  "You too were with the Nazarene, Jesus."
But he denied it saying,
  "I neither know nor understand what you are talking about."
So he went out into the outer court.
Then the cock crowed.
The maid saw him and began again to say to the bystanders,
  "This man is one of them."
Once again he denied it.
A little later the bystanders said to Peter once more,
  "Surely you are one of them; for you too are a Galilean."
He began to curse and to swear,
  "I do not know this man about whom you are talking."
And immediately a cock crowed a second time.
Then Peter remembered the word that Jesus had said to him,
  "Before the cock crows twice you will deny me three times."
He broke down and wept.

As soon as morning came,
  the chief priests with the elders and the scribes,
  that is, the whole Sanhedrin, held a council.
They bound Jesus, led him away, and handed him over to Pilate.
Pilate questioned him,
  "Are you the king of the Jews?"
He said to him in reply, "You say so."
The chief priests accused him of many things.
Again Pilate questioned him,
  "Have you no answer?
See how many things they accuse you of."
Jesus gave him no further answer, so that Pilate was amazed.

Now on the occasion of the feast he used to release to them
  one prisoner whom they requested.
A man called Barabbas was then in prison
  along with the rebels who had committed murder in a rebellion.
The crowd came forward and began to ask him
  to do for them as he was accustomed.
Pilate answered,
  "Do you want me to release to you the king of the Jews?"
For he knew that it was out of envy
  that the chief priests had handed him over.
But the chief priests stirred up the crowd
  to have him release Barabbas for them instead.
Pilate again said to them in reply,
  "Then what do you want me to do
  with the man you call the king of the Jews?"
They shouted again, "Crucify him."
Pilate said to them, "Why? What evil has he done?"
They only shouted the louder, "Crucify him."
So Pilate, wishing to satisfy the crowd,
  released Barabbas to them and, after he had Jesus scourged,
  handed him over to be crucified.

The soldiers led him away inside the palace,
  that is, the praetorium, and assembled the whole cohort.

They clothed him in purple and,
  weaving a crown of thorns, placed it on him.
They began to salute him with, "Hail, King of the Jews!"
  and kept striking his head with a reed and spitting upon him.
They knelt before him in homage.
And when they had mocked him,
  they stripped him of the purple cloak,
  dressed him in his own clothes,
  and led him out to crucify him.

They pressed into service a passer-by, Simon,
  a Cyrenian, who was coming in from the country,
  the father of Alexander and Rufus,
  to carry his cross.

They brought him to the place of Golgotha
  —which is translated Place of the Skull—.
They gave him wine drugged with myrrh,
  but he did not take it.
Then they crucified him and divided his garments
  by casting lots for them to see what each should take.
It was nine o'clock in the morning when they crucified him.
The inscription of the charge against him read,
  "The King of the Jews."
With him they crucified two revolutionaries,
  one on his right and one on his left.
Those passing by reviled him,
  shaking their heads and saying,
  "Aha! You who would destroy the temple
  and rebuild it in three days,
  save yourself by coming down from the cross."
Likewise the chief priests, with the scribes,
  mocked him among themselves and said,
  "He saved others; he cannot save himself.
Let the Christ, the King of Israel,
  come down now from the cross
  that we may see and believe."
Those who were crucified with him also kept abusing him.

At noon darkness came over the whole land
  until three in the afternoon.
And at three o'clock Jesus cried out in a loud voice,
  "Eloi, Eloi, lema sabachthani?"
  which is translated,
  "My God, my God, why have you forsaken me?"
Some of the bystanders who heard it said,
  "Look, he is calling Elijah."
One of them ran, soaked a sponge with wine, put it on a reed
  and gave it to him to drink saying,
  "Wait, let us see if Elijah comes to take him down."
Jesus gave a loud cry and breathed his last.

Here all kneel and pause for a short time.

The veil of the sanctuary was torn in two from top to bottom.
When the centurion who stood facing him
  saw how he breathed his last he said,
  "Truly this man was the Son of God!"
There were also women looking on from a distance.
Among them were Mary Magdalene,
  Mary the mother of the younger James and of Joses,
    and Salome.

These women had followed him when he was in Galilee
  and ministered to him.
There were also many other women
  who had come up with him to Jerusalem.

When it was already evening,
  since it was the day of preparation,
  the day before the sabbath, Joseph of Arimathea,
  a distinguished member of the council,
  who was himself awaiting the kingdom of God,
  came and courageously went to Pilate
  and asked for the body of Jesus.
Pilate was amazed that he was already dead.
He summoned the centurion
  and asked him if Jesus had already died.
And when he learned of it from the centurion,
  he gave the body to Joseph.
Having bought a linen cloth, he took him down,
  wrapped him in the linen cloth,
  and laid him in a tomb that had been hewn out of the rock.
Then he rolled a stone against the entrance to the tomb.
Mary Magdalene and Mary the mother of Joses
  watched where he was laid.

or Mark 15:1-39; L38B

As soon as morning came,
  the chief priests with the elders and the scribes,
  that is, the whole Sanhedrin, held a council.
They bound Jesus, led him away, and handed him over to Pilate.
Pilate questioned him,
  "Are you the king of the Jews?"
He said to him in reply, "You say so."
The chief priests accused him of many things.
Again Pilate questioned him,
  "Have you no answer?
See how many things they accuse you of."
Jesus gave him no further answer, so that Pilate was amazed.

Now on the occasion of the feast he used to release to them
  one prisoner whom they requested.
A man called Barabbas was then in prison
  along with the rebels who had committed murder in a rebellion.
The crowd came forward and began to ask him
  to do for them as he was accustomed.
Pilate answered,
  "Do you want me to release to you the king of the Jews?"
For he knew that it was out of envy
  that the chief priests had handed him over.
But the chief priests stirred up the crowd
  to have him release Barabbas for them instead.
Pilate again said to them in reply,
  "Then what do you want me to do
  with the man you call the king of the Jews?"
They shouted again, "Crucify him."
Pilate said to them, "Why? What evil has he done?"
They only shouted the louder, "Crucify him."
So Pilate, wishing to satisfy the crowd,
  released Barabbas to them and, after he had Jesus scourged,
  handed him over to be crucified.

The soldiers led him away inside the palace,
  that is, the praetorium, and assembled the whole cohort.
They clothed him in purple and,
  weaving a crown of thorns, placed it on him.
They began to salute him with, "Hail, King of the Jews!"
  and kept striking his head with a reed and spitting upon him.
They knelt before him in homage.
And when they had mocked him,
  they stripped him of the purple cloak,
  dressed him in his own clothes,
  and led him out to crucify him.

They pressed into service a passer-by, Simon,
  a Cyrenian, who was coming in from the country,
  the father of Alexander and Rufus,
  to carry his cross.

They brought him to the place of Golgotha
  —which is translated Place of the Skull—.
They gave him wine drugged with myrrh,
  but he did not take it.
Then they crucified him and divided his garments
  by casting lots for them to see what each should take.
It was nine o'clock in the morning when they crucified him.
The inscription of the charge against him read,
  "The King of the Jews."
With him they crucified two revolutionaries,
  one on his right and one on his left.
Those passing by reviled him,
  shaking their heads and saying,

"Aha! You who would destroy the temple
  and rebuild it in three days,
  save yourself by coming down from the cross."
Likewise the chief priests, with the scribes,
  mocked him among themselves and said,
  "He saved others; he cannot save himself.
Let the Christ, the King of Israel,
  come down now from the cross
  that we may see and believe."
Those who were crucified with him also kept abusing him.

At noon darkness came over the whole land
  until three in the afternoon.
And at three o'clock Jesus cried out in a loud voice,
  "Eloi, Eloi, lema sabachthani?"
  which is translated,
  "My God, my God, why have you forsaken me?"
Some of the bystanders who heard it said,
  "Look, he is calling Elijah."
One of them ran, soaked a sponge with wine, put it on a reed
  and gave it to him to drink saying,
  "Wait, let us see if Elijah comes to take him down."
Jesus gave a loud cry and breathed his last.

Here all kneel and pause for a short time.

The veil of the sanctuary was torn in two from top to bottom.
When the centurion who stood facing him
  saw how he breathed his last he said,
  "Truly this man was the Son of God!"

Gospel (cont.)
John 13:1-15; L39ABC

So when he had washed their feet
  and put his garments back on and reclined at table again,
  he said to them, "Do you realize what I have done for you?
You call me 'teacher' and 'master,' and rightly so, for indeed I am.
If I, therefore, the master and teacher, have washed your feet,
  you ought to wash one another's feet.
I have given you a model to follow,
  so that as I have done for you, you should also do."

FIRST READING
Exod 12:1-8, 11-14

The LORD said to Moses and Aaron in the land
  of Egypt,
  "This month shall stand at the head of
    your calendar;
  you shall reckon it the first month of the
    year.
Tell the whole community of Israel:
  On the tenth of this month every one of
    your families
  must procure for itself a lamb, one apiece
    for each household.
If a family is too small for a whole lamb,
  it shall join the nearest household in
    procuring one
  and shall share in the lamb
  in proportion to the number of persons
    who partake of it.
The lamb must be a year-old male and
  without blemish.
You may take it from either the sheep or the
  goats.
You shall keep it until the fourteenth day of
  this month,
  and then, with the whole assembly of Israel
    present,
  it shall be slaughtered during the evening
    twilight.
They shall take some of its blood
  and apply it to the two doorposts and the
    lintel
  of every house in which they partake of
    the lamb.
That same night they shall eat its roasted
  flesh
  with unleavened bread and bitter herbs.

"This is how you are to eat it:
  with your loins girt, sandals on your feet
    and your staff in hand,
  you shall eat like those who are in flight.
It is the Passover of the LORD.
For on this same night I will go through Egypt,
  striking down every firstborn of the land,
    both man and beast,
  and executing judgment on all the gods of
    Egypt—I, the LORD!
But the blood will mark the houses where you
  are.
Seeing the blood, I will pass over you;
  thus, when I strike the land of Egypt,
  no destructive blow will come upon you.

"This day shall be a memorial feast for you,
  which all your generations shall celebrate
  with pilgrimage to the LORD, as a perpetual
    institution."

RESPONSORIAL PSALM
Ps 116:12-13, 15-16bc, 17-18

R̸. (cf. 1 Cor 10:16) Our blessing-cup is a communion with the Blood of Christ.

How shall I make a return to the LORD
  for all the good he has done for me?
The cup of salvation I will take up,
  and I will call upon the name of the LORD.

R̸. Our blessing-cup is a communion with the Blood of Christ.

Precious in the eyes of the LORD
  is the death of his faithful ones.
I am your servant, the son of your handmaid;
  you have loosed my bonds.

R̸. Our blessing-cup is a communion with the Blood of Christ.

To you will I offer sacrifice of thanksgiving,
  and I will call upon the name of the LORD.
My vows to the LORD I will pay
  in the presence of all his people.

R̸. Our blessing-cup is a communion with the Blood of Christ.

SECOND READING
1 Cor 11:23-26

Brothers and sisters:
I received from the Lord what I also handed
  on to you,
  that the Lord Jesus, on the night he was
    handed over,
  took bread, and, after he had given thanks,
  broke it and said, "This is my body that is
    for you.
Do this in remembrance of me."
In the same way also the cup, after supper,
  saying,
  "This cup is the new covenant in my blood.
Do this, as often as you drink it, in
  remembrance of me."
For as often as you eat this bread and drink
  the cup,
  you proclaim the death of the Lord until he
    comes.

Gospel (cont.)
John 18:1–19:42; L40ABC

So the band of soldiers, the tribune, and the Jewish guards seized Jesus,
    bound him, and brought him to Annas first.
He was the father-in-law of Caiaphas,
    who was high priest that year.
It was Caiaphas who had counseled the Jews
    that it was better that one man should die rather than the people.

Simon Peter and another disciple followed Jesus.
Now the other disciple was known to the high priest,
    and he entered the courtyard of the high priest with Jesus.
But Peter stood at the gate outside.
So the other disciple, the acquaintance of the high priest,
    went out and spoke to the gatekeeper and brought Peter in.
Then the maid who was the gatekeeper said to Peter,
    "You are not one of this man's disciples, are you?"
He said, "I am not."
Now the slaves and the guards were standing around a charcoal fire
    that they had made, because it was cold,
    and were warming themselves.
Peter was also standing there keeping warm.

The high priest questioned Jesus
    about his disciples and about his doctrine.
Jesus answered him,
    "I have spoken publicly to the world.
I have always taught in a synagogue
    or in the temple area where all the Jews gather,
    and in secret I have said nothing. Why ask me?
Ask those who heard me what I said to them.
They know what I said."
When he had said this,
    one of the temple guards standing there struck Jesus and said,
    "Is this the way you answer the high priest?"
Jesus answered him,
    "If I have spoken wrongly, testify to the wrong;
    but if I have spoken rightly, why do you strike me?"
Then Annas sent him bound to Caiaphas the high priest.

Now Simon Peter was standing there keeping warm.
And they said to him,
    "You are not one of his disciples, are you?"
He denied it and said,
    "I am not."
One of the slaves of the high priest,
    a relative of the one whose ear Peter had cut off, said,
    "Didn't I see you in the garden with him?"
Again Peter denied it.
And immediately the cock crowed.

Then they brought Jesus from Caiaphas to the praetorium.
It was morning.
And they themselves did not enter the praetorium,
    in order not to be defiled so that they could eat the Passover.
So Pilate came out to them and said,
    "What charge do you bring against this man?"
They answered and said to him,
    "If he were not a criminal,
    we would not have handed him over to you."
At this, Pilate said to them,
    "Take him yourselves, and judge him according to your law."

The Jews answered him,
    "We do not have the right to execute anyone,"
in order that the word of Jesus might be fulfilled
that he said indicating the kind of death he would die.
So Pilate went back into the praetorium
    and summoned Jesus and said to him,
    "Are you the King of the Jews?"
Jesus answered,
    "Do you say this on your own
    or have others told you about me?"
Pilate answered,
    "I am not a Jew, am I?
Your own nation and the chief priests handed you over to me.
What have you done?"
Jesus answered,
    "My kingdom does not belong to this world.
If my kingdom did belong to this world,
    my attendants would be fighting
    to keep me from being handed over to the Jews.
But as it is, my kingdom is not here."
So Pilate said to him,
    "Then you are a king?"
Jesus answered,
    "You say I am a king.
For this I was born and for this I came into the world,
    to testify to the truth.
Everyone who belongs to the truth listens to my voice."
Pilate said to him, "What is truth?"

When he had said this,
    he again went out to the Jews and said to them,
    "I find no guilt in him.
But you have a custom that I release one prisoner to you at Passover.
Do you want me to release to you the King of the Jews?"
They cried out again,
    "Not this one but Barabbas!"
Now Barabbas was a revolutionary.

Then Pilate took Jesus and had him scourged.
And the soldiers wove a crown out of thorns and placed it on his head,
    and clothed him in a purple cloak,
    and they came to him and said,
    "Hail, King of the Jews!"
And they struck him repeatedly.
Once more Pilate went out and said to them,
    "Look, I am bringing him out to you,
    so that you may know that I find no guilt in him."
So Jesus came out,
    wearing the crown of thorns and the purple cloak.
And he said to them, "Behold, the man!"
When the chief priests and the guards saw him they cried out,
    "Crucify him, crucify him!"
Pilate said to them,
    "Take him yourselves and crucify him.
I find no guilt in him."
The Jews answered,
    "We have a law, and according to that law he ought to die,
    because he made himself the Son of God."

Now when Pilate heard this statement,
   he became even more afraid,
   and went back into the praetorium and said to Jesus,
   "Where are you from?"
Jesus did not answer him.
So Pilate said to him,
   "Do you not speak to me?
Do you not know that I have power to release you
   and I have power to crucify you?"
Jesus answered him,
   "You would have no power over me
   if it had not been given to you from above.
For this reason the one who handed me over to you
   has the greater sin."
Consequently, Pilate tried to release him; but the Jews cried out,
   "If you release him, you are not a Friend of Caesar.
Everyone who makes himself a king opposes Caesar."

When Pilate heard these words he brought Jesus out
   and seated him on the judge's bench
   in the place called Stone Pavement, in Hebrew, Gabbatha.
It was preparation day for Passover, and it was about noon.
And he said to the Jews,
   "Behold, your king!"
They cried out,
   "Take him away, take him away! Crucify him!"
Pilate said to them,
   "Shall I crucify your king?"
The chief priests answered,
   "We have no king but Caesar."
Then he handed him over to them to be crucified.

So they took Jesus, and, carrying the cross himself,
   he went out to what is called the Place of the Skull,
   in Hebrew, Golgotha.
There they crucified him, and with him two others,
   one on either side, with Jesus in the middle.
Pilate also had an inscription written and put on the cross.
It read,
   "Jesus the Nazorean, the King of the Jews."
Now many of the Jews read this inscription,
   because the place where Jesus was crucified was near the city;
   and it was written in Hebrew, Latin, and Greek.
So the chief priests of the Jews said to Pilate,
   "Do not write 'The King of the Jews,'
   but that he said, 'I am the King of the Jews.'"
Pilate answered,
   "What I have written, I have written."

When the soldiers had crucified Jesus,
   they took his clothes and divided them into four shares,
   a share for each soldier.
They also took his tunic, but the tunic was seamless,
   woven in one piece from the top down.
So they said to one another,
   "Let's not tear it, but cast lots for it to see whose it will be,"
   in order that the passage of Scripture might be fulfilled that says:
    They divided my garments among them,
     and for my vesture they cast lots.

This is what the soldiers did.
Standing by the cross of Jesus were his mother
   and his mother's sister, Mary the wife of Clopas,
   and Mary of Magdala.
When Jesus saw his mother and the disciple there whom he loved
   he said to his mother, "Woman, behold, your son."
Then he said to the disciple,
   "Behold, your mother."
And from that hour the disciple took her into his home.

After this, aware that everything was now finished,
   in order that the Scripture might be fulfilled,
   Jesus said, "I thirst."
There was a vessel filled with common wine.
So they put a sponge soaked in wine on a sprig of hyssop
   and put it up to his mouth.
When Jesus had taken the wine, he said,
   "It is finished."
And bowing his head, he handed over the spirit.

Here all kneel and pause for a short time.

Now since it was preparation day,
   in order that the bodies might not remain
    on the cross on the sabbath,
   for the sabbath day of that week was a solemn one,
   the Jews asked Pilate that their legs be broken
   and that they be taken down.
So the soldiers came and broke the legs of the first
   and then of the other one who was crucified with Jesus.
But when they came to Jesus and saw that he was already dead,
   they did not break his legs,
   but one soldier thrust his lance into his side,
   and immediately blood and water flowed out.
An eyewitness has testified, and his testimony is true;
   he knows that he is speaking the truth,
   so that you also may come to believe.
For this happened so that the Scripture passage might be fulfilled:
   Not a bone of it will be broken.
And again another passage says:
   They will look upon him whom they have pierced.

After this, Joseph of Arimathea,
   secretly a disciple of Jesus for fear of the Jews,
   asked Pilate if he could remove the body of Jesus.
And Pilate permitted it.
So he came and took his body.
Nicodemus, the one who had first come to him at night,
   also came bringing a mixture of myrrh and aloes
   weighing about one hundred pounds.
They took the body of Jesus
   and bound it with burial cloths along with the spices,
   according to the Jewish burial custom.
Now in the place where he had been crucified there was a garden,
   and in the garden a new tomb, in which no one had yet been
    buried.
So they laid Jesus there because of the Jewish preparation day;
   for the tomb was close by.

FIRST READING

Isa 52:13–53:12

See, my servant shall prosper,
  he shall be raised high and greatly exalted.
Even as many were amazed at him—
  so marred was his look beyond human
    semblance
  and his appearance beyond that of the sons
    of man—
so shall he startle many nations,
  because of him kings shall stand speechless;
for those who have not been told shall see,
  those who have not heard shall ponder it.

Who would believe what we have heard?
  To whom has the arm of the LORD been
    revealed?
He grew up like a sapling before him,
  like a shoot from the parched earth;
there was in him no stately bearing to make
  us look at him,
  nor appearance that would attract us to him.
He was spurned and avoided by people,
  a man of suffering, accustomed to infirmity,
one of those from whom people hide their faces,
  spurned, and we held him in no esteem.

Yet it was our infirmities that he bore,
  our sufferings that he endured,
while we thought of him as stricken,
  as one smitten by God and afflicted.
But he was pierced for our offenses,
  crushed for our sins;
upon him was the chastisement that makes
  us whole,
  by his stripes we were healed.
We had all gone astray like sheep,
  each following his own way;
but the LORD laid upon him
  the guilt of us all.

Though he was harshly treated, he submitted
  and opened not his mouth;
like a lamb led to the slaughter
  or a sheep before the shearers,
  he was silent and opened not his mouth.
Oppressed and condemned, he was taken away,
  and who would have thought any more of
    his destiny?
When he was cut off from the land of the living,
  and smitten for the sin of his people,
a grave was assigned him among the wicked
  and a burial place with evildoers,
though he had done no wrong
  nor spoken any falsehood.
But the LORD was pleased
  to crush him in infirmity.

If he gives his life as an offering for sin,
  he shall see his descendants in a long life,
  and the will of the LORD shall be
    accomplished through him.

Because of his affliction
  he shall see the light
  in fullness of days;
through his suffering, my servant shall justify
  many,
  and their guilt he shall bear.
Therefore I will give him his portion among
  the great,
  and he shall divide the spoils with the
    mighty,
because he surrendered himself to death
  and was counted among the wicked;
and he shall take away the sins of many,
  and win pardon for their offenses.

RESPONSORIAL PSALM

Ps 31:2, 6, 12-13, 15-16, 17, 25

R℣. (Luke 23:46) Father, into your hands I
commend my spirit.

In you, O LORD, I take refuge;
  let me never be put to shame.
In your justice rescue me.
Into your hands I commend my spirit;
  you will redeem me, O LORD, O faithful God.

R℣. Father, into your hands I commend my
spirit.

For all my foes I am an object of reproach,
  a laughingstock to my neighbors, and a
    dread to my friends;
  they who see me abroad flee from me.
I am forgotten like the unremembered dead;
  I am like a dish that is broken.

R℣. Father, into your hands I commend my
spirit.

But my trust is in you, O LORD;
  I say, "You are my God.
In your hands is my destiny; rescue me
  from the clutches of my enemies and my
    persecutors."

R℣. Father, into your hands I commend my
spirit.

Let your face shine upon your servant;
  save me in your kindness.
Take courage and be stouthearted,
  all you who hope in the LORD.

R℣. Father, into your hands I commend my
spirit.

SECOND READING

Heb 4:14-16; 5:7-9

Brothers and sisters:
Since we have a great high priest who has
    passed through the heavens,
  Jesus, the Son of God,
  let us hold fast to our confession.
For we do not have a high priest
  who is unable to sympathize with our
    weaknesses,
  but one who has similarly been tested in
    every way,
  yet without sin.
So let us confidently approach the throne of
    grace
  to receive mercy and to find grace for
    timely help.

In the days when Christ was in the flesh,
  he offered prayers and supplications with
    loud cries and tears
  to the one who was able to save him from
    death,
  and he was heard because of his reverence.
Son though he was, he learned obedience
  from what he suffered;
  and when he was made perfect,
  he became the source of eternal salvation
    for all who obey him.

At the Easter Vigil in the Holy Night of Easter, April 4, 2015

FIRST READING
Gen 1:1–2:2

In the beginning, when God created the
    heavens and the earth,
    the earth was a formless wasteland, and
        darkness covered the abyss,
    while a mighty wind swept over the waters.

Then God said,
    "Let there be light," and there was light.
God saw how good the light was.
God then separated the light from the darkness.
God called the light "day," and the darkness
    he called "night."
Thus evening came, and morning followed—
    the first day.

Then God said,
    "Let there be a dome in the middle of the
        waters,
    to separate one body of water from the
        other."
And so it happened:
    God made the dome,
    and it separated the water above the dome
        from the water below it.
God called the dome "the sky."
Evening came, and morning followed—the
    second day.

Then God said,
    "Let the water under the sky be gathered
        into a single basin,
    so that the dry land may appear."
And so it happened:
    the water under the sky was gathered into
        its basin,
    and the dry land appeared.
God called the dry land "the earth,"
    and the basin of the water he called "the
        sea."
God saw how good it was.
Then God said,
    "Let the earth bring forth vegetation:
    every kind of plant that bears seed
    and every kind of fruit tree on earth
    that bears fruit with its seed in it."
And so it happened:
    the earth brought forth every kind of plant
        that bears seed
    and every kind of fruit tree on earth
    that bears fruit with its seed in it.
God saw how good it was.
Evening came, and morning followed—the
    third day.

Then God said:
    "Let there be lights in the dome of the sky,
    to separate day from night.
Let them mark the fixed times, the days and
    the years,

and serve as luminaries in the dome of the
    sky,
    to shed light upon the earth."
And so it happened:
    God made the two great lights,
    the greater one to govern the day,
    and the lesser one to govern the night;
    and he made the stars.
God set them in the dome of the sky,
    to shed light upon the earth,
    to govern the day and the night,
    and to separate the light from the darkness.
God saw how good it was.
Evening came, and morning followed—the
    fourth day.

Then God said,
    "Let the water teem with an abundance of
        living creatures,
    and on the earth let birds fly beneath the
        dome of the sky."
And so it happened:
    God created the great sea monsters
    and all kinds of swimming creatures with
        which the water teems,
    and all kinds of winged birds.
God saw how good it was, and God blessed
    them, saying,
    "Be fertile, multiply, and fill the water of
        the seas;
    and let the birds multiply on the earth."
Evening came, and morning followed—the
    fifth day.

Then God said,
    "Let the earth bring forth all kinds of
        living creatures:
    cattle, creeping things, and wild animals of
        all kinds."
And so it happened:
    God made all kinds of wild animals, all
        kinds of cattle,
    and all kinds of creeping things of the earth.
God saw how good it was.
Then God said:
    "Let us make man in our image, after our
        likeness.
Let them have dominion over the fish of the sea,
    the birds of the air, and the cattle,
    and over all the wild animals
    and all the creatures that crawl on the
        ground."
God created man in his image;
    in the image of God he created him;
    male and female he created them.
God blessed them, saying:
    "Be fertile and multiply;
    fill the earth and subdue it.
Have dominion over the fish of the sea, the
    birds of the air,

and all the living things that move on the
    earth."
God also said:
    "See, I give you every seed-bearing plant all
        over the earth
    and every tree that has seed-bearing fruit
        on it to be your food;
    and to all the animals of the land, all the
        birds of the air,
    and all the living creatures that crawl on
        the ground,
    I give all the green plants for food."
And so it happened.
God looked at everything he had made, and
    he found it very good.
Evening came, and morning followed—the
    sixth day.

Thus the heavens and the earth and all their
    array were completed.
Since on the seventh day God was finished
    with the work he had been doing,
    he rested on the seventh day from all the
        work he had undertaken.

or

Gen 1:1, 26-31a

In the beginning, when God created the
    heavens and the earth,
    God said: "Let us make man in our image,
        after our likeness.
Let them have dominion over the fish of the sea,
    the birds of the air, and the cattle,
    and over all the wild animals
    and all the creatures that crawl on the
        ground."
God created man in his image;
    in the image of God he created him;
    male and female he created them.
God blessed them, saying:
    "Be fertile and multiply;
    fill the earth and subdue it.
Have dominion over the fish of the sea, the
    birds of the air,
    and all the living things that move on the
        earth."
God also said:
    "See, I give you every seed-bearing plant all
        over the earth
    and every tree that has seed-bearing fruit
        on it to be your food;
    and to all the animals of the land, all the
        birds of the air,
    and all the living creatures that crawl on
        the ground,
    I give all the green plants for food."
And so it happened.
God looked at everything he had made, and
    found it very good.

RESPONSORIAL PSALM

Ps 104:1-2, 5-6, 10, 12, 13-14, 24, 35

℟. (30) Lord, send out your Spirit, and renew the face of the earth.

Bless the Lord, O my soul!
  O Lord, my God, you are great indeed!
You are clothed with majesty and glory,
  robed in light as with a cloak.

℟. Lord, send out your Spirit, and renew the face of the earth.

You fixed the earth upon its foundation,
  not to be moved forever;
with the ocean, as with a garment, you
    covered it;
  above the mountains the waters stood.

℟. Lord, send out your Spirit, and renew the face of the earth.

You send forth springs into the watercourses
  that wind among the mountains.
Beside them the birds of heaven dwell;
  from among the branches they send forth
    their song.

℟. Lord, send out your Spirit, and renew the face of the earth.

You water the mountains from your palace;
  the earth is replete with the fruit of your
    works.
You raise grass for the cattle,
  and vegetation for man's use,
producing bread from the earth.

℟. Lord, send out your Spirit, and renew the face of the earth.

How manifold are your works, O Lord!
  In wisdom you have wrought them all—
the earth is full of your creatures.
  Bless the Lord, O my soul!

℟. Lord, send out your Spirit, and renew the face of the earth.

or

Ps 33:4-5, 6-7, 12-13, 20, 22

℟. (5b) The earth is full of the goodness of the Lord.

Upright is the word of the Lord,
  and all his works are trustworthy.
He loves justice and right;
  of the kindness of the Lord the earth is full.

℟. The earth is full of the goodness of the Lord.

By the word of the Lord the heavens were
    made;
  by the breath of his mouth all their host.
He gathers the waters of the sea as in a
    flask;
  in cellars he confines the deep.

℟. The earth is full of the goodness of the Lord.

Blessed the nation whose God is the Lord,
  the people he has chosen for his own
    inheritance.
From heaven the Lord looks down;
  he sees all mankind.

℟. The earth is full of the goodness of the Lord.

Our soul waits for the Lord,
  who is our help and our shield.
May your kindness, O Lord, be upon us
  who have put our hope in you.

℟. The earth is full of the goodness of the Lord.

SECOND READING

Gen 22:1-18

God put Abraham to the test.
He called to him, "Abraham!"
"Here I am," he replied.
Then God said:
  "Take your son Isaac, your only one, whom
      you love,
  and go to the land of Moriah.
There you shall offer him up as a holocaust
  on a height that I will point out to you."
Early the next morning Abraham saddled his
    donkey,
  took with him his son Isaac and two of his
      servants as well,
  and with the wood that he had cut for the
      holocaust,
  set out for the place of which God had told
      him.

On the third day Abraham got sight of the
    place from afar.
Then he said to his servants:
  "Both of you stay here with the donkey,
  while the boy and I go on over yonder.
We will worship and then come back to you."
Thereupon Abraham took the wood for the
    holocaust
  and laid it on his son Isaac's shoulders,
  while he himself carried the fire and the
      knife.
As the two walked on together, Isaac spoke to
    his father Abraham:
  "Father!" Isaac said.
"Yes, son," he replied.
Isaac continued, "Here are the fire and the
    wood,
  but where is the sheep for the holocaust?"
"Son," Abraham answered,
  "God himself will provide the sheep for the
      holocaust."
Then the two continued going forward.

When they came to the place of which God
    had told him,

Abraham built an altar there and arranged
    the wood on it.
Next he tied up his son Isaac,
  and put him on top of the wood on the altar.
Then he reached out and took the knife to
    slaughter his son.
But the Lord's messenger called to him from
    heaven,
  "Abraham, Abraham!"
"Here I am," he answered.
"Do not lay your hand on the boy," said the
    messenger.
"Do not do the least thing to him.
I know now how devoted you are to God,
  since you did not withhold from me your
      own beloved son."
As Abraham looked about,
  he spied a ram caught by its horns in the
      thicket.
So he went and took the ram
  and offered it up as a holocaust in place of
      his son.
Abraham named the site Yahweh-yireh;
  hence people now say, "On the mountain
      the Lord will see."

Again the Lord's messenger called to
    Abraham from heaven and said:
  "I swear by myself, declares the Lord,
  that because you acted as you did
  in not withholding from me your beloved
      son,
  I will bless you abundantly
  and make your descendants as countless
  as the stars of the sky and the sands of the
      seashore;
  your descendants shall take possession
  of the gates of their enemies,
  and in your descendants all the nations of
      the earth
    shall find blessing—
  all this because you obeyed my
      command."

or

Gen 22:1-2, 9a, 10-13, 15-18

God put Abraham to the test.
He called to him, "Abraham!"
"Here I am," he replied.
Then God said:
  "Take your son Isaac, your only one, whom
      you love,
  and go to the land of Moriah.
There you shall offer him up as a holocaust
  on a height that I will point out to you."

When they came to the place of which God
    had told him,
  Abraham built an altar there and arranged
      the wood on it.

Then he reached out and took the knife to
  slaughter his son.
But the Lord's messenger called to him from
  heaven,
  "Abraham, Abraham!"
"Here I am," he answered.
"Do not lay your hand on the boy," said the
  messenger.
"Do not do the least thing to him.
I know now how devoted you are to God,
  since you did not withhold from me your
    own beloved son."
As Abraham looked about,
  he spied a ram caught by its horns in the
    thicket.
So he went and took the ram
  and offered it up as a holocaust in place of
    his son.

Again the Lord's messenger called to
  Abraham from heaven and said:
"I swear by myself, declares the Lord,
  that because you acted as you did
  in not withholding from me your beloved son,
  I will bless you abundantly
  and make your descendants as countless
  as the stars of the sky and the sands of the
    seashore;
  your descendants shall take possession
  of the gates of their enemies,
  and in your descendants all the nations of
    the earth
    shall find blessing—
  all this because you obeyed my command."

RESPONSORIAL PSALM
Ps 16:5, 8, 9-10, 11

℟. (1) You are my inheritance, O Lord.

O Lord, my allotted portion and my cup,
  you it is who hold fast my lot.
I set the Lord ever before me;
  with him at my right hand I shall not be
    disturbed.

℟. You are my inheritance, O Lord.

Therefore my heart is glad and my soul rejoices,
  my body, too, abides in confidence;
because you will not abandon my soul to the
  netherworld,
  nor will you suffer your faithful one to
    undergo corruption.

℟. You are my inheritance, O Lord.

You will show me the path to life,
  fullness of joys in your presence,
  the delights at your right hand forever.

℟. You are my inheritance, O Lord.

THIRD READING
Exod 14:15–15:1

The Lord said to Moses, "Why are you crying
  out to me?
Tell the Israelites to go forward.
And you, lift up your staff and, with hand
  outstretched over the sea,
  split the sea in two,
  that the Israelites may pass through it on
    dry land.
But I will make the Egyptians so obstinate
  that they will go in after them.
Then I will receive glory through Pharaoh
  and all his army,
  his chariots and charioteers.
The Egyptians shall know that I am the Lord,
  when I receive glory through Pharaoh
  and his chariots and charioteers."

The angel of God, who had been leading
  Israel's camp,
  now moved and went around behind them.
The column of cloud also, leaving the front,
  took up its place behind them,
  so that it came between the camp of the
    Egyptians
  and that of Israel.
But the cloud now became dark, and thus the
  night passed
  without the rival camps coming any closer
    together all night long.
Then Moses stretched out his hand over the
  sea,
  and the Lord swept the sea
  with a strong east wind throughout the night
  and so turned it into dry land.
When the water was thus divided,
  the Israelites marched into the midst of the
    sea on dry land,
  with the water like a wall to their right and
    to their left.

The Egyptians followed in pursuit;
  all Pharaoh's horses and chariots and
    charioteers went after them
  right into the midst of the sea.
In the night watch just before dawn
  the Lord cast through the column of the
    fiery cloud
  upon the Egyptian force a glance that
    threw it into a panic;
  and he so clogged their chariot wheels
  that they could hardly drive.
With that the Egyptians sounded the retreat
  before Israel,
  because the Lord was fighting for them
    against the Egyptians.

Then the Lord told Moses, "Stretch out your
  hand over the sea,
  that the water may flow back upon the
    Egyptians,
  upon their chariots and their charioteers."
So Moses stretched out his hand over the sea,
  and at dawn the sea flowed back to its
    normal depth.
The Egyptians were fleeing head on toward
  the sea,
  when the Lord hurled them into its midst.
As the water flowed back,
  it covered the chariots and the charioteers
    of Pharaoh's whole army
  which had followed the Israelites into the sea.
Not a single one of them escaped.
But the Israelites had marched on dry land
  through the midst of the sea,
  with the water like a wall to their right and
    to their left.
Thus the Lord saved Israel on that day
  from the power of the Egyptians.
When Israel saw the Egyptians lying dead on
  the seashore
  and beheld the great power that the Lord
    had shown against the Egyptians,
  they feared the Lord and believed in him
    and in his servant Moses.

Then Moses and the Israelites sang this song
  to the Lord:
  I will sing to the Lord, for he is gloriously
    triumphant;
  horse and chariot he has cast into the sea.

RESPONSORIAL PSALM
Exod 15:1-2, 3-4, 5-6, 17-18

℟. (1b) Let us sing to the Lord; he has covered
himself in glory.

I will sing to the Lord, for he is gloriously
    triumphant;
  horse and chariot he has cast into the sea.
My strength and my courage is the Lord,
  and he has been my savior.
He is my God, I praise him;
  the God of my father, I extol him.

℟. Let us sing to the Lord; he has covered
himself in glory.

The Lord is a warrior,
  Lord is his name!
Pharaoh's chariots and army he hurled into
  the sea;
  the elite of his officers were submerged in
    the Red Sea.

℟. Let us sing to the Lord; he has covered
himself in glory.

The flood waters covered them,
    they sank into the depths like a stone.
Your right hand, O LORD, magnificent in
    power,
    your right hand, O LORD, has shattered the
    enemy.

R℣. Let us sing to the Lord; he has covered
himself in glory.

You brought in the people you redeemed
    and planted them on the mountain of your
    inheritance—
the place where you made your seat, O LORD,
    the sanctuary, LORD, which your hands
    established.
The LORD shall reign forever and ever.

R℣. Let us sing to the Lord; he has covered
himself in glory.

FOURTH READING
Isa 54:5-14

The One who has become your husband is
    your Maker;
    his name is the LORD of hosts;
your redeemer is the Holy One of Israel,
    called God of all the earth.
The LORD calls you back,
    like a wife forsaken and grieved in spirit,
    a wife married in youth and then cast off,
    says your God.
For a brief moment I abandoned you,
    but with great tenderness I will take you
    back.
In an outburst of wrath, for a moment
    I hid my face from you;
but with enduring love I take pity on you,
    says the LORD, your redeemer.
This is for me like the days of Noah,
    when I swore that the waters of Noah
    should never again deluge the earth;
so I have sworn not to be angry with you,
    or to rebuke you.
Though the mountains leave their place
    and the hills be shaken,
my love shall never leave you
    nor my covenant of peace be shaken,
    says the LORD, who has mercy on you.
O afflicted one, storm-battered and
    unconsoled,
    I lay your pavements in carnelians,
    and your foundations in sapphires;
I will make your battlements of rubies,
    your gates of carbuncles,
    and all your walls of precious stones.
All your children shall be taught by the LORD,
    and great shall be the peace of your children.

In justice shall you be established,
    far from the fear of oppression,
    where destruction cannot come near you.

RESPONSORIAL PSALM
Ps 30:2, 4, 5-6, 11-12, 13

R℣. (2a) I will praise you, Lord, for you have
rescued me.

I will extol you, O LORD, for you drew me
    clear
    and did not let my enemies rejoice over me.
O LORD, you brought me up from the
    netherworld;
    you preserved me from among those going
    down into the pit.

R℣. I will praise you, Lord, for you have
rescued me.

Sing praise to the LORD, you his faithful ones,
    and give thanks to his holy name.
For his anger lasts but a moment;
    a lifetime, his good will.
At nightfall, weeping enters in,
    but with the dawn, rejoicing.

R℣. I will praise you, Lord, for you have
rescued me.

Hear, O LORD, and have pity on me;
    O LORD, be my helper.
You changed my mourning into dancing;
    O LORD, my God, forever will I give you
    thanks.

R℣. I will praise you, Lord, for you have
rescued me.

FIFTH READING
Isa 55:1-11

Thus says the LORD:
All you who are thirsty,
    come to the water!
You who have no money,
    come, receive grain and eat;
come, without paying and without cost,
    drink wine and milk!
Why spend your money for what is not bread,
    your wages for what fails to satisfy?
Heed me, and you shall eat well,
    you shall delight in rich fare.
Come to me heedfully,
    listen, that you may have life.
I will renew with you the everlasting
    covenant,
    the benefits assured to David.
As I made him a witness to the peoples,
    a leader and commander of nations,
so shall you summon a nation you knew not,

and nations that knew you not shall run
    to you,
because of the LORD, your God,
    the Holy One of Israel, who has glorified you.

Seek the LORD while he may be found,
    call him while he is near.
Let the scoundrel forsake his way,
    and the wicked man his thoughts;
let him turn to the LORD for mercy;
    to our God, who is generous in forgiving.
For my thoughts are not your thoughts,
    nor are your ways my ways, says the LORD.
As high as the heavens are above the earth,
    so high are my ways above your ways
    and my thoughts above your thoughts.

For just as from the heavens
    the rain and snow come down
and do not return there
    till they have watered the earth,
    making it fertile and fruitful,
giving seed to the one who sows
    and bread to the one who eats,
so shall my word be
    that goes forth from my mouth;
my word shall not return to me void,
    but shall do my will,
    achieving the end for which I sent it.

RESPONSORIAL PSALM
Isa 12:2-3, 4, 5-6

R℣. (3) You will draw water joyfully from the
springs of salvation.

God indeed is my savior;
    I am confident and unafraid.
My strength and my courage is the LORD,
    and he has been my savior.
With joy you will draw water
    at the fountain of salvation.

R℣. You will draw water joyfully from the
springs of salvation.

Give thanks to the LORD, acclaim his name;
    among the nations make known his deeds,
    proclaim how exalted is his name.

R℣. You will draw water joyfully from the
springs of salvation.

Sing praise to the LORD for his glorious
    achievement;
    let this be known throughout all the earth.
Shout with exultation, O city of Zion,
    for great in your midst
    is the Holy One of Israel!

R℣. You will draw water joyfully from the
springs of salvation.

SIXTH READING

Bar 3:9-15, 32—4:4

Hear, O Israel, the commandments of life:
  listen, and know prudence!
How is it, Israel,
    that you are in the land of your foes,
    grown old in a foreign land,
defiled with the dead,
    accounted with those destined for the
      netherworld?
You have forsaken the fountain of wisdom!
  Had you walked in the way of God,
  you would have dwelt in enduring peace.
Learn where prudence is,
  where strength, where understanding;
that you may know also
  where are length of days, and life,
  where light of the eyes, and peace.
Who has found the place of wisdom,
  who has entered into her treasuries?

The One who knows all things knows her;
  he has probed her by his knowledge—
the One who established the earth for all
      time,
    and filled it with four-footed beasts;
  he who dismisses the light, and it departs,
  calls it, and it obeys him trembling;
before whom the stars at their posts
  shine and rejoice;
when he calls them, they answer, "Here we
    are!"
  shining with joy for their Maker.
Such is our God;
  no other is to be compared to him:
he has traced out the whole way of
    understanding,
  and has given her to Jacob, his servant,
  to Israel, his beloved son.

Since then she has appeared on earth,
  and moved among people.
She is the book of the precepts of God,
  the law that endures forever;
all who cling to her will live,
  but those will die who forsake her.
Turn, O Jacob, and receive her:
  walk by her light toward splendor.
Give not your glory to another,
  your privileges to an alien race.
Blessed are we, O Israel;
  for what pleases God is known to us!

RESPONSORIAL PSALM

Ps 19:8, 9, 10, 11

R⁊. (John 6:68c) Lord, you have the words of
everlasting life.

The law of the LORD is perfect,
  refreshing the soul;
the decree of the LORD is trustworthy,
  giving wisdom to the simple.

R⁊. Lord, you have the words of everlasting life.

The precepts of the LORD are right,
  rejoicing the heart;
the command of the LORD is clear,
  enlightening the eye.

R⁊. Lord, you have the words of everlasting life.

The fear of the LORD is pure,
  enduring forever;
the ordinances of the LORD are true,
  all of them just.

R⁊. Lord, you have the words of everlasting life.

They are more precious than gold,
  than a heap of purest gold;
sweeter also than syrup
  or honey from the comb.

R⁊. Lord, you have the words of everlasting life.

SEVENTH READING

Ezek 36:16-17a, 18-28

The word of the LORD came to me, saying:
  Son of man, when the house of Israel lived
    in their land,
  they defiled it by their conduct and deeds.
Therefore I poured out my fury upon them
  because of the blood that they poured out
    on the ground,
  and because they defiled it with idols.
I scattered them among the nations,
  dispersing them over foreign lands;
  according to their conduct and deeds I
    judged them.
But when they came among the nations
    wherever they came,
  they served to profane my holy name,
  because it was said of them: "These are the
    people of the LORD,
  yet they had to leave their land."
So I have relented because of my holy name
  which the house of Israel profaned
  among the nations where they came.
Therefore say to the house of Israel: Thus
    says the Lord GOD:
  Not for your sakes do I act, house of Israel,
  but for the sake of my holy name,
  which you profaned among the nations to
    which you came.
I will prove the holiness of my great name,
  profaned among the nations,
  in whose midst you have profaned it.
Thus the nations shall know that I am the
    LORD, says the Lord GOD,
  when in their sight I prove my holiness
    through you.
For I will take you away from among the
    nations,

gather you from all the foreign lands,
  and bring you back to your own land.
I will sprinkle clean water upon you
  to cleanse you from all your impurities,
  and from all your idols I will cleanse you.
I will give you a new heart and place a new
    spirit within you,
  taking from your bodies your stony hearts
  and giving you natural hearts.
I will put my spirit within you and make you
    live by my statutes,
  careful to observe my decrees.
You shall live in the land I gave your fathers;
  you shall be my people, and I will be your
    God.

RESPONSORIAL PSALM

Ps 42:3, 5; 43:3, 4

R⁊. (42:2) Like a deer that longs for running
streams, my soul longs for you, my God.

Athirst is my soul for God, the living God.
  When shall I go and behold the face of God?

R⁊. Like a deer that longs for running streams,
my soul longs for you, my God.

I went with the throng
  and led them in procession to the house of
    God,
  amid loud cries of joy and thanksgiving,
  with the multitude keeping festival.

R⁊. Like a deer that longs for running streams,
my soul longs for you, my God.

Send forth your light and your fidelity;
  they shall lead me on
and bring me to your holy mountain,
  to your dwelling-place.

R⁊. Like a deer that longs for running streams,
my soul longs for you, my God.

Then will I go in to the altar of God,
  the God of my gladness and joy;
then will I give you thanks upon the harp,
  O God, my God!

R⁊. Like a deer that longs for running streams,
my soul longs for you, my God.

or

Isa 12:2-3, 4bcd, 5-6

R⁊. (3) You will draw water joyfully from the
springs of salvation.

God indeed is my savior;
  I am confident and unafraid.
My strength and my courage is the LORD,
  and he has been my savior.
With joy you will draw water
  at the fountain of salvation.

R⁊. You will draw water joyfully from the
springs of salvation.

At the Easter Vigil in the Holy Night of Easter, *April 4, 2015*

Give thanks to the LORD, acclaim his name;
    among the nations make known his deeds,
    proclaim how exalted is his name.

R∕. You will draw water joyfully from the springs of salvation.

Sing praise to the LORD for his glorious achievement;
    let this be known throughout all the earth.
Shout with exultation, O city of Zion,
    for great in your midst
    is the Holy One of Israel!

R∕. You will draw water joyfully from the springs of salvation.

or

Ps 51:12-13, 14-15, 18-19

R∕. (12a) Create a clean heart in me, O God.

A clean heart create for me, O God,
    and a steadfast spirit renew within me.
Cast me not out from your presence,
    and your Holy Spirit take not from me.

R∕. Create a clean heart in me, O God.

Give me back the joy of your salvation,
    and a willing spirit sustain in me.
I will teach transgressors your ways,
    and sinners shall return to you.

R∕. Create a clean heart in me, O God.

For you are not pleased with sacrifices;
    should I offer a holocaust, you would not accept it.
My sacrifice, O God, is a contrite spirit;
    a heart contrite and humbled, O God, you will not spurn.

R∕. Create a clean heart in me, O God.

EPISTLE
Rom 6:3-11

Brothers and sisters:
Are you unaware that we who were baptized
    into Christ Jesus
    were baptized into his death?
We were indeed buried with him through
    baptism into death,
    so that, just as Christ was raised from the dead
    by the glory of the Father,
    we too might live in newness of life.

For if we have grown into union with him
    through a death like his,
    we shall also be united with him in the resurrection.
We know that our old self was crucified with him,
    so that our sinful body might be done away with,
    that we might no longer be in slavery to sin.
For a dead person has been absolved from sin.
If, then, we have died with Christ,
    we believe that we shall also live with him.
We know that Christ, raised from the dead, dies no more;
    death no longer has power over him.
As to his death, he died to sin once and for all;
    as to his life, he lives for God.
Consequently, you too must think of
    yourselves as being dead to sin
    and living for God in Christ Jesus.

RESPONSORIAL PSALM
Ps 118:1-2, 16-17, 22-23

R∕. Alleluia, alleluia, alleluia.

Give thanks to the LORD, for he is good,
    for his mercy endures forever.
Let the house of Israel say,
    "His mercy endures forever."

R∕. Alleluia, alleluia, alleluia.

The right hand of the LORD has struck with power;
    the right hand of the LORD is exalted.
I shall not die, but live,
    and declare the works of the LORD.

R∕. Alleluia, alleluia, alleluia.

The stone which the builders rejected
    has become the cornerstone.
By the LORD has this been done;
    it is wonderful in our eyes.

R∕. Alleluia, alleluia, alleluia.

Gospel
Mark 16:1-7; L41B

When the sabbath was over,
   Mary Magdalene, Mary, the mother of James, and Salome
   bought spices so that they might go and anoint him.
Very early when the sun had risen,
   on the first day of the week, they came to the tomb.
They were saying to one another,
   "Who will roll back the stone for us
   from the entrance to the tomb?"
When they looked up,
   they saw that the stone had been rolled back;
   it was very large.

On entering the tomb they saw a young man
   sitting on the right side, clothed in a white robe,
   and they were utterly amazed.
He said to them, "Do not be amazed!
You seek Jesus of Nazareth, the crucified.
He has been raised; he is not here.
Behold the place where they laid him.
But go and tell his disciples and Peter,
   'He is going before you to Galilee;
   there you will see him, as he told you.'"

or, at an afternoon or evening Mass

Gospel
Luke 24:13-35; L46

That very day, the first day of the week,
   two of Jesus' disciples were going
   to a village seven miles from Jerusalem called Emmaus,
   and they were conversing about all the things that had occurred.
And it happened that while they were conversing and debating,
   Jesus himself drew near and walked with them,
   but their eyes were prevented from recognizing him.
He asked them,
   "What are you discussing as you walk along?"
They stopped, looking downcast.
One of them, named Cleopas, said to him in reply,
   "Are you the only visitor to Jerusalem
   who does not know of the things
   that have taken place there in these days?"
And he replied to them, "What sort of things?"
They said to him,
   "The things that happened to Jesus the Nazarene,
   who was a prophet mighty in deed and word
   before God and all the people,
   how our chief priests and rulers both handed him over
   to a sentence of death and crucified him.
But we were hoping that he would be the one to redeem Israel;
   and besides all this,
   it is now the third day since this took place.
Some women from our group, however, have astounded us:
   they were at the tomb early in the morning
   and did not find his body;
   they came back and reported
   that they had indeed seen a vision of angels
   who announced that he was alive.
Then some of those with us went to the tomb
   and found things just as the women had described,
   but him they did not see."

And he said to them, "Oh, how foolish you are!
How slow of heart to believe all that the prophets spoke!
Was it not necessary that the Christ should suffer these things
   and enter into his glory?"
Then beginning with Moses and all the prophets,
   he interpreted to them what referred to him
   in all the Scriptures.
As they approached the village to which they were going,
   he gave the impression that he was going on farther.
But they urged him, "Stay with us,
   for it is nearly evening and the day is almost over."
So he went in to stay with them.
And it happened that, while he was with them at table,
   he took bread, said the blessing,
   broke it, and gave it to them.
With that their eyes were opened and they recognized him,
   but he vanished from their sight.
Then they said to each other,
   "Were not our hearts burning within us
   while he spoke to us on the way and opened the Scriptures to us?"
So they set out at once and returned to Jerusalem
   where they found gathered together
   the eleven and those with them who were saying,
   "The Lord has truly been raised and has appeared to Simon!"
Then the two recounted
   what had taken place on the way
   and how he was made known to them in the breaking of the bread.

Easter Sunday, *April 5, 2015*

FIRST READING
Acts 10:34a, 37-43

Peter proceeded to speak and said:
    "You know what has happened all over
        Judea,
    beginning in Galilee after the baptism
        that John preached,
    how God anointed Jesus of Nazareth
        with the Holy Spirit and power.
He went about doing good
    and healing all those oppressed by the devil,
        for God was with him.
We are witnesses of all that he did
    both in the country of the Jews and in
        Jerusalem.
They put him to death by hanging him on a
    tree.
This man God raised on the third day and
        granted that he be visible,
    not to all the people, but to us,
    the witnesses chosen by God in advance,
    who ate and drank with him after he rose
        from the dead.
He commissioned us to preach to the people
    and testify that he is the one appointed by
        God
    as judge of the living and the dead.
To him all the prophets bear witness,
    that everyone who believes in him
    will receive forgiveness of sins through his
        name."

RESPONSORIAL PSALM
Ps 118:1-2, 16-17, 22-23

℟. (24) This is the day the Lord has made; let
us rejoice and be glad.
        or:
℟. Alleluia.

Give thanks to the LORD, for he is good,
    for his mercy endures forever.
Let the house of Israel say,
    "His mercy endures forever."

℟. This is the day the Lord has made; let us
rejoice and be glad.
        or:
℟. Alleluia.

"The right hand of the LORD has struck with
    power;
    the right hand of the LORD is exalted.
I shall not die, but live,
    and declare the works of the LORD."

℟. This is the day the Lord has made; let us
rejoice and be glad.
        or:
℟. Alleluia.

The stone which the builders rejected
    has become the cornerstone.
By the LORD has this been done;
    it is wonderful in our eyes.

℟. This is the day the Lord has made; let us
rejoice and be glad.
        or:
℟. Alleluia.

SECOND READING
1 Cor 5:6b-8

Brothers and sisters:
Do you not know that a little yeast leavens all
    the dough?
Clear out the old yeast,
    so that you may become a fresh batch of
        dough,
    inasmuch as you are unleavened.
For our paschal lamb, Christ, has been
    sacrificed.
Therefore, let us celebrate the feast,
    not with the old yeast, the yeast of malice
        and wickedness,
    but with the unleavened bread of sincerity
        and truth.

or

Col 3:1-4

Brothers and sisters:
If then you were raised with Christ, seek what
        is above,
    where Christ is seated at the right hand of
        God.
Think of what is above, not of what is on earth.
For you have died, and your life is hidden
    with Christ in God.
When Christ your life appears,
    then you too will appear with him in glory.

SEQUENCE
Victimae paschali laudes

Christians, to the Paschal Victim
    Offer your thankful praises!
A Lamb the sheep redeems;
    Christ, who only is sinless,
    Reconciles sinners to the Father.
Death and life have contended in that combat
        stupendous:
    The Prince of life, who died, reigns
        immortal.
Speak, Mary, declaring
    What you saw, wayfaring.
"The tomb of Christ, who is living,
    The glory of Jesus' resurrection;
Bright angels attesting,
    The shroud and napkin resting.
Yes, Christ my hope is arisen;
    To Galilee he goes before you."
Christ indeed from death is risen, our new life
        obtaining.
    Have mercy, victor King, ever reigning!
    Amen. Alleluia.

Second Sunday of Easter (or Sunday of Divine Mercy), *April 12, 2015*

Gospel (cont.)
John 20:19-31; L44B

Then he said to Thomas, "Put your finger here and see my hands,
   and bring your hand and put it into my side,
   and do not be unbelieving, but believe."
Thomas answered and said to him, "My Lord and my God!"
Jesus said to him, "Have you come to believe because you have seen
      me?
Blessed are those who have not seen and have believed."

Now Jesus did many other signs in the presence of his disciples
   that are not written in this book.
But these are written that you may come to believe
   that Jesus is the Christ, the Son of God,
   and that through this belief you may have life in his name.

The Ascension of the Lord, *May 14, 2015 (Thursday) or May 17, 2015*

SECOND READING
Eph 1:17-23

Brothers and sisters:
May the God of our Lord Jesus Christ, the
      Father of glory,
   give you a Spirit of wisdom and revelation
   resulting in knowledge of him.
May the eyes of your hearts be enlightened,
   that you may know what is the hope that
         belongs to his call,
   what are the riches of glory
   in his inheritance among the holy ones,
   and what is the surpassing greatness of
      his power
   for us who believe,
   in accord with the exercise of his great
      might,
   which he worked in Christ,
   raising him from the dead
   and seating him at his right hand in the
      heavens,
   far above every principality, authority,
      power, and dominion,
   and every name that is named
   not only in this age but also in the one to
      come.
And he put all things beneath his feet
   and gave him as head over all things to the
      church,
   which is his body,
   the fullness of the one who fills all things
      in every way.

or

Eph 4:1-13

Brothers and sisters,
I, a prisoner for the Lord,
   urge you to live in a manner worthy of the
      call you have received,
   with all humility and gentleness, with
      patience,
   bearing with one another through love,
   striving to preserve the unity of the Spirit
   through the bond of peace:
   one body and one Spirit,
   as you were also called to the one hope of
      your call;
   one Lord, one faith, one baptism;
   one God and Father of all,
   who is over all and through all and in all.

But grace was given to each of us
   according to the measure of Christ's gift.
Therefore, it says:
      *He ascended on high and took prisoners
         captive;*
      he gave gifts to men.
What does "he ascended" mean except that he
      also descended
   into the lower regions of the earth?
The one who descended is also the one who
      ascended
   far above all the heavens,
   that he might fill all things.

And he gave some as apostles, others as
      prophets,
   others as evangelists, others as pastors and
      teachers,
   to equip the holy ones for the work of
      ministry,

for building up the body of Christ,
   until we all attain the unity of faith
   and knowledge of the Son of God, to
      mature to manhood,
   to the extent of the full stature of Christ.

or

Eph 4:1-7, 11-13

Brothers and sisters,
I, a prisoner for the Lord,
   urge you to live in a manner worthy of the
      call you have received,
   with all humility and gentleness, with
      patience,
   bearing with one another through love,
   striving to preserve the unity of the Spirit
   through the bond of peace:
   one body and one Spirit,
   as you were also called to the one hope of
      your call;
   one Lord, one faith, one baptism;
   one God and Father of all,
   who is over all and through all and in all.

But grace was given to each of us
   according to the measure of Christ's gift.

And he gave some as apostles, others as
      prophets,
   others as evangelists, others as pastors and
      teachers,
   to equip the holy ones for the work of
      ministry,
   for building up the body of Christ,
   until we all attain the unity of faith
   and knowledge of the Son of God, to
      mature to manhood,
   to the extent of the full stature of Christ.

SECOND READING

1 Cor 12:3b-7, 12-13

Brothers and sisters:
No one can say, "Jesus is Lord," except by the
    Holy Spirit.

There are different kinds of spiritual gifts but
    the same Spirit;
    there are different forms of service but the
        same Lord;
    there are different workings but the same God
    who produces all of them in everyone.
To each individual the manifestation of the
    Spirit
    is given for some benefit.

As a body is one though it has many parts,
    and all the parts of the body, though many,
        are one body,
    so also Christ.
For in one Spirit we were all baptized into one
        body,
    whether Jews or Greeks, slaves or free
        persons,
    and we were all given to drink of one Spirit.

or

Gal 5:16-25

Brothers and sisters, live by the Spirit
    and you will certainly not gratify the desire
        of the flesh.
For the flesh has desires against the Spirit,
    and the Spirit against the flesh;
    these are opposed to each other,
    so that you may not do what you want.
But if you are guided by the Spirit, you are
    not under the law.
Now the works of the flesh are obvious:
    immorality, impurity, lust, idolatry,
    sorcery, hatreds, rivalry, jealousy,
    outbursts of fury, acts of selfishness,
    dissensions, factions, occasions of envy,
    drinking bouts, orgies, and the like.
I warn you, as I warned you before,
    that those who do such things will not
        inherit the kingdom of God.
In contrast, the fruit of the Spirit is love, joy,
        peace,
    patience, kindness, generosity,
    faithfulness, gentleness, self-control.
Against such there is no law.
Now those who belong to Christ Jesus have
    crucified their flesh
    with its passions and desires.
If we live in the Spirit, let us also follow the
        Spirit.

SEQUENCE

Veni, Sancte Spiritus

Come, Holy Spirit, come!
And from your celestial home
    Shed a ray of light divine!
Come, Father of the poor!
Come, source of all our store!
    Come, within our bosoms shine.
You, of comforters the best;
You, the soul's most welcome guest;
    Sweet refreshment here below;
In our labor, rest most sweet;
Grateful coolness in the heat;
    Solace in the midst of woe.
O most blessed Light divine,
Shine within these hearts of yours,
    And our inmost being fill!
Where you are not, we have naught,
Nothing good in deed or thought,
    Nothing free from taint of ill.
Heal our wounds, our strength renew;
On our dryness pour your dew;
    Wash the stains of guilt away:
Bend the stubborn heart and will;
Melt the frozen, warm the chill;
    Guide the steps that go astray.
On the faithful, who adore
And confess you, evermore
    In your sevenfold gift descend;
Give them virtue's sure reward;
Give them your salvation, Lord;
    Give them joys that never end. Amen.
    Alleluia.

SECOND READING

Heb 9:11-15

Brothers and sisters:
When Christ came as high priest
    of the good things that have come to be,
    passing through the greater and more
        perfect tabernacle
    not made by hands, that is, not belonging
        to this creation,
    he entered once for all into the sanctuary,
    not with the blood of goats and calves
    but with his own blood, thus obtaining
        eternal redemption.
For if the blood of goats and bulls
    and the sprinkling of a heifer's ashes
    can sanctify those who are defiled
    so that their flesh is cleansed,
    how much more will the blood of Christ,
    who through the eternal Spirit offered
        himself unblemished to God,
    cleanse our consciences from dead works
    to worship the living God.

For this reason he is mediator of a new
        covenant:
    since a death has taken place for
        deliverance
    from transgressions under the first
        covenant,
    those who are called may receive the
        promised eternal inheritance.

OPTIONAL SEQUENCE

Lauda Sion

Laud, O Zion, your salvation,
Laud with hymns of exultation,
    Christ, your king and shepherd true:

Bring him all the praise you know,
He is more than you bestow.
    Never can you reach his due.

Special theme for glad thanksgiving
Is the quick'ning and the living
    Bread today before you set:

From his hands of old partaken,
As we know, by faith unshaken,
    Where the Twelve at supper met.

Full and clear ring out your chanting,
Joy nor sweetest grace be wanting,
    From your heart let praises burst:

For today the feast is holden,
When the institution olden
    Of that supper was rehearsed.

Here the new law's new oblation,
By the new king's revelation,
    Ends the form of ancient rite:

Now the new the old effaces,
Truth away the shadow chases,
    Light dispels the gloom of night.

What he did at supper seated,
Christ ordained to be repeated,
    His memorial ne'er to cease:

And his rule for guidance taking,
Bread and wine we hallow, making
    Thus our sacrifice of peace.

This the truth each Christian learns,
Bread into his flesh he turns,
    To his precious blood the wine:

Sight has fail'd, nor thought conceives,
But a dauntless faith believes,
    Resting on a pow'r divine.

Here beneath these signs are hidden
Priceless things to sense forbidden;
    Signs, not things are all we see:

Blood is poured and flesh is broken,
Yet in either wondrous token
    Christ entire we know to be.

Whoso of this food partakes,
Does not rend the Lord nor breaks;
    Christ is whole to all that taste:

Thousands are, as one, receivers,
One, as thousands of believers,
    Eats of him who cannot waste.

Bad and good the feast are sharing,
Of what divers dooms preparing,
    Endless death, or endless life.

Life to these, to those damnation,
See how like participation
    Is with unlike issues rife.

When the sacrament is broken,
Doubt not, but believe 'tis spoken,
    That each sever'd outward token
        Doth the very whole contain.

Nought the precious gift divides,
Breaking but the sign betides
    Jesus still the same abides,
        Still unbroken does remain.

The shorter form of the sequence begins here.

Lo! the angel's food is given
To the pilgrim who has striven;
    See the children's bread from heaven,
        Which on dogs may not be spent.

Truth the ancient types fulfilling,
Isaac bound, a victim willing,
    Paschal lamb, its lifeblood spilling,
        Manna to the fathers sent.

Very bread, good shepherd, tend us,
Jesu, of your love befriend us,
    You refresh us, you defend us,
        Your eternal goodness send us
In the land of life to see.

You who all things can and know,
Who on earth such food bestow,
    Grant us with your saints, though lowest,
    Where the heav'nly feast you show,
Fellow heirs and guests to be. Amen. Alleluia.

The Solemnity of the Most Sacred Heart of Jesus, June 12, 2015

FIRST READING

Hos 11:1, 3-4, 8c-9

Thus says the Lord:
When Israel was a child I loved him,
    out of Egypt I called my son.
Yet it was I who taught Ephraim to walk,
    who took them in my arms;
I drew them with human cords,
    with bands of love;
I fostered them like one
    who raises an infant to his cheeks;
Yet, though I stooped to feed my child,
    they did not know that I was their healer.

My heart is overwhelmed,
    my pity is stirred.
I will not give vent to my blazing anger,
    I will not destroy Ephraim again;
For I am God and not a man,
    the Holy One present among you;
    I will not let the flames consume you.

RESPONSORIAL PSALM

Isa 12:2-3, 4, 5-6

R̶℣. (3)You will draw water joyfully from the
springs of salvation.

God indeed is my savior;
    I am confident and unafraid.
My strength and my courage is the Lord,
    and he has been my savior.
With joy you will draw water
    at the fountain of salvation.

R̶℣. You will draw water joyfully from the
springs of salvation.

Give thanks to the Lord, acclaim his name;
    among the nations make known his deeds,
    proclaim how exalted is his name.

R̶℣. You will draw water joyfully from the
springs of salvation.

Sing praise to the Lord for his glorious
    achievement;
    let this be known throughout all the earth.
Shout with exultation, O city of Zion,
    for great in your midst
    is the Holy One of Israel!

R̶℣. You will draw water joyfully from the
springs of salvation.

SECOND READING

Eph 3:8-12, 14-19

Brothers and sisters:
To me, the very least of all the holy ones, this
    grace was given,
    to preach to the Gentiles the inscrutable
        riches of Christ,
    and to bring to light for all what is the plan
        of the mystery
    hidden from ages past in God who created
        all things,
    so that the manifold wisdom of God
    might now be made known through the
        church
    to the principalities and authorities in the
        heavens.
This was according to the eternal purpose
    that he accomplished in Christ Jesus our
        Lord,
    in whom we have boldness of speech
    and confidence of access through faith in
        him.

For this reason I kneel before the Father,
    from whom every family in heaven and on
        earth is named,
    that he may grant you in accord with the
        riches of his glory
    to be strengthened with power through his
        Spirit in the inner self,
    and that Christ may dwell in your hearts
        through faith;
    that you, rooted and grounded in love,
    may have strength to comprehend with all
        the holy ones
    what is the breadth and length and height
        and depth,
    and to know the love of Christ which
        surpasses knowledge,
    so that you may be filled with all the
        fullness of God.

FIRST READING

Isa 49:1-6

Hear me, O coastlands,
 listen, O distant peoples.
The Lord called me from birth,
 from my mother's womb he gave me my
 name.
He made of me a sharp-edged sword
 and concealed me in the shadow of his arm.
He made me a polished arrow,
 in his quiver he hid me.
You are my servant, he said to me,
 Israel, through whom I show my glory.

Though I thought I had toiled in vain,
 and for nothing, uselessly, spent my strength,
yet my reward is with the Lord,
 my recompense is with my God.
For now the Lord has spoken
 who formed me as his servant from the
 womb,
that Jacob may be brought back to him
 and Israel gathered to him;
and I am made glorious in the sight of the Lord,
 and my God is now my strength!
It is too little, he says, for you to be my servant,
 to raise up the tribes of Jacob,
 and restore the survivors of Israel;
I will make you a light to the nations,
 that my salvation may reach to the ends of
 the earth.

RESPONSORIAL PSALM

Ps 139:1b-3, 13-14ab, 14c-15

℟. (14a) I praise you, for I am wonderfully
made.

O Lord, you have probed me, you know me;
 you know when I sit and when I stand;
 you understand my thoughts from afar.
My journeys and my rest you scrutinize,
 with all my ways you are familiar.

℟. I praise you, for I am wonderfully made.

Truly you have formed my inmost being;
 you knit me in my mother's womb.
I give you thanks that I am fearfully,
 wonderfully made;
 wonderful are your works.

℟. I praise you, for I am wonderfully made.

My soul also you knew full well;
 nor was my frame unknown to you
When I was made in secret,
 when I was fashioned in the depths of the
 earth.

℟. I praise you, for I am wonderfully made.

SECOND READING

Acts 13:22-26

In those days, Paul said:
"God raised up David as their king;
 of him God testified,
 *I have found David, son of Jesse, a man
 after my own heart;*
 he will carry out my every wish.
From this man's descendants God, according to
 his promise,
 has brought to Israel a savior, Jesus.
John heralded his coming by proclaiming a
 baptism of repentance
 to all the people of Israel;
 and as John was completing his course, he
 would say,
 'What do you suppose that I am? I am not he.
Behold, one is coming after me;
 I am not worthy to unfasten the sandals of
 his feet.'

"My brothers, sons of the family of Abraham,
 and those others among you who are God-
 fearing,
 to us this word of salvation has been sent."

Gospel (cont.)
Mark 5:21-43; L98B

But his disciples said to Jesus,
  "You see how the crowd is pressing upon you,
  and yet you ask, 'Who touched me?'"
And he looked around to see who had done it.
The woman, realizing what had happened to her,
  approached in fear and trembling.
She fell down before Jesus and told him the whole truth.
He said to her, "Daughter, your faith has saved you.
Go in peace and be cured of your affliction."

While he was still speaking,
  people from the synagogue official's house arrived and said,
  "Your daughter has died; why trouble the teacher any longer?"
Disregarding the message that was reported,
  Jesus said to the synagogue official,
  "Do not be afraid; just have faith."
He did not allow anyone to accompany him inside
  except Peter, James, and John, the brother of James.
When they arrived at the house of the synagogue official,
  he caught sight of a commotion,
  people weeping and wailing loudly.
So he went in and said to them,
  "Why this commotion and weeping?
The child is not dead but asleep."
And they ridiculed him.
Then he put them all out.
He took along the child's father and mother
  and those who were with him
  and entered the room where the child was.
He took the child by the hand and said to her, *"Talitha koum,"*
  which means, "Little girl, I say to you, arise!"
The girl, a child of twelve, arose immediately and walked around.
At that they were utterly astounded.
He gave strict orders that no one should know this
  and said that she should be given something to eat.

or Mark 5:21-24, 35b-43; L98B

When Jesus had crossed again in the boat
  to the other side,
  a large crowd gathered around him, and he stayed close to the sea.
One of the synagogue officials, named Jairus, came forward.
Seeing him he fell at his feet and pleaded earnestly with him, saying,
  "My daughter is at the point of death.
Please, come lay your hands on her
  that she may get well and live."
He went off with him,
  and a large crowd followed him and pressed upon him.

While he was still speaking, people from the synagogue official's house
    arrived and said,
  "Your daughter has died; why trouble the teacher any longer?"
Disregarding the message that was reported,
  Jesus said to the synagogue official,
  "Do not be afraid; just have faith."
He did not allow anyone to accompany him inside
  except Peter, James, and John, the brother of James.
When they arrived at the house of the synagogue official,
  he caught sight of a commotion,
  people weeping and wailing loudly.
So he went in and said to them,
  "Why this commotion and weeping?
The child is not dead but asleep."
And they ridiculed him.
Then he put them all out.
He took along the child's father and mother
  and those who were with him
  and entered the room where the child was.
He took the child by the hand and said to her, *"Talitha koum,"*
  which means, "Little girl, I say to you, arise!"
The girl, a child of twelve, arose immediately and walked around.
At that they were utterly astounded.
He gave strict orders that no one should know this
  and said that she should be given something to eat.

FIRST READING

Acts 12:1-11

In those days, King Herod laid hands upon
    some members of the Church to harm
    them.
He had James, the brother of John, killed by
    the sword,
    and when he saw that this was pleasing to
    the Jews
    he proceeded to arrest Peter also.
—It was the feast of Unleavened Bread.—
He had him taken into custody and put in
    prison
    under the guard of four squads of four
    soldiers each.
He intended to bring him before the people
    after Passover.
Peter thus was being kept in prison,
    but prayer by the Church was fervently
    being made
    to God on his behalf.

On the very night before Herod was to bring
    him to trial,
    Peter, secured by double chains,
    was sleeping between two soldiers,
    while outside the door guards kept watch
    on the prison.
Suddenly the angel of the Lord stood by him,
    and a light shone in the cell.
He tapped Peter on the side and awakened
    him, saying,
    "Get up quickly."
The chains fell from his wrists.
The angel said to him, "Put on your belt and
    your sandals."
He did so.
Then he said to him, "Put on your cloak and
    follow me."

So he followed him out,
    not realizing that what was happening
    through the angel was real;
    he thought he was seeing a vision.
They passed the first guard, then the second,
    and came to the iron gate leading out to
    the city,
    which opened for them by itself.
They emerged and made their way down an
    alley,
    and suddenly the angel left him.
Then Peter recovered his senses and said,
    "Now I know for certain
    that the Lord sent his angel
    and rescued me from the hand of Herod
    and from all that the Jewish people had
    been expecting."

RESPONSORIAL PSALM

Ps 34:2-3, 4-5, 6-7, 8-9

R̸. (5) The angel of the Lord will rescue those
who fear him.

I will bless the Lord at all times;
    his praise shall be ever in my mouth.
Let my soul glory in the Lord;
    the lowly will hear me and be glad.

R̸. The angel of the Lord will rescue those
who fear him.

Glorify the Lord with me,
    let us together extol his name.
I sought the Lord, and he answered me
    and delivered me from all my fears.

R̸. The angel of the Lord will rescue those
who fear him.

Look to him that you may be radiant with joy,
    and your faces may not blush with shame.

When the poor one called out, the Lord heard,
    and from all his distress he saved him.

R̸. The angel of the Lord will rescue those
who fear him.

The angel of the Lord encamps
    around those who fear him, and delivers
    them.
Taste and see how good the Lord is;
    blessed the man who takes refuge in him.

R̸. The angel of the Lord will rescue those
who fear him.

SECOND READING

2 Tim 4:6-8, 17-18

I, Paul, am already being poured out like a
    libation,
    and the time of my departure is at hand.
I have competed well; I have finished the race;
    I have kept the faith.
From now on the crown of righteousness
    awaits me,
    which the Lord, the just judge,
    will award to me on that day, and not only
    to me,
    but to all who have longed for his
    appearance.

The Lord stood by me and gave me strength,
    so that through me the proclamation might
    be completed
    and all the Gentiles might hear it.
And I was rescued from the lion's mouth.
The Lord will rescue me from every evil
    threat
    and will bring me safe to his heavenly
    Kingdom.
To him be glory forever and ever. Amen.

Fifteenth Sunday in Ordinary Time, July 12, 2015

SECOND READING
Eph 1:3-10

Blessed be the God and Father of our Lord
    Jesus Christ,
  who has blessed us in Christ
  with every spiritual blessing in the
    heavens,
  as he chose us in him, before the foundation
    of the world,
  to be holy and without blemish before him.
In love he destined us for adoption to himself
    through Jesus Christ,
  in accord with the favor of his will,
  for the praise of the glory of his grace
  that he granted us in the beloved.

In him we have redemption by his blood,
  the forgiveness of transgressions,
  in accord with the riches of his grace that
    he lavished upon us.
In all wisdom and insight, he has made
    known to us
  the mystery of his will in accord with his
    favor
  that he set forth in him as a plan for the
    fullness of times,
  to sum up all things in Christ, in heaven
    and on earth.

Seventeenth Sunday in Ordinary Time, July 26, 2015

Gospel (cont.)
John 6:1-15; L110B

When they had had their fill, he said to his disciples,
  "Gather the fragments left over,
  so that nothing will be wasted."
So they collected them,
  and filled twelve wicker baskets with fragments
  from the five barley loaves
  that had been more than they could eat.
When the people saw the sign he had done, they said,
  "This is truly the Prophet, the one who is to come into the world."
Since Jesus knew that they were going to come and carry him off
    to make him king,
  he withdrew again to the mountain alone.

Eighteenth Sunday in Ordinary Time, August 2, 2015

Gospel (cont.)
John 6:24-35; L113B

So Jesus said to them,
  "Amen, amen, I say to you,
  it was not Moses who gave the bread from heaven;
  my Father gives you the true bread from heaven.
For the bread of God is that which comes down from heaven
  and gives life to the world."

So they said to him,
  "Sir, give us this bread always."
Jesus said to them,
  "I am the bread of life;
  whoever comes to me will never hunger,
  and whoever believes in me will never thirst."

Gospel (cont.)
Luke 1:39-56; L622

He has cast down the mighty from their thrones,
and has lifted up the lowly.
He has filled the hungry with good things,
and the rich he has sent away empty.
He has come to the help of his servant Israel
for he has remembered his promise of mercy,
the promise he made to our fathers,
to Abraham and his children forever."

Mary remained with her about three months
and then returned to her home.

FIRST READING
Rev 11:19a; 12:1-6a, 10ab

God's temple in heaven was opened,
and the ark of his covenant could be seen
in the temple.

A great sign appeared in the sky, a woman
clothed with the sun,
with the moon under her feet,
and on her head a crown of twelve stars.
She was with child and wailed aloud in pain
as she labored to give birth.
Then another sign appeared in the sky;
it was a huge red dragon, with seven heads
and ten horns,
and on its heads were seven diadems.
Its tail swept away a third of the stars in the
sky
and hurled them down to the earth.
Then the dragon stood before the woman
about to give birth,
to devour her child when she gave birth.
She gave birth to a son, a male child,
destined to rule all the nations with an iron
rod.
Her child was caught up to God and his
throne.
The woman herself fled into the desert
where she had a place prepared by God.

Then I heard a loud voice in heaven say:
"Now have salvation and power come,
and the Kingdom of our God
and the authority of his Anointed One."

RESPONSORIAL PSALM
Ps 45:10, 11, 12, 16

R̸. (10bc) The queen stands at your right
hand, arrayed in gold.

The queen takes her place at your right hand
in gold of Ophir.

R̸. The queen stands at your right hand,
arrayed in gold.

Hear, O daughter, and see; turn your ear,
forget your people and your father's house.

R̸. The queen stands at your right hand,
arrayed in gold.

So shall the king desire your beauty;
for he is your lord.

R̸. The queen stands at your right hand,
arrayed in gold.

They are borne in with gladness and joy;
they enter the palace of the king.

R̸. The queen stands at your right hand,
arrayed in gold.

SECOND READING
1 Cor 15:20-27

Brothers and sisters:
Christ has been raised from the dead,
the firstfruits of those who have fallen
asleep.
For since death came through man,
the resurrection of the dead came also
through man.
For just as in Adam all die,
so too in Christ shall all be brought to life,
but each one in proper order:
Christ the firstfruits;
then, at his coming, those who belong to
Christ;
then comes the end,
when he hands over the Kingdom to his
God and Father,
when he has destroyed every sovereignty
and every authority and power.
For he must reign until he has put all his
enemies under his feet.
The last enemy to be destroyed is death,
for "he subjected everything under his feet."

Twenty-First Sunday in Ordinary Time, *August 23, 2015*

SECOND READING

or Eph 5:2a, 25-32

Brothers and sisters:
Live in love, as Christ loved us.
Husbands, love your wives,
  even as Christ loved the church
  and handed himself over for her to sanctify
    her,
  cleansing her by the bath of water with the
    word,
  that he might present to himself the church
    in splendor,
  without spot or wrinkle or any such thing,
  that she might be holy and without
    blemish.

So also husbands should love their wives as
    their own bodies.
He who loves his wife loves himself.
For no one hates his own flesh
  but rather nourishes and cherishes it,
  even as Christ does the church,
  because we are members of his body.
*For this reason a man shall leave his father
    and his mother and be joined to his wife,
  and the two shall become one flesh.*
This is a great mystery,
  but I speak in reference to Christ and the
    church.

Twenty-Second Sunday in Ordinary Time, *August 30, 2015*

Gospel (cont.)
Mark 7:1-8, 14-15, 21-23; L125B

You disregard God's commandment but cling to human tradition."

He summoned the crowd again and said to them,
  "Hear me, all of you, and understand.
Nothing that enters one from outside can defile that person;
  but the things that come out from within are what defile.

"From within people, from their hearts,
  come evil thoughts, unchastity, theft, murder,
  adultery, greed, malice, deceit,
  licentiousness, envy, blasphemy, arrogance, folly.
All these evils come from within and they defile."

Twenty-Seventh Sunday in Ordinary Time, *October 4, 2015*

Gospel (cont.)
Mark 10:2-16; L140B

And people were bringing children to him that he might touch them,
  but the disciples rebuked them.
When Jesus saw this he became indignant and said to them,
  "Let the children come to me;
  do not prevent them, for the kingdom of God belongs to such as
    these.
Amen, I say to you,
  whoever does not accept the kingdom of God like a child
  will not enter it."
Then he embraced them and blessed them,
  placing his hands on them.

or Mark 10:2-12; L140B

The Pharisees approached Jesus and asked,
  "Is it lawful for a husband to divorce his wife?"
They were testing him.
He said to them in reply, "What did Moses command you?"
They replied,
  "Moses permitted a husband to write a bill of divorce
  and dismiss her."
But Jesus told them,
  "Because of the hardness of your hearts
  he wrote you this commandment.
But from the beginning of creation, *God made them male and female.*
For this reason a man shall leave his father and mother
  and be joined to his wife,
  and the two shall become one flesh.
So they are no longer two but one flesh.
Therefore what God has joined together,
  no human being must separate."
In the house the disciples again questioned Jesus about this.
He said to them,
  "Whoever divorces his wife and marries another
  commits adultery against her;
  and if she divorces her husband and marries another,
  she commits adultery."

Twenty-Eighth Sunday in Ordinary Time, *October 11, 2015*

Gospel (cont.)
Mark 10:17-30; L143B

It is easier for a camel to pass through the eye of a needle
  than for one who is rich to enter the kingdom of God."
They were exceedingly astonished and said among themselves,
  "Then who can be saved?"
Jesus looked at them and said,
  "For human beings it is impossible, but not for God.
All things are possible for God."
Peter began to say to him,
  "We have given up everything and followed you."
Jesus said, "Amen, I say to you,
  there is no one who has given up house or brothers or sisters
  or mother or father or children or lands
  for my sake and for the sake of the gospel
  who will not receive a hundred times more now in this present age:
  houses and brothers and sisters
  and mothers and children and lands,
  with persecutions, and eternal life in the age to come."

or Mark 10:17-27

As Jesus was setting out on a journey, a man ran up,
  knelt down before him, and asked him,
  "Good teacher, what must I do to inherit eternal life?"
Jesus answered him, "Why do you call me good?

No one is good but God alone.
You know the commandments: *You shall not kill;*
  you shall not commit adultery;
  you shall not steal;
  you shall not bear false witness;
  you shall not defraud;
  honor your father and your mother."
He replied and said to him,
  "Teacher, all of these I have observed from my youth."
Jesus, looking at him, loved him and said to him,
  "You are lacking in one thing.
Go, sell what you have, and give to the poor
  and you will have treasure in heaven; then come, follow me."
At that statement his face fell,
  and he went away sad, for he had many possessions.

Jesus looked around and said to his disciples,
  "How hard it is for those who have wealth
  to enter the kingdom of God!"
The disciples were amazed at his words.
So Jesus again said to them in reply,
  "Children, how hard it is to enter the kingdom of God!
It is easier for a camel to pass through the eye of a needle
  than for one who is rich to enter the kingdom of God."
They were exceedingly astonished and said among themselves,
  "Then who can be saved?"
Jesus looked at them and said,
  "For human beings it is impossible, but not for God.
All things are possible for God."

Twenty-Ninth Sunday in Ordinary Time, *October 18, 2015*

Gospel
Mark 10:42-45; L146B

Jesus summoned them and said to them,
  "You know that those who are recognized as rulers over the Gentiles
    lord it over them,
    and their great ones make their authority over them felt.
But it shall not be so among you.
Rather, whoever wishes to be great among you will be your servant;
  whoever wishes to be first among you will be the slave of all.
For the Son of Man did not come to be served
  but to serve and to give his life as a ransom for many."

All Souls, *November 2, 2015*

FIRST READING
Dan 12:1-3; L1011.7

In those days, I, Daniel, mourned
  and heard this word of the Lord:
At that time there shall arise
  Michael, the great prince,
  guardian of your people;
It shall be a time unsurpassed in distress
  since nations began until that time.
At that time your people shall escape,
  everyone who is found written in the book.

Many of those who sleep in the dust of the
    earth shall awake;
Some shall live forever,
  others shall be an everlasting horror and
    disgrace.
But the wise shall shine brightly
  like the splendor of the firmament,
And those who lead the many to justice
  shall be like the stars forever.

RESPONSORIAL PSALM
Ps 27:1, 4, 7, and 8b, and 9a, 13-14; L1013.3

R̸. (1a) The Lord is my light and my
salvation.
  or:
R̸. (13) I believe that I shall see the good things
of the Lord in the land of the living.

The Lord is my light and my salvation;
  whom should I fear?
The Lord is my life's refuge;
  of whom should I be afraid?

R̸. The Lord is my light and my salvation.
  or:
R̸. I believe that I shall see the good things of
the Lord in the land of the living.

One thing I ask of the Lord;
  this I seek:
To dwell in the house of the Lord
  all the days of my life,
That I may gaze on the loveliness of the Lord
  and contemplate his temple.

R̸. The Lord is my light and my salvation.
  or:
R̸. I believe that I shall see the good things of
the Lord in the land of the living.

Hear, O Lord, the sound of my call;
  have pity on me and answer me.
Your presence, O Lord, I seek.
  Hide not your face from me.

R̸. The Lord is my light and my salvation.
  or:
R̸. I believe that I shall see the good things of
the Lord in the land of the living.

I believe that I shall see the bounty of the
    Lord
  in the land of the living.
Wait for the Lord with courage;
  be stouthearted, and wait for the Lord.

R̸. The Lord is my light and my salvation.
  or:
R̸. I believe that I shall see the good things of
the Lord in the land of the living.

SECOND READING
Rom 6:3-9; L1014.3

Brothers and sisters:
Are you unaware that we who were baptized
    into Christ Jesus
  were baptized into his death?
We were indeed buried with him through
    baptism into death,
  so that, just as Christ was raised from the
    dead
  by the glory of the Father,
  we too might live in newness of life.

For if we have grown into union with him
    through a death like his,
  we shall also be united with him in the
    resurrection.
We know that our old self was crucified with
    him,
  so that our sinful body might be done away
    with,
  that we might no longer be in slavery to
    sin.
For a dead person has been absolved from sin.
If, then, we have died with Christ,
  we believe that we shall also live with him.
We know that Christ, raised from the dead,
    dies no more;
  death no longer has power over him.

Thirty-Second Sunday in Ordinary Time, *November 8, 2015*

Gospel
Mark 12:41-44; L155B

Jesus sat down opposite the treasury
    and observed how the crowd put money into the treasury.
Many rich people put in large sums.
A poor widow also came and put in two small coins worth a few cents.
Calling his disciples to himself, he said to them,
    "Amen, I say to you, this poor widow put in more
    than all the other contributors to the treasury.
For they have all contributed from their surplus wealth,
    but she, from her poverty, has contributed all she had,
    her whole livelihood."

Thanksgiving Day, *November 26, 2015*

FIRST READING
Sir 50:22-24; L943.2

And now, bless the God of all,
    who has done wondrous things on earth;
Who fosters people's growth from their
        mother's womb,
    and fashions them according to his will!
May he grant you joy of heart
    and may peace abide among you;
May his goodness toward us endure in Israel
    to deliver us in our days.

RESPONSORIAL PSALM
Ps 138:1-2a, 2bc-3, 4-5; L945.3

R. (2bc) Lord, I thank you for your faithfulness and love.

I will give thanks to you, O Lord, with all of
        my heart,
    for you have heard the words of my mouth;
    in the presence of the angels I will sing
        your praise;
I will worship at your holy temple.

R. Lord, I thank you for your faithfulness and
love.

I will give thanks to your name,
Because of your kindness and your truth.
When I called, you answered me;
    you built up strength within me.

R. Lord, I thank you for your faithfulness and
love.

All the kings of the earth shall give thanks to
        you, O Lord,
    when they hear the words of your mouth;
And they shall sing of the ways of the Lord:
    "Great is the glory of the Lord."

R. Lord, I thank you for your faithfulness and
love.

SECOND READING
1 Cor 1:3-9; L944.1

Brothers and sisters:
Grace to you and peace from God our Father
    and the Lord Jesus Christ.

I give thanks to my God always on your
        account
    for the grace of God bestowed on you in
        Christ Jesus,
    that in him you were enriched in every way,
    with all discourse and all knowledge,
    as the testimony to Christ was confirmed
        among you,
    so that you are not lacking in any spiritual
        gift
    as you wait for the revelation of our Lord
        Jesus Christ.
He will keep you firm to the end,
    irreproachable on the day of our Lord Jesus
        Christ.
God is faithful,
    and by him you were called to fellowship
        with his Son, Jesus Christ our Lord.

Choral Settings for the Model Universal Prayer (Prayer of the Faithful)

Purchasers of this volume may reproduce these choral arrangements for use in their parish or community. The music must be reproduced as given below, with composer's name and copyright line.

ORDINARY TIME, WEEKS 2-6

Cantor:

we pray to the Lord,

SATB Response:

Descant

Lord, hear our prayer.

Lord, hear our prayer.

ORDINARY TIME, WEEKS 11-23

Cantor:

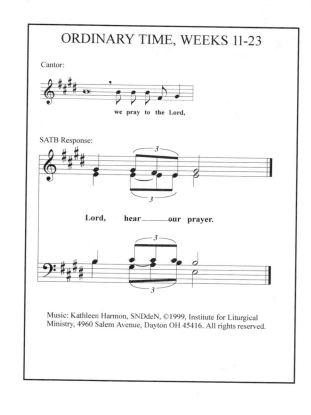

we pray to the Lord,

SATB Response:

Lord, hear our prayer.

ORDINARY TIME, WEEKS 24-33

Cantor:

we pray to the Lord,

SATB Response:

Lord, hear our prayer.

APPENDIX C

Lectionary Pronunciation Guide

Lectionary Word	Pronunciation
Aaron	EHR-uhn
Abana	AB-uh-nuh
Abednego	uh-BEHD-nee-go
Abel-Keramin	AY-b'l-KEHR-uh-mihn
Abel-meholah	AY-b'l-mee-HO-lah
Abiathar	uh-BAI-uh-ther
Abiel	AY-bee-ehl
Abiezrite	ay-bai-EHZ-rait
Abijah	uh-BAI-dzhuh
Abilene	ab-uh-LEE-neh
Abishai	uh-BIHSH-ay-ai
Abiud	uh-BAI-uhd
Abner	AHB-ner
Abraham	AY-bruh-ham
Abram	AY-br'm
Achaia	uh-KAY-yuh
Achim	AY-kihm
Aeneas	uh-NEE-uhs
Aenon	AY-nuhn
Agrippa	uh-GRIH-puh
Ahaz	AY-haz
Ahijah	uh-HAI-dzhuh
Ai	AY-ee
Alexandria	al-ehg-ZAN-dree-uh
Alexandrian	al-ehg-ZAN-dree-uhn
Alpha	AHL-fuh
Alphaeus	AL-fee-uhs
Amalek	AM-uh-lehk
Amaziah	am-uh-ZAI-uh
Amminadab	ah-MIHN-uh-dab
Ammonites	AM-uh-naitz
Amorites	AM-uh-raits
Amos	AY-muhs
Amoz	AY-muhz
Ampliatus	am-plee-AY-tuhs
Ananias	an-uh-NAI-uhs
Andronicus	an-draw-NAI-kuhs
Annas	AN-uhs
Antioch	AN-tih-ahk
Antiochus	an-TAI-uh-kuhs
Aphiah	uh-FAI-uh
Apollos	uh-PAH-luhs
Appius	AP-ee-uhs
Aquila	uh-KWIHL-uh
Arabah	EHR-uh-buh
Aram	AY-ram
Arameans	ehr-uh-MEE-uhnz
Areopagus	ehr-ee-AH-puh-guhs
Arimathea	ehr-uh-muh-THEE-uh
Aroer	uh-RO-er

Lectionary Word	Pronunciation
Asaph	AY-saf
Asher	ASH-er
Ashpenaz	ASH-pee-naz
Assyria	a-SIHR-ee-uh
Astarte	as-TAHR-tee
Attalia	at-TAH-lee-uh
Augustus	uh-GUHS-tuhs
Azariah	az-uh-RAI-uh
Azor	AY-sawr
Azotus	uh-ZO-tus
Baal-shalishah	BAY-uhl-shuh-LAI-shuh
Baal-Zephon	BAY-uhl-ZEE-fuhn
Babel	BAY-bl
Babylon	BAB-ih-luhn
Babylonian	bab-ih-LO-nih-uhn
Balaam	BAY-lm
Barabbas	beh-REH-buhs
Barak	BEHR-ak
Barnabas	BAHR-nuh-buhs
Barsabbas	BAHR-suh-buhs
Bartholomew	bar-THAHL-uh-myoo
Bartimaeus	bar-tih-MEE-uhs
Baruch	BEHR-ook
Bashan	BAY-shan
Becorath	bee-KO-rath
Beelzebul	bee-EHL-zee-buhl
Beer-sheba	BEE-er-SHEE-buh
Belshazzar	behl-SHAZ-er
Benjamin	BEHN-dzhuh-mihn
Beor	BEE-awr
Bethany	BEHTH-uh-nee
Bethel	BETH-el
Bethesda	beh-THEHZ-duh
Bethlehem	BEHTH-leh-hehm
Bethphage	BEHTH-fuh-dzhee
Bethsaida	behth-SAY-ih-duh
Beth-zur	behth-ZER
Bildad	BIHL-dad
Bithynia	bih-THIHN-ih-uh
Boanerges	bo-uh-NER-dzheez
Boaz	BO-az
Caesar	SEE-zer
Caesarea	zeh-suh-REE-uh
Caiaphas	KAY-uh-fuhs
Cain	kayn
Cana	KAY-nuh
Canaan	KAY-nuhn
Canaanite	KAY-nuh-nait
Canaanites	KAY-nuh-naits

Lectionary Word	Pronunciation
Candace	kan-DAY-see
Capernaum	kuh-PERR-nay-uhm
Cappadocia	kap-ih-DO-shee-u
Carmel	KAHR-muhl
Carnelians	kahr-NEEL-yuhnz
Cenchreae	SEHN-kree-ay
Cephas	SEE-fuhs
Chaldeans	kal-DEE-uhnz
Chemosh	KEE-mahsh
Cherubim	TSHEHR-oo-bihm
Chislev	KIHS-lehv
Chloe	KLO-ee
Chorazin	kor-AY-sihn
Cilicia	sih-LIHSH-ee-uh
Cleopas	KLEE-o-pas
Clopas	KLO-pas
Corinth	KAWR-ihnth
Corinthians	kawr-IHN-thee-uhnz
Cornelius	kawr-NEE-lee-uhs
Crete	kreet
Crispus	KRIHS-puhs
Cushite	CUHSH-ait
Cypriot	SIH-pree-at
Cyrene	sai-REE-nee
Cyreneans	sai-REE-nih-uhnz
Cyrenian	sai-REE-nih-uhn
Cyrenians	sai-REE-nih-uhnz
Cyrus	SAI-ruhs
Damaris	DAM-uh-rihs
Damascus	duh-MAS-kuhs
Danites	DAN-aits
Decapolis	duh-KAP-o-lis
Derbe	DER-bee
Deuteronomy	dyoo-ter-AH-num-mee
Didymus	DID-I-mus
Dionysius	dai-o-NIHSH-ih-uhs
Dioscuri	dai-O-sky-ri
Dorcas	DAWR-kuhs
Dothan	DO-thuhn
dromedaries	DRAH-muh-dher-eez
Ebed-melech	EE-behd-MEE-lehk
Eden	EE-dn
Edom	EE-duhm
Elamites	EE-luh-maitz
Eldad	EHL-dad
Eleazar	ehl-ee-AY-zer
Eli	EE-lai
Eli Eli Lema Sabachthani	AY-lee AY-lee luh-MAH sah-BAHK-tah-nee

Lectionary Word	Pronunciation	Lectionary Word	Pronunciation	Lectionary Word	Pronunciation
Eliab	ee-LAI-ab	Gilead	GIHL-ee-uhd	Joppa	DZHAH-puh
Eliakim	ee-LAI-uh-kihm	Gilgal	GIHL-gal	Joram	DZHO-ram
Eliezer	ehl-ih-EE-zer	Golgotha	GAHL-guh-thuh	Jordan	DZHAWR-dn
Elihu	ee-LAI-hyoo	Gomorrah	guh-MAWR-uh	Joseph	DZHO-zf
Elijah	ee-LAI-dzhuh	Goshen	GO-shuhn	Joses	DZHO-seez
Elim	EE-lihm	Habakkuk	huh-BAK-uhk	Joshua	DZHAH-shou-ah
Elimelech	ee-LIHM-eh-lehk	Hadadrimmon	hay-dad-RIHM-uhn	Josiah	dzho-SAI-uh
Elisha	ee-LAI-shuh	Hades	HAY-deez	Jotham	DZHO-thuhm
Eliud	ee-LAI-uhd	Hagar	HAH-gar	Judah	DZHOU-duh
Elizabeth	ee-LIHZ-uh-bth	Hananiah	han-uh-NAI-uh	Judas	DZHOU-duhs
Elkanah	el-KAY-nuh	Hannah	HAN-uh	Judea	dzhou-DEE-uh
Eloi Eloi Lama Sabechthani	AY-lo-ee AY-lo-ee LAH-mah sah- BAHK-tah-nee	Haran	HAY-ruhn	Judean	dzhou-DEE-uhn
		Hebron	HEE-bruhn	Junia	dzhou-nih-uh
		Hermes	HER-meez	Justus	DZHUHS-tuhs
Elymais	ehl-ih-MAY-ihs	Herod	HEHR-uhd	Kephas	KEF-uhs
Emmanuel	eh-MAN-yoo-ehl	Herodians	hehr-O-dee-uhnz	Kidron	KIHD-ruhn
Emmaus	eh-MAY-uhs	Herodias	hehr-O-dee-uhs	Kiriatharba	kihr-ee-ath-AHR-buh
Epaenetus	ee-PEE-nee-tuhs	Hezekiah	heh-zeh-KAI-uh	Kish	kihsh
Epaphras	EH-puh-fras	Hezron	HEHZ-ruhn	Laodicea	lay-o-dih-SEE-uh
ephah	EE-fuh	Hilkiah	hihl-KAI-uh	Lateran	LAT-er-uhn
Ephah	EE-fuh	Hittite	HIH-tait	Lazarus	LAZ-er-uhs
Ephesians	eh-FEE-zhuhnz	Hivites	HAI-vaitz	Leah	LEE-uh
Ephesus	EH-fuh-suhs	Hophni	HAHF-nai	Lebanon	LEH-buh-nuhn
Ephphatha	EHF-uh-thuh	Hor	HAWR	Levi	LEE-vai
Ephraim	EE-fray-ihm	Horeb	HAWR-ehb	Levite	LEE-vait
Ephrathah	EHF-ruh-thuh	Hosea	ho-ZEE-uh	Levites	LEE-vaits
Ephron	EE-frawn	Hur	her	Leviticus	leh-VIH-tih-kous
Epiphanes	eh-PIHF-uh-neez	hyssop	HIH-suhp	Lucius	LOO-shih-uhs
Erastus	ee-RAS-tuhs	Iconium	ai-KO-nih-uhm	Lud	luhd
Esau	EE-saw	Isaac	AI-zuhk	Luke	look
Esther	EHS-ter	Isaiah	ai-ZAY-uh	Luz	luhz
Ethanim	EHTH-uh-nihm	Iscariot	ihs-KEHR-ee-uht	Lycaonian	lihk-ay-O-nih-uhn
Ethiopian	ee-thee-O-pee-uhn	Ishmael	ISH-may-ehl	Lydda	LIH-duh
Euphrates	yoo-FRAY-teez	Ishmaelites	ISH-mayehl-aits	Lydia	LIH-dih-uh
Exodus	EHK-so-duhs	Israel	IHZ-ray-ehl	Lysanias	lai-SAY-nih-uhs
Ezekiel	eh-ZEE-kee-uhl	Ituraea	ih-TSHOOR-ree-uh	Lystra	LIHS-truh
Ezra	EHZ-ruh	Jaar	DZHAY-ahr	Maccabees	MAK-uh-beez
frankincense	FRANGK-ihn-sehns	Jabbok	DZHAB-uhk	Macedonia	mas-eh-DO-nih-uh
Gabbatha	GAB-uh-thuh	Jacob	DZHAY-kuhb	Macedonian	mas-eh-DO-nih-uhn
Gabriel	GAY-bree-ul	Jairus	DZH-hr-uhs	Machir	MAY-kih
Gadarenes	GAD-uh-reenz	Javan	DZHAY-van	Machpelah	mak-PEE-luh
Galatian	guh-LAY-shih-uhn	Jebusites	DZHEHB-oo-zaits	Magdala	MAG-duh-luh
Galatians	guh-LAY-shih-uhnz	Jechoniah	dzhehk-o-NAI-uh	Magdalene	MAG-duh-lehn
Galilee	GAL-ih-lee	Jehoiakim	dzhee-HOI-uh-kihm	magi	MAY-dzhai
Gallio	GAL-ih-o	Jehoshaphat	dzhee-HAHSH-uh-fat	Malachi	MAL-uh-kai
Gamaliel	guh-MAY-lih-ehl	Jephthah	DZHEHF-thuh	Malchiah	mal-KAI-uh
Gaza	GAH-zuh	Jeremiah	dzhehr-eh-MAI-uh	Malchus	MAL-kuhz
Gehazi	gee-HAY-zai	Jericho	DZHEHR-ih-ko	Mamre	MAM-ree
Gehenna	geh-HEHN-uh	Jeroham	dzhehr-RO-ham	Manaen	MAN-uh-ehn
Genesis	DZHEHN-uh-sihs	Jerusalem	dzheh-ROU-suh-lehm	Manasseh	man-AS-eh
Gennesaret	gehn-NEHS-uh-reht	Jesse	DZHEH-see	Manoah	muh-NO-uh
Gentiles	DZHEHN-tailz	Jethro	DZHEHTH-ro	Mark	mahrk
Gerasenes	DZHEHR-uh-seenz	Joakim	DZHO-uh-kihm	Mary	MEHR-ee
Gethsemane	gehth-SEHM-uh-ne	Job	DZHOB	Massah	MAH-suh
Gideon	GIHD-ee-uhn	Jonah	DZHO-nuh	Mattathias	mat-uh-THAI-uhs

Lectionary Word	Pronunciation	Lectionary Word	Pronunciation	Lectionary Word	Pronunciation
Matthan	MAT-than	Parmenas	PAHR-mee-nas	Sabbath	SAB-uhth
Matthew	MATH-yoo	Parthians	PAHR-thee-uhnz	Sadducees	SAD-dzhoo-seez
Matthias	muh-THAI-uhs	Patmos	PAT-mos	Salem	SAY-lehm
Medad	MEE-dad	Peninnah	pee-NIHN-uh	Salim	SAY-lim
Mede	meed	Pentecost	PEHN-tee-kawst	Salmon	SAL-muhn
Medes	meedz	Penuel	pee-NYOO-ehl	Salome	suh-LO-mee
Megiddo	mee-GIH-do	Perez	PEE-rehz	Salu	SAYL-yoo
Melchizedek	mehl-KIHZ-eh-dehk	Perga	PER-guh	Samaria	suh-MEHR-ih-uh
Mene	MEE-nee	Perizzites	PEHR-ih-zaits	Samaritan	suh-MEHR-ih-tuhn
Meribah	MEHR-ih-bah	Persia	PER-zhuh	Samothrace	SAM-o-thrays
Meshach	MEE-shak	Peter	PEE-ter	Samson	SAM-s'n
Mesopotamia	mehs-o-po-TAY-mih-uh	Phanuel	FAN-yoo-ehl	Samuel	SAM-yoo-uhl
Micah	MAI-kuh	Pharaoh	FEHR-o	Sanhedrin	san-HEE-drihn
Midian	MIH-dih-uhn	Pharisees	FEHR-ih-seez	Sarah	SEHR-uh
Milcom	MIHL-kahm	Pharpar	FAHR-pahr	Sarai	SAY-rai
Miletus	mai-LEE-tuhs	Philemon	fih-LEE-muhn	saraph	SAY-raf
Minnith	MIHN-ihth	Philippi	fil-LIH-pai	Sardis	SAHR-dihs
Mishael	MIHSH-ay-ehl	Philippians	fih-LIHP-ih-uhnz	Saul	sawl
Mizpah	MIHZ-puh	Philistines	fih-LIHS-tihnz	Scythian	SIH-thee-uihn
Moreh	MO-reh	Phinehas	FEHN-ee-uhs	Seba	SEE-buh
Moriah	maw-RAI-uh	Phoenicia	fee-NIHSH-ih-uh	Seth	sehth
Mosoch	MAH-sahk	Phrygia	FRIH-dzhih-uh	Shaalim	SHAY-uh-lihm
myrrh	mer	Phrygian	FRIH-dzhih-uhn	Shadrach	SHAY-drak
Mysia	MIH-shih-uh	phylacteries	fih-LAK-ter-eez	Shalishah	shuh-LEE-shuh
Naaman	NAY-uh-muhn	Pi-Hahiroth	pai-huh-HAI-rahth	Shaphat	Shay-fat
Nahshon	NAY-shuhn	Pilate	PAI-luht	Sharon	SHEHR-uhn
Naomi	NAY-o-mai	Pisidia	pih-SIH-dih-uh	Shealtiel	shee-AL-tih-ehl
Naphtali	NAF-tuh-lai	Pithom	PAI-thahm	Sheba	SHEE-buh
Nathan	NAY-thuhn	Pontius	PAHN-shus	Shebna	SHEB-nuh
Nathanael	nuh-THAN-ay-ehl	Pontus	PAHN-tus	Shechem	SHEE-kehm
Nazarene	NAZ-awr-een	Praetorium	pray-TAWR-ih-uhm	shekel	SHEHK-uhl
Nazareth	NAZ-uh-rehth	Priscilla	PRIHS-kill-uh	Shiloh	SHAI-lo
nazirite	NAZ-uh-rait	Prochorus	PRAH-kaw-ruhs	Shinar	SHAI-nahr
Nazorean	naz-aw-REE-uhn	Psalm	Sahm	Shittim	sheh-TEEM
Neapolis	nee-AP-o-lihs	Put	puht	Shuhite	SHOO-ait
Nebuchadnezzar	neh-byoo-kuhd-NEHZ-er	Puteoli	pyoo-TEE-o-lai	Shunammite	SHOO-nam-ait
Negeb	NEH-gehb	Qoheleth	ko-HEHL-ehth	Shunem	SHOO-nehm
Nehemiah	nee-hee-MAI-uh	qorban	KAWR-bahn	Sidon	SAI-duhn
Ner	ner	Quartus	KWAR-tuhs	Silas	SAI-luhs
Nicanor	nai-KAY-nawr	Quirinius	kwai-RIHN-ih-uhs	Siloam	sih-LO-uhm
Nicodemus	nih-ko-DEE-muhs	Raamses	ray-AM-seez	Silvanus	sihl-VAY-nuhs
Niger	NAI-dzher	Rabbi	RAB-ai	Simeon	SIHM-ee-uhn
Nineveh	NIHN-eh-veh	Rabbouni	ra-BO-nai	Simon	SAI-muhn
Noah	NO-uh	Rahab	RAY-hab	Sin (desert)	sihn
Nun	nuhn	Ram	ram	Sinai	SAI-nai
Obed	O-behd	Ramah	RAY-muh	Sirach	SAI-rak
Olivet	AH-lih-veht	Ramathaim	ray-muh-THAY-ihm	Sodom	SAH-duhm
Omega	o-MEE-guh	Raqa	RA-kuh	Solomon	SAH-lo-muhn
Onesimus	o-NEH-sih-muhs	Rebekah	ree-BEHK-uh	Sosthenes	SAHS-thee-neez
Ophir	O-fer	Rehoboam	ree-ho-BO-am	Stachys	STAY-kihs
Orpah	AWR-puh	Rephidim	REHF-ih-dihm	Succoth	SUHK-ahth
Pamphylia	pam-FIHL-ih-uh	Reuben	ROO-b'n	Sychar	SI-kar
Paphos	PAY-fuhs	Revelation	reh-veh-LAY-shuhn	Syene	sai-EE-nee
		Rhegium	REE-dzhee-uhm	Symeon	SIHM-ee-uhn
		Rufus	ROO-fuhs	synagogues	SIHN-uh-gahgz

Lectionary Word	Pronunciation	Lectionary Word	Pronunciation	Lectionary Word	Pronunciation
Syrophoenician	SIHR-o fee-NIHSH-ih-uhn	Timon	TAI-muhn	Zebedee	ZEH-beh-dee
		Titus	TAI-tuhs	Zebulun	ZEH-byoo-luhn
Tabitha	TAB-ih-thuh	Tohu	TO-hyoo	Zechariah	zeh-kuh-RAI-uh
Talitha koum	TAL-ih-thuh-KOOM	Trachonitis	trak-o-NAI-tis	Zedekiah	zeh-duh-KAI-uh
Tamar	TAY-mer	Troas	TRO-ahs	Zephaniah	zeh-fuh-NAI-uh
Tarshish	TAHR-shihsh	Tubal	TYOO-b'l	Zerah	ZEE-ruh
Tarsus	TAHR-suhs	Tyre	TAI-er	Zeror	ZEE-rawr
Tekel	TEH-keel	Ur	er	Zerubbabel	zeh-RUH-buh-behl
Terebinth	TEHR-ee-bihnth	Urbanus	er-BAY-nuhs	Zeus	zyoos
Thaddeus	THAD-dee-uhs	Uriah	you-RAI-uh	Zimri	ZIHM-rai
Theophilus	thee-AH-fih-luhs	Uzziah	yoo-ZAI-uh	Zion	ZAI-uhn
Thessalonians	theh-suh-LO-nih-uhnz	Wadi	WAH-dee	Ziph	zihf
Theudas	THU-duhs	Yahweh-yireh	YAH-weh-yer-AY	Zoar	ZO-er
Thyatira	thai-uh-TAI-ruh	Zacchaeus	zak-KEE-uhs	Zorah	ZAWR-uh
Tiberias	tai-BIHR-ih-uhs	Zadok	ZAY-dahk	Zuphite	ZUHF-ait
Timaeus	tai-MEE-uhs	Zarephath	ZEHR-ee-fath		